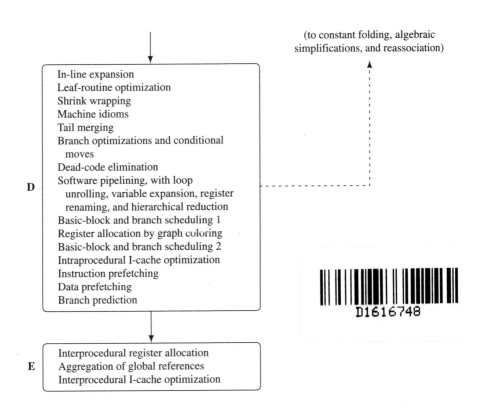

(to constant folding, algebraic simplifications, and reassociation)

D

In-line expansion
Leaf-routine optimization
Shrink wrapping
Machine idioms
Tail merging
Branch optimizations and conditional
    moves
Dead-code elimination
Software pipelining, with loop
    unrolling, variable expansion, register
    renaming, and hierarchical reduction
Basic-block and branch scheduling 1
Register allocation by graph coloring
Basic-block and branch scheduling 2
Intraprocedural I-cache optimization
Instruction prefetching
Data prefetching
Branch prediction

D1616748

E

Interprocedural register allocation
Aggregation of global references
Interprocedural I-cache optimization

B, C These optimizations are typically performed on medium- or low-level intermediate code, depending on the overall organization of the compiler. If code selection is done before all optimizations other than those in box **A** (known as the "low-level" model of optimizer structure), then these optimizations are performed on low-level code. If, on the other hand, some optimizations are performed on a medium-level, relatively machine-independent intermediate code and others are performed on low-level code after code generation (known as the "mixed" model), then these optimizations are generally done on the medium-level intermediate code.

The branches from **C1** to **C2** and **C3** represent a choice of the method used to perform essentially the same optimization (namely, moving computations to places where they are performed less frequently without changing the semantics of the program). They also represent a choice of the data-flow analyses used to perform the optimization.

D These optimizations are almost always done on a low-level form of code—one that may be quite machine-dependent (e.g., a structured assembly language) or that may be somewhat more general, such as the low-level intermediate code used in this book—because they require that addresses have been turned into the form required by the target processor and because several of them require low-level control-flow code.

E These optimizations are performed at link time, so they operate on relocatable object code.

Three optimizations, namely, constant folding, algebraic simplification, and reassociation, are in boxes connected to the other phases of the optimization process by *dotted* lines because they are best structured as subroutines that can be invoked whenever they are needed.

A version of this diagram appears in Chapters 1 and 11 through 20 to guide the reader in ordering optimizer components in a compiler.

Advanced Compiler Design
and Implementation

Advanced Compiler Design and Implementation

Steven S. Muchnick

Morgan Kaufmann Publishers
San Francisco, California

Senior Editor   Denise E. M. Penrose
Production Manager   Yonie Overton
Production Editor   Cheri Palmer
Editorial Coordinator   Jane Elliott
Cover Design   Ross Carron Design
Text Design, Composition, and Illustrations   Windfall Software
Copyeditor   Jeff Van Bueren
Proofreader   Jennifer McClain
Indexer   Ty Koontz
Printer   Quebecor Printing

Morgan Kaufmann Publishers, Inc.
Editorial and Sales Office
340 Pine Street, Sixth Floor
San Francisco, CA 94104-3205
USA
Telephone 415 / 392-2665
Facsimile 415 / 982-2665
Email mkp@mkp.com
Web Site www.mkp.com

Order toll free 800 / 745-7323

Library of Congress Cataloging-in-Publication Data

Muchnick, Steven S., date.
   Advanced compiler design and implementation / Steve Muchnick.
      p.   cm.
   Includes bibliographical references and index.
   ISBN 1-55860-320-4
   1. Compilers (Computer programs)   2. Systems programming (Computer science).   I. Title.
   QA76.76.C65M8   1997
   005.4'53—dc21   97-13063
                                                                         CIP

To Eric, *nihil sine quō*

Compiler design has been an active topic of research and development since the mid-1950s. Fortran, the first widely used higher-level language, succeeded, in large part, because of the high quality of its early compilers. John Backus and his colleagues at IBM recognized that programmers would not give up the detailed design control they had with assembly language unless the performance of compiled code was sufficiently close to the performance of handwritten machine code. Backus's group invented several key concepts that underlie the topics in this book. Among them are the treatment of array indexes in loop optimization and methods for local register allocation. Since that time, both researchers and practitioners have improved and supplanted them (repeatedly) with more effective ones.

In light of the long history of compiler design, and its standing as a relatively mature computing technology, why, one might ask, should there be a new book in the field? The answer is clear. Compilers are tools that generate efficient mappings from programs to machines. The language designs continue to change, the target architectures continue to change, and the programs become ever more ambitious in their scale and complexity. Thus, while the compiler design problem remains the same at a high level, as we zoom in, it is continually changing. Furthermore, the computational resources we can bring to bear in the compilers themselves are increasing. Consequently, modern compilers use more time- and space-intensive algorithms than were possible before. And, of course, researchers continue to invent new and better techniques for solving conventional compiler design problems. In fact, an entire collection of topics in this book are direct consequences of changes in computer architecture.

This book takes on the challenges of contemporary languages and architectures and prepares the reader for the new compiling problems that will inevitably arise in the future. For example, in Chapter 3 the book builds on the reader's knowledge of symbol tables and local scope structure to describe how to deal with imported and exported scopes as found in Ada, Modula-2, and other modern languages. And, since run-time environments model the dynamic semantics of source languages, the discussion of advanced issues in run-time support in Chapter 5, such as compiling shared objects, is particularly valuable. That chapter also addresses the rich type systems found in some modern languages and the diverse strategies for parameter passing dictated by modern architectures.

No compiler book would be complete without a chapter on code generation. The early work in code generation provided approaches to designing handcrafted instruction-selection routines and intermixing instruction selection with register management. The treatment of code generation in Chapter 6 describes automated techniques based on pattern matching, made possible not only by compiler research but also by simpler and more orthogonal instruction sets and by the feasibility of constructing and traversing intermediate-code trees in a compiler.

Optimization is the heart of advanced compiler design and the core of this book. Much theoretical work has gone into program analysis, both for the sake of optimization and for other purposes. Chapters 7 through 10 revisit what are, by now, the classic analysis methods, along with newer and more efficient ones previously described only in research papers. These chapters take a collection of diverse techniques and organize them into a unified whole. This synthesis is, in itself, a significant contribution to compiler design. Most of the chapters that follow use the analyses to perform optimizing transformations.

The large register sets in recent systems motivate the material on register allocation in Chapter 16, which synthesizes over a decade of advances in algorithms and heuristics for this problem. Also, an important source of increased speed is concurrency—the ability to do several things at once. In order to translate a sequential program into one that can exploit hardware concurrency, the compiler may need to rearrange parts of the computation in a way that preserves correctness and increases parallelism. Although a full treatment of concurrency is beyond the scope of this book, it does focus on instruction-level parallelism, which motivates the discussion of dependence analysis in Chapter 9 and the vital topic of code scheduling in Chapter 17.

Chapter 20, on optimization for the memory hierarchy, is also motivated by modern target machines, which introduce a diversity of relative speeds of data access in order to cope with the increasing gap between processor and memory speeds. An additional chapter available from the publisher's World Wide Web site discusses object-code translation, which builds on compiler technology to translate programs for new architectures, even when the source programs are unavailable.

The importance of interprocedural analysis and optimization has increased as new language designs have encouraged programmers to use more sophisticated methods for structuring large programs. Its feasibility has increased as the analysis methods have been refined and tuned and as faster computers have made the requisite analyses acceptably fast. Chapter 19 is devoted to the determination and use of interprocedural information.

Compiler design is, in its essence, an engineering activity. The methods that are used must be ones that provide good solutions to the translation situations that arise in practice—namely, real programs written in real languages executing on real machines. Most of the time, the compiler writer must take the languages and the machines as they come. Rarely is it possible to influence or improve the design of either. It is the engineering choices of what analyses and transformations to perform and when to perform them that determine the speed and quality of an optimizing compiler. Both in the treatment of the optimization material throughout the book and in the case studies in Chapter 21, these design choices are paramount.

One of the great strengths of the author, Steve Muchnick, is the wealth and diversity of his experience. After an early career as a professor of computer science, Dr. Muchnick applied his knowledge of compilers as a vital member of the teams that developed two important computer architectures, namely, PA-RISC at Hewlett-Packard and SPARC at Sun Microsystems. After the initial work on each architecture was completed, he served as the leader of the advanced compiler design and implementation groups for these systems. Those credentials stand him in good stead in deciding what the reader needs to know about advanced compiler design. His research experience, coupled with his hands-on development experience, are invaluable in guiding the reader through the many design decisions that a compiler designer must make.

Susan Graham
University of California, Berkeley

6 Producing Code Generators Automatically   137

7 Control-Flow Analysis   169

8 Data-Flow Analysis   217

9   Dependence Analysis and Dependence Graphs   267

10   Alias Analysis   293

19   Interprocedural Analysis and Optimization   607

20   Optimization for the Memory Hierarchy   669

This book concerns advanced issues in the design and implementation of compilers, for uniprocessors, with its major emphasis (over 60% of the text) on optimization. While it does consider machines with instruction-level parallelism, we ignore almost completely the issues of large-scale parallelization and vectorization.

It begins with material on compiler structure, symbol-table management (including languages that allow scopes to be imported and exported), intermediate code structure, run-time support issues (including shared objects that can be linked to at run time), and automatic generation of code generators from machine descriptions. Next it explores methods for intraprocedural (conventionally called *global*) control-flow, data-flow, dependence, and alias analyses. Then a series of groups of global optimizations are described, including ones that apply to program components from simple expressions to whole procedures. Next, interprocedural analyses of control flow, data flow, and aliases are described, followed by interprocedural optimizations and use of interprocedural information to improve global optimizations. We then discuss optimizations designed to make effective use of the memory hierarchy. Finally, we describe four commercial compiler systems in detail, namely, ones from Digital Equipment Corporation, IBM, Intel, and Sun Microsysytems, to provide specific examples of approaches to compiler structure, intermediate-code design, optimization choices, and effectiveness. As we shall see, these compiler systems represent a wide range of approaches and often achieve similar results in different ways.

How This Book Came to Be Written

In June 1990 and 1991, while a Distinguished Engineer at Sun Microsystems, I presented a half-day tutorial entitled "Advanced Compiling Techniques for RISC Systems" at the annual ACM SIGPLAN Conference on Programming Language Design and Implementation. The tutorial was based on approximately 130 transparencies on RISC architectures and relevant issues in compilers, particularly optimization. I left that experience with the idea that somewhere within the material covered there was a seed (the mental image was, in fact, of an acorn) yearning for sun, soil, and water to help it grow into the mature oak tree of a book you have before you. Over a year later I discussed this idea with Wayne Rosing, then President of Sun Microsystems Laboratories, and within a few weeks he decided to nurture this project with a year-and-a-half's worth of partial funding.

The first draft that resulted included quite a lot of material on RISC architectures, as well as material on advanced compilation issues. Before long (with the help of three reviewers) I had decided that there was little point in including the architecture material in the book. New RISC architectures are being developed quite frequently, the kind of coverage of them that is needed is provided in architecture courses at most universities, and the real strengths of the text were in the compiler material.

This resulted in a major change of direction. Most of the architecture material was dropped, keeping just those parts that support decisions on how to proceed in compilation; the focus of the compiler material was broadened to provide equal coverage of CISCs; and it was decided to focus entirely on uniprocessors and to leave it to other texts to discuss parallelization and vectorization. The focus of the compilation material was deepened and, in some respects narrowed and in others broadened (for example, material on hand-crafted code generation was dropped almost entirely, while advanced methods of scheduling, such as trace and percolation scheduling, were added). The result is what you see before you.

About the Cover

The design on the cover is of a Chilkat blanket from the author's collection of Northwest Coast native art. The blanket was woven of fine strands of red-cedar inner bark and mountain-goat wool in the late 19th century by a Tlingit woman from southeastern Alaska. It generally took six to nine months of work to complete such a blanket. The blanket design is divided into three panels, and the center panel depicts a diving whale. The head is the split image at the bottom; the body is the panel with the face in the center (a panel that looks like a face never represents the face in this iconography); the lateral fins are at the sides of the body; and the tail flukes are at the top. Each part of the design is, in itself, functional but meaningless; assembled together in the right way, the elements combine to depict a diving whale and proclaim the rights and prerogatives of the village chief who owned the blanket.

In a similar way, each component of a compiler is functional, but it is only when the components are put together in the proper way that they serve their overall purpose. Designing and weaving such a blanket requires skills that are akin to those involved in constructing industrial-strength compilers—each discipline has a set of required tools, materials, design elements, and overall patterns that must be combined in a way that meets the prospective users' needs and desires.

Audience for This Book

This book is intended for computer professionals, graduate students, and advanced undergraduates who need to understand the issues involved in designing and constructing advanced compilers for uniprocessors. The reader is assumed to have had introductory courses in data structures, algorithms, compiler design and implementation, computer architecture, and assembly-language programming, or equivalent work experience.

Overview of the Book's Contents

This volume is divided into 21 chapters and three appendices as follows:

Chapter 1. Introduction to Advanced Topics

This chapter introduces the subject of the book, namely, advanced topics in the design and construction of compilers, and discusses compiler structure, the importance of optimization, and how the rest of the material in the book works together.

Chapter 2. Informal Compiler Algorithm Notation (ICAN)

Chapter 2 describes and gives examples of an informal programming notation called ICAN that is used to present algorithms in the text. After describing the notation used to express the language's syntax, it gives a brief overview of ICAN, followed by a detailed description of the language. The brief description should be sufficient for reading most of the algorithms presented and the full description should need to be referred to only rarely.

Chapter 3. Symbol-Table Structure

Chapter 3 first discusses the attributes of variables, such as storage class, visibility, volatility, scope, size, type, alignment, structure, addressing method, and so on. Then it describes effective methods for structuring and managing local and global symbol tables, including importation and exportation of scopes (as found, e.g., in Ada, Mesa, and Modula-2); storage binding; and approaches to generating load and store instructions that take the above characteristics into account.

Chapter 4. Intermediate Representations

This chapter focuses on intermediate language design, three specific intermediate languages used in the remainder of the book, and other basic forms of intermediate code that might be used in a compiler. We use three closely related intermediate forms, one high-level, one medium-level, and one low-level, to allow us to demonstrate virtually all the optimizations discussed. We also discuss the relative importance and usefulness of our chosen forms and the others.

Two other more elaborate forms of intermediate code, namely, static single-assignment (SSA) form and program dependence graphs, are discussed in Sections 8.11 and 9.5, respectively.

Chapter 5. Run-Time Support

Chapter 5 concerns the issues involved in supporting programs written in high-level languages at run time. It discusses data representation, register usage, design of the stack frame and overall run-time stack, parameter passing, procedure structure and linkage, procedure-valued variables, code sharing, position-independent code, and issues involved in supporting symbolic and polymorphic languages.

Chapter 6. Producing Code Generators Automatically

Chapter 6 discusses automatic approaches for producing code generators from machine descriptions. We present the Graham-Glanville syntax-directed technique in detail and introduce two other approaches, namely, semantics-directed parsing and tree pattern matching.

Chapter 7. Control-Flow Analysis

This and the following three chapters discuss four types of analyses that apply to procedures and that are vital to doing correct and ambitious optimization.

Chapter 7 concentrates on approaches to determining the control flow within a procedure and to constructing a control-flow graph (CFG). It begins with an overview of the possible approaches and then discusses three of them in detail. The first is the classic approach of using depth-first search and dominators. In this area we also discuss flowgraph traversals, such as preorder and postorder, of the CFG and finding the strongly connected components of a CFG. The other two approaches depend on the concept of reducibility, which allows the control flow of a procedure to be composed hierarchically. One of the two is called interval analysis and the other is called structural analysis, and the two differ in what types of structural units they distinguish. We also discuss the representation of a procedure's hierarchical structure by a so-called control tree.

Chapter 8. Data-Flow Analysis

Chapter 8 discusses approaches to determining the flow of data in a procedure. It begins with an example and next discusses the basic mathematical concepts underlying data-flow analysis, namely, lattices, flow functions, and fixed points. It continues with a taxonomy of data-flow problems and solution methods and then proceeds to discuss in detail three techniques for solving data-flow problems that correspond to the three approaches to control-flow analysis presented in the preceding chapter. The first approach is iterative data-flow analysis, which corresponds to the use of depth-first search and dominators. The other two approaches correspond to the control-tree-based approaches to control-flow analysis and are known by the same names as those analyses: interval analysis and structural analysis. This is followed by an overview of a new sparse technique known as slotwise analysis, and descriptions of methods of representing data-flow information, namely, du-chains, ud-chains, webs, and static single-assignment (or SSA) form. The chapter concludes with thoughts on how to deal with arrays, structures, and pointers and with a discussion of a method for automating construction of data-flow analyzers.

Chapter 9. Dependence Analysis and Dependence Graphs

Chapter 9 concerns dependence analysis, which is a poor-man's version of data-flow analysis for arrays and low-level storage references, and a closely related intermediate code form known as the program dependence graph. It first discusses dependence relations and then how to compute dependence relations within a basic block, which is vital to the code-scheduling techniques discussed in Chapter 17. Next it discusses dependence in loops and methods of doing dependence testing, which are essential to the data-storage optimizations discussed in Chapter 20. Finally, it discusses the program dependence graph, which is an intermediate-code form that represents control and data dependences directly, and that can be used to perform a series of optimizations more effectively than on an intermediate code that leaves such information implicit.

Chapter 10. Alias Analysis

Chapter 10 discusses alias analysis, which determines whether a storage location may be accessible by more than one access path, such as by name and through a pointer. It discusses how aliases may impact programs in specific languages, such as Fortran 77, Pascal, C, and Fortran 90. Next it discusses a very general approach to determining the aliases present in a procedure that consists of a language-specific alias gatherer and a language-independent alias propagator. The alias gatherer and propagator can be tailored to provide information that depends or not on the control flow of the procedure and that also provides information in a variety of other ways, making it a general approach that can be suited to the needs and time constraints of a particular programming language and compiler.

Chapter 11. Introduction to Optimization

Chapter 11 introduces the subject of code optimization, discusses the fact that the applicability and effectiveness of most optimizations are recursively undecidable but still worthwhile for programs for which they are determinable, and provides a quick survey of the intraprocedural optimizations covered in Chapters 12 through 18. It then discusses flow sensitivity and may vs. must information and how they apply to optimization, the relative importance of particular optimizations, and the order in which they should be performed.

Chapter 12. Early Optimizations

Chapter 12 discusses optimizations that are usually performed early in the optimization process, namely, scalar replacement of aggregates, local and global value numbering (performed on SSA-form code), local and global copy propagation, and sparse conditional constant propagation (also performed on SSA-form code). It also discusses constant expression evaluation (or constant folding) and algebraic simplification and how they are best included in an optimizer as subroutines that can be called from wherever they are needed.

Chapter 13. Redundancy Elimination

Chapter 13 concerns several types of redundancy elimination, which, in essence, delete computations that are performed more than once on a path through a procedure. It describes local and global common-subexpression elimination, forward substitution, loop-invariant code motion, partial-redundancy elimination, and code hoisting.

Chapter 14. Loop Optimizations

Chapter 14 deals with optimizations that apply to loops, including identification of induction variables, strength reduction, removal of induction variables, linear-function test replacement, elimination of unnecessary bounds checking.

Chapter 15. Procedure Optimizations

Chapter 15 presents optimizations that apply to procedures as units of code. It discusses tail-call optimization (including tail-recursion elimination), procedure integration, in-line expansion, leaf-routine optimization, and shrink wrapping.

Chapter 16. Register Allocation

Chapter 16 concerns intraprocedural register allocation and assignment. First it discusses local, cost-based methods and then an approach that uses graph coloring. We discuss webs as the allocatable objects, the interference graph, coloring the interference graph, and generating spill code. This is followed by a brief presentation of approaches to register allocation that use a procedure's control tree.

Chapter 17. Code Scheduling

Chapter 17 concerns local and global instruction scheduling, which reorders instructions to take best advantage of the pipelines built into modern processors. There are two issues in local scheduling, namely, list scheduling, which deals with the sequence of instructions within a basic block, and branch scheduling, which deals with connections between blocks. We next consider approaches to scheduling across basic-block boundaries, including speculative loads and boosting. Next we discuss two approaches to software pipelining, called window scheduling and unroll and compact. Next we discuss loop unrolling, variable expansion, and register renaming, all of which increase the freedom available to scheduling, and hierarchical reduction, which deals with control structures embedded in loops. We finish the chapter with two global approaches to scheduling, namely, trace scheduling and percolation scheduling.

Chapter 18. Control-Flow and Low-Level Optimizations

Chapter 18 deals with control-flow optimizations and ones that are generally performed on a low-level form of intermediate code or on an assembly-language-like representation. These include unreachable-code elimination, straightening, if simplification, loop simplifications, loop inversion, unswitching, branch optimizations, tail merging (also called cross jumping), use of conditional move instructions, dead-code elimination, in-line expansion, branch prediction, machine idioms, instruction combining, and register coalescing or subsumption.

Chapter 19. Interprocedural Analysis and Optimization

Chapter 19 concerns extending analysis and optimization to deal with whole programs. It discusses interprocedural control-flow analysis, data-flow analysis, alias analysis, and transformations. It presents two approaches each to flow-insensitive side effect and alias analysis, along with approaches to computing flow-sensitive side effects and doing interprocedural constant propagation. Next it discusses interprocedural optimizations and applying interprocedural information to optimization within procedures, followed by interprocedural register allocation and aggregation of global references. It concludes with a discussion of how to integrate interprocedural analysis and optimization into the order of optimizations.

Chapter 20. Optimization for the Memory Hierarchy

Chapter 20 discusses optimization to take better advantage of the memory hierarchy found in most systems and specifically of cache memories. We first discuss the impact of data and instruction caches on program performance. We next consider instruction-cache optimization, including instruction prefetching, procedure sorting, procedure and block placement, intraprocedural code positioning, procedure splitting, and combining intra- and interprocedural methods.

Next we discuss data-cache optimization, focusing mostly on loop transformations. Rather than providing a full treatment of this topic, we cover some parts of it in detail, such as scalar replacement of array elements and data prefetching, and for others give only an outline of the definitions, terminology, and techniques, and issues involved and examples of the techniques. The latter topics include data reuse, locality, tiling, and the interaction of scalar and memory-oriented optimizations. We take this approach because the research on this subject is still too new to warrant selection of a definitive method.

Chapter 21. Case Studies of Compilers and Future Trends

Chapter 21 presents four case studies of commercial compiling systems that include a wide range of target architectures, compiler designs, intermediate-code representations, and optimizations. The four architectures are Sun Microsystems' SPARC, IBM's POWER (and PowerPC), the Digital Equipment Alpha, and the Intel 386 family. For each, we first discuss the architecture briefly and then present the hardware vendor's compilers for it.

Appendix A. Guide to Assembly Languages Used in This Book

Appendix A presents a short description of each of the assembly languages used in the text, so as to make the code examples more easily accessible. This includes discussion of the SPARC, POWER (and PowerPC), Alpha, Intel 386 architecture family, and PA-RISC assembly languages.

Appendix B. Representation of Sets, Sequences, Trees, DAGs, and Functions

Appendix B provides a quick review of concrete representations for most of the abstract data structures in the text. It is not a substitute for a course in data structures, but a ready reference to some of the issues and approaches.

Appendix C. Software Resources

Appendix C is concerned with software accessible via anonymous FTP or on the World Wide Web that can be used as a basis for compiler implementation projects in the classroom and, in some cases, in industrial settings also.

Bibliography

Finally, the bibliography presents a wide range of sources for further reading in the topics covered in the text.

Indexes

The book ends with two indexes, one of which lists mathematical formulas, ICAN functions, and major ICAN data structures.

Supplements, Resources, and Web Extensions

Several exercises appear at the end of each chapter. Advanced exercises are marked "ADV" in the left margin, and research exercises are marked "RSCH." Solutions for the exercises and an Instructor's Guide are available electronically from the publisher. The Instructor's Guide can be found on the World Wide Web at the URL for this book http://www.mkp.com/books_catalog/1-55860-320-4.asp. Instructors should contact the publisher directly to obtain solutions to exercises.

Resources

Appendix C, as described above, concerns free software designed for student compiler-construction projects and how to obtain it electronically. The entire appendix, with links to these addresses, can be accessed at the URL listed above.

Web Extension

Additional material concerned with object-code translation, an approach to producing machine code for an architecture from code for another architecture, rather than from source code, is available from the publisher's World Wide Web site, at the URL listed above. The Web Extension discusses the principles of object-code compilation and then focuses on three examples, Hewlett-Packard's HP3000–to–PA-RISC translator OCT and Digital Equipment Corporation's VAX VMS-to-Alpha translator VEST and its MIPS-to-Alpha translator mx.

Acknowledgments

First and foremost, I would like to thank my former colleagues at Sun Microsystems without whose support and encouragement this book would not have been possible. Chief among them are Peter Deutsch, Dave Ditzel, Jon Kannegaard, Wayne Rosing, Eric Schmidt, Bob Sproull, Bert Sutherland, Ivan Sutherland, and the members of the Programming Languages departments, particularly Sharokh Mortazavi, Peter Damron, and Vinod Grover. I particularly thank Wayne Rosing for the faith to fund my time working on the book for its first one and a half years.

Second, I would like to thank the reviewers, all of whom have provided valuable comments on drafts of the book, namely, J. Randy Allen, Bill Appelbe, Preston Briggs, Fabian E. Bustamante, Siddhartha Chatterjee, Bob Colwell, Subhendu Raja Das, Krishna Kunchithapadam, Jim Larus, Ion Mandoiu, Allan Porterfield, Francisco J. Torres-Rojas, and Michael Wolfe.

I am also indebted to colleagues in other companies and organizations who have shared information about their compilers and other technical topics, whether they appear directly in the book or not, namely, Michael Tiemann, James Wilson, and Torbjörn Granlund of Cygnus Support; Richard Grove, Neil Faiman, Maurice Marks, and Anton Chernoff of Digital Equipment; Craig Franklin of Green Hills Software; Keith Keilman, Michael Mahon, James Miller, and Carol Thompson of Hewlett-Packard; Robert Colwell, Suresh Rao, William Savage, and Kevin J. Smith of Intel; Bill Hay, Kevin O'Brien, and F. Kenneth Zadeck of International Business Machines; Fred Chow, John Mashey, and Alex Wu of MIPS Technologies; Andrew Johnson of the Open Software Foundation; Keith Cooper and his colleagues at Rice University; John Hennessy, Monica Lam, and their colleagues at Stanford University; and Nic Peeling of the UK Defense Research Agency.

I am particularly indebted to my parents, Samuel and Dorothy Muchnick, who created a homelife for me that was filled with possibilities, that encouraged me to ask and to try to answer hard questions, and that stimulated an appreciation for the beauty to be found in both the gifts of simplicity and in complexity, be it natural or made by the hand of man.

The staff at Morgan Kaufmann have shepherded this project through the stages of the publishing process with skill and aplomb. They include Bruce Spatz, Doug Sery, Jennifer Mann, Denise Penrose, Yonie Overton, Cheri Palmer, Jane Elliott, and Lisa Schneider. I thank them all and look forward to working with them again.

The compositor, Paul Anagnostopoulos of Windfall Software, designed the special symbols used in ICAN and did a thorough and knowledgeable job of typesetting the book. He made my day one morning when he sent me email saying that he looked forward to reading the product of our joint labor.

Last, but by no means least, I would like to thank my long-time lover, Eric Milliren, for putting up with my spending so much time writing this book during the last five years, for providing a nourishing home life for me, and for deferring several of his own major projects until completion of the book was in sight.

CHAPTER 1

Introduction to Advanced Topics

We begin by reviewing the structure of compilers and then proceed to lay the groundwork for our exploration of the advanced topics in compiler design and implementation discussed in the remainder of the book. In particular, we first review the basics of compiler structure and then give an overview of the advanced material about symbol-table structure and access, intermediate-code forms, run-time representations, and automatic generation of code generators contained in Chapters 3 through 6. Next we describe the importance of optimization to achieving fast code, possible structures for optimizing compilers, and the organization of optimizations in an aggressive optimizing compiler. Then we discuss the reading flow relationships among the chapters. We conclude with a list of related topics not covered in this book, two short sections on target machines used in examples and notations for numbers and the names we use for various data sizes, and a wrap-up of this chapter, followed by a Further Reading section and exercises, as will be found at the end of all but the last chapter.

1.1   Review of Compiler Structure

Strictly speaking, compilers are software systems that translate programs written in higher-level languages into equivalent programs in object code or machine language for execution on a computer. Thus, a particular compiler might run on an IBM-compatible personal computer and translate programs written in Fortran 77 into Intel 386–architecture object code to be run on a PC. The definition can be widened to include systems that translate from one higher-level language to another, from one machine language to another, from a higher-level language to an intermediate-level form, etc. With the wider definition, we might have, for example, a compiler that runs on an Apple Macintosh and translates Motorola M68000 Macintosh object code to PowerPC object code to be run on a PowerPC-based Macintosh.

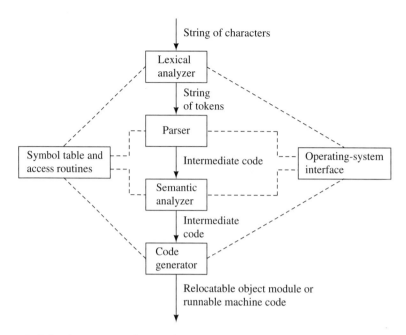

FIG. 1.1 High-level structure of a simple compiler.

A compiler, as narrowly defined, consists of a series of phases that sequentially analyze given forms of a program and synthesize new ones, beginning with the sequence of characters constituting a source program to be compiled and producing ultimately, in most cases, a relocatable object module that can be linked with others and loaded into a machine's memory to be executed. As any basic text on compiler construction tells us, there are at least four phases in the compilation process, as shown in Figure 1.1, namely,

1. *lexical analysis,* which analyzes the character string presented to it and divides it up into tokens that are legal members of the vocabulary of the language in which the program is written (and may produce error messages if the character string is not parseable into a string of legal tokens);

2. *syntactic analysis* or *parsing,* which processes the sequence of tokens and produces an intermediate-level representation, such as a parse tree or a sequential intermediate code (for an example, see the definition of MIR in Section 4.6.1), and a symbol table that records the identifiers used in the program and their attributes (and may produce error messages if the token string contains syntax errors);

3. checking of the program for *static-semantic validity* (or *semantic checking*), which takes as input the intermediate code and symbol table and determines whether the program satisfies the static-semantic properties required by the source language, e.g., whether identifiers are consistently declared and used (and may produce error messages if the program is semantically inconsistent or fails in some other way to satisfy the requirements of the language's definition); and

4. *code generation,* which transforms the intermediate code into equivalent machine code in the form of a relocatable object module or directly runnable object code.

Any detected errors may be warnings or definite errors and, in the latter case, may terminate compilation.

In addition to the four phases, a compiler includes a symbol table and its access routines and an interface to the operating system and user environment (to read and write files, read user input, output messages to the user, etc.) that are available to all phases of the compilation process (as shown in Figure 1.1). The latter can be structured to allow the compiler to run under multiple operating systems without changing how it interfaces with them. The compiler structure diagrams from here on, except in Chapter 21, do not include the symbol table or operating-system interface.

For many higher-level languages, the four phases can be combined into one pass over the source program to produce a fast, one-pass compiler. Such a compiler may be entirely appropriate for a casual user or as an alternative to incremental compilation in a software-development environment, where the goal is to provide quick turnaround for program changes in the edit-compile-debug cycle. It is generally not possible for such a compiler to produce very efficient code, however.

Alternatively, the lexical and syntactic analysis phases can be combined into a pass that produces a symbol table and some form of intermediate code,[1] and the semantic checking and generation of object code from the intermediate code may be done as a separate, second pass, or as two separate passes (or semantic checking may be done largely as part of the first pass). The object code produced by the compiler may be relocatable target-machine code or assembly language, which, in turn, needs to be processed by an assembler to produce relocatable object code. Once a program or its parts have been compiled, they generally need to be linked to interconnect them and any needed library routines, and read and relocated by a loader to produce a runnable image in memory. Linking may be done either before execution (statically) or during execution (dynamically), or may be split between the two, e.g., with the user's program components linked statically and system libraries linked dynamically.

1.2   Advanced Issues in Elementary Topics

Here we provide an introduction to the advanced topics in symbol-table design and access, intermediate-code design, run-time representations, and automatic generation of code generators discussed in Chapters 3 through 6. These are topics whose basic issues are generally among the major focuses of first courses in compiler design

---

1. Some languages, such as Fortran, *require* that lexical and syntactic analysis be done cooperatively to correctly analyze programs. For example, given a line of Fortran code that begins "do 32 i = 1" it is not possible to tell, without further lookahead, whether the characters before the equals sign make up three tokens or one. If the 1 is followed by a comma, there are three tokens before the equals sign and the statement begins a do loop, whereas if the line ends with the 1, there is one token before the equals sign, which may be equivalently written "do32i", and the statement is an assignment.

and development. However, they all have complexities that are introduced when one considers supporting a language whose flavor is not strictly vanilla.

Design of symbol tables has been largely a matter more of occult arts than scientific principles. In part this is because the attributes of symbols vary from one language to another and because it is clear that the most important aspects of a global symbol table are its interface and its performance. There are several ways to organize a symbol table for speed depending on the choice of the underlying data structures, such as stacks, various sorts of trees, hash tables, and so on, each having strong points to recommend it. We discuss some of these possibilities in Chapter 3, but we primarily focus on a combination of stacks, hashing, and linked lists that deals with the requirements of languages such as Ada, Mesa, Modula-2, and C++ to be able to import and export scopes in ways that expand on the simple stack model of languages like Fortran, C, and Pascal.

Intermediate-code design is also, to a significant degree, a matter of wizardry rather than science. It has been suggested that there are as many intermediate-language designs as there are different compiler suites—but this is probably off by a factor of two or so. In fact, given that many compilers use two or more distinct intermediate codes, there may be about twice as many intermediate-code designs as compiler suites!

So Chapter 4 explores the issues encountered in designing intermediate codes and the advantages and disadvantages of various choices. In the interest of moving on to describe algorithms that operate on intermediate code, we must ultimately choose one or more of them as concrete examples. We choose four: HIR, a high-level one that preserves loop structure and bounds and array subscripting for use in data-cache-related optimization; MIR, a medium-level one for most of the remainder of the book; LIR, a low-level one for optimizations that must deal with aspects of real machines, with a subvariety that has symbolic, rather than real, machine registers for use in global register allocation; and SSA form, which can be thought of as a version of MIR with an additional operation, namely, the ϕ-function, although we almost always use it in flowgraphs, rather than sequential programs. Figure 1.2 shows a HIR loop, and a translation of it to MIR, and to LIR with symbolic registers.

Figure 1.3 shows the SSA form of the loop; its code is identical to that in Figure 1.2(c), except that it has been turned into a flowgraph and the symbolic register s2 has been split into three—namely, $s2_1$, $s2_2$, and $s2_3$—and a ϕ-function has been added at the beginning of block B2 where $s2_1$ and $s2_3$ come together. SSA form has the major advantage of making several optimizations that previously worked on basic blocks or extended basic blocks[2] apply, as well, to whole procedures, often with significantly improved effectiveness.

Another intermediate-code form, the program dependence graph, that is useful in performing several types of optimizations is discussed in Section 9.5.

Chapter 5 focuses on issues of structuring the run-time environment in which programs execute. Along with code generation, it is one of the few things that are essential to get right if a language implementation is to be both correct and efficient.

---

2. An extended basic block is a tree of basic blocks that can be entered only at its root and left only from a leaf.

```
for v ← v1 by v2 to v3 do
   a[i] := 2
endfor
```
(a)

```
     v ← v1                          s2 ← s1
     t2 ← v2                         s4 ← s3
     t3 ← v3                         s6 ← s5
L1: if v > t3 goto L2      L1: if s2 > s6 goto L2
     t4 ← addr a                    s7 ← addr a
     t5 ← 4 * i                     s8 ← 4 * s9
     t6 ← t4 + t5                   s10 ← s7 + s8
     *t6 ← 2                        [s10] ← 2
     v ← v + t2                     s2 ← s2 + s4
     goto L1                        goto L1
L2:                        L2:
```
(b)   (c)

FIG. 1.2   A code fragment (assuming v2 is positive) in (a) HIR, (b) MIR, and (c) LIR with symbolic registers.

If the run-time model as designed doesn't support some of the operations of the language, clearly one has failed in the design. If it works, but is slower than it needs to be, it will have a major impact on performance, and one that generally will not be fixable by optimizations. The essential issues are representation of source data types, allocation and use of registers, the run-time stack, access to nonlocal symbols, and procedure calling, entry, exit, and return. In addition, we cover extensions to the run-time model that are necessary to support position-independent code, and

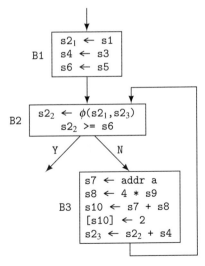

FIG. 1.3   SSA form of the example in Figure 1.2. Note the splitting of s2 into three variables $s2_1$, $s2_2$, and $s2_3$, and the ϕ-function at the entry to block B2.

their use in making possible and efficient the dynamic linking of shared code objects at run time, and we provide an overview of the additional issues that must be considered in compiling dynamic and polymorphic languages, such as incrementally changing running code, heap storage management, and run-time type checking (and its optimization or, where possible, elimination).

Finally, Chapter 6 concerns methods for automatically generating code generators from machine descriptions. It describes one technique, namely, the syntax-directed Graham-Glanville approach, in detail, and introduces two others, Ganapathi and Fischer's semantics-directed parsing and Aho, Ganapathi, and Tjiang's *twig*, which uses tree pattern matching and dynamic programming. All of these approaches have the advantage over hand-generated code generators of allowing the programmer to think at a higher level and to more easily modify a code generator over time, either to fix it, to improve it, or to adapt it to a new target.

1.3   The Importance of Code Optimization

Generally, the result of using a one-pass compiler structured as described in Section 1.1 is object code that executes much less efficiently than it might if more effort were expended in its compilation. For example, it might generate code on an expression-by-expression basis, so that the C code fragment in Figure 1.4(a) might result in the SPARC assembly code[3] in Figure 1.4(b), while it could be turned into the much more efficient code in Figure 1.4(c) if the compiler optimized it, including allocating the variables to registers. Even if the variables are not allocated to registers, at least the redundant load of the value of c could be eliminated. In a typical early one-scalar SPARC implementation, the code in Figure 1.4(b) requires 10 cycles to execute, while that in Figure 1.4(c) requires only two cycles.

Among the most important optimizations, in general, are those that operate on loops (such as moving loop-invariant computations out of them and simplifying or eliminating computations on induction variables), global register allocation, and instruction scheduling, all of which are discussed (along with many other optimizations) in Chapters 12 through 20.

However, there are many kinds of optimizations that may be relevant to a particular program, and the ones that are vary according to the structure and details of the program.

A highly recursive program, for example, may benefit significantly from tail-call optimization (see Section 15.1), which turns recursions into loops, and may only then benefit from loop optimizations. On the other hand, a program with only a few loops but with very large basic blocks within them may derive significant benefit from loop distribution (which splits one loop into several, with each loop body doing part of the work of the original one) or register allocation, but only modest improvement from other loop optimizations. Similarly, procedure integration or inlining, i.e., replacing subroutine calls with copies of their bodies, not only decreases the overhead of calling them but also may enable any or all of the intraprocedural optimizations to be applied to the result, with marked improvements that would

---

3. A guide to reading SPARC assembly language can be found in Appendix A.

```
int a, b, c, d;     ldw    a,r1        add    r1,r2,r3
c = a + b;          ldw    b,r2        add    r3,1,r4
d = c + 1;          add    r1,r2,r3
                    stw    r3,c
                    ldw    c,r3
                    add    r3,1,r4
                    stw    r4,d
(a)                 (b)                (c)
```

FIG. 1.4   A C code fragment in (a) with naive SPARC code generated for it in (b) and optimized code in (c).

not have been possible without inlining or (the typically much more expensive) techniques of interprocedural analysis and optimization (see Chapter 19). On the other hand, inlining usually increases code size, and that may have negative effects on performance, e.g., by increasing cache misses. As a result, it is desirable to measure the effects of the provided optimization options in a compiler and to select the ones that provide the best performance for each program.

These and other optimizations can make large differences in the performance of programs—frequently a factor of two or three and, occasionally, much more, in execution time.

An important design principle for large software projects, including compilers, is to design and construct programs consisting of small, functionally distinct modules and make each module as simple as one reasonably can, so that it can be easily designed, coded, understood, and maintained. Thus, it is entirely possible that unoptimized compilation does very local code generation, producing code similar to that in Figure 1.4(b), and that optimization is necessary to produce the much faster code in Figure 1.4(c).

1.4   Structure of Optimizing Compilers

A compiler designed to produce fast object code includes optimizer components. There are two main models for doing so, as shown in Figure 1.5(a) and (b).[4] In Figure 1.5(a), the source code is translated to a low-level intermediate code, such as our LIR (Section 4.6.3), and all optimization is done on that form of code; we call this the *low-level model* of optimization. In Figure 1.5(b), the source code is translated to a medium-level intermediate code, such as our MIR (Section 4.6.1), and optimizations that are largely architecture-independent are done on it; then the code is translated to a low-level form and further optimizations that are mostly architecture-dependent are done on it; we call this the *mixed model* of optimization. In either model, the optimizer phase(s) analyze and transform the intermediate code to eliminate unused generality and to take advantage of faster ways to perform given tasks. For example, the optimizer might determine that a computation performed

---

4. Again, lexical analysis, parsing, semantic analysis, and either translation or intermediate-code generation might be performed in a single step.

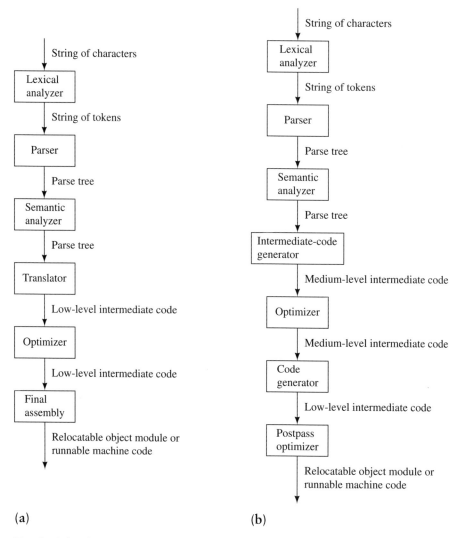

FIG. 1.5 Two high-level structures for an optimizing compiler: (a) with all optimization done on low-level intermediate code, and (b) with optimization divided into two phases, one operating on each of medium-level and low-level intermediate code.

in a loop produces the same result every time it is executed, so that moving the computation out of the loop would cause the program to execute faster. In the mixed model, the so-called postpass optimizer performs low-level optimizations, such as taking advantage of machine idioms and the target machine's addressing modes, while this would be done by the unitary optimizer in the low-level model.

A mixed-model optimizer is likely to be more easily adapted to a new architecture and may be more efficient at compilation time, while a low-level-model optimizer is less likely to be easily ported to another architecture, unless the second architecture resembles the first very closely—for example, if it is an upward-compatible extension of the first. The choice between the mixed and low-level models is largely one of investment and development focus.

The mixed model is used in Sun Microsystems' compilers for SPARC (see Section 21.1), Digital Equipment Corporation's compilers for Alpha (see Section 21.3), Intel's compilers for the 386 architecture family (see Section 21.4), and Silicon Graphics' compilers for MIPS. The low-level model is used in IBM's compilers for POWER and PowerPC (see Section 21.2) and Hewlett-Packard's compilers for PA-RISC.

The low-level model has the advantage of making it easier to avoid phase-ordering problems in optimization and exposes all address computations to the entire optimizer. For these and other reasons, we recommend using the low-level model in building an optimizer from scratch, unless there are strong expectations that it will be ported to a significantly different architecture later. Nevertheless, in the text we describe optimizations that might be done on either medium- or low-level code as being done on medium-level code. They can easily be adapted to work on low-level code.

As mentioned above, Sun's and Hewlett-Packard's compilers, for example, represent contrasting approaches in this regard. The Sun global optimizer was originally written for the Fortran 77 compiler for the Motorola MC68010-based Sun-2 series of workstations and was then adapted to the other compilers that shared a common intermediate representation, with the certain knowledge that it would need to be ported to future architectures. It was then ported to the very similar MC68020-based Sun-3 series, and more recently to SPARC and SPARC-V9. While considerable investment has been devoted to making the optimizer very effective for SPARC in particular, by migrating some optimizer components from before code generation to after it, much of it remains comparatively easy to port to a new architecture.

The Hewlett-Packard global optimizer for PA-RISC, on the other hand, was designed as part of a major investment to unify most of the company's computer products around a single new architecture. The benefits of having a single optimizer and the unification effort amply justified designing a global optimizer specifically tailored to PA-RISC.

Unless an architecture is intended only for very special uses, e.g., as an embedded processor, it is insufficient to support only a single programming language for it. This makes it desirable to share as many of the compiler components for an architecture as possible, both to reduce the effort of writing and maintaining them and to derive the widest benefit from one's efforts at improving the performance of compiled code. Whether the mixed or the low-level model of optimization is used makes no difference in this instance. Thus, all the real compilers we discuss in Chapter 21 are members of compiler suites for a particular architecture that share multiple components, including code generators, optimizers, assemblers, and possibly other components, but that have distinct front ends to deal with the lexical, syntactic, and static-semantic differences among the supported languages.

In other cases, compilers for the same language are provided by a software vendor for multiple architectures. Here we can expect to see the same front end used, and usually the same optimizer components, but different code generators and possibly additional optimizer phases to deal with the particular features of each architecture. The mixed model of optimization is the more appropriate one in this case. Often the code generators are structured identically, independent of the target machine, in a way appropriate either to the source language or, more frequently, the common intermediate code, and differ only in the instructions generated for each target.

Yet another option is the use of a *preprocessor* to transform programs in one language into equivalent programs in another language and to compile them from there. This is how the early implementations of C++ worked, using a program named cfront to translate C++ code to C code, performing, in the process (among other things), what has come to be known as *name mangling*—the transformation of readable C++ identifiers into virtually unreadable—but compilable—C identifiers. Another example of this is the use of a preprocessor to transform Fortran programs to ones that can take better advantage of vector or multiprocessing systems. A third example is to translate object code for an as-yet-unbuilt processor into code for an existing machine so as to emulate the prospective one.

One issue we have ignored so far in our discussion of optimizer structure and its place in a compiler or compiler suite is that some optimizations, particularly the data-cache-related ones discussed in Section 20.4, are usually most effective when applied to a source-language or high-level intermediate form, such as our HIR (Section 4.6.2). This can be done as the first step in the optimization process, as shown in Figure 1.6, where the final arrow goes to the translator in the low-level model and

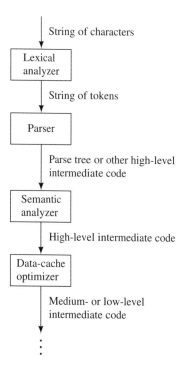

FIG. 1.6 Adding data-cache optimization to an optimizing compiler. The continuation is to either the translator in the low-level model in Figure 1.5(a) or to the intermediate-code generator in the mixed model in Figure 1.5(b).

to the intermediate-code generator in the mixed model. An alternative approach, used in the IBM compilers for POWER and PowerPC, first translates to a low-level code (called XIL) and then generates a high-level representation (called YIL) from it to do data-cache optimization. Following the data-cache optimization, the resulting YIL code is converted back to XIL.

1.5   Placement of Optimizations in Aggressive Optimizing Compilers

In the last section we discussed the placement of optimizations in the overall compilation process. In what follows, the wrap-up section of each chapter devoted to optimization includes a diagram like the one in Figure 1.7 that specifies a reasonable sequence for performing almost all the optimizations discussed in the text in an aggressive optimizing compiler. Note that we say "aggressive" because we assume that the goal is to improve performance as much as is reasonably possible without compromising correctness. In each of those chapters, the optimizations discussed there are highlighted by being in **bold** type. Note that the diagram includes only optimizations, not the other phases of compilation.

The letters at the left in Figure 1.7 specify the type of code that the optimizations to its right are usually applied to, as follows:

A   These optimizations are typically applied either to source code or to a high-level intermediate code that preserves loop structure and sequencing and array accesses in essentially their source-code form. Usually, in a compiler that performs these optimizations, they are done very early in the compiling process, since the overall process tends to lower the level of the code as we move along from one pass to the next.

B,C These optimizations are typically performed on medium- or low-level intermediate code, depending on whether the mixed or low-level model is used.

D   These optimizations are almost always done on a low-level form of code—one that may be quite machine-dependent (e.g., a structured assembly language) or that may be somewhat more general, such as our LIR—because they require that addresses have been turned into base register + offset form (or something similar, depending on the addressing modes available on the target processor) and because several of them require low-level control-flow code.

E   These optimizations are performed at link time, so they operate on relocatable object code. One interesting project in this area is Srivastava and Wall's OM system, which is a pilot study for a compiler system that does all optimization at link time.

The boxes in Figure 1.7, in addition to corresponding to the levels of code appropriate for the corresponding optimizations, represent the gross-level flow among the optimizations. For example, constant folding and algebraic simplifications are in a box connected to other phases by dotted arrows because they are best structured as subroutines that can be invoked anywhere they are needed.

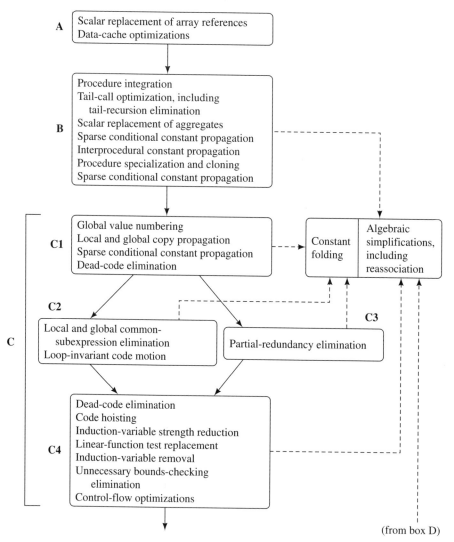

FIG. 1.7 Order of optimizations.

The branches from C1 to either C2 or C3 represent a choice of the methods one uses to perform essentially the same optimization (namely, moving computations to places where they are computed less frequently without changing the semantics of the program). They also represent a choice of the data-flow analyses used to perform the optimizations.

The detailed flow within the boxes is much freer than between the boxes. For example, in box B, doing scalar replacement of aggregates after sparse conditional constant propagation may allow one to determine that the scalar replacement is worthwhile, while doing it before constant propagation may make the latter more effective. An example of the former is shown in Figure 1.8(a), and of the latter in

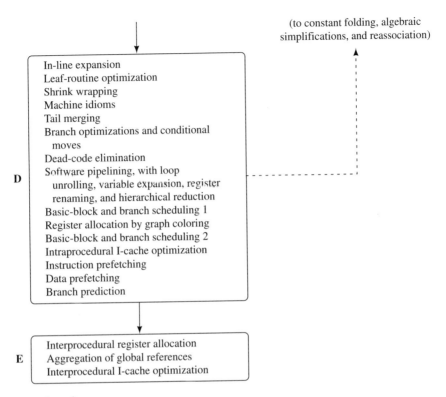

FIG. 1.7   *(continued)*

Figure 1.8(b). In (a), upon propagating the value 1 assigned to a to the test a = 1, we determine that the Y branch from block B1 is taken, so scalar replacement of aggregates causes the second pass of constant propagation to determine that the Y branch from block B4 is also taken. In (b), scalar replacement of aggregates allows sparse conditional constant propagation to determine that the Y exit from B1 is taken.

Similarly, one ordering of global value numbering, global and local copy propagation, and sparse conditional constant propagation may work better for some programs and another ordering for others.

Further study of Figure 1.7 shows that we recommend doing both sparse conditional constant propagation and dead-code elimination three times each, and instruction scheduling twice. The reasons are somewhat different in each case:

1. Sparse conditional constant propagation discovers operands whose values are constant each time such an operand is used—doing it before interprocedural constant propagation helps to transmit constant-valued arguments into and through procedures, and interprocedural constants can help to discover more intraprocedural ones.

2. We recommend doing dead-code elimination repeatedly because several optimizations and groups of optimizations typically create dead code and eliminating it as soon as reasonably possible or appropriate reduces the amount of code that other

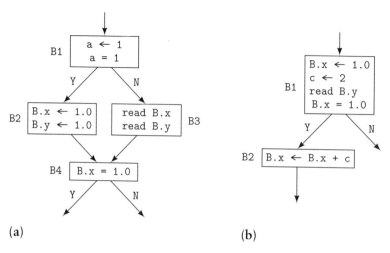

FIG. 1.8 Examples of (a) the effect of doing scalar replacement of aggregates after constant propagation, and (b) before constant propagation.

compiler phases—be they optimizations or other tasks, such as lowering the level of the code from one form to another—have to process.

3. Instruction scheduling is recommended to be performed both before and after register allocation because the first pass takes advantage of the relative freedom of code with many symbolic registers, rather than few real registers, while the second pass includes any register spills and restores that may have been inserted by register allocation.

Finally, we must emphasize that implementing the full list of optimizations in the diagram results in a compiler that is both very aggressive at producing high-performance code for a single-processor system and that is quite large, but does not deal at all with issues such as code reorganization for parallel and vector machines.

1.6   Reading Flow Among the Chapters

There are several approaches one might take to reading this book, depending on your background, needs, and several other factors. Figure 1.9 shows some possible paths through the text, which we discuss below.

1. First, we suggest you read this chapter (as you're presumably already doing) and Chapter 2. They provide the introduction to the rest of the book and the definition of the language ICAN in which all algorithms in the book are written.

2. If you intend to read the whole book, we suggest reading the remaining chapters in order. While other orders are possible, this is the order the chapters were designed to be read.

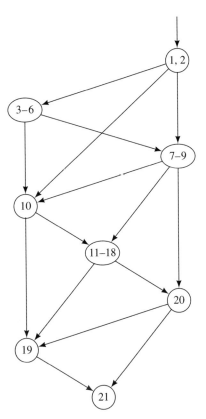

FIG. 1.9 Reading flow among the chapters in this book.

3. If you need more information on advanced aspects of the basics of compiler design and implementation, but may skip some of the other areas, we suggest you continue with Chapters 3 through 6.

4. If your primary concern is optimization, are you interested in data-related optimization for the memory hierarchy, as well as other kinds of optimization?

    (a) If yes, then continue with Chapters 7 through 10, followed by Chapters 11 through 18 and 20.

    (b) If not, then continue with Chapters 7 through 10, followed by Chapters 11 through 18.

5. If you are interested in interprocedural optimization, read Chapter 19, which covers interprocedural control-flow, data-flow, alias, and constant-propagation analyses, and several forms of interprocedural optimization, most notably interprocedural register allocation.

6. Then read Chapter 21, which provides descriptions of four production compiler suites from Digital Equipment Corporation, IBM, Intel, and Sun Microsystems and includes examples of other intermediate-code designs, choices and orders of

optimizations to perform, and techniques for performing optimizations and some of the other tasks that are parts of the compilation process. You may also wish to refer to the examples in Chapter 21 as you read the other chapters.

The three appendixes contain supporting material on the assembly languages used in the text, concrete representations of data structures, and access to resources for compiler projects via `ftp` and the World Wide Web.

1.7   Related Topics Not Covered in This Text

There is a series of other topics we might have covered in the text, but which we omit for a variety of reasons, such as not expanding the book beyond its already considerable size, having only tangential relationships to the primary subject matter, or being covered well in other texts. (In Section 1.11 we provide references that the reader can use as entry points to material on these areas.) These include, among other areas, the following:

1. The *interaction of optimization and debugging* is an area that has been under investigation since about 1980. Progress has been relatively slow, but there is an impressive body of work by now. The work of Adl-Tabatabai and Gross and of Wismüller provides excellent entry points into the literature.

2. *Parallelization and vectorization* and their relationship to scalar optimization are not covered because they would require a lot more space and because there are already several good texts on parallelization and vectorization, for example, those by Wolfe, Banerjee, and Zima and Chapman. However, the technique of dependence analysis covered in Chapter 9 and the loop transformations discussed in Section 20.4.2 are fundamental to parallelization and vectorization.

3. *Profiling feedback to the compilation process* is important and is referred to several times in the remainder of the book. A good introduction to the techniques, interpretation of their results, and their application in compilers can be found in the work of Ball and Larus and of Wall, along with references to previous work.

1.8   Target Machines Used in Examples

Most of our examples of target-machine code are in SPARC assembly language. We use a simplified version that does not have register windows. Occasionally there are examples for SPARC-V9 or in other assembly languages, such as for POWER or the Intel 386 architecture family. In all cases, the assembly languages are described well enough in Appendix A to enable one to read the examples.

1.9   Number Notations and Data Sizes

The terms *byte* and *word* are usually reserved for the natural sizes of a character and a register datum on a particular system. Since we are concerned primarily with 32-bit systems with 8-bit bytes and with 64-bit systems designed as extensions of

TABLE 1.1 Sizes of data types.

Term	Size (bits)
Byte	8
Halfword	16
Word	32
Doubleword	64
Quadword	128

32-bit systems, we use these and other terms for storage sizes uniformly as shown in Table 1.1.

Almost all the numbers in this book are in decimal notation and are written in the ordinary way. We occasionally use hexadecimal notation, however. An integer represented in hexadecimal is written as "0x" followed by a string of hexadecimal digits (namely, 0–9 and either a–f or A–F) and is always to be interpreted as an unsigned number (unless it is specifically indicated to represent a signed value) of length equal to the number of the leftmost one bit counting the rightmost as number one. For example, 0x3a is an 8-bit representation of the number 58 and 0xfffffffe is a 32-bit representation of the number $4294967294 = 2^{32} - 2$.

1.10   Wrap-Up

In this chapter we have concentrated on reviewing some of the basic aspects of compilers and on providing a setting for launching into the chapters that follow.

After discussing what to expect in Chapters 3 through 6, which concern advanced aspects of what are generally considered elementary topics, we next described the importance of optimization; structures for optimizing compilers, including the mixed and low-level models; and the organization of optimizations in an aggressive optimizing compiler.

Next we discussed possible orderings for reading the remaining chapters, and concluded with a list of related topics not covered here, and short sections on target machines used in examples and on notations for numbers and the names we use for various data sizes.

The primary lessons to take away from this chapter are five in number, namely,

1. that there are advanced issues in what are usually considered elementary topics in compiler construction, such as dealing with imported and exported scopes, design or selection of intermediate languages, and position-independent code and shared code objects, that need to be taken into consideration in designing and building real-world compilers;

2. that there are several reasonable ways to organize both a compiler as a whole and the optimization components within it;

3. that there are two primary models (mixed and low-level) for dividing up the optimization process, that the low-level model is generally preferable, but that the one to choose varies with the circumstances of a particular compiler/optimization project;

4. that there are new optimizations and improved methods of performing traditional ones being developed continually; and

5. that there are important topics, such as debugging of optimized code and the integration of scalar optimization with parallelization and vectorization, that deserve careful study but are beyond the scope of this book.

1.11   Further Reading

Unlike the history of programming languages, for which there are two excellent books available, namely, [Wexe81] and [BerG95], there is very little published material on the history of compilers. A history of the very earliest stages of compiler development is given in Knuth [Knut62]; some more recent material is included in the two volumes noted above, i.e., [Wexe81] and [BerG95].

Among the better recent introductory texts on compiler construction are [AhoS86] and [FisL91].

Name mangling, as used in the encoding of C++ programs as C programs, is described as the "function name encoding scheme" in [Stro88].

[GhoM86] describes the origins, structure, and function of the Sun global optimizer, and [JohM86] describes the structure and performance of the Hewlett-Packard global optimizer for PA-RISC.

Srivastava and Wall's OM system is described in [SriW93].

A starting reference to Adl-Tabatabai and Gross's work on optimization and debugging is [AdlG93]. Wismüller's [Wism94] is a reference to another thread of work in this area.

The texts available on compiling for parallel systems are [Bane88], [Bane93], [Bane94], [Wolf96], and [ZimC91].

The work of Ball and Larus on profiling is covered in [BalL92]. Wall's work in [Wall91] concerns the effect of feedback from profiling on recompilation and the resulting performance effects.

1.12   Exercises

1.1 Determine and describe the large-scale structure and intermediate codes of a compiler in use in your computing environment. What sections of the compiler are optionally executed under user control?

RSCH 1.2 Pick a paper from among [GhoM86], [JohM86], [SriW93], [AdlG93], [Wism94], [BalL92], and [Wall91] and write a three- to five-page synopsis of the issues or problems it concerns, the findings or conclusions, and the support for them offered in the paper.

CHAPTER 2

Informal Compiler Algorithm Notation (ICAN)

I n this chapter we discuss ICAN, the Informal Compiler Algorithm Notation we use in this text to express compiler algorithms. First we discuss the extended Backus-Naur form that is used to express the syntax of both ICAN and the intermediate languages discussed in the following chapter. Next we provide an introduction to the language and its relationship to common programming languages, an informal overview of the language, and then a formal description of the syntax of ICAN and an informal English description of its semantics. It is hoped that, in general, the informal overview will be sufficient for the reader to understand ICAN programs, but the full definition is provided to deal with those instances where it is not.

2.1 Extended Backus–Naur Form Syntax Notation

To describe the syntax of programming languages we use a version of Backus-Naur Form that we call Extended Backus-Naur Form, or XBNF. In XBNF terminals are written in `typewriter font` (e.g., "type" and "["), nonterminals are written in *italic font* with initial capital letters and other uppercase letters interspersed for readability (e.g., "*ProgUnit*", not "*Progunit*"). A production consists of a nonterminal followed by a long right arrow ("$\longrightarrow$") and a sequence of nonterminals, terminals, and operators. The symbol "ϵ" represents the empty string of characters.

The operators are listed in Table 2.1. The operators superscript "*", superscript "+", and "$\bowtie$" all have higher precedence than concatenation, which has higher precedence than alternation "|". The curly braces "{" . . . "}" and square brackets "[" . . . "]" act as grouping operators, in addition to brackets indicating that what they contain is optional. Note that the XBNF operators are written in our ordinary text font. When the same symbols appear in `typewriter font`, they are terminal symbols in the language being defined. Thus, for example,

TABLE 2.1 Operators used in Extended Backus-Naur Form syntax descriptions.

Symbol	Meaning
|	Separates alternatives
{ and }	Grouping
[and]	Optional
*	Zero or more repetitions
+	One or more repetitions
⋈	One or more repetitions of the left operand separated by occurrences of the right operand

$$KnittingInst \longrightarrow \{\{\texttt{knit} \mid \texttt{purl}\}\ Integer \mid \texttt{castoff}\}^{+}$$

describes a *KnittingInst* as a sequence of one or more of any of three possibilities, namely, knit followed by an integer, purl followed by an integer, or castoff; and

$$Wall \longrightarrow \texttt{brick} \bowtie \texttt{mortar} \mid \texttt{cementblock} \bowtie \texttt{mortar}$$

describes a *Wall* as a sequence of bricks separated (or, perhaps more appropriately, joined) by occurrences of mortar or as a sequence of cementblocks separated by occurrences of mortar.

As a more relevant example, consider

$$\begin{aligned} ArrayTypeExpr &\longrightarrow \texttt{array [} ArrayBounds \texttt{] of } TypeExpr \\ ArrayBounds &\longrightarrow \{[Expr]\ \cdot\cdot\ [Expr]\} \bowtie , \end{aligned}$$

The first line describes an *ArrayTypeExpr* as the keyword array, followed by a left bracket "[", followed by an occurrence of something that conforms to the syntax of *ArrayBounds*, followed by a right bracket "]", followed by the keyword of, followed by an occurrence of something conforming to the syntax of *TypeExpr*. The second line describes *ArrayBounds* as a series of one or more triples of the form of an optional *Expr*, followed by "··", followed by an optional *Expr*, with the triples separated by commas ",". The following are examples of *ArrayTypeExpr*s:

```
array [··] of integer
array [1··10] of real
array [1··2,1··2] of real
array [m··n+2] of boolean
```

2.2   Introduction to ICAN

Algorithms in this text are written in a relatively transparent, informal notation[1] called ICAN (Informal Compiler Algorithm Notation) that derives features from

---

1. One measure of the informality of ICAN is that many facets of the language that are considered to be errors, such as accessing an array with an out-of-range subscript, have their effects undefined.

```
 1      Struc: Node  ⟶  set of Node
 2
 3      procedure Example_1(N,r)
 4         N: in set of Node
 5         r: in Node
 6      begin
 7         change := true: boolean
 8         D, t: set of Node
 9         n, p: Node
10         Struc(r) := {r}
11         for each n ∈ N (n ≠ r) do
12            Struc(n) := N
13         od
14         while change do
15            change := false
16            for each n ∈ N - {r} do
17               t := N
18               for each p ∈ Pred[n] do
19                  t ∩= Struc(p)
20               od
21               D := {n} ∪ t
22               if D ≠ Struc(n) then
23                  change := true; Struc(n) := D
24               fi
25            od
26         od
27      end    || Example_1
```

FIG. 2.1 A sample ICAN global declaration and procedure (the line numbers at left are not part of the code).

several programming languages, such as C, Pascal, and Modula-2, and that extends them with natural notations for objects such as sets, tuples, sequences, functions, arrays, and compiler-specific types. Figures 2.1 and 2.2 give examples of ICAN code.

The syntax of ICAN is designed so that every variety of compound statement includes an ending delimiter, such as "fi" to end an if statement. As a result, separators are not needed between statements. However, as a convention to improve readability, when two or more statements are written on the same line we separate them with semicolons (Figure 2.1, line 23). Similarly, if a definition, declaration, or statement extends beyond a single line, the continuation lines are indented (Figure 2.2, lines 1 and 2 and lines 4 and 5).

A comment begins with the delimiter "||" and runs to the end of the line (Figure 2.1, line 27).

Lexically, an ICAN program is a sequence of ASCII characters. Tabs, comments, line ends, and sequences of one or more spaces are called "whitespace." Each occurrence of whitespace may be turned into a single space without affecting the meaning of a program. Keywords are preceded and followed by whitespace, but operators need not be.

```
1       webrecord = record {defs: set of Def,
2                           uses: set of Use}
3
4       procedure Example_2(nwebs,Symreg,nregs,
5          Edges) returns boolean
6          nwebs: inout integer
7          nregs: in integer
8          Symreg: out array [1··nwebs] of webrecord
9          Edges: out set of (integer × integer)
10      begin
11         s1, s2, r1, r2: integer
12         for r1 := 1 to nregs (odd(r1)) do
13             Symreg[nwebs+r1] := nil
14         od
15         Edges := ∅
16         for r1 := 1 to nregs do
17             for r2 := 1 to nregs do
18                 if r1 ≠ r2 then
19                     Edges ∪= {⟨nwebs+r1,nwebs+r2⟩}
20                 fi
21             od
22         od
23         for s1 := 1 to nwebs do
24             repeat
25                 case s1 of
26      1:              s2 := s1 * nregs
27      2:              s2 := s1 - 1
28      3:              s2 := nregs - nwebs
29                      return false
30      default:    s2 := 0
31                 esac
32             until s2 = 0
33             for r2 := 1 to nregs do
34                 if Interfere(Symreg[s1],r2) then
35                     goto L1
36                 fi
37             od
38  L1:    od
39         nwebs += nregs
40         return true
41      end    || Example_2
```

FIG. 2.2   A second example of ICAN code (the line numbers at left are not part of the code).

Lexical analysis proceeds left to right, and characters are accumulated to form tokens that are as long as they can be. Thus, for example, the code

```
for I37_6a:=-12 by 1 to n17a do
```

consists of nine tokens, as follows:

```
for   I37_6a   :=   -12   by   1   to   n17a   do
```

2.3   A Quick Overview of ICAN

In this section we give a quick overview of ICAN, which should be sufficient for the reader to begin reading and understanding programs in the text. The following sections define the syntax of the language formally and the semantics informally.

An ICAN program consists of a series of type definitions, followed by a series of variable declarations, followed by a series of procedure declarations, followed by an optional main program.

A type definition consists of a type name followed by an equals sign and a type expression, such as

```
intset = set of integer
```

Types may be either generic or compiler-specific, and either simple or constructed. The generic simple types are `boolean`, `integer`, `real`, and `character`. The type constructors are listed in the following table:

Constructor	Name	Example Declaration
enum	Enumeration	`enum {left,right}`
array ... of	Array	`array [1··10] of integer`
set of	Set	`set of MIRInst`
sequence of	Sequence	`sequence of boolean`
×	Tuple	`integer × set of real`
record	Record	`record {x: real, y: real}`
∪	Union	`integer ∪ boolean`
⟶	Function	`integer ⟶ set of real`

A variable declaration consists of the name of the variable, followed by an optional initialization, followed by a colon and the variable's type, e.g.,

```
is := {1,3,7}: intset
```

A procedure declaration consists of the procedure's name, followed by its parameter list in parentheses, followed by an optional return type, followed by its parameter declarations and its body. A parameter declaration consists of a comma-separated sequence of variable names; followed by a colon; one of `in` (call by value), `out` (call by result), or `inout` (call by value-result); and the type of the parameters. A procedure body consists of the keyword `begin`, followed by a series of variable declarations, followed by a series of statements, followed by the keyword `end`. For example, Figures 2.1, 2.2, and 2.3 all give examples of procedure declarations.

An expression is either a constant, a variable, `nil`, a unary operator followed by an expression, two expressions separated by a binary operator, a parenthesized expression, an array expression, a sequence expression, a set expression, a tuple expression, a record expression, a procedure or function call, an array element, a tuple element, a record field, a size expression, or a quantified expression. The operands and operators must be of compatible types.

```
procedure exam(x,y,is) returns boolean
   x, y: out integer
   is: in intset
begin
   tv := true: boolean
   z: integer
   for each z ∈ is (z > 0) do
      if x = z then
         return tv
      fi
   od
   return y ∈ is
end     || exam
```

FIG. 2.3 An example ICAN procedure declaration.

The operators appropriate to specific types may be found in Section 2.7. A few of the less obvious ones are discussed below. The following are examples of constants of constructed types:

Type	Example Constant
array [1··2,1··2] of real	[[1.0,2.0],[3.0,4.0]]
sequence of integer	[2,3,5,7,9,11]
integer × boolean	⟨3,true⟩
set of (integer × real)	{⟨3,3.0⟩,⟨2,2.0⟩}
record {x: real, y: real}	⟨x:1.0,y:-1.0⟩
(integer × real) ⟶ boolean	{⟨1,2.0,true⟩,⟨1,3.0,false⟩}

The integer and real types include ∞ and -∞. The empty set is denoted ∅ and the empty sequence []. The value nil is a member of every type and is the value of any uninitialized variable. The expression $|x|$ produces the size of x if x is a member of any constructed type—cardinality for sets, length for sequences, etc.

The unary operator "♦" when applied to a set yields an arbitrary member of the set. The expression $sq \downarrow i$ yields the ith member of the sequence sq, $sq1 \oplus sq2$ yields the concatenation of $sq1$ and $sq2$, and $sq \ominus i$ yields sq with the ith element removed; if i is negative, it counts backward from the end of sq. The expression $tpl @ i$ yields the ith element of tuple tpl.

Compiler-specific types are defined as needed. For example,

```
Block = array [··] of array [··] of MIRInst
Edge = Node × Node
```

Statements include assignments, calls, returns, gotos, ifs, cases; and for, while, and repeat loops. The basic assignment operator is ":=". As in C, the colon may be replaced by any binary operator whose left-hand operand and result have the same type; for example, the following assignments both do the same thing:

```
Seq := Seq ⊕ [9,11]
Seq ⊕= [9,11]
```

Each compound statement has an ending delimiter. The beginning, internal, and ending delimiters of the compound statements are as follows:

Beginning	Internal	Ending
if	elif, else	fi
case	of, default	esac
for	do	od
while	do	od
repeat		until

Case labels are also internal delimiters in case statements.

All keywords used in the language are reserved—they may not be used as identifiers. They are listed in Table 2.8.

The following sections describe ICAN in detail.

2.4   Whole Programs

An ICAN program consists of a series of type definitions, followed by a series of variable declarations, followed by a series of procedure declarations, followed by an optional main program. The main program has the form of a procedure body. The syntax of ICAN programs is given in Table 2.2.

TABLE 2.2   Syntax of whole ICAN programs.

Program	$\longrightarrow$	*TypeDef* VarDecl* ProcDecl* [MainProg]*
MainProg	$\longrightarrow$	*ProcBody*

2.5   Type Definitions

A type definition consists of one or more pairs of a type name followed by an equals sign "=", followed by the definition (Figure 2.2, lines 1 and 2). The syntax of type definitions is given in Table 2.3. Type definitions may be recursive. The type defined by a recursive type definition is the smallest set that satisfies the definition, i.e., it is the least fixed point of the definition. For example, the type defined by

```
IntPair = integer ∪ (IntPair × IntPair)
```

is the set containing all integers and all pairs each of whose elements is either an integer or a pair of elements of the type.

TABLE 2.3 Syntax of ICAN type definitions.

TypeDef	$\longrightarrow$	{*TypeName* =}* *TypeExpr*
TypeName	$\longrightarrow$	*Identifier*
TypeExpr	$\longrightarrow$	*SimpleTypeExpr* | *ConstrTypeExpr* | (*TypeExpr*)
		| *TypeName* | $\emptyset$
SimpleTypeExpr	$\longrightarrow$	`boolean` | `integer` | `real` | `character`
ConstrTypeExpr	$\longrightarrow$	*EnumTypeExpr* | *ArrayTypeExpr* | *SetTypeExpr*
		| *SequenceTypeExpr* | *TupleTypeExpr* | *RecordTypeExpr*
		| *UnionTypeExpr* | *FuncTypeExpr*
EnumTypeExpr	$\longrightarrow$	`enum {` *Identifier* $\bowtie$ `, }`
ArrayTypeExpr	$\longrightarrow$	`array [` *ArrayBounds* `] of` *TypeExpr*
ArrayBounds	$\longrightarrow$	{[*Expr*] $\cdots$ [*Expr*]} $\bowtie$,
SetTypeExpr	$\longrightarrow$	`set of` *TypeExpr*
SequenceTypeExpr	$\longrightarrow$	`sequence of` *TypeExpr*
TupleTypeExpr	$\longrightarrow$	*TypeExpr* $\bowtie$ ×
RecordTypeExpr	$\longrightarrow$	`record {` {*Identifier* $\bowtie$, : *TypeExpr*} $\bowtie$ `, }`
UnionTypeExpr	$\longrightarrow$	*TypeExpr* $\bowtie$ ∪
FuncTypeExpr	$\longrightarrow$	*TypeExpr* $\bowtie$ × $\longrightarrow$ [*TypeExpr* | $\emptyset$]

2.6   Declarations

The syntax of ICAN variable and procedure declarations is given in Table 2.4. The syntax includes the nonterminal *ConstExpr*, which is not defined in the grammar. It denotes an expression none of whose components is a variable.

A variable declaration consists of the name of the identifier being declared followed by an optional initialization, followed by a colon and its type (Figure 2.1, lines 1, 4, 5, and 7 through 9). An array's dimensions are part of its type and are specified by placing a list of the ranges of values of each of the subscripts in square

TABLE 2.4 Syntax of ICAN declarations.

VarDecl	$\longrightarrow$	{*Variable* [:= *ConstExpr*]} $\bowtie$, : *TypeExpr*
Variable	$\longrightarrow$	*Identifier*
ProcDecl	$\longrightarrow$	`procedure` *ProcName* *ParamList* [`returns` *TypeExpr*]
		ParamDecls *ProcBody*
ProcName	$\longrightarrow$	*Identifier*
ParamList	$\longrightarrow$	([*Parameter* $\bowtie$,])
Parameter	$\longrightarrow$	*Identifier*
ParamDecls	$\longrightarrow$	*ParamDecl**
ParamDecl	$\longrightarrow$	*Variable* $\bowtie$, : {`in` | `out` | `inout`} *TypeExpr*
ProcBody	$\longrightarrow$	`begin` *VarDecl** *Statement** `end`

brackets after the keyword `array` (Figure 2.2, line 8). An initial value for an identifier is specified by following it with the assignment operator ":=" and the value (which may be any expression constructed solely from constants, as long as it is of the right type) following the identifier (Figure 2.1, line 7). Several identifiers of the same type may be declared in a single declaration by separating their names and optional initializations with commas (Figure 2.1, lines 8 and 9).

A procedure is declared by the keyword `procedure` followed by its name, followed by a series of parameters in parentheses, followed by an optional return type, followed by a series of indented lines that declare the types of the parameters (Figure 2.1, lines 4 and 5), followed by the procedure's body (Figure 2.1, lines 6 through 27). The return type consists of the keyword `returns` followed by a type expression (Figure 2.2, line 5). Parameters are declared "`in`" (call by value), "`out`" (call by result), or "`inout`" (call by value-result) (see Figure 2.2, lines 6 through 9). A procedure's text is indented between the keywords `begin` and `end` (Figure 2.1, lines 6 and 27).

A type definition or variable declaration may be made global to a group of procedures by placing it before their declarations (Figure 2.1, line 1 and Figure 2.2, lines 1 and 2).

2.7   Data Types and Expressions

The syntax of ICAN expressions and generic simple constants are given in Tables 2.5 and 2.6, respectively.

TABLE 2.5   Syntax of ICAN expressions.

Expr	$\longrightarrow$	*Variable* | *SimpleConst* | (*Expr*) | *UnaryOper Expr*
		| *Expr BinaryOper Expr* | *ArrayExpr* | *SequenceExpr*
		| *SetExpr* | *TupleExpr* | *RecordExpr* | *ProcFuncExpr*
		| *ArrayEltExpr* | *SizeExpr* | *QuantExpr* | *Expr* ∈ *TypeExpr*
		| nil
UnaryOper	$\longrightarrow$	! | − | ♦
BinaryOper	$\longrightarrow$	= | ≠ | & | ∨ | + | − | * | / | % | ↑ | < | ≤ | > | ≥ | ∪ | ∩
		| ∈ | ∉ | ⊕ | ↓ | ⊖ | @ | .
ArrayExpr	$\longrightarrow$	[*Expr* ⋈ ,]
SequenceExpr	$\longrightarrow$	[*Expr* ⋈ ,] | " *ASCIICharacter** "
SetExpr	$\longrightarrow$	∅ | { *Expr* ⋈ , | [*Variable* ∈] *Expr* where *SetDefClause* }
TupleExpr	$\longrightarrow$	⟨ *Expr* ⋈ , ⟩
RecordExpr	$\longrightarrow$	⟨ {*Identifier* : *Expr*} ⋈ , ⟩
ProcFuncExpr	$\longrightarrow$	*ProcName ArgList*
ArgList	$\longrightarrow$	([*Expr* ⋈ ,])
ArrayEltExpr	$\longrightarrow$	*Expr* [*Expr* ⋈ ,]
QuantExpr	$\longrightarrow$	{∃ | ∀} *Variable* ∈ [*Expr* | *TypeExpr*] (*Expr*)
SizeExpr	$\longrightarrow$	| *Expr* |

TABLE 2.6 Syntax of ICAN constants of generic simple types.

SimpleConst	$\longrightarrow$	*IntConst* | *RealConst* | *BoolConst* | *CharConst*
IntConst	$\longrightarrow$	0 | [-] *NZDigit Digit** | [-] ∞
NZDigit	$\longrightarrow$	1 | 2 | 3 | 4 | 5 | 6 | 7 | 8 | 9
Digit	$\longrightarrow$	0 | *NZDigit*
RealConst	$\longrightarrow$	[-] {*IntConst* . [*IntConst*] | [*IntConst*] . *IntConst*}
		[E *IntConst*] | [-] ∞
BoolConst	$\longrightarrow$	true | false
CharConst	$\longrightarrow$	' *ASCIICharacter* '
Identifier	$\longrightarrow$	*Letter* {*Letter* | *Digit* | _ }*
Letter	$\longrightarrow$	a | ... | z | A | ... | Z

A type corresponds to the set of its members. It may be either simple or constructed. Also, a type may be generic or compiler-specific.

The generic simple types are boolean, integer, real, and character.

A constructed type is defined by using one or more type constructors. The type constructors are enum, array ... of, set of, sequence of, record, "∪", "×", and "→". The symbol "∪" constructs union types, "×" constructs tuple types, and "→" constructs function types.

An expression is either a constant, a variable, nil, a unary operator followed by an expression, two expressions separated by a binary operator, a parenthesized expression, an array expression, a sequence expression, a set expression, a tuple expression, a record expression, a procedure or function call, an array element, a quantified expression, or a size expression. The operands and operators must be of compatible types, as described below.

2.7.1   Generic Simple Types

The Boolean values are true and false. The following binary operators apply to Booleans:

Operation	Symbol
Equals	=
Not equals	≠
Logical and	&
Logical or	∨

The prefix unary operator negation "!" applies to Booleans.

A quantified expression is Boolean-valued. It consists of the symbol "∃" or "∀" followed by a variable, followed by "∈", followed by a type- or set-valued expression, followed by a parenthesized Boolean-valued expression. For example,

```
∃v ∈ Var (Opnd(inst,v))
```

is a quantified expression that evaluates to true if and only if there is some variable v such that Opnd(inst,v) is true.

An integer value is either 0, an optional minus sign followed by a series of one or more decimal digits the first of which is nonzero, ∞, or $-\infty$.

A real value is an integer followed by a period, followed by an integer (either but not both of the integers may be absent), followed by an optional exponent, ∞, or $-\infty$.[2] An exponent is the letter "E" followed by an integer.

The following binary operators apply to finite integers and reals:

Operation	Symbol
Plus	+
Minus	−
Times	*
Divide	/
Modulo	%
Exponentiation	↑
Equals	=
Not equals	≠
Less than	<
Less than or equal to	≤
Greater than	>
Greater than or equal to	≥

The prefix unary operator negation "−" applies to finite integers and reals. Only the relational operators apply to infinite values.

A character value is an allowed ASCII character enclosed in single quotation marks, e.g., 'a' or 'G'. The allowed ASCII characters (represented by the otherwise undefined nonterminal *ASCIICharacter* in the syntax) are all the printing ASCII characters, space, tab, and carriage return. Several of the characters require escape sequences to represent them, as follows:

Escape Sequence	Meaning
%r	Carriage return
%"	"
%'	'
%%	%

The binary operators equals ("=") and not equals ("≠") apply to characters.

2.7.2   Enumerated Types

An enumerated type is a non-empty finite set of identifiers. A variable *var* is declared to be of an enumerated type by a declaration of the form

$$var: \text{enum } \{element_1, \ldots, element_n\}$$

where each *element$_i$* is an identifier.

---

2. ICAN real values are *not* floating-point numbers—they are mathematical real numbers.

The following example declares `action` to be a variable of an enumerated type:

```
action: enum {Shift, Reduce, Accept, Error}
```

The binary operators equals ("=") and not equals ("≠") apply to members of an enumerated type.

Elements of an enumerated type may appear as case labels (see Section 2.8.6).

2.7.3 Arrays

A variable *var* is declared to be of an array type by a declaration of the form

> *var*: array [*subslist*] of *basetype*

where *subslist* is a comma-separated list of subscript ranges, each of which may be just "··", and *basetype* is the type of the array's elements. For example, the code fragment

```
U: array [5··8] of real
V: array [1··2,1··3] of real
      .
      .
      .
U := [1.0,0.1,0.01,0.001]
V := [[1.0,2.0,3.0],[4.0,5.0,6.0]]
```

declares U to be a one-dimensional array whose subscript ranges over the integers 5 through 8, and V to be a two-dimensional array whose first subscript ranges over the integers 1 through 2, whose second subscript ranges over the integers 1 through 3, and both of whose elements are of type `real`. It also assigns particular array constants to be their values.

Of course, an array may be viewed as a finite function from the product of some number of copies of the integers to another type.

A constant of a one-dimensional array type is a comma-separated series of constants of the element type, enclosed in square brackets, whose length is $hi - lo + 1$, where *lo* and *hi* are the minimal and maximal subscript values. A constant of an *n*-dimensional array type for $n > 1$ is a comma-separated series of constants in square brackets whose type is that of the $(n - 1)$-dimensional array obtained by deleting the first subscript. The series is enclosed in square brackets and its length is $hi - lo + 1$, where *lo* and *hi* are the minimal and maximal values of the first subscript. Thus, arrays are represented in row-major order.

The binary operators equals ("=") and not equals ("≠") apply to whole arrays. An array-valued expression of dimension *n* followed by a comma-separated list of at most *n* subscript values enclosed in square brackets is an expression.

Note that the two array types

```
array [1··10,1··10] of integer
array [1··10] of array [1··10] of integer
```

are different, even though constants of the two types are indistinguishable. The first is a two-dimensional array, and the second is a one-dimensional array of one-dimensional arrays.

2.7.4   Sets

A variable *var* of a set type may have as its value any subset of its base type declared as follows:

    var: set of *basetype*

where *basetype* is the type of the set's elements.

A set constant is either the empty set "∅", a comma-separated series of elements enclosed by left and right curly braces, or an intentionally defined set constant. The elements must all be of the same type. For example, the following are set constants:

    ∅   {1}   {1,2,100}   {⟨true,1.0⟩,⟨false,-2.3⟩}
    {n ∈ integer where 0 ≤ n & n ≤ 20 & n % 2 = 0}

Further, in the program fragment

    B: set of integer
    B := {1,4,9,16}
    B := {n ∈ integer where ∃m ∈ integer (1 ≤ m & m ≤ 4 & n = m * m)}

both assignments are valid, and both assign the same value to B.

The following binary operators apply to sets:

Operation	Symbol
Union	∪
Intersection	∩
Difference	−
Member of	∈
Not member of	∉

The last two of these, "∈" and "∉", take a value of a type *ty* as their left operand and a value of type "set of *ty*" as their right operand, and produce a Boolean result. For "∈", the result is true if the left operand is a member of the right operand and false otherwise. For "∉", the result is false if the left operand is a member of the right and true otherwise.

The prefix unary operator "♦" selects, at random, an element from its set operand, and the selected element is the result, e.g., ♦{1,2,7} may have any of 1, 2, or 7 as its value.

Note that the binary operator "∈" and the same symbol used in for-loop iterators are different. The former produces a Boolean value, while the latter is part of a larger expression that generates a sequence of values, as shown in Figure 2.4. The code in (a) is equivalent in meaning to that in (b), where Tmp is a new temporary of the same type as A.

The otherwise undefined nonterminal *SetDefClause* in the syntax description is a clause that defines the members of a set intentionally, such as the text between where and "}" in the following code:

    S := {n ∈ N where ∃e ∈ E (e@2 = n)}

```
                          Tmp := A
for each a ∈ A do         while Tmp ≠ ∅ do
     body                      a := ◆Tmp
od                             Tmp -= {a}
                               body
                          od
(a)                       (b)
```

FIG. 2.4 (a) An ICAN for loop that iterates over a set, and (b) equivalent code using a while loop.

Note that a set definition containing a *SetDefClause* can always be replaced by a nest of loops, such as the following for the assignment above, assuming that the type of E is the product of the type of N with itself:

```
S := ∅
for each n ∈ N do
     for each e ∈ E do
          if e@2 = n then
               S ∪= {n}
          fi
     od
od
```

2.7.5   Sequences

A variable *var* is declared to be of a sequence type by a declaration of the form

   var: sequence of *basetype*

where *basetype* is the element type of the sequences that may be *var*'s value.

A constant of a sequence type is a finite comma-separated series of members of its base type enclosed in square brackets. The elements must all be of the same type. The empty sequence is denoted "[]". For example, the following are sequence constants:

   []   [1]   [1,2,1]   [true,false]

Sequence concatenation is represented by the binary operator "⊕". The binary operator "↓" when applied to a sequence and a nonzero integer selects an element of the sequence; in particular, the positive integer n selects the nth element of the sequence, and the negative integer $-n$ selects the nth element from the end of the sequence. For example, $[2,3,5,7] \downarrow 2 = 3$ and $[2,3,5,7] \downarrow -2 = 5$. The binary operator ⊖ when applied to a sequence s and a nonzero integer n produces a copy of the sequence with the nth element removed. For example, $[2,3,5,7] \ominus 2 = [2,5,7]$ and $[2,3,5,7] \ominus -2 = [2,3,7]$.

The type CharString is an abbreviation for sequence of character. For example, "ab CD" is identical to ['a','b',' ','C','D']. The empty CharString is denoted interchangeably by [] and by "", and for any character x, ['x'] = "x".

Note that the array constants are a subset of the sequence constants—the only difference is that in an array constant, all members at each nesting level must have the same length.

2.7.6   Tuples

A variable *var* is declared to be of a tuple type by a declaration of the form

$$var: basetype_1 \times \ldots \times basetype_n$$

where $basetype_i$ is the type of the ith component.

A tuple constant is a fixed-length comma-separated series enclosed in angle brackets. As an example of a tuple type, consider

```
integer × integer × boolean
```

An element of this type is a triple whose first and second elements are integers and whose third element is a Boolean, such as ⟨1,7,true⟩. The following are also examples of tuple constants:

⟨1⟩   ⟨1,2,true⟩   ⟨true,false⟩

The binary operator @ when applied to a tuple and a positive integer index produces the element of the tuple with that index. Thus, for example, ⟨1,2,true⟩@3 = true.

2.7.7   Records

A variable *var* is declared to be of a record type by a declaration of the form

$$var: \text{record } \{idents_1 : basetype_1, \ldots, idents_n : basetype_n\}$$

where $idents_i$ is a comma-separated list of component selectors and $basetype_i$ is the corresponding components' type.

A record constant is a tuple, each of whose elements is a pair consisting of an identifier (called the *selector*) and a value, separated by a colon. All values of a particular record type must have the same set of identifiers and, for each identifier, the values must be of the same type, but the values corresponding to different selectors may be of different types. For example, the type ibpair defined by the type definition

```
ibpair = record {int: integer,
                 bool: boolean}
```

has as its members pairs of the form ⟨int:i,bool:b⟩, where i is an integer and b is a Boolean. The order of the pairs in a member of a record type is immaterial; thus, for example, ⟨int:3,bool:true⟩ and ⟨bool:true,int:3⟩ are identical record constants. The following are also examples of record constants:

⟨rl:1.0,im:-1.0⟩   ⟨left:1,right:2,val:true⟩

The binary operator "." when applied to a record and an expression whose value is one of the record's selectors produces the corresponding component's value. For example, in the code sequence

```
ibpair = record {int: integer,
                 bool: boolean}
. . .
b: boolean
ibp: ibpair
. . .
ibp := ⟨int:2,bool:true⟩
ibp.int := 3
b := ibp.bool
```

the final values of ibp and b are ⟨int:3,bool:true⟩ and true, respectively.

2.7.8   Unions

A union type is the union of the sets of values in the types that make up the union. A variable *var* is declared to be of a union type by a declaration of the form

$$var: \; basetype_1 \; \cup \; \ldots \; \cup \; basetype_n$$

where $basetype_i$ ranges over the types of the sets making up the union type.

As an example of a union type, consider integer ∪ boolean. An element of this type is either an integer or a Boolean.

All the operators that apply to sets apply to unions. If the sets making up a union type are disjoint, then the set an element of the union belongs to may be determined by using the "member of" operator "∈".

2.7.9   Functions

A function type has a *domain* type (written to the left of the arrow) and a *range* type (written to the right of the arrow).

A variable *var* is declared to be of a function type by a declaration of the form

$$var: \; basetype_1 \; \times \; \ldots \; \times \; basetype_n \; \longrightarrow \; basetype_0$$

where for $i = 1, \ldots, n$, $basetype_i$ is the type of the ith component of the domain and $basetype_0$ is the type of the range.

A function constant with n argument positions is a set each of whose elements is an $(n + 1)$-tuple whose first n members are of the 1st through n^{th} domain types, respectively, and whose $(n + 1)^{st}$ member is of the range type. To be a function, the set of tuples must be *one-to-one*, i.e., if two tuples have the same first n members, they must have the same $(n + 1)^{st}$ member also.

As an example of a function type, consider boolean ⟶ integer. A variable or constant of this type is a set of pairs whose first member is a Boolean and whose second is an integer. It may also be expressed by an assignment or assignments involving the name of the type. Thus, given the declaration

    A: boolean ⟶ integer

we could write, for example, either

    A := {⟨true,3⟩,⟨false,2⟩}

or

    A(true) := 3
    A(false) := 2

to assign a particular function to be the value of A.

A function need not have a defined value for every element of its domain.

2.7.10 Compiler-Specific Types

The compiler-specific types are all named with an uppercase initial letter and are introduced as needed in the text. They may be either simple or constructed, as necessary. For example, the types Var, Vocab, and Operator are all simple types, while the types Procedure, Block, and Edge defined by

    Block = array [··] of array [··] of MIRInst
    Procedure = Block
    Edge = Node × Node

are constructed. The type MIRInst is also constructed and is defined in Section 4.6.1.

2.7.11 The Value nil

The value nil is a member of every type. It is the value of any variable that has not been initialized. In most contexts, using it as an operand in an expression causes the result to be nil. For example, 3 + nil equals nil.

The only expressions in which using nil as an operand in an expression does not produce nil as the result are equality and inequality comparisons, as follows:

Expression	Result
nil = nil	true
a = nil	false
nil ≠ nil	false
a ≠ nil	true

where a is any value other than nil.

In addition, nil may appear as the right-hand side of an assignment (Figure 2.2, line 13) and as an argument to or return value from a procedure.

2.7.12   The Size Operator

The operator "| |" applies to objects of all constructed types. In each case, its value is the number of elements in its argument, as long as its argument is of finite size. For example, if A is declared to be

```
A: array [1··5,1··5] of boolean
```

and f is declared and defined to be

```
f: integer × integer ⟶ boolean
.  .  .
f(1,1) := true
f(1,2) := false
f(3,4) := true
```

then

```
|{1,7,23}| = 3
|['a','b','e','c','b']| = 5
|⟨rl:1.0,im:-1.0⟩| = 2
|A| = 25
|f| = 3
```

If x is of infinite size, $|x|$ is undefined.

2.8   Statements

Statements include assignments (e.g., Figure 2.1, lines 12 and 19), procedure and function calls (Figure 2.1, line 19 and Figure 2.2, line 34), returns (Figure 2.2, lines 29 and 40), gotos (Figure 2.2, line 35), ifs (Figure 2.1, lines 22 through 24), cases (Figure 2.2, lines 25 through 31), and for loops (Figure 2.1, lines 16 through 25), while loops (Figure 2.1, lines 14 through 26), and repeat loops (Figure 2.2, lines 24 through 32). Their syntax is given in Table 2.7.

A statement may be labeled (Figure 2.2, line 38) with an identifier followed by a colon.

Each structured statement's body is delimited by keywords, such as if and fi.

2.8.1   Assignment Statements

An assignment statement consists of a series of one or more left-hand parts, each followed by an assignment operator, and a right-hand part (Figure 2.1, lines 10, 12, 15, 19, and 21). Each left-hand part may be a variable name or the name of an element of a variable, such as a member of a record, array, sequence, or tuple, or a function value. The assignment operator in each of the left-hand parts except the last must be ":=". The last assignment operator may be either ":=" (Figure 2.1, lines 10 and 17 and Figure 2.2, lines 26 through 28) or an extended assignment operator in which the colon is replaced by a binary operator whose left-hand operand and result have the same type (Figure 2.1, line 19 and Figure 2.2, lines 19 and 39). For example, all the assignments in the following code are legal:

TABLE 2.7 Syntax of ICAN statements.

Statement	$\longrightarrow$	*AssignStmt* | *ProcFuncStmt* | *ReturnStmt*
		| *GotoStmt* | *IfStmt* | *CaseStmt* | *WhileStmt*
		| *ForStmt* | *RepeatStmt* | *Label* : *Statement*
		| *Statement* ;
Label	$\longrightarrow$	*Identifier*
AssignStmt	$\longrightarrow$	{*LeftSide* :=}* *LeftSide* {: | *BinaryOper*} = *Expr*
LeftSide	$\longrightarrow$	*Variable* | *ArrayElt* | *SequenceElt* | *TupleElt* | *RecordElt*
		| *FuncElt*
ArrayElt	$\longrightarrow$	*LeftSide* [*Expr* ⋈ ,]
SequenceElt	$\longrightarrow$	*LeftSide* ↓ *Expr*
TupleElt	$\longrightarrow$	*LeftSide* @ *Expr*
RecordElt	$\longrightarrow$	*LeftSide* . *Expr*
FuncElt	$\longrightarrow$	*LeftSide* *ArgList*
ProcFuncStmt	$\longrightarrow$	*ProcFuncExpr*
ReturnStmt	$\longrightarrow$	return [*Expr*]
GotoStmt	$\longrightarrow$	goto *Label*
IfStmt	$\longrightarrow$	if *Expr* then *Statement** {elif *Statement**}*
		[else *Statement**] fi
CaseStmt	$\longrightarrow$	case *Expr* of {*CaseLabel* : *Statement**}$^+$
		[default : *Statement**] esac
WhileStmt	$\longrightarrow$	while *Expr* do *Statement** od
ForStmt	$\longrightarrow$	for *Iterator* do *Statement** od
Iterator	$\longrightarrow$	{*Variable* := *Expr* [by *Expr*] to *Expr*
		| each *Variable* ⋈ , ∈ {*Expr* | *TypeExpr*}} [(*Expr*)]
RepeatStmt	$\longrightarrow$	repeat *Statement** until *Expr*

```
recex = record {lt,rt: boolean}
i, j: integer
f: integer ⟶ (boolean ⟶ integer)
g: integer ⟶ sequence of recex
p: sequence of integer
t: boolean × boolean
r: recex
. . .
i := 3
j := i += 1
f(3)(true) := true
g(0)↓2.lt := true
p↓2 := 3
t@1 := true
r.rt := r.lt := false
```

The right-hand part may be any type-compatible expression (see Section 2.7). The left- and right-hand parts of an assignment must be of the same type when an extended assignment operator is expanded to its ordinary form. The right-hand side following an extended assignment operator is evaluated as if it had parentheses around it. For example, the assignment

```
S := S1 ∪= {a} ∩ X
```

is equivalent to

```
S := S1 := S1 ∪ ({a} ∩ X)
```

which, in turn, is equivalent to

```
S1 := S1 ∪ ({a} ∩ X)
S  := S1
```

and not to

```
S1 := (S1 ∪ {a}) ∩ X
S  := S1
```

2.8.2   Procedure Call Statements

A procedure call statement has the form of a procedure expression, i.e., *ProcFuncExpr* in Table 2.5. It consists of a procedure name followed by a parenthesized list of arguments separated by commas. It causes the named procedure to be invoked with the given arguments.

2.8.3   Return Statements

A return statement consists of the keyword `return` followed optionally by an expression.

2.8.4   Goto Statements

A goto statement consists of the keyword `goto` followed by a label.

2.8.5   If Statements

An if statement has the form

```
if condition₀ then
    then_body
elif condition₁ then
    elif_body₁
    . . .
elif conditionₙ then
    elif_bodyₙ
```

```
else
     else_body
fi
```

with the `elif` and `else` parts optional. The conditions are Boolean-valued expressions and are evaluated in the short-circuit manner, e.g., given $p \vee q$, q is evaluated if and only if p evaluates to `false`. Each of the bodies is a sequence of zero or more statements.

2.8.6   Case Statements

A case statement has the form

```
          case selector of
label₁:      body₁
label₂:      body₂
    . . .
labelₙ:      bodyₙ
default:  body₀
     esac
```

with the default part optional. Each label is a constant of the same type as the selector expression, which must be of a simple type or an enumerated type. Each body is a sequence of zero or more statements. As in Pascal, after executing one of the bodies, execution continues with the statement following the "esac" closing delimiter. There must be at least one non-`default` case label and corresponding body.

2.8.7   While Statements

A while statement has the form

```
while condition do
     while_body
od
```

The condition is a Boolean-valued expression and is evaluated in the short-circuit manner. The body is a sequence of zero or more statements.

2.8.8   For Statements

A for statement has the form

```
for iterator do
     for_body
od
```

The iterator may be numerical or enumerative. A numerical iterator specifies a variable, a range of values, and a parenthesized Boolean expression, such as "`i := n by -1 to 1 (A[i] = 0)`" (see Figure 2.2, lines 12 through 14). The "by" part is optional if it is "by 1". The Boolean expression is optional and, if not supplied, the value true is used. The value of the variable may not be changed in the body of the loop.

An enumerative iterator, such as "each n ∈ N (n ≠ abc)" (see Figure 2.1, lines 11 through 13 and lines 16 through 25), or "each p,q ∈ T (p ≠ q)", selects all and only the elements of its set operand that satisfy the parenthesized Boolean expression following the set operand, in an indeterminate order. If the parenthesized Boolean expression is missing, the value true is used. If the variable series has more than one element, they all must satisfy the same criteria. For example, "each m,n ∈ N (1 ≤ m & m ≤ n & n ≤ 2)" causes the pair of variables ⟨m,n⟩ to range over ⟨1,1⟩, ⟨1,2⟩, and ⟨2,2⟩, in some order. For any set S that appears in the iterator, the body of the for statement must not change S's value.

The body is a sequence of zero or more statements.

2.8.9   Repeat Statements

A repeat statement has the form

```
repeat
    repeat_body
until condition
```

The body is a sequence of zero or more statements. The condition is a Boolean-valued expression and is evaluated in the short-circuit manner.

2.8.10   Keywords in ICAN

The keywords in ICAN are given in Table 2.8. They are all reserved and may not be used as identifiers.

TABLE 2.8   The keywords in ICAN.

array	begin	boolean	by
case	character	default	do
each	elif	else	end
enum	esac	false	fi
for	goto	if	in
inout	integer	nil	od
of	out	procedure	real
record	repeat	return	returns
sequence	set	to	true
until	where	while	

2.9   Wrap-Up

This chapter is devoted to describing ICAN, the informal notation used to present algorithms in this book.

The language allows for a rich set of predefined and constructed types, including ones that are specific to compiler construction, and is an expressive notation for expressions and statements. Each compound statement has an ending delimiter, and some, such as while and case statements, have internal delimiters too.

The informality of the language lies primarily in its not being specific about the semantics of constructions that are syntactically valid but semantically ambiguous, undefined, or otherwise invalid.

2.10   Further Reading

There are no references for ICAN, as it was invented for use in this book.

2.11   Exercises

2.1 (a) Describe how to translate an XBNF syntax representation into a representation that uses only concatenation. (b) Apply your method to rewrite the XBNF description

$$
\begin{array}{lcl}
E & \longrightarrow & V \mid AE \mid (\ E\ ) \mid ST \mid SE \mid TE \\
AE & \longrightarrow & [\ \{\ E \mid \texttt{nil}\}\ ] \\
ST & \longrightarrow & "\ AC^+\ " \\
SE & \longrightarrow & \emptyset \mid \{\ E^*\ \} \\
TE & \longrightarrow & \langle\ E \bowtie\ ,\ \rangle
\end{array}
$$

2.2 Show that arrays, sets, records, tuples, products, and functions are all "syntactic sugar" in ICAN by describing how to implement them and their operations in a version of ICAN that does not include them (i.e., express the other type constructors in terms of the union and sequence constructors).

2.3 (a) Write an ICAN algorithm to run a maze. That is, given a set of nodes N ⊆ Node, a set of undirected arcs E ⊆ Node × Node, and start and finish nodes start, goal ∈ N, the algorithm should return a list of nodes that make up a path from start to goal, or nil if there is no such path. (b) What is the time complexity of your algorithm in terms of n = |N| and e = |E|?

2.4 Adapt your algorithm from the preceding exercise to solve the traveling salesman problem. That is, return a list of nodes beginning and ending with start that passes through every node other than start exactly once, or return nil if there is no such path.

2.5 Given a binary relation R on a set A, i.e., R ⊆ A × A, write an ICAN procedure RTC(R,x,y) to compute its reflexive transitive closure. The reflexive transitive closure of R, written R*, satisfies a R* b if and only if a = b or there exists a c such that a R c and c R* b, so RTC(R,x,y) returns true if x R* y and false otherwise.

ADV 2.6   We have purposely omitted pointers from ICAN because they present several serious issues that can be avoided entirely by excluding them. These include, for example, pointer aliasing, in which two or more pointers point to the same object, so that changing the referent of one of them affects the referents of the others also, and the possibility of creating circular structures, i.e., structures in which following a series of pointers can bring us back to where we started. On the other hand, excluding pointers may result in algorithms' being less efficient than they would otherwise be. Suppose we were to decide to extend ICAN to create a language, call it PICAN, that includes pointers. (a) List advantages and disadvantages of doing so. (b) Discuss the needed additions to the language and the issues these additions would create for programmers and implementers of the language.

CHAPTER 3

Symbol-Table Structure

In this chapter we explore issues involved in structuring symbol tables to accommodate the features of modern programming languages and to make them efficient for compiled implementations of the languages.

We begin with a discussion of the storage classes that symbols may belong to and the rules governing their visibility, or scope rules, in various parts of a program. Next we discuss symbol attributes and how to structure a local symbol table, i.e., one appropriate for a single scope. This is followed by a description of a representation for global symbol tables that includes importing and exporting of scopes, a programming interface to global and local symbol tables, and ICAN implementations of routines to generate loads and stores for variables according to their attributes.

3.1 Storage Classes, Visibility, and Lifetimes

Most programming languages allow the user to assign variables to storage classes that prescribe scope, visibility, and lifetime characteristics for them. The rules governing scoping also prescribe principles for structuring symbol tables and for representing variable access at run time, as discussed below.

A *scope* is a unit of static program structure that may have one or more variables declared within it. In many languages, scopes may be nested: procedures are scoping units in Pascal, as are blocks, functions, and files in C. The closely related concept of *visibility* of a variable indicates in what scopes the variable's name refers to a particular instance of the name. For example, in Pascal, if a variable named a is declared in the outermost scope, it is visible everywhere in the program[1] except

---

1. In many languages, such as C, the scope of a variable begins at its declaration point in the code and extends to the end of the program unit, while in others, such as PL/I, it encompasses the entire relevant program unit.

within functions that also declare a variable a and any functions nested within them, where the local a is visible (unless it is superseded by another declaration of a variable with the same name). If a variable in an inner scope makes a variable with the same name in a containing scope temporarily invisible, we say the inner one *shadows* the outer one.

The *extent* or *lifetime* of a variable is the part of the execution period of the program in which it is declared from when it first becomes visible to when it is last visible. Thus, a variable declared in the outermost scope of a Pascal program has a lifetime that extends throughout the execution of the program, while one declared within a nested procedure may have multiple lifetimes, each extending from an entry to the procedure to the corresponding exit from it. A Fortran variable with the save attribute or a C static local variable has a noncontiguous lifetime—if it is declared within procedure f ( ), its lifetime consists of the periods during which f ( ) is executing, and its value is preserved from each execution period to the next.

Almost all languages have a *global* storage class that gives variables assigned to it an extent that covers the entire execution of the program and global scope, i.e., it makes them visible throughout the program, or in languages in which the visibility rules allow one variable to shadow another, it makes them visible wherever they are not shadowed. Examples of global scope include variables declared extern in C and those declared in the outermost scope in Pascal.

Fortran has the common storage class, which differs from most scoping concepts in that an object may be visible in multiple program units that are not related by nesting and it may have different names in any or all of them. For example, given the common declarations

```
common /block1/i1,j1
```

and

```
common /block1/i2,j2
```

in routines f1( ) and f2( ), respectively, variables i1 and i2 refer to the same storage in their respective routines, as do j1 and j2, and their extent is the whole execution of the program.

Some languages, such as C, have a *file* or *module* storage class that makes a variable visible within a particular file or module and makes its extent the whole period of execution of the program.

Most languages support an *automatic* or *stack* storage class that gives a variable a scope that is the program unit in which it is declared and an extent that lasts for a particular activation of that program unit. This may be associated with procedures, as in Pascal, or with both procedures and blocks within them, as in C and PL/I.

Some languages allow storage classes that are *static* modifications of those described above. In particular, C allows variables to be declared static, which causes them to be allocated storage for the duration of execution, even though they are declared within a particular function. They are accessible only within the function, and they retain their values from one execution of it to the next, like Fortran save variables.

Some languages allow data objects (and in a few languages, variable names) to have dynamic extent, i.e., to extend from their points of explicit allocation to their points of destruction. Some, particularly LISP, allow *dynamic scoping,* i.e., scopes may nest according to calling relationships, rather than static nesting. With dynamic scoping, if procedure f( ) calls g( ) and g( ) uses a variable x that it doesn't declare, then the x declared in its caller f( ) is used, or if there is none, in the caller of f( ), and so on, regardless of the static structure of the program.

Some languages, such as C, have an explicit volatile storage class modifier that specifies that a variable declared volatile may be modified asynchronously, e.g., by an I/O device. This imposes restrictions on optimizations that may be performed on constructs that access the variable.

3.2   Symbol Attributes and Symbol-Table Entries

Each symbol in a program has associated with it a series of attributes that are derived both from the syntax and semantics of the source language and from the symbol's declaration and use in the particular program. The typical attributes include a series of relatively obvious things, such as the symbol's name, type, scope, and size. Others, such as its addressing method, may be less obvious.

Our purpose in this section is to enumerate possible attributes and to explain the less obvious ones. In this way, we provide a description of the constituents of a symbol table, namely, the symbol-table entries. A *symbol-table entry* collects together the attributes of a particular symbol in a way that allows them to be easily set and retrieved.

Table 3.1 lists a typical set of attributes for a symbol. The provision of both size and boundary on the one hand and bitsize and bitbdry on the other allows for both unpacked and packed data representations.

A type referent is either a pointer to or the name of a structure representing a constructed type (in ICAN, lacking pointers, we would use the latter). The provision of type, basetype, and machtype allows us to specify, for example, that the Pascal type

    array [1..3,1..5] of char

has for its type field a type referent such as t2, whose associated value is ⟨array,2,[⟨1,3⟩,⟨1,5⟩],char⟩, for its basetype simply char, and for its machtype the value byte. Also, the value of nelts for it is 15. The presence of the basereg and disp fields allows us to specify that, for example, to access the beginning of our Pascal array we should form the address [r7+8] if basereg is r7 and disp is 8 for it.

The most complex aspect of a symbol-table record is usually the value of the type attribute. Source-language types typically consist of the predefined ones, such as integer, char, real, etc. in Pascal, and the constructed ones, such as Pascal's enumerated, array, record, and set types. The predefined ones can be represented by an enumeration, and the constructed ones by tuples. Thus, the Pascal type template

    array [*t*1,...,*tn*] of *t*0

TABLE 3.1 Typical fields in symbol-table entries.

Name	Type	Meaning
name	Character string	The symbol's identifier
class	Enumeration	Storage class
volatile	Boolean	Asynchronously accessed
size	Integer	Size in bytes
bitsize	Integer	Size in bits if not an integral number of bytes
boundary	Integer	Alignment in bytes
bitbdry	Integer	Alignment in bits if not an integral number of bytes
type	Enumeration or type referent	Source-language data type
basetype	Enumeration or type referent	Source-language type of the elements of a constructed type
machtype	Enumeration	Machine type corresponding to the source type, if simple, or of the elements, if constructed
nelts	Integer	Number of elements
register	Boolean	True if the symbol's value is in a register
reg	Character string	Name of register containing the symbol's value
basereg	Character string	Name of the base register used to compute the symbol's address
disp	Integer	Displacement of symbol's storage from value in base register

can be represented by a tuple consisting of an enumerated value representing its constructor (array), the number of dimensions, and a sequence of representations of each of the dimensions $t1$ through tn, and the representation of its base type $t0$, i.e., the ICAN triple

$$\langle \text{array}, n, [t1, \ldots, tn, t0] \rangle$$

as in the example above. Similarly, a record type template

record $f1: t1; \ldots; \ fn: tn$ end

```
t1 = array [0..5,1..10] of integer;
t2 = record
            t2a: integer;
            t2b: ↑t2;
            t2c: array [1..3] of char;
        end;
t3 = array [1..100] of t2;
```
(a)
```
t1 = ⟨array,2,[⟨0,5⟩,⟨1,10⟩],integer⟩
t2 = ⟨record,3,[⟨t2a,integer⟩,⟨t2b,⟨pointer,t2⟩⟩,
        ⟨t2c,⟨array,1,[⟨1,3⟩],char⟩⟩]⟩
t3 = ⟨array,1,[⟨1,100⟩],t2⟩
```
(b)

FIG. 3.1   (a) A series of Pascal type declarations, and (b) its representation by ICAN tuples.

can be represented by a tuple consisting of an enumerated value representing its constructor (record), the number of fields, and a sequence of pairs comprising representations of the field identifiers fi and types ti, i.e.,

$$⟨record, n, [⟨f1, t1⟩, ..., ⟨fn, tn⟩]⟩$$

Uses of names of constructed types in type definitions are represented by references to the definitions of those types. As a specific example, consider the Pascal type declarations in Figure 3.1(a), which are represented by ICAN structures like those shown in Figure 3.1(b). Note that they are recursive: the definition of t2 includes a reference to t2.

In all languages we are aware of, the predefined types are global and the user-defined types follow scoping rules identical to those for variables, so they can be represented by type tables (or graphs) that parallel the local and global symbol-table structures discussed below.

3.3   Local Symbol-Table Management

We next consider how to manage a symbol table that is local to a specific procedure, an issue that is fundamental to any approach to code generation.

The interfaces of a set of procedures that create, destroy, and manipulate the symbol table and its entries are as follows (SymTab is the type representing symbol tables and Symbol is the type of symbols):

New_Sym_Tab: SymTab ⟶ SymTab
> Creates a new local symbol table with the given symbol table as its parent, or nil if there is none (see the discussion of global symbol-table structure in Section 3.4), and returns the new (empty) local symbol table.

Dest_Sym_Tab: SymTab ⟶ SymTab
> Destroys the current local symbol table and returns its parent (or nil if there is no parent).

`Insert_Sym: SymTab × Symbol ⟶ boolean`
> Inserts an entry for the given symbol into the given symbol table and returns `true`, or if the symbol is already present, does not insert a new entry and returns `false`.

`Locate_Sym: SymTab × Symbol ⟶ boolean`
> Searches the given symbol table for the given symbol and returns `true` if it is found, or `false` if it is not.

`Get_Sym_Attr: SymTab × Symbol × Attr ⟶ Value`
> Returns the value associated with the given attribute of the given symbol in the given symbol table, if it is found, or `nil` if not.

`Set_Sym_Attr: SymTab × Symbol × Attr × Value ⟶ boolean`
> Sets the given attribute of the given symbol in the given symbol table to the given value and returns `true`, if it is found, or returns `false` if not; each of the fields listed in Table 3.1 is considered an attribute, and there may be others as needed.

`Next_Sym: SymTab × Symbol ⟶ Symbol`
> Iterates over the symbol table, in some order, returning the symbol following the one that is its second argument; when called with the second argument set to `nil`, it returns the first symbol in the symbol table or `nil` if the symbol table is empty; when called with the second argument set to the last symbol, it returns `nil`.

`More_Syms: SymTab × Symbol ⟶ boolean`
> Returns `true` if there are more symbols to iterate over and `false` otherwise; if the symbol argument is `nil`, it returns `true` if the symbol table is non-empty, or `false` if the symbol table is empty.

Note the use of the type `Value` in the definitions of `Get_Sym_Attr( )` and `Set_Sym_Attr( )`. It is intended to be a union type that encompasses all the types that attributes might have. Note, also, that the last two routines can be used to iterate over the symbols in a symbol table by being used in the following way:

```
s := nil
while More_Syms(symtab,s) do
    s := Next_Sym(symtab,s)
    if s ≠ nil then
        process symbol s
    fi
od
```

A major consideration in designing a symbol table is implementing it so that symbol and attribute insertion and retrieval are both as fast as possible. We could structure the symbol table as a one-dimensional array of entries, but that would make searching relatively slow. Two alternatives suggest themselves, namely, a balanced binary tree or hashing. Both provide quick insertion, searching, and retrieval, at the expense of some work to keep the tree balanced or to compute hash keys. As discussed in Section 3.4 below, hashing with a chain of entries for each hash key is generally the better approach. The most appropriate implementation of it to deal with the scope rules of languages such as Modula-2, Mesa, Ada, and object-oriented

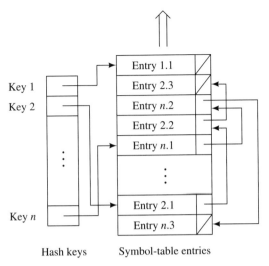

Hash keys	Symbol-table entries

FIG. 3.2 Hashed local symbol table with a chain of buckets for each hash key.

languages is to combine an array with hashing. Figure 3.2 shows a schematic view of how such a symbol table might be organized ("Entry $i.j$" represents the jth entry in the ith hash chain). The hash function should be chosen so as to distribute identifiers relatively evenly across the key values.

3.4   Global Symbol-Table Structure

The scoping and visibility rules of the source language dictate the structure of the global symbol table. For many languages, such as ALGOL 60, Pascal, and PL/I, the scoping rules have the effect of structuring the entire global symbol table as a tree of local symbol tables with the local table for the global scope as its root and the local tables for nested scopes as the children of the table for the scope they are nested in. Thus, for example, if we have a Pascal program with the structure given in Figure 3.3, then the structure of its global symbol table is as shown in Figure 3.4.

However, a simpler structure can be used for such languages in a compiler since, at any point during compilation, we are processing a particular node of this tree and only need access to the symbol tables on the path from that node to the root of the tree. Thus, a stack containing the local symbol tables on a path is sufficient. When we enter a new, more deeply nested scope, we push a local table onto the stack, and when we exit a scope, we pop its table from the stack. Figure 3.5 shows the sequence of global symbol tables that occurs during the processing of the program in Figure 3.3. Now any reference to a variable not found in the current local scope can be searched for in the ancestor scopes. For example, focusing on procedure i( ), the use of variable b refers to the local b declared in i( ), while the use of a refers to the one declared in g( ), and the use of c refers to the global c declared in the outermost scope e( ).

```
program e;
   var a, b, c: integer;
   procedure f;
      var a, b, c: integer;
   begin
      a := b + c
   end;
   procedure g;
         var a, b: integer;
      procedure h;
         var c, d: integer;
      begin
         c := a + d;
      end;
      procedure i;
         var b, d: integer;
      begin
         b := a + c
      end;
   begin
      b := a + c
   end;
   procedure j;
      var b, d: integer;
   begin
      b := a + d
   end;
begin
   a := b + c
end .
```

FIG. 3.3 Nesting structure of an example Pascal program.

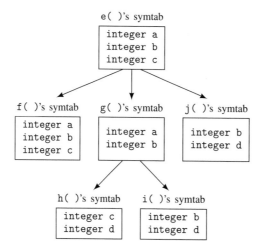

FIG. 3.4 Tree of local symbol tables for the Pascal code in Figure 3.3.

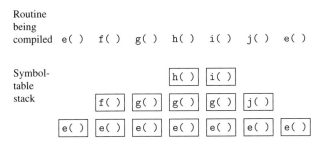

FIG. 3.5 Symbol-table stacks occurring during compiling the Pascal code in Figure 3.3.

The stack of local symbol tables can be implemented as a stack of arrays and hash tables, with each of them implemented as described in Section 3.3. A better structure uses two stacks, one to contain identifiers and the other to indicate the base of each local table, with a single hash table accessed by hashing a symbol's name as before. If we take this approach, New_Sym_Tab( ) pushes a new entry onto the block stack, Insert_Sym( ) adds an entry at the top of the symbol stack and puts it at the beginning of its hash chain, and Locate_Sym( ) needs to search only along the chain the symbol hashes to. Dest_Sym_Tab( ) removes from all chains the entries above the current entry in the block stack, all of which are at the heads of the chains, and deallocates the top entry on the block stack. Figure 3.6 gives an example of this scoping model, assuming e and f have the same hash value.

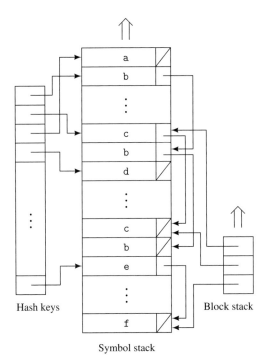

FIG. 3.6 Hashed global symbol table with a block stack.

The only remaining issue is dealing with scoping constructs that do not obey the tree structure discussed above, such as Modula-2's `import` and `export`, Ada's packages and `use` statement, and C++'s inheritance mechanism. Compilation systems for the first two languages must provide a mechanism for saving and retrieving interface definitions for modules and packages, respectively. A useful distinction due to Graham, Joy, and Roubine [GraJ79], on which the following model of scoping is based, is between *open* scopes, for which the visibility rules correspond directly to the nesting of the scopes, and *closed* scopes, for which visibility is explicitly specified in a program. For open scopes, the mechanism we have described above is sufficient.

Closed scopes, on the other hand, make a specified set of names visible in certain other scopes, independent of nesting. For example, in Modula-2 a module may include a list of names of objects it exports, and other modules may import any or all of those names by listing them explicitly. Ada's package mechanism allows a package to export a set of objects and allows other modules to import them by indicating explicitly that they use the package. These and the other explicit scoping mechanisms can be implemented in the stack-plus-hashing symbol-table model by keeping, for each identifier, a list of the scope level numbers of scopes in which the identifier is visible. This would be simple to maintain, but it can be done with less space overhead.

A simplification results from noting that the level numbers in such a list must be consecutive, since a scope can export an identifier only if it is visible in it and can import it only explicitly or if it is visible in the containing scope. The process can be further simplified by making sure that each entry is removed from the symbol table when the outermost scope in which it is visible is exited—then we need only record the level of the innermost scope in which it is visible and update the level number on entry to and exit from such a scope. This provides fast implementations for scope entry, symbol insertion, and attribute setting and retrieval, but could require searching the entire symbol table upon leaving a scope to find the entries that need to be deleted.

The most effective adaptation of the stack-plus-hashing model to closed scopes uses the stack structure to reflect the scope that a symbol is declared in or the outermost level it is exported to, and the hash structure to implement visibility rules. It reorders the elements of the hash chain into which an imported symbol is to be entered to bring it to the front before setting its innermost-level-number field, and does the same reordering for each symbol the scope exports. It then enters locally declared symbols ahead of those already in the hash chain. The reader can verify that the symbols in each chain are kept in an order that reflects the visibility rules. On exiting a scope, we must remove from the hash chains the local symbols that are not exported, which are among those whose stored level numbers match the level number of the current scope. If such a symbol is declared in a scope containing the current one or is exported to such a scope, then we can determine that from the stack structure of the symbol table and can leave the symbol in the hash chain, subtracting one from its innermost level number; otherwise, we remove the symbol from its hash chain.

As an example, consider the code shown in Figure 3.7. Upon entering procedure f( ), the symbol table is as shown in Figure 3.8(a). Upon entering g( ), we have a newly declared d and variables a and b (note that we assume that b and d have the

```
program
   var a, b, c, d
   procedure f( )
      var b
      procedure g( )
         var d
         import a, b from P
      end
   end
end
package P
   export a, b
end
```

FIG. 3.7 An example of code with an import.

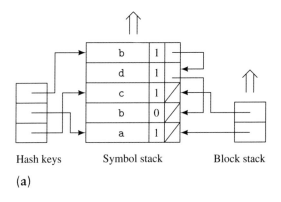

Hash keys   Symbol stack   Block stack

(a)

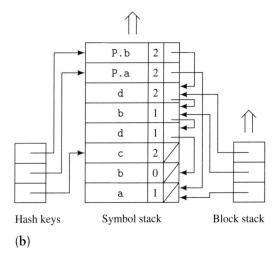

Hash keys   Symbol stack   Block stack

(b)

FIG. 3.8 (a) Hashed global symbol table with innermost level numbers, and (b) after entering
g( ), a scope with local variable d and imported symbols a and b.

same hash value) imported from package P. The resulting symbol-table structure is as shown in Figure 3.8(b). Note that the hash chain containing the bs and d in (a) has been reordered so that the imported b comes first, followed by the newly declared d, and then the other three previous entries. The innermost level numbers have been adjusted to indicate that the imported a and b, g( )'s d, and the global a are visible inside g( ). To return to the previous state, i.e., the state represented in (a), we pop the top entry off the block stack and all the symbol entries above the point it indicates in the symbol stack and adjust the hash chains to reflect deletion of those symbols. Since we did not reorder the hash chains for the enclosing scopes when we entered g( ), this returns the symbol table to its previous state.

To support the global symbol-table structure, we add two routines to the interface described in Section 3.3:

Encl_Sym_Tab: SymTab × Symbol ⟶ SymTab
Returns the nearest enclosing symbol table that declares its second argument, or nil if there is none.

Depth_Sym_Tab: SymTab ⟶ integer
Returns the depth of the given symbol table relative to the current one, which, by convention, has depth zero.

3.5   Storage Binding and Symbolic Registers

Storage binding translates variable names into addresses, a process that must occur either before or during code generation. In our intermediate-language hierarchy, it is part of the process of translating a routine from MIR to LIR (see Chapter 4), which, in addition to translating names to addresses, expands MIR assignments into loads, operations, and stores, and expands calls to instruction sequences.

Each variable is assigned an address, or more accurately an *addressing method*, appropriate to its storage class. We use the latter term because, for example, a local variable in a procedure is not assigned a fixed machine address (or a fixed address relative to the base of a module), but rather a stack location that is accessed by an offset from a register whose value generally does not point to the same location each time the procedure is invoked.

For storage binding, variables are divided into four major categories: global, global static, stack, and stack static variables. In languages that allow variables or a whole scope to be imported, we must consider that case as well.

Global variables and those with static storage class are generally assigned either to fixed relocatable addresses or to offsets from a base register known as the global pointer.[2] Some compilers, such as those provided by MIPS for the MIPS architecture, use offsets from a base register for all globals up to a maximum size the programmer can control and, thus, achieve single-instruction access for all the globals that fit into the available range. Stack variables are assigned offsets from the stack pointer or

---

2. In generating position-independent code, the latter approach is used, as discussed in Section 5.7.

frame pointer, so they appear and disappear with procedure invocations and, thus, their locations may change from one invocation to another.

In most languages, heap objects are allocated space dynamically and are accessed by means of pointers whose values are set by the memory allocator. However, in some languages, such as LISP, such objects may be "interned," i.e., assigned names that access them directly.

An alternative approach for stack variables and, in some cases, for global variables as well, is to allocate them to registers, rather than to memory locations. Of course, it is essential that such variables fit into a register and registers are not generally indexable, so this approach cannot be used for arrays. Also, one cannot generally assign many variables to registers before or during code generation, since there is only a fixed set of registers available. However, one can assign scalar variables to an unbounded set of *symbolic registers,* i.e., to names that can be assigned to real registers or to memory locations later in the compilation process. This is done in compilers that use the graph-coloring approach to global register allocation discussed in Section 16.3. Symbolic registers are allocated by simply incrementing a counter, so the first variable is assigned to s0, the next to s1, and so on. Alternatively, the register allocator can pack variables assigned to storage locations into registers and then delete the associated storage accesses, as is done in the priority-based graph-coloring approach discussed in Section 16.4.

Figure 3.9 gives an ICAN routine named Bind_Local_Vars( ) that binds local variables to storage locations using the symbol-table manipulation routines described in Sections 3.3 and 3.4. The fields in symbol-table entries include at least the ones described in Table 3.1.

Bind_Local_Vars( ) assigns each static variable a displacement and, for stack-allocated variables, assigns a displacement and the frame pointer as the base register. For records, we cycle through the elements, assigning them displacements and base registers. The value of initdisp is the displacement of the first location in the stack frame that is available to allocate. We assume that Initdisp and the bases of the stack frame and static storage area are doubleword-aligned to begin with. Note that we assign negative offsets from fp to local symbols, as discussed below in Chapter 5, and positive offsets to statics. We ignore the possibility of packed records, as discussed in Section 5.1. Round_Abs_Up( ) is used to ensure proper boundary alignment. The function abs( ) returns the absolute value of its argument, and the function ceil( ) returns the least integer greater than or equal to its argument. Binding to symbolic registers is virtually the same and handling global variables is similar, except that it may need to be spread out across a series of compilation units, depending on the source language's structure.

As an example of storage binding, consider the MIR fragment in Figure 3.10(a), where a is a global integer variable, b is a local integer variable, and c[0..9] is a local variable holding an array of integers. Let gp be the register pointing to the global area and fp be the frame pointer. Then we might assign a to offset 8 beyond gp, b to fp-20, and c to fp-24 (note that fetching c[1] results in loading from location fp-28: this is the case because c[0] is located at fp-24 and the elements of c[ ] are 4 bytes long); binding each variable to its location in the MIR code would result in the LIR code shown in Figure 3.10(b). (Of course, the

```
procedure Bind_Local_Vars(symtab,Initdisp)
   symtab: in SymTab
   Initdisp: in integer
begin
   symclass: enum {local, local_static}
   symbasetype: Type
   i, symsize, staticloc := 0, stackloc := Initdisp,
      symnelts: integer
   s := nil: Symbol
   while More_Syms(symtab,s) do
      s := Next_Sym(symtab,s)
      symclass := Get_Sym_Attr(symtab,s,class)
      symsize := Get_Sym_Attr(symtab,s,size)
      symbasetype := Get_Sym_Attr(symtab,s,basetype)
      case symclass of
local:   if symbasetype = record then
            symnelts := Get_Sym_Attr(symtab,s,nelts)
            for i := 1 to symnelts do
               symsize := Get_Sym_Attr(symtab,s,⟨i,size⟩)
               || allocate local symbols at negative offsets
               || from the frame pointer
               stackloc -= symsize
               stackloc := Round_Abs_Up(stackloc,symsize)
               Set_Sym_Attr(symtab,s,reg,"fp")
               Set_Sym_Attr(symtab,s,⟨i,disp⟩,stackloc)
            od
         else
            stackloc -= symsize
            stackloc := Round_Abs_Up(stackloc,symsize)
            Set_Sym_Attr(symtab,s,reg,"fp")
            Set_Sym_Attr(symtab,s,disp,stackloc)
         fi
```

FIG. 3.9 Routines to do storage binding of local variables.

fourth instruction is redundant, since the value it loads is stored by the preceding instruction. The MIR-to-LIR translator might recognize this, or the task might be left to the postpass optimizer, as described in Section 18.11.)

If we were using symbolic registers, b would be assigned to one, say s2. Global variable a might also be, depending on whether the register allocator assigns globals to registers or not; we assume for now that it does. The resulting LIR code would be as shown in Figure 3.10(c). Note that c[1] has not been assigned a symbolic register because it is an array element.

There are several possible approaches to arranging local variables in the stack frame. We could simply assign them to consecutive locations in the frame, allowing enough space for each, but this might require us to put variables on boundaries in memory that are inappropriate for accessing them quickly—e.g., it might result in a word-sized object being put on a halfword boundary, requiring two halfword loads,

```
local_static:
        if symbasetype = record then
            symnelts := Get_Sym_Attr(symtab,s,nelts)
            for i := 1 to symnelts do
                symsize := Get_Sym_Attr(symtab,s,⟨i,size⟩)
                || allocate local static symbols at positive offsets
                || from the beginning of static storage
                staticloc := Round_Abs_Up(staticloc,symsize)
                Set_Sym_Attr(symtab,s,⟨i,disp⟩,staticloc)
                staticloc += symsize
            od
        else
            staticloc := Round_Abs_Up(staticloc,symsize)
            Set_Sym_Attr(symtab,s,disp,staticloc)
            staticloc += symsize
        fi
    esac
  od
end     || Bind_Local_Vars

procedure Round_Abs_Up(m,n) returns integer
    m, n: in integer
begin
    return sign(m) * ceil(abs(float(m)/float(n))) * abs(n)
end     || Round_Abs_Up
```

FIG. 3.9 *(continued)*

a shift, and an "or" at worst, in place of a single word load. If there are no half-word loads, as in the Alpha architecture, an "and" would be needed also. We might remedy this by guaranteeing that each stack frame starts on a doubleword boundary and leaving gaps between objects to cause them to appear on the appropriate boundaries, but this wastes space, which may be important because RISC loads and stores provide only short offsets and CISC instructions require use of longer offsets and may impact cache performance.

```
a ← a * 2          r1 ← [gp+8]        s0 ← s0 * 2
                   r2 ← r1 * 2
                   [gp+8] ← r2
b ← a + c[1]       r3 ← [gp+8]        s1 ← [fp-28]
                   r4 ← [fp-28]       s2 ← s0 + s1
                   r5 ← r3 + r4
                   [fp-20] ← r5

(a)                (b)                (c)
```

FIG. 3.10 (a) A MIR fragment and two translations to LIR, one with names bound to storage locations (b) and the other with simple variables bound to symbolic registers (c).

```
int i;
double float x;
short int j;
float y;
```

FIG. 3.11   C local variable declarations.

We can do better by sorting variables by the alignments they need, largest first, and by guaranteeing that each stack frame is aligned in memory on a boundary that provides the most efficient access. We would sort all quantities needing double-word alignment at the beginning of the frame, followed by word-aligned quantities, then halfwords, and finally bytes. If the beginning of the stack frame is doubleword-aligned, this guarantees that each variable is on an appropriate boundary. For example, given the C variable declarations shown in Figure 3.11, we could store them in declaration order as shown in Figure 3.12(a) or store them sorted by size as shown in Figure 3.12(b). Note that sorting them not only makes access to them faster, it also frequently saves space. Since no language definition we know of permits one to rely on the arrangement in memory of local variables, this sorting is safe.

A third approach is to sort by size, but to allocate smallest first, respecting boundary alignment. This may use somewhat more space than the preceding approach, but for large stack frames it makes more variables accessible with short offsets.

How to store large local data structures, such as arrays, requires more thought. We could store them directly in the stack frame, and some compilers do so, but this might require offsets larger than the immediate field allowed in instructions to access array elements and other variables. Note that if we put large objects near the beginning of the stack frame, then other objects require large offsets from fp, while if we put them at the end of the frame, the same thing occurs relative to sp. We could allocate a second base register (and, perhaps, more) to extend the stack frame, but even that might not make it large enough. An alternative is to allocate large objects in the middle of the stack frame (or possibly elsewhere), and to store pointers to them in the stack frame at small offsets from fp. This requires an extra load to access an array, but the cost of the load is frequently amortizable over many array accesses, especially if the array is used heavily in one or more loops.

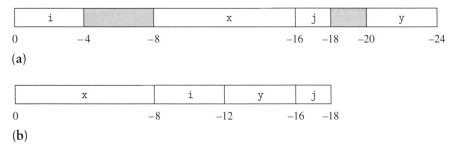

FIG. 3.12   (a) Unsorted aligned and (b) sorted frame layouts for the declarations shown in Figure 3.11 (offsets in bytes).

3.6   Approaches to Generating Loads and Stores

For concreteness, we assume for now that we are generating assembly code for a 32-bit SPARC-V9 system, except that we use a flat register file, rather than register windows.

The procedures described below generate the loads needed to put values into registers to be used and the stores to put computed values into the appropriate memory locations. They could also modify the corresponding symbol-table entries to reflect the location of each value, i.e., whether it is in a register and, if so, which register and generate moves between the integer and floating-point registers, as necessary, so that values are in the type of registers they need to be in to be used.

`Sym_to_Reg: SymTab × Var ⟶ Register`
Generates a load from the storage location corresponding to a given variable to a register, register pair, or register quadruple of the appropriate type, and returns the name of the first register. The global data types and structures used in the process are given in Figure 3.13; a straightforward version of `Sym_to_Reg( )` is given in Figure 3.14 and auxiliary routines used in the process are given in Figure 3.15. The variable `GloSymtab` has as its value the global symbol table. The variable `StaticLinkOffset` holds the offset from register `fp` of the current procedure's static link. The following functions are used in the code:

1. `Locate_Sym`(*symtab*,*v*) returns `true` if variable *v* is in symbol table *symtab* and `false` otherwise (see Section 3.3).

2. `Encl_Sym_Tab`(*symtab*,*v*) returns the symbol table, stepping outward from *symtab*, in which variable *v* is found or `nil` if it is not found (see Section 3.4).

3. `Depth_Sym_Tab`(*symtab*1,*symtab*) returns the difference in depths from the current symbol table *symtab* to the enclosing one *symtab*1 (see Section 3.4).

4. `Get_Sym_Attr`(*symtab*,*v*,*attr*) returns the value of the *attr* attribute of variable *v* in symbol table *symtab* (see Section 3.3).

5. `Short_Const`(*c*) returns `true` if *c* fits into 13 bits (the length of a SPARC short constant operand) and `false` otherwise.

6. `Gen_Inst`(*opc*,*opds*) outputs the instruction with opcode *opc* and argument list *opds*.

7. `Reg_Char`(*reg*) converts its `Register` operand *reg* to the corresponding character string.

`Sym_to_Reg_Force: SymTab × Var × Register`
Generates a load from the storage location corresponding to a given symbol to the named register, register pair, or register quadruple of the appropriate type. This routine can be used, for example, to force procedure arguments to the appropriate registers.

`Alloc_Reg: SymTab × Var ⟶ Register`
Allocates a register, register pair, or register quadruple of the appropriate type to hold the value of its variable argument and sets the `reg` field in the variable's symbol-table entry, unless there already is a register allocated, and (in either case) returns the name of the first register.

```
SymType = enum {byte, uns_byte, short, uns_short, int,
    uns_int, long_int, uns_long_int, float, dbl_float,
    quad_float}
LdStType = array [1··11] of record
                {type: SymType,
                 LdOp, StOp: CharString}
LdStType :=
    || types, load instructions, and store instructions
    [⟨type:byte,         LdOp:"ldsb",  StOp:"stsb"⟩,
     ⟨type:uns_byte,     LdOp:"ldub",  StOp:"stub"⟩,
     ⟨type:short,        LdOp:"ldsh",  StOp:"stsh"⟩,
     ⟨type:uns_short,    LdOp:"lduh",  StOp:"stuh"⟩,
     ⟨type:int,          LdOp:"ldsw",  StOp:"stsw"⟩,
     ⟨type:uns_int,      LdOp:"lduw",  StOp:"stuw"⟩,
     ⟨type:long_int,     LdOp:"ldd",   StOp:"std"⟩,
     ⟨type:uns_long_int, LdOp:"ldd",   StOp:"std"⟩,
     ⟨type:float,        LdOp:"ldf",   StOp:"stf"⟩,
     ⟨type:dbl_float,    LdOp:"lddf",  StOp:"stdf"⟩,
     ⟨type:quad_float,   LdOp:"ldqf",  StOp:"stqf"⟩]
GloSymtab: SymTab
StaticLinkOffset: integer
Depth: integer
```

FIG. 3.13 Global types and data structures used to generate loads and stores.

Reg_to_Sym: SymTab × Register ⟶ Var
    Generates a store of the second argument's value (a register name) to the variable's storage location. Code for a straightforward version of Reg_to_Sym( ) is given in Figure 3.14 and uses the global types and data structures in Figure 3.13 and the auxiliary routines in Figure 3.15.

Alloc_Reg_Anon: enum {int,flt} × integer ⟶ Register
    Allocates a register, register pair, or register quadruple of the appropriate type (according to the value of the second argument, which may be 1, 2, or 4) and returns the name of the first register. It does not associate the register with a symbol, unlike Alloc_Reg( ).

Free_Reg: Register ⟶ ∅
    Returns its argument register to the pool of available registers.

Rather than simply loading a value into a register before using it and storing a value as soon as it has been computed, we can easily provide more sophisticated versions of the routines that move values to and from registers. The first improvement is to track what is in each register and, if a needed value is already in a register of the appropriate type, to use it without redundantly loading it; if the value is already in a register, but of the wrong type, we can generate a move instead of a load if the target architecture supports moves between the integer and floating-point registers. If we run out of registers, we select one for reuse (we assign this task to Alloc_Reg( )). Similarly, instead of storing each value as soon as it has been computed, we can defer

```
procedure Sym_to_Reg(symtab,v) returns Register
   symtab: in SymTab
   v: in Var
begin
   symtab1: SymTab
   symdisp: integer
   Opcode: CharString
   reg: Register
   symtype: SymType
   symtab1 := Find_Sym_Tab(symtab,v)
   if Get_Sym_Attr(symtab1,v,register) then
      return Get_Sym_Attr(symtab1,v,reg)
   fi
   symtype := Get_Sym_Attr(symtab1,v,type)
   Opcode := LdStType[Find_Opcode(symtype)].LdOp
   reg := Alloc_Reg(symtab1,v)
   symdisp := Get_Sym_Attr(symtab1,v,disp)
   || generate load instruction and return loaded register
   Gen_LdSt(symtab1,Opcode,reg,symdisp,false)
   return  reg
end    || Sym_to_Reg

procedure Reg_to_Sym(symtab,r,v)
   symtab: in SymTab
   r: in Register
   v: in Var
begin
   symtab1: SymTab
   disp: integer
   Opcode: CharString
   symtype: SymType
   symtab1 := Find_Sym_Tab(symtab,v)
   symtype := Get_Sym_Attr(symtab1,v,type)
   Opcode := LdStType[Find_Opcode(symtype)].StOp
   symdisp := Get_Sym_Attr(symtab1,v,disp)
   || generate store from register that is the value of r
   Gen_LdSt(symtab1,Opcode,r,symdisp,true)
end    || Reg_to_Sym
```

FIG. 3.14 Routines to load and store, respectively, a variable's value to or from a register, register pair, or quadruple.

stores to the end of the basic block, or until we run out of registers. Alternatively, if there are more registers needed than available, we could implement Reg_to_Sym( ) so that it stores each computed quantity as early as it reasonably can, so as to minimize both the number of stores needed and the number of registers in use at once.

The last two strategies above can be carried a step further. Namely, we can do register allocation for basic blocks in a sequence that allows us to take into account,

```
procedure Find_Sym_Tab(symtab,v) returns SymTab
   symtab: in SymTab
   v: in Var
begin
   symtab1: SymTab
   || determine correct symbol table for symbol
   || and set Depth if neither local nor global
   Depth := 0
   if Locate_Sym(symtab,v) then
      return symtab
   elif Locate_Sym(GloSymtab,v) then
      return GloSymtab
   else
      symtab1 := Encl_Sym_Tab(symtab,v)
      Depth := Depth_Sym_Tab(symtab1,symtab)
      return symtab1
   fi
end     || Find_Sym_Tab

procedure Find_Opcode(symtype) returns integer
   symtype: in SymType
begin
   for i := 1 to 11 do
      if type = LdStType[i].symtype then
         return i
      fi
   od
end     || Find_Opcode
```

FIG. 3.15 Auxiliary routines used in generating loads and stores.

for most blocks, the contents of the registers on entry to the block. If a block has a single predecessor, the register state on entry to it is the exit state of its predecessor. If it has multiple predecessors, the appropriate choice is the intersection of the register states on exit from the predecessors. This allows quite efficient register allocation and minimization of loads and stores for structures such as if-then-elses, but it does not help for loops, since one of the predecessors of a loop body is the loop body itself. To do much better than this we need the global register-allocation techniques discussed in Chapter 16, which also discusses the local approach we have just described in more detail.

Another alternative is to assign symbolic registers during code generation and leave it to the global register allocator to assign memory locations for those symbolic registers requiring them.

It is a relatively easy generalization to generate loads and stores for variables in closed scopes imported into the current scope. Doing so involves adding attributes to each symbol table (*not* symbol-table entries) to indicate what kind of scope it represents and what register to use (i.e., other than fp and gp) to access the symbols in it.

```
procedure Gen_LdSt(symtab1,OpCode,reg,disp,stflag)
   symtab1: in SymTab
   OpCode: in CharString
   reg: in Register
   symdisp: in integer
   stflag: in boolean
begin
   i: integer
   reg1, regc: CharString
   if symtab1 = GloSymtab then
      || set reg1 to base address
      reg1 := "ɤρ"
      regc := Reg_Char(reg)
   else
      reg1 := "fp"
      if stflag then
         reg := Alloc_Reg_Anon(int,4)
      fi
      regc := Reg_Char(reg)
      || generate loads to get to the right stack frame
      for i := 1 to Depth do
         Gen_Inst("lduw","[" ⊕ reg1 ⊕ "+"
            ⊕ StaticLinkOffset ⊕ "]," ⊕ regc)
         reg1 := regc
      od
      if stflag then
         Free_Reg(reg)
      fi
   fi
   if Short_Const(symdisp) then
      || generate load or store
      Gen_Inst(Opcode,"[" ⊕ reg1 ⊕ "+" ⊕ symdisp
         ⊕ "]," ⊕ regc)
   else
      || generate sethi and load or store
      Gen_Inst("sethi","%hi(" ⊕ symdisp ⊕ ")," ⊕ regc)
      Gen_Inst(Opcode,"[" ⊕ reg1 ⊕ "+%lo("
         ⊕ symdisp ⊕ ")]," ⊕ regc)
   fi
end    || Gen_LdSt
```

FIG. 3.15 *(continued)*

3.7   Wrap-Up

In this chapter we have been concerned with issues involved in structuring local and global symbol tables to accommodate the features of modern programming languages and to make them efficient for use in compiled language implementations.

We began with a discussion of storage classes and visibility or scoping rules. Next we discussed symbol attributes and how to structure a local symbol table, followed by a description of a way to organize a global symbol table that includes importing and exporting scopes, so as to support languages like Modula-2, Ada, and C++.

Then we specified a programming interface to global and local symbol tables that allows them to be structured in any way one desires, as long as it satisfies the interface. Next we explored issues involved in binding variables to storage locations and symbolic registers, and we presented ICAN implementations of routines to generate loads and stores for variables in accord with their attributes and the symbol-table interface mentioned above.

The primary lessons in this chapter are (1) that there are many ways to implement symbol tables, some more efficient than others, (2) that it is important to make operations on symbol tables efficient, (3) that careful thought about the data structures used can produce both highly efficient and relatively simple implementations, (4) that the structure of the symbol table can be hidden from other parts of a compiler by a sufficiently specified interface, and (5) that there are several approaches to generating loads and stores that can be more or less efficient in terms of tracking register contents and minimizing memory traffic.

3.8   Further Reading

The programming language Mesa is described in [MitM79].

[Knut73] provides a wealth of information and techniques for designing hash functions.

The paper by Graham, Joy, and Roubine on which our scoping model is based is [GraJ79].

3.9   Exercises

3.1 Give examples from real programming languages of as many of the following pairs of scopes and lifetimes as actually occur. For each, cite the language and give example code.

	Entire program	File or module	Set of procedures	One procedure	One block
Entire execution					
Execution in a module					
All executions of a procedure					
Single execution of a procedure					
Execution of a block					

3.2 Write an ICAN routine Struct_Equiv(*tn*1,*tn*2,*td*) that takes two type names *tn*1 and *tn*2 and an ICAN representation of a set of Pascal type definitions *td*, such that each of *tn*1 and *tn*2 is either a simple type or one of the types defined in *td* and returns true if the types named *tn*1 and *tn*2 are structurally equivalent or false if they are not. *td* is an ICAN list of pairs, each of whose members consists of a type name and a type representation, where, for example, the type definitions in Figure 3.1(b) are represented by the following list:

```
[⟨t1,⟨array,2,[⟨0,5⟩,⟨1,10⟩],integer⟩⟩,
 ⟨t2,⟨record,3,[⟨t2a,integer⟩,⟨t2b,⟨pointer,t2⟩⟩,
          ⟨t2c,⟨array,1,[⟨1,3⟩],char⟩⟩]⟩⟩,
 ⟨t3,⟨array,1,[⟨1,100⟩],t2⟩⟩]
```

Two types are structurally equivalent if (1) they are the same simple type or (2) their definitions are identical, except for possibly using different names for types from which they are composed. For example, given the Pascal type definitions

```
t1 = integer;
t2 = array [1..10] of integer;
t3 = array [1..10] of t1;
t4 = record f1: integer; f2: ↑t4 end;
t5 = record f1: t1;      f2: ↑t4 end;
t6 = record f1: t2;      f2: ↑t4 end;
```

each of the pairs t1 and integer, t2 and t3, and t4 and t5 are structurally equivalent, while t6 is inequivalent to all the other types.

3.3 Write routines to assign stack variables to offsets from the frame pointer (a) in the order given in the symbol table, (b) ordered by the length of the data, longest first, and (c) ordered shortest first.

3.4 Write register-tracking versions of (a) Sym_to_Reg( ), (b) Reg_to_Sym( ), and (c) Alloc_Reg( ).

3.5 Design an ICAN symbol-table entry that includes at least the fields described at the beginning of Section 3.3 and write the routines Get_Sym_Attr( ) and Set_Sym_Attr( ) in ICAN.

3.6 Design a structure for a local symbol table, using your entry design from the preceding exercise, and write ICAN implementations of Insert_Sym( ), Locate_Sym( ), Next_Sym( ), and More_Syms( ).

3.7 Design a structure for a global symbol table, using your local-table design from the preceding exercise, and write ICAN implementations of New_Sym_Tab( ), Dest_Sym_Tab( ), Encl_Sym_Tab( ), and Depth_Sym_Tab( ) that take closed scopes into account.

CHAPTER 4

Intermediate Representations

I n this chapter we explore issues involved in the design of intermediate-code
representations. As we shall see, there are numerous feasible choices for
intermediate-code structure.

While we discuss several intermediate-code forms and their relative advantages,
we shall finally need to select and use a particular intermediate-code design for
concreteness in our presentation of optimization and code-generation issues. Our
primary intermediate language is called MIR, for Medium-level Intermediate Representation. In addition, we also describe a somewhat higher-level form called HIR, for
High-level Intermediate Representation, and a lower-level form called LIR, for Low-
level Intermediate Representation. The basic MIR is suitable for most optimizations
(as is LIR), while HIR is used for dependence analysis and some of the code transformations based on it, and LIR is used for optimizations that require that registers and
addressing be explicit.

4.1   Issues in Designing an Intermediate Language

Intermediate-language design is largely an art, not a science. There are several principles that apply and a large body of experience to draw on, but there is always a
decision about whether to use or adapt an existing representation or, if an existing
language is not used, there are many decisions to be made in the design of a new one.
If an existing one is to be used, there are considerations of its appropriateness for the
new application—both the languages to be compiled and the target architecture—
and any resulting porting costs, versus the savings inherent in reuse of an existing
design and code. There is also the issue of whether the intermediate form is appropriate for the kinds and degree of optimization to be performed. Some optimizations
may be very hard to do at all on a given intermediate representation, and some may
take much longer to do than they would on another representation. For example,
the UCODE intermediate language, forms of which are used in the PA-RISC and MIPS

compilers, is very well suited to an architecture that evaluates expressions on a stack, as that is its model of expression evaluation. It is less well suited *a priori* to a load-store architecture with a large register set instead of an evaluation stack. Thus, both Hewlett-Packard's and MIPS's compilers translate UCODE into another form for optimization. HP translates it to a very low-level representation, while MIPS translates it within its optimizer to a medium-level triples form, optimizes it, and then translates it back to UCODE for the code generator.

If a new intermediate representation is to be designed, the issues include its level (and, most particularly, how machine-dependent it is), its structure, its expressiveness (i.e., the constructs needed to cover the appropriate range of languages), its appropriateness for optimization or for particular optimizations, and its appropriateness for code generation for the target architecture or architectures.

There is also the possibility of using more than one intermediate form, translating from one to another in the compilation process, either to preserve an existing technology investment or to do the tasks appropriate to each level at the corresponding time (or both), or the possibility of having a multi-level intermediate form. The former is what Hewlett-Packard does in their compilers for PA-RISC. They first translate to a version of UCODE, which was the intermediate form used for the previous generation of HP3000s (for which it was very appropriate, since they were stack machines). Then, in two steps, they translate to a very low-level representation called SLLIC[1] on which they do virtually all their optimization. It is essential to doing optimization effectively at that level, however, that they preserve information gathered about the code in the language-specific front ends and the intermediate stages.

In the latter approach, some constructs typically have more than one possible representation, and each may be appropriate for a particular task. One common example of this is being able to represent subscripted expressions by lists of subscripts (a relatively high-level form) and by linearized expressions that make explicit the computation of the offset in memory from the base address of the array or another element's address (a lower-level form). The list form is desirable for doing dependence analysis (see Section 9.1) and the various optimizations based on it, while the linearized form is appropriate for constant folding, strength reduction, loop-invariant code motion, and other more basic optimizations.

For example, using the notation described in Section 4.6 below, a use of the C expression a[i][j+2] with the array declared to be

```
float a[20][10]
```

might be represented in a high-level form (HIR) as shown in Figure 4.1(a), in a medium-level form (MIR) as shown in Figure 4.1(b), and in a low-level form (LIR) as shown in Figure 4.1(c). Use of a variable name in the high-level and medium-level forms indicates the symbol-table entry for it, and the unary operators addr and * in the medium-level form indicate "address of" and pointer indirection, respectively. The high-level form indicates that it is a reference to an element of an array with

---

1. SLLIC is an abbreviation for Spectrum Low-Level Intermediate Code. Spectrum was the internal name for PA-RISC during its development.

```
t1 ← a[i,j+2]            t1 ← j + 2              r1 ← [fp-4]
                         t2 ← i * 20             r2 ← r1 + 2
                         t3 ← t1 + t2            r3 ← [fp-8]
                         t4 ← 4 * t3             r4 ← r3 * 20
                         t5 ← addr a             r5 ← r4 + r2
                         t6 ← t5 + t4            r6 ← 4 * r5
                         t7 ← *t6                r7 ← fp - 216
                                                 f1 ← [r7+r6]

    (a)                      (b)                     (c)
```

FIG. 4.1 (a) High-, (b) medium-, and (c) low-level representations of a C array reference.

two subscripts, the first of which is i and the second of which is the expression j + 2. The medium-level form computes

(addr a) + 4 * (i * 20 + j + 2)

as the address of the array element and then loads the value with that address into the temporary t7. The low-level form fetches the values of i and j from memory (assumed to be at offsets -4 and -8, respectively, from the contents of the frame pointer register fp), computes the offset into the array, and then fetches the value of the array element into floating-point register f1.

Note that intermediate codes are typically represented within a compiler in a binary form and symbols, such as variables, are usually pointers to symbol-table entries, so as to achieve both speed and compactness. In our examples, we use external text representations designed for readability. Most compilers include a debugging output form of their intermediate code(s), at least for the benefit of the compiler writers. In some cases, such as in compilers that save intermediate code to enable cross-module procedure integration (see Section 15.2), there needs to be a form that not only can be printed out for debugging, but that can also be read back in and used. The three main issues encountered in designing such an external representation are (1) how to represent pointers in a position-independent way in the external form; (2) how to represent compiler-generated objects, such as temporaries, in a way that makes them unique to the module in which they appear; and (3) how to make the external representation both compact and fast to write and read. One possibility is to use two external representations—a character-based one for human consumption (and, possibly, human generation) and a binary one to support cross-module procedure integration and other interprocedural analyses and optimizations. In the binary form, pointers can be made position-independent by making them relative to the locations of the pointer references. To make each temporary unique to the module that uses it, it can be made to include the module name.

4.2   High-Level Intermediate Languages

High-level intermediate languages (ILs) are used almost entirely in the earliest stages of the compilation process, or in preprocessors before compilation. In the former case, they are produced by compiler front ends and are usually transformed shortly

```
int f(a,b)
int a, b;
{   int c;
    c = a + 2;
    print(b,c);
}
```

FIG. 4.2 A tiny C routine whose abstract syntax tree is given in Figure 4.3.

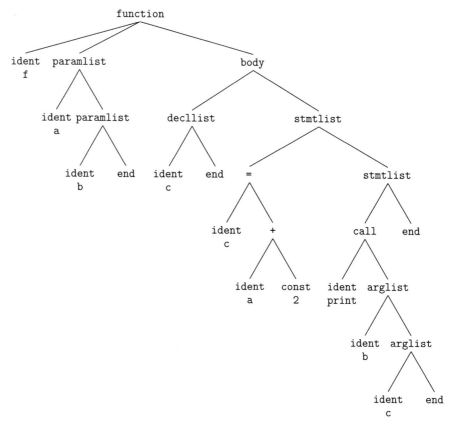

FIG. 4.3 Abstract syntax tree for the C routine in Figure 4.2.

thereafter into lower-level forms; in the latter, they are often transformed back into source code in the original language or another language.

One frequently occurring form of high-level IL is the abstract syntax tree, which makes explicit the structure of a program, usually with just enough information available to reconstruct its source form or a close facsimile thereof. A major use for abstract syntax trees is in language-sensitive or syntax-directed editors for programming languages, in which they usually are the standard internal representation for programs. As an example, consider the simple C routine in Figure 4.2 and its abstract syntax tree representation in Figure 4.3. The tree, along with a symbol table indicating the types of the variables, provides all the information necessary to reconstruct the source (except information about the details of its layout, which could be included as annotations in the tree if desired).

A single tree traversal by a compiler component that is knowledgeable about the semantics of the source language is all that is necessary to transform the abstract syntax tree into a medium-level intermediate-code representation, such as those discussed in the next section.

Another form of high-level IL is one that is designed for dependence analysis, as discussed in Section 9.1. Such an IL is usually linear, rather than tree-like, but preserves some of the features of the source language, such as array subscripts and loop structure, in essentially their source forms. Our HIR described below in Section 4.6.2 has high-level features of this sort, but also includes many medium-level features.

4.3 Medium-Level Intermediate Languages

Medium-level intermediate languages are generally designed to reflect the range of features in a set of source languages, but in a language-independent way, and are designed to be good bases for generation of efficient machine code for one or more architectures. They provide a way to represent source variables, temporaries, and registers; to reduce control flow to simple conditional and unconditional branches, calls, and returns; and to make explicit the operations necessary to support block structure and procedures.

Our MIR (Section 4.6.1) and Sun IR (Section 21.1) are both good examples of medium-level ILs.

Medium-level ILs are appropriate for most of the optimizations done in compilers, such as common-subexpression elimination (Section 13.1), code motion (Section 13.2), and algebraic simplification (Section 12.3).

4.4 Low-Level Intermediate Languages

Low-level intermediate languages frequently correspond almost one-to-one to target-machine instructions and, hence, are often quite architecture-dependent. They deviate from one-to-one correspondence generally in cases where there are alternatives for the most effective code to generate for them. For example, a low-level intermediate language may have an integer multiply operator, while the target architecture may not have a multiply instruction, or the multiply instruction may not be the best choice of code to generate for some combinations of operands. Or, the intermediate code may have only simple addressing modes, such as register + register and register + constant, while the target architecture has more complex ones, such as scaled indexing or index register modification. In either case, it becomes the function of the final instruction-selection phase of the compilation process or of a postpass optimizer to select the appropriate instruction or instruction sequence to generate from the intermediate code. The use of such representations allows maximal optimization to be performed on the intermediate code and in the final phases of compilation,

```
L1:   t2 ← *t1
      t1 ← t1 + 4
      . . .
      t3 ← t3 + 1
      t5 ← t3 < t4
      if t5 goto L1
(a)
```

```
L1:   LDWM    4(0,r2),r3          L1:   LDWX    r2(0,r1),r3
      . . .                             . . .
      ADDI    1,r4,r4                   ADDIB,< 4,r2,L1
      COMB,<  r4,r5,L1
(b)                                (c)
```

FIG. 4.4 A MIR fragment in (a) with alternative PA-RISC code sequences generated for it in (b) and (c).

to either expand intermediate-code instructions into code sequences or to combine related ones into more powerful instructions.

For example, suppose the target architecture has a load instruction that optionally updates the base address used to fetch the data in parallel with fetching it, but that doing such an update fails to set the machine's condition codes or does not allow for its use in an add and (conditional) branch instruction, and so it cannot be used to count the containing loop. We then have available the possibility of combining intermediate-code instructions that fetch the data and increment the data address into a fetch with increment. On the other hand, if the loop control variable has been determined to be an induction variable and eliminated, we might need to keep the address update separate from the data fetch to use it to test for termination of the loop. An example of this is shown in Figure 4.4. The MIR in Figure 4.4(a) separately loads the data, increments the address loaded from, increments the loop counter, tests for completion of the loop, and branches based on the result of the test. The operands are temporaries and constants. The PA-RISC code in Figure 4.4(b) does a load word with modify that updates the address in r2 to point to the next array element, then does an add immediate to increment the loop counter, and a compare and branch to close the loop. The alternative code in Figure 4.4(c) does a load word indexed to access the data, and an add immediate and branch to update the address and close the loop.

4.5 Multi-Level Intermediate Languages

Some of the intermediate languages we consider include features that are best viewed as representing multiple levels in the same language. For example, the medium-level Sun IR has some high-level features, such as a way to represent multiply subscripted array references with the multiple subscripts, as well as with the several subscripts linearized to a single offset. The former representation is valuable for some varieties of dependence analysis (see Section 9.3) and hence valuable to vectorization, parallelization, and data-cache optimizations, while the latter form is more susceptible to the traditional loop optimizations.

At the other end of the spectrum, the low-level SLLIC includes integer multiply and divide operators, despite the fact that no PA-RISC hardware includes an integer multiply instruction that operates on integer registers (although PA-RISC 1.1 does provide one that operates on integers held in floating-point registers) or any integer divide instruction at all. This provides the opportunity to do optimizations (such as algebraic simplifications and strength reductions) that depend on recognizing that a multiplication or division is being performed and thus allows the module that generates the final code to determine that a particular multiplication, for example, can be done most efficiently using shift and add instructions, rather than by the hardware multiply.

4.6   Our Intermediate Languages: MIR, HIR, and LIR

In most of our examples expressed in an intermediate language from here on we use a language called MIR (Medium-level Intermediate Representation, pronounced "meer"), which we describe next. Where appropriate we use an enhanced version of MIR called HIR (High-level Intermediate Representation, pronounced "heer"), with some higher-level features, such as representing subscripted references to array elements by lists, rather than by linear expressions representing offsets from the base of the array. Correspondingly, where appropriate we use an adaptation of MIR called LIR (Low-level Intermediate Representation, pronounced "leer"), when lower-level features, such as explicit representation of registers, memory addresses, and the like are appropriate. On occasion we mix features of MIR and HIR or MIR and LIR in the same program to make a specific point or to represent a stage in the translation from one level to the next.

4.6.1   Medium-Level Intermediate Representation (MIR)

Basically MIR consists of a symbol table and quadruples consisting of an operator and three operands, each representing operations, plus a few additional operators that have fewer or more than three operands. A few categories of special symbols are reserved to denote temporary variables, registers, and labels. We write MIR instructions, wherever it is appropriate, as assignments, using "←" as the assignment operator. We use the XBNF notation described in Section 2.1 to present the syntax of MIR and the other intermediate languages, HIR and LIR, that are defined below.

We begin our description of MIR by giving the syntax of programs in XBNF, which appears in Table 4.1. A program consists of a sequence of program units. Each program unit consists of an optional label, followed by a sequence of (possibly labeled) instructions delimited by begin and end.

Next, we give the syntax of MIR instructions in Table 4.2, which implicitly declares the ICAN type MIRInst, and describe their semantics. A MIR instruction may

TABLE 4.1 XBNF syntax of MIR programs and program units.

Program	$\longrightarrow$	[*Label* :] *ProgUnit**
ProgUnit	$\longrightarrow$	[*Label* :] begin *MIRInsts* end
MIRInsts	$\longrightarrow$	{[*Label* :] *MIRInst* [│ │ *Comment*]}*
Label	$\longrightarrow$	*Identifier*

TABLE 4.2 XBNF syntax of MIR instructions.

MIRInst	$\longrightarrow$	*ReceiveInst* │ *AssignInst* │ *GotoInst* │ *IfInst* │ *CallInst*
		│ *ReturnInst* │ *SequenceInst* │ *Label* : *MIRInst*
ReceiveInst	$\longrightarrow$	receive *VarName* (*ParamType*)
AssignInst	$\longrightarrow$	*VarName* ← *Expression*
		│ *VarName* ←(*VarName*) *Operand*
		│ [*] *VarName* [. *EltName*] ← *Operand*
GotoInst	$\longrightarrow$	goto *Label*
IfInst	$\longrightarrow$	if *RelExpr* {goto *Label* │ trap *Const*}
CallInst	$\longrightarrow$	[call │ *VarName* ←] *ProcName* , *ArgList*
ArgList	$\longrightarrow$	([{*Operand* , *TypeName*} ⋈ ;])
ReturnInst	$\longrightarrow$	return [*Operand*]
SequenceInst	$\longrightarrow$	sequence
Expression	$\longrightarrow$	*Operand BinOper Operand*
		│ *UnaryOper Operand* │ *Operand*
RelExpr	$\longrightarrow$	*Operand RelOper Operand* │ [!] *Operand*
Operand	$\longrightarrow$	*VarName* │ *Const*
BinOper	$\longrightarrow$	+ │ - │ * │ / │ mod │ min │ max │ *RelOper*
		│ shl │ shr │ shra │ and │ or │ xor │ . │ *.
RelOper	$\longrightarrow$	= │ != │ < │ <= │ > │ >=
UnaryOper	$\longrightarrow$	- │ ! │ addr │ (*TypeName*) │ *
Const	$\longrightarrow$	*Integer* │ *FloatNumber* │ *Boolean*
Integer	$\longrightarrow$	0 │ [-] *NZDecDigit DecDigit** │ 0x *HexDigit*$^+$
FloatNumber	$\longrightarrow$	[-] *DecDigit*$^+$. *DecDigit*$^+$ [E [-] *DecDigit*$^+$] [D]
Boolean	$\longrightarrow$	true │ false
Label	$\longrightarrow$	*Identifier*
VarName	$\longrightarrow$	*Identifier*
EltName	$\longrightarrow$	*Identifier*
ParamType	$\longrightarrow$	val │ res │ valres │ ref
Identifier	$\longrightarrow$	*Letter* {*Letter* │ *Digit* │ _}*
Letter	$\longrightarrow$	a │ ... │ z │ A │ ... │ Z
NZDecDigit	$\longrightarrow$	1 │ 2 │ 3 │ 4 │ 5 │ 6 │ 7 │ 8 │ 9
DecDigit	$\longrightarrow$	0 │ *NZDecDigit*
HexDigit	$\longrightarrow$	*DecDigit* │ a │ ... │ f │ A │ ... │ F

be a receive, an assignment, a goto, an if, a call, a return, or a sequence, and it may be labeled.

A receive specifies the reception of a parameter from a calling routine. Receives may appear only as the first executable instructions in a program. The instruction specifies the parameter and the parameter-passing discipline used, namely, value (val), result (res), value-result (valres), or reference (ref).

An assignment either computes an expression and assigns its value to a variable, conditionally assigns the value of an operand to a variable, or assigns a value through a pointer or to a component of a structure. The target of the first two types of assignments is a variable. In a conditional assignment, the value of the variable in parentheses after the arrow must be Boolean, and the assignment is performed only if its value is true. An expression may consist of two operands combined by a binary operator, a unary operator followed by an operand, or just an operand. A binary operator may be any of the arithmetic operators

```
+  -  *  /  mod  min  max
```

or the relational operators

```
=  !=  <  <=  >  >=
```

or the shift and logical operators

```
shl  shr  shra  and  or  xor
```

or the component-selection operators

```
.  *.
```

A unary operator may be any of the symbols shown in Table 4.3.

The target of the second type of assignment is composed of an optional indirection operator "*" (which indicates assignment through a pointer), a variable name, and an optional component selection operator ("." followed by a member name of the given structure). It can be used to assign a value to an object accessed by means of a pointer, or to a component of a structure, or to an object that is both.

A goto instruction causes a transfer of control to the instruction labeled by its target, which must be in the current procedure. An if instruction tests a relation or a condition or its negation and, if it is satisfied, causes a transfer of control. The transfer of control may be either identical to that caused by a goto instruction or

TABLE 4.3 Unary operators in MIR.

Symbol	Meaning
–	Arithmetic minus
!	Logical negation
addr	Address of
(*TypeName*)	Type conversion
*	Pointer indirection

may be to an underlying run-time system (a "trap"). In the latter case, it specifies an integer trap number.

A call instruction gives the name of the procedure being called and a list of actual arguments and may specify a variable to be assigned the result of the call (if there is one). It causes the named procedure to be invoked with the arguments given and, if appropriate, the returned value to be assigned to the variable.

A return specifies execution of a return to the procedure that invoked the current one and may include an operand whose value is returned to the caller.

A sequence instruction represents a barrier in the intermediate code. Instructions with one or more operands with the volatile storage class modifier must not be moved across a sequence instruction, either forward or backward. This restricts the optimizations that can be performed on code that contains such instructions.

Identifiers consist of a letter followed by a sequence of zero or more letters, digits, or underscores. The name of a variable, type, or procedure may be any identifier, except those reserved for labels, temporaries, and symbolic registers, as described next. Identifiers consisting of an uppercase "L" followed by a non-negative decimal integer, e.g., L0, L32, and L7701, denote labels. For the names of temporaries, we reserve names consisting of a lowercase "t" followed by a non-negative decimal integer, e.g., t0, t32, and t7701. For symbolic registers, we reserve names consisting of a lowercase "s" followed by a non-negative decimal integer, and for real registers we reserve r0, ..., r31 and f0, ..., f31.

Integer constants may be in either decimal or hexadecimal notation. A decimal integer is either "0" or consists of an optional minus sign followed by a nonzero decimal digit, followed by zero or more decimal digits. A hexadecimal integer consists of "0x" followed by a sequence of hexadecimal digits, where a hexadecimal digit is either a decimal digit, any of the uppercase letters "A" through "F", or the lowercase letters "a" through "f". For example, the following are all legal integers:

```
0    1    3462    -2    -49    0x0    0x137A    0x2fffffffc
```

In a floating-point number, the part beginning with "E" indicates that the preceding value is to be multiplied by 10 to the value of the integer following the "E", and the optional "D" indicates a double-precision value. Thus, for example,

```
0.0    3.2E10    -0.5    -2.0E-22
```

are all single-precision floating-point numbers, and

```
0.0D    3.2E102D    -0.5D    -2.0E-22D
```

are all double-precision floating-point numbers.

Comments in MIR programs begin with the characters "||" and run to the end of the current line.

We use full MIR programs where appropriate, but most of the time we use only fragments, since they are enough to satisfy our needs.

As an example of MIR, the pair of C procedures in Figure 4.5 corresponds to the code in Figure 4.6.

Note that some of the operators in MIR, such as min and max, are not generally included in machine instruction sets. We include them in our intermediate code because they occur frequently in higher-level languages and some architectures provide

```
void make_node(p,n)
   struct node *p;
   int n;
{  struct node *q;
   q = malloc(sizeof(struct node));
   q->next = nil;
   q->value = n;
   p->next = q;
}

void insert_node(n,l)
   int n;
   struct node *l;
{  if (n > l->value)
      if (l->next == nil) make_node(l,n);
      else insert_node(n,l->next);
}
```

FIG. 4.5 Example pair of C procedures.

```
make_node:
   begin
      receive p(val)
      receive n(val)
      q ← call malloc,(8,int)
      *q.next ← nil
      *q.value ← n
      *p.next ← q
      return
   end
insert_node:
   begin
      receive n(val)
      receive l(val)
      t1 ← l*.value
      if n <= t1 goto L1
      t2 ← l*.next
      if t2 != nil goto L2
      call make_node(l,type1;n,int)
      return
L2:      t4 ← l*.next
      call insert_node,(n,int;t4,type1)
      return
L1:      return
   end
```

FIG. 4.6 MIR code for the pair of C procedures in Figure 4.5.

ways to compute them very efficiently and, in particular, without any branches. For example, for PA-RISC, the MIR instruction t1 ← t2 min t3 can be translated (assuming that ti is in register ri) to [2]

```
MOVE      r2,r1  /* copy r2 to r1 */
COM,>=    r3,r2  /* compare r3 to r2, nullify next if >= */
MOVE      r3,r1  /* copy r3 to r1 if not nullified */
```

Also, note that we have provided two ways to represent conditional tests and branches: either (1) by computing the value of a condition and then branching based on it or its negation, e.g.,

```
t3 ← t1 < t2
if t3 goto L1
```

or (2) by computing the condition and branching in the same MIR instruction, e.g.,

```
if t1 < t2 goto L1
```

The former approach is well suited to an architecture with condition codes, such as SPARC, POWER, or the Intel 386 architecture family. For such machines, the comparison can sometimes be subsumed by a previous subtract instruction, since t1 < t2 if and only if 0 < t2 − t1, and it may be desirable to move the compare or subtract away from the conditional branch to allow the condition codes to be determined in time to know whether the branch will be taken or not. The latter approach is well suited to an architecture with compare and branch instructions, such as PA-RISC or MIPS, since the MIR instruction can usually be translated to a single machine instruction.

4.6.2   High-Level Intermediate Representation (HIR)

In this section we describe the extensions to MIR that make it into the higher-level intermediate representation HIR.

An array element may be referenced with multiple subscripts and with its subscripts represented explicitly in HIR. Arrays are stored in row-major order, i.e., with the last subscript varying fastest. We also include a high-level looping construct, the for loop, and a compound if. Thus, *MIRInst* needs to be replaced by *HIRInst*, and the syntax of *AssignInst* and *Operand* need to be changed as shown in Table 4.4. An *IntExpr* is any expression whose value is an integer.

The semantics of the for loop are similar to those of Fortran's do, rather than C's for statement. In particular, the meaning of the HIR for loop in Figure 4.7(a) is given by the MIR code in Figure 4.7(b), with the additional proviso that the body of the loop must not change the value of the control variable v. Note that Figure 4.7(b) selects one or the other loop body (beginning with L1 or L2), depending on whether opd2 > 0 or not.

---

2. The MOVE and COM opcodes are both pseudo-ops, not actual PA-RISC instructions. MOVE can be implemented as an ADD or OR and COM as a COMCLR.

TABLE 4.4 Changes to xbnf description of instructions and operands to turn MIR into HIR.

HIRInst	$\longrightarrow$	*AssignInst* | *GotoInst* | *IfInst* | *CallInst* | *ReturnInst*
		| *ReceiveInst* | *SequenceInst* | *ForInst* | *IfInst*
		| *TrapInst* | *Label* : *HIRInst*
ForInst	$\longrightarrow$	for *VarName* $\leftarrow$ *Operand* [by *Operand*] to *Operand* do
		*HIRInst** endfor
IfInst	$\longrightarrow$	if *RelExpr* then *HIRInst** [else *HIRInst**] endif
AssignInst	$\longrightarrow$	[*VarName* | *ArrayRef*] $\leftarrow$ *Expression*
		| [*] *VarName* [. *EltName*] $\leftarrow$ *Operand*
TrapInst	$\longrightarrow$	trap *Const*
Operand	$\longrightarrow$	*VarName* | *ArrayRef* | *Const*
ArrayRef	$\longrightarrow$	*VarName* [{*Subscript* $\bowtie$,}]
Subscript	$\longrightarrow$	*IntExpr*

```
for v ← opd1 by opd2 to opd3
    instructions
endfor
```

```
        v ← opd1
        t2 ← opd2
        t3 ← opd3
        if t2 > 0 goto L2
L1: if v < t3 goto L3
        instructions
        v ← v + t2
        goto L1
L2: if v > t3 goto L3
        instructions
        v ← v + t2
        goto L2
L3:
```

(a)   (b)

FIG. 4.7 (a) Form of the HIR for loop, and (b) its semantics in MIR.

4.6.3   Low-Level Intermediate Representation (LIR)

In this section we describe the changes to MIR that make it into the lower-level intermediate code LIR. We give only the necessary changes to the syntax and semantics of MIR by providing replacements for productions in the syntax of MIR (and additional ones, as needed) and descriptions of the additional features. The changes to the xbnf description are as shown in Table 4.5. Assignments and operands need to be changed to replace variable names by registers and memory addresses. Calls need to be changed to delete the argument list, since we assume that parameters are

TABLE 4.5 Changes in the XBNF description of MIR instructions and expressions to create LIR.

LIRInst	$\longrightarrow$	*RegAsgnInst* | *CondAsgnInst* | *StoreInst* | *LoadInst*
		| *GotoInst* | *IfInst* | *CallInst* |*ReturnInst*
		| *SequenceInst* | *Label* : *LIRInst*
RegAsgnInst	$\longrightarrow$	*RegName* ← *Expression*
		| *RegName* (*Const* , *Const*) ← *Operand*
CondAsgnInst	$\longrightarrow$	*RegName* ←(*RegName*) *Operand*
StoreInst	$\longrightarrow$	*MemAddr* [(*Length*)] ← *Operand*
LoadInst	$\longrightarrow$	*RegName* ← *MemAddr* [(*Length*)]
GotoInst	$\longrightarrow$	goto {*Label* | *RegName* [{+ | -} *Const*]}
CallInst	$\longrightarrow$	[*RegName* ←] call {*ProcName* | *RegName*} , *RegName*
Operand	$\longrightarrow$	*RegName* | *Const*
MemAddr	$\longrightarrow$	[*RegName*] [(*Length*)]
		| [*RegName* + *RegName*] [(*Length*)]
		| [*RegName* [+ | -] *Const*] [(*Length*)]
Length	$\longrightarrow$	*Const*

passed in the run-time stack or in registers (or, if there are more than a predetermined number of parameters, the excess ones are also passed in the run-time stack).

There are five types of assignment instructions, namely, those that

1. assign an expression to a register;

2. assign an operand to an element of a register (in LIR, the element is represented by two integers, namely, the first bit position and the width in bits of the element separated by a comma and enclosed in parentheses);

3. conditionally assign an operand to a register depending on the value in a register;

4. store an operand at a memory address; or

5. load a register from a memory address.

A memory address is given in square brackets ("[" and "]") as the contents of a register, the sum of the contents of two registers, or a register's contents plus or minus an integer constant. The length specification, if it appears, is an integer number of bytes.

In a call instruction that has two or more register operands, the next to last contains the address to be branched to and the last names the register to be used to store the return address.

For the names of registers, we reserve r0, r1, ... , r31 for integer or general-purpose registers, f0, f1, ... , f31 for floating-point registers, and s0, s1, ... for symbolic registers.

4.7   Representing MIR, HIR, and LIR in ICAN

So as to be able to conveniently manipulate MIR, HIR, and LIR code in ICAN programs, we next discuss a means of representing the former in the latter, which constitutes the definition of the ICAN types MIRInst, HIRInst, LIRInst, and a series of others. This representation can be thought of as an internal form, i.e., ICAN structures, corresponding to the external printed forms of the intermediate representations that are defined in the preceding section.

We begin with Table 4.6, which gives, for each intermediate-language operator (including the ones that represent operations that are thought of as applying to the left-hand side in an assignment), its representation by an element of the enumerated type IROper, which is defined as follows:

```
IROper = enum {
        add,      sub,      mul,      div,      mod,      min,
        max,      eql,      neql,     less,     lseq,     grtr,
        gteq,     shl,      shr,      shra,     and,      or,
        xor,      ind,      elt,      indelt,   neg,      not,
        addr,     val,      cast,     lind,     lcond,    lindelt,
        lelt}
```

Next we define the ICAN types Var, Const, Register, Symbol, Operand, and LIROperand.

```
Var = CharString
Const = CharString
Register = CharString
Symbol = Var ∪ Const
Operand = Var ∪ Const ∪ TypeName
LIROperand = Register ∪ Const ∪ TypeName
```

Actually, each type is a subset of the type it is declared to be. In particular:

1. A member of Var is a quoted sequence of alphanumeric characters and underscores, the first of which must be a letter. Temporaries are variables that begin with a lowercase "t" and follow it by a sequence of one or more decimal digits. Symbols that begin with one of "s", "r", or "f" followed by one or more decimal digits denote registers and are not members of Var.

2. A member of Const is a quoted sequence of characters representing an integer or a floating-point number.

TABLE 4.6 Names of MIR, HIR, and LIR operators as members of the ICAN enumerated type IROper.

Intermediate-Code Operator	ICAN Identifier	Intermediate-Code Operator	ICAN Identifier
+	add	– (binary)	sub
* (binary)	mul	/	div
mod	mod	min	min
max	max	=	eql
!=	neql	<	less
<=	lseq	>	grtr
>=	gteq	shl	shl
shr	shr	shra	shra
and	and	or	or
xor	xor	* (unary)	ind
.	elt	*.	indelt
– (unary)	neg	!	not
addr	addr	(none)	val
(type cast)	cast		

Intermediate-Code Operator	ICAN Identifier
(indirect assignment)	lind
(conditional assignment)	lcond
(indirect element assignment)	lindelt
(element assignment)	lelt

3. A Register is a symbol that begins with one of "s", "r", or "f" followed by one or more decimal digits. Symbolic registers begin with "s", integer registers with "r", and floating-point registers with "f".

The remaining parts of the representation of the intermediate codes in ICAN depend on the particular intermediate code—MIR, HIR, or LIR—so we divide up the presentation into the following three subsections. First we define Instruction to be

    Instruction = HIRInst ∪ MIRInst ∪ LIRInst

4.7.1   Representing MIR in ICAN

We represent each kind of MIR instruction by an ICAN tuple, as shown in Table 4.7, which implicitly declares the type MIRInst. The enumerated types MIRKind,

TABLE 4.7   MIR instructions represented as ICAN tuples.

Label:
⟨kind:label,lbl:*Label*⟩

receive *VarName*(*ParamType*)
⟨kind:receive,left:*VarName*,ptype:*ParamType*⟩

VarName ← *Operand1 Binop Operand2*
⟨kind:binasgn,left:*VarName*,opr:*Binop*,opd1:*Operand1*,opd2:*Operand2*⟩

VarName ← *Unop Operand*
⟨kind:unasgn,left:*VarName*,opr:*Unop*,opd:*Operand*⟩

VarName ← *Operand*
⟨kind:valasgn,left:*VarName*,opd:*Operand*⟩

VarName1 ←(*VarName2*) *Operand*
⟨kind:condasgn,left:*VarName1*,cond:*VarName2*,opd:*Operand*⟩

VarName ← (*TypeName*) *Operand*
⟨kind:castasgn,left:*VarName*,type:*TypeName*,opd:*Operand*⟩

VarName ← *Operand*
⟨kind:indasgn,left:*VarName*,opd:*Operand*⟩

VarName.*EltName* ← *Operand*
⟨kind:eltasgn,left:*VarName*,elt:*EltName*,opd:*Operand*⟩

VarName.*EltName* ← *Operand*
⟨kind:indeltasgn,left:*VarName*,elt:*EltName*,opd:*Operand*⟩

goto *Label*
⟨kind:goto,lbl:*Label*⟩

if *Operand1 Binop Operand2* goto *Label*
⟨kind:binif,opr:*Binop*,opd1:*Operand1*,opd2:*Operand2*,lbl:*Label*⟩

if *Unop Operand* goto *Label*
⟨kind:unif,opr:*Unop*,opd:*Operand*,lbl:*Label*⟩

if *Operand* goto *Label*
⟨kind:valif,opr:*Operand*,lbl:*Label*⟩

if *Operand1 Binop Operand2* trap *Const*
⟨kind:bintrap,opr:*Binop*,opd1:*Operand1*,opd2:*Operand2*,trapno:*Const*⟩

if *Unop Operand* trap *Const*
⟨kind:untrap,opr:*Unop*,opd:*Operand*,trapno:*Const*⟩

if *Operand* trap *Const*
⟨kind:valtrap,opr:*Operand*,trapno:*Const*⟩

call *ProcName*,(*Opd1*,*TN1*; ...;*Opdn*,*TNn*)
⟨kind:call,proc:*ProcName*,args:[⟨*Opd1*,*TN1*⟩,...,⟨*Opdn*,*TNn*⟩]⟩

(continued)

TABLE 4.7 *(continued)*

VarName ← *ProcName*, (*Opd1*, *TN1*; ...; *Opdn*, *TNn*)
    ⟨kind:callasgn,left:*VarName*,proc:*ProcName*,
      args:[⟨*Opd1*,*TN1*⟩,...,⟨*Opdn*,*TNn*⟩]⟩

return
    ⟨kind:return⟩

return *Operand*
    ⟨kind:retval,opd:*Operand*⟩

sequence
    ⟨kind:sequence⟩

VarName
    ⟨kind:var,val:*VarName*⟩

Const
    ⟨kind:const,val:*Const*⟩

TNi
        ptype:*TNi*

OpdKind, and ExpKind and the functions Exp_Kind( ) and Has_Left( ) are defined in Figure 4.8.

Exp_Kind(k) indicates whether a MIR instruction of kind k contains a binary expression, a unary expression, a list of expressions, or no expression, and Has_Left(k) returns true if a MIR instruction of kind k has a left field and false otherwise. From here until we begin to need the basic-block structure of procedures in Chapter 12, we represent sequences of intermediate-code instructions by the array Inst[$1 \cdot \cdot n$] for some n, which is declared as

```
Inst: array [1··n] of Instruction
```

For example, the MIR instruction sequence

```
L1:    b ← a
       c ← b + 1
```

is represented by the array of tuples

```
Inst[1] = ⟨kind:label,lbl:"L1"⟩
Inst[2] = ⟨kind:valasgn,left:"b",opd:⟨kind:var,val:"a"⟩⟩
Inst[3] = ⟨kind:binasgn,left:"c",opr:add,
              opd1:⟨kind:var,val:"b"⟩,opd2:⟨kind:const,val:"1"⟩⟩
```

As a larger example, Figure 4.9 shows the MIR code for the body of the second program unit, labeled "insert_node", in Figure 4.6 represented as ICAN tuples.

```
MIRKind = enum {
    label,     receive,  binasgn, unasgn,   valasgn,
    condasgn, castasgn, indasgn, eltasgn,  indeltasgn,
    goto,      binif,    unif,     valif,     bintrap,
    untrap,    valtrap,  call,     callasgn, return,
    retval,    sequence}

OpdKind = enum {var,const,type}
ExpKind = enum {binexp,unexp,noexp,listexp}
Exp_Kind: MIRKind ⟶ ExpKind
Has_Left: MIRKind ‐ > boolean

Exp_Kind := {
    ⟨label,noexp⟩,        ⟨receive,noexp⟩,   ⟨binasgn,binexp⟩,
    ⟨unasgn,unexp⟩,       ⟨valasgn,unexp⟩,   ⟨condasgn,unexp⟩,
    ⟨castasgn,unexp⟩,     ⟨indasgn,unexp⟩,   ⟨eltasgn,unexp⟩,
    ⟨indeltasgn,unexp⟩, ⟨goto,noexp⟩,        ⟨binif,binexp⟩,
    ⟨unif,unexp⟩,         ⟨valif,unexp⟩,     ⟨bintrap,binexp⟩,
    ⟨untrap,unexp⟩,       ⟨valtrap,unexp⟩,   ⟨call,listexp⟩,
    ⟨callasgn,listexp⟩, ⟨return,noexp⟩,      ⟨retval,unexp⟩,
    ⟨sequence,noexp⟩}

Has_Left := {
    ⟨label,false⟩,        ⟨receive,true⟩,    ⟨binasgn,true⟩,
    ⟨unasgn,true⟩,        ⟨valasgn,true⟩,    ⟨condasgn,true⟩,
    ⟨castasgn,true⟩,      ⟨indasgn,true⟩,    ⟨eltasgn,true⟩,
    ⟨indeltasgn,true⟩, ⟨goto,false⟩,         ⟨binif,false⟩,
    ⟨unif,false⟩,         ⟨valif,false⟩,     ⟨bintrap,false⟩,
    ⟨untrap,false⟩,       ⟨valtrap,false⟩,   ⟨call,false⟩,
    ⟨callasgn,true⟩,      ⟨return,false⟩,    ⟨retval,false⟩,
    ⟨sequence,false⟩}
```

FIG. 4.8 Types and functions used to determine properties of MIR instructions.

Note that the TNi occurring in the argument list of a call or callasgn instruction are type names: a pair $\langle Opdi, TNi \rangle$ indicates the value and type of the ith argument.

4.7.2   Representing HIR in ICAN

To represent HIR in ICAN, we proceed essentially as for MIR. Table 4.8 shows the correspondence between HIR instructions and ICAN tuples and implicitly declares the type HIRInst. HIR needs no additional operators, so we use IROper to represent the type of its operands.

The enumerated types HIRKind, HIROpdKind, and HIRExpKind and the functions HIR_Exp_Kind( ) and HIR_Has_Left( ) are somewhat different from the ones for

```
Inst[1]  = ⟨kind:receive,left:"n",ptype:val⟩
Inst[2]  = ⟨kind:receive,left:"l",ptype:val⟩
Inst[3]  = ⟨kind:binasgn,left:"t1",opr:indelt,
             opd1:⟨kind:var,val:"l"⟩,
             opd2:⟨kind:const,val:"value"⟩⟩
Inst[4]  = ⟨kind:if,opr:lseq,opd1:⟨kind:var,val:"n"⟩,
             opd2:⟨kind:var,val:"t1"⟩,lbl:"L1"⟩
Inst[5]  = ⟨kind:binasgn,left:"t2",opr:indelt,
             opd1:⟨kind:var,val:"l"⟩,
             opd2:⟨kind:const,val:"value"⟩⟩
Inst[6]  = ⟨kind:if,opr:neql,opd1:⟨kind:var,val:"t2"⟩,
             opd2:⟨kind:const,val:"nil"⟩,lbl:"L2"⟩
Inst[7]  = ⟨kind:call,proc:"make_node",
             args:[⟨⟨kind:var,val:"t3"⟩,ptype:"type1"⟩,
             ⟨⟨kind:var,val:"n"⟩,ptype:"int"⟩]⟩
Inst[8]  = ⟨kind:return⟩
Inst[9]  = ⟨kind:label,lbl:"L2"⟩
Inst[10] = ⟨kind:binasgn,left:"t4",opr:indelt,
             opd1:⟨kind:var,val:"l"⟩,
             opd2:⟨kind:const,val:"next"⟩⟩
Inst[11] = ⟨kind:call,proc:"insert_node",
             args:[⟨⟨kind:var,val:"n"⟩,ptype:"int"⟩,
               ⟨⟨kind:var,val:"t4"⟩,ptype:"type1"⟩]⟩
Inst[12] = ⟨kind:return⟩
Inst[13] = ⟨kind:label,lbl:"L1"⟩
Inst[14] = ⟨kind:return⟩
```

FIG. 4.9 The body of the MIR program unit insert_node in Figure 4.6 represented by ICAN tuples.

MIR and are defined in Figure 4.10. HIR_Exp_Kind(k) indicates whether a HIR instruction of kind k contains a ternary expression,[3] a binary expression, a unary expression, a list of expressions, or no expression, and HIR_Has_Left(k) returns true if a HIR instruction of kind k has a left field and false otherwise.

4.7.3   Representing LIR in ICAN

Table 4.9 shows the correspondence between LIR instructions and ICAN structures. The last three items represent operands. As in the representation of MIR and HIR code in ICAN, we use the type IROper to represent LIR operators.

The enumerated types LIRKind, LIROpdKind, and LIRExpKind and the functions LIR_Exp_Kind( ) and LIR_Has_Left( ) are declared in Figure 4.11. LIR_Exp_Kind(k) indicates whether a LIR instruction of kind k contains a binary

---

3. Only for instructions have ternary expressions.

TABLE 4.8 Representation of HIR instructions that are not in MIR in ICAN.

---

for *VarName* ← *Operand1* by *Operand2* to *Operand3* do
      ⟨kind:for,left:*VarName*,opd1:*Operand1*,opd2:*Operand2*,opd3:*Operand3*⟩

endfor
      ⟨kind:endfor⟩

if *Operand1 Binop Operand2* then
      ⟨kind:strbinif,opr:*Binop*,opd1:*Operand1*,opd2:*Operand2*⟩

if *Unop Operand* then
      ⟨kind:strunif,opr:*Unop*,opd:*Operand*⟩

if *Operand* then
      ⟨kind:strvalif,opd:*Operand*⟩

else
      ⟨kind:else⟩

endif
      ⟨kind:endif⟩

VarName[*Expr1*,...,*Exprn*] ← *Operand1 Binop Operand2*
      ⟨kind:arybinasgn,left:*VarName*,subs:[*Expr1*,...,*Exprn*],opr:*Binop*,
      opd1:*Operand1*,opd2:*Operand2*⟩

VarName[*Expr1*,...,*Exprn*] ← *Unop Operand*
      ⟨kind:aryunasgn,left:*VarName*,subs:[*Expr1*,...,*Exprn*],opr:*Unop*,
      opd:*Operand*⟩

VarName[*Expr1*,...,*Exprn*] ← *Operand*
      ⟨kind:aryvalasgn,left:*VarName*,subs:[*Expr1*,...,*Exprn*],opd:*Operand*⟩

VarName[*Expr1*,...,*Exprn*]
      ⟨kind:aryref,var:*VarName*,subs:[*Expr1*,...,*Exprn*]⟩

---

expression, a unary expression, or no expression, and LIR_Has_Left(k) returns
true if a LIR instruction of kind k has a left field and false otherwise.

A *RegName* operand may have as its value an integer register (written ri), a
floating-point register (written fi), or a symbolic register (written si). The enumeration and function declared by

```
RegType = enum {reg,freg,symreg}
Reg_Type: Register ⟶ RegType
```

can be used to distinguish the three varieties. Memory addresses (denoted by
tran(*MemAddr*) in Table 4.9) are represented as shown in Table 4.10.

As an example of the representation of LIR code in ICAN, consider the code
shown in Figure 4.12. The corresponding sequence of ICAN structures is shown in
Figure 4.13.

```
HIRKind = enum {
    label,     receive,   binasgn, unasgn,  valasgn,
    condasgn,  castasgn,  indasgn, eltasgn, indeltasgn,
    goto,      trap,      call,    callasgn, return,
    retval,    sequence,  for,     endfor,  strbinif,
    strunif,   strvalif,  else,    endif,   arybinasgn,
    aryunasgn, aryvalasgn}

HIROpdKind = enum {var,const,type,aryref}
HIRExpKind = enum {terexp,binexp,unexp,noexp,listexp}
HIR_Exp_Kind: HIRKind ⟶ HIRExpKind
HIR_Has_Left: HIRKind ⟶ boolean

HIR_Exp_Kind := {
    ⟨label,noexp⟩,          ⟨receive,noexp⟩,
    ⟨binasgn,binexp⟩,       ⟨unasgn,unexp⟩,
    ⟨valasgn,unexp⟩,        ⟨condasgn,unexp⟩,
    ⟨castasgn,unexp⟩,       ⟨indasgn,unexp⟩,
    ⟨eltasgn,unexp⟩,        ⟨indeltasgn,unexp⟩,
    ⟨goto,noexp⟩,           ⟨trap,noexp⟩,
    ⟨call,listexp⟩,         ⟨callasgn,listexp⟩,
    ⟨return,noexp⟩,         ⟨retval,unexp⟩,
    ⟨sequence,noexp⟩,       ⟨for,terexp⟩,
    ⟨endfor,noexp⟩,         ⟨strbinif,binexp⟩,
    ⟨strunif,unexp⟩,        ⟨strvalif,unexp⟩,
    ⟨else,noexp⟩,           ⟨endif,noexp⟩,
    ⟨arybinasgn,binexp⟩, ⟨aryunasagn,unexp⟩,
    ⟨aryvalasagn,unexp⟩
}

HIR_Has_Left := {
    ⟨label,false⟩,      ⟨receive,true⟩,
    ⟨binasgn,true⟩,     ⟨unasgn,true⟩,
    ⟨valasgn,true⟩,     ⟨condasgn,true⟩,
    ⟨castasgn,true⟩,    ⟨indasgn,true⟩,
    ⟨eltasgn,true⟩,     ⟨indeltasgn,true⟩,
    ⟨goto,false⟩,       ⟨trap,false⟩,
    ⟨call,false⟩,       ⟨callasgn,true⟩,
    ⟨return,false⟩,     ⟨retval,false⟩,
    ⟨sequence,false⟩,   ⟨for,true⟩,
    ⟨endfor,false⟩,     ⟨strbinif,false⟩,
    ⟨strunif,false⟩,    ⟨strvalif,false⟩,
    ⟨else,false⟩,       ⟨endif,false⟩,
    ⟨arybinasgn,true⟩, ⟨aryunasagn,true⟩,
    ⟨aryvalasagn,true⟩
}
```

FIG. 4.10 ICAN types and functions to determine properties of HIR instructions.

TABLE 4.9 Representation of LIR instructions in ICAN.

Label:
    ⟨kind:label,lbl:*Label*⟩

RegName ← Operand1 Binop Operand2
    ⟨kind:regbin,left:*RegName*,opr:*Binop*,opd1:*Operand1*,opd2:*Operand2*⟩

RegName ← Unop Operand
    ⟨kind:regun,left:*RegName*,opr:*Unop*,opd:*Operand*⟩

RegName ← Operand
    ⟨kind:regval,left:*RegName*,opd.*Operand*⟩

RegName1 ← (RegName2) Operand
    ⟨kind:regcond,left:*RegName1*,cond:*RegName2*,opd:*Operand*⟩

RegName(Const1,Const2) ← Operand
    ⟨kind:regelt,left:*RegName*,fst:*Const1*,blen:*Const2*,opd:*Operand*⟩

MemAddr ← Operand
    ⟨kind:stormem,addr:tran(*MemAddr*),opd:*Operand*⟩

RegName ←MemAddr
    ⟨kind:loadmem,left:*RegName*,addr:tran(*MemAddr*)⟩

goto *Label*
    ⟨kind:goto,lbl:*Label*⟩

goto *RegName + Const*
    ⟨kind:gotoaddr,reg:*RegName*,disp:*Const*⟩

if *Operand1 Binop Operand2* goto *Label*
    ⟨kind:regbinif,opr:*Binop*,opd1:*Operand1*,opd2:*Operand2*,lbl:*Label*⟩

if *Unop Operand* goto *Label*
    ⟨kind:regunif,opr:*Unop*,opd:*Operand*,lbl:*Label*⟩

if *Operand* goto *Label*
    ⟨kind:regvalif,opr:*Operand*,lbl:*Label*⟩

if *Operand1 Binop Operand2* trap *Const*
    ⟨kind:regbintrap,opr:*Binop*,opd1:*Operand1*,opd2:*Operand2*,
    trapno:*Const*⟩

if *Unop Operand* trap *Const*
    ⟨kind:reguntrap,opr:*Unop*,opd:*Operand*,trapno:*Const*⟩

if *Operand* trap *Const*
    ⟨kind:regvaltrap,opr:*Operand*,trapno:*Const*⟩

call *ProcName,RegName*
    kind:callreg,proc:*ProcName*,rreg:*RegName*⟩

call *RegName1,RegName2*
    ⟨kind:callreg2,creg:*RegName1*,rreg:*RegName2*⟩

(continued)

TABLE 4.9 *(continued)*

RegName1 ← call *ProcName*,*RegName2*
        ⟨kind:callregasgn,left:*RegName1*,proc:*ProcName*,rreg:*RegName2*⟩

RegName1 ← call *RegName2*,*RegName3*
        ⟨kind:callreg3,left:*RegName1*,creg:*RegName2*,rreg:*RegName3*⟩

return
        ⟨kind:return⟩

return *Operand*
        ⟨kind:retval,opd:*Operand*⟩

sequence
        ⟨kind:sequence⟩

RegName
        ⟨kind:regno,val:*RegName*⟩

Const
        ⟨kind:const,val:*Const*⟩

TypeName
        ⟨kind:type,val:*TypeName*⟩

```
LIRKind = enum {
    label,      regbin,   regun,     regval,     regcond,
    regelt,     stormem,  loadmem,   goto,       gotoaddr,
    regbinif,   regunif,  regvalif,  regbintrap, reguntrap,
    regvaltrap, callreg,  callreg2,  callregasgn, callreg3,
    return,     retval,   sequence}

LIROpdKind = enum {regno,const,type}
LIRExpKind = enum {binexp,unexp,noexp}
LIR_Exp_Kind: LIRKind ⟶ LIRExpKind
LIR_Has_Left: LIRKind ⟶ boolean

LIR_Exp_Kind := {
    ⟨label,noexp⟩,        ⟨regbin,binexp⟩,
    ⟨regun,unexp⟩,        ⟨regval,unexp⟩,
    ⟨regcond,unexp⟩,      ⟨regelt,unexp⟩,
    ⟨stormem,unexp⟩,      ⟨loadmem,noexp⟩,
    ⟨goto,noexp⟩,         ⟨gotoaddr,noexp⟩,
    ⟨regbinif,binexp⟩,    ⟨regunif,unexp⟩,
    ⟨regvalif,unexp⟩,     ⟨regbintrap,binexp⟩,
    ⟨reguntrap,unexp⟩,    ⟨regvaltrap,unexp⟩,
    ⟨callreg,noexp⟩,      ⟨callreg2,noexp⟩,
    ⟨callregasgn,noexp⟩,  ⟨callreg3,noexp⟩,
    ⟨return,noexp⟩,       ⟨retval,unexp⟩,
    ⟨sequence,noexp⟩}
```

FIG. 4.11 ICAN data types and functions to determine properties of LIR instructions.

```
LIR_Has_Left := {
    ⟨label,false⟩,         ⟨regbin,true⟩,
    ⟨regun,true⟩,          ⟨regval,true⟩,
    ⟨regcond,false⟩,       ⟨regelt,false⟩,
    ⟨stormem,false⟩,       ⟨loadmem,true⟩,
    ⟨goto,false⟩,          ⟨gotoaddr,false⟩,
    ⟨regbinif,false⟩,      ⟨regunif,false⟩,
    ⟨regvalif,false⟩,      ⟨regbintrap,false⟩,
    ⟨reguntrap,false⟩,     ⟨regvaltrap,false⟩,
    ⟨callreg,false⟩,       ⟨callreg2,false⟩,
    ⟨callregasgn,truc⟩,    ⟨callreg3,true⟩,
    ⟨return,false⟩,        ⟨retval,false⟩,
    ⟨sequence,false⟩}
```

FIG. 4.11 *(continued)*

TABLE 4.10 Representation of memory addresses (denoted by tran(*MemAddr*) in Table 4.9).

[*RegName*] (*Length*)
    ⟨kind:addr1r,reg:*RegName*,len:*Length*⟩

[*RegName1+RegName2*] (*Length*)
    ⟨kind:addr2r,reg:*RegName1*,reg2:*RegName2*,len:*Length*⟩

[*RegName+Const*] (*Length*)
    ⟨kind:addrrc,reg:*RegName*,disp:*Const*,len:*Length*⟩

```
L1:  r1 ← [r7+4]
     r2 ← [r7+r8]
     r3 ← r1 + r2
     r4 ← -r3
     if r3 > 0 goto L2
     r5 ←(r9) r1
     [r7-8](2) ← r5
L2:  return r4
```

FIG. 4.12 An example of LIR code to be represented by ICAN tuples.

```
Inst[1]  = ⟨kind:label,lbl:"L1"⟩
Inst[2]  = ⟨kind:loadmem,left:"r1",
           addr:⟨kind:addrrc,reg:"r7",disp:"4",len:4⟩⟩
Inst[3]  = ⟨kind:loadmem,left:"r2",
           addr:⟨kind:addr2r,reg:"r7",reg2:"r8",len:4⟩⟩
Inst[4]  = ⟨kind:regbin,left:"r3",opr:add,opd1:⟨kind:regno,
           val:"r1"⟩,opd2:⟨kind:regno,val:"r2"⟩⟩
```

(continued)

FIG. 4.13 The sequence of ICAN tuples corresponding to the LIR code in Figure 4.12.

```
Inst[5]   = ⟨kind:regun,left:"r4",opr:neg,
              opd:⟨kind:regno,val:"r3"⟩⟩
Inst[6]   = ⟨kind:regbinif,opr:grtr,
              opd1:⟨kind:regno,val:"r3"⟩,
              opd2:⟨kind:const,val:"0"⟩,lbl:"L2"⟩
Inst[7]   = ⟨kind:regcond,left:"r5",sel:"r9",
              opd:⟨kind:regno,val:"r1"⟩⟩
Inst[8]   = ⟨kind:stormem,
              addr:⟨kind:addrrc,reg:"r7",disp:"-8",len:2⟩,
              opd:⟨kind:regno,val:"r5"⟩⟩
Inst[9]   = ⟨kind:label,lbl:"L2"⟩
Inst[10]  = ⟨kind:retval,opd:⟨kind:regno,val:"r4"⟩⟩
```

FIG. 4.13 *(continued)*

4.8   ICAN Naming of Data Structures and Routines that Manipulate Intermediate Code

From here on in the text, in almost every case, we view a procedure as consisting of several data structures, as follows:

1. ProcName: Procedure, the name of the procedure.

2. nblocks: integer, the number of basic blocks making up the procedure.

3. ninsts: array [1··nblocks] of integer, an array such that for $i = 1, \ldots,$ nblocks, ninsts[i] is the number of instructions in basic block i.

4. Block, LBlock: array [1··nblocks] of array [··] of Instruction, the array of arrays of HIR or MIR instructions (for Block) or LIR instructions (for LBlock) that make up the basic blocks, i.e., Block[i] [1··ninsts[i]] is the array of instructions in basic block i, and similarly for LBlock.

5. Succ, Pred: integer $\longrightarrow$ set of integer, the functions that map each basic block index i to the sets of indexes of the successor and predecessor basic blocks, respectively, of block i.

In a few instances, such as sparse conditional constant propagation (Section 12.6), where we focus on individual instructions, rather than blocks, we use slightly different naming conventions.

The procedures

```
insert_before(i,j,ninsts,Block,inst)
insert_after(i,j,ninsts,Block,inst)
append_block(i,ninsts,Block,inst)
```

defined in Figure 4.14 insert instruction *inst* before or after Block[i] [j] or append *inst* to Block[i] and adjust the data structures accordingly. Note that a request to insert an instruction after the last instruction of a block is handled specially if the last instruction is a goto or an if—i.e., the instruction is inserted just before the control-transfer instruction.

```
procedure insert_before(i,j,ninsts,Block,inst)
   i, j: in integer
   ninsts: inout array [··] of integer
   Block: inout array [··] of array [··] of Instruction
   inst: in Instruction
begin
   || insert an instruction after position j in block i
   || and adjust data structures accordingly
   k: integer
   for k := j to ninsts[i] do
      Block[i][k+1] := Block[i][k]
   od
   ninsts[i] += 1
   Block[i][j] := inst
end    || insert_before

procedure insert_after(i,j,ninsts,Block,inst)
   i, j: in integer
   ninsts: inout array [··] of integer
   Block: inout array [··] of array [··] of Instruction
   inst: in Instruction
begin
   || insert an instruction after position j in block i
   || and adjust data structures accordingly
   k: integer
   if j = ninsts[i] & Control_Transfer(Block[i][j]) then
      ninsts[i] := j += 1
      Block[i][j] := Block[i][j-1]
      Block[i][j-1] := inst
   else
      for k := j+1 to ninsts[i] do
         Block[i][k+1] := Block[i][k]
      od
      ninsts[i] += 1
      Block[i][j+1] := inst
   fi
end    || insert_after

procedure append_block(i,ninsts,Block,inst)
   i: in integer
   ninsts: inout array [··] of integer
   Block: inout array [··] of array [··] of Instruction
   inst: in Instruction
begin
   || add an instruction at the end of block i
   insert_after(i,ninsts[i],Block,inst)
end    || append_block
```

FIG. 4.14 The ICAN routines insert_before( ), insert_after( ), and append_block( ) that insert an instruction into a basic block before or after a given position or append an instruction to a block.

```
procedure delete_inst(i,j,nblocks,ninsts,Block,Succ,Pred)
    i, j: in integer
    nblocks: inout integer
    ninsts: inout array [··] of integer
    Block: inout array [··] of array [··] of Instruction
    Succ, Pred: inout integer ⟶ set of integer
begin
    || delete instruction j from block i and adjust data structures
    k: integer
    for k := j to ninsts[i]-1 do
        Block[i][k] := Block[i][k+1]
    od
    ninsts[i] -= 1
    if ninsts[i] = 0 then
        delete_block(i,nblocks,ninsts,Block,Succ,Pred)
    fi
end    || delete_inst
```

FIG. 4.15 The ICAN routine delete_inst( ) that deletes an instruction at a given position from a basic block.

```
procedure insert_block(i,j,nblocks,ninsts,Succ,Pred)
    i, j: in integer
    nblocks: inout integer
    ninsts: inout array [··] of integer
    Succ, Pred: inout integer ⟶ set of integer
begin
    || insert a new block between block i and block j
    nblocks += 1
    ninsts[nblocks] := 0
    Succ(i) := (Succ(i) ∪ {nblocks}) - {j}
    Succ(nblocks) := {j}
    Pred(j) := (Pred(j) ∪ {nblocks}) - {i}
    Pred(nblocks) := {i}
end    || insert_block
```

FIG. 4.16 The ICAN routine insert_block( ) that splits an edge by inserting a block between the two given blocks.

The procedure

delete_inst(i,j,nblocks,ninsts,Block,Succ,Pred)

defined in Figure 4.15 deletes instruction j from block i and adjusts the other data structures that are used to represent programs.

The procedure

insert_block(i,j,nblocks,ninsts,Succ,Pred)

defined in Figure 4.16 splits the edge $i \rightarrow j$ by inserting a new empty block between block i and block j.

```
procedure delete_block(i,nblocks,ninsts,Block,Succ,Pred)
   i: in integer
   nblocks: inout integer
   ninsts: inout array [··] of integer
   Block: inout array [··] of array [··] of Instruction
   Succ, Pred: inout integer ⟶ set of integer
begin
   || delete block i and adjust data structures
   j, k: integer
   if i ∈ Succ(i) then
      Succ(i) -= {i}
      Pred(i) -= {i}
   fi
   for each j ∈ Pred(i) do
      Succ(j) := (Succ(j) - {i}) ∪ Succ(i)
   od
   for each j ∈ Succ(i) do
      Pred(j) := (Pred(j) - {i}) ∪ Pred(i)
   od
   nblocks -= 1
   for j := i to nblocks do
      Block[j] := Block[j+1]
      Succ(j) := Succ(j+1)
      Pred(j) := Pred(j+1)
   od
   for j := 1 to nblocks do
      for each k ∈ Succ(j) do
         if k > i then
            Succ(j) := (Succ(j) - {k}) ∪ {k-1}
         fi
      od
      for each k ∈ Pred(j) do
         if k > i then
            Pred(j) := (Pred(j) - {k}) ∪ {k-1}
         fi
      od
   od
end    || delete_block
```

FIG. 4.17   The ICAN routine delete_block( ) that removes an empty basic block.

The procedure

delete_block(i,nblocks,ninsts,Block,Succ,Pred)

defined in Figure 4.17 deletes basic block i and adjusts the data structures that represent a program.

4.9   Other Intermediate-Language Forms

In this section, we describe several alternative representations of the instructions in a basic block of medium-level intermediate code (namely, triples; trees; directed acyclic graphs, or DAGs; and Polish prefix), how they are related to MIR, and their advantages and disadvantages relative to it. In the output of a compiler's front end, the control structure connecting the basic blocks is most often represented in a form similar to the one we use in MIR, i.e., by simple explicit gotos, ifs, and labels. It remains for control-flow analysis (see Chapter 7) to provide more information about the nature of the control flow in a procedure, such as whether a set of blocks forms an if-then-else construct, a while loop, or whatever.

Two further important intermediate-code forms are static single-assignment form and the program dependence graph, described in Sections 8.11 and 9.5.

First, note that the form we are using for MIR and its relatives is not the conventional one for quadruples. The conventional form is written with the operator first, followed by the three operands, usually with the result operand first, so that our

```
t1 ← x + 3
```

would typically be written as

```
+    t1,x,3
```

We have chosen to use the infix form simply because it is easier to read. Also, recall that the form shown here is designed as an external or printable notation, while the corresponding ICAN form discussed above can be thought of as an internal representation, although even it is designed for reading convenience—if it were truly an internal form, it would be a lot more compact and the symbols would most likely be replaced by pointers to symbol-table entries.

It should also be noted that there is nothing inherently medium-level about any of the alternative representations in this section—they would function equally well as low-level representations.

Figure 4.18(a) gives an example MIR code fragment that we use in comparing MIR to the other code forms.

4.9.1   Triples

Triples are similar to quadruples, except that the results are not named explicitly in a triples representation. Instead, the results of the triples have implicit names that are used in other triples when they are needed as operands, and an explicit store operation must be provided, since there is no way to name a variable or storage location as the result of a triple. We might, for example, use "*a* sto *b*" to mean store *b* in location *a* and "*a* *sto *b*" for the corresponding indirect store through a pointer. In internal representations, triple numbers are usually either pointers to or index numbers of the triples they correspond to. This can significantly complicate insertion and deletion of triples, unless the targets of control transfers are nodes in a representation of the basic-block structure of the procedure, rather than references to specific triples.

```
L1:  i ← i + 1              (1)  i + 1
                            (2)  i sto (1)
     t1 ← i + 1             (3)  i + 1
     t2 ← p + 4             (4)  p + 4
     t3 ← *t2               (5)  *(4)
     p ← t2                 (6)  p sto (4)
     t4 ← t1 < 10           (7)  (3) < 10
     *r ← t3                (8)  r *sto (5)
     if t4 goto L1          (9)  if (7), (1)

(a)                        (b)
```

FIG. 4.18 (a) A MIR code fragment for comparison to other intermediate-code forms, and (b) its translation to triples.

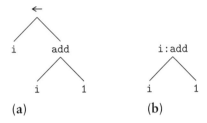

(a)   (b)

FIG. 4.19 Alternative forms of trees: (a) with an explicit assignment operator, and (b) with the result variable labeling the root node of its computation tree.

In external representations, the triple number is usually listed in parentheses at the beginning of each line and the same form is used to refer to it in the triples, providing a simple way to distinguish triple numbers from integer constants. Figure 4.18(b) shows a translation of the MIR code in Figure 4.18(a) to triples.

Translation back and forth between quadruples and triples is straightforward. Going from quadruples to triples requires replacing temporaries and labels by triple numbers and introducing explicit store triples. The reverse direction replaces triple numbers by temporaries and labels and may absorb store triples into quadruples that compute the result being stored.

Using triples has no particular advantage in optimization, except that it simplifies somewhat the creation of the DAG for a basic block before code generation (see Section 4.9.3), performing local value numbering (see Section 12.4.1) in the process. The triples provide direct references to their operands and so simplify determining the descendants of a node.

4.9.2   Trees

To represent intermediate code by trees, we may choose either to have explicit assignment operators in the trees or to label the root node of an expression computation with the result variable (or variables), as shown by Figure 4.19(a) and (b), respectively, a choice somewhat analogous to using quadruples or triples. We choose to use the second form, since it corresponds more closely than the other form to the DAGs discussed in the following section. We label the interior nodes with the operation names given in Figure 4.6 that make up the ICAN type IROper.

Trees are almost always used in intermediate code to represent the portions of the code that do non-control-flow computation, and control flow is represented in a form that connects sequences of trees to each other. A simple translation of the (non-control-flow) MIR code in Figure 4.18(a) to tree form is shown in Figure 4.20. Note that this translation is, in itself, virtually useless—it provides one tree for each quadruple that contains no more or less information than the quadruple.

A more ambitious translation would determine that the t1 computed by the second tree is used only as an operand in the sixth tree and that, since t1 is a temporary, there is no need to store into it if the second tree is grafted into the sixth tree in place of the occurrence of t1 there. Similar observations apply to combining the third tree into the fifth. Notice, however, that the fourth tree cannot be grafted into the seventh, since the value of p is changed between them. Performing these transformations results in the sequence of trees shown in Figure 4.21.

This version of the tree representation has clear advantages over the quadruples: (1) it has eliminated two temporaries (t1 and t2) and the stores to them; (2) it provides the desired input form for the algebraic simplifications discussed in Section 12.3.1; (3) locally optimal code can be generated from it for many machine architectures by using Sethi-Ullman numbers, which prescribe the order in which instructions should be generated to minimize the number of registers used; and (4) it provides a form that is easy to translate to Polish-prefix code (see Section 4.9.4) for input to a syntax-directed code generator (see Section 6.2).

Translating from quadruples to trees can be done with varying degrees of effort, as exemplified by the sequences of trees in Figures 4.20 and 4.21. Translation to the first form should be obvious, and achieving the second form can be viewed as an optimization of the first. The only points about which we need to be careful are that, in grafting a tree into a later one in the sequence, we must make sure that there

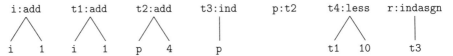

FIG. 4.20 Translation of the (non-control-flow) MIR code in Figure 4.18(a) to a sequence of simple trees.

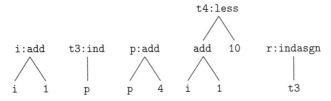

FIG. 4.21 Minimized tree form of the (non-control-flow) MIR code in Figure 4.18(a).

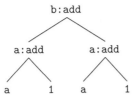

FIG. 4.22 Result of trying to translate the MIR instructions a ← a + 1; b ← a + a to a single tree.

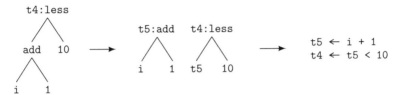

FIG. 4.23 Example of translation from minimized tree form to MIR code.

are no uses of any of the result variables that label nodes in the first one between its original location and the tree it is grafted into and that its operands are also not recomputed between the two locations.

Note that a sequence of MIR instructions may not correspond to a single tree for two distinct reasons—it may not be connected, or it may result in evaluating an instruction several times, rather than once. As an example of the latter situation, consider the code sequence

```
a ← a + 1
b ← a + a
```

This would result in the tree shown in Figure 4.22, which corresponds to evaluating the first instruction twice. We could, however, remove the label from the second "a:add" node.

Translation from trees to quadruples is simple. We may proceed by either a pre-order traversal or a postorder one. In the first case, we perform a preorder traversal of each tree, in the order they appear. For each *interior node* (i.e., non-leaf node) with at least one descendant that is an interior node, we create a new temporary and divide the tree into two (call them the "upper tree" and the "lower tree") along the edge connecting the two interior nodes. We label the root of the lower tree with the new temporary, and insert the pair of trees in sequence (with the lower tree first) in place of the one we are dividing. We repair the upper tree by putting the new tempo-rary in place of the lower tree. An example from Figure 4.21 appears in Figure 4.23. When we no longer have any interior nodes with interior-node descendants, each tree corresponds to a single MIR instruction, and the remainder of the translation is obvious.

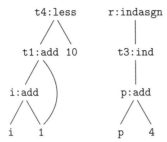

DAG for the non-control-flow code of MIR code in Figure 4.18(a).

In the second approach to translating from trees to MIR, we perform a postorder traversal of the given tree, generating a MIR instruction for each subtree that contains only a single operator and replacing its root by the left-hand side of the MIR instruction.

4.9.3 Directed Acyclic Graphs (DAGs)

The DAG representation of a basic block can be thought of as compressing the minimal sequence of trees that represents it still further. The leaves of such a DAG represent the values of the variables and constants available on entry to the block that are used within it. The other nodes of the DAG all represent operations and may also be annotated with variable names, indicating values computed in the basic block. We draw DAG nodes like the tree nodes in the preceding section. As an example of a DAG for a basic block, see Figure 4.24, which corresponds to the first seven instructions in Figure 4.18(a). In the DAG, the lower left "add" node represents the MIR assignment "i ← i + 1", while the "add" node above it represents the computation of "i + 1" that is compared to 10 to compute a value for t4. Note that the DAG reuses values, and so is generally a more compact representation than either trees or the linear notations.

To translate a sequence of MIR assignment instructions to a DAG, we process the instructions in order. For each one, we check whether each operand is already represented by a DAG node. If it is not, we make a DAG leaf for it. Then we check whether there is a parent of the operand node(s) that represents the current operation; if not, we create one. Then we label the node representing the result with the name of the result variable and remove that name as a label of any other node in the DAG.

Figure 4.25 is a sequence of MIR instructions and the graphic form of the corresponding DAG is shown in Figure 4.26. Note that, in the DAG, the neg node is an operator node that has no labels (it is created for instruction 4 and labeled d, but that label is then moved by instruction 7 to the mul node), so no code need be generated for it.

As mentioned above, the DAG form is useful for performing local value numbering, but it is a comparatively difficult form on which to perform most other optimizations. On the other hand, there are node-listing algorithms that guide code generation from DAGs to produce quite efficient code.

```
1    c ← a
2    b ← a + 1
3    c ← 2 * a
4    d ← -c
5    c ← a + 1
6    c ← b + a
7    d ← 2 * a
8    b ← c
```

FIG. 4.25 Example basic block of MIR code to be converted to a DAG.

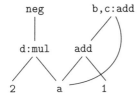

FIG. 4.26 Graphic form of the DAG corresponding to the MIR code in Figure 4.25.

```
binasgn  i  add  i  1
unasgn   t3 ind  p
binasgn  p  add  p  4
binasgn  t4 less add  i  1  10
indasgn  r  t3
```

FIG. 4.27 Polish-prefix form of the trees in Figure 4.21 divided into instructions.

4.9.4   Polish–Prefix Notation

Polish-prefix notation is essentially the result of a preorder traversal of one tree form or another. Translation between it and trees in both directions is a quite straightforward recursive process.

For the minimal tree form given in Figure 4.21, the Polish-prefix form is the code shown in Figure 4.27 (note that we assume that the one descendant of a unary node is its left child). The second line, for example, represents a unary assignment with t3 as its left-hand side and the result of indirecting through p as its right-hand side.

Polish-prefix notation is most useful as input to syntax-directed code generators (see Section 6.2). On the other hand, it is of little use in optimization because its recursive structure is only implicit.

4.10   Wrap–Up

In this chapter, we have discussed the design of intermediate-code representations; compared and contrasted several, including abstract syntax trees, quadruples, triples, trees, DAGs, and Polish-prefix notation; and selected three to use in our examples in the rest of the book. We have chosen to use HIR, MIR, and LIR and have given both an external ASCII form and an internal ICAN structure form for each.

The concerns in selecting an intermediate-code form include expressiveness (the ability to represent the relevant concepts), appropriateness for the tasks to be performed on it, compactness and speed of access (so as not to waste space and/or time), ease of translating from source code to intermediate code and subsequently to relocatable machine language or another lower-level form, and development cost (whether it is already implemented or what it will cost to implement it).

The basic MIR is suitable for most optimizations (as is LIR), while the higher-level HIR is used for dependence analysis (Chapter 9) and for some of the code transformations based on it, and the lower-level LIR is used for optimizations that require that registers and addressing be explicit.

Two other important intermediate code forms, static single-assignment (SSA) form and program dependence graphs, are discussed in Sections 8.11 and 9.5, respectively. We use the former in several optimizations, such as global value numbering (Section 12.4.2) and sparse conditional constant propagation (Section 12.6).

4.11   Further Reading

Sethi-Ullman numbers are discussed first in [SetU70] and more recently in [AhoS86].

The primary description of Hewlett-Packard's compilers for PA-RISC is [CouH86].

4.12   Exercises

4.1 Construct an abstract syntax tree that represents the C function

```
double sumorprod(a,n,i)
    double a[100];
    int n;
    int i;
{   double acc;
    int j;
    if (i = 0)
    {   acc = 0.0;
        for (j = 0; j < 100; j++)
            acc += a[j];
    } else
    {   acc = 1.0;
        for (j = 99; j >= 0; j--)
            if (a[j] != 0)
                acc *= a[j];
    }
    return acc;
}
```

4.2 Construct a HIR representation of the C function in Exercise 4.1.

4.3 Construct a MIR representation of the C function in Exercise 4.1.

4.4 Construct a LIR representation of the C function in Exercise 4.1.

4.5 Construct the ICAN representation of the MIR code in Exercise 4.3.

4.6 Translate the MIR representation of the C function in Exercise 4.3 into (a) triples, (b) trees, (c) DAGs, and (d) Polish-prefix notation.

4.7 Write an ICAN routine MIR_to_Triples(n,Inst,TInst) that translates the array Inst[1], ..., Inst[n] of MIR instructions to the array TInst[1], ..., TInst[m] of triples and returns m as its value. Assume that triples are represented by records similar to those used for MIR instructions, except that (1) the additional kinds store and indstore correspond, respectively, to the operators sto and *sto discussed in Section 4.9.1, (2) the other kinds of triples have no left fields, and (3) there is an additional type of operand ⟨kind:trpl,val:*num*⟩ that names the result of the triple that is stored in TInst[*num*].

4.8 Write an ICAN routine MIR_to_Trees(n,Inst,Root) that translates the array Inst[1], ..., Inst[n] of MIR instructions to a collection of trees whose roots it stores in Root[1], ..., Root[m] and that returns m as its value. A tree node is an element of the type Node defined by

```
Leaf = record {kind: enum {var,const},
               val: Var ∪ Const,
               names: set of Var}
Interior = record {kind: IROper,
               lt, rt: Node,
               names: set of Var}
Node = Leaf ∪ Interior
```

If an interior node's kind is a unary operator, its operand is its lt field and its rt field is nil.

4.9 Write an ICAN routine Prefix_to_MIR(PP,Inst) that translates the sequence PP of Polish-prefix operators and operands to an array Inst[1], ..., Inst[n] of MIR instructions and returns n as its value. Assume PP is of type sequence of (MIRKind ∪ IROper ∪ Var ∪ Const), and Polish-prefix code is written as shown in Figure 4.27.

4.10 Write an ICAN routine DAG_to_MIR(R,Inst) that translates the DAG with set of roots R to an array Inst[1], ..., Inst[n] of MIR instructions and returns n as its value. Assume that nodes in a DAG are represented by the type Node defined above in Exercise 4.8.

CHAPTER 5

Run-Time Support

In this chapter, we undertake a quick review of the basic issues involved in supporting at run time the concepts commonly embodied in higher-level languages. Since most of these concepts are covered well and in considerable detail in introductory texts on compilers, we do not explore most of them in great detail. Our main purpose is to remind the reader of the issues and alternatives, to suggest appropriate ways of handling run-time issues, and to provide references for further reading where they may be useful. Some of the more advanced concepts, such as position-independent code and heap storage management, are discussed in the final sections of this chapter.

In general, our concerns in this chapter are the software conventions necessary to support various source languages, including data representation, storage allocation for the various storage classes of variables, visibility rules, procedure calling, entry, exit, and return, and so on.

One issue that helps determine[1] the organization of many run-time data structures is the existence of Application Binary Interface (ABI) standards for many architectures. Such standards specify the layout and characteristics of numerous aspects of the run-time environment, thus easing the task of software producers by making interoperability much more likely for software that satisfies the standards. Some examples of such documents are the UNIX System V ABI and its processor-specific supplements for various architectures, such as SPARC and the Intel 386 architecture family.

We begin by considering data types and approaches to representing them efficiently at run time in Section 5.1. Next, we briefly discuss register usage and elementary methods for managing it in Section 5.2 (approaches to globally optimizing register usage are discussed in Chapter 16), and we discuss the structure of the stack frame for a single procedure in Section 5.3. This is followed by a discussion of the

---

1. Some would say "hinders creativity in determining."

overall organization of the run-time stack in Section 5.4. In Sections 5.5 and 5.6, we discuss issues involved in supporting parameter passing and procedure calls. In Section 5.7, we discuss support for code sharing by means of dynamic linking and position-independent code. Finally, in Section 5.8, we discuss support for dynamic and polymorphic languages.

5.1   Data Representations and Instructions

To implement a higher-level language, we must provide mechanisms to represent its data types and data-structuring concepts and to support its storage-management concepts. The fundamental data types generally include at least integers, characters, and floating-point values, each with one or more sizes and formats, enumerated values, and Booleans.

We expect integer values to be mapped to an architecture's fundamental integer type or types. At least one size and format, usually 32-bit signed two's-complement, is supported directly by loads, stores, and computational operations on each of the real-world target architectures. Most also support 32-bit unsigned integers, either with a complete set of computational operations or very nearly so. Byte and half-word signed and unsigned integers are supported either by loads and stores for those lengths or by loads and stores of word-sized data and extract and insert operations that create word-sized values, appropriately sign- or zero-extended, and the corresponding fundamental integer operations. Operations on longer integer types generally require multiple loads and stores (except, for some architectures, for doubleword quantities) and are generally supported by add with carry and subtract with borrow operations, from which the full set of multiple-precision arithmetic and relational operations can be constructed.

Characters, until recently, have generally been byte-sized quantities, although there is now, more frequently, support for halfword character representations, such as Unicode, that encompass syllabic writing systems such as Katakana and Hiragana and logographic systems such as Chinese and Kanji. The support needed for individual characters consists of loads, stores, and comparisons, and these operations are provided by the corresponding integer (signed or unsigned) byte and halfword loads and stores (or their constructed equivalents), integer comparisons, and occasionally by more complex instructions such as POWER's load signed byte and compare indexed instruction. While many CISCs have some built-in support for one character representation or another (e.g., ASCII for the DEC VAX series and EBCDIC for the IBM System/370), more modern architectures generally do not favor a particular character set and leave it to the programmer to craft the appropriate operations in software.

Floating-point values generally have two or three formats corresponding to ANSI/IEEE Std 754-1985—single, double, and (less frequently) extended precision, that generally occupy a word, a doubleword, and from 80 bits to a quadword, respectively. In all cases, the hardware directly supports single-precision loads and stores and, in most cases, double-precision ones as well, although extended loads and stores are usually not supported. Most current architectures, with the notable exception of POWER and the Intel 386 architecture family, provide a full complement of arithmetic and comparison operations for single- and double-precision values, except that some omit the square root operation, and some, such as SPARC Version 8, include the quad-precision operations also. POWER provides only double-precision operations and converts single-precision values to and from double in the process of performing loads and stores, respectively, although PowerPC supports both single- and double-precision formats directly. The Intel 386 architecture supports only an 80-bit format in its floating-point registers; loads and stores convert single- and double-precision values to and from that format. For most architectures, the complex system of exceptions and exceptional values mandated by the standard requires some amount of software assistance, and in some cases, such as Alpha, it requires a lot.

Enumerated values are generally represented by consecutive unsigned integers and the only operations required on them are loads, stores, and comparisons, except for Pascal and Ada, which allow one to iterate over the elements of an enumerated type. Booleans may be an enumerated type, as in Pascal, Modula-2, and Ada; integers, as in C; or simply a separate type, as in Fortran 77.

Arrays of values generally may have more than one dimension and, depending on the source language, may have elements that are of a fundamental type or almost any type. In either case, they may be thought of as n-dimensional rectangular solids with each of the n dimensions corresponding to a subscript position. They are most often represented by conceptually slicing them either in *row-major* order (as in most languages), or vice versa, in *column-major* order (as in Fortran), and then assigning a storage block to each element according to its position in the slicing. Thus, for example, a Pascal array declared

```
var a: array[1..10,0..5] of integer
```

occupies $(10 - 1 + 1) \times (5 - 0 + 1) = 60$ words of storage, with, e.g., a[1,0] in the zeroth word, a[1,1] in the first, a[2,0] in the sixth, and a[10,5] in the 59th. In general, for a Pascal array exam declared

```
var exam: array[lo₁..hi₁,lo₂..hi₂,...,loₙ..hiₙ] of type
```

the address of element exam[$sub_1, sub_2, \ldots, sub_n$] is

$$base(\text{exam}) + size(type) \cdot \sum_{i=1}^{n}(sub_i - lo_i) \prod_{j=i+1}^{n}(hi_j - lo_j + 1)$$

where $base(\text{exam})$ is the address of the first element of the array and $size(type)$ is the number of bytes occupied by each element.[2] Similar formulas apply for other languages, except that for Fortran the product runs from $j = 1$ to $j = i - 1$.

Some architectures provide instructions that simplify processing of multiple arrays. For example, the Intel 386 architecture family provides loads and stores (and memory-to-memory moves) that use a base register, an index register scaled by 1, 2,

---

2. Actually, for the sake of time efficiency, the compiler may round the size of each element up to a unit that can be efficiently accessed in memory.

```
struct s1 {                    struct s2 {
    int large1;                    int large2: 18;
    short int small1;              int small2: 10;
};                             };
(a)                            (b)
```

FIG. 5.1 Two C structs, one unpacked in (a) and the other packed in (b).

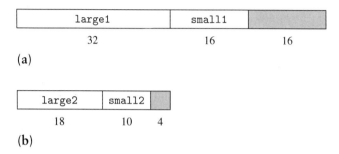

(a)

(b)

FIG. 5.2 Representation of the structures in Figure 5.1.

4, or 8, and a displacement. Some architectures, such as POWER and PA-RISC, provide loads and stores with base-register updating and, in the case of PA-RISC, scaling, that simplify access to consecutive array elements and to parallel arrays with different-sized elements.

Records consisting of multiple named fields are generally not supported directly by machine operations. In most higher-level languages that provide them, they may be either *packed,* i.e., with consecutive elements stored directly adjacent to each other without regard to boundaries that would make access to them more efficient, or *unpacked,* taking alignment into account. As an example, in C the structure declarations in Figure 5.1(a) and (b), where the numbers after the colons represent lengths in bits, would require a doubleword and a word, respectively. An object of type struct s1 would be stored as shown in Figure 5.2(a), while an object of type struct s2 would be stored as shown in (b). Obviously, fields whose sizes and boundary alignments correspond to implemented loads and stores can be accessed and manipulated more easily than packed fields, which may require multiple loads and stores to access an element and either shift and mask or extract and insert operations, depending on the machine architecture.

Pointers generally occupy a word or a doubleword and are supported by loads, stores, and comparisons. The object referenced by a pointer is usually accessed by loading the pointer into an integer register and specifying that register to be used to form the address in another load or a store instruction. Some languages, such as C and C++, provide addition and subtraction of integers from a pointer to access array elements.

Character strings are represented in various ways, depending on the source language. For example, the Pascal and PL/I representations of a character string include

```
type color = set of (red, orange, yellow, green,
                      blue, indigo, violet);
var  primary: color;
 . . .
primary := [red, yellow, blue]
```

FIG. 5.3 An example of sets in Pascal.

a count of the number of characters it contains, while C strings are terminated with a null character, i.e., one with the value 0. The Intel 386 architecture provides move, compare, and scan string instructions. Of RISC architectures, only POWER and PowerPC provide instructions specifically designed for string operations, namely, the load and store string (lsx, lsi, stsx, and stsi) and load string and compare (lscbx) instructions that use multiple registers and a byte offset to indicate the beginning address of the string. The others provide less support, such as MIPS's unaligned load and store instructions, or only the basic load and store instructions.

Sets are generally represented by bit strings, with each bit indicating whether a particular element is in a set value or not. Thus, for example, given the Pascal set type color and variable primary in Figure 5.3, the representation of primary would usually be a word with the hexadecimal value 0x54, i.e., the third, fifth, and seventh bits from the right would be ones. An alternate representation is sometimes used if the sets are expected to be *sparse,* that is, to have many more possible elements than actual elements. In this representation, the set is a list of the bit positions that are ones, usually sorted in increasing order. Our example set would consist of four storage units, the first containing 3 (the number of elements) and the others containing the values 3, 5, and 7; the size of the storage units might be chosen based on the number of elements in the set type or might always be a word.

Various higher-level languages provide a series of other types that can be represented in terms of the types and type constructors we have discussed. For example, complex numbers can be represented as records consisting of two floating-point components, one each for the real and imaginary parts; and rationals can be represented as records consisting of two integers, one each for the numerator and denominator, usually with the proviso that the greatest common factor of the two integers be one. Of course, languages with rich sets of type constructors can provide vast collections of types.

The representations discussed above all assume that types are associated with variables and are known at compile time. Some languages, such as LISP and Smalltalk, associate types with data objects rather than variables, and may require type determination at run time. We leave consideration of this issue to Section 5.8.

5.2   Register Usage

The use of registers is among the most important issues in designing a compiler for any machine in which access to registers is faster than access to other levels of the memory hierarchy—a category that includes all current machines we are aware of and most of the machines that have ever been built. Ideally, we would allocate all objects to registers and avoid accessing memory entirely, if that were possible. While this objective applies to almost all CISCs, it is even more important for recent CISC implementations such as the Intel Pentium and its successors, which are biased toward making RISC-style instructions fast, and for RISCs, since almost all operations in a RISC require their operands to be in registers and place their results in registers. Unfortunately, registers are always comparatively few in number, since they are among the most expensive resources in most implementations, both because of the area and interconnection complexity they require and because the number of registers affects the structure of instructions and the space available in instructions for specifying opcodes, offsets, conditions, and so on. In addition, arrays require indexing, a capability not supported by most register-set designs, so they cannot generally be held in registers.

Of course, it is rarely the case that all data can be kept in registers all the time, so it is essential to manage carefully use of the registers and access to variables that are not in registers. In particular, there are four issues of concern:

1. to allocate the most frequently used variables to registers for as much of a program's execution as possible;

2. to access variables that are not currently in registers as efficiently as possible;

3. to minimize the number of registers used for bookkeeping, e.g., to manage access to variables in memory, so as to make as many registers as possible available to hold variables' values; and

4. to maximize the efficiency of procedure calls and related operations, such as entering and exiting a scoping unit, so as to reduce their overhead to a minimum.

Of course, these objectives usually conflict with each other. In particular, efficient access to variables that are not in registers and efficient procedure calling may require more registers than we might otherwise want to devote to them, so this is an area where careful design is very important and where some architectural support may be appropriate. Very effective techniques for allocating frequently used variables to registers are covered in Chapter 16, so we will not consider that topic here.

Among the things that may contend for registers are the following:

stack pointer
The stack pointer points to the current top of the run-time stack, which is usually what would be the beginning of the next procedure invocation's local storage (i.e., its stack frame) on the run-time stack.

frame pointer
The frame pointer (which may not be necessary) points to the beginning of the current procedure invocation's stack frame on the run-time stack.

dynamic link
The dynamic link points to the beginning of the preceding frame on the run-time stack (or, if no frame pointer is used, to the end of the preceding frame) and is used to reestablish the caller's stack frame when the current procedure invocation returns.

Alternatively this may be an integer in an instruction that represents the distance between the current and previous frame pointers, or, if frame pointers are not used, stack pointers.

static link
> The static link points to the stack frame for the closest invocation of the lexically enclosing scope and is used to access nonlocal variables (some languages, such as C and Fortran, do not require static links).

global offset table pointer
> The global offset table pointer points to a table used in code shared among multiple processes (see Section 5.7) to establish and access private (per process) copies of external variables (this is unnecessary if such sharing does not occur).

arguments
> Arguments passed to a procedure called by the one currently active.

return values
> Results returned by a procedure called by the one currently active.

frequently used variables
> The most frequently used local (and possibly nonlocal or global) variables.

temporaries
> Temporary values computed and used during expression evaluation and other short-term activities.

Each of these categories will be discussed in the sections that follow.

Depending on the design of the instruction set and registers, some operations may require register pairs or quadruples. Integer register pairs are frequently used for the results of multiply and divide operations, in the former case because the length of a product is the sum of the lengths of its operands and in the latter to provide space for both the quotient and the remainder; and for double-length shift operations, which some architectures, such as PA-RISC, provide in place of the rotate operations commonly found in CISCs.

5.3   The Local Stack Frame

Despite the desirability of keeping all operands in registers, many procedures require an area in memory for several purposes, namely,

1. to provide homes for variables that either don't fit into the register file or may not be kept in registers, because their addresses are taken (either explicitly or implicitly, as for call-by-reference parameters) or because they must be indexable;

2. to provide a standard place for values from registers to be stored when a procedure call is executed (or when a register window is flushed); and

3. to provide a way for a debugger to trace the chain of currently active procedures.

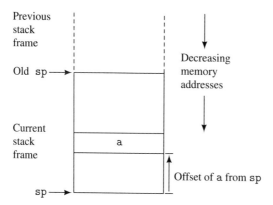

Previous stack frame

Old sp →

Current stack frame

a

sp →

Decreasing memory addresses

Offset of a from sp

FIG. 5.4 A stack frame with the current and old stack pointers.

Since many such quantities come into existence on entry to a procedure and are no longer accessible after returning from it, they are generally grouped together into an area called a *frame,* and the frames are organized into a stack. Most often the frames are called *stack frames.* A stack frame might contain values of parameters passed to the current routine that don't fit into the registers allotted for receiving them, some or all of its local variables, a register save area, compiler-allocated temporaries, a display (see Section 5.4), etc.

To be able to access the contents of the current stack frame at run time, we assign them memory offsets one after the other, in some order (described below), and make the offsets relative to a pointer kept in a register. The pointer may be either the *frame pointer* fp, which points to the first location of the current frame, or the *stack pointer* sp, which points to the current top of stack, i.e., just beyond the last location in the current frame. Most compilers choose to arrange stack frames in memory so the beginning of the frame is at a higher address than the end of it. In this way, offsets from the stack pointer into the current frame are always non-negative, as shown in Figure 5.4.

Some compilers use both a frame pointer and a stack pointer, with some variables addressed relative to each (Figure 5.5). Whether one should choose to use the stack pointer alone, the frame pointer alone, or both to access the contents of the current stack frame depends on characteristics of both the hardware and the languages being supported. The issues are (1) whether having a separate frame pointer wastes a register or is free; (2) whether the short offset range from a single register provided in load and store instructions is sufficient to cover the size of most frames; and (3) whether one must support memory allocation functions like the C library's alloca( ), which dynamically allocates space in the current frame and returns a pointer to that space. Using the frame pointer alone is generally not a good idea, since we need to save the stack pointer or the size of the stack frame somewhere anyway, so as to be able to call further procedures from the current one. For most architectures, the offset field in load and store instructions is sufficient for most stack frames and there is a cost for using an extra register for a frame pointer, namely,

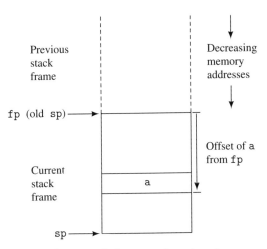

FIG. 5.5 A stack frame with frame and stack pointers.

saving it to memory and restoring it and not having it available to hold the value of a variable. Thus, using only the stack pointer is appropriate and desirable if it has sufficient range and we need not deal with functions like alloca( ).

The effect of alloca( ) is to extend the current stack frame, thus making the stack pointer point to a different location from where it previously pointed. This, of course, changes the offsets of locations accessed by means of the stack pointer, so they must be copied to the locations that now have the corresponding offsets. Since one may compute the address of a local variable in C and store it anywhere, this dictates that the quantities accessed relative to sp must not be addressable by the user and that, preferably, they must be things that are needed only while the procedure invocation owning the frame is suspended by a call to another procedure. Thus, sp-relative addressing can be used for such things as short-lived temporaries, arguments being passed to another procedure, registers saved across a call, and return values. So, if we must support alloca( ), we need both a frame pointer and a stack pointer. While this costs a register, it has relatively low instruction overhead, since on entry to a procedure, we (1) save the old frame pointer in the new frame, (2) set the frame pointer with the old stack pointer's value, and (3) add the length of the current frame to the stack pointer, and, essentially, reverse this process on exit from the procedure. On an architecture with register windows, such as SPARC, this can be done even more simply. If we choose the stack pointer to be one of the *out* registers and the frame pointer to be the corresponding *in* register, as the SPARC UNIX System V ABI specifies, then the save and restore instructions can be used to perform the entry and exit operations, with saving registers to memory and restoring left to the register-window spill and fill trap handlers.

An alternative that increases the range addressable from sp is to make it point some fixed distance below the top of the stack (i.e., within the current stack frame), so that part of the negative offset range from it is usable, in addition to positive offsets. This increases the size of stack frames that can be accessed with single load or store instructions in return for a small amount of extra arithmetic to find the real top of the stack in the debugger and any other tools that may need it. Similar things can be done with `fp` to increase its usable range.

5.4   The Run-Time Stack

At run time we do not have all the symbol-table structure present, if any. Instead, we must assign addresses to variables during compilation that reflect their scopes and use the resulting addressing information in the compiled code. As discussed in Section 5.3, there are several kinds of information present in the stack; the kind of interest to us here is support for addressing visible nonlocal variables. As indicated above, we assume that visibility is controlled by static nesting. The structure of the stack includes a stack frame for each active procedure,[3] where a procedure is defined to be *active* if an invocation of it has been entered but not yet exited. Thus, there may be several frames in the stack at once for a given procedure if it is recursive, and the nearest frame for the procedure statically containing the current one may be several levels back in the stack. Each stack frame contains a *dynamic link* to the base of the frame preceding it in the stack, i.e., the value of `fp` for that frame.[4]

In addition, if the source language supports statically nested scopes, the frame contains a *static link* to the nearest invocation of the statically containing procedure, which is the stack frame in which to look up the value of a variable declared in that procedure. That stack frame, in turn, contains a static link to the nearest frame for an invocation of its enclosing scope, and so on, until we come to the global scope. To set the static link in a stack frame, we need a mechanism for finding the nearest invocation of the procedure that the current procedure is statically nested in. Note that the invocation of a procedure not nested in the current procedure is itself a nonlocal reference, and the value needed for the new frame's static link is the scope containing that nonlocal reference. Thus,

1. if the procedure being called is nested directly within its caller, its static link points to its caller's frame;

2. if the procedure is at the same level of nesting as its caller, then its static link is a copy of its caller's static link; and

3. if the procedure being called is *n* levels higher than the caller in the nesting structure, then its static link can be determined by following *n* static links back from the caller's static link and copying the static link found there.

An example of this is shown in Figures 5.6 and 5.7. For the first call, from f( ) to g( ), the static link for g( ) is set to point to f( )'s frame. For the call from g( )

---

3. We assume this until Chapter 15, where we optimize away some stack frames.
4. If the stack model uses only a stack pointer to access the current stack frame and no frame pointer, then the dynamic link points to the end of the preceding frame, i.e., to the value of `sp` for that frame.

```
procedure f( )
begin
   procedure g( )
   begin
      call h( )
   end
   procedure h( )
   begin
      call i( )
   end
   procedure i( )
   begin
      procedure j( )
      begin
         procedure k( )
         begin
            procedure l( )
            begin
               call g( )
            end
            call l( )
         end
         call k( )
      end
      call j( )
   end
   call g( )
end
```

FIG. 5.6 An example of nested procedures for static link determination.

to h( ), the two routines are nested at the same level in the same routine, so h( )'s
static link is a copy of g( )'s. Finally, for the call from l( ) to g( ), g( ) is nested
three levels higher in f( ) than l( ) is, so we follow three static links back from
l( )'s and copy the static link found there.

As discussed below in Section 5.6.4, a call to an imported routine or to one in a
separate package must be provided a static link along with the address used to call it.

Having set the static link for the current frame, we can now do *up-level addressing* of nonlocal variables by following static links to the appropriate frame. For
now, we assume that the static link is stored at offset sl_off from the frame pointer
fp (note that sl_off is the value stored in the variable StaticLinkOffset used in
Section 3.6). Suppose we have procedure h( ) nested in procedure g( ), which in
turn is nested in f( ). To load the value of f( )'s variable i at offset i_off in its
frame while executing h( ), we would execute a sequence of instructions such as the
following LIR:

```
r1 ← [fp+sl_off]     || get frame pointer of g( )
r2 ← [r1+sl_off]     || get frame pointer of f( )
r3 ← [r2+i_off]      || load value of i
```

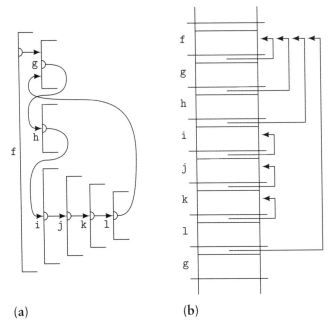

(a)   (b)

FIG. 5.7 (a) Static nesting structure of the seven procedures and calls among them in Figure 5.6, and (b) their static links during execution (after entering g( ) from l( )).

While this appears to be quite expensive, it isn't necessarily. First, accessing nonlocal variables is generally infrequent. Second, if nonlocal accesses are common, a mechanism called a *display* can amortize the cost over multiple references. A display keeps all or part of the current sequence of static links in either an array of memory locations or a series of registers. If the display is kept in registers, nonlocal references are no more expensive than references to local variables, once the display has been set up. Of course, dedicating registers to holding the display may be disadvantageous, since it reduces the number of registers available for other purposes. If the display is kept in memory, each reference costs at most one extra load to get the frame pointer for the desired frame into a register. The choice regarding whether to keep the display in memory or in registers, or some in each, is best left to a global register allocator, as discussed in Chapter 16.

5.5   Parameter-Passing Disciplines

There are several mechanisms for passing arguments to and returning results from procedures embodied in existing higher-level languages, including (1) call by value, (2) call by result, (3) call by value-result, (4) call by reference, and (5) call by name. In this section, we describe each of them and how to implement them, and mention some languages that use each. In addition, we discuss the handling of label parameters, which some languages allow to be passed to procedures. We use the term *arguments* or *actual arguments* to refer to the values or variables being passed to a routine and the term *parameters* or *formal parameters* to refer to the variables they are associated with in the called routine.

Conceptually, *call by value* passes an argument by simply making its value available to the procedure being called as the value of the corresponding formal parameter. While the called procedure is executing, there is no interaction with the caller's variables, unless an argument is a pointer, in which case the callee can use it to change the value of whatever it points to. Call by value is usually implemented by copying each argument's value to the corresponding parameter on entry to the called routine. This is simple and efficient for arguments that fit into registers, but it can be very expensive for large arrays, since it may require massive amounts of memory traffic. If we have the caller and callee both available to analyze when we compile either of them, we may be able to determine that the callee does not store into a call-by-value array parameter and either it does not pass it on to any routines it calls or the routines it calls also do not store into the parameter (see Section 19.2.1); in that case, we can implement call by value by passing the address of an array argument and allowing the callee to access the argument directly, rather than having to copy it.

Versions of call by value are found in C, C++, ALGOL 60, and ALGOL 68. In C, C++, and ALGOL 68, it is the only parameter-passing mechanism, but in all three, the parameter passed may be (and for some C and C++ types, always is) the address of an object, so it may have the effect of call by reference, as discussed below. Ada in parameters are a modified form of call by value—they are passed by value, but are read-only within the called procedure.

Call by result is similar to call by value, except that it returns values from the callee to the caller rather than passing them from the caller to the callee. On entry to the callee, it does nothing; when the callee returns, the value of a call-by-result parameter is made available to the caller, usually by copying it to the actual argument associated with it. Call by result has the same efficiency considerations as call by value. It is implemented in Ada as out parameters.

Call by value-result is precisely the union of call by value and call by result. On entry to the callee, the argument's value is copied to the parameter and on return, the parameter's value is copied back to the argument. It is implemented in Ada as inout parameters and is a valid parameter-passing mechanism for Fortran.

Call by reference establishes an association between an actual argument and the corresponding parameter on entry to a procedure. At that time, it determines the address of the argument and provides it to the callee as a means for accessing the argument. The callee then has full access to the argument for the duration of the call; it can change the actual argument arbitrarily often and can pass it on to other routines. Call by reference is usually implemented by passing the address of the actual argument to the callee, which then accesses the argument by means of the address. It is very efficient for array parameters, since it requires no copying, but it can be inefficient for small arguments, i.e., those that fit into registers, since it precludes their being passed in registers. This can be seen by considering a call-by-reference argument that is also accessible as a global variable. If the argument's address is passed to a called routine, accesses to it as a parameter and as a global variable both use the same location; if its value is passed in a register, access to it as a global variable will generally use its memory location, rather than the register.

A problem may arise when a constant is passed as a call-by-reference parameter. If the compiler implements a constant as a shared location containing its value that is accessed by all uses of the constant in a procedure, and if it is passed by reference to another routine, that routine may alter the value in the location and hence alter the value of the constant for the remainder of the caller's execution. The usual remedy is to copy constant parameters to new anonymous locations and to pass the addresses of those locations.

Call by reference is a valid parameter-passing mechanism for Fortran. Since C, C++, and ALGOL 68 allow addresses of objects to be passed as value parameters, they, in effect, provide call by reference also.

The semantics of parameter passing in Fortran allow either call by value-result or call by reference to be used for each argument. Thus, call by value-result can be used for values that fit into registers and call by reference can be used for arrays, providing the efficiency of both mechanisms for the kinds of arguments for which they perform best.

Call by name is the most complex parameter-passing mechanism, both conceptually and in its implementation, and it is really only of historical significance since ALGOL 60 is the only well-known language that provides it. It is similar to call by reference in that it allows the callee access to the caller's argument, but differs in that the address of the argument is (conceptually) computed at each access to the argument, rather than once on entry to the callee. Thus, for example, if the argument is the expression a[i] and the value of i changes between two uses of the argument, then the two uses access different elements of the array. This is illustrated in Figure 5.8, where i and a[i] are passed by the main program to procedure f( ). The first use of the parameter x fetches the value of a[1], while the second use sets a[2]. The call to outinteger( ) prints 5 5 2. If call by reference were being used, both uses would access a[1] and the program would print 5 5 8. Implementing call by name requires a mechanism for computing the address of the argument at each access; this is generally done by providing a parameterless procedure called a *thunk*. Each call to an argument's thunk returns its current address. This, of course, can be a very expensive mechanism. However, many simple cases can be recognized by a compiler as identical to call by reference. For example, passing a simple variable, a whole array, or a fixed element of an array always results in the same address, so a thunk is not needed for such cases.

Labels may be passed as arguments to procedures in some languages, such as ALGOL 60 and Fortran, and they may be used as the targets of gotos in the procedures they are passed to. Implementing this functionality requires that we pass both the code address of the point marked by the label and the dynamic link of the corresponding frame. A goto whose target is a label parameter executes a series of

```
begin
    integer array a[1:2]; integer i;
    procedure f(x,j);
        integer x, j;
        begin integer k;
            k := x;
            j := j + 1;
            x = j;
            f := k;
        end;
    i := 1;
    a[1] := 5;
    a[2] := 8;
    outinteger(a[1],f(a[i],i),a[2]);
end
```

FIG. 5.8 Call by name parameter-passing mechanism in ALGOL 60.

one or more return operations, until the appropriate stack frame (indicated by the
dynamic link) is reached, and then executes a branch to the instruction indicated by
the label.

5.6   Procedure Prologues, Epilogues, Calls, and Returns

Invoking a procedure from another procedure involves a handshake to pass control
and argument values from the caller to the callee and another to return control and
results from the callee to the caller. In the simplest of run-time models, executing a
procedure consists of five major phases (each of which, in turn, consists of a series
of steps), as follows:

1. The procedure *call* assembles the arguments to be passed to the procedure and
    transfers control to it.

    (a) Each argument is evaluated and put in the appropriate register or stack location;
         "evaluation" may mean computing its address (for reference parameters), its
         value (for value parameters), etc.

    (b) The address of the code for the procedure is determined (or, for most languages,
         was determined at compile time or at link time).

    (c) Registers that are in use and saved by the caller are stored in memory.

    (d) If needed, the static link of the called procedure is computed.

    (e) The return address is saved in a register and a branch to the procedure's code is
         executed (usually these are done by a single `call` instruction).

2. The procedure's *prologue*, executed on entry to the procedure, establishes the ap-
    propriate addressing environment for the procedure and may serve other functions,
    such as saving registers the procedure uses for its own purposes.

(a) The old frame pointer is saved, the old stack pointer becomes the new frame pointer, and the new stack pointer is computed.

(b) Registers used by the callee and saved by the callee are stored to memory.

(c) If the run-time model uses a display, it is constructed.

3. The procedure does its work, possibly including calling other procedures.

4. The procedure's *epilogue* restores register values and the addressing environment of the caller, assembles the value to be returned, and returns control to the caller.

(a) Registers saved by the callee are restored from memory.

(b) The old stack and frame pointers are recovered.

(c) The value (if any) to be returned is put in the appropriate place.

(d) A branch to the return address is executed.

5. Finally, the code in the caller following the call finishes restoring its execution environment and receives the returned value.

(a) Registers saved by the caller are restored from memory.

(b) The returned value is used.

Several issues complicate this model, including: how the parameter-passing mechanism varies with the number and types of arguments, dividing up the registers into sets saved by the caller, saved by the callee, or neither ("scratch" registers); the possibility of calling a procedure whose address is the value of a variable; and whether a procedure is private to the process containing it or shared (discussed in the next section).

Managing registers efficiently across the procedure call interface is essential to achieving high performance. If the caller assumes that the callee may use any register (other than those dedicated to particular purposes, such as the stack pointer) for its own purposes, then it must save and restore all the registers it may have useful values in—potentially almost all the registers. Similarly, if the callee assumes that all the undedicated registers are in use by the caller, then it must save and restore all the registers the caller may have useful values in—again, potentially almost all the registers. Thus, it is very important to divide the register set in an optimal way into four classes, namely, (1) dedicated (manipulated only by the calling conventions), (2) caller-saved, (3) callee-saved, and (4) scratch (not saved across procedure calls at all). Of course, the optimal division depends on architectural features, such as register windows, as in SPARC; sharing one register set for integer and floating-point data, as in the Motorola 88000; and architectural restrictions, such as the Intel 386 architecture family's small number of registers and their inhomogeneity. The optimal division may vary from program to program. Interprocedural register allocation, as described in Section 19.6, can mitigate the impact of the variation from one program to another. Lacking that, experiment and experience are the best guides for determining a satisfactory partition. Some examples of ways to divide the register set are provided in the UNIX ABI processor supplements.

Note that both of the methods that pass parameters in registers need to incorporate a stack-based approach as well—if there are too many parameters to pass in the available registers, they are passed on the stack instead.

5.6.1   Parameters Passed in Registers: Flat Register File

In architectures with large general-purpose register files, parameters are usually passed in registers. A sequence of integer registers and a sequence of floating-point registers are designated to contain the first *ia* integer arguments and the first *fa* floating-point arguments, for some small values of *ia* and *fa*,[5] with the arguments divided in order between the two register sets according to their types, and the remaining arguments, if any, passed in storage at an agreed point in the stack. Suppose we have a call f(i,x,j) with parameters passed by value, where the first and third parameters are integers and the second is a single-precision floating-point value. Thus, for our example, the arguments i and j would be passed in the first two integer parameter registers, and x would be passed in the first floating-point parameter register. The procedure-invocation handshake includes making the code generated for f( ) receive its parameters this way (this example is used in Exercises 5.4–5.6 in Section 5.11).

This mechanism is adequate for value parameters that fit into single registers or into pairs of registers and for all reference parameters. Beyond that size, another convention is typically used for value parameters, namely, the address of the argument is passed to the called procedure and it is responsible for copying the parameter's value into its own stack frame or into other storage. The size of the argument may also be passed, if needed.

If more than *ia* integer arguments or more than *fa* floating-point arguments are passed, the additional ones are typically passed on the stack just beyond the current stack pointer and, hence, can be accessed by the called routine with non-negative offsets from the new frame pointer.

Returning a value from a procedure is typically done in the same way that arguments are passed, except that, in most languages, there may not be more than one return value and some care is required to make procedures *reentrant*, i.e., executable by more than one thread of control at the same time. Reentrancy is achieved by returning values that are too large to fit into a register (or two registers) in storage provided by the caller, rather than storage provided by the callee. To make this work, the caller must provide, usually as an extra hidden argument, a pointer to an area of storage where it will receive such a value.[6] The callee can then put it there, rather than having to provide storage for the value itself.

---

5. Weicker found that the average number of arguments passed to a procedure is about 2, and other studies have substantially agreed with that result, so the value of *n* is typically in the range 5 to 8. However, some system specifications allow many more; in particular, the UNIX System V ABI for the Intel i860 makes available 12 integer and 8 floating-point registers for parameter passing.

6. If the caller also provides the size of the area as a hidden argument, the callee can check that the value it returns fits into the provided area.

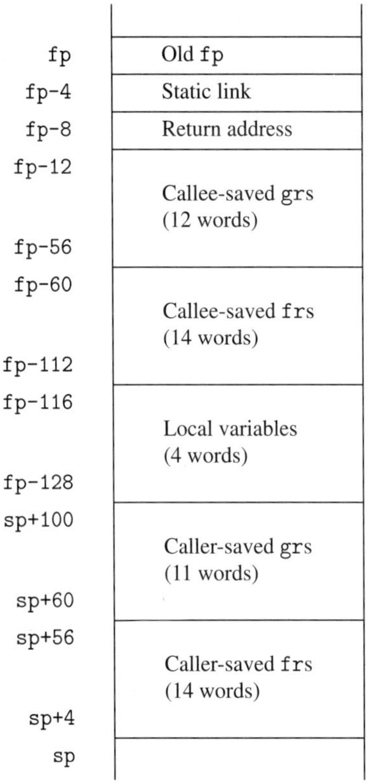

fp	Old fp
fp-4	Static link
fp-8	Return address
fp-12	
	Callee-saved grs (12 words)
fp-56	
fp-60	
	Callee-saved frs (14 words)
fp-112	
fp-116	
	Local variables (4 words)
fp-128	
sp+100	
	Caller-saved grs (11 words)
sp+60	
sp+56	
	Caller-saved frs (14 words)
sp+4	
sp	

FIG. 5.9 Structure of the stack frame for the procedure-calling example with parameters passed in registers.

A typical register usage might be as follows:

Registers	Usage
r0	0
r1—r5	Parameter passing
r6	Frame pointer
r7	Stack pointer
r8—r19	Caller-saved
r20—r30	Callee-saved
r31	Return address
f0—f4	Parameter passing
f5—f18	Caller-saved
f19—f31	Callee-saved

and might return a result in r1 or f0, according to its type. We choose the stack structure shown in Figure 5.9, where we assume that the local variables occupy four words and that gr and fr abbreviate "general register" and "floating-point register," respectively. Were it necessary to pass some parameters on the stack because there are too many of them to all be passed in registers or if the called routine were to traverse the parameter list, space would be allocated between fp-128 and sp+104 to accommodate them. Exercise 5.4 requests that you produce code for a procedure call, prologue, parameter use, epilogue, and return for this model.

5.6.2   Parameters Passed on the Run-Time Stack

In the stack-based model, the arguments are pushed onto the run-time stack and used from there. In a machine with few registers and stack-manipulation instructions, such as the VAX and the Intel 386 architecture, we use those instructions to store the arguments in the stack. This would, for example, replace

```
    r1 ← 5              || put third argument on stack
    sp ← sp - 4
```

by

```
    pushl   5           ; push third argument onto stack
```

for the Intel 386 architecture family. Also, we would not need to adjust the stack pointer after putting the arguments on the stack—the pushes would do it for us. The return value could either be passed in a register or on the stack; we use the top of the floating-point register stack in our example.

For the Intel 386 and its successors, the architecture provides eight 32-bit integer registers. Six of the registers are named eax, ebx, ecx, edx, esi, and edi and are, for most instructions, general-purpose. The other two, ebp and esp, are the base (i.e., frame) pointer and stack pointer, respectively. The architecture also provides eight 80-bit floating-point registers known as st(0) (or just st) through st(7) that function as a stack, with st(0) as the current top of stack. In particular, a floating-point return value is placed in st(0). The run-time stack layout is shown in Figure 5.10.

Exercise 5.5 requests that you produce code for a procedure call, prologue, parameter use, epilogue, and return for this model.

5.6.3   Parameter Passing in Registers with Register Windows

Register windows, as provided in SPARC, simplify the process of passing arguments to and returning results from procedures. They also frequently result in a significant reduction in the number of loads and stores executed, since they make it possible to provide a much larger register file without increasing the number of bits required to specify register numbers (typical SPARC implementations provide seven or eight windows, or a total of 128 or 144 integer registers) and take advantage of locality of procedure calls through time.

The use of register windows prescribes, in part, the division of the integer registers into caller- and callee-saved: the caller's *local* registers are not accessible to the callee, and vice versa for the callee's *local* registers; the caller's *out* registers are the callee's *in* registers and so are primarily dedicated (including the return address

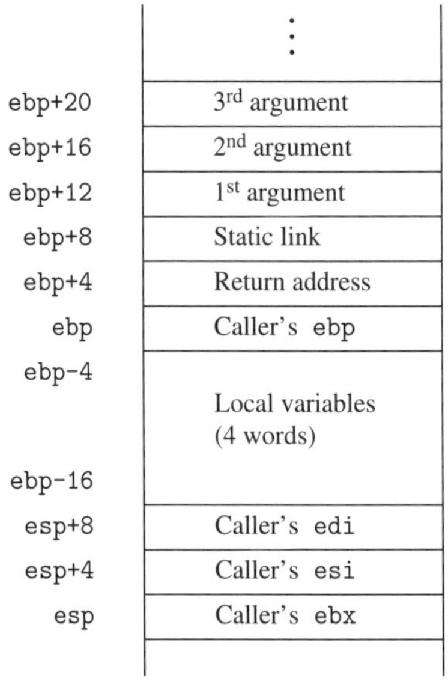

	⋮
ebp+20	3rd argument
ebp+16	2nd argument
ebp+12	1st argument
ebp+8	Static link
ebp+4	Return address
ebp	Caller's ebp
ebp-4	Local variables (4 words)
ebp-16	
esp+8	Caller's edi
esp+4	Caller's esi
esp	Caller's ebx

FIG. 5.10 Structure of the stack frame for the procedure-calling example with parameters passed on the run-time stack for the Intel 386 architecture family.

and the caller's stack pointer, which becomes the callee's frame pointer) or used for receiving parameters; the callee's *out* registers can be used as temporaries and are used to pass arguments to routines the callee calls. Saving values in the windowed registers to memory and restoring them is done by the window spill and fill trap handlers, rather than by user code. Figure 5.11 shows the overlapping relationships among three routines' register windows.

When a procedure call is executed, *out* registers o0 through o5 conventionally contain integer arguments that are being passed to the current procedure (floating-point arguments are passed in the floating-point registers). The stack pointer sp is conventionally in o6 and the frame pointer fp is in i6, so that a save executed in a called procedure causes the old sp to become the new fp. Additional arguments, if any, are passed on the run-time stack, as in the flat register model. When a procedure returns, it places its return value in one (or a pair) of its *in* registers if it is an integer value or in floating-point register f0 if it is a floating-point value. Then it restores the caller's stack pointer by issuing a restore instruction to move to the previous register window.

Figure 5.12 shows a typical stack frame layout for SPARC. The 16 words of storage at sp through sp+60 are for use by the register-window spill trap handler, which stores the contents of the current window's *in*s and *local*s there. Because of this, sp *must* always point to a valid spill area; it is modified only by the indivisible save and restore instructions. The former can be used to advance to a new window and to allocate a new stack frame at once and the latter reverses this process. The word at sp+64 is used to return structures and unions to the caller. It is set up by the caller with the address of the area to receive the value.

Caller's window

```
r31 (i7)
   .
   .        ins
   .
r24 (i0)

r23 (l7)
   .
   .        locals
   .
r16 (l0)          Current window

r15 (o7)          r31 (i7)
   .                 .
   .      outs       .      ins
   .                 .
r8 (o0)           r24 (i0)

                  r23 (l7)
                     .
                     .      locals
                     .
                  r16 (l0)          Callee's window

                  r15 (o7)          r31 (i7)
                     .                 .
                     .      outs       .      ins
                     .                 .
                  r8 (o0)           r24 (i0)

                                    r23 (l7)
                                       .
                                       .      locals
                                       .
                                    r16 (l0)

                                    r15 (o7)
                                       .
                                       .      outs
                                       .
                                    r8 (o0)
```

```
r7 (g7)
   .
   .        globals
   .
r1 (g1)

r0 (g0)   0
```

FIG. 5.11 SPARC register windows for three successive procedures.

The first six words of integer arguments are passed in registers. Succeeding arguments are passed in the stack frame. If it should be necessary to traverse a variable-length argument list, the entry-point code stores the first six arguments beginning at sp+68. The area beginning at sp+92 is used to hold additional arguments and temporaries and to store the global and floating-point registers when they need to be saved. For our example, b in Figure 5.12 is 32, so the size of the entire stack frame is 148 bytes.

Exercise 5.6 requests that you produce code for a procedure call, prologue, parameter use, epilogue, and return for this model.

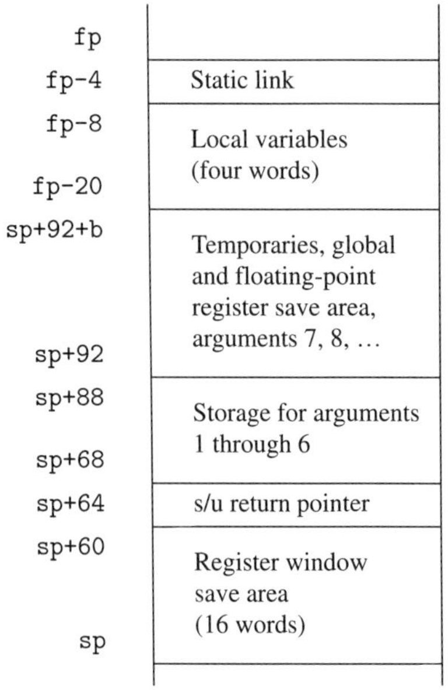

fp	
fp-4	Static link
fp-8	Local variables
fp-20	(four words)
sp+92+b	Temporaries, global and floating-point register save area,
sp+92	arguments 7, 8, ...
sp+88	Storage for arguments
sp+68	1 through 6
sp+64	s/u return pointer
sp+60	Register window save area
sp	(16 words)

FIG. 5.12 Structure of the stack frame for the procedure-calling example with register windows (s/u means *structure or union*).

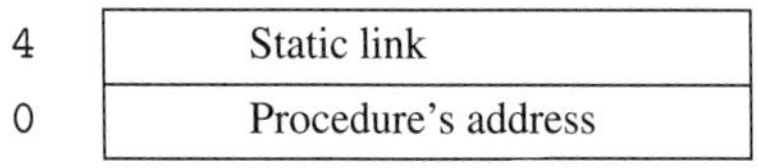

4	Static link
0	Procedure's address

FIG. 5.13 A procedure descriptor containing a procedure's address and its static link.

5.6.4   Procedure-Valued Variables

Calling a procedure that is the value of a variable requires special care in setting up its environment. If the target procedure is local, it must be passed a static link that is appropriate for it. This is best handled by making the value of the variable not be the address of the procedure's code, but rather a pointer to a *procedure descriptor* that includes the code address and the static link. We show such a descriptor in Figure 5.13. Given this descriptor design, the "call" code, regardless of the parameter-passing model, must be modified to get the static link and address of the called routine from the descriptor. To call the procedure, we load the address of the procedure into a register, load the static link into the appropriate register, and perform a register-based call. Alternately, since this code sequence is short and invariant, we could make one copy of it, do all calls to procedure variables by calling it, and replace the register-based call that terminates it by a register-based branch, since the correct return address is the one used to call this code sequence.

5.7   Code Sharing and Position-Independent Code

We have implicitly assumed above that a running program is a self-contained process, except possibly for calls to operating system services, i.e., any library routines that are called are linked statically (before execution) with the user's code, and all that needs to be done to enable execution is to load the executable image of the program into memory, to initialize the environment as appropriate to the operating system's standard programming model, and to call the program's main procedure with the appropriate arguments. There are several drawbacks to this model, having to do with space utilization and the time at which users' programs and libraries are bound together, that can all be solved by using so-called *shared libraries* that are loaded and linked dynamically on demand during execution and whose code is shared by all the programs that reference them. The issues, presented as advantages of the shared library model, are as follows:

1. A shared library need exist in the file system as only a single copy, rather than as part of each executable program that uses it.

2. A shared library's code need exist in memory as only one copy, rather than as part of every executing program that uses it.

3. Should an error be discovered in the implementation of a shared library, it can be replaced with a new version, as long as it preserves the library's interface, without requiring programs that use it to be relinked—an already executing program continues to use the copy of the library that was present in the file system when it demanded it, but new invocations of that program and others use the new copy.

Note that linking a program with a nonshared library typically results in acquiring only the routines the program calls, plus the transitive closure of routines they call, rather than the whole library, but this usually does not result in a large space savings—especially for large, complex libraries such as those that implement windowing or graphics systems—and spreading this effect over all programs that link with a given library almost always favors shared libraries.

   A subtle issue is the need to keep the semantics of linking the same, as much as possible, as with static linking. The most important component of this is being able to determine before execution that the needed routines are present in the library, so that one can indicate whether dynamic linking will succeed, i.e., whether undefined and/or multiply defined external symbols will be encountered. This functionality is obtained by providing, for each shared library, a table of contents that lists its entry points and external symbols and those used by each routine in it (see Figure 5.14 for an example). The first column lists entry points and externally known names in this shared library and the second and third columns list entry points and externals they reference and the shared libraries they are located in. The pre-execution linking operation then merely checks the tables of contents corresponding to the libraries to be linked dynamically, and so can report the same undefined symbols that static linking would. The run-time *dynamic linker* is then guaranteed to fail if and only if the pre-execution static linker would. Still, some minor differences may be seen

Entry Points and External Symbols Provided	Shared Library Used	Entry Points and External Symbols Used
entry1	library1	extern1
		entry2
	library2	entry3
entry2	library1	entry1
	library2	entry4
		entry5
extern1		

FIG. 5.14   An example of a shared library's table of contents.

when one links a dynamic library ahead of a static library, when both were originally linked statically.

Also, the code that is shared need not constitute a library in the sense in which that term has traditionally been used. It is merely a unit that the programmer chooses to link in at run time, rather than in advance of it. In the remainder of this section, we call the unit a *shared object* rather than a shared library, to reflect this fact.

Shared objects do incur a small performance impact when a program is running alone, but on a multiprogrammed system, this impact may be balanced entirely or nearly so by the reduced working set size, which results in better paging and cache performance. The performance impact has two sources, namely, the cost of run-time linking and the fact that shared objects must consist of *position-independent* code, i.e., code that can be loaded at different addresses in different programs, and each shared object's private data must be allocated one copy per linked program, resulting in somewhat higher overhead to access it.

We next consider the issues and non-issues involved in supporting shared objects. Position independence must be achieved so that each user of a shared object is free to map it to any address in memory, possibly subject to an alignment condition such as the page size, since programs may be of various sizes and may demand shared objects in any order. Accessing local variables within a shared object is not an issue, since they are either in registers or in an area accessed by means of a register, and so are private to each process. Accessing global variables is an issue, since they are often placed at absolute rather than register-relative addresses. Calling a routine in a shared object is an issue, since one does not know until the routine has been loaded what address to use for it. This results in four problems that need to be solved to make objects position-independent and hence sharable, namely, (1) how control is passed within an object, (2) how an object addresses its own external variables, (3) how control is passed between objects, and (4) how an object addresses external variables belonging to other objects.

In most systems, transferring control within an object is easy, since they provide program-counter-relative (i.e., position-based) branches and calls. Even though the

object as a whole needs to be compiled in such a way as to be positioned at any
location when it is loaded, the relative offsets of locations within it are fixed at
compile time, so PC-relative control transfers are exactly what is needed. If no PC-
relative call is provided by the architecture, it can be simulated by a sequence of
instructions that constructs the address of a call's target from its offset from the
current point, as shown below.

For an instance of a shared object to address its own external variables, it needs
a position-independent way to do so. Since processors do not generally provide PC-
relative loads and stores, a different technique must be used. The most common
approach uses a so-called *global offset table,* or GOT, that initially contains offsets
of external symbols within a so-called dynamic area that resides in the object's data
space. When the object is dynamically linked, the offsets in the GOT are turned
into absolute addresses within the current process's data space. It only remains for
procedures that reference externals to gain addressability to the GOT. This is done
by a code sequence such as the following LIR code:

```
        gp ← GOT_off + 8
        call    next,r31
next:   gp ← gp + r31
```

where GOT_off is the address of the GOT relative to the instruction that uses it. The
code sets the global pointer gp to point to the base of the GOT. Now the procedure
can access external variables by means of their addresses in the GOT; for example,
to load the value of an external integer variable named a, whose address is stored at
offset a_off in the GOT, into register r3, it would execute

```
    r2 ← [gp+a_off]
    r3 ← [r2]
```

The first instruction loads the address of a into r2 and the second loads its value into
r3. Note that for this to work, the GOT can be no larger than the non-negative part
of the range of the offset in load and store instructions. For a RISC, if a larger range
is needed, additional instructions must be generated before the first load to set the
high-order part of the address, as follows:

```
    r3 ← high_part(a_off)
    r2 ← gp + r3
    r2 ← [r2+low_part(a_off)]
    r3 ← [r2]
```

where high_part( ) and low_part( ) provide the upper and lower bits of their argument, divided into two contiguous pieces. For this reason, compilers may provide
two options for generating position-independent code—one with and one without
the additional instructions.

Transferring control between objects is not as simple as within an object, since
the objects' relative positions are not known at compile time, or even when the
program is initially loaded. The standard approach is to provide, for each routine
called from an object, a *stub* that is the target of calls to that routine. The stub is
placed in the calling object's data space, not its read-only code space, so it can be

modified when the called routine is invoked during execution, causing the routine to be loaded (if this is its first use in the called object) and linked.

There are several possible strategies for how the stubs work. For example, each stub might contain the name of the routine it corresponds to and a call to the dynamic linker, which would replace the beginning of the stub with a call to the actual routine. Alternately, given a register-relative branch instruction, we could organize the stubs into a structure called a *procedure linkage table,* or PLT, reserve the first stub to call the dynamic linker, the second one to identify the calling object, and the others to each construct the index of the relocation information for the routine the stub is for, and branch to the first one (thus invoking the dynamic linker). This approach allows the stubs to be resolved lazily, i.e., only as needed, and versions of it are used in several dynamic linking systems. For SPARC, assuming that we have stubs for three procedures, the form of the PLT before loading and after the first and third routines have been dynamically linked are as shown in Figure 5.15(a) and (b), respectively. Before loading, the first two PLT entries are empty and each of the others contains instructions that compute a shifted version of the entry's index in the PLT and branch to the first entry. During loading of the shared object into memory, the dynamic linker sets the first two entries as shown in Figure 5.15(b)—the second one identifies the shared object and the first creates a stack frame and invokes the dynamic linker—and leaves the others unchanged, as shown by the .PLT3 entry. When the procedure, say f( ), corresponding to entry 2 in the PLT is first called, the stub at .PLT2—which still has the form shown in Figure 5.15(a) at this point— is invoked; it puts the shifted index computed by the sethi in g1 and branches to .PLT0, which calls the dynamic linker. The dynamic linker uses the object identifier and the value in g1 to obtain the relocation information for f( ), and modifies entry .PLT2 correspondingly to create a jmpl to the code for f( ) that discards the return address (note that the sethi that begins the next entry is executed—harmlessly—in the delay slot of the jmpl). Thus, a call from this object to the PLT entry for f( ) henceforth branches to the beginning of the code for f( ) with the correct return address.

Accessing another object's external variables is essentially identical to accessing one's own, except that one uses that object's GOT.

A somewhat subtle issue is the ability to form the address of a procedure at run time, to store it as the value of a variable, and to compare it to another procedure address. If the address of a procedure in a shared object, when computed within the shared object, is the address of its first instruction, while its address when computed from outside the object is the address of the first instruction in a stub for it, then we have broken a feature found in C and several other languages. The solution is simple: both within shared code and outside it, we use procedure descriptors (as described in the preceding section) but we modify them to contain the PLT entry address rather than the code's address, and we extend them to include the address of the GOT for the object containing the callee. The code sequence used to perform a call through a procedure variable needs to save and restore the GOT pointer, but the result is that such descriptors can be used uniformly as the values of procedure variables, and comparisons of them work correctly.

```
 .PLT0: unimp                          .PLT0: save   sp,-64,sp
        unimp                                 call   dyn_linker
        unimp                                 nop
 .PLT1: unimp                          .PLT1: .word object_id
        unimp                                 unimp
        unimp                                 unimp
 .PLT2: sethi (.-.PLT0),g1             .PLT2: sethi (.-.PLT0),g1
        ba,a  .PLT0                           sethi %hi(f),g1
        nop                                   jmpl  g1+%lo(f),r0
 .PLT3: sethi (.-.PLT0),g1             .PLT3: sethi (.-.PLT0),g1
        ba,a  .PLT0                           ba,a  .PLT0
        nop                                   nop
 .PLT4: sethi (.-.PLT0),g1             .PLT4: sethi (.-.PLT0),g1
        ba,a  .PLT0                           sethi %hi(h),g1
        nop                                   jmpl  g1+%lo(h),r0
        nop                                   nop

   (a)                                   (b)
```

FIG. 5.15 SPARC PLT (a) before loading, and (b) after two routines have been dynamically linked.

5.8   Symbolic and Polymorphic Language Support

Most of the compiler material in this book is devoted to languages that are well suited to compilation: languages that have static, compile-time type systems, that do not allow the user to incrementally change the code, and that typically make much heavier use of stack storage than heap storage.

In this section, we briefly consider the issues involved in compiling programs written in more dynamic languages, such as LISP, ML, Prolog, Scheme, SELF, Smalltalk, SNOBOL, Java, and so on, that are generally used to manipulate symbolic data and have run-time typing and polymorphic operations. We refer the reader to [Lee91] for a more expansive treatment of some of these issues. There are five main problems in producing efficient code for such a language, beyond those considered in the remainder of this book, namely,

1. an efficient way to deal with run-time type checking and function polymorphism,

2. fast implementations of the language's basic operations,

3. fast function calls and ways to optimize them to be even faster,

4. heap storage management, and

5. efficient ways of dealing with incremental changes to running programs.

Run-time type checking is required by most of these languages because they assign types to data, not to variables. Thus, when we encounter at compile time an operation of the form "a + b", or "(plus a b)", or however it might be written in a particular language, we do not, in general, have any way of knowing whether the operation being performed is addition of integers, floating-point numbers, rationals, or arbitrary-precision reals; whether it might be concatenation of lists or strings; or whether it is some other operation determined by the types of its two operands. So we need to compile code that includes type information for constants and that checks the types of operands and branches to the appropriate code to implement each operation. In general, the most common cases that need to be detected and dispatched on quickly are integer arithmetic and operations on one other data type, namely, list cells in LISP and ML, strings in SNOBOL, and so on.

Architectural support for type checking is minimal in most systems. SPARC, however, provides tagged add and subtract instructions that, in parallel with performing an add or subtract, check that the low-order two bits of both 32-bit operands are zeros. If they are not, either a trap or a condition code setting can result, at the user's option, and the result is not written to the target register. Thus, by putting at least part of the tag information in the two low-order bits of a word, one gets a very inexpensive way to check that an add or subtract has integer operands. Some other RISCs, such as MIPS and PA-RISC, support somewhat slower type checking by providing compare-immediate-and-branch instructions. Such instructions can be used to check the tag of each operand in a single instruction, so the overhead is only two to four cycles, depending on the filling of branch-delay slots.

The low-order two bits of a word can also be used to do type checking in SPARC for at least one more data type, such as list cells in LISP. Assuming that list cells are doublewords, if one uses the address of the first word plus 3 as the pointer to a list cell (say in register r1), then word accesses to the car and cdr fields use addresses of the form r1 - 3 and r1 + 1, and the addresses are valid if and only if the pointers used in loads or stores to access them have a 3 in the low-order two bits, i.e., a tag of 3 (see Figure 5.16). Note that this leaves two other tag values (1 and 2) available for another type and an indicator that more detailed type information needs to be accessed elsewhere.

The odd-address facet of the tagging scheme can be used in several other RISC architectures. Other efficient means of tagging data are discussed in Chapter 1 of [Lee91].

The work discussed in Section 9.6 concerns, among other things, software techniques for assigning, where possible, types to variables in languages in which, strictly speaking, only data objects have types.

Fast function calling is essential for these languages because they strongly encourage dividing programs up into many small functions. Polymorphism affects function-calling overhead because it causes determination at run time of the code to invoke for a particular call, based on the types of its arguments. RISCs are ideal

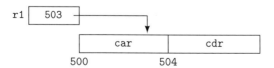

FIG. 5.16 A LISP list cell and a SPARC tagged pointer to it.

in this regard, since they generally provide fast function calls by branch-and-link instructions, pass arguments in registers, and, in most cases, provide quick ways to dispatch on the type of one or more arguments. One can move the type of an argument into a register, convert it to an offset of the proper size, and branch into a table of branches to code that implements a function for the corresponding type.

Dynamic and symbolic languages generally make heavy use of heap storage, largely because the objects they are designed to operate on are very dynamic in size and shape. Thus, it is essential to have a very efficient mechanism for allocating heap storage and for recovering it. Storage recovery is uniformly by garbage collection, not by explicit freeing. The most efficient method of garbage collection for general use for such languages is *generation scavenging,* which is based on the principle that the longer an object lives, the longer it is likely to live.

Finally, the ability to incrementally change the code of a running program is a characteristic of most of these languages. This is usually implemented in compiled implementations by a combination of run-time compilation and indirect access to functions. If the name of a function in a running program is the address of a cell that contains the address of its code, as in the procedure descriptors discussed in Sections 5.6 and 5.7, then one can change the code and its location, at least when it is not active, by changing the address in the indirect cell to point to the new code for the function. Having the compiler available at run time also enables on-the-fly recompilation, i.e., the ability to recompile an existing routine, perhaps because one had previously cached a compiled copy of the routine that assumed that its arguments had particular types and that information no longer applies. This approach was used to good advantage in Deutsch and Schiffman's implementation of Smalltalk-80 for a Motorola M68000-based system [DeuS84] and has been used repeatedly since in other polymorphic-language implementations.

The above discussion only scratches the surface of the issues involved in designing an efficient implementation of a dynamic language. See Section 5.10 for references to further sources in this area.

5.9   Wrap-Up

In this chapter, we have reviewed the basic issues in supporting the concepts that are commonly embodied in higher-level languages at run time, including data types and approaches to representing them efficiently at run time, storage allocation and addressing methods, visibility and scope rules, register usage and elementary methods for managing it, the structure of a single procedure's stack frame and the overall organization of the run-time stack, and the issues involved in supporting parameter passing and procedure calling, entry, exit, and return.

Since most of this material is covered well in introductory texts on compilers, our purpose has been to remind the reader of the issues and of appropriate ways of handling them and to provide references for further reading. More advanced concepts, such as position-independent code and support for dynamic and polymorphic languages, are discussed in the final sections in greater detail.

The existence of Application Binary Interface standards for many architectures determines how some of these issues must be handled (if it is necessary for a project to conform to the standard), and thus eases the task of achieving interoperability with other software.

In the latter sections of the chapter, we have discussed issues that are generally not covered in introductory courses at all. In Section 5.7, we provided a detailed account of how to support code sharing between processes, by means of position-independent code and dynamic linking. Finally, in Section 5.8, we surveyed the issues in supporting dynamic and polymorphic languages, a subject that could easily take another whole volume if it were covered in detail.

5.10   Further Reading

The UNIX System V ABI documents referred to at the beginning of this chapter are the general specification [UNIX90a], and its processor-specific supplements for, e.g., SPARC [UNIX90c], the Motorola 88000 [UNIX90b], and the Intel 386 architecture family [UNIX93]. Hewlett-Packard's [HewP91] specifies the stack structure and calling conventions for PA-RISC.

The Unicode specification, which encompasses 16-bit character representations for the Latin, Cyrillic, Arabic, Hebrew, and Korean (Hangul) alphabets; the alphabets of several languages spoken in India; Chinese and Kanji characters; and Katakana and Hiragana is [Unic90].

The idea of using thunks to compute the addresses of call-by-name parameters is first described in [Inge61].

Weicker's statistics on the average number of arguments passed to a procedure are given in [Weic84], along with the code for the original version of the dhrystone benchmark.

Statistics on the power of register windows to reduce the number of loads and stores executed in a RISC architecture are given in [CmeK91].

[GinL87] gives an exposition of the advantages of shared libraries or objects and an overview of their implementation in a specific operating system, SunOS for SPARC. It also describes the minor differences that may be observed between loading a program statically and dynamically.

The symbolic and polymorphic languages mentioned in Section 5.8 are described in detail in [Stee84] (LISP), [MilT90] (ML), [CloM87] (Prolog), [CliR91] (Scheme), [UngS91] (SELF), [Gold84] (Smalltalk), [GriP68] (SNOBOL), and [GosJ96] (Java).

The generation scavenging approach to garbage collection is described in [Unga87] and [Lee89].

The first published description of on-the-fly compilation is Deutsch and Schiffman's implementation of Smalltalk-80 [DeuS84] for a Motorola M68000-based system. Other issues in implementing dynamic and polymorphic languages, such as inferring control- and data-flow information, are discussed in [Lee91] and in numerous papers in the proceedings of the annual programming languages and functional programming conferences.

5.11   Exercises

5.1 Suppose that MIR contained neither byte nor halfword loads and stores. (a) Write an efficient MIR routine that moves a byte string from the address in register r1 to the address in r2 with the length in r3. (b) Now assume the C convention that a string is terminated by a null character, i.e., 0x00, and rewrite the routines to move such strings efficiently.

5.2 Write ICAN routines to scan the entries in a local symbol table and assign them storage addresses (offsets from the frame pointer fp) in three orders: (a) as ordered in the symbol table, (b) in decreasing order by size, and (c) in increasing order by size.

5.3 Determine how one of the compilers in your computing environment divides up register usage. This may require simply reading a manual, or it may require a series of experiments.

5.4 Suppose we have a call f(i,x,j), with parameters passed by value, where the first and third parameters are integers and the second is a single-precision floating-point value. The call is executed in the procedure g( ), which is nested within the same scope as f( ), so they have the same static link. Write LIR code that implements the procedure-calling and return handshake, assuming that parameters are passed in registers with a flat register file, as discussed in Section 5.6.1. The answer should have five parts, as follows: (1) the call, (2) f( )'s prologue, (3) use of the first parameter, (4) f( )'s epilogue, and (5) the return point.

5.5 Write either LIR code or Intel 386 architecture family assembly language for the preceding exercise, assuming that parameters are passed on the run-time stack, as discussed in Section 5.6.2.

5.6 Write LIR code for the preceding exercise, assuming that parameters are passed in registers with register windowing, as discussed in Section 5.6.3.

ADV 5.7 Devise a language extension to Pascal or a similar language that requires (some) stack frames to be preserved, presumably in heap storage, independent of the original calling conventions. Why might such a language extension be useful?

5.8 Write a LIR version of the routine alloca( ) described in Section 5.3.

5.9 Write a (single) program that demonstrates that all the parameter-passing disciplines are distinct. That is, write a program in a language of your choice and show that using each of the five parameter-passing methods results in different output from your program.

5.10 Describe (or write in ICAN) a procedure to be used at run time to distinguish which of a series of methods with the same name is to be invoked in Java, based on the overloading and overriding found in the language.

ADV 5.11 Write sample code for the procedure-calling handshake for a language with call by name. Specifically, write LIR code for a call f(n,a[n]) where both parameters are called by name.

5.12 Describe and give code examples for an approach to handling shared objects that uses only a GOT and no PLTs.

RSCH 5.13 Explore the issues involved in supporting a polymorphic language by mixing on-the-fly compilation (discussed briefly in Section 5.8) with interpretation of an intermediate code. The issues include, for example, transfers of control between interpreted and compiled code (in both directions), how to tell when it is worthwhile to compile a routine, and how to tell when to recompile a routine or to switch back to interpreting it.

CHAPTER 6

Producing Code Generators Automatically

In this chapter, we explore briefly the issues involved in generating machine or assembly code from intermediate code, and then delve into automatic methods for generating code generators from machine descriptions.

There are several sorts of issues to consider in generating code, including

1. the register, addressing, and instruction architecture of the target machine,

2. software conventions that must be observed,

3. a method for binding variables to memory locations or so-called symbolic registers,

4. the structure and characteristics of the intermediate language,

5. the implementations of intermediate-language operators that don't correspond directly to target-machine instructions,

6. a method for translating from intermediate code to machine code, and

7. whether to target assembly language or a directly linkable or relocatable version of machine code.

The importance of and choices made for some of these issues vary according to whether we are writing a compiler for a single language and target architecture; for several languages for one architecture; for one language for several architectures; or for several languages and several architectures. Also, it is usually prudent to take into account that a given compiler may need to be adapted to support additional source languages and machine architectures over its lifetime.

If we are certain that our job is to produce compilers for a single architecture, there may be no advantage in using automatic methods to generate a code generator from a machine description. In such a case, we would use a hand-crafted approach, such as those described in the typical introductory compiler text. If, on the other hand, we expect to be producing compilers for several architectures, generating code generators automatically from machine descriptions may be of great value. It is generally easier to write or modify a machine description than to produce a code generator from scratch or to adapt an existing code generator to a new architecture.

The machine architecture needs to be understood for obvious reasons—although some reasons may not be so obvious. It is the target that the code we generate must aim for—if we miss it, the code simply will not run. Less obviously, there may not be a good match between some language features and the target architecture. For example, if we must handle 64-bit integer arithmetic on a machine with a 32-bit word length, we need to write open or closed routines (i.e., in-line code or subroutines) to perform the 64-bit operations. A similar situation arises almost universally for complex numbers. If the machine has PC-relative conditional branches with a displacement too short to cover the sizes of programs, we need to devise a means for branching to locations far enough away to cover the class of expected programs, perhaps by branching on the negation of a condition around an unconditional jump with a broader range.

The software conventions have a similar importance. They must be designed to support the source language's features and to coincide with any published standard that must be adhered to, such as an Application Binary Interface (ABI) definition (see the beginning of Chapter 5), or the generated code will not meet its requirements. Understanding the details of the software conventions and how to implement code that satisfies them efficiently is essential to producing efficient code.

The structure of the intermediate language we are working from is not essential to determining whether we are generating correct code, but it is a major determining factor in selecting the method to use. There are code-generation approaches designed to work on DAGs, trees, quadruples, triples, Polish-prefix code, and several other forms, including several different representations of control structure.

Whether to target assembly language or a relocatable binary form of object code is mostly a question of convenience and the importance of compilation-time performance. Generating assembly code requires that we include an assembly phase in the compilation process, and hence requires additional time (both for running the assembler and for writing and reading the assembly code), but it makes the output of the code generator easier to read and check, and it allows us to leave to the assembler the handling of such issues as generating a branch to a currently unknown future location in the code by producing a symbolic label now and leaving it to the assembler to locate it in the code later. If, on the other hand, we generate linkable code directly, we generally need a way to output a symbolic form of the code for debugging anyway, although it need not be full assembly language and it might be generated from the object code by a disassembler, as IBM does for its POWER and PowerPC compilers (see Section 21.2.2).

6.1   Introduction to Automatic Generation of Code Generators

While hand-crafted code generators are effective and fast, they have the disadvantage of being implemented by hand and so are much more difficult to modify and port than a code generator that is automatically generated. Several approaches have been developed that construct a machine description from a code generator. We describe three of them to varying levels of detail here. All begin with a low-level intermediate code that has addressing computations exposed.

In all three cases, the code generator does pattern matching on trees, although that will not be immediately apparent in the first two—they both work on a Polish-prefix intermediate representation. Of course, as noted in Section 4.9.4, Polish prefix results from a preorder tree traversal, so the tree is simply hidden in a linear presentation.

6.2   A Syntax-Directed Technique

The first approach to generating a code generator from a machine description is known as the Graham-Glanville method after its originators. It represents machine operations by rules similar to those in a context-free grammar, along with corresponding machine instruction templates. When a rule matches a substring of a Polish-prefix intermediate-code string (which represents a preorder traversal of a sequence of trees) and its associated semantic constraints are met, the part matched is replaced by an instantiation of the left-hand symbol of the rule and a corresponding instantiation of the instruction template is emitted.

A Graham-Glanville code generator consists of three components, namely, intermediate-language transformations, the pattern matcher, and instruction generation. The first transforms, as necessary, the output of a compiler front end into a form suitable for pattern matching; for example, source-language operators not representable by machine operations might be transformed into subroutine calls, and calls are transformed into sequences of explicit state-changing instructions. The second component actually does the pattern matching, determining what sequence of reductions is appropriate to consume an input string of intermediate code. The third, which is meshed with the second in its execution, actually generates an appropriate sequence of instructions and performs register allocation. In the remainder of this section, we concentrate on the pattern-matching phase and, to a lesser degree, on instruction generation.

As an example, consider the subset of LIR instructions in Figure 6.1(a), where each argument position is qualified with a number that is used to match intermediate-code substrings with code-generation rules and instruction templates. The corresponding rules and SPARC instruction templates are shown in Figure 6.1(b) and (c). In the figure, "r.n" denotes a register, "k.n" a constant, and "ϵ" the empty string. The numbers are used both to coordinate matching with code emission and to express syntactic restrictions in the rules—for example, if the first and second operands in a string must be the same register for the match to succeed, then they would both have the same number.

We use "↑" to denote a load, "←" to denote a store, and mov to denote a register-to-register move in the Polish-prefix code.

As an example, suppose we have the LIR code shown in Figure 6.2. Then, assuming r3 and r4 are dead at the end of this code sequence, there is no need to include them explicitly in the tree representation, as shown in Figure 6.3, but we do need to retain r1 and r2. The resulting Polish-prefix form is

```
r.2 ← r.1              r.2 ⇒ r.1              or  r.1,0,r.2
r.2 ← k.1              r.2 ⇒ k.1              or  0,k.1,r.2
r.2 ← r.1              r.2 ⇒ mov r.2 r.1      or  r.1,0,r.2


r.3 ← r.1 + r.2        r.3 ⇒ + r.1 r.2        add r.1,r.2,r.3
r.3 ← r.1 + k.2        r.3 ⇒ + r.1 k.2        add r.1,k.2,r.3
r.3 ← k.2 + r.1        r.3 ⇒ + k.2 r.1        add r.1,k.2,r.3


r.3 ← r.1 - r.2        r.3 ⇒ - r.1 r.2        sub r.1,r.2,r.3
r.3 ← r.1 - k.2        r.3 ⇒ - r.1 k.2        sub r.1,k.2,r.3


r.3 ← [r.1+r.2]        r.3 ⇒ ↑ + r.1 r.2      ld  [r.1,r.2],r.3
r.3 ← [r.1+k.2]        r.3 ⇒ ↑ + r.1 k.2      ld  [r.1,k.2],r.3
r.2 ← [r.1]            ε ⇒ ↑ r.2 r.1          ld  [r.1],r.2


[r.2+r.3] ← r.1        ε ⇒ ← + r.2 r.3 r.1    st  r.1,[r.2,r.3]
[r.2+k.1] ← r.1        ε ⇒ ← + r.2 k.1 r.1    st  r.1,[r.2,k.1]
[r2] ← r.1             ε ⇒ ← r.2 r.1          st  r.1,[r.2]
(a)                    (b)                    (c)
```

FIG. 6.1 (a) LIR instructions, (b) Graham-Glanville machine-description rules, and (c) corresponding SPARC instruction templates.

```
r2 ← [r8]
r1 ← [r8+4]
r3 ← r2 + r1
[r8+8] ← r3
r4 ← r1 - 1
[r8+4] ← r4
```

FIG. 6.2 A LIR code sequence for Graham-Glanville code generation.

$$\uparrow \text{r2 r8} \leftarrow + \text{r8 8} + \text{r2 mov r1} \uparrow + \text{r8 4} \leftarrow + \text{r8 4} - \text{r1 1}$$

The pattern matching that occurs during its parsing is shown in Figure 6.4, along with the SPARC instructions generated for it. The underlining indicates the portion of the string that is matched, and the symbol underneath it shows what replaces the matched substring; for loads and arithmetic operators, the resulting register is determined by the register allocator used during code generation.

6.2.1   The Code Generator

The code generator is essentially an SLR(1) parser that performs the usual shift and reduce actions, but that emits machine instructions instead of parse trees or intermediate code. In essence, the parser recognizes a language whose productions are the machine-description rules with "ϵ" replaced by a nonterminal N and the additional production $S \Rightarrow N^*$. There are, however, a few important differences from SLR parsing.

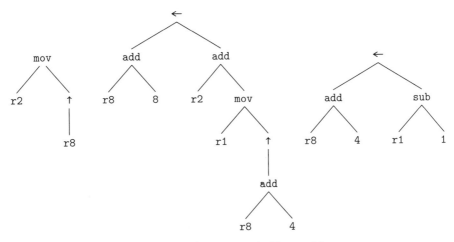

FIG. 6.3 Trees corresponding to the LIR code sequence in Figure 6.2.

```
↑ r2 r8 ← + r8 8 + r2 mov r1 ↑ + r8 4 ← + r8 4 - r1 1
ϵ                                                          ld    [r8],r2
← + r8 8 + r2 mov r1 ↑ + r8 4 ← + r8 4 - r1 1
                    r3                                     ld    [r8,4],r3
← + r8 8 + r2 mov r1 r3 ← + r8 4 - r1 1
                r1                                         or    r3,0,r1
← + r8 8 + r2 r1 ← + r8 4 - r1 1
            r4                                            add    r2,r1,r4
← + r8 4 r4 ← + r8 4 - r1 1
ϵ                                                         st    r4,[r8,4]
← + r8 4 - r1 1
            r5                                            sub    r1,1,r5
← + r8 4 r5
ϵ                                                         st    r5,[r8,4]
(a)                                                      (b)
```

FIG. 6.4 (a) Parsing process and (b) emitted instructions for the trees in Figure 6.3.

Rules with "ϵ" on the left-hand side are allowed, and the "ϵ" is treated as a nonterminal symbol. Unlike in parsing, machine-description grammars are almost always ambiguous. The ambiguities are resolved in two ways. One is by favoring shift actions over reduce actions (i.e., the algorithm is *greedy* or *maximal munch*) and longer reductions over shorter ones, so as to match the longest possible string. The other is by ordering the rules when the parsing tables are produced so that the code generator picks the first rule that matches when it performs a reduction during code generation. Thus, in specifying the rules, one can bias code generation to particular choices by ordering the rules in a particular way or by building a cost evaluation into the code generator.

The code-generation algorithm uses seven global data types, a stack, and two functions that are constructed by the code-generator generator, as follows:

```
Vocab = Terminal ∪ Nonterminal
ExtVocab = Vocab ∪ {'ε','$'}
VocabSeq = sequence of Vocab
ActionType = enum {Shift,Reduce,Accept,Error}
|| type of machine grammar rules
Rule = record {lt: Nonterminal ∪ {'ε'},
               rt: VocabSeq}
|| type of parsing automaton items that make up its states
Item = record {lt: Nonterminal ∪ {'ε'},
               rt: VocabSeq,
               pos: integer}
ActionRedn = ActionType × set of Item
Stack: sequence of (integer ∪ ExtVocab)
Action: State × ExtVocab ⟶ ActionRedn
Next: State × ExtVocab ⟶ State
```

It takes as input a Polish-prefix intermediate-code string InterCode, which must be a sequence of members of Terminal. An element of type ActionRedn is a pair ⟨a,r⟩ consisting of a member a of ActionType and r in set of Item such that $r \neq \emptyset$ if and only if a = Reduce. The algorithm is shown in Figure 6.5. Get_Symbol( ) returns the first symbol in its argument, and Discard_Symbol( ) removes that symbol.

The function Emit_Instrs(*reduction*,*left*,*right*) selects a rule from among those encoded in *reduction*, emits one or more corresponding instructions using the information on the stack to instantiate the corresponding template, sets *left* to the instantiated symbol on the left-hand side of the rule used, and sets *right* to the length of the rule's right-hand side. To understand why Emit_Instrs( ) needs to use information on the stack to decide what instruction sequence to emit, consider the second rule in Figure 6.1. There is no problem with using it, as long as the constant matched by k.1 fits into the 13-bit signed immediate field found in most SPARC instructions. If it doesn't fit, Emit_Instrs( ) needs to generate a sethi and an or to construct the constant in a register, followed by the corresponding three-register instruction given in the first rule in Figure 6.1. We can introduce this alternative into the rules by providing the additional rule and instruction template

```
(empty)              r.2 ⇒ k.1          sethi %hi(k.1),r.2
                                         or    %lo(k.1),r.2,r.2
```

However, we would still need to check the lengths of constant operands, since otherwise this rule would not be used when needed—it matches a shorter substring than does any rule that includes an operator and a constant operand, so we would always shift on finding a constant operand, rather than reduce.

```
procedure Generate(InterCode) returns boolean
   Intercode: in VocabSeq
begin
   state := 0, right: integer
   action: ActionType
   reduction: set of Item
   left, lookahead: ExtVocab
   Stack := [0]
   lookahead := Lookahead(InterCode)
   while true do
      action := Action(state,lookahead)↓1
      reduction := Action(state,lookahead)↓2
      case action of
Shift:    Stack ⊕= [lookahead]
          state := Next(state,lookahead)
          Stack ⊕= [state]
          Discard_Symbol(InterCode)
          if InterCode = [] then
              lookahead := '$'
          else
              lookahead := Get_Symbol(InterCode)
          fi
Reduce:   Emit_Instrs(reduction,left,right)
          for i := 1 to 2 * right do
              Stack ⊖= -1
          od
          state := Stack↓-1
          if left ≠ 'ε' then
              Stack ⊕= [left]
              state := Next(state,left)
              Stack ⊕= [state]
          fi
Accept:   return true
Error:    return false
      esac
   od
end    || Generate
```

FIG. 6.5 The code-generation algorithm.

Another issue hidden in `Emit_Instrs( )` is register allocation. It can be handled by the method described in Section 3.6, or preferably by assigning scalar variables and temporaries to an unlimited set of symbolic registers that the register allocator (see Section 16.3) will eventually assign to machine registers or storage locations.

6.2.2   The Code-Generator Generator

The code-generator generator, shown in Figures 6.6 and 6.7, is based on the sets-of-items construction used in building SLR parsing tables (where an *item* is a production in the grammar with a dot "•" in its right-hand side), but with several modifications. Items are represented by the global type `Item` declared above; an item $[l \Rightarrow r_1 \ldots r_i \cdot r_{i+1} \ldots r_n]$ corresponds to the record $\langle \texttt{lt}:l, \texttt{rt}:r_1 \ldots r_n, \texttt{pos}:i \rangle$. The main routine `Gen_Tables( )` returns `true` if the set of rules in `MGrammar` is uniform (see Figure 6.7) and all syntactic blocks (see Subsection 6.2.4) could be repaired; and `false` otherwise. The global variables in Figure 6.6 are global to all the

```
MaxStateNo: integer
MGrammar: set of Rule
ItemSet: array [··] of set of Item

procedure Gen_Tables( ) returns boolean
begin
   StateNo := 0: integer
   unif: boolean
   item: Item
   rule: Rule
   || remove cycles of nonterminals from machine grammar
   Elim_Chain_Loops( )
   MaxStateNo := 0
   || generate action/next tables
   ItemSet[0] := Closure({<lt:rule.lt,rt:rule.rt,pos:0>
                          where rule ∈ MGrammar
   while StateNo ≤ MaxStateNo do
      Successors(StateNo)
      || process fails if some state is not uniform
      if !Uniform(StateNo) then
          return false
      fi
      StateNo += 1
   od
   || process fails if some syntactic blockage is not repairable
   unif := Fix_Synt_Blocks( )
   Action(0,'$') := <Accept,∅>
   return unif
end    || Gen_Tables
```

FIG. 6.6 Constructing the SLR(1) parsing tables.

```
procedure Successors(s)
   s: in integer
begin
   NextItems: set of Item
   v: Vocab
   x: ExtVocab
   j: integer
   item, item1: Item
   for each v ∈ Vocab do
      || if there is an item [x ⇒ α•vβ] in ItemSet[s],
      || set action to shift and compute next state
      if ∃item ∈ ItemSet[s] (v = item.rt↓(itom.pos+1)) then
         Action(s,v) := ⟨Shift,∅⟩
         NextItems := Closure(Advance({item1 ∈ Itemset[s]
            where v =item1.rt↓(item1.pos+1)}))
         if ∃j ∈ integer (ItemSet[j] = NextItems) then
            Next(s,v) := j
         else
            MaxStateNo += 1
            ItemSet[MaxStateNo] := NextItems
            Next(s,v) := MaxStateNo
         fi
      || if there is an item [x ⇒ α•] in ItemSet[s],
      || set action to reduce and compute the reduction
      elif ∃item ∈ ItemSet[s] (item.pos = |item.rt|+1) then
         Reduction := {item ∈ ItemSet[s]
            where item.pos = |item.rt|+1 & v ∈ Follow(item.lt)
            & ∀item1 ∈ ItemSet[s] (item1.pos ≤ |item.rt|
               ∨ v ∉ Follow(item1.lt))
         Action(s,v) := ⟨Reduce,Reduction⟩
      || otherwise set action to error
      else
         Action(s,v) := ⟨Error,∅⟩
      fi
   od
end      || Successors
```

FIG. 6.6 *(continued)*

routines in this section. The array `ItemSet[ ]` is indexed by state numbers and is used to hold the sets of items as they are constructed. Vocab is the vocabulary of terminal and nonterminal symbols that occurs in the rules. Like a parser generator, the code-generator generator proceeds by constructing sets of items and associating each of them with a state. The function `Successors( )` computes the sets of items corresponding to the successors of each state and fills in the `Action( )` and `Next( )` values for each transition.

The functions `Elim_Chain_Loops( )` and `Fix_Synt_Blocks( )` are described below. The function `Uniform( )` determines whether the set of rules satisfies a

```
procedure Uniform(s) returns boolean
    s: in integer
begin
    u, v, x: Vocab
    item: Item
    for each item ∈ ItemSet[s] (item.pos ≤ |item.rt|) do
        if item.pos ≠ 0 then
            x := Parent(item.rt↓item.pos,item.rt)
            if Left_Child(item.rt↓item.pos,item.rt) then
                for each u ∈ Vocab do
                    if Action(s,u) = ⟨Error,∅⟩
                        & (Left_First(x,u) V Right_First(x,u)) then
                        return false
                    fi
                od
            fi
        fi
    od
    return true
end     || Uniform

procedure Closure(S) returns set of Item
    S: in set of Item
begin
    OldS: set of Item
    item, s: Item
    repeat
        || compute the set of items [x ⇒ αv·β]
        || such that [x ⇒ α·vβ] is in S
        OldS := S
        S ∪= {item ∈ Item where ∃s ∈ S (s.pos < |s.rt|
            & s.(s.pos+1) ∈ Nonterminal
            & item.lt = s.(s.pos+1) & item.pos = 0)}
    until S = OldS
    return S
end     || Closure

procedure Advance(S) returns set of Item
    S: in set of Item
begin
    s: Item
    || advance the dot one position in each item
    || that does not have the dot at its right end
    return {item ∈ Item where ∃s ∈ S (item.lt = s.lt
        & s.pos ≤ |s.rt| & item.rt = s.rt
        & item.pos = s.pos+1)}
end     || Advance
```

FIG. 6.7 The functions Uniform( ), Closure( ), and Advance( ) used in constructing the SLR(1) parsing tables.

property called uniformity defined as follows: a set of rules is *uniform* if and only if any left operand of a binary operator is a valid left operand of that operator in any Polish-prefix string containing the operator, and similarly for right operands and operands of unary operators. To be suitable for Graham-Glanville code generation, the set of rules must be uniform. The procedure `Uniform( )` uses two functions that are defined below, namely, `Parent( )` and `Left_Child( )` and two functions that are defined from the relations discussed in the next two paragraphs, namely, `Left_First`(x,u) and `Right_First`(x,u), which return `true` if x *Left First* u and x *Right First* u, respectively, and `false` otherwise.

The function

$$Parent : Vocab \times DottedPrefix \longrightarrow Nonterminal \cup \{'\epsilon'\}$$

where *DottedPrefix* is the set of prefixes of sentences generated by the rules each with a dot inserted in its right-hand side, returns the parent of its first argument in the tree form of its second argument, and

$$Left\_Child : Vocab \times DottedPrefix \longrightarrow boolean$$

returns a Boolean value indicating whether its first argument is the left child of its parent in the tree form of its second argument.

The relations used in the algorithm and in defining the functions and relations used in it are as follows (where *BinOp* and *UnOp* are the sets of binary and unary operator symbols and the lowercase Greek letters other than ϵ stand for strings of symbols, respectively):

Left $\subseteq$ (*BinOp* $\cup$ *UnOp*) $\times$ *Vocab*
   x *Left* y if and only if there is a rule $r \Rightarrow \alpha xy\beta$, where r may be ϵ.

Right $\subseteq$ *BinOp* $\times$ *Vocab*
   x *Right* y if and only if there is a rule $r \Rightarrow \alpha x\beta y\gamma$ for some $\beta \neq \epsilon$, where r may be ϵ.

First $\subseteq$ *Vocab* $\times$ *Vocab*
   x *First* y if and only if there is a derivation $x \overset{*}{\Rightarrow} y\alpha$, where α may be ϵ.

Last $\subseteq$ *Vocab* $\times$ *Vocab*
   x *Last* y if and only if there is a derivation $x \overset{*}{\Rightarrow} \alpha y$, where α may be ϵ.

EpsLast $\subseteq$ *Vocab*
   EpsLast = $\{x \mid \exists$ a rule $\epsilon \Rightarrow \alpha y$ and y *Last* $x\}$.

RootOps $\subseteq$ *BinOp* $\cup$ *UnOp*
   RootOps = $\{x \mid \exists$ a rule $\epsilon \Rightarrow x\alpha$ and $x \in BinOp \cup UnOp\}$.

The function *Follow* : *Vocab* $\longrightarrow$ *Vocab* can be defined from the auxiliary function *Follow*1 : *Vocab* $\longrightarrow$ *Vocab* and sets *EpsLast* and *RootOps* as follows:

$$Follow1(u) = \{v \mid \exists \text{ a rule } r \Rightarrow \alpha xy\beta \text{ such that } x \text{ Last } u \text{ and } y \text{ First } v\}$$

$$Follow(u) = \begin{cases} Follow1(u) \cup RootOps & \text{if } u \in EpsLast \\ Follow1(u) & \text{otherwise} \end{cases}$$

r.2 ← r.1	r.2 ⇒ r.1	or r.1,0,r.2
r.3 ← r.1 + r.2	r.3 ⇒ + r.1 r.2	add r.1,r.2,r.3
r.3 ← r.1 + k.2	r.3 ⇒ + r.1 k.2	add r.1,k.2,r.3
r.2 ← [r.1]	r.2 ⇒ ↑ r.1	ld [r.1],r.2
[r2] ← r.1	ϵ ⇒ ← r.2 r.1	st r.1,[r.2]
(a)	(b)	(c)

FIG. 6.8 (a) LIR instructions, (b) Graham-Glanville machine-description rules, and (c) corresponding SPARC instruction templates.

As an example of a Graham-Glanville code generator, consider the very simple machine-description rules in Figure 6.8. In the example, we write items in their traditional notation, that is, we write $[x \Rightarrow \alpha \cdot y\beta]$ in place of $\langle \text{lt:}x, \text{rt:}\alpha y\beta, \text{pos:}|\alpha| \rangle$. First, the *Left*, *Right*, and so on relations, sets, and functions are as given in Figure 6.9. Next, we trace several stages of Gen_Tables( ) for the given grammar. Initially we have StateNo = MaxStateNo = 0 and ItemSet[0] = {[ϵ ⇒ • ← r r]}. Next we call Successors(0), which sets v = 'ϵ', computes Action(0,'←') = ⟨Shift,∅⟩, and sets NextItems to

Closure(Advance({[ϵ ⇒ • ← r r]}))

which evaluates to

NextItems = {[ϵ ⇒ ← • r r], [r ⇒ • r], [r ⇒ • + r r],
            [r ⇒ • + r k], [r ⇒ • ↑ r]}

Now MaxStateNo is increased to 1, ItemSet[1] is set to the value just computed for NextItems, and Next(0,'←') is set to 1.

Next we compute Uniform(1). All items in ItemSet[1] have the dot at the beginning, so this is vacuously true. In the following steps, Uniform( ) always returns true.

Next, StateNo is set to 1 and we call Successors(1). It first sets v = 'r', computes Action(1,'r') = ⟨Shift,∅⟩, and sets NextItems to

Closure(Advance({[ϵ ⇒ ← • r r],[r ⇒ • r]}))

which evaluates to

NextItems = {[ϵ ⇒ ← r • r], [r ⇒ r •], [r ⇒ • r],
            [r ⇒ • + r r], [r ⇒ • + r k], [r ⇒ • ↑ r]}

Now MaxStateNo is increased to 2, ItemSet[2] is set to the value just computed for NextItems, and Next(1,'r') is set to 2.

Next, Successors(1) sets v = '+', computes Action(1,'+') = ⟨Shift,∅⟩, and sets NextItems to

Closure(Advance({[r ⇒ • + r r],[r ⇒ • + r k]}))

$$'+'\ \textit{Left}\ 'r' \qquad '\uparrow'\ \textit{Left}\ 'r' \qquad '\leftarrow'\ \textit{Left}\ 'r'$$

$$'+'\ \textit{Right}\ 'r' \qquad '+'\ \textit{Right}\ 'k' \qquad '\leftarrow'\ \textit{Right}\ 'r'$$

$$'r'\ \textit{First}\ 'r' \qquad 'r'\ \textit{First}\ '+' \qquad 'r'\ \textit{First}\ '\uparrow'$$
$$'\epsilon'\ \textit{First}\ '\epsilon' \qquad '\epsilon'\ \textit{First}\ '\leftarrow'$$

$$'r'\ \textit{Last}\ 'r' \qquad 'r'\ \textit{Last}\ 'k' \qquad '\epsilon'\ \textit{Last}\ '\epsilon'$$
$$'\epsilon'\ \textit{Last}\ 'r' \qquad '\epsilon'\ \textit{Last}\ 'k'$$

$$\textit{EpsLast} = \{'r','k'\} \qquad \textit{RootOps} = \{'\leftarrow'\}$$

$$\textit{Follow1}('\epsilon') = \{'r','+','\uparrow','\leftarrow'\}$$
$$\textit{Follow1}('r') = \{'r','+','\uparrow','\leftarrow'\}$$
$$\textit{Follow1}('k') = \{'r','+','\uparrow','\leftarrow'\}$$
$$\textit{Follow1}('+') = \{'r','+','\uparrow','\leftarrow'\}$$
$$\textit{Follow1}('\uparrow') = \emptyset$$
$$\textit{Follow1}('\leftarrow') = \emptyset$$

$$\textit{Follow}('\epsilon') = \{'r','+','\uparrow','\leftarrow'\}$$
$$\textit{Follow}('r') = \{'r','+','\uparrow','\leftarrow'\}$$
$$\textit{Follow}('k') = \{'r','+','\uparrow','\leftarrow'\}$$
$$\textit{Follow}('+') = \{'r','+','\uparrow','\leftarrow'\}$$
$$\textit{Follow}('\uparrow') = \emptyset$$
$$\textit{Follow}('\leftarrow') = \emptyset$$

FIG. 6.9 Relations, sets, and functions for our example machine-description grammar in Figure 6.8.

which evaluates to

```
NextItems = {[r ⇒ + · r r], [r ⇒ + · r k], [r ⇒ · r],
             [r ⇒ · + r r], [r ⇒ · + r k], [r ⇒ · ↑ r]}
```

Now MaxStateNo is increased to 3, ItemSet[3] is set to the value just computed for NextItems, and Next(1,'+') is set to 3.

The code-generator generator continues producing Shift actions until it reaches MaxStateNo = 9, for which ItemSet[9] is {[ϵ ⇒ + r k ·], [r ⇒ k ·]}, which results in a Reduce action, namely,

⟨Reduce,{[ϵ ⇒ + r k ·]}⟩

The resulting Action/Next table is shown in Figure 6.10 and a graphic presentation of the parsing automaton appears in Figure 6.11. In both the table and the diagram, only non-error transitions are shown. The entries in the table that contain a number correspond to shift actions, e.g., in state 3 with lookahead 'r', we shift and go to state 6. The entries for reduce actions are given as the set of items to reduce by, e.g., in state 5 for lookahead '←', '↑', '+', or 'r', reduce by the item set {[ϵ ⇒ ← r r ·]}. In the diagram, a shift transition is represented by an arrow from one state to another labeled with the corresponding lookahead symbol. Thus,

State	Lookahead Symbol					
Number	←	↑	+	r	k	$
0	1					Accept
1		4	3	2		
2		4	3	5		
3		4	3	6		
4		4	3	7		
5	{[ε ⇒ ← r r •]}					
6		4	3	8	9	
7	{[r ⇒ ↑ r •]}					
8	{[r ⇒ + r r •]}					
9	{[r ⇒ + r k •]}					

FIG. 6.10 Action/Next table for the machine-description grammar given in Figure 6.8.

for example, the arrow from state 3 to state 6 labeled with an 'r' corresponds to the transition just described for the tabular form.

Next, we trace the action of the code generator with the above Action/Next table on the intermediate-code string

    ← + r1 2 + ↑ r3 3 $

The process begins by setting state to 0, pushing 0 onto the stack, and fetching the symbol '←' as the value of lookahead. The action for '←' in state 0 is to shift, so the symbol is pushed onto the stack, the next state is fetched from the Action/Next table and pushed onto the stack, the lookahead symbol is discarded from the input string, and the lookahead symbol is set to the next symbol, namely, '+'. The stack now has the contents

    | 1 '←' 0 |

The action for '+' in state 1 is to shift and the next state is 3. The resulting stack is

    | 3 '+' 1 '←' 0 |

The action for lookahead r1 in state 3 is to shift and enter state 6, so the stack becomes

    | 6 r1 3 '+' 1 '←' 0 |

Two more shift actions put the parser in state 9, with the lookahead set to '+' and the stack

    | 9 2 6 r1 3 '+' 1 '←' 0 |

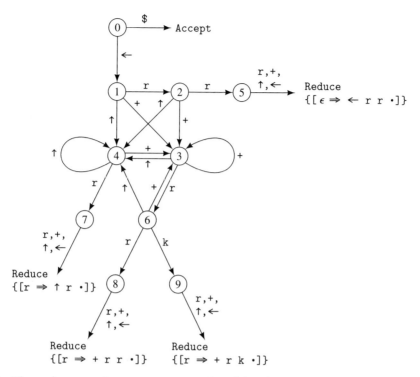

FIG. 6.11 The code-generation automaton produced for the machine-description grammar in Figure 6.8.

The appropriate action in state 9 is to reduce by the set of items {[r ⟹ + r k •]}, so Emit_Instrs( ) is called. It allocates a register for the result of the addition operation, namely, r2, and outputs the instruction

        add   r1,2,r2

The value of left is set to r2 and right is set to 3, so six items are popped off the stack and discarded, and r2 and the next state (2) are pushed onto the stack, resulting in

2	r2	1	'+'	0

We leave it to the reader to continue the process and to verify that the following sequence of instructions is produced, assuming registers r4 and r5 are allocated as shown:

        add   r1,2,r2
        ld   [r3],r4
        add   r4,3,r5
        st   r2,[r5]

6.2.3   Eliminating Chain Loops

In a parsing grammar, it is relatively rare to find chain loops, i.e., sets of nonterminals such that each of them can derive the others. On the other hand, such loops are extremely common in machine descriptions. As an example of the effect of chain loops, consider the simple grammar consisting of the following rules (the fact that the language generated by this grammar is empty is irrelevant—adding productions that generate terminals does not affect the presence of the chain loop):

$$r \Rightarrow \uparrow r$$
$$r \Rightarrow s$$
$$s \Rightarrow t$$
$$t \Rightarrow r$$
$$\epsilon \Rightarrow \leftarrow s \ t$$

The parsing automaton for this grammar is shown in Figure 6.12. Now, if we take as input the intermediate-code string $\leftarrow$ r1 $\uparrow$ r2, then, after processing $\leftarrow$ r1, the automaton is in state 1, the stack is

| 1 | '$\leftarrow$' | 0 |

and the lookahead symbol is '$\uparrow$'. From this state, the code generator emits a register-to-register move and returns to the same state, stack, and lookahead—i.e., it's stuck.

Eliminating loops can be done as a preprocessing step applied to the machine-description grammar or during construction of the Action/Next table. The code in Figure 6.13 provides a way to do this as a grammar preprocessor. The procedure Elim_Chain_Loops( ) finds productions $\langle \text{lt}:l, \text{rt}:r \rangle$ in MGrammar that have a

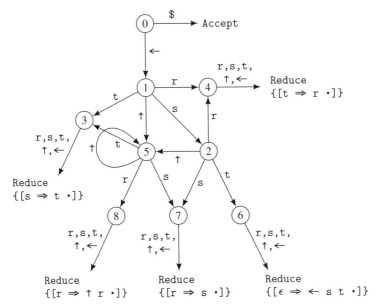

FIG. 6.12 Parsing automaton for the example grammar that has a chain loop.

```
procedure Elim_Chain_Loops( )
begin
    r1, r2: Rule
    CMG: set of Rule
    R: set of Nonterminal
    MG := MGrammar
    for each r1 ∈ MG do
        if r1.lt ≠ ε & |r1.rt| = 1 then
            if Close(r1,C,R) then
                for each r2 ∈ C do
                    MGrammar := (MGrammar - {r2})
                        ∪ Replace(R,r2,r1.lι)
                od
            fi
        fi
        MG -= {r1}
    od
end     || Elim_Chain_Loops

procedure Close(rule,C,R) returns boolean
    rule: in Rule
    C: out set of Rule
    R: out set of Nonterminal
begin
    r1: Rule
    || determine set of grammar rules making up a chain loop
    R := Reach(rule.rt)
    if rule.lt ∈ R then
        Prune(rule.lt,R)
    fi
    C := ∅
    for each r1 ∈ MGrammar do
        if r.lt ∈ R & |r1.rt| = 1 & r1.rt ∈ R then
            C ∪= {r1}
        fi
    od
    return C ≠ ∅
end     || Close
```

FIG. 6.13 The procedure Elim_Chain_Loops( ) to eliminate chain loops of nonterminals and the procedure Close( ) used by this procedure.

single nonterminal on both the left-hand and right-hand sides. For each of them, it uses Close (⟨lt:l,rt:r⟩, C,R) to determine whether the set of nonterminals derivable from r is a loop; if so, Close( ) returns in R the set of nonterminals in the loop and in C the set of productions making it up. Close( ) uses the procedures Reach( ) and Prune( ) defined in Figure 6.14 to determine the set of nonterminals reachable from its argument and to prune nonterminals from which the initial nonterminal is not reachable, respectively. Elim_Chain_Loops( ) then removes all but one of the nonterminals in the loop from the grammar, removes the rules making up the loop,

```
procedure Reach(r) returns set of Nonterminal
      r: in  Nonterminal
begin
      r1: Rule
      R := {r}: set of Nonterminal
      change := true: boolean
      || determine the set of nonterminals reachable from r
      || without generating any terminal symbols
      while change do
            change := false
            for each r1 ∈ MGrammar do
                  if r1.lt ∈ R & |r1.rt| = 1 & r1.rt↓1 ∈ Nonterminal & r1.rt ∉ R then
                        R ∪= {r1.rt}
                        change := true
                  fi
            od
      od
      return R
end    || Reach

procedure Prune(l,R)
      l: in Nonterminal
      R: inout set of Nonterminal
begin
      r: Nonterminal
      || prune from R the set of nonterminals from which
      || the initial nonterminal is not reachable
      for each r ∈ R do
            if l ∉ Reach(r) then
                  R -= {r}
            fi
      od
end    || Prune
```

FIG. 6.14 The procedures Reach( ) and Prune( ) used by Close( ).

and modifies the remaining rules to use the remaining nonterminal in place of the others. The function Replace(R,r,x) replaces all occurrences of symbols in R in the rule r by the symbol x.

There are situations in which chain loops might seem to be desirable, such as for moving values between the integer and floating-point registers in either direction. Such situations can easily be accommodated by explicit unary operators.

6.2.4   Eliminating Syntactic Blocks

There are usually also situations in which the greedy strategy of always preferring to shift rather than to reduce can result in the code generator's blocking, i.e., entering

```
ε ⇒ ← a r
s ⇒ r
r ⇒ ↑ a
r ⇒ + r s
r ⇒ * r s
r ⇒ c
a ⇒ r
a ⇒ + r r
a ⇒ + r * 2 r
a ⇒ + r * 4 r
a ⇒ + r * 8 r
```

FIG. 6.15 Fragment of a machine-description grammar for Hewlett-Packard's PA-RISC addressing modes.

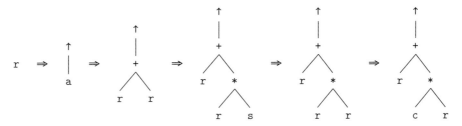

FIG. 6.16 Derivation sequence for the tree form of ↑ + r * c r.

the Error state unnecessarily. For example, consider the machine-description fragment in Figure 6.15, which focuses on an addressing mode of Hewlett-Packard's PA-RISC, and in which c represents an arbitrary integer constant. The addressing mode uses a base register plus an index register whose value may be left shifted by 0, 1, 2, or 3 bit positions (represented by the last four lines in the figure). Blocking occurs for this grammar fragment in the states containing the items [s ⇒ ↑ + r * • n r] (where n = 2, 4, and 8) for any input symbol other than 2, 4, or 8. However, an address of the form + r * c r, for an arbitrary c, or + r * r r is legal—it just requires a series of instructions to compute it, rather than one instruction. In particular, in tree form, we have the derivation shown in Figure 6.16 for the first case, corresponding to performing a multiply, followed by an add, followed by a fetch. To achieve this in the code generator, we need to add transitions out of the states containing the items [s ⇒ ↑ + r * • n r] that shift on an arbitrary constant or a register, rather than just on 2, 4, or 8. In accord with the derivation above, we add a transition on r to a new state and another shift transition from there under s to another new state that reduces by [s ⇒ ↑ + r * r s •] and generates the corresponding sequence of instructions.

Fix_Synt_Blocks( ) and auxiliary routines to repair syntactic blocking are given in Figure 6.17. Fix_Synt_Blocks( ) acts by generalizing the symbol that causes the blocking by following the inverses of chain productions as long as it can.

```
procedure Fix_Synt_Blocks( ) returns boolean
begin
  i, j: integer
  x, y: Nonterminal
  item, item1: Item
  NextItems, I: set of Item
  i := 1
  while i ≤ MaxStateNo do
  I := ItemSet[i]
    for each item ∈ I do
      || if there is a derivation that blocks for some inputs and
      || not for others similar to it, attempt to generalize it by
      || adding states and transitions to cover all similar inputs
      if ∃x ∈ Nonterminal
        (Derives([x],1,[item.rt↓(item.pos+1)])
        & Action(i,item.rt↓(item.pos+1)) = ⟨Error,∅⟩
        & Derives([item.lt],0,Subst(item.rt,item.pos+1,x))
        & ∀y ∈ Nonterminal (!Derives([y],1,[x]))
          ∨ !Derives([item.lt],0,
          Subst(item.rt,item.pos+1,[y]))) then
        item := Generalize(⟨lt:item.lt,
          rt:Subst(item.rt,item.pos+1,x),pos:item.pos⟩,
          item.pos+1,|item.rt|)
        if item = nil then
          return false
        fi
        ItemSet[i] ∪= {item}
        Action(i,x) := ⟨Shift,∅⟩
        NextItems := Closure(Advance({item1 ∈ ItemSet[i]
          where item1.lt = item.lt & item1.rt = Subst(item.rt,pos+1,x)
          & item1.pos = item.pos}))
        if ∃j ∈ integer (ItemSet[j] = NextItems) then
          Next(i,x) := j
        || add new states and transitions where needed
        else
          StateNo := i
          MaxStateNo += 1
          ItemSet[MaxStateNo] := NextItems
          Next(StateNo,x) := MaxStateNo
```

FIG. 6.17 Routines to repair syntactic blocking by generalizing one or more nonterminals.

This algorithm may result in an item that needs further repair, as in this particular case, for which the final symbol also needs to be generalized to prevent blocking. Note that it is essential to the correct operation of Derives( ) that we have already eliminated chain loops—otherwise it could recurse forever for some inputs.

As an example of the action of Fix_Synt_Blocks( ), suppose that the item [s ⇒ ↑ + r * • 2 r] discussed above is in ItemSet[26] and that MaxStateNo is 33. Code generation blocks in state 26 for any lookahead other than 2, so we apply the

```
                    while StateNo <= MaxStateNo do
                       Successors(StateNo)
                       if !Uniform(StateNo) then
                            return false
                       fi
                    od
              fi
          else
              return false
          fi
          I -= {item}
       od
       i += 1
    od
    return true
end    || Fix_Synt_Blocks

procedure Generalize(item,lo,hi) returns Item
    item: in Item
    lo, hi: in integer
begin
    i: integer
    l, x, y: Nonterminal
    || attempt to find a generalization of the blocking item
    for i := lo to hi do
       if ∃x ∈ Nonterminal (Derives([x],1,[item.rt↓i])
             & Derives([item.lt],0,Subst(item.rt,i,x))
           & ∀y ∈ Nonterminal (!Derives([y],1,[x])
               V !Derives([item.lt],0,Subst(item.rt,i,y)))) then
            item.rt↓i := x
       fi
    od
    return item
end    || Generalize
```

(continued)

FIG. 6.17 *(continued)*

routine to discover whether other nonblocking actions are possible. The routine sets x to r and determines that there is a derivation s $\overset{*}{\Rightarrow}$ ↑ + r * r r. So it calls

```
Generalize([s ⇒ ↑ + r * • r r],6,6)
```

which returns `[s ⇒ ↑ + r * • r s]`. That item becomes the value of `item` and is added to `ItemSet[26]`. Now `Action(26,r)` is set to ⟨Shift,∅⟩ and `NextItems` becomes

```
{[s ⇒ ↑ + r * r • s],[s ⇒ • r]}
```

`MaxStateNo` is increased to 34, `ItemSet[34]` is set to the above set, and `Next(26,r)` is set to 34. Finally, the routine uses `Successors( )` and `Uniform( )` to

```
procedure Derives(x,i,s) returns boolean
   x, s: in VocabSeq
   i: in integer
begin
   j: integer
   if i = 0 & x = s then
      return true
   fi
   for each rule ∈ MGrammar do
      for j := 1 to |x| do
         if rule.lt = x↓j then
            return Derives(rule.rt,0,s)
         fi
      od
   od
   return false
end     || Derives

procedure Subst(s,i,x) returns VocabSeq
   s: in VocabSeq
   i: in integer
   x: in Vocab
begin
   t := []: VocabSeq
   j: integer
   for j := 1 to |s| do
      if j = i then
         t ⊕= [x]
      else
         t ⊕= [s↓j]
      fi
   od
   return t
end     || Subst
```

FIG. 6.17 *(continued)*

produce the additional states and transitions necessary to process the new item and
to ensure uniformity of the new states.

6.2.5   Final Considerations

One issue that was a problem for early Graham-Glanville code generators is that the
Action/Next tables for machines with many instruction types and addressing modes
were huge (for the VAX, about 8,000,000 rules resulted). Henry [Henr84] devised
methods for significantly compressing the tables and, in any case, the problem is
nowhere near as severe for the typical RISC machine because of the small number of
addressing modes provided by most of them.

6.3   Introduction to Semantics-Directed Parsing

In this section, we give an overview of a second, more powerful, and more complex approach to code generation from Polish-prefix intermediate code, namely, the *attribute-* or *affix-grammar* method developed by Ganapathi and Fischer, which adds semantics to the code-generation rules through the use of attributes. We sketch the idea here and leave it to the reader to consult the literature for the details.

We assume familiarity with the basics of attribute grammars. We denote inherited attributes by preceding them with a down arrow "↓" and synthesized attributes with an up arrow "↑". Attribute values are written after the arrows. In addition to passing values up and down in the code-generation process, attributes are used to control code generation and to compute new attribute values and produce side effects. Control is achieved through attributes written in capitalized italics (e.g., *IsShort* in the example below) that represent predicates. A rule is applicable in a given situation if and only if it syntactically matches the subject string and all its predicates are satisfied. Actions, written in uppercase typewriter font (e.g., EMIT3 in the example), compute new attribute values and produce side effects. The most important side effect in an affix-grammar code generator is, of course, emitting code.

Thus, for example, the Graham-Glanville rules for addition of the contents of a register and a constant from Figure 6.1

```
r.3 ⇒ + r.1 k.2        add r.1,k.2,r.3
r.3 ⇒ + k.2 r.1        add r.1,k.2,r.3
```

can be turned into affix-grammar rules that check that the constant is within the allowed range and that subsume code emission and register allocation in the rules, as follows:

$$r \uparrow r2 \Rightarrow + \ r \downarrow r1 \ k \downarrow k1 \ \textit{IsShort}(k1) \ \texttt{ALLOC}(r2) \ \texttt{EMIT3}(\texttt{"add"}, r1, k1, r2)$$
$$r \uparrow r2 \Rightarrow + \ k \downarrow k1 \ r \downarrow r1 \ \textit{IsShort}(k1) \ \texttt{ALLOC}(r2) \ \texttt{EMIT3}(\texttt{"add"}, r1, k1, r2)$$

The first of these should be read as follows: Given a Polish-prefix string of the form + r k with the register number having the value $r1$ and the constant $k1$, if the constant satisfies the predicate *IsShort*($k1$), then allocate a register $r2$ to hold the result, emit the three-operand add instruction obtained by substituting the values associated with the registers and the constant, reduce the string to r, and pass the value $r2$ upward as a synthesized attribute of the nonterminal r.

In addition to generating code from a low-level intermediate language, affix grammars can be used to do storage binding (i.e., to generate code from a higher-level intermediate form), to integrate several kinds of peephole optimizations into code generation, and to factor machine-description rule sets so as to significantly reduce their size. Since affix grammars can do storage binding, we could start with a somewhat higher-level intermediate code, such as a Polish-prefix translation of MIR. In fact, since the predicates and functions may be coded arbitrarily, they can be used to do virtually anything a compiler back end can do—for example, one could accumulate all the code to be emitted as the value of some attribute until the entire input string has been reduced and then do essentially any transformation on it for which sufficient information is available (and one could accumulate that information during the code-generation process, also).

Ganapathi and Fischer report having built three affix-grammar-based code-generator generators (one from the UNIX parser generator YACC, the second from ECP, and a third *ab initio*) and have used them to produce code generators in compilers for Fortran, Pascal, BASIC, and Ada for nearly a dozen architectures.

6.4   Tree Pattern Matching and Dynamic Programming

In this section, we give an introduction to a third approach to automatically generating code generators that was developed by Aho, Ganapathi, and Tjiang [AhoG89]. Their approach uses tree pattern matching and dynamic programming. The resulting system is known as *twig*.

Dynamic programming is an approach to decision making in a computational process that depends on an *optimality principle* that applies to the domain under consideration. The optimality principle asserts that if all subproblems have been solved optimally, then the overall problem can be solved optimally by a particular method of combining the solutions to the subproblems. Using dynamic programming contrasts sharply with the greedy approach taken by Graham-Glanville code generators—rather than trying only one way to match a tree, we may try many, but only those that are optimal for the parts already matched, since only they can be combined to produce code sequences that are optimal overall, given an applicable optimality principle.

When *twig* matches a subtree with a pattern, it generally replaces it by another tree. The sequence of subtrees rewritten in a matching process that succeeds in reducing a tree to a single node is called a *cover* of the tree. A *minimal-cost cover* is a cover such that the sum of the costs (see below for details) for the matching operations that produced the cover is as small as it can be. Code emission and register allocation are performed as side effects of the matching process.

The input for *twig* consists of tree-rewriting rules of the form

label: *pattern* [{*cost*}] [= {*action*}]

where *label* is an identifier that corresponds to the nonterminal on the left-hand side of a grammar rule; *pattern* is a parenthesized prefix representation of a tree pattern; *cost* is C code to be executed by the code generator when a subtree matches the pattern, and that both returns a cost for use by the dynamic programming algorithm and determines whether the pattern meets the semantic criteria for matching the subtree; and *action* is C code to be executed if the pattern match succeeds and the dynamic programming algorithm determines that the pattern is part of the minimal-cost cover of the overall tree. The *action* part may include replacing the matched subtree with another, emitting code, or other actions.

The *cost* and *action* parts are both optional, as indicated by the brackets around them. If the *cost* is omitted, a default cost specified elsewhere is returned and the pattern is assumed to match. If the *action* is omitted, the default is to do nothing.

Rule Number	Rewriting Rule	Cost	Instruction
1	reg.$i \Rightarrow$ con.c	*IsShort*(c);1	`or` c,r0,ri
2	reg.$i \Rightarrow$ $\overset{\uparrow}{\diagup \diagdown}$ reg.j reg.k	1	`ld` [rj,rk],ri
3	reg.$i \Rightarrow$ $\overset{\uparrow}{\diagup \diagdown}$ reg.j con.c	*IsShort*(c);1	`ld` [rj,c],ri
4	$\epsilon \Rightarrow$ $\overset{\leftarrow}{\diagup | \diagdown}$ reg.i reg.j reg.k	1	`st` ri,[rj,rk]
5	$\epsilon \Rightarrow$ $\overset{\leftarrow}{\diagup | \diagdown}$ reg.i reg.j con.c	*IsShort*(c);1	`st` ri,[rj,c]
6	reg.$k \Rightarrow$ $\overset{+}{\diagup \diagdown}$ reg.i reg.j	1	`add` ri,rj,rk

FIG. 6.18   A simple tree-rewriting system.

As an example of the pattern-matching process, consider the tree-rewriting system in Figure 6.18, which includes the tree forms of some of the rules in Figure 6.1. The predicate *IsShort*( ) determines whether its argument fits into the 13-bit constant field in SPARC instructions. The corresponding *twig* specification is shown in Figure 6.19. The `prologue` implements the function *IsShort*( ). The `label` declaration lists all the identifiers that can appear as labels, and the `node` declaration lists all the identifiers that can occur in the patterns, in addition to those listed as labels.[1] The string $$ is a pointer to the root of the tree matched by the pattern, and a string of the form $$i$$ points to the ith child of the root. `ABORT` causes pattern matching to be aborted, in effect by returning an infinite cost. `NODEPTR` is the type of nodes, and `getreg`( ) is the register allocator. The various `emit_...`( ) routines emit particular types of instructions.

Now, suppose we are generating code for the parenthesized prefix expression

```
st(add(ld(r8,8),add(r2,ld(r8,4))))
```

which is designed to resemble the second tree in Figure 6.3, but using only the operations defined in Figure 6.19. The pattern matcher would descend through the tree structure of the expression until it finds that pattern 1 matches the subexpression "8" and pattern 3 matches "ld(r8,8)". Using the first of these matches would

---

1. Alphabetic identifiers are used instead of symbols such as "↑" and "+" because *twig* is not designed to handle the latter.

```
prologue { int IsShort(NODEPTR p);
    { return value(p) >= -4096 && value(p) <= 4095; }  }
node  con ld st add;
label reg no_value;

reg : con
      { if (IsShort($$)) cost = 1;
        else ABORT; }
    = { NODEPTR regnode = getreg( );
        emit_3("or",$$,"r0",regnode);
        return regnode; }

reg : ld(reg,reg,reg)
      { cost = 1; }
    = { NODEPTR regnode = getreg( );
        emit_ld($2$,$3$,regnode);
        return regnode; }

reg : ld(reg,reg,con)
      { cost = 1; }
    = { NODEPTR regnode = getreg( );
        emit_ld($2$,$3$,regnode);
        return regnode; }

no_value : st(reg,reg,reg)
      { cost = 1; }
    = { emit_st($1$,$2$,$3$);
        return NULL; }

no_value : st(reg,con,reg)
      { cost = 1; }
    = { emit_st($1$,$2$,$3$);
        return NULL; }

reg : add(reg,reg,reg)
      { cost = 1; }
    = { NODEPTR regnode = getreg( );
        emit_3("add",$1$,$2$,regnode);
        return regnode; }
```

FIG. 6.19 Specification in *twig* corresponding to the tree-rewriting system in Figure 6.18.

result in a subtree that matches pattern 2, but its cost would be 2, rather than the 1 resulting from using pattern 3 alone, so pattern 3 would be used. The subexpression "ld(r8,4)" would be matched similarly. However, neither of the implied reductions would be done immediately, since there might be alternative matches that would have lower cost; instead, an indication of each match would be stored in the node that is the root of the matched subexpression. Once the matching process has been completed, the reductions and actions are performed.

Path String	Rules
c	1
↑ 1 r	2, 3
↑ 2 r	2
↑ 2 c	3
← 1 r	4, 5
← 2 r	4, 5
← 3 r	4
← 3 c	5
+ 1 r	6
+ 2 r	6

FIG. 6.20   Tree-matching path strings for the rules in Figure 6.18.

The method *twig* uses to do code generation is a combination of top-down tree pattern matching and dynamic programming, as indicated above. The basic idea is that a tree can be characterized by the set of labeled paths from its root to its leaves, where the labeling numbers the descendants of each node consecutively. A *path string* alternates node identifiers with integer labels. For example, the third tree in Figure 6.3 can be represented uniquely by the path strings

$$← 1 + 1 \text{ r8}$$
$$← 1 + 2 \text{ } 4$$
$$← 2 - 1 \text{ r1}$$
$$← 2 - 2 \text{ } 1$$

and similar sets of strings can be constructed for the tree patterns. The path strings for a set of tree patterns can, in turn, be used to construct a pattern-matching automaton that is a generalization of a finite automaton. The automaton matches the various tree patterns in parallel and each accepting state indicates which paths through which tree patterns it corresponds to. A subtree matches a tree pattern if and only if there is a traversal of the automaton that results in an accepting state for each path string corresponding to the tree pattern.

As an example of such an automaton, we construct one for the rules in Figure 6.18. The path strings and the rules they correspond to are listed in Figure 6.20, and the resulting automaton is shown in Figure 6.21. The initial state is 0, the states with double circles are accepting states, and each non-accepting state has an additional unshown transition, namely, for "other," go to the error state (labeled "error"). The labels near the accepting states give the numbers of the rules for which some path string produces that state. Thus, for example, the pattern in rule 5 is matched if and only if running the automaton in parallel results in halting in states 9, 11, and 14. Details of the construction of the automaton and how it is turned into code can be found in the literature.

The dynamic programming algorithm assumes that it is given a *uniform register machine* with n interchangeable registers ri and instructions of the form $ri ← E$, where E is an expression consisting of operators, registers, and memory locations. The cost associated with a sequence of instructions is the sum of the costs of the

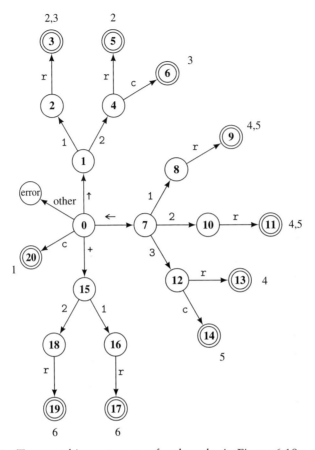

FIG. 6.21 Tree-matching automaton for the rules in Figure 6.18.

individual instructions. The algorithm partitions the code-generation problem for an expression E into subproblems, one for each of E's subexpressions, and solves the subproblems recursively. The key to making dynamic programming applicable is to evaluate each expression *contiguously*, i.e., first those of its subtrees that need to have their values stored in memory locations are evaluated, and then the expression is evaluated either in the order left subtree, right subtree, root; or right subtree, left subtree, root. Thus, there is no oscillation between the subtrees of an operator once the parts of the expression that have to be stored to memory have been evaluated. Then for any sequence of instructions for the uniform register machine that evaluates a given expression, there is a sequence that evaluates the same expression at no greater cost, with a minimal number of registers, and is contiguous.

Note that most real machines do not have uniform registers. In particular, they have operations that use even-odd register pairs, and one can give examples of expressions whose optimal evaluation sequences require arbitrary numbers of oscillations between their subexpressions. However, such examples are very unusual in that the size of the expressions grows at least linearly with the number of oscillations required, and expressions in practice are generally not very big. Thus, contiguity is only mildly violated, and the algorithm produces near-optimal instruction sequences almost all the time in practice.

Aho and Johnson's algorithm [AhoJ76] (1) computes bottom-up, for each node N of an expression tree, entries in a table of costs $c[N, i]$ for computing the tree rooted at N, using at most i registers; (2) uses the cost table to determine which subtrees must have their values stored to memory; and (3) recursively determines a sequence of instructions that does an optimal evaluation of the tree.

Experience with *twig* shows that it is relatively easy to write and modify *twig* specifications, and that it produces code generators that compare favorably in both code quality and performance with code generators designed to be easily retargeted, such as the one in the pcc2 portable C compiler.

Bottom-up tree matching can also be used to automatically produce, from machine descriptions, code generators that generate optimal code. One such approach was developed by Pelegri-Llopart and is based on *bottom-up rewriting systems,* or BURS.

6.5   Wrap-Up

In this chapter, we have briefly discussed the issues in generating machine code from intermediate code, and then we have explored automatic methods for generating code generators from machine descriptions.

The basic issues include the architecture of the target machine, software conventions that must be observed, the structure and characteristics of the intermediate language, the implementations of intermediate-language operations that don't correspond directly to target-machine instructions, whether to target assembly language or relocatable machine code, and the approach to translating intermediate code to the chosen target-code form.

Whether we are writing a compiler for a single language and a single target architecture, or multiple source languages, multiple target architectures, or both determine the importance of the choices made for most of these issues. In particular, the more target architectures involved, the more important it is to use automated methods.

While hand-crafted code generators are effective and fast, they have the (obvious) disadvantage of being implemented by hand and so are usually much more difficult to modify or port than a code generator that is automatically generated from a machine description.

Several approaches have been developed that produce a code generator from a machine description. We have described three of them in varying levels of detail. All begin with a low-level intermediate code that has addressing computations exposed, and in all cases the code generator does pattern matching on trees, either explicitly in one case or implicitly in the other two cases, namely, on Polish-prefix intermediate code that represents a preorder traversal of a sequence of trees.

6.6   Further Reading

The first significantly successful project to generate code generators automatically is reported in [Catt79].

The Graham-Glanville approach to code generation is first described in [GlaG78] and developed further in [AigG84] and [Henr84]. Other implementations of Graham-Glanville code-generator generators are described in [GraH82], [Bird82], [LanJ82], and [ChrH84].

The attribute-grammar approach to code generation was developed by Ganapathi and Fischer and is described in [GanF82], [GanF84], and [GanF85], among other papers. The ECP error-correcting parser, which served as the basis of one of Ganapathi and Fischer's implementations, is described in [MauF81].

An excellent introduction to tree automata and their uses can be found in [Enge75]. The tree-pattern matching approach to code generation developed by Aho, Ganapathi, and Tjiang is described in [AhoG89]. The tree pattern matcher is a generalization of a linear-time string-matching algorithm due to Aho and Corasick [AhoC75], incorporating some ideas from Hoffman and O'Donnell [HofO82] that extend it to trees. The dynamic programming algorithm is based on one developed by Aho and Johnson [AhoJ76]. The pcc2 portable C compiler that Aho, Ganapathi, and Tjiang compared *twig* to is described in [John78]. Pelegri-Llopart's approach to generating locally optimal code by bottom-up tree matching is described in [Pele88] and [PelG88]. A tree-automata-based approach to code generation that begins with a high-level intermediate code is described in [Ahal93].

Henry and Damron ([HenD89a] and [HenD89b]) provide an excellent overview of about a dozen approaches to automatically generating code generators from machine descriptions, giving detailed discussions and evaluations of eight of them and a comparison of their performance, both in terms of the speed of the code generators they produce and the quality of the resulting code.

6.7   Exercises

6.1 Write an ICAN version of Emit_Instrs( ) (see Section 6.2.1) sufficient for the grammar in Figure 6.1, including distinguishing short constants.

6.2 (a) Construct the Graham-Glanville parsing tables for the machine-description rules and machine instructions below, where fr.*n* denotes a floating-point constant.

```
fr.2 ⇒ fr.1                fmov   fr.1,fr.2
fr.2 ⇒ mov fr.2 fr.1       fmov   fr.1,fr.2

r.3 ⇒ + r.1 r.2            add    r.1,r.2,r.3
r.3 ⇒ - r.1 r.2            sub    r.1,r.2,r.3

fr.3 ⇒ +f fr.1 fr.2        fadd   fr.1,fr.2,fr.3
fr.3 ⇒ -f fr.1 fr.2        fsub   fr.1,fr.2,fr.3
fr.3 ⇒ *f fr.1 fr.2        fmuls  fr.1,fr.2,fr.3
```

```
fr.3 ⇒ /f fr.1 fr.2         fdivs  fr.1,fr.2,fr.3
fr.2 ⇒ sqrt fr.1            fsqrts fr.1,fr.2

fr.2 ⇒ cvti fr.1 fr.2       fstoi  fr.1,fr.2
fr.2 ⇒ cvtf fr.1 fr.2       fitos  fr.1,fr.2

fr.3 ⇒ ↑ + r.1 r.2          ldf    [r.1,r.2],fr.3
fr.3 ⇒ ↑ + r.1 k.2          ldf    [r.1,k.2],fr.3
fr.2 ⇒ fr.1                 ldf    fr.1,fr.2

ε ⇒ ← + r.2 r.3 fr.1        stf    fr.1,[r.2,r.3]
ε ⇒ ← + r.2 k.1 fr.1        stf    fr.1,[r.2,k.3]
```

(b) Check your parsing automaton by generating code for the Polish-prefix sequence

```
← + r1 4 cvti -f fr2
mov fr2 *f fr3 ↑ + r1 8
← + r1 12 sqrt ↑ + r7 0
```

6.3 Construct the relations (*Left, Right*, etc.) and functions (*Parent*( ), *Follow*( ), etc.) for the grammar in the preceding exercise.

6.4 Give a more complex example of chain loops than that found at the beginning of Section 6.2.3, and use the algorithm in Figure 6.13 to eliminate it.

6.5 Write a chain-loop eliminator that can be used during or after the Graham-Glanville parsing tables have been constructed.

6.6 Give an example of the use of dynamic programming in computer science other than the one in Section 6.4.

RSCH 6.7 Read Pelegri-Llopart and Graham's article [PelG88] and write a BURS-based code-generator generator in ICAN.

CHAPTER 7

Control-Flow Analysis

Optimization requires that we have compiler components that can construct a global "understanding" of how programs use the available resources.[1] The compiler must characterize the control flow of programs and the manipulations they perform on their data, so that any unused generality that would ordinarily result from unoptimized compilation can be stripped away; thus, less efficient but more general mechanisms are replaced by more efficient, specialized ones.

When a program is read by a compiler, it is initially seen as simply a sequence of characters. The lexical analyzer turns the sequence of characters into tokens, and the parser discovers a further level of syntactic structure. The result produced by the compiler front end may be a syntax tree or some lower-level form of intermediate code. However, the result, whatever its form, still provides relatively few hints about what the program does or how it does it. It remains for control-flow analysis to discover the hierarchical flow of control within each procedure and for data-flow analysis to determine global (i.e., procedure-wide) information about the manipulation of data.

Before we consider the formal techniques used in control-flow and data-flow analysis, we present a simple example. We begin with the C routine in Figure 7.1, which computes, for a given $m \geq 0$, the mth Fibonacci number. Given an input value m, it checks whether it is less than or equal to 1 and returns the argument value if so; otherwise, it iterates until it has computed the mth member of the sequence and returns it. In Figure 7.2, we give a translation of the C routine into MIR.

Our first task in analyzing this program is to discover its control structure. One might protest at this point that the control structure is obvious in the source code—

---

1. We put quotation marks around "understanding" because we feel it is important to guard against anthropomorphizing the optimization process, or, for that matter, computing in general.

```
      unsigned int fib(m)
         unsigned int m;
      {  unsigned int f0 = 0, f1 = 1, f2, i;
         if (m <= 1) {
            return m;
         }
         else {
            for (i = 2; i <= m; i++) {
               f2 = f0 + f1;
               f0 = f1;
               f1 = f2;
            }
            return f2;
         }
      }
```

FIG. 7.1 A C routine that computes Fibonacci numbers.

```
      1          receive m
      2          f0 ← 0
      3          f1 ← 1
      4          if m <= 1 goto L3
      5          i ← 2
      6    L1: if i <= m goto L2
      7          return f2
      8    L2: f2 ← f0 + f1
      9          f0 ← f1
     10          f1 ← f2
     11          i ← i + 1
     12          goto L1
     13    L3: return m
```

FIG. 7.2 MIR intermediate code for the C routine in Figure 7.1.

the routine's body consists of an if-then-else with a loop in the else part; but this structure is no longer obvious in the intermediate code. Further, the loop might have been constructed of ifs and gotos, so that the control structure might not have been obvious in the source code. Thus, the formal methods of control-flow analysis are definitely not useless. To make their application to the program clearer to the eye, we first transform it into an alternate visual representation, namely, a flowchart, as shown in Figure 7.3.

Next, we identify basic blocks, where a basic block is, informally, a straight-line sequence of code that can be entered only at the beginning and exited only at the end. Clearly, nodes 1 through 4 form a basic block, which we call B1, and nodes 8 through 11 form another, which we call B6. Each of the other nodes is a basic block

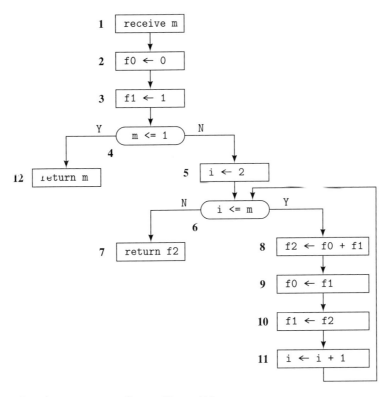

FIG. 7.3 Flowchart corresponding to Figure 7.2.

unto itself; we make node 12 into B2, node 5 into B3, node 6 into B4, and node 7 into B5. Next we collapse the nodes that form a basic block into a node representing the whole sequence of MIR instructions, resulting in the so-called flowgraph of the routine shown in Figure 7.4. For technical reasons that will become clear when we discuss backward data-flow analysis problems, we add an entry block with the first real basic block as its only successor, an exit block at the end, and branches following each actual exit from the routine (blocks B2 and B5) to the exit block.

Next, we identify the loops in the routine by using what are called dominators. In essence, a node A in the flowgraph dominates a node B if every path from the entry node to B includes A. It is easily shown that the dominance relation on the nodes of a flowgraph is antisymmetric, reflexive, and transitive, with the result that it can be displayed by a tree with the entry node as the root. For our flowgraph in Figure 7.4, the dominance tree is shown in Figure 7.5.

Now we can use the dominance tree to identify loops. A back edge in the flowgraph is an edge whose head dominates its tail, for example, the edge from B6 to B4. A loop consists of all nodes dominated by its entry node (the head of the back edge) from which the entry node can be reached (and the corresponding edges) and

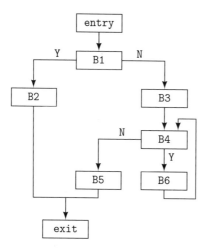

FIG. 7.4 Flowgraph corresponding to Figure 7.3.

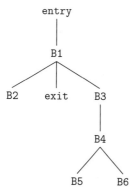

FIG. 7.5 Dominance tree for the flowgraph in Figure 7.4.

having exactly one back edge within it. Thus, B4 and B6 form a loop with B4 as its entry node, as expected, and no other set of nodes in the flowgraph does.

We shall continue with this example in Chapter 8 as our initial example of data-flow analysis. We now proceed to a more formal exposition of the concepts encountered in the example and several elaborations of and alternatives to them.

7.1   Approaches to Control-Flow Analysis

There are two main approaches to control-flow analysis of single routines, both of which start by determining the basic blocks that make up the routine and then constructing its flowgraph. The first approach uses dominators to discover loops and simply notes the loops it finds for use in optimization. This approach is sufficient for use by optimizers that do data-flow analysis by iteration, as in our example in Section 8.1, or that concentrate their attention strictly on the loops in a routine.

The second approach, called interval analysis, includes a series of methods that analyze the overall structure of the routine and that decompose it into nested regions called intervals. The nesting structure of the intervals forms a tree called a control tree, which is useful in structuring and speeding up data-flow analysis. The most sophisticated variety of interval analysis, called structural analysis, classifies essentially all the control-flow structures in a routine. It is sufficiently important that we devote a separate section to it. The data-flow analysis methods based on the use of intervals are generally called *elimination methods*, because of a broad similarity between them and Gaussian elimination methods for problems in linear algebra.

Most current optimizing compilers use dominators and iterative data-flow analysis. And, while this approach is the least time-intensive to implement and is sufficient to provide the information needed to perform most of the optimizations discussed below, it is inferior to the other approaches in three ways, as follows:

1. The interval-based approaches are faster at performing the actual data-flow analyses, especially for structural analysis and programs that use only the simpler types of structures.

2. The interval-based approaches (particularly structural analysis) make it easier to update already computed data-flow information in response to changes to a program (changes made either by an optimizer or by the compiler user), so that such information need not be recomputed from scratch.

3. Structural analysis makes it particularly easy to perform the control-flow transformations discussed in Chapter 18.

Thus, we feel that it is essential to present all three approaches and to leave it to the compiler implementer to choose the combination of implementation effort and optimization speed and capabilities desired.

Since all the approaches require identification of basic blocks and construction of the flowgraph of the routine, we discuss these topics next. Formally, a *basic block* is a maximal sequence of instructions that can be entered only at the first of them and exited only from the last of them. Thus, the first instruction in a basic block may be (1) the entry point of the routine, (2) a target of a branch, or (3) an instruction immediately following a branch or a return.[2] Such instructions are called *leaders*. To determine the basic blocks that compose a routine, we first identify all the leaders,

---

2. If we consider RISC machine instructions, rather than intermediate-code instructions, we may need to modify this definition slightly: if the architecture has delayed branches, the instruction in the delay slot of a branch may be in the basic block ended by the preceding branch and may *also* begin a new basic block itself, if it is the target of a branch. Branches with two delay slots, as in MIPS-X, complicate this still further. Our intermediate codes do *not* include this complication.

and then, for each leader, include in its basic block all the instructions from the leader to the next leader or the end of the routine, in sequence.

In almost all cases, the above approach is sufficient to determine the basic-block structure of a procedure. On the other hand, note that we have not indicated whether a call instruction should be considered a branch in determining the leaders in a routine. In most cases, it need not be considered a branch, resulting in longer and fewer basic blocks, which is desirable for optimization. However, if a procedure call has alternate returns as it may in Fortran, then it must be considered a basic-block boundary. Similarly, in some special cases in C, a call needs to be considered a basic-block boundary. The best-known example is C's setjump( ) function, which provides a crude exception-handling mechanism. The problem with a setjump( ) call is that, not only does it return to just after where it was called from, but a later use of the exception-handling mechanism, i.e., a call to longjmp( ), also passes control from wherever it is called to the return point of the dynamically enclosing setjump( ) call. This requires the call to setjump( ) to be considered a basic-block boundary and, even worse, introduces phantom edges into the flowgraph: in general, any call from the routine that did the setjump( ) needs a control-flow edge inserted from its return point to the return point of the setjump( ), since potentially any of these calls could return to that point by invoking longjmp( ). In practice, this is usually handled by not attempting to optimize routines that include calls to setjump( ), but putting in the phantom control-flow edges is a (usually very pessimistic) alternative.

In Pascal, a goto that exits a procedure and passes control to a labeled statement in a statically enclosing one results in similar extra edges in the flowgraph of the containing procedure. However, since such gotos can always be identified by processing nested procedures from the innermost ones outward, they do not cause as serious a problem as setjump( ) does in C.

Some optimizations will make it desirable to consider calls as behaving like basic-block boundaries also. In particular, instruction scheduling (see Section 17.1) may need to consider calls to be basic-block boundaries to fill delay slots properly, but may also benefit from having longer blocks to work on. Thus, calls may be desirable to be considered to be both block boundaries and not in the same optimization.

Now, having identified the basic blocks, we characterize the control flow in a procedure by a rooted, directed graph (hereafter called simply a graph) with a set of nodes, one for each basic block plus two distinguished ones called entry and exit, and a set of (control-flow) edges running from basic blocks to others in the same way that the control-flow edges of the original flowchart connected the final instructions in the basic blocks to the leaders of basic blocks; in addition, we introduce an edge from entry to the initial basic block(s)[3] of the routine and an edge from each final basic block (i.e., a basic block with no successors) to exit. The entry and exit

---

3. There is usually only one initial basic block per routine. However, some language constructs, such as Fortran 77's multiple entry points, allow there to be more than one.

blocks are not essential and are added for technical reasons—they make many of our algorithms simpler to describe. (See, for example, Section 13.1.2, where, in the data-flow analysis performed for global common-subexpression elimination, we need to initialize the data-flow information for the entry block differently from all other blocks if we do not ensure that the entry block has no edges entering it; a similar distinction occurs for the exit block in the data-flow analysis for code hoisting in Section 13.5.) The resulting directed graph is the *flowgraph* of the routine. A strongly connected subgraph of a flowgraph is called a *region*.

Throughout the remainder of the book, we assume that we are given a flowgraph $G = \langle N, E \rangle$ with node set N and edge set $E \subseteq N \times N$, where entry $\in N$ and exit $\in N$. We generally write edges in the form $a \rightarrow b$, rather than $\langle a, b \rangle$.

Further, we define the sets of *successor* and *predecessor* basic blocks of a basic block in the obvious way, a *branch node* as one that has more than one successor, and a *join node* as one that has more than one predecessor. We denote the set of successors of a basic block $b \in N$ by $Succ(b)$ and the set of predecessors by $Pred(b)$. Formally,

$$Succ(b) = \{n \in N \mid \exists e \in E \text{ such that } e = b \rightarrow n\}$$

$$Pred(b) = \{n \in N \mid \exists e \in E \text{ such that } e = n \rightarrow b\}$$

An *extended basic block* is a maximal sequence of instructions beginning with a leader that contains no join nodes other than its first node (which need not be a join node itself if, e.g., it is the entry node). Since an extended basic block has a single entry and possibly multiple exits, it can be thought of as a tree with its entry basic block as the root. We refer to the basic blocks that make up an extended basic block in this way in some contexts. As we shall see in succeeding chapters, some local optimizations, such as instruction scheduling (Section 17.1), are more effective when done on extended basic blocks than on basic blocks. In our example in Figure 7.4, blocks B1, B2, and B3 make up an extended basic block that is not a basic block.

An ICAN algorithm named Build_Ebb(r, Succ, Pred) that constructs the set of indexes of the blocks in an extended basic block with block r as its root is given in Figure 7.6. The algorithm Build_All_Ebbs(r, Succ, Pred) in Figure 7.7 constructs the set of all extended basic blocks for a flowgraph with entry node r. It sets AllEbbs to a set of pairs with each pair consisting of the index of its root block and the set of indexes of blocks in an extended basic block. Together the two algorithms use the global variable EbbRoots to record the root basic blocks of the extended basic blocks.

As an example of Build_Ebb( ) and Build_All_Ebbs( ), consider the flow-graph in Figure 7.8. The extended basic blocks discovered by the algorithms are {entry}, {B1,B2,B3}, {B4,B6}, {B5,B7}, and {exit}, as indicated by the dashed boxes in the figure.

Similarly, a *reverse extended basic block* is a maximal sequence of instructions ending with a branch node that contains no branch nodes other than its last node.

```
EbbRoots: set of Node
AllEbbs: set of (Node × set of Node)

procedure Build_Ebb(r,Succ,Pred) returns set of Node
   r: in Node
   Succ, Pred: in Node ⟶ set of Node
begin
   Ebb := ∅: set of Node
   Add_Bbs(r,Ebb,Succ,Pred)
   return Ebb
end    || Build_Ebb

procedure Add_Bbs(r,Ebb,Succ,Pred)
   r: in Node
   Ebb: inout set of Node
   Succ, Pred: in Node ⟶ set of Node
begin
   change: boolean
   x: Node
   Ebb ∪= {r}
   repeat
      change := false
      for each x ∈ Succ(r) do
         if |Pred(x)| = 1 & x ∉ Ebb then
            Add_Bbs(x,Ebb,Succ,Pred)
            change := true
         elif x ∉ EbbRoots then
            EbbRoots ∪= {x}
            change := true
         fi
      od
   until !change
end    || Add_Bbs
```

FIG. 7.6 A pair of routines to construct the set of blocks in the extended basic block with a given root.

```
entry: Node

procedure Build_All_Ebbs(r,Succ,Pred)
   r: in Node
   Succ, Pred: in Node ⟶ set of Node
begin
   x: Node
   s: Node × set of Node
   EbbRoots := {r}
   AllEbbs := ∅
```

FIG. 7.7 A routine to construct all the extended basic blocks in a given flowgraph.

```
    while EbbRoots ≠ ∅ do
       x := ◆ EbbRoots
       EbbRoots -= {x}
       if ∀s ∈ AllEbbs (s@1 ≠ x) then
          AllEbbs ∪= {⟨x,Build_Ebb(x,Succ,Pred)⟩}
       fi
    od
end      || Build_All_Ebbs

begin
    Build_All_Ebbs(entry,Succ,Pred)
end
```

FIG. 7.7 *(continued)*

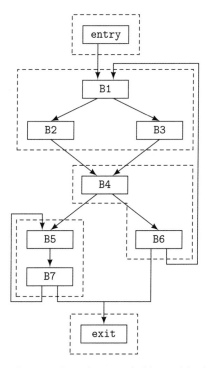

FIG. 7.8 Flowgraph with extended basic blocks indicated by the dashed boxes.

7.2   Depth–First Search, Preorder Traversal, Postorder Traversal, and Breadth–First Search

This section concerns four graph-theoretic concepts that are important to several of the algorithms we use below. All four apply to rooted, directed graphs and, thus, to

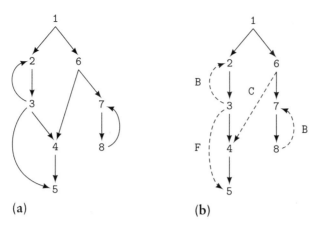

(a)   (b)

FIG. 7.9 (a) A rooted directed graph, and (b) a depth-first presentation of it.

flowgraphs. The first is *depth-first search*, which visits the descendants of a node in the graph before visiting any of its siblings. For example, given the graph in Figure 7.9(a), Figure 7.9(b) is a depth-first presentation of it. The number assigned to each node in a depth-first search is the node's *depth-first number*.

The algorithm in Figure 7.10 constructs a depth-first presentation of the graph. The *depth-first presentation* includes all the graph's nodes and the edges that make up the depth-first order displayed as a tree (called a *depth-first spanning tree*) and the other edges—the ones that are not part of the depth-first order—displayed in such a way as to distinguish them from the tree edges (we use dashed lines instead of solid lines for them). The edges that are part of the depth-first spanning tree are called *tree edges*. The edges that are not part of the depth-first spanning tree are divided into three classes called *forward edges* (which we label "F" in examples) that go from a node to a direct descendant, but not along a tree edge; *back edges* (which we label "B") that go from a node to one of its ancestors in the tree; and *cross edges* (which we label "C") that connect nodes such that neither is an ancestor of the other.

Note that the depth-first presentation of a graph is not unique. For example, the graph in Figure 7.11(a) has the two different depth-first presentations shown in Figure 7.11(b) and (c).

The routine Depth_First_Search( ) in Figure 7.10 does a generic depth-first search of a flowgraph and provides four points to perform actions:

1. Process_Before( ) allows us to perform an action before visiting each node.

2. Process_After( ) allows us to perform an action after visiting each node.

3. Process_Succ_Before( ) allows us to perform an action before visiting each successor of a node.

4. Process_Succ_After( ) allows us to perform an action after visiting each successor of a node.

```
N: set of Node
r, i: Node
Visit: Node ⟶ boolean

procedure Depth_First_Search(N,Succ,x)
    N: in set of Node
    Succ: in Node ⟶ set of Node
    x: in Node
begin
    y: Node
    Process_Before(x)
    Visit(x) := true
    for each y ∈ Succ(x) do
        if !Visit(y) then
            Process_Succ_Before(y)
            Depth_First_Search(N,Succ,y)
            Process_Succ_After(y)
        fi
    od
    Process_After(x)
end    || Depth_First_Search

begin
    for each i ∈ N do
        Visit(i) := false
    od
    Depth_First_Search(N,Succ,r)
end
```

FIG. 7.10 A generic depth-first search routine.

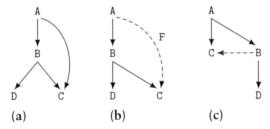

(a)   (b)   (c)

FIG. 7.11 (a) A rooted directed graph and (b) and (c) two distinct depth-first presentations of it.

The second and third notions we need are two traversals of the nodes of a rooted, directed graph and the orders they induce in the set of nodes of the graph. Let $G = \langle N, E, r \rangle$ be a rooted, directed graph. Let $E' \subseteq E$ be the set of edges in a depth-first presentation of G without the back edges. Then a *preorder traversal* of the graph G is a traversal in which each node is processed before its descendants, as defined by E'. For example, entry, B1, B2, B3, B4, B5, B6, exit is a preorder

```
N: set of Node
r, x: Node
i := 1, j := 1: integer
Pre, Post: Node —→ integer
Visit: Node —→ boolean
EType: (Node × Node) —→ enum {tree,forward,back,cross}

procedure Depth_First_Search_PP(N,Succ,x)
   N: in set of Node
   Succ: in Node —→ set of Node
   x: in Node
begin
   y: in Node
   Visit(x) := true
   Pre(x) := j
   j += 1
   for each y ∈ Succ(x) do
      if !Visit(y) then
         Depth_First_Search_PP(N,Succ,y)
         EType(x → y) := tree
      elif Pre(x) < Pre(y) then
         Etype(x → y) := forward
      elif Post(y) = 0 then
         EType(x → y) := back
      else
         EType(x → y) := cross
      fi
   od
   Post(x) := i
   i += 1
end    || Depth_First_Search_PP

begin
   for each x ∈ N do
      Visit(x) := false
   od
   Depth_First_Search_PP(N,Succ,r)
end
```

FIG. 7.12 Computing a depth-first spanning tree, preorder traversal, and postorder traversal.

traversal of the graph in Figure 7.4. The sequence entry, B1, B3, B2, B4, B6, B5, exit is another preorder traversal of the graph in Figure 7.4.

Let G and E' be as above. Then a *postorder traversal* of the graph G is a traversal in which each node is processed after its descendants, as defined by E'. For example, exit, B5, B6, B4, B3, B2, B1, entry is a postorder traversal of the graph in Figure 7.4, and exit, B6, B5, B2, B4, B3, B1, entry is another one.

The routine Depth_First_Search_PP( ) given in Figure 7.12 is a specific instance of depth-first search that computes both a depth-first spanning tree and

```
procedure Breadth_First(N,Succ,s) returns Node ⟶ integer
   N: in set of Node
   Succ: in Node ⟶ set of Node
   s: in Node
begin
   i := 2: integer
   t: Node
   T := ∅: set of Node
   Order: Node ⟶ integer
   Order(r) := 1
   for each t ∈ Succ(s) do
      if Order(t) = nil then
         Order(t) := i
         i += 1
         T ∪= {t}
      fi
   od
   for each t ∈ T do
      Breadth_First(N,Succ,t)
   od
   return Order
end     || Breadth_First
```

FIG. 7.13   Computing a breadth-first order.

preorder and postorder traversals of the graph $G = \langle N, E \rangle$ with root $r \in N$. After Depth_First_Search_PP( ) has been executed, the depth-first spanning tree is given by starting at the root and following the edges e with Etype(e) = tree. The preorder and postorder numbers assigned to the nodes are the integers stored into Pre( ) and Post( ), respectively.

The fourth notion is *breadth-first search,* in which all of a node's immediate descendants are processed before any of their unprocessed descendants. The order in which nodes are visited in a breadth-first search is a *breadth-first order.* For our example in Figure 7.9, the order 1, 2, 6, 3, 4, 5, 7, 8 is a breadth-first order.

The ICAN code in Figure 7.13 constructs a breadth-first ordering of the nodes of a flowgraph when it is called as Breadth_First(N,Succ,r).

7.3   Dominators and Postdominators

To determine the loops in a flowgraph, we first define a binary relation called dominance on flowgraph nodes. We say that node *d dominates* node *i,* written *d dom i,* if every possible execution path from entry to *i* includes *d.* Clearly, *dom* is reflexive (every node dominates itself), transitive (if *a dom b* and *b dom c,* then *a dom c*), and antisymmetric (if *a dom b* and *b dom a,* then *b = a*). We further define the subrelation called *immediate dominance* (*idom*) such that for $a \neq b,$

```
procedure Dom_Comp(N,Pred,r) returns Node ⟶ set of Node
    N: in set of Node
    Pred: in Node ⟶ set of Node
    r: in Node
begin
    D, T: set of Node
    n, p: Node
    change := true: boolean
    Domin: Node ⟶ set of Node
    Domin(r) := {r}
    for each n ∈ N - {r} do
        Domin(n) := N
    od
    repeat
        change := false
*       for each n ∈ N - {r} do
            T := N
            for each p ∈ Pred(n) do
                T ∩= Domin(p)
            od
            D := {n} ∪ T
            if D ≠ Domin(n) then
                change := true
                Domin(n) := D
            fi
        od
    until !change
    return Domin
end     || Dom_Comp
```

FIG. 7.14 A simple approach to computing all the dominators of each node in a flowgraph.

a idom b if and only if *a dom b* and there does not exist a node *c* such that $c \neq a$ and $c \neq b$ for which *a dom c* and *c dom b*, and we write *idom(b)* to denote the immediate dominator of *b*. Clearly the immediate dominator of a node is unique. The immediate dominance relation forms a tree of the nodes of a flowgraph whose root is the entry node, whose edges are the immediate dominances, and whose paths display all the dominance relationships. Further, we say that *d strictly dominates i*, written *d sdom i*, if *d* dominates *i* and $d \neq i$.

We also say that node *p postdominates* node *i*, written *p pdom i*, if every possible execution path from *i* to exit includes *p*, i.e., *i dom p* in the flowgraph with all the edges reversed and entry and exit interchanged.

We give two approaches to computing the set of dominators of each node in a flowgraph. The basic idea of the first approach is that node *a* dominates node *b* if and only if $a = b$, or *a* is the unique immediate predecessor of *b*, or *b* has more than one predecessor and for all immediate predecessors *c* of *b*, $c \neq a$ and *a* dominates *c*. The algorithm is Dom_Comp( ) given in Figure 7.14, which stores in

Domin(i) the set of all nodes that dominate node i. It is most efficient if the for loop marked with an asterisk processes the nodes of the flowgraph in a depth-first order.

As an example of the use of Dom_Comp( ), we apply it to the flowgraph in Figure 7.4. The algorithm first initializes change = true, Domin(entry) = {entry}, and Domin(i) = {entry,B1,B2,B3,B4,B5,B6,exit} for each node i other than entry. Then it enters the repeat loop, where it sets change = false and enters the for loop within it. The for loop sets n = B1 and T = {entry,B1,B2,B3,B4,B5,B6,exit} and enters the inner for loop. The inner for loop sets p = entry (the only member of Pred(B1)) and so sets T = {entry}. The inner for loop then terminates, D is set to {entry,B1}, change to true, and Domin(B1) = {entry,B1}. Next the outer for loop sets n = B2, T = {entry,B1,B2,B3,B4,B5,B6,exit}, and enters the inner for loop. Since Pred(B2) = {B1}, the inner for loop sets T to {entry,B1}. Then D is set to {entry,B1,B2} and Domin(B2) = {entry,B1,B2}. Continuing the process results in the following:

i	Domin(i)
entry	{entry}
B1	{entry,B1}
B2	{entry,B1,B2}
B3	{entry,B1,B3}
B4	{entry,B1,B3,B4}
B5	{entry,B1,B3,B4,B5}
B6	{entry,B1,B3,B4,B6}
exit	{entry,B1,exit}

If we need the immediate dominator of each node, we can compute it by the routine given in Figure 7.15. As for the previous algorithm, the greatest efficiency is achieved by having the for loop that is marked with an asterisk process the nodes of the flowgraph in depth-first order. The algorithm can be implemented with reasonable efficiency by representing the sets by bit vectors, with a running time that is $O(n^2 e)$ for a flowgraph with n nodes and e edges. In essence, the algorithm first sets Tmp(i) to Domin(i) − {i} and then checks for each node i whether each element in Tmp(i) has dominators other than itself and, if so, removes them from Tmp(i). As an example of the use of Idom_Comp( ), we apply it to the just computed dominator sets for the flowgraph in Figure 7.4. The algorithm initializes the Tmp( ) array to the following:

i	Tmp(i)
entry	∅
B1	{entry}
B2	{entry,B1}
B3	{entry,B1}
B4	{entry,B1,B3}
B5	{entry,B1,B3,B4}
B6	{entry,B1,B3,B4}
exit	{entry,B1}

```
procedure Idom_Comp(N,Domin,r) returns Node ⟶ Node
    N: in set of Node
    Domin: in Node ⟶ set of Node
    r: in Node
begin
    n, s, t: Node
    Tmp: Node ⟶ set of Node
    Idom: Node ⟶ Node
    for each n ∈ N do
        Tmp(n) := Domin(n) - {n}
    od
*   for each n ∈ N - {r} do
        for each s ∈ Tmp(n) do
            for each t ∈ Tmp(n) - {s} do
                if t ∈ Tmp(s) then
                    Tmp(n) -= {t}
                fi
            od
        od
    od
    for each n ∈ N - {r} do
        Idom(n) := ◆Tmp(n)
    od
    return Idom
end     || Idom_Comp
```

FIG. 7.15 Computing immediate dominators, given sets of dominators.

Next it sets n = B1 and s = entry and finds that Tmp(B1) - {entry} = ∅, so Tmp(B1) is left unchanged. Then it sets n = B2. For s = entry, Tmp(entry) is empty, so Tmp(B2) is not changed. On the other hand, for s = B1, Tmp(B1) is {entry} and it is removed from Tmp(B2), leaving Tmp(B2) = {B1}, and so on. The final values of Tmp( ) are as follows:

i	Tmp(i)
entry	∅
B1	{entry}
B2	{B1}
B3	{B1}
B4	{B3}
B5	{B4}
B6	{B4}
exit	{B1}

The last action of Idom_Comp( ) before returning is to set Idom(n) to the single element of Tmp(n) for $n \neq r$.

The second approach to computing dominators was developed by Lengauer and Tarjan [LenT79]. It is more complicated than the first approach, but it has the advantage of running significantly faster on all but the smallest flowgraphs.

Note that, for a rooted directed graph $\langle N, E, r \rangle$, node v is an *ancestor* of node w if $v = w$ or there is a path from v to w in the graph's depth-first spanning tree, and v is a *proper ancestor* of w if v is an ancestor of w and $v \neq w$. Also, we use $Dfn(v)$ to denote the depth-first number of node v.

The algorithm `Domin_Fast( )` is given in Figure 7.16, and Figures 7.17 and 7.18 contain auxiliary procedures. Given a flowgraph with its $Succ(\ )$ and $Pred(\ )$ functions, the algorithm ultimately stores in $Idom(v)$ the immediate dominator of each node $v \neq r$.

The algorithm first initializes some data structures (discussed below) and then performs a depth-first search of the graph, numbering the nodes as they are encountered, i.e., in a depth-first order. It uses a node $no \notin N$.

Next it computes, for each node $w \neq r$, a so-called semidominator of w and sets $Sdno(w)$ to the semidominator's depth-first number. The *semidominator* of a node w other than r is the node v with minimal depth-first number such that there is a path from $v = v_0$ to $w = v_k$, say $v_0 \rightarrow v_1, \ldots, v_{k-1} \rightarrow v_k$, such that $Dfn(v_i) > Dfn(w)$ for $1 \leq i \leq k - 1$.

Depth-first ordering and semidominators have several useful properties, as follows:

1. For any two nodes v and w in a rooted directed graph with $Dfn(v) \leq Dfn(w)$, any path from v to w must include a common ancestor of v and w in the flowgraph's depth-first spanning tree. Figure 7.19 shows the relationship between v and w for $Dfn(v) \leq Dfn(w)$ to be satisfied, where w may be in any of the positions of v, a, b, or c, where b is a descendant of an ancestor u of v such that $Dfn(b) > Dfn(v)$. A dotted arrow indicates a possibly empty path, and a dashed arrow represents a non-empty path. If $w = v$ or a, then v is the common ancestor. Otherwise, u is the common ancestor.

2. For any node $w \neq r$, w's semidominator is a proper ancestor of w and the immediate dominator of w is an ancestor of its semidominator.

3. Let E' denote E with the non-tree edges replaced by edges from the semidominator of each node to the node. Then the dominators of the nodes in $\langle N, E', r \rangle$ are the same as the dominators in $\langle N, E, r \rangle$.

4. Let

    $$V(w) = \{Dfn(v) \mid v \rightarrow w \in E \text{ and } Dfn(v) < Dfn(w)\}$$

    and

    $$S(w) = \{Sdno(u) \mid Dfn(u) > Dfn(w) \text{ and for some } v \in N, v \rightarrow w \in E$$

    $$\text{and there is a path from } u \text{ to } v \in E\}$$

    Then the semidominator of w is the node with depth-first number $\min(V(w) \cup S(w))$.

Note that we do not actually compute the semidominator of each node v, but, rather, just its depth-first number $Sdno(v)$.

```
      Label, Parent, Ancestor, Child: Node —→ Node
      Ndfs: integer —→ Node
      Dfn, Sdno, Size: Node —→ integer
      n: integer
      Succ, Pred, Bucket: Node —→ set of Node

      procedure Domin_Fast(N,r,Idom)
         N: in set of Node
         r: in Node
         Idom: out Node —→ Node
      begin
         u, v, w: Node
         i: integer
         || initialize data structures and perform depth-first search
         for each v ∈ N ∪ {n0} do
            Bucket(v) := ∅
            Sdno(v) := 0
         od
         Size(n0) := Sdno(n0) := 0
         Ancestor(n0) := Label(n0) := n0
         n := 0
         Depth_First_Search_Dom(r)
   *1    for i := n by -1 to 2 do
            || compute initial values for semidominators and store
            || nodes with the same semidominator in the same bucket
            w := Ndfs(i)
            for each v ∈ Pred(w) do
               u := Eval(v)
               if Sdno(u) < Sdno(w) then
                  Sdno(w) := Sdno(u)
               fi
            od
            Bucket(Ndfs(Sdno(w))) ∪= {w}
            Link(Parent(w),w)
            || compute immediate dominators for nodes in the bucket
            || of w's parent
   *2       while Bucket(Parent(w)) ≠ ∅ do
               v := ♦Bucket(Parent(w)); Bucket(Parent(w)) -= {v}
               u := Eval(v)
               if Sdno(u) < Sdno(v) then
                  Idom(v) := u
               else
                  Idom(v) := Parent(w)
               fi
            od
         od
      end
```

FIG. 7.16   A more complicated but faster approach to computing dominators.

```
      || adjust immediate dominators of nodes whose current version of
      || the immediate dominator differs from the node with the depth-first
      || number of the node's semidominator
*3    for i := 2 to n do
      w := Ndfs(i)
      if Idom(w) ≠ Ndfs(Sdno(w)) then
          Idom(w) := Idom(Idom(w))
      fi
*4    od
end    || Domin_Fast
```

FIG. 7.16 *(continued)*

```
procedure Depth_First_Search_Dom(v)
   v: in Node
begin
   w: Node
   || perform depth-first search and initialize data structures
   Sdno(v) := n += 1
   Ndfs(n) := Label(v) := v
   Ancestor(v) := Child(v) := n0
   Size(v) := 1
   for each w ∈ Succ(v) do
      if Sdno(w) = 0 then
         Parent(w) := v
         Depth_First_Search_Dom(w)
      fi
   od
end    || Depth_First_Search_Dom

procedure Compress(v)
   v: in Node
begin
   || compress ancestor path to node v to the node whose
   || label has the maximal semidominator number
   if Ancestor(Ancestor(v)) ≠ n0 then
      Compress(Ancestor(v))
      if Sdno(Label(Ancestor(v))) < Sdno(Label(v)) then
         Label(v) := Label(Ancestor(v))
      fi
      Ancestor(v) := Ancestor(Ancestor(v))
   fi
end    || Compress
```

FIG. 7.17 Depth-first search and path-compression algorithms used in computing dominators.

```
procedure Eval(v) returns Node
   v: in Node
begin
   || determine the ancestor of v whose semidominator
   || has the minimal depth-first number
   if Ancestor(v) = n0 then
       return Label(v)
   else
      Compress(v)
      if Sdno(Label(Ancestor(v))) >= Sdno(Label(v)) then
         return Label(v)
      else
         return Label(Ancestor(v))
      fi
   fi
end    || Eval

procedure Link(v,w)
   v, w: in Node
begin
   s := w, tmp: Node
   || rebalance the forest of trees maintained
   || by the Child and Ancestor data structures
   while Sdno(Label(w)) < Sdno(Label(Child(s))) do
       if Size(s) + Size(Child(Child(s)))
          >= 2*Size(Child(s)) then
          Ancestor(Child(s)) := s
          Child(s) := Child(Child(s))
       else
          Size(Child(s)) := Size(s)
          s := Ancestor(s) := Child(s)
       fi
   od
   Label(s) := Label(w)
   Size(v) += Size(w)
   if Size(v) < 2*Size(w) then
      tmp := s
      s := Child(v)
      Child(v) := tmp
   fi
   while s ≠ n0 do
      Ancestor(s) := v
      s := Child(s)
   od
end    || Link
```

FIG. 7.18 Label evaluation and linking algorithms used in computing dominators.

FIG. 7.19 For v and w to satisfy $Dfn(v) \leq Dfn(w)$, w may be in any of the positions of v, a, b, or c, where b is some descendant of u visited after all the tree descendants of v. A dotted arrow represents a possibly empty path, and a dashed arrow represents a non-empty path.

After computing $Sdno(v)$, for each non-root node v, the algorithm implicitly defines its immediate dominator as follows: Let u be a node whose semidominator w has minimal depth-first number among all nodes u such that there is a non-empty path from w to u and a path from u to v, both in the depth-first spanning tree. Then the immediate dominator $Idom(v)$ of v is the semidominator of v if $Sdno(v) = Sdno(u)$, or else it is $Idom(u)$.

Finally, the algorithm explicitly sets $Idom(v)$ for each v, processing the nodes in depth-first order.

The main data structures used in the algorithm are as follows:

1. `Ndfs(`i`)` is the node whose depth-first number is i.

2. `Succ(`v`)` is the set of successors of node v.

3. `Pred(`v`)` is the set of predecessors of node v.

4. `Parent(`v`)` is the node that is the parent of node v in the depth-first spanning tree.

5. `Sdno(`v`)` is the depth-first number of the semidominator of node v.

6. `Idom(`v`)` is the immediate dominator of node v.

7. `Bucket(`v`)` is the set of nodes whose semidominator is `Ndfs(`v`)`.

The routines `Link( )` and `Eval( )` maintain an auxiliary data structure, namely, a forest of trees within the depth-first spanning tree that keeps track of nodes that have been processed. `Eval( )` uses `Compress( )` to perform path compression on paths leading from a node by means of the `Ancestor( )` function (see below) to the root of the depth-first spanning tree. It consists of two data structures, namely,

1. `Ancestor(`v`)` is an ancestor of v in the forest or is n0 if v is a tree root in the forest, and

2. `Label(`v`)` is a node in the ancestor chain of v such that the depth-first number of its semidominator is minimal.

Finally, `Child(`v`)` and `Size(`v`)` are two data structures that are used to keep the trees in the forest balanced, and thus achieve the low time bound of the algorithm. With the use of balanced trees and path compression, this dominator-finding algorithm has a run-time bound of $O(e \cdot \alpha(e, n))$, where n and e are the numbers of nodes and edges, respectively, in the graph, and $\alpha( )$ is a very slowly growing function—essentially a functional inverse of Ackermann's function. Without the use of balanced trees, the `Link( )` and `Eval( )` functions are significantly simpler, but the running time is $O(e \cdot \log n)$.

For a more detailed description of how this algorithm works, see Lengauer and Tarjan [LenT79].

As an example of using the `Domin_Fast( )` algorithm, we apply it to the flow-graph in Figure 7.4.

After the call from `Domin_Fast( )` to `Depth_First_Search_Dom( )` has returned (i.e., at the point marked *1 in Figure 7.16), the values of `Ndfs( )`, `Sdom( )`, and `Idom( )` are as follows:

j	Ndfs(j)	Sdno(Ndfs(j))	Idom(Ndfs(j))
1	entry	1	n0
2	B1	2	n0
3	B2	3	n0
4	exit	4	n0
5	B3	5	n0
6	B4	6	n0
7	B5	7	n0
8	B6	8	n0

Next we show a series of snapshots of values that have changed from the previous listing, all at the point labeled *2. For i = 8, the changed line is

j	Ndfs(j)	Sdno(Ndfs(j))	Idom(Ndfs(j))
8	B6	8	B5

For i = 7, the changed lines are

j	Ndfs(j)	Sdno(Ndfs(j))	Idom(Ndfs(j))
7	B5	6	n0
8	B6	8	B4

For i = 6, the changed lines are

j	Ndfs(j)	Sdno(Ndfs(j))	Idom(Ndfs(j))
6	B4	5	n0
7	B5	6	B4

For i = 5, the changed lines are

j	Ndfs(j)	Sdno(Ndfs(j))	Idom(Ndfs(j))
5	B3	2	n0
6	B4	5	B3

For i = 4, the changed lines are

j	Ndfs(j)	Sdno(Ndfs(j))	Idom(Ndfs(j))
4	exit	2	n0
5	B3	2	B1

For i = 3, the changed lines are

j	Ndfs(j)	Sdno(Ndfs(j))	Idom(Ndfs(j))
3	B2	3	n0
4	exit	2	n0

For i = 2, the changed lines are

j	Ndfs(j)	Sdno(Ndfs(j))	Idom(Ndfs(j))
2	B1	2	n0
3	B2	2	B1

At both point *3 and point *4 in Domin_Fast( ), the values for all nodes are as follows:

j	Ndfs(j)	Sdno(Ndfs(j))	Idom(Ndfs(j))
1	entry	1	n0
2	B1	1	entry
3	B2	2	B1
4	exit	2	B1
5	B3	2	B1
6	B4	5	B3
7	B5	6	B4
8	B6	6	B4

and the values of Idom( ) match those computed by the first method.

Alstrup and Lauridsen [AlsL96] describe a technique for incrementally updating a dominator tree as the control flow of a procedure is modified. For the first time, the computational complexity of their technique makes it better than rebuilding the dominator tree from scratch.

7.4   Loops and Strongly Connected Components

Next, we define a *back edge* in a flowgraph as one whose head dominates its tail. Note that this notion of back edge is more restrictive than the one defined in Section 7.2. For example, the rooted directed graph in Figure 7.20(a) has as one of its depth-first presentations the graph in Figure 7.20(b), which has a back edge from d to c such that c does not dominate d. While this back edge does define a loop, the loop has two entry points (c and d), so it is not a natural loop.

Given a back edge $m{\to}n$, the *natural loop* of $m{\to}n$ is the subgraph consisting of the set of nodes containing n and all the nodes from which m can be reached in the flowgraph without passing through n and the edge set connecting all the nodes in its node set. Node n is the *loop header*. We can construct the node set of the natural loop of $m{\to}n$ by the algorithm Nat_Loop( ) in Figure 7.21. Given the graph and the back edge, this algorithm stores the set of nodes in the loop in Loop. Computing the set of edges of the loop, if needed, is easy from there.

Many of the optimizations we consider require moving code from inside a loop to just before its header. To guarantee that we uniformly have such a place available,

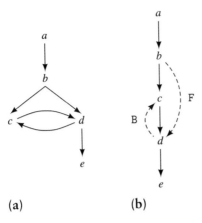

(a)   **(b)**

FIG. 7.20   (a) A rooted directed graph and (b) a depth-first presentation of it.

```
procedure Nat_Loop(m,n,Pred) returns set of Node
    m, n: in Node
    Pred: in Node ⟶ set of Node
begin
    Loop: set of Node
    Stack: sequence of Node
    p, q: Node
    Stack := []
    Loop := {m,n}
    if m = n then
        return Loop
    fi
    while Stack ≠ [] do
        || add predecessors of m that are not predecessors of n
        || to the set of nodes in the loop; since n dominates m,
        || this only adds nodes in the loop
        p := Stack↓-1
        Stack ⊖= -1
        for each q ∈ Pred(p) do
            if q ∉ Loop then
                Loop ∪= {q}
                Stack ⊕= [q]
            fi
        od
    od
    return Loop
end     || Nat_Loop
```

FIG. 7.21   Computing the natural loop of back edge $m \rightarrow n$.

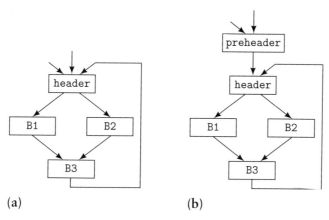

FIG. 7.22 Example loop (a) without and (b) with preheader.

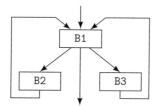

FIG. 7.23 Two natural loops with the same header B1.

we introduce the concept of a *preheader*, which is a new (initially empty) block placed just before the header of a loop, such that all the edges that previously went to the header from outside the loop now go to the preheader, and there is a single new edge from the preheader to the header. Figure 7.22(b) shows the result of introducing a preheader for the loop in Figure 7.22(a).

It is not hard to see that unless two natural loops have the same header they are either disjoint or one is nested within the other. On the other hand, given two loops with the same header, as in Figure 7.23, it is often not clear whether one is nested in the other (and if so, which is nested in which), or whether they make up just one loop. If they resulted from the code in Figure 7.24(a), it would be clear that the left loop was the inner one; if, on the other hand, they resulted from the code in Figure 7.24(b), they more likely make up one loop together. Given that we cannot distinguish these two situations without knowing more about the source code, we treat such situations in this section as comprising single loops (structural analysis, discussed in Section 7.7, will treat them differently).

A natural loop is only one type of strongly connected component of a flowgraph. There may be other looping structures that have more than one entry point, as we will see in Section 7.5. While such multiple-entry loops occur rarely in practice, they do occur, so we must take them into account.

The most general looping structure that may occur is a *strongly connected component* (SCC) of a flowgraph, which is a subgraph $G_S = \langle N_S, E_S \rangle$ such that every

```
        i = 1;                        B1:  if (i < j)
B1:  if (i >= 100)                         goto B2;
         goto b4;                          else if (i > j)
         else if ((i % 10) == 0)               goto B3;
             goto B3;                      else goto B4;
         else                       B2:  ...
B2:      ...                              i++;
         i++;                             goto B1;
         goto B1;                   B3:  ...
B3:  ...                                  i--;
     i++;                                 goto B1;
     goto B1;                      B4:  ...
B4:  ...
(a)                                (b)
```

FIG. 7.24 Alternative C code sequences that would both produce the flowgraph in Figure 7.23.

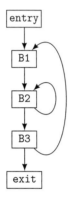

FIG. 7.25 A flowgraph with two strongly connected components, one maximal and one not maximal.

node in N_S is reachable from every other node by a path that includes only edges in E_S.

A strongly connected component is *maximal* if every strongly connected component containing it is the component itself. As an example, consider the flowgraph in Figure 7.25. The subgraph consisting of B1, B2, and B3 and the edges connecting them make up a maximal strongly connected component, while the subgraph consisting of the node B2 and the edge B2→B2 is a strongly connected component, but not a maximal one.

The algorithm Strong_Components(r) in Figure 7.26 gives a method for computing all the maximal SCCs of a flowgraph with entry node r. It is a version of Tarjan's algorithm, and it computes the SCCs in time linear in the number of nodes and edges in the flowgraph. The function Dfn: Node $\longrightarrow$ integer is a depth-first order of the nodes in N.

```
NextDfn: integer
All_SCC: set of set of Node
LowLink, Dfn: Node ⟶ integer
Stack: sequence of Node

procedure Strong_Components(x,Succ)
   x: in Node
   Succ: Node ⟶ set of Node
begin
   i: integer
   y, z: Node
   SCC: set of Node
   LowLink(x) := Dfn(x) := NextDfn += 1
   Stack ⊕= [x]
   for each y ∈ Succ(x) do
      if Dfn(y) = 0 then
         Strong_Components(y)
         LowLink(x) := min(LowLink(x),LowLink(y))
      elif Dfn(y) < Dfn(x) then
         LowLink(x) := min(LowLink(x),Dfn(y))
      fi
   od
   if LowLink(x) = Dfn(x) then || x is the root of an SCC
      SCC := ∅
      while Stack ≠ [] do
         z := Stack↓-1
         if Dfn(z) < Dfn(x) then
            All_SCC ∪= {SCC}
            return
         fi
         Stack ⊖= -1
         SCC ∪= {z}
      od
      All_SCC ∪= {SCC}
   fi
end    || Strong_Components

begin
   x: Node
   for each x ∈ N do
      Dfn(x) := 0
      LowLink(x) := 0
   od
   NextDfn := 0
   Stack := []
   All_SCC := ∅
   for each x ∈ N do
      if Dfn(x) = 0 then
         Strong_Components(x,Succ)
      fi
   od
end
```

FIG. 7.26   Computing strongly connected components.

The idea of the algorithm is as follows: For any node n in an SCC, let LowLink(n) be the smallest preorder number of any node m in the SCC such that there is a path from n to m in the depth-first spanning tree of the containing graph with at most one back or cross edge in the path. Let LL(n) be the node with preorder value LowLink(n), and let n_0 be n and n_{i+1} be LL(n_i). Eventually we must have, for some i, $n_{i+1} = n_i$; call this node LLend(n). Tarjan shows that LLend(n) is the lowest-numbered node in preorder in the maximal SCC containing n, and so it is the root in the given depth-first spanning tree of the graph whose set of nodes is the SCC containing n. Computing LLend(n) separately for each n would require more than linear time; Tarjan modifies this approach to make it work in linear time by computing LowLink(n) and using it to determine the nodes n that satisfy $n = $ LL(n), and hence $n = $ LLend(n).

7.5   Reducibility

Reducibility is a very important property of flowgraphs, and one that is most likely misnamed. The term *reducible* results from several kinds of transformations that can be applied to flowgraphs that collapse subgraphs into single nodes and, hence, "reduce" the flowgraph successively to simpler graphs, with a flowgraph considered to be reducible if applying a sequence of such transformations ultimately reduces it to a single node. A better name would be *well-structured* and the definition of reducibility we use makes this notion clear, but, given the weight of history, we use the term reducible interchangeably. A flowgraph $G = \langle N, E \rangle$ is reducible or *well-structured* if and only if E can be partitioned into disjoint sets E_F, the *forward* edge set, and E_B, the *back* edge set, such that $\langle N, E_F \rangle$ forms a DAG in which each node can be reached from the entry node, and the edges in E_B are all back edges as defined in Section 7.4. Another way of saying this is that if a flowgraph is reducible, then all the loops in it are natural loops characterized by their back edges and vice versa. It follows from this definition that in a reducible flowgraph there are no jumps into the middles of loops—each loop is entered only through its header.

Certain control-flow patterns make flowgraphs irreducible. Such patterns are called *improper regions,* and, in general, they are multiple-entry strongly connected components of a flowgraph. In fact, the simplest improper region is the two-entry loop shown in Figure 7.27(a), and the one in Figure 7.27(b) generalizes it to a three-entry loop; it's easy to see how to produce an infinite sequence of (comparatively simple) distinct improper regions beginning with these two.

The syntax rules of some programming languages, such as Modula-2 and its descendants and BLISS, allow only procedures with reducible flowgraphs to be constructed. This is true in most other languages as well, as long as we avoid gotos, specifically gotos into loop bodies. Statistical studies of flowgraph structure have shown that irreducibility is infrequent, even in languages like Fortran 77 that make no effort to restrict control-flow constructs[4] and in programs written over 20 years ago, before structured programming became a serious concern: two studies have

---

4. This is not quite true. The Fortran 77 standard does specifically prohibit branching into do loops, but it places no restrictions on branching into loops made up of ifs and gotos.

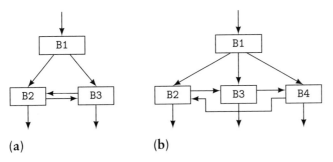

FIG. 7.27 Simple improper regions.

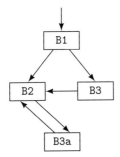

FIG. 7.28 Result of applying node splitting to B3 in the improper region shown in Figure 7.27(a).

found that over 90% of a selection of real-world Fortran 77 programs have reducible control flow and that *all* of a set of 50 large Fortran 66 programs are reducible. Thus, irreducible flowgraphs occur only rarely in practice, and so one could almost ignore their existence. However, they do occur, so we must make sure our approaches to control- and data-flow analysis are capable of dealing with them.

There are three practical approaches to dealing with irreducibility in the control-tree-based approaches to data-flow analysis discussed in Section 8.6 (which depend on flowgraphs being reducible). One is to do iterative data-flow analysis, as described in Section 8.4, on irreducible regions and to plug the results into the data-flow equations for the rest of the flowgraph. The second is to use a technique called *node splitting* that transforms irreducible regions into reducible ones. If we split node B3 in the example in Figure 7.27(a), the result is the flowgraph in Figure 7.28: B3 has become a pair of nodes, B3 and B3a, and the loop is now a proper one with entry B2. If irreducibility were common, node splitting could be very expensive, since it could exponentially increase the size of the flowgraph; fortunately, this is not the case in practice. The third approach is to perform an induced iteration on the lattice of monotone functions from the lattice to itself (see Sections 8.5 and 8.6).

7.6   Interval Analysis and Control Trees

Interval analysis is a name given to several approaches to both control- and data-flow analysis. In control-flow analysis, interval analysis refers to dividing up the flowgraph into regions of various sorts (depending on the particular approach),

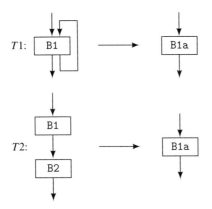

FIG. 7.29 *T1-T2 transformations.*

consolidating each region into a new node (often called an *abstract node,* since it abstracts away the internal structure of the region it represents), and replacing the edges entering or leaving the region with edges entering or leaving the corresponding abstract node. A flowgraph resulting from one or more such transformations is called an *abstract flowgraph.* Since the transformations are applied either one at a time or to disjoint subgraphs in parallel, the resulting regions are *nested* in the sense that each abstract node corresponds to a subgraph. Thus, the result of applying a sequence of such transformations produces a *control tree,* defined as follows:

1. The root of the control tree is an abstract graph representing the original flowgraph.

2. The leaves of the control tree are individual basic blocks.

3. The nodes between the root and the leaves are abstract nodes representing regions of the flowgraph.

4. The edges of the tree represent the relationship between each abstract node and the regions that are its descendants (and that were abstracted to form it).

For example, one of the simplest and historically earliest forms of interval analysis is known as *T1-T2* analysis. It is composed of just two transformations: *T1* collapses a one-node self loop to a single node, and *T2* collapses a sequence of two nodes such that the first is the only predecessor of the second to a single node, as shown in Figure 7.29.

Now suppose we are given the flowgraph shown on the left in Figure 7.30. Applying *T1* and *T2* repeatedly, we get the sequence of reductions shown in that figure. The corresponding control tree is shown in Figure 7.31.

As originally defined, interval analysis used what are known as maximal intervals and ignored the existence of irreducible or improper regions. A *maximal interval* $I_M(h)$ with header h is the maximal, single-entry subgraph with h as its only entry node and with all closed paths in the subgraph containing h. In essence, $I_M(h)$ is the natural loop with entry h, plus some acyclic structure dangling from its exits. For example, in Figure 7.4, $I_M(\text{B4})$ is {B4,B6,B5,exit}; B6 is included because the only

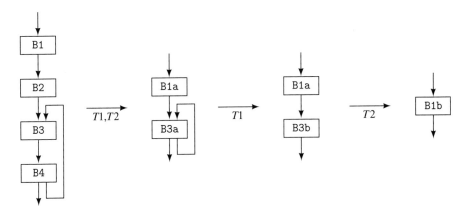

FIG. 7.30 Example of $T1$-$T2$ transformations.

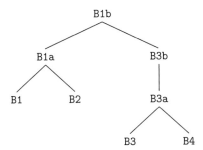

FIG. 7.31 $T1$-$T2$ control tree for the flowgraph in Figure 7.30.

closed path containing B4 is the one consisting of B4 → B6 and B6 → B4, and B5 and `exit` are included because the subgraph would not be maximal otherwise.

A more modern form of interval analysis, which we concentrate on in the remainder of this section, identifies the loops in the flowgraph without classifying other types of control structures. In this context, a *minimal interval* (or simply an *interval*) I is defined to be (1) a natural loop, (2) a maximal acyclic subgraph, or (3) a minimal irreducible region. Thus, a minimal interval that is a natural loop differs from the corresponding maximal interval in that the latter includes successors of the nodes in the loop that are not themselves in the loop and that are also not headers of maximal intervals, while the former excludes them. For example, Figure 7.32(a) and (b) shows the maximal and minimal intervals, respectively, in the same flowgraph.

A somewhat more complex example is shown in Figure 7.33. In this example, rather than naming the abstract subgraphs, we simply give the set of nodes comprising each of them—this makes the control tree (shown in Figure 7.34) obvious. Basic blocks B2 and B4 form a loop, as do B5 and B6. After they have been collapsed to single nodes, B3 and {B5,B6} are found to make an irreducible region, which is collapsed. The remaining abstract graph is acyclic, and hence forms a single interval.

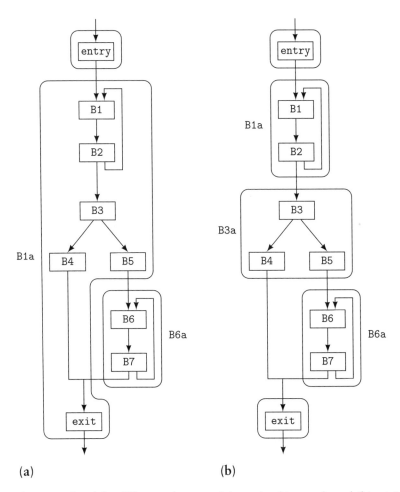

FIG. 7.32 An example of the difference between (a) maximal intervals and (b) minimal intervals.

Since we consider structural analysis (covered in detail in Section 7.7) to be superior to interval analysis, we give here only an outline of how to perform interval analysis.[5] The basic steps are as follows:

1. Perform a postorder traversal of the node set of the flowgraph, looking for loop headers (each a single node) and headers of improper regions (each a set of more than one node).

2. For each loop header found, construct its natural loop using the algorithm Nat_Loop( ) given in Figure 7.21 and reduce it to an abstract region of type "natural loop."

---

5. Actually, interval analysis can be viewed as a cut-down version of structural analysis that uses fewer types of regions or intervals. Thus, an algorithm for performing interval analysis can be derived from the one for structural analysis.

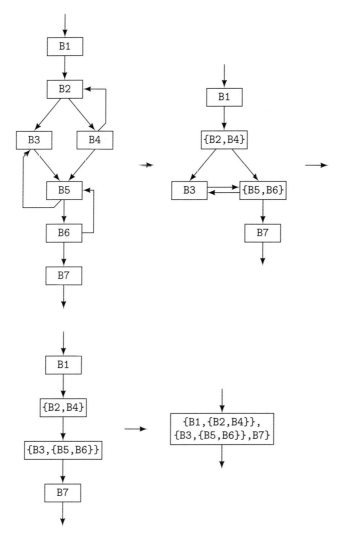

FIG. 7.33 Example of interval analysis.

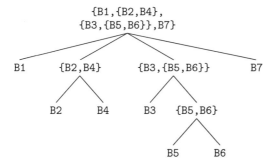

FIG. 7.34 Control tree for the flowgraph in Figure 7.33.

3. For each set of entries of an improper region, construct the minimal strongly connected component (the algorithm given in Figure 7.26 can be modified to construct the minimal SCC) of the flowgraph containing all the entries and reduce it to an abstract region of type "improper region."

4. For the entry node and for each immediate descendant of a node in a natural loop or in an irreducible region, construct the maximal acyclic graph with that node as its root; if the resulting graph has more than one node in it, reduce it to an abstract region of type "acyclic region."

5. Iterate this process until it terminates.

Note that termination is guaranteed since either the flowgraph is acyclic or it contains one or the other type of loop: if it is acyclic, the process terminates with the current iteration; if it includes one or more cycles, at least one natural-loop or improper-region reduction will occur during each iteration, reducing the number of cycles in the graph by at least one, and every flowgraph contains only a finite number of cycles to begin with.

7.7   Structural Analysis

Structural analysis is a more refined form of interval analysis. Its goal is to make the syntax-directed method of data-flow analysis (developed by Rosen for use on syntax trees) applicable to lower-level intermediate code. Rosen's method, called *high-level data-flow analysis,* has the advantage that it gives, for each type of structured control-flow construct in a source language, a set of formulas that perform conventional (bit-vector) data-flow analyses across and through them much more efficiently than iteration does. Thus, this method extends one of the goals of optimization, namely, to move work from execution time to compilation time, by moving work from compilation time to language-definition time—in particular, the data-flow equations for structured control-flow constructs are determined by the syntax and semantics of the language.

Structural analysis extends this approach to arbitrary flowgraphs by discovering their control-flow structure and providing a way to handle improper regions. Thus, for example, it can take a loop made up of ifs, gotos, and assignments and discover that it has the form of a while or repeat loop, even though its syntax gives no hint of that.

It differs from basic interval analysis in that it identifies many more types of control structures than just loops, forming each into a region and, as a result, provides a basis for doing very efficient data-flow analysis. The control tree it builds is typically larger than for interval analysis—since more types of regions, and hence more regions, are identified—but the individual regions are correspondingly simpler and smaller. One critical concept in structural analysis is that every region it identifies has exactly one entry point, so that, for example, an irreducible or improper region will always include the lowest common dominator of the set of entries to the strongly connected component that is the multiple-entry cycle within the improper region.

Figures 7.35 and 7.36 give examples of typical acyclic and cyclic control structures, respectively, that structural analysis can recognize. Note that which of these

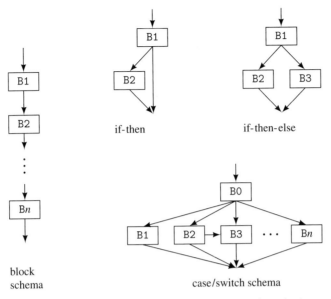

FIG. 7.35 Some types of acyclic regions used in structural analysis.

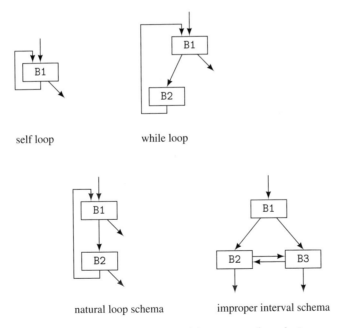

FIG. 7.36 Some types of cyclic regions used in structural analysis.

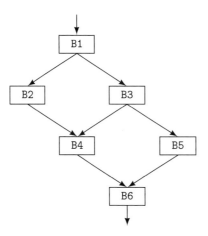

FIG. 7.37 An acyclic region that does not fit any of the simple categories and so is identified as a proper interval.

are appropriate for a given source language may vary with the choice of language and that there may be others. In particular, the case/switch construct in a particular language may or may not allow each of the cases to fall through to the next case, rather than branching directly to the construct's exit—in C's switch, any case may fall through or branch to the exit, while in Pascal's case, all cases branch to the exit. Thus, the case/switch structure is really intended to be a schema that covers the range of possibilities. Note that a natural loop represents any reducible loop that is not one of the other specific reducible looping constructs (i.e., not a self or while loop). It too is schematic, since the loop may have more than two exit edges.

Similarly, the improper (or irreducible) interval is schematic, since its entry block may have more than two successors and it may contain more than three blocks. One more type of interval is used in structural analysis, namely, a *proper interval*, which is an arbitrary acyclic structure, i.e., one that contains no cycles and that cannot be reduced by any of the simple acyclic cases. An example of such a structure is shown in Figure 7.37.

Also, the situation represented in Figure 7.23 in which there are two back edges entering B1 is recognized by structural analysis as two nested while loops. Which one it makes the inner loop depends on the order in which they are encountered.

Structural analysis proceeds by constructing a depth-first spanning tree for the flowgraph in question and then examining the flowgraph's nodes in preorder for instances of the various region types, forming abstract nodes from them and collapsing the connecting edges, and constructing the corresponding control tree in the process. The order in which the checking for regions of various types is done and the way in which it is done are important: for example, a sequence of $n \geq 3$ regions that make up a block can be collapsed in one step to one block if we follow the sequence to the end before forming the region, or it can be collapsed in $n - 1$ steps to a hierarchy of $n - 1$ blocks if we only inspect the first block and its successor at each step. Clearly, the former approach is preferred.

```
RegionType = enum {Block,IfThen,IfThenElse,Case,Proper,SelfLoop,
    WhileLoop,NaturalLoop,Improper}
|| Structof(n) = the region containing node n
StructOf: Node —→ Node
|| StrucType(n) = the member of RegionType that is the type of
|| the region denoted by region node n
StructType: Node —→ RegionType
|| the set of all region nodes
Structures: set of Node
|| StructNodes(n) = the set of nodes making up the region
|| abstracted to node n
StructNodes: Node —→ set of Node
|| node and edge sets of the control tree
CTNodes: set of Node
CTEdges: set of (Node × Node)
PreCtr: integer
|| preorder traversal of the flowgraph
Pre: Node —→ integer
```

FIG. 7.38   Global data structures used in structural analysis.

Following Sharir [Shar80], we construct four data structures, called StructOf, StructType, Structures, and StructNodes as we analyze a flowgraph (Figure 7.38). StructOf gives, for each node, the (abstract) region node immediately containing it. StructType gives, for each region node, its type. Structures is the set of all region nodes. StructNodes gives, for each region, the list of nodes in it.

The structural analysis algorithm Structural_Analysis( ) given in Figure 7.39 first initializes the data structures described above that record the structure of the flowgraph and the structures that represent the control tree (CTNodes and CTEdges), and then it does a depth-first search of the flowgraph so as to determine a preorder traversal of the flowgraph's nodes. It identifies each region and collapses it to a single node; it assumes that the region types are those shown in Figures 7.35 and 7.36, plus the others described above, although others can be used as appropriate to the language(s) being processed. If a reduction has been performed, it rebuilds the preorder traversal and processes the flowgraph again; note that we could repair the tree incrementally as we reduce flowgraph structures rather than rebuilding it *ab initio*, but this would complicate presentation of the algorithm. The algorithm replaces the edges entering a region with edges to the new node and edges leaving the region with edges from the new node. In parallel, it constructs the corresponding control tree.

The set ReachUnder is used to determine the nodes contained in a cyclic control structure. If it contains one node, the loop must be a self loop or an improper (or irreducible) region. If it contains two nodes, it can be a while loop or a natural loop with exit edges from both nodes. If it contains three or more nodes, the loop is a natural loop. Note that for an improper region, the entry node is *not* part of the cyclic structure; the routine Smallest_Improper( ) in Figure 7.45 determines the set of nodes contained in the region.

```
procedure Structural_Analysis(N,E,entry)
   N: in set of Node
   E: in set of (Node × Node)
   entry: in Node
begin
   reduction: boolean
   m, n: Node
   rtype: RegionType
   NodeSet, ReachUnder, NonEntries: set of Node
   StructOf := ∅
   StructType := ∅
   Structures := ∅
   StructNodes := ∅
   CTNodes := N
   CTEdges := ∅
   repeat
      reduction := false
      NonEntries := ∅
      DFS_Preorder(N,E,entry)
      || locate an acyclic region, if present
      while |N| > 1 & !reduction do
         n := ◆N
         for each m ∈ N - {n} do
            if Pre(m) < Pre(n) then
               n := m
            fi
         od
         rtype := Acyclic_Region_Type(N,E,n,NodeSet)
         if rtype ≠ nil then
            Reduce(N,E,n,rtype,NodeSet)
            reduction := true
         else
            || locate an cyclic region, if present
            ReachUnder := {n}
            for each m ∈ N do
               if StructOf(m) = ∅ & Path_Back(m,n) then
                  ReachUnder ∪= {m}
               fi
            od
            rtype := Cyclic_Region_Type(N,E,n,ReachUnder)
            if rtype ≠ nil then
               Reduce(N,E,n,rtype,ReachUnder)
               reduction := true
            else
               N -= {n}
               NonEntries ∪= {n}
            fi
         fi
      od
```

FIG. 7.39 Structural analysis algorithm.

```
          if reduce & NonEntries ≠ Ø then
              N ∪= NonEntries
          fi
      until !reduction
  end    || Structural_Analysis
```

FIG. 7.39 *(continued)*

```
procedure DFS_Preorder(N,E,x)
    N: in set of Node
    E: in set of (Node × Node)
    x: in Node
begin
    y: in Node
    PreCtr := 0
    for each y ∈ N do
        Pre(y) := nil
    od
    PreCtr += 1
    Pre(x) := PreCtr
    fr each y ∈ Succ(x) do
        if PreCtr(y) = nil then
            DFS_Preorder(N,E,y)
        fi
    od
end    || DFS_Preorder
```

FIG. 7.40 Computing a preorder traversal of the nodes in a flowgraph.

The algorithm terminates when it has reduced the flowgraph to the trivial graph with a single node and no edges. The routine DFS_Preorder( ) given in Figure 7.40 constructs a preorder traversal of the nodes in the flowgraph. The routine Acyclic_Region_Type($N,E,node,nset$) given in Figure 7.41 determines whether *node* is the entry node of an acyclic control structure and returns either its type or nil (if it is not such an entry node); the routine also stores in *nset* the set of nodes in the identified control structure. The function Path_Back(m,n) returns true if there is a node k such that there is a (possibly empty) path from m to k and an edge from k to n such that $k{\to}n$ is a back edge and the path does not pass through n; otherwise it returns false.

The routine Cyclic_Region_Type($N,E,node,nset$) given in Figure 7.42 determines whether *node* is the entry node of a cyclic control structure and either returns its type or nil (if it is not such an entry node); it similarly stores in *nset* the set of nodes in the identified control structure.

The routine Reduce($N,E,n,rtype,NodeSet$), defined in Figure 7.43, calls Create_Node( ) to create a region node to represent the identified region and sets the StructType, Structures, StructOf, and StructNodes data structures accord-

```
procedure Acyclic_Region_Type(N,E,node,nset)
   returns RegionType
   N: in set of Node
   E: in set of (Node × Node)
   node: inout Node
   nset : out set of Node
begin
   m, n: Node
   p, s: boolean
   nset := ∅
   || check for a Block
   p := true
   s := |Succ(node)| = 1
   while p & s do
      nset ∪= {node}
      node := ◆Succ(node)
      p := |Pred(node)| = 1
      s := |Succ(node)| = 1
   od
   if p then
      nset ∪= {node}
   fi
   if |nset| ≥ 2 then
      return Block
   elif |Succ(node)| = 2 then
      || check for an IfThenElse
      m := ◆Succ(node)
      n := ◆(Succ(node) - {m})
      if Succ(m) = Succ(n) & |Succ(m)| = 1
         & |Pred(m)| = 1 & |Pred(n)| = 1 then
         nset := {node,m,n}
         return IfThenElse
      || other cases
      elif . . .
         . . .
      else
         return nil
      fi
   fi
end    || Acyclic_Region_Type
```

FIG. 7.41 Routine to identify the type of an acyclic structure.

```
procedure Cyclic_Region_Type(N,E,node,nset)
   returns RegionType
   N, nset: in set of Node
   E: in set of (Node × Node)
   node: in Node
begin
   m: Node
```

FIG. 7.42 Routine to identify the type of a cyclic structure.

```
      size := |nset|: integer
      || check for a SelfLoop
      if size = 1 then
          if node→node ∈ E then
             return SelfLoop
          else
             || it's an Improper region
             nset := Smallest_Improper(N,E,node)
             return Improper
          fi
      || check for a WhileLoop
      elif size = 2 then
          m := ◆(nset - {node})
          if |Succ(node)| = 2 & |Succ(m)| = 1 &
             |Pred(node)| = 2 & |Pred(m)| = 1 then
             return WhileLoop
          fi
      || it's a Natural Loop
      elif size > 2 then
          . . .
          return NaturalLoop
      fi
   end    || Cyclic_Entry_Type
```

FIG. 7.42 *(continued)*

```
procedure Reduce(N,E,n,rtype,NodeSet)
   N: in set of Node
   E: in set of (Node × Node)
   n: in Node
   rtype: in RegionType
   NodeSet: inout set of Node
begin
   node, m: Node
   if rtype = Improper then
      || determine set of nodes in Improper region
      NodeSet := Smallest_Improper(N,E,n)
   fi
   node := Create_Node( )
   Pre(node) := min{Pre(n) where n ∈ NodeSet}
   || replace node set by an abstract region node and
   || set data structures
   Replace(N,E,node,NodeSet)
   StructType(node) := rtype
   Structures ∪= {node}
   for each m ∈ NodeSet do
      StructOf(m) := node
   od
   StructNodes(node) := NodeSet
end    || Reduce
```

FIG. 7.43 Region reduction routine for structural analysis.

```
procedure Replace(N,E,node,NodeSet)
   N: inout set of Node
   E: inout set of (Node × Node)
   node: in Node
   NodeSet: in set of Node
begin
   || link region node into abstracted flowgraph and augment
   ||   the control tree
   m: Node
   e: Node × Node
   N := (N - NodeSet) ∪ {node}
   for each e ∈ E do
      if e@1 ∈ NodeSet ∨ e@2 ∈ NodeSet then
         E -= {e}
         if e@1 ∈ N & e@1 ≠ node then
            E ∪= {e@1→node}
         elif e@2 ∈ N & e@2 ≠ node then
            E ∪= {node→e@2}
         fi
      fi
   od
   CTNodes ∪= {node}
   for each n ∈ NodeSet do
      CTEdges ∪= {node→n}
   od
end    || Replace
```

FIG. 7.44 Routine to do node and edge replacement and control-tree building for structural analysis.

ingly. It uses Replace($N,E,node,NodeSet$), shown in Figure 7.44 to replace the identified region by the new node, to adjust the incoming and outgoing edges correspondingly, and to build the control tree, given by CTNodes and CTEdges.

The routine Smallest_Improper($N,E,node$) given in Figure 7.45 is used to determine the smallest improper region headed by *node*; it limits the improper region to the smallest subgraph containing *node* such that *node* dominates all nodes in it and any node other than *node* on a non-empty path from *node* to some other node in the improper region is also in it. This approach almost always results in smaller improper intervals than Sharir's original method. The function Path(n,m,I) returns true if there is a path from n to m such that all the nodes in it are in I and false otherwise.

As an example of structural analysis, consider the flowgraph in Figure 7.46(a). Figure 7.47 shows a depth-first spanning tree for the flowgraph. The first stage of the analysis,[6] shown in Figure 7.46(b), does two reductions: B2 is recognized as a

---

6. The figure actually shows what can be thought of as a parallel version of structural analysis that may make several reductions in each pass. This is done in the figure to save space, but could be implemented in the algorithm at the expense of significantly decreasing its understandability.

```
procedure Smallest_Improper(N,E,node) returns set of Node
   N: in set of Node
   E: in set of (Node × Node)
   node: in Node
begin
   I: set of Node
   m, n: Node
   I := {n ∈ N where n ≠ node & node dom n}
   for each n ∈ I do
      for each m ∈ I do
         if !Path(n,m,I) then
            I -= {n}
         fi
      od
   od
   return I ∪ {node}
end    || Smallest_Improper
```

FIG. 7.45 Improper interval minimization routine for structural analysis.

self loop and reduced accordingly, and B5 and B6 are recognized as an if-then and reduced. It sets the data structures as follows:

```
StructType(B2a) = SelfLoop
StructOf(B2) = B2a
StructNodes(B2a) = {B2}
StructType(B5a) = IfThen
StructOf(B5) = StructOf(B6) = B5a
StructNodes(B5a) = {B5,B6}
Structures = {B2a,B5a}
```

The next stage, shown in Figure 7.46(c), recognizes and reduces the if-then made up of B1 and B2a and the block made up of B5a and B7. It sets the data structures as follows:

```
StructType(B1a) = IfThen
StructOf(B1) = StructOf(B2a) = B1a
StructNodes(B1a) = {B1,B2a}
StructType(B5b) = BasicBlock
StructOf(B5a) = StructOf(B7) = B5b
StructNodes(B5b) = {B5a,B7}
Structures = {B2a,B5a,B1a,B5b}
```

In the next stage, shown in Figure 7.46(d), B3, B4, and B5b are reduced as an if-then-else. The data structures are set as follows:

```
StructType(B3a) = IfThenElse
StructOf(B3) = StructOf(B4) = StructOf(B5b) = B3a
StructNodes(B3a) = {B3,B4,B5b}
Structures = {B2a,B5a,B1a,B5b,B3a}
```

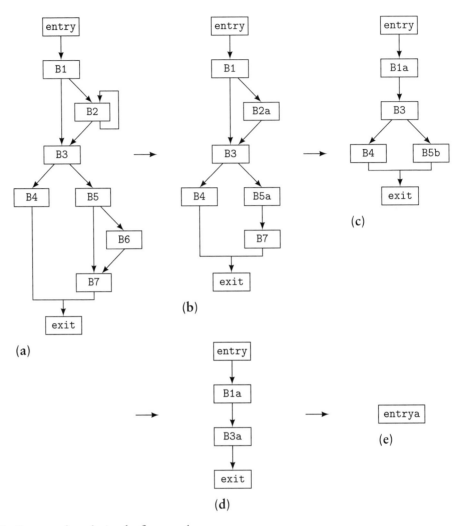

FIG. 7.46 Structural analysis of a flowgraph.

In the final stage, entry, B1a, B3a, and exit are reduced as a block, resulting in Figure 7.46(e). The data structures are set as follows:

```
StructType(entrya) = BasicBlock
StructOf(entry) = StructOf(B1a) = StructOf(B3a)
    = StructOf(exita) = entrya
StructNodes(entrya) = {entry,B1a,B3a,exit}
Structures = {B2a,B5a,B1a,B5b,B3a,entrya}
```

The resulting control tree is given in Figure 7.48.

Figure 7.49 gives two examples of flowgraphs that contain improper intervals. In example (a), the routine Smallest_Improper( ) recognizes the subgraph consisting of all nodes except B6 as the improper interval. In (b), it recognizes an improper

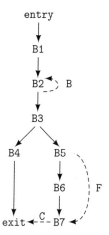

FIG. 7.47 Depth-first spanning tree for the flowgraph in Figure 7.46(a).

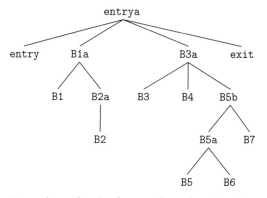

FIG. 7.48 Control tree for the flowgraph analyzed in Figure 7.46.

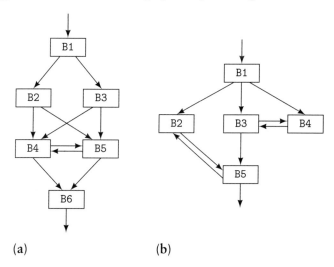

(a)   (b)

FIG. 7.49 Two examples of improper intervals.

interval consisting of B1, B3, and B4 and then another consisting of the reduced node for that interval along with B2 and B5.

7.8   Wrap-Up

Control-flow analysis is our first foray into material that relates directly to optimization.

Optimization requires that we be able to characterize the control flow of programs and the manipulations they perform on their data, so that any unused generality can be removed and operations can be replaced by faster ones.

As discussed above, there are two main approaches to control-flow analysis, both of which start by determining the basic blocks that make up the routine and constructing its flowgraph. The first approach uses dominators to discover loops and simply notes the loops it finds for use in optimization. We also identify extended basic blocks and reverse extended basic blocks for those optimizations that can be applied to them. This is sufficient for use by iterative data-flow analyzers.

The second approach, called interval analysis, includes a series of methods that analyze the overall structure of the routine and that decompose it into nested regions called intervals. The nesting structure of the intervals forms the control tree, which is useful in structuring and speeding up data-flow analysis. The most sophisticated form of interval analysis, called structural analysis, classifies essentially all the control-flow structures in a routine. It is sufficiently important that we devoted a separate section to it.

In the past, most optimizing compilers used dominators and iterative data-flow analysis, but this is changing because the interval-based approaches are faster, they make it easier to update already computed data-flow information, and structural analysis makes it particularly easy to perform the control-flow transformations discussed in Chapter 18.

7.9   Further Reading

Lengauer and Tarjan's approach to computing dominators is described in [LenT79]. It uses path-compression methods that are described more fully in [Tarj81]. Tarjan's algorithm for finding strongly connected components is described in [Tarj72]. Alstrup and Lauridsen's dominator-tree update algorithm is described in [AlsL96].

An overview of the flowgraph transformations that are responsible for the notion of flowgraph reducibility's being called that can be found in [Kenn81]. The studies of reducibility in Fortran programs are from Allen and Cocke [AllC72b]; and Knuth [Knut71]. $T1$-$T2$ analysis is described in [Ullm73]. The definition of maximal interval is from Allen and Cocke [AllC76]; Aho, Sethi, and Ullman [AhoS86] also use maximal intervals. Both give algorithms for partitioning a reducible flowgraph into maximal intervals.

Structural analysis was originally formulated by Sharir [Shar80]. The syntax-tree-based method of data-flow analysis is due to Rosen (see [Rose77] and [Rose79]) and was extended by Schwartz and Sharir [SchS79]. The modern approach to analyzing and minimizing improper intervals is described in [JaiT88].

7.10   Exercises

7.1 Specify the set of flowgraph edges that must be added to a C function because it includes a call to `setjump( )`.

7.2 (a) Divide the ICAN procedure `Domin_Fast( )` in Figure 7.16 into basic blocks. You might find it useful to construct a flowgraph of it. (b) Then divide it into extended basic blocks.

7.3 Construct (a) a depth-first presentation, (b) depth-first ordering, (c) preorder, and (d) postorder of the flowchart nodes for the routine `Depth_First_Search_PP( )` in Figure 7.12.

7.4 Suppose that for each pair of nodes a and b in a flowgraph a dom b if and only if b pdom a. What is the structure of the flowgraph?

7.5 Implement `Dom_Comp( )`, `Idom_Comp( )`, and `Domin_Fast( )` in a language available to you and run them on the flowgraph in Figure 7.32.

7.6 Explain what the procedure `Compress( )` in Figure 7.17 does.

7.7 Explain what the procedure `Link( )` in Figure 7.18 does.

7.8 Apply the algorithm `Strong_Components( )` in Figure 7.26 to the graph in Figure 7.50.

7.9 Define an infinite sequence of distinct improper regions R_1, R_2, R_3, . . . , with each R_i consisting of a set of nodes N_i and a set of edges E_i.

7.10 Give an infinite sequence of irreducible regions R_1, R_2, R_3, . . . such that R_i consists of i nodes and such that performing node splitting on R_i results in a flowgraph whose number of nodes is exponential in i.

7.11 Write an ICAN program to compute the maximal intervals in a reducible flowgraph.

7.12 Write an ICAN program to compute the minimal intervals in a reducible flowgraph.

RSCH 7.13 Read Rosen's articles ([Rose77] and [Rose79]) and show the formulas he would construct for an if-then-else construct and a repeat loop.

7.14 Write a formal specification of the case/switch schema in Figure 7.35 as a set of graphs.

7.15 Are there any other types of acyclic regions that are not reducible to the ones in Figure 7.35? If so, give an example. If not, prove it.

7.16 Write a formal specification of the set of natural loops (see Figure 7.36), where a natural loop is defined to be a single-entry, multiple-exit loop, with only a single branch back to the entry from within it.

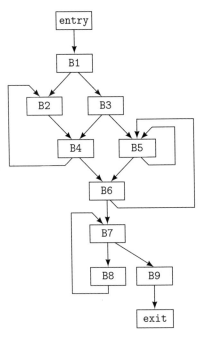

FIG. 7.50 An example graph to which to apply the algorithm Strong_Components( ) in Figure 7.26.

RSCH 7.17 Modify the ICAN routine Structural_Analysis( ) in Figure 7.39 and its subroutines to incrementally update the depth-first search tree as part of performing each reduction.

   7.18 Perform a structural control-flow analysis of the routine (a) Make_Webs( ) in Figure 16.7 and (b) Gen_Spill_Code( ) in Figure 16.24.

CHAPTER 8

Data-Flow Analysis

T he purpose of data-flow analysis is to provide global information about how a procedure (or a larger segment of a program) manipulates its data. For example, constant-propagation analysis seeks to determine whether all assignments to a particular variable that may provide the value of that variable at some particular point necessarily give it the same constant value. If so, a use of the variable at that point can be replaced by the constant.

The spectrum of possible data-flow analyses ranges from abstract execution of a procedure, which might determine, for example, that it computes the factorial function (as discussed in Section 8.14), to much simpler and easier analyses such as the reaching definitions problem discussed in the next section.

In all cases, we must be certain that a data-flow analysis gives us information that does not misrepresent what the procedure being analyzed does, in the sense that it must not tell us that a transformation of the code is safe to perform that, in fact, is not safe. We must guarantee this by careful design of the data-flow equations and by being sure that the solution to them that we compute is, if not an exact representation of the procedure's manipulation of its data, at least a conservative approximation of it. For example, for the reaching definitions problem, where we determine what definitions of variables may reach a particular use, the analysis must not tell us that no definitions reach a particular use if there are some that may. The analysis is conservative if it may give us a larger set of reaching definitions than it might if it could produce the minimal result.

However, to obtain the maximum possible benefit from optimization, we seek to pose data-flow problems that are both conservative and, at the same time, as aggressive as we can make them. Thus, we shall always attempt to walk the fine line between being as aggressive as possible in the information we compute and being conservative, so as to get the greatest possible benefit from the analyses and code-improvement transformations we perform without ever transforming correct code to incorrect code.

Finally, as you will recall, in Section 7.1 we discussed three approaches to control- and data-flow analysis and our reasons for presenting all three of them in the text. It is worth referring to that section to refresh your memory as to why we choose to present all three.

8.1   An Example: Reaching Definitions

As an introduction to data-flow analysis, we continue the informal example we began at the beginning of Chapter 7 by performing a simple data-flow analysis called reaching definitions on the procedure given there that computed Fibonacci numbers. Our starting point consists of the flowchart in Figure 7.3 and the flowgraph in Figure 7.4.

A definition is an assignment of some value to a variable. A particular definition of a variable is said to reach a given point in a procedure if there is an execution path from the definition to that point such that the variable may have, at that point, the value assigned by the definition. Our goal is to determine which particular definitions of (i.e., assignments to) each variable may, by some control-flow path, reach any particular point in the procedure. We take the term *control-flow path* to mean any directed path in the flowchart for a procedure, usually irrespective of whether predicates controlling branching along the path are satisfied or not.

We could perform data-flow analysis on the flowchart of a procedure, but it is more efficient in general to divide it up into local flow analysis, done within each basic block, and global flow analysis, done on the flowgraph. To do so, we summarize the effect of each basic block to produce the local information and then use it in the global analysis, producing information that corresponds to the entry and exit of each basic block. The resulting global information can then be combined with the local information to produce the set of definitions that reach the beginning of each intermediate-language construct within any basic block. This has the effect of reducing the number of steps needed to compute the data-flow information, often significantly, in return for the generally small expense of propagating the information from the beginning (or end) of a block to a point within it when it is needed there.

Similarly, most of the data-flow analyses we consider concern sets of various kinds of program objects (constants, variables, definitions, expressions, etc.) and the determination of what set of such objects is valid at any particular point in a procedure. What kind of objects and what is meant by valid depend on the particular problem. In the next few paragraphs, we formulate the reaching definitions problem in two ways, as a problem over sets and as a problem over bit vectors, which are simply a convenient representation for sets for use in a computer, since set union, intersection, and complement correspond directly to bitwise or, and, and not on bit vectors.

Reaching definitions analysis can be done in the classic form known as an iterative forward bit-vector problem—"iterative" because we construct a collection of data-flow equations to represent the information flow and solve it by iteration from an appropriate set of initial values; "forward" because the information flow is in the direction of execution along the control-flow edges in the program; and "bit-

```
1    int g(int m, int i);

2    int f(n)
3        int n;
4    {   int i = 0, j;
5        if (n == 1) i = 2;
6        while (n > 0) {
7            j = i + 1;
8            n = g(n,i);
9        }
10       return j;
11   }
```

FIG. 8.1 Example of undecidability of reaching definitions and dependence on input values.

vector" because we can represent each definition by a 1 (meaning it may reach the given point) or a 0 (meaning it does not) and, hence, the collection of all definitions that may reach a point by a sequence or vector of bits.

In general, as for most of the data-flow analysis problems we deal with, it is recursively undecidable whether a definition *actually* reaches some other point. Also, whether a definition reaches a particular point may depend on the input data. For example, in the C code in Figure 8.1, whether the definition of i in the declaration in line 4 actually reaches the uses in lines 7 and 8 depends on the value of the parameter n of function f( ), and whether the definition of j in line 7 actually reaches the use in the return in line 10 depends on whether the while loop terminates, which is, in general, recursively undecidable. Thus, we distinguish between what we can determine to be false on the one hand and what we either know to be true or cannot determine on the other. Since optimizations based on reaching definitions depend on what may be true, we keep to the side of conservatism, putting the preservation of correctness of the program ahead of aggressiveness of optimization.

Table 8.1 gives the correspondence between bit positions and definitions in the flowchart in Figure 7.3. Thus, a vector of eight bits can be used to represent which definitions reach the beginning of each basic block in the program.

Clearly, the appropriate initial condition is that none of the definitions reaches the entry node, so the set of definitions valid on entry to the entry block is

$$RCHin(\text{entry}) = \emptyset$$

or as an eight-bit vector,

$$RCHin(\text{entry}) = \langle 00000000 \rangle$$

Further, since we are trying to determine which definitions *may* reach a particular point, it is a conservative (but unnecessary) assumption to initialize

$$RCHin(i) = \emptyset \quad \text{for all } i$$

or

$$RCHin(i) = \langle 00000000 \rangle \quad \text{for all } i$$

TABLE 8.1 Correspondence between bit-vector positions, definitions, and basic blocks for the flowchart in Figure 7.3.

Bit Position	Definition	Basic Block
1	m in node 1	B1
2	f0 in node 2	
3	f1 in node 3	
4	i in node 5	B3
5	f2 in node 8	B6
6	f0 in node 9	
7	f1 in node 10	
8	i in node 11	

Now we must figure out what effect each node in the flowgraph has on each bit in the bit vectors. If a MIR instruction redefines the variable represented by the given bit position, then it is said to *kill* the definition; otherwise it *preserves* it. This suggests that we define sets (and corresponding bit vectors) called $PRSV(i)$ that represent the definitions preserved by block i. It is easy to see that, as sets (using the bit positions to represent the definitions),

$$PRSV(\text{B1}) = \{4, 5, 8\}$$
$$PRSV(\text{B3}) = \{1, 2, 3, 5, 6, 7\}$$
$$PRSV(\text{B6}) = \{1\}$$
$$PRSV(i) \quad = \{1, 2, 3, 4, 5, 6, 7, 8\} \quad \text{for } i \neq \text{B1}, \text{B3}, \text{B6}$$

and, as bit vectors (counting from the left end),

$$PRSV(\text{B1}) = \langle 00011001 \rangle$$
$$PRSV(\text{B3}) = \langle 11101110 \rangle$$
$$PRSV(\text{B6}) = \langle 10000000 \rangle$$
$$PRSV(i) \quad = \langle 11111111 \rangle \quad \text{for } i \neq \text{B1}, \text{B3}, \text{B6}$$

For example, the 0 in bit position seven of $PRSV(\text{B1})$ indicates that basic block B1 kills the definition of f1 in node 10,[1] while the 1 in bit position 5 of $PRSV(\text{B1})$ indicates that B1 does not kill the definition of f2 in node 8. Some texts, such as [AhoS86], use $KILL(\ )$—the negation of $PRSV(\ )$—instead of $PRSV(\ )$.

---

1. In fact, since there is no way for control to flow from the basic block containing node 10, namely, block B6, to block B1, we need not make this bit a 0, but it certainly does not hurt to do so.

Correspondingly, we define sets and bit vectors $GEN(i)$ that give the definitions generated by block i,[2] i.e., that are assigned values in the block and not subsequently killed in it. As sets, the $GEN(\ )$ values are

$GEN(\text{B1}) = \{1, 2, 3\}$

$GEN(\text{B3}) = \{4\}$

$GEN(\text{B6}) = \{5, 6, 7, 8\}$

$GEN(i) \ \ = \emptyset \ \ \text{for } i \neq \text{B1}, \text{B3}, \text{B6}$

and as bit vectors they are

$GEN(\text{B1}) = \langle 11100000 \rangle$

$GEN(\text{B3}) = \langle 00010000 \rangle$

$GEN(\text{B6}) = \langle 00001111 \rangle$

$GEN(i) \ \ = \langle 00000000 \rangle \ \ \text{for } i \neq \text{B1}, \text{B3}, \text{B6}$

Finally, we define sets and corresponding bit vectors $RCHout(i)$ that represent the definitions that reach the end of basic block i. As for $RCHin(i)$, it is sufficient to initialize $RCHout(i)$ by[3]

$RCHout(i) = \emptyset$

or

$RCHout(i) = \langle 00000000 \rangle \ \ \text{for all } i$

Now a definition may reach the end of basic block i if and only if either it occurs in block i and the variable it defines is not redefined in i or it may reach the beginning of i and is preserved by i; or symbolically, using sets and set operations, this is represented by

$RCHout(i) = GEN(i) \cup (RCHin(i) \cap PRSV(i)) \ \ \text{for all } i$

or, using bitwise logical operations on bit vectors, by

$RCHout(i) = GEN(i) \vee (RCHin(i) \wedge PRSV(i)) \ \ \text{for all } i$

A definition may reach the beginning of block i if it may reach the end of some predecessor of i, i.e., for sets,

$$RCHin(i) = \bigcup_{j \in Pred(i)} RCHout(j) \ \ \text{for all } i$$

---

2. We ignore, for the moment, the fact that some definitions of a variable are unambiguous, such as explicit assignments, while others, such as assignments through pointers and procedure calls, are ambiguous in the sense that they may or may not affect a particular variable, and we may not be able to determine whether they do. No ambiguous definitions occur in this procedure.

3. As we shall see, this is actually unnecessary: since each $RCHout(i)$ is computed from the $RCHin(i)$, $GEN(i)$, and $PRSV(i)$ for the same block, we really need not initialize the $RCHout(\ )$ values at all.

or, for bit vectors,

$$RCHin(i) = \bigvee_{j \in Pred(i)} RCHout(j) \quad \text{for all } i$$

To solve the system of (bit-vector) equations for $RCHin(i)$ and $RCHout(i)$, we simply initialize the $RCHin(i)$ to the values given above and iterate application of the equations until no further changes result. To understand why iteration produces an acceptable solution to the system of equations, we require a general introduction to lattices and fixed-point iteration, which is given in the next section. After one application of the equations, we have

$RCHout(\text{entry})$	$= \langle 00000000 \rangle$	$RCHin(\text{entry})$	$= \langle 00000000 \rangle$
$RCHout(\text{B1})$	$= \langle 11100000 \rangle$	$RCHin(\text{B1})$	$= \langle 00000000 \rangle$
$RCHout(\text{B2})$	$= \langle 11100000 \rangle$	$RCHin(\text{B2})$	$= \langle 11100000 \rangle$
$RCHout(\text{B3})$	$= \langle 11110000 \rangle$	$RCHin(\text{B3})$	$= \langle 11100000 \rangle$
$RCHout(\text{B4})$	$= \langle 11110000 \rangle$	$RCHin(\text{B4})$	$= \langle 11110000 \rangle$
$RCHout(\text{B5})$	$= \langle 11110000 \rangle$	$RCHin(\text{B5})$	$= \langle 11110000 \rangle$
$RCHout(\text{B6})$	$= \langle 10001111 \rangle$	$RCHin(\text{B6})$	$= \langle 11110000 \rangle$
$RCHout(\text{exit})$	$= \langle 11110000 \rangle$	$RCHin(\text{exit})$	$= \langle 11110000 \rangle$

After iterating one more time, we have

$RCHout(\text{entry})$	$= \langle 00000000 \rangle$	$RCHin(\text{entry})$	$= \langle 00000000 \rangle$
$RCHout(\text{B1})$	$= \langle 11100000 \rangle$	$RCHin(\text{B1})$	$= \langle 00000000 \rangle$
$RCHout(\text{B2})$	$= \langle 11100000 \rangle$	$RCHin(\text{B2})$	$= \langle 11100000 \rangle$
$RCHout(\text{B3})$	$= \langle 11110000 \rangle$	$RCHin(\text{B3})$	$= \langle 11100000 \rangle$
$RCHout(\text{B4})$	$= \langle 11111111 \rangle$	$RCHin(\text{B4})$	$= \langle 11111111 \rangle$
$RCHout(\text{B5})$	$= \langle 11111111 \rangle$	$RCHin(\text{B5})$	$= \langle 11111111 \rangle$
$RCHout(\text{B6})$	$= \langle 10001111 \rangle$	$RCHin(\text{B6})$	$= \langle 11111111 \rangle$
$RCHout(\text{exit})$	$= \langle 11111111 \rangle$	$RCHin(\text{exit})$	$= \langle 11111111 \rangle$

and iterating one more time produces no more changes, so the above values are the solution.

Note that the rules for performing the iteration never change a 1 to a 0, i.e., they are monotone, so we are guaranteed that the iteration process ultimately does terminate.

The solution to the data-flow equations gives us a global view of which definitions of variables may reach which uses. For example, it shows that the definition of f0 in basic block B1 may reach the first use of f0 in block B6 and that along the execution path through basic block B2, the variables i and f2 are never defined. One way we might use this information to optimize the program is to avoid allocation of storage (and registers) for i and f2 along the path through B2.

Note that, while it may be easier to understand the data-flow equations as presented above, there is actually no theoretical reason to have both $RCHin(\ )$ and

RCHout( ) functions. Instead, we can substitute the equations for *RCHout( )* into the equations for *RCHin( )* to get the simpler system of equations

$$RCHin(i) = \bigcup_{j \in Pred(i)} (GEN(j) \cup (RCHin(j) \cap PRSV(j))) \quad \text{for all } i$$

or

$$RCHin(i) = \bigvee_{j \in Pred(i)} (GEN(j) \vee (RCHin(j) \wedge PRSV(j))) \quad \text{for all } i$$

with exactly the same solution. However, there is a practical trade-off involved in choosing to use both *RCHin( )* and *RCHout( )* functions or only one of them. If we employ both, we double the space required to represent the data-flow information, but we reduce the amount of computation required; with only the *RCHin( )* functions saved, we need to compute

$$GEN(j) \cup (RCHin(j) \cap PRSV(j))$$

repeatedly, even if *RCHin(j)* has not changed, while if we use both functions, we have its value available immediately.

8.2   Basic Concepts: Lattices, Flow Functions, and Fixed Points

We now proceed to define the conceptual framework underlying data-flow analysis. In each case, a data-flow analysis is performed by operating on elements of an algebraic structure called a lattice. Elements of the lattice represent abstract properties of variables, expressions, or other programming constructs for all possible executions of a procedure—independent of the values of the input data and, usually, independent of the control-flow paths through the procedure. In particular, most data-flow analyses take no account of whether a conditional is true or false and, thus, of whether the `then` or `else` branch of an `if` is taken, or of how many times a loop is executed. We associate with each of the possible control-flow and computational constructs in a procedure a so-called flow function that abstracts the effect of the construct to its effect on the corresponding lattice elements.

In general, a *lattice* L consists of a set of values and two operations called *meet*, denoted $\sqcap$, and *join,* denoted $\sqcup$, that satisfy several properties, as follows:

1. For all $x, y \in L$, there exist unique z and $w \in L$ such that $x \sqcap y = z$ and $x \sqcup y = w$ (closure).

2. For all $x, y \in L$, $x \sqcap y = y \sqcap x$ and $x \sqcup y = y \sqcup x$ (commutativity).

3. For all $x, y, z \in L$, $(x \sqcap y) \sqcap z = x \sqcap (y \sqcap z)$ and $(x \sqcup y) \sqcup z = x \sqcup (y \sqcup z)$ (associativity).

4. There are two unique elements of L called *bottom*, denoted $\bot$, and *top*, denoted $\top$, such that for all $x \in L$, $x \sqcap \bot = \bot$ and $x \sqcup \top = \top$ (existence of unique top and bottom elements).

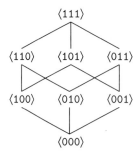

FIG. 8.2 **BV**^{3}, the lattice of three-element bit vectors.

Many lattices, including all the ones we use except the one for constant propagation (see Section 12.6), are also *distributive*, i.e., for all x, y, $z \in L$,

$$(x \sqcap y) \sqcup z = (x \sqcap z) \sqcup (y \sqcap z) \quad \text{and} \quad (x \sqcup y) \sqcap z = (x \sqcap z) \sqcup (y \sqcap z)$$

Most of the lattices we use have bit vectors as their elements and meet and join are bitwise and and or, respectively. The bottom element of such a lattice is the bit vector of all zeros and top is the vector of all ones. We use **BV**^{n} to denote the lattice of bit vectors of length n. For example, the eight-bit vectors in our example in Section 8.1 form a lattice with $\bot = \langle 00000000 \rangle$ and $\top = \langle 11111111 \rangle$. The join of two bit vectors is the bit vector that has a one wherever either of them has a one and a zero otherwise. For example,

$$\langle 00101111 \rangle \sqcup \langle 01100001 \rangle = \langle 01101111 \rangle$$

A lattice similar to the one in the reaching definitions example, but with vectors of only three bits, is shown in Figure 8.2.

There are several ways to construct lattices by combining simpler ones. The first of these methods is the product operation, which combines lattices elementwise. The *product* of two lattices L_1 and L_2 with meet operators $\sqcap_1$ and $\sqcap_2$, respectively, which is written $L_1 \times L_2$, is $\{\langle x_1, x_2 \rangle \mid x_1 \in L_1, x_2 \in L_2\}$, with the meet operation defined by

$$\langle x_1, x_2 \rangle \sqcap \langle y_1, y_2 \rangle = \langle x_1 \sqcap_1 y_1, x_2 \sqcap_2 y_2 \rangle$$

The join operator is defined analogously. The product operation generalizes in the natural way to more than two lattices and, in particular, what we have already referred to as **BV**^{n} is just the product of n copies of the trivial lattice **BV** $=$ **BV**$^1 = \{0, 1\}$ with bottom 0 and top 1.

In some cases, bit vectors are undesirable or insufficient to represent the needed information. A simple example for which they are undesirable is for constant propagation of integer values, for which we use a lattice based on the one called **ICP** shown in Figure 8.3. Its elements are $\bot$, $\top$, all the integers, and the Booleans, and it is defined by the following properties:

1. For all $n \in$ **ICP**, $n \sqcap \bot = \bot$.

2. For all $n \in$ **ICP**, $n \sqcup \top = \top$.

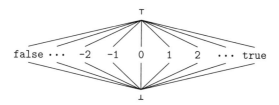

FIG. 8.3 Integer constant-propagation lattice ICP.

3. For all $n \in$ ICP, $n \sqcap n = n \sqcup n = n$.

4. For all integers and Booleans $m, n \in$ ICP, if $m \neq n$, then $m \sqcap n = \bot$ and $m \sqcup n = \top$.

In Figure 8.3, the meet of any two elements is found by following the lines downward from them until they meet, and the join is found by following the lines upward until they join.

Bit vectors could be used for constant propagation, as follows. Define *Var* to be the set of variable names of interest, and let **Z** denote the set of integers. The set of functions from finite subsets of *Var* to **Z** includes a representative for each possible assignment of constant values to the variables used in any program. Each such function can be represented as an infinite bit vector consisting of a position for each $\langle v, c \rangle$ pair for some $v \in$ *Var* and constant $c \in$ **Z**, where the position contains a 1 if v has value c and a 0 otherwise. The set of such infinite bit vectors forms a lattice under the usual lattice ordering on bit vectors. Clearly this lattice is much more complex than **ICP**: its elements are infinite bit vectors, and not only is it infinitely wide, like **ICP**, but it is also infinitely high, which makes this formulation very undesirable.

Some data-flow analysis problems require very much more complex lattices than bit vectors, such as the two used by Jones and Muchnick [JonM81a] to describe the "shapes" of LISP-like data structures, one of which consists of elements that are regular tree grammars and the other of which consists of complex graphs.

It should be clear from the graphic presentation of the lattices that the meet and join operations induce a partial order on the values, which is written $\sqsubseteq$. It can be defined in terms of the meet operation as

$$x \sqsubseteq y \text{ if and only if } x \sqcap y = x$$

or it can be defined dually in terms of the join operation. The related operations $\sqsubset$, $\sqsupset$, and $\sqsupseteq$ are defined correspondingly. The following properties of $\sqsubseteq$ (and corresponding ones for the other ordering relations) are easily derived from the definitions of meet and join:

1. For all x, y, z, if $x \sqsubseteq y$ and $y \sqsubseteq z$, then $x \sqsubseteq z$ (transitivity).

2. For all x, y, if $x \sqsubseteq y$ and $y \sqsubseteq x$, then $x = y$ (antisymmetry).

3. For all x, $x \sqsubseteq x$ (reflexivity).

A function mapping a lattice to itself, written as $f: \mathbf{L} \to \mathbf{L}$, is *monotone* if for all x, y $x \sqsubseteq y \Rightarrow f(x) \sqsubseteq f(y)$. For example, the function $f: \mathbf{BV}^3 \to \mathbf{BV}^3$ as defined by

$$f(\langle x_1 x_2 x_3 \rangle) = \langle x_1 1 x_3 \rangle$$

is monotone, while the function $g: \mathbf{BV}^3 \to \mathbf{BV}^3$ as defined by $g(\langle 000 \rangle) = \langle 100 \rangle$ and $g(\langle x_1 x_2 x_3 \rangle) = \langle 000 \rangle$ otherwise is not.

The *height* of a lattice is the length of the longest strictly ascending chain in it, i.e., the maximal n such that there exist $x_1, x_2, \ldots, x_n$ such that

$$\perp = x_1 \sqsubset x_2 \sqsubset \ldots \sqsubset x_n = \top$$

For example, the heights of the lattices in Figures 8.2 and 8.3 are 4 and 3, respectively. As for other lattice-related concepts, height may be dually defined by descending chains. Almost all the lattices we use have finite height, and this, combined with monotonicity, guarantees termination of our data-flow analysis algorithms. For lattices of infinite height, it is essential to show that the analysis algorithms halt.

In considering the computational complexity of a data-flow algorithm, another notion is important, namely, effective height relative to one or more functions. The *effective height* of a lattice $\mathbf{L}$ relative to a function $f: \mathbf{L} \to \mathbf{L}$ is the length of the longest strictly ascending chain obtained by iterating application of $f(\ )$, i.e., the maximal n such that there exist $x_1, x_2 = f(x_1), x_3 = f(x_2), \ldots, x_n = f(x_{n-1})$ such that

$$x_1 \sqsubset x_2 \sqsubset x_3 \sqsubset \ldots \sqsubset x_n \sqsubseteq \top$$

The effective height of a lattice relative to a set of functions is the maximum of its effective heights for each function.

A *flow function* models, for a particular data-flow analysis problem, the effect of a programming language construct as a mapping from the lattice used in the analysis to itself. For example, the flow function for block B1 in the reaching definitions analysis in Section 8.1 is the function $F_{B1}: \mathbf{BV}^8 \to \mathbf{BV}^8$ given by

$$F_{B1}(\langle x_1 x_2 x_3 x_4 x_5 x_6 x_7 x_8 \rangle) = \langle 1 1 x_3 x_4 x_5 x_6 x_7 x_8 \rangle$$

We require that all flow functions be monotone. This is reasonable in that the purpose of a flow function is to model the information about a data-flow problem provided by a programming construct and, hence, it should not decrease the information already obtained. Monotonicity is also essential to demonstrating that each analysis we consider halts and to providing computational complexity bounds for it.

The programming construct modeled by a particular flow function may vary, according to our requirements, from a single expression to an entire procedure. Thus, the function that transforms each $RCHin(i)$ to $RCHout(i)$ in the example in Section 8.1 may be viewed as a flow function, as may the function that transforms the entire set of $RCHin(i)$s to $RCHout(i)$s.

A *fixed point* of a function $f: \mathbf{L} \to \mathbf{L}$ is an element $z \in \mathbf{L}$ such that $f(z) = z$. For a set of data-flow equations, a fixed point is a solution of the set of equations, since applying the right-hand sides of the equations to the fixed point produces the same value. In many cases, a function defined on a lattice may have more than one fixed point. The simplest example of this is the function $f: \mathbf{BV} \to \mathbf{BV}$ with $f(0) = 0$ and $f(1) = 1$. Clearly, both 0 and 1 are fixed points of this function.

The value that we wish to compute in solving data-flow equations is the so-called *meet-over-all-paths* (MOP) solution. Intuitively, this results from beginning with some prescribed information *Init* at the entry node of a flowgraph (or the exit node for backward flow problems), applying the composition of the appropriate flow functions along all possible paths from the entry (or exit) node to each node in the flowgraph, and forming, for each node, the meet of the results. Expressed in equations, we have the following for a forward flow problem. Let $G = \langle N, E \rangle$ be a flowgraph. Let $Path(B)$ represent the set of all paths from entry to any node $B \in N$ and let p be any element of $Path(B)$. Let $F_B(\ )$ be the flow function representing flow through block B and $F_p(\ )$ represent the composition of the flow functions encountered in following the path p, i.e., if $B1 = \text{entry}, \ldots, Bn = B$ are the blocks making up a particular path p to B, then

$$F_p = F_{Bn} \circ \cdots \circ F_{B1}$$

Let *Init* be the lattice value associated with the entry block. Then the meet-over-all-paths solution is

$$MOP(B) = \bigsqcap_{p \in Path(B)} F_p(Init) \text{ for } B = \text{entry}, B1, \ldots, Bn, \text{exit}$$

Analogous equations express the meet-over-all-paths solution for a backward flow problem.

Unfortunately, it is not difficult to show that for an arbitrary data-flow analysis problem in which the flow functions are only guaranteed to be monotone, there may be no algorithm that computes the meet-over-all-paths solution for all possible flowgraphs. What our algorithms do compute is called the *maximum fixed point* (MFP) solution, which is simply the solution to the data-flow equations that is maximal in the ordering of the underlying lattice, i.e., the solution that provides the most information. Kildall [Kild73] showed that for data-flow problems in which all the flow functions are distributive, the general iterative algorithm that we give in Section 8.4 computes the MFP solution and that, in that case, the MFP and MOP solutions are identical. Kam and Ullman [KamU75] generalized this result to show that for data-flow problems in which the flow functions are all monotone but not necessarily distributive, the iterative algorithm produces the MFP solution (but not necessarily the MOP solution).

Before moving on to discuss the types of data-flow problems that are of interest to us and how to solve them, we take a moment to discuss the issue of associating data-flow information with the entry points of basic blocks in the flowgraph, rather than with edges. The former is standard practice in most of the literature and all the compilers we are aware of. However, a few papers associate data-flow information with edges in the flowgraph. This has the effect of producing better information in some cases, essentially because it does not force information at a node with multiple predecessors (or, for backward flow problems, a node with multiple successors) to be merged before it enters the node.

A simple example of a situation in which this produces improved information is the constant-propagation instance shown in Figure 8.4. Clearly, the value assigned to

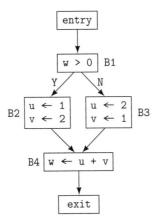

FIG. 8.4 Flowgraph for which associating data-flow information with edges produces better results than associating it with node entries.

w in B4 is the constant 3. Regardless of whether we associate information with node entries or with edges, we know that on exit from both B2 and B3, both u and v have constant values. If we do constant propagation and associate data-flow information with the edges, then we preserve the fact that, on the edge from B2 to B4, u has value 1 and v has value 2, and on the edge from B3 to B4, u has value 2 and v has value 1. This allows the flow function for B4 to combine the distinct values to determine that B4 in turn assigns the constant value 3 to w. On the other hand, if we associate the data-flow information with node entries, then all we know at entry to B4 is that neither u's value nor v's value is a constant (in both cases, the value is either 1 or 2, but the lattice **ICP** doesn't provide a way to distinguish that information from ⊤, and even if it did, it would not be enough for us to determine that w's value is a constant).

8.3   Taxonomy of Data-Flow Problems and Solution Methods

Data-flow analysis problems are categorized along several dimensions, including the following:

1. the information they are designed to provide;

2. whether they are relational or involve independent attributes;

3. the types of lattices used in them and the meanings attached to the lattice elements and functions defined on them; and

4. the direction of information flow: in the direction of program execution (forward problems), opposite the direction of execution (backward problems), or in both directions (bidirectional problems).

Almost all the problems we consider are examples of the *independent-attribute* type, i.e., they assign a lattice element to each object of interest, be it a variable definition, expression computation, or whatever. Only a few, such as the structure type determination problem described in Section 8.14, require that the data-flow state of a procedure at each point be expressed by a relation that describes the relationships among the values of the variables, or something similar. The relational problems have much greater computational complexity than the independent-attribute problems.

Similarly, almost all the problems we consider are one-directional, either *forward* or *backward*. *Bidirectional* problems require forward and backward propagation at the same time and are significantly more complicated to formulate, understand, and solve than one-directional problems. Happily, in optimization, bidirectional problems are rare. The most important instance is the classic formulation of partial-redundancy elimination, mentioned in Section 13.3, and even it has been superseded by the more modern version presented there, which uses only unidirectional analyses.

Among the most important data-flow analyses for program optimization are those described below. In each case, we give a fuller characterization of the problem and the equations for it when we describe the first optimization for which it is useful.

Reaching Definitions

This determines which definitions of a variable (i.e., assignments to it) may reach each use of the variable in a procedure. As we have seen, it is a forward problem that uses a lattice of bit vectors with one bit corresponding to each definition of a variable.

Available Expressions

This determines which expressions are available at each point in a procedure, in the sense that on every path from the entry to the point there is an evaluation of the expression, and none of the variables occurring in the expression are assigned values between the last such evaluation on a path and the point. Available expressions is a forward problem that uses a lattice of bit vectors in which a bit is assigned to each definition of an expression.

Live Variables

This determines for a given variable and a given point in a program whether there is a use of the variable along some path from the point to the exit. This is a backward problem that uses bit vectors in which each use of a variable is assigned a bit position.

Upwards Exposed Uses

This determines what uses of variables at particular points are reached by particular definitions. It is a backward problem that uses bit vectors with a bit position corresponding to each use of a variable. It is the dual of reaching definitions in that one connects definitions to uses, while the other connects uses to definitions. Note that these are typically different, as shown by the example in Figure 8.5, where the definition of x in B2 reaches the uses in B4 and B5, while the use in B5 is reached by the definitions in B2 and B3.

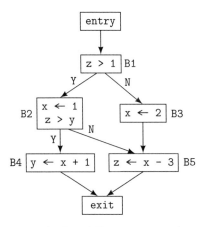

FIG. 8.5 Example that differentiates reaching definitions from upwards exposed uses.

Copy-Propagation Analysis

This determines that on every path from a copy assignment, say $x \leftarrow y$, to a use of variable x there are no assignments to y. This is a forward problem that uses bit vectors in which each bit position represents a copy assignment.

Constant-Propagation Analysis

This determines that on every path from an assignment of a constant to a variable, say, $x \leftarrow const$, to a use of x the only assignments to x assign it the value *const*. This is a forward flow problem. In its classic formulation, it uses vectors with one position per variable and values drawn from the lattice $\mathbf{ICP}^n$ discussed in Section 8.2, or from a similar lattice with elements chosen from another appropriate data type. In its sparse conditional form (see Section 12.6) it uses a similar lattice, but one lattice value per definition and symbolic execution, rather than simple data-flow analysis.

Partial-Redundancy Analysis

This determines what computations are performed twice (or more times) on some execution path without the operands being modified between the computations. As originally formulated by Morel and Renvoise, it is a bidirectional flow problem that uses bit vectors in which each position represents an expression computation. Their formulation also determines redundant variable definitions and assignments. A more recent formulation of the problem has shown that it can be performed as a series of forward and backward data-flow computations.

The flow-analysis problems listed above are not the only ones encountered in optimization, but they are among the most important.

There are many approaches to solving data-flow problems, including the following (see Section 8.16 for detailed source information):

1. Allen's strongly connected region method;

2. Kildall's iterative algorithm (see Section 8.4);

3. Ullman's $T1$-$T2$ analysis;

4. Kennedy's node-listing algorithm;

5. Farrow, Kennedy, and Zucconi's graph-grammar approach;

6. elimination methods, e.g., interval analysis (see Section 8.8);

7. Rosen's high-level (syntax-directed) approach;

8. structural analysis (see Section 8.7); and

9. slotwise analysis (see Section 8.9).

Here we concentrate on three approaches: (1) the simple iterative approach, with several strategies for determining the order of the iterations; (2) an elimination or control-tree-based method using intervals; and (3) another control-tree-based method using structural analysis. As we shall see, these methods present a range of ease of implementation, speed and space requirements, and ease of incrementally updating the data-flow information to avoid totally recomputing it. We then make a few remarks about other approaches, such as the recently introduced slotwise analysis.

8.4   Iterative Data-Flow Analysis

Iterative analysis is the method we used in the example in Section 8.1 to perform reaching definitions analysis. We present it first because it is the easiest method to implement and, as a result, the one most frequently used. It is also of primary importance because the control-tree-based methods discussed in Section 8.6 need to be able to do iterative analysis (or node splitting or data-flow analysis over a lattice of functions) on improper (or irreducible) regions of code.

We first present an iterative implementation of forward analysis. Methods for backward and bidirectional problems are easy generalizations.

We assume that we are given a flowgraph $G = \langle N, E \rangle$ with `entry` and `exit` blocks in N and desire to compute $in(B), out(B) \in L$ for each $B \in N$ where $in(B)$ represents the data-flow information on entry to B and $out(B)$ represents the data-flow information on exit from B, given by the data-flow equations

$$in(B) = \begin{cases} Init & \text{for } B = \text{entry} \\ \displaystyle\bigcap_{P \in Pred(B)} out(P) & \text{otherwise} \end{cases}$$

$$out(B) = F_B(in(B))$$

where $Init$ represents the appropriate initial value for the data-flow information on entry to the procedure, $F_B(\ )$ represents the transformation of the data-flow information corresponding to executing block B, and $\sqcap$ models the effect of combining the data-flow information on the edges entering a block. Of course, this can also be expressed with just $in(\ )$ functions as

```
      procedure Worklist_Iterate(N,entry,FP,dfin,Init)
          N: in set of Node
          entry: in Node
          FP: in Node ──→ L
          dfin: out Node ──→ L
          Init: in L
      begin
          B, P: Node
          Worklist: set of Node
          effect, totaleffect:L
          dfin(entry) := Init
 *        Worklist := N - {entry}
          for each B ∈ N do
              dfin(B) := ⊤
          od
          repeat
 *            B := ♦Worklist
              Worklist -= {B}
              totaleffect := ⊤
              for each P ∈ Pred(B) do
                  effect := F(P,dfin(P))
                  totaleffect ⊓= effect
                  if dfin(B) ≠ totaleffect then
                      dfin(B) := totaleffect
 *                    Worklist ∪= {B}
                  fi
              od
          until Worklist = ∅
      end    || Worklist_Iterate
```

FIG. 8.6 Worklist algorithm for iterative data-flow analysis (statements that manage the worklist are marked with asterisks).

$$
in(B) = \begin{cases} Init & \text{for } B = \text{entry} \\ \displaystyle\bigcap_{P \in Pred(B)} F_P(in(P)) & \text{otherwise} \end{cases}
$$

If ⊔ models the effect of combining flow information, it is used in place of ⊓ in the algorithm. The value of *Init* is usually ⊤ or ⊥.

The algorithm Worklist_Iterate( ), given in Figure 8.6, uses just *in*( ) functions; the reader can easily modify it to use both *in*( )s and *out*( )s. The strategy is to iterate application of the defining equations given above, maintaining a worklist of blocks whose *in*( ) values have changed on the last iteration, until the worklist is empty; initially the worklist contains all blocks in the flowgraph except entry, since its information will never change. Since the effect of combining information from edges entering a node is being modeled by ⊓, the appropriate initialization for totaleffect is ⊤. The function $F_B(x)$ is represented by F(B,x).

The computational efficiency of this algorithm depends on several things: the lattice **L**, the flow functions $F_B(\ )$, and how we manage the worklist. While the lattice

TABLE 8.2 Flow functions for the flowgraph in Figure 7.4.

$$F_{\text{entry}} = id$$
$$F_{B1}(\langle x_1 x_2 x_3 x_4 x_5 x_6 x_7 x_8 \rangle) = \langle 111 x_4 x_5 00 x_8 \rangle$$
$$F_{B2} = id$$
$$F_{B3}(\langle x_1 x_2 x_3 x_4 x_5 x_6 x_7 x_8 \rangle) = \langle x_1 x_2 x_3 1 x_5 x_6 x_7 0 \rangle$$
$$F_{B4} = id$$
$$F_{B5} = id$$
$$F_{B6}(\langle x_1 x_2 x_3 x_4 x_5 x_6 x_7 x_8 \rangle) = \langle x_1 0001111 \rangle$$

and flow functions are determined by the data-flow problem we are solving, the management of the worklist is independent of it. Note that managing the worklist corresponds to how we implement the statements marked with asterisks in Figure 8.6. The easiest implementation would use a stack or queue for the worklist, without regard to how the blocks are related to each other by the flowgraph structure. On the other hand, if we process all predecessors of a block before processing it, then we can expect to have the maximal effect on the information for that block each time we encounter it. This can be achieved by beginning with an ordering we encountered in the preceding chapter, namely, reverse postorder, and continuing with a queue. Since in postorder a node is not visited until all its depth-first spanning-tree successors have been visited, in reverse postorder it is visited before any of its successors have been. If A is the maximal number of back edges on any acyclic path in a flowgraph G, then $A + 2$ passes through the `repeat` loop are sufficient if we use reverse postorder.[4] Note that it is possible to construct flowgraphs with A on the order of $|N|$, but that this is very rare in practice. In almost all cases $A \leq 3$, and frequently $A = 1$.

As an example of the iterative forward algorithm, we repeat the example we did informally in Section 8.1. The flow functions for the individual blocks are given in Table 8.2, where *id* represents the identity function. The initial value of *dfin(B)* for all blocks is $\langle 00000000 \rangle$. The path-combining operator is ⊔ or bitwise logical or on the bit vectors. The initial worklist is {B1, B2, B3, B4, B5, B6, exit}, in reverse postorder.

Entering the `repeat` loop, the initial value of B is B1, with the worklist becoming {B2, B3, B4, B5, B6, exit}. B1's only predecessor is P = entry, and the result of computing `effect` and `totaleffect` is $\langle 00000000 \rangle$, unchanged from the initial value of dfin(B1), so B1 is not put back into the worklist.

Next, we get B = B2 and the worklist becomes {B3, B4, B5, B6, exit}. The only predecessor of B2 is P = B1, and the result of computing `effect` and `totaleffect` is $\langle 11100000 \rangle$, which becomes the new value of dfin(B2), and B2 is added onto the end of the worklist to produce {B3, B4, B5, B6, exit, B2}.

Next, we get B = B3, and the worklist becomes {B4, B5, B6, exit, B2}. B3 has one predecessor, namely, B1, and the result of computing `effect` and `totaleffect` is $\langle 11100000 \rangle$, which becomes the new value of dfin(B3), and B3 is put back on the end of the worklist.

Then we get B = B4, and the worklist becomes {B5, B6, exit, B2, B3}. B4 has two predecessors, B3 and B6, with B3 contributing $\langle 11110000 \rangle$ to effect, totaleffect, and dfin(B4), and B6 contributing $\langle 00001111 \rangle$, so that the final result of this iteration is dfin(B4) = $\langle 11111111 \rangle$ and the worklist becomes {B5, B6, exit, B2, B3, B4}.

Next, B = B5, and the worklist becomes {B6, exit, B2, B3, B4}. B5 has one predecessor, B4, which contributes $\langle 11111111 \rangle$ to effect, totaleffect, and dfin(B5), and B5 is added onto the end of the worklist.

Next, B = B6, and the worklist becomes {exit, B2, B3, B4, B5}. B6's one predecessor, B4, contributes $\langle 11111111 \rangle$ to dfin(B6), and B6 is put back onto the end of the worklist.

Now exit is removed from the worklist, resulting in {B2, B3, B4, B5, B6}, and its two predecessors, B2 and B5, result in dfin(exit) = $\langle 11111111 \rangle$, and exit is put back onto the end of the worklist.

The reader can check that the body of the repeat loop is executed one more time for each element of the worklist, but that no further changes result in the dfin( ) values computed. One can also check that the results are identical to those computed in Section 8.1.

Converting the algorithm above to handle backward problems is trivial, once we have properly posed a backward problem. We can either choose to associate the data-flow information for a backward problem with the entry to each block or with its exit. To take advantage of the duality between forward and backward problems, we choose to associate it with the exit.

As for a forward analysis problem, we assume that we are given a flowgraph $G = \langle N, E \rangle$ with entry and exit blocks in N and that we desire to compute $out(B) \in L$ for each $B \in N$ where $out(B)$ represents the data-flow information on exit from B, given by the data-flow equations

$$out(B) = \begin{cases} Init & \text{for } B = \text{exit} \\ \displaystyle\prod_{P \in Succ(B)} in(P) & \text{otherwise} \end{cases}$$

$$in(B) = F_B(out(B))$$

where $Init$ represents the appropriate initial value for the data-flow information on exit from the procedure, $F_B( )$ represents the transformation of the data-flow information corresponding to executing block B in reverse, and $\sqcap$ models the effect of combining the data-flow information on the edges exiting a block. As for forward-flow problems, they can also be expressed with just $out( )$ functions as

$$out(B) = \begin{cases} Init & \text{for } B = \text{exit} \\ \displaystyle\prod_{P \in Succ(B)} F_P(out(P)) & \text{otherwise} \end{cases}$$

If $\sqcup$ models the effect of combining flow information, it is used in place of $\sqcap$ in the algorithm.

Now the iterative algorithm for backward problems is identical to that given for forward problems in Figure 8.6, with the appropriate substitutions: *out*( ) for *in*( ), exit for entry, and *Succ*( ) for *Pred*( ). The most effective way to manage the worklist is by initializing it in reverse preorder, and the computational efficiency bound is the same as for the forward iterative algorithm.

8.5   Lattices of Flow Functions

Just as the objects on which we perform a data-flow analysis are best viewed as elements of a lattice, the set of flow functions we use in performing such an analysis also forms a lattice with its meet and join induced by those of the underlying lattice. As we shall see in Section 8.6, the induced lattice of monotone flow functions is very important to formulating the control-tree-based approaches to data-flow analysis.

In particular, let L be a given lattice and let L^F denote the set of all monotone functions from L to L, i.e.,

$f \in L^F$ if and only if $\forall x, y \in L \; x \sqsubseteq y$ implies $f(x) \sqsubseteq f(y)$

Then the induced pointwise meet operation on L^F given by

$\forall f, g \in L^F, \; \forall x \in L \; (f \sqcap g)(x) = f(x) \sqcap g(x)$

and the corresponding induced join and order functions are all easily checked to be well defined, establishing that L^F is indeed a lattice. The bottom and top elements of L^F are $\bot^F$ and $\top^F$, defined by

$\forall x \in L \; \bot^F(x) = \bot$ and $\top^F(x) = \top$

To provide the operations necessary to do control-tree-based data-flow analysis, we need to define one more function in and two more operations on L^F. The additional function is simply the *identity* function *id*, defined by $id(x) = x$, $\forall x \in L$. The two operations are composition and Kleene (or iterative) closure. For any two functions $f, g \in L^F$, the *composition* of f and g, written $f \circ g$, is defined by

$(f \circ g)(x) = f(g(x))$

It is easily shown that L^F is closed under composition. Also, for any $f \in L^F$, we define f^n by

$f^0 = id$ and for $n \geq 1$, $f^n = f \circ f^{n-1}$

The *Kleene closure* of $f \in L^F$, written $f^\star$, is defined by

$\forall x \in L \; f^\star(x) = \lim_{n \to \infty} (id \sqcap f)^n(x)$

Also, as is usual, we define $f^+ = f \circ f^\star$. To show that L^F is closed under Kleene closure, we rely on the fact that our lattices all have finite effective heights under all the functions we use. This implies that if we compute for any $x_0 \in L$ the sequence

$x_{i+1} = (id \sqcap f)(x_i)$

there is an i such that $x_i = x_{i+1}$ and so, clearly, $f^\star(x_0) = x_i$.

It is easy to show that if $\mathbf{L}$ is a lattice of bit vectors, say $\mathbf{BV}^n$, then for every function $f: \mathbf{BV}^n \to \mathbf{BV}^n$, f is *distributive* over meet and join, i.e.,

$$\forall x, y, \ f(x \sqcup y) = f(x) \sqcup f(y) \ \text{ and } \ f(x \sqcap y) = f(x) \sqcap f(y)$$

Also, as long as the various bit positions change independently of each other, as is the case for all the bit-vector analyses we consider, $\mathbf{BV}^n$ has effective height 1, i.e., $f \circ f = f$, so $f^* = id \sqcap f$. As we shall see in the next section, this makes control-tree-based data-flow analyses that are representable by bit vectors very efficient.

8.6 Control-Tree-Based Data-Flow Analysis

The algorithms for *control-tree-based data-flow analysis,* namely, interval analysis and structural analysis, are very similar in that they are both based on the use of the control trees discussed in Sections 7.6 and 7.7. They are significantly harder to implement than iterative methods—requiring node splitting, iteration, or solving of a data-flow problem on the lattice of monotone functions to handle improper regions, if they occur—but they have the advantage of being more easily adapted to a form that allows for incremental updating of the data-flow information as a program is changed by optimizing transformations.

As a whole, control-tree-based methods are known, for historical reasons, as *elimination methods*. They involve making two passes over the control tree for a procedure, which is assumed to have been built by either structural or interval control-flow analysis, as mentioned above. In each pass, they visit each node in the control tree: in the first pass, performed bottom up, i.e., starting from the basic blocks, they construct a flow function that represents the effect of executing the part of the procedure that is represented by that portion of the control tree; in the second pass, performed top down, i.e., starting from the abstract node representing the whole procedure and from initial information corresponding to either the entry (for forward problems) or the exit (for backward problems), they construct and evaluate data-flow equations that propagate the data-flow information into and through the region represented by each control-tree node, using the flow functions constructed in the first pass.

8.7 Structural Analysis

Structural analysis uses the detailed information about control structures developed by structural control-flow analysis to produce corresponding data-flow equations that represent the data-flow effects of the control structures. We begin with it because it is simpler to describe and understand, and because, once we have all the mechanisms we need for it, those needed for interval analysis are simply a subset of them.

8.7.1 Structural Analysis: Forward Problems

To begin with, we assume that we are performing a forward analysis—as we shall see, backward analyses are a bit trickier since the control-flow constructs each have

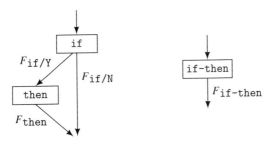

FIG. 8.7 Flow functions for structural analysis of an `if-then` construct.

a single entry, but may have multiple exits. Also, we assume, as for our iterative algorithm, that the effect of combining data-flow information where several control-flow paths merge is modeled by $\sqcap$.

In performing a structural data-flow analysis, most of the abstract graphs we encounter in the first pass are simple regions of the types shown schematically in Figures 7.35 and 7.36. The flow function F_B for a basic block is the same as it is for iterative analysis—it depends only on the problem being solved and on the contents of the basic block.

Now, assume that we have an `if-then` construct, as shown in Figure 8.7, with the flow functions for each construct given on the edges leaving it. Then, the flow function $F_{if\text{-}then}$ constructed for it in the first pass is related to the flow functions for the components of the `if-then` as follows:

$$F_{if\text{-}then} = (F_{then} \circ F_{if/Y}) \sqcap F_{if/N}$$

i.e., the effect of executing the `if-then` construct is the result of combining (by the path-combining operator $\sqcap$) the effect of executing the `if` part and exiting it on the Y branch followed by executing the `then` part, with the effect of executing the `if` part and exiting it on the N branch.

Note that we can choose either to distinguish the Y and N exits from the `if` and to have distinct flow functions $F_{if/Y}$ and $F_{if/N}$ for them, or not. Had we chosen not to distinguish them, as in our presentation of iterative analysis above, we would simply have a single flow function for the `if`, namely, F_{if}, rather than $F_{if/Y}$ and $F_{if/N}$, i.e., we would have

$$F_{if\text{-}then} = (F_{then} \circ F_{if}) \sqcap F_{if} = (F_{then} \sqcap id) \circ F_{if}$$

Either approach is legitimate—the former may yield more precise information than the latter, in case the branches of the `if` discriminate among data-flow values of interest to us, as for example in constant propagation or bounds-checking analysis. In our examples below, however, we use the latter approach, as is customary.

The data-flow equations constructed in the second pass tell us how, given data-flow information entering the `if-then` construct, to propagate it to the entry of each of the substructures. They are relatively transparent:

$$in(\text{if}) \quad = in(\text{if-then})$$

$$in(\text{then}) = F_{if/Y}(in(\text{if}))$$

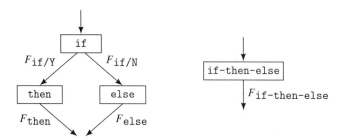

FIG. 8.8 Flow functions for structural analysis of an `if-then-else` construct.

or, if we choose not to distinguish exits:

$$in(\texttt{if}) \quad = in(\texttt{if-then})$$

$$in(\texttt{then}) = F_{\texttt{if}}(in(\texttt{if}))$$

The first of these equations can be read as saying that on entry to the `if` part, we have the same data-flow information that we have on entry to the `if-then` construct, and the second as saying that on entry to the `then` part, we have the result of transforming the information on entry to the `if` by the data-flow effect of the `if` part, exiting it on the Y branch. The second pair is identical, except for not distinguishing the exits from the `if` part.

Next, we consider how to extend this to an `if-then-else` construct, and then to a `while` loop. The form of an `if-then-else` is shown in Figure 8.8 and the functions are an easy generalization of those for the `if-then` case. The flow function $F_{\texttt{if-then-else}}$ constructed in the first pass is related to the flow functions for the components as follows:

$$F_{\texttt{if-then-else}} = (F_{\texttt{then}} \circ F_{\texttt{if/Y}}) \sqcap (F_{\texttt{else}} \circ F_{\texttt{if/N}})$$

and the propagation functions constructed in the second pass are

$$in(\texttt{if}) \quad = in(\texttt{if-then-else})$$

$$in(\texttt{then}) = F_{\texttt{if/Y}}(in(\texttt{if}))$$

$$in(\texttt{else}) = F_{\texttt{if/N}}(in(\texttt{if}))$$

For a `while` loop, we have the form shown in Figure 8.9. In the bottom-up pass, the flow function that expresses the result of iterating the loop once and coming back to its entry is $F_{\texttt{body}} \circ F_{\texttt{while/Y}}$, so the result of doing this an arbitrary number of times is given by this function's Kleene closure

$$F_{\texttt{loop}} = (F_{\texttt{body}} \circ F_{\texttt{while/Y}})^{\star}$$

and the result of executing the entire `while` loop is given by executing the `while` and body blocks repetitively, followed by executing the `while` block and exiting it on the N branch, i.e.,

$$F_{\texttt{while-loop}} = F_{\texttt{while/N}} \circ F_{\texttt{loop}}$$

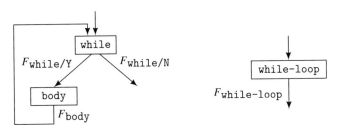

FIG. 8.9 Flow functions for structural analysis of a while loop.

Note that in the most common case, namely, a bit-vector problem,

$$(F_{\text{body}} \circ F_{\text{while/Y}})^*$$

is simply

$$id \sqcap (F_{\text{body}} \circ F_{\text{while/Y}})$$

but that the equations above are valid regardless of the forward-flow problem being solved. In the top-down pass, we have for the while loop

$$in(\text{while}) = F_{\text{loop}}(in(\text{while-loop}))$$

$$in(\text{body}) \ = F_{\text{while/Y}}(in(\text{while}))$$

since the while part can be reached either from outside the loop or by iterating it, and the body can be reached only by entering the loop, executing the while and body blocks some number of times (possibly zero), and exiting the while block through the Y branch.

Again, if we don't distinguish between the exits, we have

$$F_{\text{loop}} = (F_{\text{body}} \circ F_{\text{while}})^*$$

and the result of executing the entire while loop is given by executing the while and body blocks repetitively, followed by executing the while block and exiting it on the N branch, i.e.,

$$F_{\text{while-loop}} = F_{\text{while}} \circ F_{\text{loop}}$$

$$= F_{\text{while}} \circ (F_{\text{body}} \circ F_{\text{while}})^*$$

$$in(\text{while}) \quad = F_{\text{loop}}(in(\text{while-loop}))$$

$$in(\text{body}) \quad = F_{\text{while}}(in(\text{while}))$$

It should be clear from the if-then and if-then-else cases how to generalize the construction of the equations to a general acyclic region A. In particular, suppose that the abstract nodes making up the acyclic region are $B0, B1, \ldots, Bn$, with $B0$ as the entry node of the region, and with each Bi having exits $Bi/1, \ldots, Bi/e_i$ (of course, in most cases $e_i = 1$, and only very rarely is it larger than 2). Associate a forward-flow function $F_{Bi/e}$ with each Bi/e from it, in the usual way, and let $P(A, Bi_k/e_k)$

denote the set of all possible paths from the entry of A to some abstract node's exit Bi_k/e_k in A. For the bottom-up pass, given the path

$$p = B0/e_0, Bi_1/e_1, \ldots, Bi_k/e_k \in P(A, Bi_k/e_k)$$

the composite flow function for the path is

$$F_p = F_{Bi_k/e_k} \circ \cdots \circ F_{Bi_1/e_1} \circ F_{Bi_0/e_0}$$

and the flow function corresponding to all possible paths from the entry point of A to node exit Bi_k/e_k is

$$F_{(A,Bi_k/e_k)} = \bigcap_{p \in P(A,Bi_k/e_k)} F_p$$

For the top-down pass, for the entry to Bi, for $i \neq 0$, let $P_p(A, Bi)$ denote the set of all $P(A, Bj/e)$ such that $Bj \in Pred(Bi)$ and exit Bj/e leads to Bi. Then

$$in(Bi) = \begin{cases} in(A) & \text{for } i = 0 \\ \bigcap\limits_{P(A,Bj/e) \in P_p(A,Bi)} F_{(A,Bj/e)}(in(A)) & \text{otherwise} \end{cases}$$

For a general cyclic but proper region C, there is a single back edge leading from some block Bc to the entry block $B0$. If we remove the back edge, the result is an acyclic region. Proceeding as above, we construct flow functions that correspond to following all possible paths from C's entry to Bi_k/e_k in the acyclic region that results from removing the back edge. This gives us a collection of flow functions $F_{(C,Bi_k/e_k)}$ and, in particular, if Bc/e is the tail of the back edge, a function

$$F_{iter} = F_{(C,Bc/e)}$$

that represents the result of performing one iteration of the body of the region. Thus,

$$F_C = F_{iter}^\star$$

represents the overall data-flow effect of executing the region and returning to its entry, and

$$F'_{(C,Bi_k/e_k)} = F_{(C,Bi_k/e_k)} \circ F_C$$

represents the effect of executing the region and exiting it from Bi_k/e_k. Correspondingly, for the top-down pass,

$$in(Bi) = \begin{cases} in(C) & \text{for } i = 0 \\ \bigcap\limits_{P(C,Bj/e) \in P_p(C,Bi)} F'_{(C,Bj/e)}(in(B0)) & \text{otherwise} \end{cases}$$

For an improper region R, in the bottom-up pass we construct a set of equations similar to those for the general acyclic region above that represent the data-flow effect of a path from the region's entry to any point within it. In the top-down pass, we use the functions constructed in the bottom-up pass to propagate the data-flow information to each point within the region in the usual way, starting with the

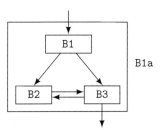

FIG. 8.10 An improper region.

information we have at its entry. The major difference between these equations and those for the acyclic case is that the top-down system for the improper region R is recursive, since the region contains multiple cycles. Given the system of equations, we can proceed in any of three ways, as follows:

1. We can use node splitting, which can turn improper regions into proper ones with (possibly many) more nodes.

2. We can solve the system of equations iteratively, using as initial data whatever the equations for the surrounding constructs yield us at the entry to R, each time we solve the data-flow problem.

3. We can view the system of equations as itself a forward data-flow problem defined, not over $\mathbf{L}$, but over $\mathbf{L}^F$ (the lattice of monotone functions from $\mathbf{L}$ to $\mathbf{L}$ that we discussed in Section 8.5), and solve it, producing flow functions that correspond to the paths within the region; this requires that the underlying lattice $\mathbf{L}$ be finite, which is sufficient for most of the problems we consider, including all the bit-vector ones, but not for constant propagation (see Section 12.6).

For example, consider the simple improper region in Figure 8.10, and suppose that it reduces to the region called B1a, as shown. Then the bottom-up equation for F_{B1a} is

$$F_{\text{B1a}} = ((F_{\text{B3}} \circ F_{\text{B2}})^+ \circ F_{\text{B1}}) \sqcap ((F_{\text{B3}} \circ F_{\text{B2}})^\star \circ F_{\text{B3}} \circ F_{\text{B1}})$$

since a trip through B1a in the forward direction goes either through B1 followed by one or more trips through either the pair made up of B2 followed by B3 or through B1 followed by B3 followed by zero or more iterations of the pair B2 followed by B3. For the top-down equations, one gets the recursive system

$$in(\text{B1}) = in(\text{B1a})$$

$$in(\text{B2}) = F_{\text{B1}}(in(\text{B1})) \sqcap F_{\text{B3}}(in(\text{B3}))$$

$$in(\text{B3}) = F_{\text{B1}}(in(\text{B1})) \sqcap F_{\text{B2}}(in(\text{B2}))$$

or we can solve the equations for $in(\text{B2})$ and $in(\text{B3})$ in the function lattice to produce

$$in(\text{B2}) = (((F_{\text{B3}} \circ F_{\text{B2}})^\star \circ F_{\text{B1}}) \sqcap ((F_{\text{B3}} \circ F_{\text{B2}})^\star \circ F_{\text{B3}} \circ F_{\text{B1}}))(in(\text{B1}))$$

$$= ((F_{\text{B3}} \circ F_{\text{B2}})^\star \circ (id \sqcap F_{\text{B3}}) \circ F_{\text{B1}})(in(\text{B1}))$$

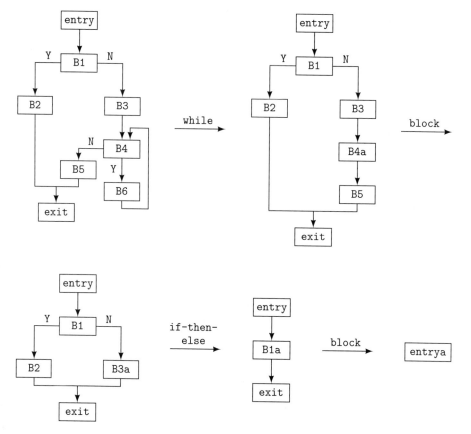

FIG. 8.11 Structural control-flow analysis of our reaching definitions example.

and

$$in(\text{B3}) = (((F_{B2} \circ F_{B3})^\star \circ F_{B1}) \sqcap ((F_{B2} \circ F_{B3})^\star \circ F_{B2} \circ F_{B1}))(in(\text{B1}))$$

$$= ((F_{B3} \circ F_{B2})^\star \circ (id \sqcap F_{B2}) \circ F_{B1})(in(\text{B1}))$$

As an example of a forward structural data-flow analysis, we continue with our reaching definitions instance. First, we must do the structural control-flow analysis for it, as shown in Figure 8.11. The first equation we construct in the bottom-up pass of the data-flow analysis is for the while loop, as follows (and since distinguishing Y and N exits makes no difference in computing reaching definitions, we omit them):

$$F_{B4a} = F_{B4} \circ (F_{B6} \circ F_{B4})^\star = F_{B4} \circ (id \sqcap (F_{B6} \circ F_{B4}))$$

The others are, for the block reduced to B3a:

$$F_{B3a} = F_{B5} \circ F_{B4a} \circ F_{B3}$$

for the if-then-else reduced to B1a:

$$F_{B1a} = (F_{B2} \circ F_{B1}) \sqcap (F_{B3a} \circ F_{B1})$$

and for the block reduced to entrya:

$$F_{\text{entrya}} = F_{\text{exit}} \circ F_{\text{B1a}} \circ F_{\text{entry}}$$

As we shall see, the last equation is actually not used in the data-flow analysis.

In the top-down pass, we construct for the components of the entrya block the equations

$$in(\text{entry}) = Init$$

$$in(\text{B1a}) \quad = F_{\text{entry}}(in(\text{entry}))$$

$$in(\text{exit}) \quad = F_{\text{B1a}}(in(\text{B1a}))$$

for the if-then-else reduced to B1a:

$$in(\text{B1}) = in(\text{B1a})$$

$$in(\text{B2}) = in(\text{B3}) = F_{\text{B1}}(in(\text{B1a}))$$

for the block reduced to B3a:

$$in(\text{B3}) \quad = in(\text{B3a})$$

$$in(\text{B4a}) = F_{\text{B3}}(in(\text{B4a}))$$

$$in(\text{B5}) \quad = F_{\text{B4a}}(in(\text{B4a}))$$

and for the while loop reduced to B4a:

$$in(\text{B4}) = (F_{\text{B6}} \circ F_{\text{B4}})^{\star}(in(\text{B4a})) = (id \sqcap (F_{\text{B6}} \circ F_{\text{B4}}))(in(\text{B4a}))$$

$$in(\text{B6}) = F_{\text{B4}}(in(\text{B4}))$$

The initial value of $in(\text{entry})$ and the flow functions for the individual blocks are identical to those in the iterative example above. Our first step in solving the equations for the $in(\,)$ values by hand is to simplify the equations for the compound flow functions, as follows:

$$
\begin{aligned}
F_{\text{B4a}} &= F_{\text{B4}} \circ (F_{\text{B6}} \circ F_{\text{B4}})^{\star} \\
&= F_{\text{B4}} \circ (id \sqcap (F_{\text{B6}} \circ F_{\text{B4}})) \\
&= id \circ (id \sqcap (F_{\text{B6}} \circ id)) \\
&= id \sqcap F_{\text{B6}}
\end{aligned}
$$

$$
\begin{aligned}
F_{\text{B3a}} &= F_{\text{B5}} \circ F_{\text{B4a}} \circ F_{\text{B3}} \\
&= id \circ (id \sqcap F_{\text{B6}}) \circ F_{\text{B3}} \\
&= (id \sqcap F_{\text{B6}}) \circ F_{\text{B3}} \\
&= F_{\text{B4a}} \circ F_{\text{B3}}
\end{aligned}
$$

$$
\begin{aligned}
F_{\text{B1a}} &= (F_{\text{B2}} \circ F_{\text{B1}}) \sqcap (F_{\text{B3a}} \circ F_{\text{B1}}) \\
&= (id \circ F_{\text{B1}}) \sqcap ((id \sqcap F_{\text{B6}}) \circ F_{\text{B3}} \circ F_{\text{B1}}) \\
&= F_{\text{B1}} \sqcap ((id \sqcap F_{\text{B6}}) \circ F_{\text{B3}} \circ F_{\text{B1}})
\end{aligned}
$$

TABLE 8.3 *in*( ) values computed by structural analysis for our reaching definitions example.

in(entry)	= ⟨00000000⟩
in(B1)	= ⟨00000000⟩
in(B2)	= ⟨11100000⟩
in(B3)	= ⟨11100000⟩
in(B4)	= ⟨11111111⟩
in(B5)	= ⟨11111111⟩
in(B6)	= ⟨11111111⟩
in(exit)	= ⟨11111111⟩

We then compute the values of *in*( ) starting from *in*(entry) and using the available values of the F_B( ) functions, which results in the values shown in Table 8.3. The reader can check that the *in*( ) values for the individual basic blocks are identical to those computed by the iterative approach (Section 8.1).

8.7.2   Structural Analysis: Backward Problems

As remarked at the beginning of the previous section, backward problems are somewhat harder for structural analysis since the control-flow constructs we use are guaranteed to each have a single entry, but not necessarily a single exit.

For constructs with a single exit, such as the if-then or if-then-else, we can simply "turn the equations around." Given the if-then-else in Figure 8.12, the equation constructed in the bottom-up pass for backward flow through the if-then-else is

$$B_{\texttt{if-then-else}} = (B_{\texttt{if/Y}} \circ B_{\texttt{then}}) \sqcap (B_{\texttt{if/N}} \circ B_{\texttt{else}})$$

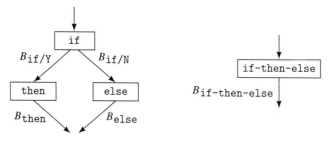

FIG. 8.12 Flow functions for backward structural analysis of an if-then-else construct.

and the equations for the top-down pass are

$$out(\texttt{then}) = out(\texttt{if-then-else})$$

$$out(\texttt{else}) = out(\texttt{if-then-else})$$

$$out(\texttt{if})\quad = B_{\texttt{then}}(out(\texttt{then})) \sqcap B_{\texttt{else}}(out(\texttt{else}))$$

For a general acyclic region A, suppose again that the abstract nodes making up the acyclic region are $B0, B1, \ldots, Bn$. Let $B0$ be the entry node of the region, and let each Bi have entries $Bi/1, \ldots, Bi/e_i$ (of course, in most cases $e_i = 1$ or 2, and only rarely is it larger than 2). Associate a backward-flow function $B_{Bi/e}$ with each Bi and entry e to it, and let $P(Bi_k/e_k, Bi_l/e_l)$ denote the set of all possible (forward) paths from some Bi_k/e_k to Bi_l/e_l. For the bottom-up pass, given some path $p \in P(Bi_k/e_k, Bi_l/e_l)$, the composite backward-flow function for the path is

$$B_p = B_{Bi_k/e_k} \circ \ldots \circ B_{Bi_l/e_l}$$

Define $Exits(A)$ to be the set of exit blocks of region A, i.e., $Bi \in Exits(A)$ if and only if there exists $Bj \in Succ(Bi)$ such that $Bj \notin A$. Then the backward-flow function corresponding to all possible paths from Bi_k/e_k to all possible exits from the region A is

$$B_{(A,Bi_k/e_k)} = \prod_{\substack{p \in P(Bi_k/e_k, Bi_l/e_l) \\ Bi_l \in Exits(A)}} B_p$$

For the top-down pass, for each exit block Bj from A, we have data-flow information $out(Bj)$ associated with it. Let $P_s(A, Bi)$ denote the set of all $P(Bj/e, Bk/f)$ such that $Bj \in Succ(Bi)$ and $Bk \in Exits(A)$. Then

$$out(Bi) = \begin{cases} out(A) & \text{if } Bi \in Exits(A) \\ \displaystyle\prod_{P(Bj/e,Bk/f)\in P_s(A,Bi)} B_{(A,Bj/e)}(out(Bk)) & \text{otherwise} \end{cases}$$

For a general cyclic but proper region C, we combine the method above for an acyclic region with that for forward problems for a cyclic proper region. Again, there is a single back edge leading from some block Bc to the entry block $B0$, and if we remove the back edge, the result is an acyclic region. We construct backward-flow functions that correspond to following all possible (backward) paths from all of C's exits to Bi_k/e_k in the acyclic region that results from removing the back edge. This gives us a collection of flow functions $B_{(C,Bi_k/e_k)}$ and, in particular, if Bc/e is the head of the back edge, a function

$$B_{iter} = B_{(C,Bc/e)}$$

that represents the result of performing one iteration of the body of the region. Thus,

$$B_C = B_{iter}^{\star}$$

represents the overall backward data-flow effect of executing the region and returning to its entry, and

$$B'_{(C,Bi_k/e_k)} = B_{(C,Bi_k/e_k)} \circ B_C$$

represents the backward data-flow effect of executing the region backward, starting from its exits to some node Bi_k within it. Correspondingly, for the top-down pass, for any exit block from Bj of C, we have data-flow information $out(Bj)$ associated with it, and for each node Bi within the region, as follows:

$$out(Bi) = \begin{cases} out(C) & \text{if } Bi \in Exits(C) \\ \displaystyle\bigcap_{P(Bj/e,Bk/f) \in P_s(C,Bi)} B_{(C,Bj/e)}(out(Bk)) & \text{otherwise} \end{cases}$$

where $P_s(C, Bi)$ and $P(Bj/e, Bk/f)$ are as defined for an acyclic region above.

The handling of improper regions for backward problems is analogous to their handling for forward problems. We construct the corresponding recursive set of data-flow equations and either use node splitting, solve them iteratively, or solve them as a data-flow problem over $\mathbf{L^F}$. The one surprise in this is that the data-flow problem over the function lattice turns out to be a forward one, rather than a backward one.

As an example of a backward problem, consider the region A consisting of B0 through B5 in Figure 8.13. Let p be the path B0/1, B1/1, B3/1, B4/1. Then B_p is given by

$$B_p = B_{B0/1} \circ B_{B1/1} \circ B_{B3/1} \circ B_{B4/1}$$

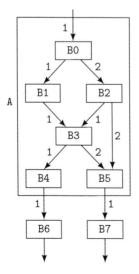

FIG. 8.13 An acyclic region A for backward structural analysis.

The paths from B0/1 to both exits from A are

$$p1 = \text{B0/1, B1/1, B3/1, B4/1}$$

$$p2 = \text{B0/1, B1/1, B3/2, B5/1}$$

$$p3 = \text{B0/2, B2/1, B3/1, B4/1}$$

$$p4 = \text{B0/2, B2/1, B3/2, B5/1}$$

$$p5 = \text{B0/2, B2/2, B5/1}$$

and the backward-flow function from all the exits of A to B0/1 is

$$B_{(A,\text{B0/1})} = B_{p1} \sqcap B_{p2} \sqcap B_{p3} \sqcap B_{p4} \sqcap B_{p5}$$

$$= B_{\text{B0/1}} \circ B_{\text{B1/1}} \circ B_{\text{B3/1}} \circ B_{\text{B4/1}}$$

$$\sqcap \; B_{\text{B0/1}} \circ B_{\text{B1/1}} \circ B_{\text{B3/2}} \circ B_{\text{B5/1}}$$

$$\sqcap \; B_{\text{B0/2}} \circ B_{\text{B2/1}} \circ B_{\text{B3/1}} \circ B_{\text{B4/1}}$$

$$\sqcap \; B_{\text{B0/2}} \circ B_{\text{B2/1}} \circ B_{\text{B3/2}} \circ B_{\text{B5/1}}$$

$$\sqcap \; B_{\text{B0/2}} \circ B_{\text{B2/2}} \circ B_{\text{B5/1}}$$

and the value of $out(\text{B0})$ is

$$out(\text{B0}) = B_{p1}(out(\text{B4})) \sqcap B_{p2}(out(\text{B5})) \sqcap B_{p3}(out(\text{B4})) \sqcap B_{p4}(out(\text{B5}))$$

$$\sqcap \; B_{p5}(out(\text{B5}))$$

$$= B_{\text{B0/1}}(B_{\text{B1/1}}(B_{\text{B3/1}}(B_{\text{B4/1}}(out(\text{B4})))))$$

$$\sqcap \; B_{\text{B0/1}}(B_{\text{B1/1}}(B_{\text{B3/2}}(B_{\text{B5/1}}(out(\text{B5})))))$$

$$\sqcap \; B_{\text{B0/2}}(B_{\text{B2/1}}(B_{\text{B3/1}}(B_{\text{B4/1}}(out(\text{B4})))))$$

$$\sqcap \; B_{\text{B0/2}}(B_{\text{B2/1}}(B_{\text{B3/2}}(B_{\text{B5/1}}(out(\text{B5})))))$$

$$\sqcap \; B_{\text{B0/2}}(B_{\text{B2/2}}(B_{\text{B5/1}}(out(\text{B5}))))$$

8.7.3   Representing Structural Analysis Equations

The equations used in structural analysis are of two kinds: (1) those for the simple forms, such as an if-then-else or while loop, which can be represented by code that implements them directly; and (2) those for the complex forms, such as improper regions.

An example of code for a simple structure is given in Figure 8.14. The type Component is intended to contain an identifier for each of the possible components of a simple structure; here we have restricted it to the components of an if-then-else. The type FlowFcn represents functions from variables to lattice values. The data-flow analysis assigns such a function to the entry point of each region. The argument r of ComputeF_if_then_else( ) holds a region number; each component of a structure has one. The function Region_No: integer x Component → integer returns the region number of the given component of the given region.

```
Component = enum {if,then,else}
FlowFcn = Var ⟶ Lattice

procedure ComputeF_if_then_else(x,r) returns FlowFcn
   x: in FlowFcn
   r: in integer
begin
   y: FlowFcn
   y := ComputeF_if(x,Region_No(r,if))
   return ComputeF_then(y,Region_No(r,then))
      ⊓ ComputeF_else(y,Region_No(r,else))
end    || ComputeF_if_then_else

procedure ComputeIn_then(x,r) returns FlowFcn
   x: in FlowFcn
   r: in integer
begin
   return ComputeF_if(ComputeIn_if(x,r),r)
end    || ComputeIn_then
```

FIG. 8.14 Code representation of some of the structural data-flow equations for an `if-then-else`.

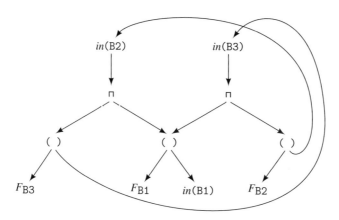

FIG. 8.15 Graphic representation of some of the structural data-flow equations for the region B1a in Figure 8.10.

The complex forms can be represented in a data-flow analyzer in a variety of ways. One relatively simple, time- and space-efficient way is to use graphs with two types of nodes, one type for $in(B)$ values and F_B values (including a special one for id), and the other type representing the operations composition "∘", meet "⊓", join "⊔", Kleene closure "*", non-empty closure "+", and function application "( )". Note that a function-application node represents the application of its left subgraph to its right, and a composition node represents the composition of its left subgraph with its right. Figure 8.15 shows the graphic representation of some of the equations for the improper region B1a in Figure 8.10. This representation can be used by a simple interpreter to apply the equations analyzing the region they correspond to.

Note that the fact that part of a flowgraph requires the interpreted representation does not mean that all of it does. If, for example, we have a simple loop whose body is an improper region that contains an `if-then-else` construct, then we can execute code for the loop and the `if-then-else` and use the interpreter for the improper region.

8.8   Interval Analysis

Now that we have built all the mechanisms to do structural data-flow analysis, performing interval analysis is trivial: it is identical to structural analysis, except that only three kinds of regions appear, namely, general acyclic, proper, and improper ones.

As an example, consider the original flowgraph from Figure 7.4, which we reproduce in Figure 8.16, along with its reduction to intervals. The first step turns the loop comprising B4 and B6 into the node B4a, and the second step reduces the resulting acyclic structure to the single node entrya. The corresponding forward data-flow functions are as follows:

$$F_{B4a} = F_{B4} \circ (F_{B6} \circ F_{B4})^\star$$
$$= F_{B4} \circ (id \sqcap (F_{B6} \circ F_{B4}))$$
$$= id \circ (id \sqcap (F_{B6} \circ id))$$
$$= id \sqcap F_{B6}$$
$$F_{entrya} = F_{exit} \circ (F_{B2} \sqcap (F_{B5} \circ F_{B4a} \circ F_{B3})) \circ F_{B1} \circ F_{entry}$$

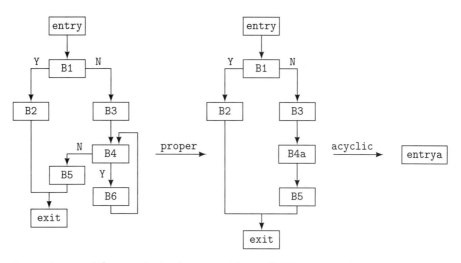

FIG. 8.16   Interval control-flow analysis of our reaching definitions example.

in( ) values computed by interval analysis for our reaching definitions example.

$in(\text{entry})$	$=$	$\langle 00000000 \rangle$
$in(\text{B1})$	$=$	$\langle 00000000 \rangle$
$in(\text{B2})$	$=$	$\langle 11100000 \rangle$
$in(\text{B3})$	$=$	$\langle 11100000 \rangle$
$in(\text{B4})$	$=$	$\langle 11111111 \rangle$
$in(\text{B5})$	$=$	$\langle 11111111 \rangle$
$in(\text{B6})$	$=$	$\langle 11111111 \rangle$
$in(\text{exit})$	$=$	$\langle 11111111 \rangle$

and the equations for *in*( ) are as follows:

$$in(\text{entry}) = in(\text{entrya}) = Init$$

$$in(\text{B1}) = F_{\text{entry}}(in(\text{entry}))$$

$$in(\text{B2}) = F_{\text{B1}}(in(\text{B1}))$$

$$in(\text{B3}) = F_{\text{B1}}(in(\text{B1}))$$

$$in(\text{B4a}) = F_{\text{B3}}(in(\text{B3}))$$

$$in(\text{B4}) = in(\text{B4a}) \sqcap (F_{\text{B6}} \circ F_{\text{B4}})^*(in(\text{B4a}))$$

$$= in(\text{B4a}) \sqcap (id \sqcap (F_{\text{B6}} \circ id))(in(\text{B4a}))$$

$$= in(\text{B4a}) \sqcap in(\text{B4a}) \sqcap F_{\text{B6}}(in(\text{B4a}))$$

$$= in(\text{B4a}) \sqcap F_{\text{B6}}(in(\text{B4a}))$$

$$in(\text{B6}) = F_{\text{B4}}(in(\text{B4}))$$

$$= in(\text{B4})$$

$$in(\text{B5}) = F_{\text{B4a}}(in(\text{B4a}))$$

$$= (F_{\text{B4}} \circ (id \sqcap (F_{\text{B6}} \circ F_{\text{B4}})))(in(\text{B4a}))$$

$$= id(in(\text{B4a})) \sqcap id(F_{\text{B6}}(id(in(\text{B4a}))))$$

$$= in(\text{B4a}) \sqcap F_{\text{B6}}(in(\text{B4a}))$$

$$in(\text{exit}) = F_{\text{B2}}(in(\text{B2})) \sqcap F_{\text{B5}}(in(\text{B5}))$$

The resulting *in*( ) values, shown in Table 8.4, are identical to those computed by the iterative and structural analyses.

8.9   Other Approaches

Dhamdhere, Rosen, and Zadeck describe a new approach to data-flow analysis that they call *slotwise analysis* [DhaR92]. Instead of developing long bit vectors to represent a data-flow characteristic of variables or some other type of program construct and operating on the bit vectors by one of the methods described above, they, in effect, consider each slot of all the bit vectors separately. That is, first they consider what happens to the first slot in all the bit vectors throughout the procedure, then the second, and so on. For some data-flow problems, this approach is useless, since they depend on combining information from different slots in two or more bit vectors to compute the value of a slot in another bit vector. But for many problems, such as reaching definitions and available expressions, each slot at a particular location in a procedure depends only on that slot at other locations. Further, for the available expressions problem, for example, the information in most slots is the default value 0 (= unavailable) in most places. This combination can make a slotwise approach very attractive.

In their paper, the authors show how to apply slotwise analysis to partial-redundancy analysis, an analysis used in several important commercial compilers.

8.10   Du-Chains, Ud-Chains, and Webs

Du- and ud-chains are a sparse representation of data-flow information about variables. A *du-chain* for a variable connects a definition of that variable to all the uses it may flow to, while a *ud-chain* connects a use to all the definitions that may flow to it. That the two are different may be seen by inspecting the example in Figure 8.5. The du-chain for the x defined in block B2 includes the uses in both blocks B4 and B5, while that for the x defined in block B3 includes only the use in block B5. The ud-chain for the use of x in block B4 includes only the definition in B2, while the ud-chain for the use of x in block B5 includes the definitions in both B2 and B3.

Abstractly a du- or ud-chain is a set of pairs of basic-block-position pairs, one for each use or definition, respectively. Concretely, they are generally represented by linked lists. They can be constructed by solving the reaching definitions data-flow problem for a procedure and then using the resulting information to build the linked lists. Once the lists have been constructed, the reaching definitions bit vectors can be deallocated, since the chains represent the same information.

For our purposes, the du- and ud-chains for a procedure are represented by functions of the ICAN type UdDuChain, where

```
UdDu = integer × integer
UdDuChain: (Symbol × UdDu) → set of UdDu
```

A *web* for a variable is the maximal union of intersecting du-chains for the variable. Thus, the web for x in Figure 8.5 includes both definitions and both uses, while in Figure 8.17, there are two webs for x, one consisting of the definitions in B2 and B3 and the uses in B4 and B5 and the other containing the definition of x in B5 and its use in B6. Webs are particularly useful in global register allocation by graph coloring (see Chapter 16)—they are the units that are candidates for allocation to registers.

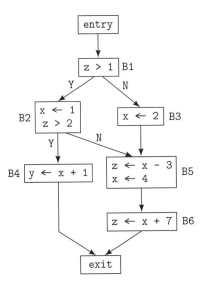

FIG. 8.17 Example of webs.

Note that one effect of constructing webs is to separate uses of a variable with a name like i that may be used over and over again in a procedure as, say, a loop index, but whose uses are disjoint from each other. This can significantly improve register allocation by reducing the range over which a variable may require a register and can improve the effectiveness of other optimizations as well. In particular, optimizations that apply to a single variable or that apply to a limited range of program text, such as strength reduction applied to induction variables, may benefit from this.

8.11   Static Single-Assignment (SSA) Form

Static single-assignment form is a relatively new intermediate representation that effectively separates the values operated on in a program from the locations they are stored in, making possible more effective versions of several optimizations.

A procedure is in *static single-assignment (SSA) form* if every variable assigned a value in it occurs as the target of only one assignment. In SSA form du-chains are explicit in the representation of a procedure: a use of a variable may use the value produced by a particular definition if and only if the definition and use have exactly the same name for the variable in the SSA form of the procedure. This simplifies and makes more effective several kinds of optimizing transformations, including constant propagation, value numbering, invariant code motion and removal, strength reduction, and partial-redundancy elimination. Thus, it is valuable to be able to translate a given representation of a procedure into SSA form, to operate on it and, when appropriate, to translate it back into the original form.

In translating to SSA form, the standard mechanism is to subscript each of the variables and to use so-called ϕ-functions at join points, such as the entry to B5 in

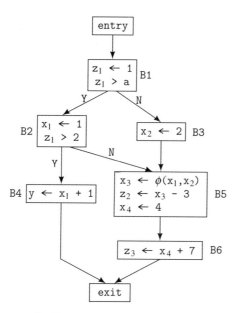

FIG. 8.18 Standard translation of the example in Figure 8.17 into SSA form.

Figure 8.18, to sort out the multiple assignments to a variable. Each ϕ-*function* has as many argument positions as there are versions of the variable coming together at that point, and each argument position corresponds to a particular control-flow predecessor of the point. Thus, the standard SSA-form representation of our example in Figure 8.17 is as shown in Figure 8.18. The variable x has been split into four variables x_1, x_2, x_3, and x_4, and z has been split into z_1, z_2, and z_3, each of which is assigned to only once.

The translation process into SSA form first figures out at what join points to insert ϕ-functions, then inserts trivial ϕ-functions (i.e., ϕ-functions of the form $\phi(x, x, \ldots, x)$) with the number of argument positions equal to the number of control-flow predecessors of the join point that some definition of the variable reaches, and then renames definitions and uses of variables (conventionally by sub-scripting them) to establish the static single-assignment property. Once we have finished doing whatever we translated to SSA form for, we need to eliminate the ϕ-functions, since they are only a conceptual tool, and are not computationally effective—i.e., when we come to a join point with a ϕ-function while executing a procedure, we have no way to determine which branch we came to it by and hence which value to use.[5]

Translating a procedure to minimal SSA form, i.e., an SSA form with a minimal number of ϕ-functions, can be done by using what are known as dominance frontiers. For a flowgraph node x, the *dominance frontier* of x, written $DF(x)$, is the set

5. An extension of SSA form called *gated single-assignment form* includes in each ϕ-function a selector that indicates which position to select according to the path taken to reach a join point.

of all nodes y in the flowgraph such that x dominates an immediate predecessor of y but does not strictly dominate y, i.e.,

$$DF(x) = \{y \mid (\exists z \in Pred(y) \text{ such that } x \text{ } dom \text{ } z) \text{ and } x \text{ } !sdom \text{ } y\}$$

Computing $DF(x)$ directly for all x would be quadratic in the number of nodes in the flowgraph. An algorithm that is linear results from breaking it into the computation of two intermediate components, $DF_{local}(x)$ and $DF_{up}(x, z)$, as follows:

$$DF_{local}(x) = \{y \in Succ(x) \mid idom(y) \neq x\}$$
$$DF_{up}(x, z) = \{y \in DF(z) \mid idom(y) \neq x\}$$

and computing $DF(x)$ as

$$DF(x) = DF_{local}(x) \cup \bigcup_{z \in N \text{ } idom(z) = x} DF_{up}(x, z)$$

To compute the dominance frontier for a given flowgraph, we turn the above equations into the code shown in Figure 8.19. The function value $\text{IDom}(x)$ is the set of nodes that x immediately dominates, and $\text{DF}(x)$, on completion, contains the dominance frontier of x. The worklist W initially contains the exit node, and in later stages enumerates the predecessors of nodes that have already had their dominance frontiers computed.

Now, we define for a set of flowgraph nodes S, the dominance frontier of S as

$$DF(S) = \bigcup_{x \in S} DF(x)$$

and the *iterated dominance frontier* $DF^+(\text{ })$ as

$$DF^+(S) = \lim_{i \to \infty} DF^i(S)$$

where $DF^1(S) = DF(S)$ and $DF^{i+1}(S) = DF(S \cup DF^i(S))$. If S is the set of nodes that assign to variable x, plus the entry node, then $DF^+(S)$ is exactly the set of nodes that need ϕ-functions for x.

To compute the iterated dominance frontier for a flowgraph, we adapt the equations given above, as shown in Figure 8.20. The value of $\text{DF\_Plus}(S)$ is the iterated dominance frontier of the set of nodes S, given that we have precomputed $\text{DF}(x)$ for all nodes x in the flowgraph. This implementation of computing $DF^+(S)$ has a time bound quadratic in the size of the procedure in the worst case, but is usually linear in practice.

As an example of translating to minimal SSA form, consider the flowgraph in Figure 8.21. The dominator tree for the flowgraph is shown in Figure 8.22. Using

```
DF, IDom, Succ, Pred: Node ⟶ set of Node

procedure Dom_Front(N,E,exit)
   N: in set of Node
   E: in set of (Node × Node)
   exit: in Node
begin
   x, y: Node
   W := {exit}, SW := ∅: set of Node
   more: boolean
   for each x ∈ N do
      DF(x) := ∅
   od
   repeat
      more := false
      while W ≠ ∅ do
         x := ◆W; W -= {x}
         SW ∪= {x}
         DF(x) := Succ(x)
         for each y ∈ IDom(x) do
            DF(x) ∪= DF(y)
         od
         DF(x) -= IDom(x)
      od
      while SW ≠ ∅ do
         x := ◆SW; SW -= {x}
         for each y ∈ Pred(x) do
            if DF(y) = ∅ then
               W ∪= {y}
               more := true
            fi
         od
      od
   until !more
end    || Dom_Front
```

FIG. 8.19 Code to compute the dominance frontier of a flowgraph.

the iterative characterization of dominance frontiers given above, we compute for variable k:

$$DF^1(\{entry, B1, B3\}) = \{B2\}$$

$$DF^2(\{entry, B1, B3\}) = DF(\{entry, B1, B2, B3\}) = \{B2\}$$

and for i:

$$DF^1(\{entry, B1, B3, B6\}) = \{B2, exit\}$$

$$DF^2(\{entry, B1, B3, B6\}) = DF(\{entry, B1, B2, B3, B6, exit\})$$

$$= \{B2, exit\}$$

```
procedure DF_Plus(S) returns set of Node
    S: in set of Node
begin
    D, DFP: set of Node
    change := true: boolean
    DFP := DF_Set(S)
    repeat
        change := false
        D := DF_Set(S ∪ DFP)
        if D ≠ DFP then
            DFP := D
            change := true
        fi
    until !change
    return DFP
end      || DF_Plus

procedure DF_Set(S) returns set of Node
    S: in set of Node
begin
    x: Node
    D := ∅: set of Node
    for each x ∈ S do
        D ∪= DF(x)
    od
    return D
end      || DF_Set
```

FIG. 8.20 Code to compute the iterated dominance frontier of a flowgraph.

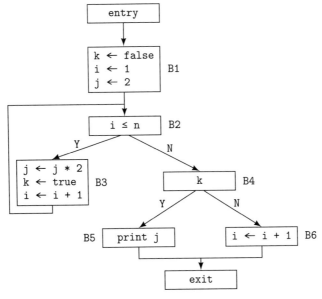

FIG. 8.21 Example flowgraph to be translated to minimal SSA form.

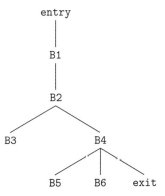

FIG. 8.22 Dominator tree for the flowgraph in Figure 8.21.

and for j (as for k):

$$DF^1(\{\text{entry}, \text{B1}, \text{B3}\}) = \{\text{B2}\}$$

$$DF^2(\{\text{entry}, \text{B1}, \text{B3}\}) = DF(\{\text{entry}, \text{B1}, \text{B2}, \text{B3}\}) = \{\text{B2}\}$$

so B2 and exit are the nodes requiring ϕ-functions. In particular, B2 requires a ϕ-function for each of i, j, and k, and exit needs one for i. The result of subscripting the variables and inserting the ϕ-functions is shown in Figure 8.23. Note that the ϕ-function inserted into the exit block is not really necessary (unless i is live on exit

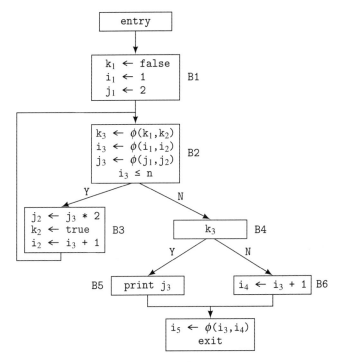

FIG. 8.23 Result of translating the flowgraph in Figure 8.21 to minimal SSA form.

from the procedure); *pruned SSA form* eliminates such unneeded ϕ-functions at the expense of somewhat increased computation cost.

Efficient algorithms are given in the literature (see Section 8.16) for translation to and from minimal SSA form. There is also experimental evidence [CytF91] of the effect of translating to SSA form: the numbers of assignments in 221 Fortran 77 procedures after translation to SSA form were anywhere from 1.3 to 3.8 times the numbers of assignments in the original forms. The occasionally large increase in program size is of some concern in using SSA form but, given that it makes some optimizations much more effective, it is usually worthwhile.

8.12   Dealing with Arrays, Structures, and Pointers

So far, we have said nothing in our discussion of data-flow analysis about dealing with values more complex than simple constants and variables whose values are restricted to such constants. Since variables (and, in some languages, constants) may also have arrays, records, pointers, and so on as their values, it is essential that we consider how to fit them into our data-flow analysis framework and how to represent them in SSA form.

One option that is used in many compilers is to simply ignore array and record assignments and to treat assignments through pointers pessimistically. In this approach, it is assumed that a pointer may point to any variable's value and, hence, that an assignment through a pointer may implicitly affect any variable. Languages like Pascal provide some help with this issue, as they restrict pointers to point only to objects of the types they are declared to be pointers to. Dealing with pointers in a way that produces much more useful information requires what is known as alias analysis, to which we devote Chapter 10. Pointers into heap storage may be modeled conservatively by considering the heap to be a single large object, like an array, with any assignment through a pointer assumed to both access and change any object in the heap. More aggressive techniques for dealing with pointers and records are discussed below in Section 8.14.

In C, pointers are not even restricted to pointing to heap storage—they may also point to objects on the stack and to statically allocated objects. The alias analysis methods discussed in Chapter 10 are important for aggressive optimization of C programs.

Some languages allow array assignments in which the values of all elements of an array are set at once. Such assignments can be handled easily by considering array variables and constants to be just like ordinary variables and constants. However, most array assignments set a single element, e.g., A[3] ← 5 or A[i] ← 2, rather than the entire array. Assignments that set a known element can also be treated like ordinary assignments, but this still does not account for most array operations. One possibility for dealing with assignments that set an array element named by a variable is to translate them to a form that uses access and update assignments that make them appear to operate on the whole array, as in Figure 8.24. While such operators permit our data-flow algorithms to work correctly, they generally produce

```
x ← a[i]              x ← access(a,i)
a[j] ← 4              a ← update(a,j,4)
(a)                   (b)
```

FIG. 8.24 Assignments involving array elements and their translation into access/update form.

information that is too crude to be very useful in optimizing array operations. The usual alternative is to do dependence analysis of array operations, as discussed in Section 9.1, which can provide more precise information about arrays, but at the expense of considerable additional computation. Relatively recently, an approach to doing data-flow analysis of array elements, called *last-write trees* (see Section 8.16), has been introduced.

In most languages, assignments involving direct references to elements of records (rather than through pointers) can only use member names that are constants. Thus, assignments to records can be treated as either accesses and updates to the whole record, as suggested for arrays above, or they can be treated as dealing with individual members. The latter approach can result in more effective optimization if records are used frequently in a program, and is discussed in Section 12.2. If the source language allows variables to be used to select members of records, then they are essentially fixed-size arrays with symbolic element names and can be handled like other arrays.

8.13   Automating Construction of Data–Flow Analyzers

Several tools have been implemented that, given a variety of types of intermediate code and a description of a data-flow problem, construct a data-flow analyzer that solves the given data-flow problem. Such tools can be used to construct data-flow analyzers for use in an optimizer, as long as the particular intermediate code is used.

The first well-known analyzer constructor of this type was developed by Kildall [Kild73]. His system constructs an iterative analyzer that operates on what he calls "pools," where a pool is, in current parlance, the data-flow information one has at a particular point in a procedure at some time during the analysis. Kildall gives a tabular form for expressing pools and rules that, according to the type of flowgraph node being processed and the data-flow problem being solved, transforms an "input pool" into the corresponding "output pool." His system allows for pools to be represented as bit vectors, linked lists, or value numbers (see Section 12.4), depending on the data-flow problem, and performs a worklist implementation of iterative analysis similar to the one presented in Section 8.4.

A much more recent and more sophisticated analyzer constructor is Tjiang and Hennessy's Sharlit [TjiH92]. In addition to performing data-flow analyses, it can be used to specify optimizing transformations. Much of what one needs to write to specify an analyzer and optimizer in Sharlit is purely declarative, but other parts, such as the optimizing transformations, require writing procedural code, which one does in C++. This analyzer constructor operates on an intermediate code of quadruples called SUIF (see Section C.3.3). The quadruple types of interest to it are loads, stores, binary operations that take two operands and place the result in a destination, and others that specify control flow. Rather than requiring a data-flow analyzer to consist of a local component that analyzes and propagates information through basic blocks and a global component that works on the flowgraph of basic blocks, Sharlit allows the analyzer specifier to vary the granularity at which the compiler writer wishes to work. One can operate on individual intermediate-code nodes, or group them into basic blocks, intervals, or other structural units—whichever may be most appropriate to the problem at hand.

The underlying technique used by Sharlit to perform a data-flow analysis is path simplification, based on Tarjan's fast algorithms for path problems, which compute a regular expression of node names, called a *path expression,* that specifies all possible execution paths from one node to or through another. For example, for the flowgraph in Figure 7.32(a), the path expression for the path from the entry through block B5 is

$$\mathtt{entry}\cdot(\mathtt{B1}\cdot\mathtt{B2})^{\star}\cdot\mathtt{B3}\cdot\mathtt{B5}$$

and the one for the path from B3 through exit is

$$\mathtt{B3}\cdot(\mathtt{B4} + (\mathtt{B5}\cdot(\mathtt{B6}\cdot\mathtt{B7})^{\star}))\cdot\mathtt{exit}$$

The "·" operator represents concatenation, "+" represents joining of paths, and "$\star$" represents repetition. The operators are interpreted in a data-flow analyzer as composition of flow functions, meet, and fixed-point computation, respectively.

To specify an optimizer to Sharlit, one must give the following:

1. a description of the flowgraphs it is to operate on (including such choices as whether to consider individual quadruples or basic blocks as the units for the analysis);

2. the set of data-flow values to be used, one of which is associated with each node in the flowgraph in the solution (which may be bit vectors, assignments of constant values to variables, or other objects);

3. flow functions that describe the effects of nodes on data-flow values; and

4. action routines that specify optimizing transformations to be performed using the results of the data-flow analysis.

Given the description of how the data-flow problem being solved interprets the flowgraph, values, and functions and a procedure to be analyzed, Sharlit computes a set of path expressions for components of a flowgraph, and then uses the flow functions and path expressions to compute the flow values constituting the solution. It then uses the resulting values and the action routines to traverse the flowgraph and perform the applicable transformations.

Tjiang and Hennessy give three examples of how Sharlit can be used to compute available expressions (iterative analysis on a flowgraph of individual nodes, local analysis to compute flow functions for basic blocks, and interval analysis). They conclude that the tool greatly simplifies the specification and debugging of an optimizer and is competitive in the results it produces with optimizers built by hand for commercial compilers.

8.14   More Ambitious Analyses

So far we have considered only relatively weak forms of data-flow analysis, which give little hint of its power or of its close relationship with such powerful methods as proving properties of programs, including correctness. In this section, we explore how the complexity of the lattices used and the reasoning power we allow ourselves about the operations performed in a program affect the properties we are able to determine.

Consider doing constant-propagation analysis on the simple example in Figure 8.25. If the arithmetic operations, such as the i + 1 that occurs here, are all considered to be uninterpreted—i.e., if we assume that we have no information about their effect at all—then we have no way of determining whether j's value is constant at the entry to B4. If, on the other hand, we strengthen our constant-propagation analysis to include the ability to do addition of constants, then we can easily determine that j has the value 2 on entry to B4.

In the example in Figure 8.26, assuming that we can reason about subtraction of 1 and comparison to 0 and that we distinguish the "Y" and "N" exits from tests, then we can conclude that, on entry to the exit block, n's value is ≤ 0. If we extend this program to the one shown in Figure 8.27, then we can conclude that n = 0 on entry to the exit block. Further, if we can reason about integer functions, then we can also determine that at the same point, if $n_0 \geq 0$, $f = n_0!$, where n_0 represents the value of n on entry to the flowgraph. This at least suggests that we can use data-flow analytic techniques to do program verification. The data-flow information we need to associate with each exit of each block to do so is the inductive assertions shown in Table 8.5. While this requires more machinery and has much greater

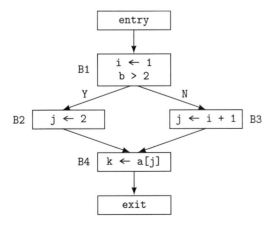

FIG. 8.25 Simple example for constant-propagation analysis.

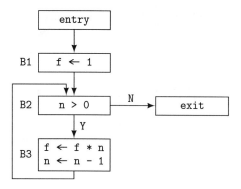

FIG. 8.26 Simple factorial computation.

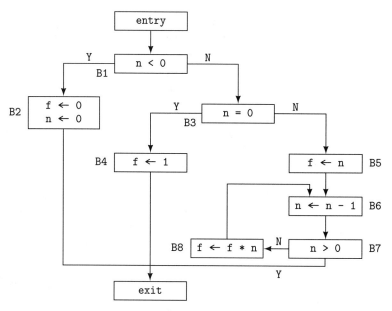

FIG. 8.27 Full factorial computation.

computational complexity than any analysis we might actually use in a compiler, it at least demonstrates the spectrum of possibilities that data-flow analysis encompasses.

Another example of a computationally expensive data-flow analysis, but one that is less so than program verification, is type determination and dependence analysis of data structures that include records and pointers. This has been investigated by a series of researchers starting in 1968 and is a problem for which there are still no entirely satisfactory solutions. Various methods have been proposed, but they all fall into three major categories, the grammar-based approach and the k-limited graphs defined in a paper of Jones and Muchnick [JonM81a] and the access-path approach of Hendren et al. described briefly in Section 9.6.

TABLE 8.5 Inductive assertions associated with the exit from each block in Figure 8.27 that are needed to determine that it computes the integer factorial function.

Block	Inductive Assertion
entry	$n = n_0$
B1/Y	$n = n_0 < 0$
B1/N	$n = n_0 \geq 0$
B2	$n = 0$ and $f = n_0!$
B3/Y	$n = n_0 = 0$ and $f = 1$
B3/N	$n = n_0 > 0$
B4	$n = n_0 = 0$ and $f = n_0!$
B5	$n = n_0 > 0$ and $f = n_0$
B6	$n \geq 0$ and $f = n_0 \times (n_0 - 1) \times \cdots \times (n + 1)$
B7/Y	$n > 0$ and $f = n_0 \times (n_0 - 1) \times \cdots \times (n + 1)$
B7/N	$n = 0$ and $f = n_0 \times (n_0 - 1) \times \cdots \times 1 = n_0!$
B8	$n > 0$ and $f = n_0 \times (n_0 - 1) \times \cdots \times n$

8.15   Wrap-Up

Data-flow analysis provides global information about how a procedure (or a larger segment of a program) manipulates its data, thus providing grist for the mill of optimization. The spectrum of possible data-flow analyses ranges from abstract execution of a procedure, which might determine that it computes a particular function, to much simpler and easier analyses such as reaching definitions. However, as for control-flow analysis, there are three main approaches, one associated with each of the control-flow approaches. The approach associated with dominators and back edges is called iterative data-flow analysis and the other two approaches have the same names as the corresponding control-flow approaches, namely, interval analysis and structural analysis. They have trade-offs as to their benefits and disadvantages similar to the control-flow approaches as well.

No matter which approach we use, we must ensure that the data-flow analysis gives us correct and conservative information, i.e., that it does not misrepresent what the procedure does by telling us that a transformation is safe to perform that, in fact, is not. We guarantee this by careful design of the data-flow equations and by being sure that the solution to them that we compute is, if not an exact representation of the desired information, at least a conservative approximation to it. For example, for reaching definitions, which determine what definitions of variables may reach a particular use, the analysis must not tell us that no definitions reach a particular use if there are some that may. The analysis is conservative if it gives us a set of reaching definitions that is no smaller than if it could produce the minimal result.

However, to maximize the benefit that can be derived from optimization, we seek to pose data-flow problems that are both conservative and as aggressive as we can make them. Thus, we walk a fine line between being as aggressive as possible in the information we compute, and being conservative, so as to get the greatest possible benefit from the analyses and transformations performed without ever transforming correct code to incorrect code.

8.16   Further Reading

An example of a text that uses $KILL(\ )$ functions rather than $PRSV(\ )$ is [AhoS86].

The lattices used by Jones and Muchnick to describe the "shapes" of LISP-like data structures are presented in [JonM81b].

Proof that there may be no algorithm that computes the meet-over-all-paths solution for a data-flow analysis involving monotone functions can be found in [Hech77] and [KamU75]. Kildall's result that for data-flow problems in which all the flow functions are distributive, the general iterative algorithm computes the MFP solution and that, in that case, the MFP and MOP solutions are identical, is found in [Kild73]. Kam and Ullman's partial generalization to monotone but not distributive functions is found in [KamU75].

Papers that associate data-flow information with edges in the flowgraph include [JonM76], [JonM81a], and [Rose81]. The second of those papers also draws the distinction between relational and independent attributes.

Morel and Renvoise's original formulation of partial-redundancy elimination is found in [MorR79] and Knoop, Rüthing, and Steffen's more recent one is given in [KnoR92].

The approaches to solving data-flow problems in Section 8.3 are described in the following papers:

Approach	Reference
Allen's strongly connected region method	[Alle69]
Kildall's iterative algorithm	[Kild73]
Ullman's $T1$-$T2$ analysis	[Ullm73]
Kennedy's node-listing algorithm	[Kenn75]
Farrow, Kennedy, and Zucconi's graph-grammar approach	[FarK75]
Elimination methods, e.g., interval analysis	[AllC76]
Rosen's high-level (syntax-directed) approach	[Rose77]
Structural analysis	[Shar80]
Slotwise analysis	[DhaR92]

The proof that, if A is the maximal number of back edges on any acyclic path in a flowgraph, then $A + 2$ passes through the repeat loop in the iterative algorithm are sufficient if we use reverse postorder, is due to Hecht and Ullman [HecU75]. Alternatives for managing the worklist include round-robin and various node listings, which are discussed in [Hech77].

A precursor of slotwise analysis is found in [Kou77]. [DhaR92] shows how to apply slotwise analysis to partial-redundancy analysis.

Static single-assignment form is described in [CytF89] and [CytF91] and is derived from an earlier form developed by Shapiro and Saint [ShaS69]. The linear-time dominance-frontier algorithm appears in[CytF91], along with efficient methods for translating to and from SSA form.

The use of last-write trees to do data-flow analysis of array elements is introduced in [Feau91].

Tjiang and Hennessy's Sharlit is described in [TjiH92] and [Tjia93]. It operates on the SUIF intermediate representation, which is described in [TjiW91] (see Appendix C for information on downloading SUIF). [TjiH92] gives three examples of the use of Sharlit.

Investigation of how to apply data-flow analysis to recursive data structures includes [Reyn68], [Tene74a], [Tene74b], [JonM81a], [Laru89], [Hend90], [ChaW90], [HumH94], [Deut94], and a variety of others. The approach used in [HumH94] is discussed in Section 9.6.

8.17   Exercises

8.1 What is the complexity in bit-vector or set operations of iteratively computing unidirectional data-flow information using (a) both *in*( ) and *out*( ) functions versus (b) using only one of them?

8.2 Give an example of a lattice that is not distributive.

8.3 Give an example of a specific data-flow problem and an instance for which the MOP and MFP solutions are different.

8.4 Evaluate the space and time complexity of associating data-flow information with edges in a flowgraph versus with node entries and exits.

RSCH 8.5 Formulate the data-flow analysis in Figure 8.4 as a relational problem, as described in [JonM81a]. Is the result as good as associating information with edges? What about the computational complexity?

RSCH 8.6 Research Kennedy's node-listing algorithm [Kenn75] or Farrow, Kennedy, and Zucconi's graph-grammar approach [FarK75] to data-flow analysis. What are their advantages and disadvantages in comparison to the methods discussed here?

8.7 What alternative ways might one use to manage the worklist in Figure 8.6? How do they compare in ease of implementation and computational effectiveness to reverse postorder for forward problems?

8.8 Draw the lattice of monotone functions from BV^2 to itself.

ADV 8.9 Is L^F distributive for any L? If not, give an example. If so, prove it.

RSCH 8.10 Research the updating of data-flow information as a flowgraph is being modified, as discussed in [Zade84]. What evidence is there that this is worth doing in a compiler, rather than recomputing data-flow information when needed?

8.11 Work an example of structural data-flow analysis on a flowgraph with an improper region. Show each of the three approaches to handling the improper region, namely, (1) node splitting, (2) iteration, and (3) solving a data-flow problem on the underlying lattice's lattice of monotone functions.

8.12 (a) Formulate a backward data-flow analysis using the structural approach. (b) Show that the iteration over the function lattice to handle an improper region is a forward analysis.

8.13 (a) Construct an example flowgraph that is a simple loop whose body is an improper region that contains an `if-then-else` construct. (b) Write the structural data-flow equations for your example. (c) Write the ICAN code to perform a forward data-flow analysis for the loop and the `if-then-else`. (d) Construct an ICAN data structure to represent the data flow in the improper region as discussed in Section 8.7.3. (e) Write an interpreter in ICAN that evaluates data-flow information using the data structure in part (d). (f) Use the code for the loop and the `if-then-else` and the interpreter for the improper region to compute reaching definitions for the flowgraph.

8.14 Suggest alternative representations for structural analysis equations (i.e., ones other than those shown in Section 8.7.3). What advantages and disadvantages do your approaches have?

8.15 Formulate and solve a $\mathbf{BV}^n$ problem, such as available expressions, slotwise.

8.16 Construct the du-chains, ud-chains, and webs for the procedure in Figure 16.7.

8.17 Compute $DF(\ )$ and $DF^+(\ )$ for the procedure in Figure 16.7.

RSCH 8.18 Investigate last-write trees [Feau91] for data-flow analysis of arrays. What do they provide, allow, and cost?

ADV 8.19 Does Sharlit produce the MOP solution of a data-flow problem?

CHAPTER 9

Dependence Analysis and Dependence Graphs

D
ependence analysis is a vital tool in instruction scheduling (see Section 17.1) and data-cache optimization (see Section 20.4).

As a tool for instruction scheduling, it determines the ordering relationships between instructions in a basic block (or larger unit of code) that must be satisfied for the code to execute correctly. This includes determining, for two given register or memory references, whether the areas of memory they access overlap and whether pairs of instructions have resource conflicts. Similarly, dependence analysis and the loop transformations it enables are the main tools for data-cache optimization and are essential to automatic vectorization and parallelization.

Also, a new intermediate form called the program dependence graph (see Section 9.5) has been proposed as a basis for doing several sorts of optimizations.

One of the final sections of this chapter is devoted to dependences between dynamically allocated objects.

9.1 Dependence Relations

In this section, we introduce the basic notions of dependence analysis. Following sections show how they are used specifically in instruction scheduling and data-cache-related analysis. In each case, we may construct a graph called the dependence graph that represents the dependences present in a code fragment—in the case of instruction scheduling as applied to a basic block, the graph has no cycles in it, and so it is known as the dependence DAG. As we shall see, dependence analysis can be applied to code at any level—source, intermediate, or object.

If statement S_1 precedes S_2 in their given execution order, we write $S_1 \lhd S_2$. A *dependence* between two statements in a program is a relation that constrains their execution order. A *control dependence* is a constraint that arises from the control flow of the program, such as S2's relationship to S3 and S4 in Figure 9.1— S3 and S4 are executed only if the condition in S2 is not satisfied. If there is a

```
S1        a ← b + c
S2        if a > 10 goto L1
S3          d ← b * e
S4          e ← d + 1
S5  L1:   d ← e / 2
```

FIG. 9.1 Example of control and data dependence in MIR code.

control dependence between statements S_1 and S_2, we write $S_1 \, \delta^c \, S_2$. So, S2 δ^c S3 and S2 δ^c S4 in Figure 9.1.

A *data dependence* is a constraint that arises from the flow of data between statements, such as between S3 and S4 in the figure—S3 sets the value of d and S4 uses it; also, S3 uses the value of e and S4 sets it. In both cases, reordering the statements could result in the code's producing incorrect results. There are four varieties of data dependences, as follows:

1. If $S_1 \lhd S_2$ and the former sets a value that the latter uses, this is called a *flow dependence* or *true dependence*, which is a binary relation denoted $S_1 \, \delta^f \, S_2$; thus, for example, the flow dependence between S3 and S4 in Figure 9.1 is written S3 δ^f S4.

2. If $S_1 \lhd S_2$, S_1 uses some variable's value, and S_2 sets it, then we say that there is an *antidependence* between them, written $S_1 \, \delta^a \, S_2$. Statements S3 and S4 in Figure 9.1 represent an antidependence, S3 δ^a S4, as well as a flow dependence, since S3 uses e and S4 sets it.

3. If $S_1 \lhd S_2$ and both statements set the value of some variable, we say there is an *output dependence* between them, written $S_1 \, \delta^o \, S_2$. In the figure, we have S3 δ^o S5.

4. Finally, if $S_1 \lhd S_2$ and both statements read the value of some variable, we say there is an *input dependence* between them, written $S_1 \, \delta^i \, S_2$; for example, in the figure, S3 δ^i S5, since both read the value of e. Note that an input dependence does not constrain the execution order of the two statements, but it is useful to have this concept in our discussion of scalar replacement of array elements in Section 20.3.

A set of dependence relationships may be represented by a directed graph called a *dependence graph*. In such a graph, the nodes represent statements and the edges represent dependences. Each edge is labeled to indicate the kind of dependence it represents, except that it is traditional to leave flow-dependence edges unlabeled. Figure 9.2 gives the dependence graph for the code in Figure 9.1. Control dependences are generally omitted in dependence graphs, unless such a dependence is the

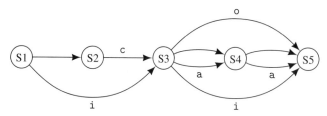

FIG. 9.2 The dependence graph for the code in Figure 9.1.

only one that connects two nodes (in our example, there is a control dependence connecting S2 and S4, but it is omitted in the graph).

9.2   Basic-Block Dependence DAGs

The method of basic-block scheduling we consider in Chapter 17 is known as list scheduling. It requires that we begin by constructing a dependence graph that represents the constraints on the possible schedules of the instructions in a block and hence, also, the degrees of freedom in the possible schedules. Since a basic block has no loops within it, its dependence graph is always a DAG known as the *dependence DAG* for the block.

The nodes in a dependence DAG represent machine instructions or low-level intermediate-code instructions and its edges represent dependences between the instructions. An edge from I_1 to I_2 may represent any of several kinds of dependences. It may be that

1. I_1 writes a register or location that I_2 uses, i.e., $I_1 \delta^f I_2$;

2. I_1 uses a register or location that I_2 changes, i.e., $I_1 \delta^a I_2$;

3. I_1 and I_2 write to the same register or location, i.e., $I_1 \delta^o I_2$;

4. we cannot determine whether I_1 can be moved beyond I_2; or

5. I_1 and I_2 have a structural hazard, as described below.

The fourth situation occurs, for example, in the case of a load followed by a store that uses different registers to address memory, and for which we cannot determine whether the addressed locations might overlap. More specifically, suppose an instruction reads from [r11](4) and the next writes to [r2+12](4). Unless we know that r2+12 and r11 point to different locations, we must assume that there is a dependence between the two instructions.

The techniques described below in Section 9.4 can be used to disambiguate many memory references in loops, and this information can be passed on as annotations in the code to increase the freedom available to the scheduler.

A node I_1 is a predecessor of another node I_2 in the dependence DAG if I_2 must not execute until I_1 has executed for some number of cycles. The type of dependence represented by an edge in the DAG is unimportant, so we omit the type labels. However, the edge from I_1 to I_2 is labeled with an integer that is the required *latency* between I_1 and I_2, except that we omit labels that are zeros. The latency is the *delay* required between the initiation times of I_1 and I_2 minus the execution time required by I_1 before any other instruction can begin executing (usually one cycle, but frequently zero in a superscalar implementation). Thus, if I_2 can begin execution in the cycle following when I_1 begins, then the latency is zero, while if two cycles must elapse between beginning I_1 and I_2, then the latency is one. For example, for the LIR code in Figure 9.3(a) with the assumption that a load has a latency of one cycle and requires two cycles to complete, the dependence DAG is as shown in Figure 9.3(b).

Condition codes and other implicit resources are treated as if they were registers for the computation of dependences.

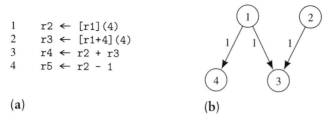

```
1    r2 ← [r1](4)
2    r3 ← [r1+4](4)
3    r4 ← r2 + r3
4    r5 ← r2 - 1
```

(a)   (b)

FIG. 9.3 (a) A basic block of LIR code, and (b) its dependence DAG.

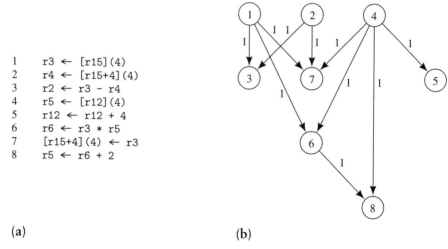

```
1    r3 ← [r15](4)
2    r4 ← [r15+4](4)
3    r2 ← r3 - r4
4    r5 ← [r12](4)
5    r12 ← r12 + 4
6    r6 ← r3 * r5
7    [r15+4](4) ← r3
8    r5 ← r6 + 2
```

(a)   (b)

FIG. 9.4 (a) A more complex LIR example, and (b) its dependence DAG.

As a second, more complex example, consider the LIR code in Figure 9.4(a) and its dependence DAG in Figure 9.4(b), again assuming a latency of one cycle for loads. Instructions 1 and 2 are independent of each other since they reference different memory addresses and different target registers. Instruction 3 must follow both of them because it uses the values loaded by both of them. Instruction 4 is independent of 1 and 2 because they are all loads to different registers. Instruction 7 must follow 1, 2, and 4 because it uses the result of 1, stores into the address loaded from by 2, and would conflict with 4 if the value in r12 is r15+4.

Note that the edge from 4 to 8 in Figure 9.4(b) is redundant, since there is an edge from 4 to 6 and another from 6 to 8. On the other hand, if the edge from 4 to 8 were labeled with a latency of 4, it would not be redundant since then

        1, 2, 4, 5, 6, 7, 8, 3

and

        1, 2, 4, 5, 6, 8, 7, 3

would both be feasible schedules, but the first would require eight cycles, while the second would require nine.

To construct the dependence DAG for a basic block we need two functions,

    Latency: LIRInst × integer × LIRInst × integer ⟶ integer

and

    Conflict: LIRInst × LIRInst ⟶ boolean

defined by

$$\text{Latency}(I_1, n_1, I_2, n_2) = \text{the number of latency cycles incurred by beginning execution of } I_2\text{'s } n_2^{\text{th}} \text{ cycle while executing cycle } n_1 \text{ of } I_1$$

and

$$\text{Conflict}(I_1, I_2) = \begin{cases} \text{true} & \text{if } I_1 \text{ must precede } I_2 \text{ for correct execution} \\ \text{false} & \text{otherwise} \end{cases}$$

Note that for any two LIR instructions I_1 and I_2 separated by a .sequence pseudo-op, $\text{Conflict}(I_1, I_2)$ is true.

To compute Latency( ), we use resource vectors. A *resource vector* for an instruction is an array of sets of computational resources such that the instruction needs the given resources in successive cycles of its execution. For example, the MIPS R4000 floating-point unit has seven resources named A (mantissa Add), E (Exception test), M (Multiplier first stage), N (Multiplier second stage), R (adder Round), S (operand Shift), and U (Unpack). The single-precision floating-point add (add.s) and multiply (mul.s) instructions have the following resource vectors:

	1	2	3	4	5	6	7
add.s	U	S,A	A,R	R,S			
mul.s	U	M	M	M	N	N,A	R

so starting an add.s in cycle four of a mul.s would result in conflicts in the sixth and seventh cycles of the mul.s—in the sixth, both instructions need resource A, and in the seventh, both need R. Competition by two or more instructions for a resource at the same time is called a *structural hazard*.

Now, to compute $\text{Latency}(I_1, I_2)$, we match the resource vector for instruction I_1 with that for I_2 (see Figure 9.5). In particular, we repeatedly check whether elements of the two resource vectors have a non-empty intersection, stepping along I_1's resource vector each time we find a resource conflict. The procedure Inst_RV( ) takes an instruction as its first argument and the length of the resource vector as its second and returns the resource vector corresponding to the type of that instruction. The function ResSet(*inst*, *i*) returns the set of resources used by cycle *i* of instruction *inst*. The constant MaxCycles is the maximum number of cycles needed by any instruction.

```
ResVec = array [1··MaxCycles] of set of Resource
MaxCycles: integer

procedure Latency(inst1,cyc1,inst2,cyc2) returns integer
    inst1, inst2: in LIRInst
    cyc1, cyc2: in integer
begin
    I1RV, I2RV: ResVec
    n := MaxCycles, i := 0, j, k: integer
    cycle: boolean
    I1RV := Inst_RV(inst1,cyc1)
    I2RV := Inst_RV(inst2,cyc2)
    || determine cycle of inst1 at which inst2 can begin
    || executing without encountering stalls
    repeat
        cycle := false
        j := 1
        while j ≤ n do
            if I1RV[j] ∩ I2RV[j] ≠ ∅ then
                for k := 1 to n - 1 do
                    I1RV[k] := I1RV[k+1]
                od
                n -= 1
                i += 1
                cycle := true
                goto L1
            fi
            j += 1
        od
L1:     until !cycle
        return i
    end     || Latency

procedure Inst_RV(inst,cyc) returns ResVec
    inst: in LIRInst
    cyc: in integer
begin
    IRV: ResVec
    i: integer
    || construct resource vector for latency computation
    || from resource set
    for i := 1 to MaxCycles do
        if cyc+i-1 < MaxCycles then
            IRV[i] := ResSet(inst,cyc+i-1)
        else
            IRV[i] := ∅
        fi
    od
    return IRV
end     || Inst_RV
```

FIG. 9.5 Computing the Latency( ) function.

For the example Latency(mul.s,4,add.s,1), we have MaxCycles = 7 and the following resource vectors:

```
I1RV[1] = {M}        I2RV[1] = {U}
I1RV[2] = {N}        I2RV[2] = {S,A}
I1RV[3] = {N,A}      I2RV[3] = {A,R}
I1RV[4] = {R}        I2RV[4] = {R,S}
I1RV[5] = ∅          I2RV[5] = ∅
I1RV[6] = ∅          I2RV[6] = ∅
I1RV[7] = ∅          I2RV[7] = ∅
```

The reader can easily check that the call to Latency( ) returns the value 2, so starting the add.s immediately would result in a two-cycle stall,[1] but the add.s can be started in cycle 6 of the mul.s with no stall cycles.

While this method of computing latency is transparent, it can be computed significantly more quickly. Proebsting and Fraser [ProF94] describe a method that uses a deterministic finite automaton whose states are similar to sets of resource vectors and whose transitions are instructions to compute the analogue of the j loop in our algorithm by a single table lookup.

Now let Inst[1··m] be the sequence of instructions (including .sequence pseudo-ops) that make up a basic block. If the basic block ends with a branch and if branches have a delay slot in the architecture, we exclude the branch from the sequence of instructions. The data structure DAG has the form shown in Figure 9.6, where Nodes = {1,..., n} and Roots ⊆ Nodes.

The algorithm to construct the scheduling DAG is called Build_DAG( ) and is given in Figure 9.6. The algorithm iterates over the instructions in order. It first determines, for each instruction, whether it conflicts with any of the ones already in the DAG. If so, the instructions it conflicts with are put into the set Conf. Then, if Conf is empty, the current instruction is added to Roots, the set of roots of the DAG. Otherwise, for each instruction in Conf, a new edge is added to the graph from it to the new instruction and the label associated with the edge is set to the corresponding latency. Constructing the DAG requires $O(n^2)$ operations, since it compares each pair of instructions in the basic block to find the dependences.

As an example of the DAG-building process, consider the sequence of eight LIR instructions given in Figure 9.4(a). Build_DAG( ) is called with n = 8 and Inst[1] through Inst[8] set to the eight instructions in sequence. For the first instruction, there are no previous instructions to conflict with, so it is made a root. The second instruction does not conflict with the first, so it is also made a root. The third instruction conflicts with both the first and second, since it uses the values loaded by them, so edges are added to the DAG running from the first and second instructions to the third, each with a latency of one. The fourth instruction does not conflict with any of its predecessors—it might be the case that [r12](4) is the same address as

---

1. A *stall* refers to the inaction (or "stalling") of a pipeline when it cannot proceed to execute the next instruction presented to it because a needed hardware resource is in use or because some condition it uses has not yet been satisfied. For example, a load instruction may stall for a cycle in some implementations if the quantity loaded is used by the next instruction.

```
DAG = record {
        Nodes, Roots: set of integer,
        Edges: set of (integer × integer),
        Label: set of (integer × integer) ⟶ integer}

procedure Build_DAG(m,Inst) returns DAG
    m: in integer
    Inst: in array [1··m] of LIRInst
begin
    D := ⟨Nodes:∅,Edges:∅,Label:∅,Roots:∅⟩: DAG
    Conf: set of integer
    j, k: integer
    || determine nodes, edges, labels, and
    || roots of a basic-block scheduling DAG
    for j := 1 to m do
        D.Nodes ∪= {j}
        Conf := ∅
        for k := 1 to j - 1 do
            if Conflict(Inst[k],Inst[j]) then
                Conf ∪= {k}
            fi
        od
        if Conf = ∅ then
            D.Roots ∪= {j}
        else
            for each k ∈ Conf do
                D.Edges ∪= {⟨k,j⟩}
                D.Label(k,j) := Latency(Inst[k],Inst[j])
            od
        fi
    od
    return D
end    || Build_DAG
```

FIG. 9.6 Algorithm to construct the dependence DAG for basic-block scheduling.

[r15] (4) or [r15+4] (4), but since they are all loads and there are no intervening stores to any of the locations, they don't conflict. The DAG that results from this process is the one shown in Figure 9.4(b).

9.3   Dependences in Loops

In studying data-cache optimization, our concern is almost entirely with data dependence, not control dependence.

While dependences among scalar variables in a single basic block are useful for instruction scheduling and as an introduction to the concepts, our next concern is dependences among statements that involve subscripted variables nested inside loops. In particular, we consider uses of subscripted variables in perfectly nested

```
for i1 ← 1 to n1 do
   for i2 ← 1 to n2 do
       . . .
           for ik ← 1 to nk do
               statements
           endfor
       . . .
   endfor
endfor
```

FIG. 9.7 A canonical loop nest.

loops in HIR that are expressed in *canonical form*, i.e., each loop's index runs from 1 to some value *n* by 1s and only the innermost loop has statements other than `for` statements within it.

The *iteration space* of the loop nest in Figure 9.7 is the *k*-dimensional polyhedron consisting of all the *k*-tuples of values of the loop indexes (called *index vectors*), which is easily seen to be the product of the index ranges of the loops, namely,

$$[1..\text{n1}] \times [1..\text{n2}] \times \ldots \times [1..\text{nk}]$$

where $[a..b]$ denotes the sequence of integers from a through b and n1, . . . , nk are the maximum values of the iteration variables.

We use "$\prec$" to denote the lexicographic ordering of index vectors. Thus,

$$\langle i1_1, \ldots, ik_1 \rangle \prec \langle i1_2, \ldots, ik_2 \rangle$$

if and only if

$$\exists j, 1 \leq j \leq k, \text{ such that } i1_1 = i1_2, \ldots, i(j-1)_1 = i(j-1)_2 \text{ and } ij_1 < ij_2$$

and, in particular, $0 \prec \langle i1, \ldots, ik \rangle$, i.e., $\bar{i}$ is *lexicographically positive*, if

$$\exists j, 1 \leq j \leq k, \text{ such that } i1 = 0, \ldots, i(j-1) = 0 \text{ and } ij > 0$$

Note that iteration $\langle i1_1, \ldots, ik_1 \rangle$ of a loop nest precedes iteration $\langle i1_2, \ldots, ik_2 \rangle$ if and only if

$$\langle i1_1, \ldots, ik_1 \rangle \prec \langle i1_2, \ldots, ik_2 \rangle$$

The *iteration-space traversal* of a loop nest is the sequence of vectors of index values encountered in executing the loops, i.e., the lexicographic enumeration of the index vectors. We represent the traversal graphically by a layout of nodes corresponding to the index vectors with dashed arrows between them indicating the traversal order. For example, for the loop in Figure 9.8, the iteration space is $[1..3] \times [1..4]$ and the iteration-space traversal is portrayed in Figure 9.9.

Note that the iteration space of a loop nest need not be rectangular. In particular, the loop nest in Figure 9.10 has the trapezoidal iteration space and traversal shown in Figure 9.11.

Given subscripted variables nested in loops, the dependence relations are more complicated than for scalar variables: the dependences are functions of the index

```
        for i1 ← 1 to 3 do
           for i2 ← 1 to 4 do
S1            t ← x + y
S2            a[i1,i2] ← b[i1,i2] + c[i1,i2]
S3            b[i1,i2] ← a[i1,i2-1] * d[i1+1,i2] + t
           endfor
        endfor
```

FIG. 9.8 An example of a doubly nested loop.

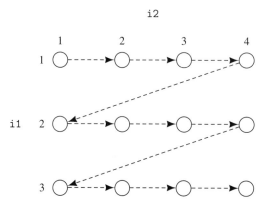

FIG. 9.9 The iteration-space traversal for the code in Figure 9.8.

```
        for i1 ← 1 to 3 do
           for i2 ← 1 to i1+1 do
S1            a[i1,i2] ← b[i1,i2] + c[i1,i2]
S2            b[i1,i2] ← a[i1,i2-1]
           endfor
        endfor
```

FIG. 9.10 A doubly nested loop with a nonrectangular iteration-space traversal.

variables, as well as of the statements. We use bracketed subscripts after a statement number to indicate the values of the index variables. We extend the "◁" notation so that $S_1[i1_1, \ldots, ik_1] \triangleleft S_2[i1_2, \ldots, ik_2]$ means that $S_1[i1_1, \ldots, ik_1]$ is executed before $S_2[i1_2, \ldots, ik_2]$, where $i1$ through ik are the loop indexes of the loops containing the statements S_1 and S_2, outermost first. Note that $S_1[i1_1, \ldots, ik_1] \triangleleft S_2[i1_2, \ldots, ik_2]$ if and only if either S_1 precedes S_2 in the program and $\langle i1_1, \ldots, ik_1 \rangle \preceq \langle i1_2, \ldots, ik_2 \rangle$ or S_1 is the same statement as or follows S_2 and $\langle i1_1, \ldots, ik_1 \rangle \prec \langle i1_2, \ldots, ik_2 \rangle$.

For our example in Figure 9.8, we have the following execution-order relationships:

$$S2[i1, i2-1] \triangleleft S3[i1, i2]$$

$$S2[i1, i2] \triangleleft S3[i1, i2]$$

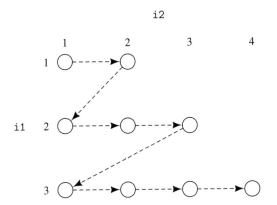

FIG. 9.11 The trapezoidal iteration-space traversal of the loop nest in Figure 9.10.

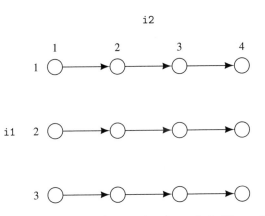

FIG. 9.12 The dependence relations for the code in Figure 9.8.

and the corresponding dependence relations:

S2[i1, i2−1] δ^f S3[i1, i2]

S2[i1, i2] δ^a S3[i1, i2]

Like the iteration-space traversal, the dependence relations for the loop body as a whole can be displayed graphically, as shown in Figure 9.12. We omit arrows that represent self-dependences. Note that each ⟨i1, 1⟩ iteration uses the value of a[i1,0], but that this is not represented in the diagram, since 0 is not a legal value for the loop index i2.

Next we introduce distance, direction, and dependence vectors as notations for loop-based dependences. A *distance vector* for a nest of k loops is a k-dimensional vector $\vec{d} = \langle d_1, \ldots, d_k \rangle$, where each d_i is an integer; it means that for each index vector $\vec{i}$, the iteration with index vector $\vec{i} + \vec{d} = \langle i_1 + d_1, \ldots, i_k + d_k \rangle$ depends on the one with index vector $\vec{i}$. A *direction vector* approximates one or more distance vectors and has elements that are ranges of integers, where each range is $[0, 0]$, $[1, \infty]$, $[-\infty, -1]$, or $[-\infty, \infty]$, or the union of two or more ranges. There are two frequently occurring notations for direction vectors, as follows:

$[0, 0]$	$[1, \infty]$	$[-\infty, -1]$	$[-\infty, \infty]$
$=$	$+$	$-$	$\pm$
$=$	$<$	$>$	$*$

In the second notation, the symbols "$\neq$", "$\leq$", and "$\geq$" are used for unions of ranges, with the obvious meanings. So the dependences described above for the loop nest in Figure 9.8 are represented by the distance vectors

S2[i1, i2-1] $\langle 0, 1 \rangle$ S3[i1, i2]

S2[i1, i2] $\langle 0, 0 \rangle$ S3[i1, i2]

which can be summarized (with significant loss of information) by the direction vector $\langle =, \leq \rangle$.

Dependence vectors generalize the other two kinds of vectors. A *dependence vector* for a nest of k loops is a k-dimensional vector $\vec{d} = \langle [d_1^-, d_1^+], \ldots, [d_k^-, d_k^+] \rangle$, where each $[d_i^-, d_i^+]$ is a (possibly infinite) range of integers and infinite values satisfying $d_i^- \in Z \cup \{-\infty\}$, $d_i^+ \in Z \cup \{\infty\}$, and $d_i^- \leq d_i^+$. Note that a dependence vector corresponds to a (possibly infinite) set of distance vectors called its *distance vector set* $DV(\vec{d})$, as follows:

$$DV(\vec{d}) = \{\langle a_1, \ldots, a_k \rangle \mid a_i \in Z \text{ and } d_i^- \leq a_i \leq d_i^+\}$$

If $d_i^- = d_i^+$ for $1 \leq i \leq k$, then the dependence vector is a distance vector. Conventionally, we write such single values in place of their ranges. As above, the ranges $[1, \infty]$, $[-\infty, -1]$, and $[-\infty, \infty]$ correspond to the directions "$+$" or "$<$", "$-$" or "$>$", and "$\pm$" or "$*$".

The dependences for the loop nest in Figure 9.8 can now be represented by the dependence vector $\langle 0, [0, 1] \rangle$.

Note that dependences with distance $\langle 0, 0, \ldots, 0 \rangle$ have no effect on loop transformations that avoid reordering the statements in the body of a loop. Accordingly, we may omit mentioning such dependences.

Further, a dependence may be *loop-independent*, i.e., independent of the loops surrounding it, or *loop-carried*, i.e., present because of the loops around it. In Figure 9.8, the dependence of S3 on S2 arising from the use of b[i1,i2] in S2 and its definition in S3 is loop-independent—even if there were no loops around the statements, the antidependence would still be valid. In contrast, the flow dependence of S2 on S3, arising from S2's setting an element of a[ ] and S3's use of it one iteration of the i2 loop later, is loop-carried and, in particular, carried by the inner loop; removing the outer loop would make no difference in this dependence. A loop-independent dependence is denoted by a subscript zero attached to the dependence symbol and a dependence carried by loop i (counting outward) by a subscript $i \geq 1$. Thus, for example, for the dependences in Figure 9.8, we have

```
for i ← 1 to n do
    for j ← 1 to n do
S1          a[i,j] ← (a[i-1,j] + a[i+1,j])/2.0
    endfor
endfor
```

FIG. 9.13 An assignment S1 with the distance vector $\langle 1, 0 \rangle$.

$$S2[i1, i2-1]\delta_1^f \; S3[i1, i2]$$

$$S2[i1, i2]\delta_0^a \; S3[i1, i2]$$

or in the distance vector notation:

$$S2[i1, i2-1] \; \langle 0, 1 \rangle_1 \; S3[i1, i2]$$

$$S2[i1, i2] \; \langle 0, 0 \rangle_0 \; S3[i1, i2]$$

These concepts are useful in doing scalar replacement of array elements (Section 20.3).

As another example, the assignment in Figure 9.13 has the distance vector $\langle 1, 0 \rangle$ and is carried by the outer loop, i.e.,

$$S1[i1-1, j] \; \langle 1, 0 \rangle_1 \; S1[i1, j]$$

9.4   Dependence Testing

In Section 20.4, we are concerned with transforming loop nests to take better advantage of the memory hierarchy. Most of the transformations we consider there are applicable only if there are no dependences (of particular kinds, depending on the transformation) between iterations of a loop nest. Thus, it is essential to be able to determine whether there are dependences present in a loop nest and, if so, what they are.

Consider the example loop in Figure 9.14(a). To determine whether there are any dependences between references to a[ ] in the same iteration, we must determine whether there exists an integer i that satisfies the equation

$$2 * i + 1 = 3 * i - 5$$

and the inequality $1 \leq i \leq 4$. The equation is easily seen to hold if and only if $i = 6$, and this value of i does not satisfy the inequality, so there are no same-iteration dependences (i.e., dependences with distance 0) in this loop.

```
for i ← 1 to 4 do              for i ← 1 to 4 do
    b[i] ← a[3*i-5] + 2.0          b[i] ← a[4*i] + 2.0
    a[2*i+1] ← 1.0/i               a[2*i+1] ← 1.0/i
endfor                         endfor
(a)                            (b)
```

FIG. 9.14 Two example HIR loops for dependence testing.

To determine whether there are any dependences between references to a[ ] in different iterations, we seek integers i_1 and i_2 that satisfy the equation

$$2 * i_1 + 1 = 3 * i_2 - 5$$

and that both satisfy the given inequality. Again, we can easily determine that for any i, $i_1 = 3 * i$ and $i_2 = 2 * i + 2$ satisfy the equation, and for $i = 1$, we get $i_1 = 3$ and $i_2 = 4$, both of which satisfy the inequality. Thus, there is a dependence with positive distance in the loop: a[7] is used in iteration 3 and set in iteration 4.

Notice that if the loop limits were nonconstant expressions, we would not be able to conclude that there was no dependence with distance 0—we could only conclude that there might be a dependence with distance 0 or a positive distance, since the inequality would no longer be applicable.

Next, suppose we change the first statement in the loop to fetch a[4*i], as in Figure 9.14(b). Now we must satisfy the equation

$$2 * i_1 + 1 = 4 * i_2$$

either for the same or different integer values of i_1 and i_2 and the same inequality as above, as well. It is easy to see that this is not possible, regardless of satisfying the inequality—the left-hand side of the equation is odd for any value of i_1, while the right-hand side is even for any value of i_2. Thus there are no dependences in the second loop, regardless of the values of the loop bounds.

In general, testing whether there are dependences present in a loop nest and, if so, what they are is a problem in *constrained Diophantine equations*—i.e., solving one or more equations with integer coefficients for integer solutions that also satisfy given inequalities, which is equivalent to *integer programming,* a problem that is known to be *NP*-complete. However, almost all subscript expressions occurring in real programs are very simple.

In particular, the subscripts are almost always linear expressions of the loop indexes, and, from this point on, we assume that this is the case. Often the subscripts are linear expressions in a single index. Accordingly, we assume that we are given a loop nest of the form shown in Figure 9.15 with n loops indexed by the variables i_1 through i_n and two references to elements of the array x[ ] with subscripts that are all linear expressions in the loop indexes. There is a dependence present if and only if for each subscript position the equation

$$a_0 + \sum_{j=1}^{n} a_j * i_{j,1} = b_0 + \sum_{j=1}^{n} b_j * i_{j,2}$$

and the inequalities

$$1 \le i_{j,1} \le h i_j \text{ and } 1 \le i_{j,2} \le h i_j \text{ for } j = 1, \dots, n$$

are jointly satisfied. Of course, the type of dependence is determined by whether each instance of x[...] is a use or a definition. There are numerous methods in use for testing for dependence or independence. We describe several in detail and give references for a list of others.

```
for i₁ ← 1 to hi₁ do
    for i₂ ← 1 to hi₂ do
        ...
            for iₙ ← 1 to hiₙ do
                ...
                ... x[..., a₀ + a₁ * i₁ + ··· + aₙ * iₙ, ...] ···
                ...
                ... x[..., b₀ + b₁ * i₁ + ··· + bₙ * iₙ, ...] ···
                ...
            endfor
        ...
    endfor
endfor
```

FIG. 9.15 Form of the HIR loop nest assumed for dependence testing.

The earliest test currently in use is known as the GCD (greatest common divisor) test and was developed by Banerjee [Bane76] and Towle [Towl76]. It is a comparatively weak test in terms of its ability to prove independence. The *GCD test* states that if, for at least one subscript position,

$$\gcd\left(\bigcup_{j=1}^{n} \text{sep}(a_j, b_j, j)\right) \nmid \sum_{j=0}^{n} (a_j - b_j)$$

where gcd( ) is the greatest common divisor function, "$a \nmid b$" means a does not divide b, and $\text{sep}(a, b, j)$ is defined by[2]

$$\text{sep}(a, b, j) = \begin{cases} \{a - b\} & \text{if direction } j \text{ is } = \\ \{a, b\} & \text{otherwise} \end{cases}$$

then the two references to x[...] are independent; or equivalently, if there is a dependence, then the GCD divides the sum. For example, for our loop in Figure 9.14(a), the test for a same-iteration dependence reduces to

$$\gcd(3 - 2) \nmid (-5 - 1 + 3 - 2)$$

or $1 \nmid -5$, which is false, and so tells us only that there may be a dependence. Similarly, for inter-iteration dependence, we have

$$\gcd(3, 2) \nmid (-5 - 1 + 3 - 2)$$

or again $1 \nmid -5$, which again fails to rule out independence. For the example in Figure 9.14(b), on the other hand, we have

$$\gcd(4, 2) \nmid (-1 + 4 - 2)$$

which reduces to $2 \nmid 1$. Since this is true, these two array references are independent.

---

2. Note that since $\gcd(a, b) = \gcd(a, a - b) = \gcd(b, a - b)$ for all a and b, the unequal direction case includes the equal direction case.

The GCD test can be generalized to arbitrary lower loop bounds and loop increments. To do so, assume the jth loop control is

for $i_j \leftarrow lo_j$ by inc_j to hi_j

Then the GCD test states that if, for at least one subscript position,

$$\gcd\left(\bigcup_{j=1}^{n} sep(a_j * inc_j, b_j * inc_j, j)\right) \nmid a_0 - b_0 + \sum_{j=1}^{n} (a_j - b_j) * lo_j$$

then the two instances of x[...] are independent.

Two important classes of array references are the separable and weakly separable ones, which are found to occur almost to the exclusion of others in a very wide range of real programs. A pair of array references is *separable* if in each pair of subscript positions the expressions found are of the form $a * i_j + b_1$ and $a * i_j + b_2$ where i_j is a loop control variable and a, b_1, and b_2 are constants. A pair of array references is *weakly separable* if each pair of subscript expressions is of the form $a_1 * i_j + b_1$ and $a_2 * i_j + b_2$ where i_j is as above and a_1, a_2, b_1, and b_2 are constants. Both of our examples in Figure 9.14 are weakly separable but not separable.

For a separable pair of array references, testing dependence is trivial: a dependence exists if either of two situations holds for each subscript position, namely,

1. $a = 0$ and $b_1 = b_2$, or

2. $(b_1 - b_2)/a \leq hi_j$.

For a weakly separable pair of array references, we have for each subscript position j a linear equation of the form

$$a_1 * y + b_1 = a_2 * x + b_2$$

or

$$a_1 * y = a_2 * x + (b_2 - b_1)$$

and there is a dependence between the two references if each set of equations for a particular value of j has a solution that satisfies the inequality given by the bounds of loop j. Now we appeal to the theory of linear equations and divide the problem into cases, as follows (in each case, the solutions represent dependences if and only if they satisfy the bounds inequalities):

(a) If the set of equations has one member, assume it is as given above. Then we have one linear equation in two unknowns and there are integer solutions if and only if $\gcd(a_1, a_2) \mid (b_2 - b_1)$.

(b) If the set of equations has two members, say,

$$a_{1,1} * y = a_{2,1} * x + (b_{2,1} - b_{1,1})$$

and

$$a_{1,2} * y = a_{2,2} * x + (b_{2,2} - b_{1,2})$$

```
for i ← 1 to n do
    for j ← 1 to n do
        f[i] ← g[2*i,j] + 1.0
        g[i+1,3*j] ← h[i,i] - 1.5
        h[i+2,2*i-2] ← 1.0/i
    endfor
endfor
```

FIG. 9.16 An example of weak separability.

then it is a system of two equations in two unknowns. If $a_{2,1}/a_{1,1} = a_{2,2}/a_{1,2}$, there are rational solutions if and only if

$$(b_{2,1} - b_{1,1})/a_{1,1} = (b_{2,2} - b_{1,2})/a_{1,2}$$

and the solutions are easily enumerated. If $a_{2,1}/a_{1,1} \neq a_{2,2}/a_{1,2}$, then there is one rational solution, and it is easily determined. In either case, we check that the solutions are integers and that the required inequalities are also satisfied.

(c) If the set of equations has $n > 2$ members, then either $n - 2$ equations are redundant and this case reduces to the preceding one or it is a system of at least three equations in two unknowns and is overdetermined.

As an example of weak separability, consider the loop nest in Figure 9.16. We first consider the g[ ] references. For there to be a dependence, we must have for the first subscript

$$2 * x = y + 1$$

and for the second

$$z = 3 * w$$

The two equations are independent of each other and each has an infinite number of integer solutions. In particular, there are dependences between the array references as long as n ≥ 3. For the h[ ] references, we must satisfy

$$x = y + 2$$

and

$$x = 2 * y - 2$$

simultaneously. This is easily seen to be true if and only if $x = 6$ and $y = 4$, so there is a dependence if and only if n ≥ 6.

As indicated above, there are numerous other dependence tests available with varying power and computational complexity (see Section 9.8 for further reading). These include:

1. the extended GCD test,

2. the strong and weak SIV (single index variable) tests,

3. the Delta test,

4. the Acyclic test,

5. the Power test,

6. the Simple Loop Residue test,

7. the Fourier-Motzkin test,

8. the Constraint-Matrix test, and

9. the Omega test.

9.5   Program-Dependence Graphs

Program-dependence graphs, or PDGs, are an intermediate-code form designed for use in optimization. The PDG for a program consists of a control-dependence graph (CDG)[3] and a data-dependence graph. Nodes in a PDG may be basic blocks, statements, individual operators, or constructs at some in-between level. The data-dependence graph is as described above in Sections 9.1 and 9.3.

The CDG, in its most basic form, is a DAG that has program predicates (or, if the nodes are basic blocks, blocks that end with predicates) as its root and internal nodes, and nonpredicates as its leaves. A leaf is executed during the execution of the program if the predicates on the path leading to it in the control-dependence graph are satisfied.

More specifically, let $G = \langle N, E \rangle$ be a flowgraph for a procedure. Recall that a node m postdominates node n, written m *pdom* n, if and only if every path from n to `exit` passes through m (see Section 7.3). Then node n is *control-dependent* on node m if and only if

1. there exists a control-flow path from m to n such that every node in the path other than m is postdominated by n and

2. n does not postdominate m.[4]

To construct the CDG, we first construct the basic CDG and then add so-called *region nodes* to it. To construct the basic CDG, we begin by adding a dummy predicate node called `start` to the flowgraph with its "Y" edge running to the `entry` node and its "N" edge to `exit`. Call the resulting graph G^+. Next, we construct the postdominance relation on G^+,[5] which can be displayed as a tree, and we define S to be the set of edges $m \rightarrow n$ in G^+ such that n does not postdominate m. Now for

---

3. [FerO87] defines two notions of the control-dependence graph, the one we discuss here (called by the authors the *exact* CDG) and the *approximate* CDG, which shows the same dependences as the exact CDG for well-structured programs and from which it is somewhat easier to generate sequential code.

4. Note that this notion of control dependence is a subrelation of the one discussed in Section 9.1.

5. This can be done by reversing the edges in the flowgraph and using either of the dominator-computation algorithms in Section 7.3.

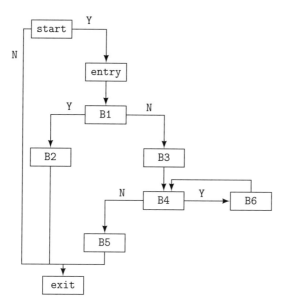

FIG. 9.17 Flowgraph from Figure 7.4 with `start` node added.

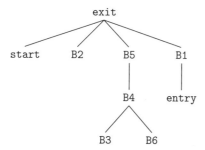

FIG. 9.18 Postdominance tree for the flowgraph in Figure 9.17.

each edge $m \to n \in S$, we determine the lowest common ancestor of m and n in the *postdominance tree* (or m itself if it is the root). The resulting node l is either m or m's parent, and all nodes in N on the path from l to n in the postdominance tree except l are control-dependent on m.

For example, consider the flowgraph shown in Figure 7.4. The result of adding the `start` node is Figure 9.17 and its postdominance tree is shown in Figure 9.18. The set S consists of `start`→`entry`, B1→B2, B1→B3, and B4→B6, and the basic CDG is as shown in Figure 9.19.

The purpose of region nodes is to group together all the nodes that have the same control dependence on a particular predicate node, giving each predicate node at most two successors, as in the original control-flow graph. The result of adding region nodes to our example is shown in Figure 9.20.

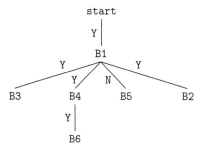

FIG. 9.19 Basic control-dependence graph for the flowgraph in Figure 9.17.

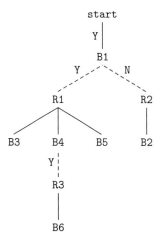

FIG. 9.20 Control-dependence graph with region nodes for the flowgraph in Figure 9.17.

An important property of PDGs is that nodes control-dependent on the same node, such as B3 and B5 in our example, can be executed in parallel as long as there are no data dependences between them.

Several other intermediate-code forms with goals similar to those of the program-dependence graph have been suggested in the literature. These include the dependence flowgraph, the program-dependence web, and the value-dependence graph.

9.6 Dependences Between Dynamically Allocated Objects

So far we have discussed dependences between machine instructions and between array accesses, plus the program-dependence graph. Another area of concern is large dynamically allocated data structures linked by pointers, e.g., lists, trees, DAGs, and other graph structures that are used in both algebraic and symbolic languages, such as LISP, Prolog, and Smalltalk. If we can determine that such a data structure or graph is, for example, a linked list, a tree, or a DAG, or that parts of it are never shared (i.e., accessible from two variables at once through a chain of pointers), we may be able to improve memory or cache allocation for it, just as for arrays.

Some of the pioneering work in this area was done in the mid 1970s by Tenenbaum and by Jones and Muchnick, designed largely as an attempt to assign data types to variables in a language in which only data objects have types *a priori;* there has been a flurry of research activity in recent years. More recent papers by Deutsch and by Hummel, Hendren, and Nicolau present approaches with impressive results, but these approaches require large amounts of computational effort to obtain their results. (See Section 9.8 for further reading.)

We describe briefly a technique developed by Hummel, Hendren, and Nicolau. What it does consists of three parts, namely, (1) it develops a naming scheme for anonymous locations in heap memory by describing the relationships between such locations; (2) it develops axioms that characterize the basic aliasing relations among locations and/or the lack thereof in the data structures; and (3) it uses a theorem prover to establish desired properties of the structures, such as that a particular structure is a queue expressed as a linked list with items added at one end and removed from the other.

The naming scheme uses the names of fixed locations and fields in records to specify relationships. Specifically it uses *handles,* which name fixed nodes (usually pointer variables) in a structure and have the form _h*var* where *var* is a variable name, and *access-path matrices,* which express relationships between handles and variables. Thus, for the C type declaration in Figure 9.21(a) and some particular programs, the axioms in (b) might be applicable. The third axiom, for example, says that any location reachable from a pointer variable p by one or more accesses of left or right components is distinct from the location denoted by p itself.

Figure 9.22 shows a C function that uses the data type defined in Figure 9.21(a) and that satisfies the given axioms. An access-path matrix for the program point

```
typedef struct node {struct node *left;
                     struct node *right;
                     int val} node;
```
(a)

```
Ax1: ∀p p.left ≠ p.right
Ax2: ∀p,q p ≠ q ⇒ p.left ≠ q.left,
                  p.left ≠ q.right,
                  p.right ≠ q.left,
                  p.right ≠ q.right
Ax3: ∀p p(.left|.right)⁺ ≠ p.ε
```
(b)

FIG. 9.21   (a) Example of a C type declaration for a recursive data structure, and (b) axioms that apply to structures built from it.

```
typedef struct node {struct node *left;
                     struct node *right;
                     int val} node;

int follow(ptr,i,j)
   struct node *ptr;
   int i, j;
{  struct node *p1, *p2;
   int n;
   p1 = ptr;
   p2 = ptr;
   for (n = 0; n < i; n++)
      p1 = p1->left;
   for (n = 0; n < j; n++)
      p2 = p2->right;
   return (p1 == p2);
}
```

FIG. 9.22 Example of a C function that uses structures of the type defined in Figure 9.21.

TABLE 9.1 Access-path matrix for the point just preceding the return in Figure 9.22. The value at the intersection of row _h$var1$ and column $var2$ represents the path from the original value of $var1$ to the current value of $var2$. A "-" entry means there is no such path.

	ptr	p1	p2
_hptr	ϵ	$left^+$	$right^+$
_hp1	–	$left^+$	$right^+$
_hp2	–	$left^+$	$right^+$

just preceding the `return` is given in Table 9.1. The theorem prover can, given the axioms in Figure 9.21(b), prove that the function returns 0.

Note that, like most powerful theories, those that describe pointer operations are undecidable. Thus the theorem prover may answer any of "yes," "no," or "maybe" for a particular problem.

9.7   Wrap-Up

As we have seen in this chapter, dependence analysis is a tool that is vital to instruction scheduling and data-cache optimization, both of which are discussed in their own chapters below.

For instruction scheduling, dependence analysis determines the ordering relationships between instructions that must be satisfied for the code to execute correctly, and so determines the freedom available to the scheduler to rearrange the code to improve performance. In doing so, it takes into account as many of the relevant resources as it can. It definitely must determine ordering among instructions that affect and depend on registers and implicit resources, such as condition codes. It usually will also disambiguate memory addresses to the degree it is able—often depending on information passed on to it from earlier phases of the compilation process—again so as to provide the maximum latitude for scheduling.

As a tool for data-cache optimization, the primary purpose of dependence analysis is to determine, for two or more given memory references—usually subscripted array references nested inside one or more loops—whether the areas of memory they access overlap and what relation they have to each other if they do overlap. This determines, for example, whether they both (or all) write to the same location, or whether one writes to it and the other reads from it, etc. Determining what dependences do hold and which loops they are carried by provides a large fraction of the information necessary to reorder or otherwise modify the loops and array references to improve data-cache performance. It is also an essential tool for compilers that do automatic vectorization and/or parallelization, but that subject is beyond the scope of this book.

Also, we discussed a relatively new intermediate-code form called the program-dependence graph that makes dependences explicit and that has been proposed as a basis for doing data-cache optimization and other sorts of optimizations. Several variations on this concept are referred to in the text, suggesting that it is not yet clear which, if any, of them will become important tools for optimization.

We devoted another of the final sections of the chapter to techniques for dependence analysis of dynamically allocated objects that are accessed by pointers. This is an area that has been the subject of research for well over 20 years, and while effective methods for performing it are becoming available, they are also very computation-intensive, leaving it in doubt as to whether such techniques will come to be important components in production compilers.

9.8   Further Reading

The reader interested in an exposition of the use of dependence analysis to drive vectorization or parallelization should consult [Wolf92], [Wolf89b], [Bane88], or [ZimC91].

The use of resource vectors to compute latency is described in [BraH91]. Our description of the pipeline of the MIPS R4000's floating-point pipeline is derived from [KanH92]. Use of a deterministic finite automaton to compute latency is described in [ProF94].

Dependence vectors are defined by Wolf and Lam in [WolL91]. The proof that general dependence testing in loop nests is *NP*-complete is found in [MayH91]. The GCD test developed by Banerjee and Towle is described in [Bane76] and [Towl76]. The classes of separable and weakly separable array references are defined in [Call86]. Among the other types of dependence tests in use are the following:

Dependence Test	References
The extended GCD test	[Bane88]
The strong and weak SIV (single index variable) tests	[GofK91]
The Delta test	[GofK91]
The Acyclic test	[MayH91]
The Power test	[WolT90]
The Simple Loop Residue test	[MayH91]
The Fourier-Motzkin test	[DanE73] and [MayH91]
The Constraint-Matrix test	[Wall88]
The Omega test	[PugW92]

[GofK91] and [MayH91] evaluate several tests for their applicability and practicality.

Program-dependence graphs are defined in [FerO87]. The alternative forms are the dependence flowgraph defined in [JohP93], the program-dependence web of [CamK93], and the value-dependence graph of [WeiC94].

The early work on assigning types to variables in dynamic languages was done by Tenenbaum ([Tene74a] and [Tene74b]) and by Jones and Muchnick ([JonM76] and [JonM78]).

Some of the pioneering work in characterizing the memory usage and dependences among recursive data structures was done by Jones and Muchnick in [JonM81a]. More recent work is reported in [WolH90], [Deut94], and [HumH94].

9.9   Exercises

9.1 (a) What are the dependences between the LIR instructions in the following basic block? (b) Use Build_DAG( ) to construct the scheduling DAG for the block and draw the resulting dependence DAG.

```
r1 ← [r7+4](4)
r2 ← [r7+8](2)
r3 ← r2 + 2
r4 ← r1 + r2
[r5](4) ← r4
r4 ← r5 - r3
[r5](4) ← r4
[r7+r2](2) ← r3
r4 ← r3 + r4
r3 ← r7 + r4
r7 ← r7 + 2
```

9.2 Let the floating-point addition instruction have the following resource vector:

1	2	3	4	5	6	7
U	S,A	A,R	R,S			

Supposing that the LIR add instruction f4 ← f3 + 1.0 is available for initiation in cycle 1, compute the latency of the instruction with the pipeline containing instructions that use the following execution resources in the following stages of the pipeline:

1	2	3	4	5	6	7	8	9	10	11
M	U,A	A	S	R,S	S	M	M,U	A	S,A	R

9.3   Hewlett-Packard's PA-RISC compilers build the basic-block scheduling DAG backward, i.e., from the leaves toward the roots, so as to track uses of condition flags and the instructions that set them. Code a version of Build_DAG( ) called Build_Back_DAG( ) that does this for LIR code.

ADV 9.4   Research the notion of extending the dependence graph from a basic block to any single-entry, single-exit subgraph of a flowgraph that contains no loops. Does this give additional freedom in instruction scheduling? If so, give an example. If not, why not?

9.5   What is the iteration-space traversal of the following triply nested HIR loop?

```
    for i ← 1 to n do
        for j ← n by -1 to 1 do
            for k ← 1 to n+1 do
S1              A[i,j,k] ← A[i,j-1,k-1] + A[i-1,j,k]
S2              B[i,j-1,k] ← A[i,j-1,k-1] * 2.0
S3              A[i,j,k+1] ← B[i,j,k] + 1.0
            endfor
        endfor
    endfor
```

9.6   Given the loop nest in the preceding exercise, what are the execution-order and dependence relationships within it?

9.7   (a) Write an algorithm that, given a distance vector, produces the minimal dependence vector that covers it, where d_1 covers d_2 if and only if any dependence expressed by d_2 is also represented by d_1. (b) Do the same thing for direction vectors.

9.8   Give a three-deep loop nest that the GCD test determines independence for.

RSCH 9.9   Research the Delta test described in [GofK91]. (a) How does it work? (b) How effective is it? (c) What does it cost?

RSCH 9.10   Research the Omega test described in [PugW92]. (a) How does it work? (b) How effective is it? (c) What does it cost?

RSCH 9.11   Research the notion of extending dependence to synchronized accesses to shared variables in a parallel language; i.e., what are appropriate meanings for $S_1 \, \delta^f \, S_2$, $S_1 \, \delta^a \, S_2$, etc. in this situation?

CHAPTER 10

Alias Analysis

A*lias analysis* refers to the determination of storage locations that may be accessed in two or more ways. For example, a C variable may have its address computed and be assigned to or read from both by name and through a pointer, as shown in Figure 10.1, a situation that can be visualized as shown in Figure 10.2, where the boxes represent the variables, with each box labeled with its name and containing its value. As hinted at in Chapter 8, determining the range of possible aliases in a program is essential to optimizing it correctly, while minimizing the sets of aliases found is important to doing optimization as aggressively as possible. If we should happen to miss identifying an alias, we can very easily produce incorrect code for a program. Consider the C code fragment in Figure 10.3. The second k = a + 5 assignment is redundant if and only if both the call to f( ) and the assignment through the pointer q leave the values of both k and a unmodified. Since the address of k is passed to f( ), it might alter k's value. Since q is external, either f( ) or some earlier unshown code in procedure exam1( ) might have set it to point to either a or k. If either of these situations is the case, the second k = a + 5 assignment is not provably redundant. If neither of them is the case, the assignment is redundant. This example shows the significance of both intraprocedural and interprocedural alias determination. In practice, intraprocedural alias determination is usually the more important of the two. We consider it here in detail and leave the interprocedural case to Chapter 19.

Despite the fact that high-quality aliasing information is essential to correct and aggressive optimization, there are many programs for which only the most minimal such information is needed. Despite the fact that a C program may contain arbitrarily complex aliasing, it is sufficient for most C programs to assume that only variables whose addresses are computed are aliased and that any pointer-valued variable may point to any of them. In most cases, this assumption places minimal restrictions on optimization. If, on the other hand, we have a C program with 200 variables such that 100 of them have their addresses computed and the other

```
main()
{  int *p;
   int n;
   p = &n;
   n = 4;
   printf("%d\n",*p);
}
```

FIG. 10.1 Simple pointer aliasing in C.

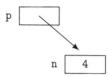

FIG. 10.2 Relationship between the variables at the call to printf( ) in Figure 10.1.

```
exam1( )
{  int a, k;
   extern int *q;
      . . .
   k = a + 5;
   f(a,&k);
   *q = 13;
   k = a + 5;   /* redundant? */
      . . .
}
```

FIG. 10.3 Example of the importance of alias computation.

100 are pointer-valued, then clearly aggressive alias analysis is essential to most optimizations that might be performed on the program.

In the following chapters on global optimization, we generally assume that alias analysis has been performed and do not mention it further. Nevertheless, the reader must be aware that alias analysis is essential to performing most optimizations correctly, as the above example suggests.

It is useful to distinguish *may* alias information from *must* alias information. The former indicates what may occur on some path through a flowgraph, while the latter indicates what must occur on all paths through the flowgraph. If, for example, every path through a procedure includes an assignment of the address of variable x to variable p and only assigns that value to p, then "p points to x" is must alias information for the procedure. On the other hand, if the procedure includes paths that assign the address of y to pointer variable q on one of the paths and the address of z on another, then "q may point to y or z" is may alias information.

It is also useful to distinguish flow-sensitive from flow-insensitive alias information. *Flow-insensitive* information is independent of the control flow encountered in a procedure, while *flow-sensitive* aliasing information depends on control flow. An example of a flow-insensitive statement about aliasing is that "p may point to x because there is a path on which p is assigned the address of x." The statement simply indicates that a particular aliasing relationship may hold anywhere in the procedure because it does hold somewhere in the procedure. A flow-sensitive example might indicate that "p points to x in block B7." The above-mentioned approach to alias analysis for C that simply distinguishes variables whose addresses are taken is flow insensitive; the method we describe in detail below is flow sensitive.

In general, the may vs. must classification is important because it tells us whether a property must hold, and hence can be counted on, or that it only may hold, and so must be allowed for but cannot be counted on. The flow-sensitivity classification is important because it determines the computational complexity of the problem under consideration. Flow-insensitive problems can usually be solved by solving subproblems and then combining their solutions to provide a solution for the whole problem, independent of control flow. Flow-sensitive problems, on the other hand, require that one follow the control-flow paths through the flowgraph to compute their solutions.

The formal characterization of aliasing depends on whether we are concerned with may or must information and whether it is flow sensitive or flow insensitive. The cases are as follows:

1. *Flow-insensitive may information*: In this case, aliasing is a binary relation on the variables in a procedure *alias* $\in$ *Var* $\times$ *Var*, such that x *alias* y if and only if x and y may, possibly at different times, refer to the same storage location. The relation is symmetric and intransitive.[1] The relation is intransitive because the fact that a and b may refer to the same storage location at some point and b and c may, likewise, refer to the same location at some point does not allow us to conclude anything about a and c—the relationships a *alias* b and b *alias* c may simply hold at different points in the procedure.

2. *Flow-insensitive must information*: In this case, aliasing is again a binary relation *alias* $\in$ *Var* $\times$ *Var*, but with a different meaning. We have x *alias* y if and only if x and y must, throughout the execution of a procedure, refer to the same storage location. This relation is symmetric and transitive. If a and b must refer to the same storage location throughout execution of a procedure and b and c must refer to the same storage location throughout execution of the procedure, then, clearly, a and c refer to the same location also.

3. *Flow-sensitive may information*: In this case, aliasing can be thought of as a set of binary relations, one for each program point (i.e., between two instructions) in a procedure that describes the relationships between variables at that point, but it is clearer and easier to reason about if we make aliasing a function from program points and variables to sets of abstract storage locations. In this formulation, for a program point p and a variable v, $Alias(p, v) = SL$ means that at point p variable v

---

1. It does not matter whether we make the relation reflexive or irreflexive, since x *alias* x provides no useful information.

may refer to any of the locations in SL. Now if $Alias(p, a) \cap Alias(p, b) \neq \emptyset$ and $Alias(p, b) \cap Alias(p, c) \neq \emptyset$, then it may be the case that $Alias(p, a) \cap Alias(p, c) \neq \emptyset$ also, but this is not necessarily the case. Also, if $p1$, $p2$, and $p3$ are distinct program points, $Alias(p1, a) \cap Alias(p2, a) \neq \emptyset$, and $Alias(p2, a) \cap Alias(p3, a) \neq \emptyset$, then, likewise, it may also be the case that $Alias(p1, a) \cap Alias(p3, a) \neq \emptyset$.

4. *Flow-sensitive must information*: In this case, aliasing is best characterized as a function from program points and variables to abstract storage locations (not sets of locations). In this formulation, for a program point p and a variable v, $Alias(p, v) = l$ means that at point p variable v must refer to location l. Now if $Alias(p, a) = Alias(p, b)$ and $Alias(p, b) = Alias(p, c)$, then it must be the case that $Alias(p, a) = Alias(p, c)$ also. Similarly, if $p1$, $p2$, and $p3$ are distinct program points, $Alias(p1, a) = Alias(p2, a)$, and $Alias(p2, a) = Alias(p3, a)$, then it must also be the case that $Alias(p1, a) = Alias(p3, a)$. Thus, flow-sensitive must aliasing information for a particular program point is a transitive relation between variables, and flow-sensitive must information for a particular variable is a transitive relation between program points. It is also easy to see that each of those relations is symmetric.

This classification is further complicated by the inclusion of pointers in a language as is the case, for example, in C. Then any object that may refer to a storage location, such as a pointer field in a record, may be aliased to any other reference to a location. Thus, in a language with pointers, aliasing is a relation or function between references to locations, where references include any objects that may have pointers as their values, not just variables.

The sources of aliases vary from language to language, but there is a common component to alias computation as well. For example, a language may allow two variables to overlay one another or may allow one to be a pointer to the other or not, but regardless of these language-specific rules, if variable a is pointed to by variable b and b is pointed to by c at a given execution point, then a is reachable by following pointers from c. Thus, we divide alias computation into two parts:

1. a language-specific component, called the *alias gatherer,* that we expect the compiler front end to provide us; and

2. a single component in the optimizer, called the *alias propagator,* that performs a data-flow analysis using the aliasing relations discovered by the front end to combine aliasing information and transfer it to the points where it is needed.

The language-specific alias gatherer may discover aliases that are present because of

1. overlapping of the memory allocated for two objects;

2. references to arrays, array sections, or array elements;

3. references through pointers;

4. parameter passing; or

5. combinations of the above mechanisms.

```
exam2( )
{  int a, b, c[100], d, i;
   extern int *q;
   . . .
   q = &a;
   a = 2;
   b = *q + 2;
   . . .
   q = &b;
   for (i = 0; i < 100; i++) {
      c[i] = c[i] + a;
      *q = i;
   }
   d = *q + a;
}
```

FIG. 10.4 Different aliases in different parts of a procedure.

Before we delve into the details, we consider the granularity of aliasing information that we might compute and its effects. In particular, it might be the case that two variables are provably not aliased in one segment of a procedure, but that they are either aliased or not determinable not to be aliased in another part of it. An example of this is shown in Figure 10.4. Here q points to a in the first section of the code, while it points to b in the second section. If we were to do flow-insensitive may alias computation for the entire procedure (assuming that no other statements affect the possible aliases), we would simply conclude that q could point to either a or b. This would prevent us from moving the assignment *q = i out of the for loop. On the other hand, if we computed aliases with finer granularity, we could conclude that q cannot point to a inside the loop, which would allow us to replace the *q = i assignment inside the loop with a single *q = 100, or even b = 100, after the loop. While this degree of discrimination is definitely valuable in many cases, it may be beyond the scope of what is acceptable in compilation time and memory space. One choice is that of the Sun compilers (see Section 21.1), namely, (optional) aggressive computation of alias information, while the other is taken in the MIPS compilers, which simply assume that any variable whose address is computed can be aliased.

Thus, we leave it to the individual compiler writer to choose the granularity appropriate for a given implementation. We describe an approach that does distinguish individual points within a procedure; the reader can easily modify it to one that does not.

10.1   Aliases in Various Real Programming Languages

Next we consider the forms of alias information that should be collected by a front end and passed on to the alias propagator. We examine four commonly used languages, namely, Fortran 77, Pascal, C, and Fortran 90. We assume that the reader is generally familiar with each of the languages. Following exploration of aliasing in these four languages, we present an approach to alias gathering that is similar in some respects to that taken in the Hewlett-Packard compilers for PA-RISC, but that differs from it significantly in alias propagation. While that compiler's propagation method is flow insensitive, ours is specifically flow sensitive—in fact, the propagation method we use is data-flow-analytic, i.e., it performs a data-flow analysis to determine the aliases.

10.1.1   Aliases in Fortran 77

In ANSI-standard Fortran 77, there are comparatively few ways to create aliases and they are mostly detectable exactly during compilation. However, one consideration we must keep in mind is that established programming practice in this area occasionally violates the Fortran 77 standard; and most compilers follow practice, at least to some degree, rather than the standard.

The EQUIVALENCE statement can be used to specify that two or more scalar variables, array variables, and/or contiguous portions of array variables begin at the same storage location. The variables are local to the subprogram in which they are equivalenced, unless they are also specified in a COMMON statement, in which case they may be accessible to several subprograms. Thus, the effects of aliases created by EQUIVALENCE statements are purely local and statically determinable, as long as the equivalenced variables are not also in common storage, as described in the next paragraph.

The COMMON statement associates variables in different subprograms with the same storage. COMMON is unusual for modern programming languages in that it associates variables by location, rather than by name. Determining the full effects of variables in common storage requires interprocedural analysis, but one can at least determine locally that a variable is potentially affected by other subprograms because it is in common storage.

In Fortran 77, parameters are passed in such a way that, as long as the actual argument is associated with a named storage location (e.g., it is a variable or an array element, rather than a constant or an expression), the called subprogram can change the value of the actual argument by assigning a value to the corresponding formal parameter.[2] It is not specified in the standard whether the mechanism of argument-parameter association is call by reference or call by value-result; both implement the Fortran 77 convention correctly.

Section 15.9.3.6 of the Fortran 77 standard says that if one passes the same actual argument to two or more formal parameters of a subprogram or if an argument is an object in common storage, then neither the subprogram nor any subprograms in the call chain below it can assign a new value to the argument. If compilers enforced this rule, the only aliases in Fortran 77 would be those created by EQUIVALENCE and COMMON statements. Unfortunately, some programs violate this rule and compilers sometimes use it to decide whether a construct can be optimized in a particular way. Thus, we might consider there to also exist a "practical" Fortran 77 that includes aliases created by parameter passing (see Section 15.2 for an example), but we would

---

2. The actual Fortran terminology is "actual argument" and "dummy argument."

be on dangerous ground in doing so—some compilers would support it consistently, others inconsistently, and some possibly not at all.

Fortran 77 has no global storage other than variables in common, so there are no other ways to create aliases with nonlocal objects than by placing them in common or by violating the parameter-passing conventions as just described.

Several Fortran 77 compilers include the Cray extensions. These provide, among other things, a limited pointer type. A pointer variable may be set to point to a scalar variable, an array variable, or an absolute storage location (called the pointer's *pointee*), and the pointer's value may be changed during execution of a program. However, it cannot point to another pointer. Also, a pointee cannot appear in a COMMON or EQUIVALENCE statement or be a formal parameter. This extension greatly increases the possibilities for alias creation, since multiple pointers may point to the same location. The Cray compiler, on the other hand, assumes during compilations performed with optimization enabled that no two pointers point to the same location and, more generally, that a pointee is never overlaid on another variable's storage. Clearly, this places the burden of alias analysis on the programmer and can cause programs to produce different results according to whether optimization is enabled or not, but it also allows the compiler to proceed without doing alias analysis on pointers or to proceed by making worst-case assumptions about them.

10.1.2   Aliases in Pascal

In ANSI-standard Pascal, there are several mechanisms for creating aliases, including variant records, pointers, variable parameters, access to nonlocal variables by nested procedures, recursion, and values returned by functions.

Variables of a user-defined record type may have multiple variants and the variants may be either tagged or untagged. Allowing multiple untagged variants is similar to having equivalenced variables in Fortran 77—if a variable is of an untagged variant-record type, its variant fields may be accessed by two or more sets of names.

A Pascal variable of a pointer type is restricted to have either the value nil or to point to objects of a particular specified type. Since the language provides no way to obtain the address of an existing object, a non-null pointer can point only to an object allocated dynamically by the procedure new( ). new(p) takes a pointer variable p as its argument, allocates an object of the type declared to be pointed to by p, and sets p to point to it.[3] Pointer variables of a given type may be assigned to other pointer variables of the same type, so multiple pointers may point to the same object. Thus, an object may be accessible through several pointers at once, but it cannot both have its own variable name and be accessible through a pointer.

Pascal procedure parameters are either value parameters or variable parameters. An actual argument passed to a value parameter cannot be changed by the called procedure through the parameter, and so value parameters do not create aliases.

---

3. new( ) may be given additional arguments that specify nested variants of the record type its first argument points to; in that case, it allocates an object of the specified variant type.

Variable parameters, on the other hand, allow the called routine to change the associated actual argument, and hence do create aliases.

Also, Pascal allows procedure definitions to be nested and inner procedures to access variables defined in outer ones, as long as they are visible, i.e., as long as no intervening procedure in the nesting sequence defines a variable with the same name. Thus, for example, a dynamically allocated object in a Pascal program may be accessible as a variable parameter, through a locally declared pointer, and through a nonlocally declared pointer all at once.

A Pascal procedure may be recursive, so that a variable declared in an inner scope may be accessible to multiple invocations and a local variable of one invocation of it may be accessible as a variable parameter of a deeper invocation.

Finally, a Pascal procedure may return a pointer and hence can create an alias for a dynamically allocated object.

10.1.3   Aliases in C

In ANSI-standard C, there is one mechanism for creating static aliases, namely, the union type specifier, which is similar in its effect to Fortran 77's EQUIVALENCE construct. A union type may have several fields declared, all of which overlap in storage. C union types differ from Fortran's equivalenced variables, however, in that a union type may be accessed by a pointer and may be dynamically allocated.

Notice that we did *not* say "dynamically allocated and so accessed by a pointer" in the last sentence. C allows objects to be dynamically allocated and, of course, references to them must be through pointers, since there is no dynamic name-creation mechanism. Such objects can be referenced through multiple pointers, so pointers may alias each other. In addition, it is legal in C to compute the address of an object with the & operator, regardless of whether it is statically, automatically, or dynamically allocated and to access or store to it through a pointer assigned its address.

C also allows arithmetic on pointers and considers it equivalent to array indexing—increasing a pointer to an array element by 1 causes it to point to the next element of the array. Suppose we have the code fragment

```
int a[100], *p;
. . .
p = a;
p = &a[0];
a[1] = 1;
*(p + 2) = 2;
```

Then the two assignments to p assign it exactly the same value, namely, the address of the zeroth element of array a[ ], and the following two assignments assign 1 to a[1] and 2 to a[2], respectively. Even though a C array b[ ] declared to be of length n contains elements numbered from 0 through $n - 1$, it is legal to address b[n], as in

```
int b[100], p;
 . . .
for (p = b; p < &b[100]; p++)
*p = 0;
```

but not valid to dereference b[*n*]. Thus, a pointer-valued expression may alias an array element, and the element it aliases may change over time. Pointer arithmetic could conceivably be used indiscriminately to sweep through memory and create arbitrary aliases, but the ANSI C standard rules the behavior of code that does this to be undefined (see Section 3.3.6 of the ANSI C standard).

C also can create aliases by parameter passing and by returning a pointer value from a function. Although all arguments in C are passed by value, they can create aliases because they may be pointers to arbitrary objects. Also, there is no restriction in C regarding passing the same object as two distinct arguments to a function, so, for example, a function such as

```
f(i,j)
int *i, *j;
{    *i = *j + 1;
}
```

can be invoked with a call such as f(&k,&k), unlike in standard Fortran 77. Further, an argument may point to a global variable, making it accessible in the procedure both by name and through the pointer. A pointer returned as the value of a function may point to any object accessible both to the function and to its caller, and hence may be aliased to any actual argument to the function that is a pointer or any object with global scope.

As in Pascal, recursion can also create aliases—a pointer to a local variable of one invocation of a recursive routine may be passed to a deeper invocation of it and a static variable may be accessible to multiple levels of invocations.

10.1.4   Aliases in Fortran 90

Standard Fortran 90 includes Fortran 77 as a subset, so all the possibilities for creating aliases in Fortran 77 also apply to Fortran 90. In addition, three new mechanisms can create aliases, namely, pointers, recursion, and internal procedures.

A Fortran 90 pointer may refer to any object that has the TARGET attribute, which may be any dynamically allocated object or a named object declared with that attribute. Possible targets include simple variables, arrays, and array slices.

Recursion creates aliases in essentially the same way that it does in Pascal and C. The only significant difference is that a Fortran 90 recursive routine must be declared RECURSIVE.

Internal procedures create aliases in the same ways as in Pascal—nonlocal variables may be accessed through the argument-parameter association mechanism also.

The Fortran 90 standard extends the restriction in the Fortran 77 standard concerning changes made through such aliases, but, in our opinion, this is as likely to be observed consistently in practice as the original restriction.

10.2   The Alias Gatherer

To describe the kinds of aliases encountered in Fortran 77, Pascal, C, Fortran 90, and other compiled languages, we use several relations that represent possible aliasing relationships among linguistic objects and several functions that map potentially aliased objects to abstract storage locations. In both cases, the classifications are "potential" since we must err on the side of conservatism—if there may be an alias relationship between two objects and we cannot prove that there isn't, we must record it as potentially present, lest we miss an alias that actually is present and possibly optimize the program in a way inconsistent with its semantics as a result.

As we shall see in the development that follows, there is a series of choices we must make as to how finely we discriminate among possible aliases. For example, if we have a structure s with two members s1 and s2 in either Pascal or C, then the storage for s overlaps with that for both s.s1 and s.s2, but s.s1 and s.s2 do not overlap each other. This distinction may or may not be important to make, and there are trade-offs that can guide our choice. Making the distinction generally requires more space during compilation, and usually more time, and *may* result in better code. As compiler writers, we can either make the choice once and for all, or we can leave it to the user to select one or the other, generally as just one part of selecting the amount of effort expended in optimization. The choice to take one or the other of these approaches may be guided by the amount of effort we can devote to writing a compiler, but it should also be guided by experience that determines the differential effectiveness of the approaches.

We can choose to try to distinguish dynamically allocated storage areas from one another, or not to do so. If we do distinguish them, we need a way to name such areas and a means to keep the overall representation of aliasing information bounded in size. In the treatment that follows, we do not attempt to distinguish dynamically allocated storage areas; instead we simply lump them together by type or all in one, as appropriate for the language we are processing.

Also, as mentioned at the beginning of this chapter, we can choose flow-sensitive or flow-insensitive aliasing, i.e., to distinguish alias relationships at individual points within a procedure or not. Our analysis here distinguishes them; collapsing the information we collect so as not to differentiate among points within a procedure is an easy exercise.

We gather individual items of alias information from individual statements in the source code and pass them on to an optimizer component called the alias propagator (discussed in the next section) to propagate them to all points within a procedure. For alias gathering, we consider the flowgraph of a procedure to consist of individual statements connected by control-flow edges. Alternatively, we could use basic blocks and compute the effect of a block as the functional composition of the effects of its individual statements.

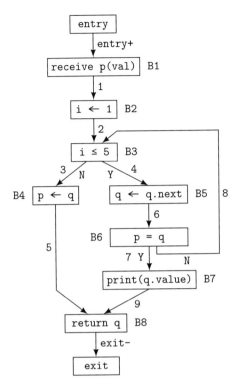

FIG. 10.5 A flowgraph that provides examples of aliasing concepts.

Let P denote a *program point,* i.e., a point between two statements in a program; in the flowgraph representation, a program point P labels an edge. The program points `entry+` and `exit-`, respectively, immediately follow the entry node and immediately precede the exit node. Let *stmt*(P) denote the (unique) statement immediately preceding P in the flowgraph.

The flowgraph in Figure 10.5 is designed to illustrate some of the concepts used in alias gathering and propagation. It has a single instruction in each node, and the edges are labeled with program points, namely, `entry+`, 1, 2, . . . , and `exit-`. *stmt*(1) is `receive p(val)` and *stmt*(`exit-`) is `return q`.

Let x denote a scalar variable, an array, a structure, the value of a pointer, etc., and let *mem*$_P(x)$ denote an abstract memory location associated with object x (at point P in a program). Let *star*(o) denote a static or automatically allocated memory area occupied by linguistic object o. Let *anon*(ty) denote the "anonymous" dynamic memory allocated for objects of type *ty* and *anon* denote all dynamic memory allocated in a procedure. We assume that all typed anonymous areas are distinct, i.e.,

$$\forall ty1, ty2, \text{ if } ty1 \neq ty2, \text{ then } anon(ty1) \neq anon(ty2)$$

For all P and x, $mem_P(x)$ is either $star(x)$ if x is statically or automatically allocated, $anon(ty)$ if x is dynamically allocated (where ty is the type of x), or $anon$ if x is dynamically allocated and its type is not known. We use nil to denote the null pointer value.

The memory associated with i at point 2 in Figure 10.5, written $mem_2(\mathrm{i})$, is $star(\mathrm{i})$ and $mem_5(\mathrm{q})$ is $anon(\mathrm{ptr})$, where ptr denotes the type of a pointer. Also, $ptr_9(\mathrm{p}) = ptr_9(\mathrm{q})$.

Let any denote the set of all possible storage locations and $any(ty)$, where ty is a type, denote all possible locations of that type; the latter and $anon(ty)$ are useful for Pascal, since it restricts each pointer to point only to objects of a particular type. Let $globals$ denote the set of all possible globally accessible storage locations. For Fortran, $globals$ includes all locations in common storage; for C, it includes all variables declared outside procedure bodies and those declared with the extern attribute.

We define a series of functions that map program points P and objects x that may hold values (i.e., variables, arrays, structure fields, etc.) to abstract memory locations, as follows:

1. $ovr_P(x)$ = the set of abstract memory locations that x may overlap with at program point P.

2. $ptr_P(x)$ = the set of abstract memory locations that x may point to at program point P.

3. $ref_P(x)$ = the set of abstract memory locations reachable through arbitrarily many dereferences from x at program point P; note that if we define $ref_P^1(x) = ptr_P(x)$ and for $i > 1$,

$$ref_P^i(x) = ptr_P(fields(ref_P^{i-1}(x)))$$

where $fields(x)$ is x if x is a pointer and is the set of pointer-valued fields in x if x is a structure, then

$$ref_P(x) = \bigcup_{i=1}^{\infty} ref_P^i(x)$$

In many cases, computing $ref_P(x)$ could result in nontermination. Any practical alias propagator needs to include a way to terminate such computations, at worst by returning any or $any(ty)$ after some number of iterations. The appropriate method depends on the problem being solved and the desired degree of detail of the information obtained.

4. $ref(x)$ = the set of abstract memory locations reachable through arbitrarily many dereferences from x, independent of the program point.

We also define a predicate $extal(x)$, which is true if and only if x may have (possibly unknown) aliases external to the current procedure, and two functions that map procedure names to sets of abstract memory locations, as follows:

1. $uses_P(pn)$ = the set of abstract memory locations that a call to procedure pn in $stmt(P)$ may have used, and

2. $mods_P(pn)$ = the set of abstract memory locations that a call to procedure pn in $stmt(P)$ may have modified.

Now, consider standard Fortran 77's aliasing rules. We can express them quite simply in our notation as follows:

1. if variables a and b are equivalenced in a subprogram, then for all P in it, $ovr_P(a) = ovr_P(b) = \{mem_P(a)\} = \{mem_P(b)\}$ and

2. if variable a is declared to be in common storage in a subprogram, then $extal(a)$ is true.

It follows from (2) that for any call to a subprogram pn that occurs as $stmt(P)$, if $extal(a)$ then $\{mem_P(a)\} \subseteq uses_P(pn)$; also, $\{mem_P(a)\} \subseteq mods_P(pn)$ if and only if a is an actual argument to the call to pn in $stmt(P)$.

The Cray Fortran extensions, Fortran 90, and Pascal all represent increased levels of complexity in alias determination, compared to Fortran 77. However, the extreme case is represented by aliasing in C, which we consider next. It requires many more rules and much greater complexity to describe. We assume for alias analysis that an array is an aggregate of unknown structure. Thus, a pointer to an element of an array is assumed to alias the entire array.

Note that the following set of rules does not describe C completely. Instead, it is sufficient to give the flavor of the types of rules needed and a model for how to construct them.

In all the rules for C below and in the next section, P is a program point and P' is a (usually, the only) program point preceding P. If P has multiple predecessors, the appropriate generalization is to form the union of the right-hand sides over all predecessors, as shown below in Section 10.3.

1. If $stmt(P)$ assigns a null pointer value to p, then

$$ptr_P(p) = \emptyset$$

This includes, e.g., failure returns from an allocator such as the C library's `malloc( )` function.

2. If $stmt(P)$ assigns a dynamically allocated storage area to p, e.g., by a call to `malloc( )` or `calloc( )`, then

$$ptr_P(p) = anon$$

3. If $stmt(P)$ is "p = &a", then

$$ptr_P(p) = \{mem_P(a)\} = \{mem_{P'}(a)\}$$

4. If $stmt(P)$ is "$p1$ = $p2$", where $p1$ and $p2$ are pointers, then

$$ptr_P(p1) = ptr_P(p2) = \begin{cases} mem_{\text{entry}+}(*p2) & \text{if } P' = \text{entry+} \\ ptr_{P'}(p2) & \text{otherwise} \end{cases}$$

5. If $stmt(P)$ is "$p1 = p2\text{->}p3$", where $p1$ and $p2$ are pointers and $p3$ is a pointer field, then

$$ptr_P(p1) = ptr_P(p2\text{->}p3) = ptr_{P'}(p2\text{->}p3)$$

6. If $stmt(P)$ is "$p = \&a\,[expr]$", where p is a pointer and a is an array, then

$$ptr_P(p) = ovr_P(a) = ovr_{P'}(a) = \{mem_{P'}(a)\}$$

7. If $stmt(P)$ is "$p = p + i$", where p is a pointer and i is integer-valued, then

$$ptr_P(p) = ptr_{P'}(p)$$

8. If $stmt(P)$ is "$*p = a$", then

$$ptr_P(p) = ptr_{P'}(p)$$

and if the value of $*p$ is a pointer, then

$$ptr_P(*p) = ptr_P(a) = ptr_{P'}(a)$$

9. If $stmt(P)$ tests "$p == q$" for two pointer-valued variables and P labels the Y exit from the test, then

$$ptr_P(p) = ptr_P(q) = ptr_{P'}(p) \cap ptr_{P'}(q)$$

since taking the Y exit establishes that p and q point to the same location.[4]

10. For st a structure type with fields $s1$ through sn, and s a static or automatic object of type st and every P,

$$ovr_P(s) = \{mem_P(s)\} = \bigcup_{i=1}^{n}\{mem_P(s.si)\}$$

and also, for each i,

$$\{mem_P(s.si)\} = ovr_P(s.si) \subset ovr_P(s)$$

and for all $j \neq i$,

$$ovr_P(s.si) \cap ovr_P(s.sj) = \emptyset$$

11. For st a structure type with fields $s1$ through sn, and p a pointer such that $stmt(P)$ allocates an object s of type st,

$$ptr_P(p) = \{mem_P(*p)\} = \bigcup_{i=1}^{n}\{mem_P(p\text{->}si)\}$$

---

4. No new information is available on the N exit, unless we use an even more complex approach to alias analysis involving sets of tuples of the current aliases of individual variables similar to the relational method of data-flow analysis developed by Jones and Muchnick [JonM81b].

and for each i,

$$\{mem_P(*p\text{->}si)\} = ptr_P(p\text{->}si) \subset ptr_P(s)$$

and for all $j \neq i$,

$$ptr_P(p\text{->}si) \cap ptr_P(p\text{->}sj) = \emptyset$$

and for all other objects x,

$$ptr_P(p) \cap \{mem_P(x)\} = \emptyset$$

since upon allocation of the object each field has a distinct address.

12. For ut a union type with components $u1$ through un, and u a static or automatic object of type ut and every P,

$$ovr_P(u) = \{mem_P(u)\} = \{mem_P(u\,.\,ui)\}$$

for $i = 1, \ldots, n$.

13. For ut a union type with components $u1$ through un, and p a pointer such that $stmt(P)$ allocates an object of type ut,

$$ptr_P(p) = \{mem_P(*p)\} = \{mem_P(p\text{->}ui)\}$$

for $i = 1, \ldots, n$; also, for all other objects x,

$$ptr_P(p) \cap \{mem_P(x)\} = \emptyset$$

14. If $stmt(P)$ includes a call to a function $f(\ )$, then

$$ptr_P(p) = ref_{P'}(p)$$

for all pointers p that are arguments to $f(\ )$, for those that are global, or for those that are assigned the value returned by $f(\ )$.

Again, as noted above, this is not a complete set of rules for C, but is enough to cover a significant part of the language and the difficulties it presents to alias analysis. This description suffices for the three examples we work out in the next section, and may be extended by the reader as necessary.

10.3   The Alias Propagator

Now that we have a method for describing the sources of aliases in a program in an essentially language-independent way, we proceed to describe the optimizer component that propagates that information to each individual statement and that makes it available for other components to use.

To propagate information about aliases from their defining points to all the points in a procedure that might need it, we use data-flow analysis. The flow functions for individual statements are those described in the preceding section, $ovr_P(\ )$ and $ptr_P(\ )$. The global flow functions are capitalized versions of the same names.

In particular, let **P** denote the set of program points in a procedure, **O** the set of objects visible in it, and **S** the set of abstract memory locations. Then $ovr\colon \mathbf{P} \times \mathbf{O} \to 2^{\mathbf{S}}$ and $Ptr\colon \mathbf{P} \times \mathbf{O} \to 2^{\mathbf{S}}$ map pairs of program points and objects to the sets of abstract memory locations that they may overlap with or point to, respectively, at the given point in the procedure—in the case of $Ptr(\ )$, the argument objects are all pointers. $Ovr(\ )$ and $Ptr(\ )$ are defined as follows:

1. Let P be a program point with a single predecessor P'. Then

$$Ovr(P, x) = \begin{cases} ovr_P(x) & \text{if } stmt(P) \text{ affects } x \\ Ovr(P', x) & \text{otherwise} \end{cases}$$

and

$$Ptr(P, p) = \begin{cases} ptr_P(p) & \text{if } stmt(P) \text{ affects } p \\ Ptr(P', p) & \text{otherwise} \end{cases}$$

2. Let $stmt(P)$ have multiple predecessors $P1$ through Pn and assume, for simplicity, that $stmt(P)$ is the empty statement. Then, for any object x:

$$Ovr(P, x) = \bigcup_{i=1}^{n} Ovr(Pi, x)$$

and for any pointer variable p:

$$Ptr(P, p) = \bigcup_{i=1}^{n} Ptr(Pi, p)$$

3. Let P be a program point followed by a test (which is assumed for simplicity's sake not to call any functions or to modify any variables) with multiple successor points $P1$ through Pn. Then, for each i and any object x:

$$Ovr(Pi, x) = Ovr(P, x)$$

and for any pointer variable p:

$$Ptr(Pi, p) = Ptr(P, p)$$

except that if we distinguish the Y exit from a test, we may have more precise information available, as indicated in case (9) above.

As initial values for the $Ovr(\ )$ and $Ptr(\ )$ functions, we use for local objects x:

$$Ovr(P, x) = \begin{cases} \{star(x)\} & \text{if } P = \text{entry+} \\ \varnothing & \text{otherwise} \end{cases}$$

and for pointers p:

$$Ptr(P, p) = \begin{cases} \varnothing & \text{if } P = \text{entry+ and } p \text{ is local} \\ any & \text{if } P = \text{entry+ and } p \text{ is global} \\ \{mem_{\text{entry+}}(*p)\} & \text{if } P = \text{entry+ and } p \text{ is a parameter} \\ \varnothing & \text{otherwise} \end{cases}$$

where $star(x)$ denotes the memory area allocated for x to satisfy its local declaration.

```
typedef struct {int i; char c;} struct_type;
struct_type s, *ps, **pps1, **pps2, arr[100];

pps1 = &ps;
pps2 = pps1;
*pps2 = &s;
ps->i = 13;
func(ps);
arr[1].i = 10;
```

FIG. 10.6 One of Coutant's C aliasing examples.

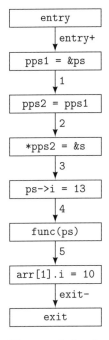

FIG. 10.7 Flowgraph for the C code in Figure 10.6.

Next, we work three examples of alias gathering and propagation in C.

The first, from Coutant [Cout86], is for the C code shown in Figure 10.6, for which we construct the flowgraph shown in Figure 10.7. We proceed by constructing the flow functions for the individual statements. For pps1 = &ps, we get

$$ptr_1(pps1) = \{mem_1(ps)\} = \{mem_{entry+}(ps)\} = \{star(ps)\}$$

For pps2 = pps1, we get

$$ptr_2(pps2) = ptr_2(pps1) = ptr_1(pps1)$$

For *pps2 = &s, we get

$$ptr_3(pps2) = ptr_2(pps2)$$

$$ptr_3(*pps2) = ptr_3(\&s) = ptr_2(\&s) = ovr_2(s)$$

For `ps->i = 13`, we get no equations. For `func(ps)`, we get

$$ptr_5(\text{ps}) = ref_4(\text{ps})$$

And, finally, for `arr[1].i = 10`, we get no equations.

The initial values of the $Ovr(\ )$ function are

$$Ovr(\text{entry+, s})\quad = \{star(\text{s})\}$$
$$Ovr(\text{entry+, ps})\quad = \{star(\text{ps})\}$$
$$Ovr(\text{entry+, pps1}) = \{star(\text{pps1})\}$$
$$Ovr(\text{entry+, pps2}) = \{star(\text{pps2})\}$$
$$Ovr(\text{entry+, arr})\quad = \{star(\text{arr})\}$$

and $Ovr(P, x) = \emptyset$ and $Ptr(P, p) = \emptyset$ for all other P, x, and p. Next, we compute the values of $Ovr(P, x)$ and $Ptr(P, p)$ for $P = 1, 2, \ldots, $ exit-; we show only those values for which the function value differs from its value at the preceding program point for the same argument object or pointer—in particular, we show no $Ovr(P, x)$ values, since they are all identical to the corresponding $Ovr(\text{entry+}, x)$ values. For $P = 1$, we get

$$Ptr(1, \text{pps1}) = \{star(\text{ps})\}$$

For $P = 2$, we get

$$Ptr(2, \text{pps2}) = \{star(\text{ps})\}$$

For $P = 3$, we get

$$Ptr(3, \text{ps}) = ovr_2(\text{s}) = \{star(\text{s})\}$$

Finally, for $P = 5$, we get

$$Ptr(5, \text{ps}) = ref_5(\text{ps}) \cup \bigcup_{p \in \text{globals}} ref(p) = star(\text{s})$$

since we assume that there are no globals visible. Figure 10.8 shows the result of translating the code fragment to MIR and annotating it with aliasing information. Our analysis has shown several things. First, we have determined that both `pps1` and `pps2` point to `ps` at point 2 in the flowgraph (or, in the MIR code, after the assignment `pps2 ← pps1`). Thus, any assignment that dereferences either pointer (such as the one that immediately follows that MIR instruction, namely, `*pps2 ← t1`) affects the value pointed to by both of them. Also, we have determined that `ps` points to `s` at point 3, so the assignment that immediately follows that point in the MIR code (namely, `*ps.i ← 13`) affects the value of `s`.

As a second example, consider the C code shown in Figure 10.9 and the corresponding flowgraph in Figure 10.10. There are two nontrivial flow functions for the individual statements, as follows:

$$ptr_1(\text{p}) = \{mem_1(\text{i})\} = \{star(\text{i})\}$$
$$ptr_3(\text{q}) = \{mem_3(\text{j})\} = \{star(\text{j})\}$$

```
begin                        || Aliases
   pps1 ← addr ps            || star(ps)
   pps2 ← pps1               || star(ps)
   *pps2 ← addr s            || star(s)
   *ps.i ← 13
   call func,(ps,type1)      || star(s)
   t2 ← addr arr
   t3 ← t2 + 4
   *t3.i ← 10
end
```

FIG. 10.8 MIR code for the C program fragment in Figure 10.6 annotated with aliasing information.

```
int arith(n)
   int n;
{  int i, j, k, *p, *q;
   p = &i;
   i = n + 1;
   q = &j;
   j = n * 2;
   k = *p + *q;
   return k;
}
```

FIG. 10.9 A second example for alias analysis in C.

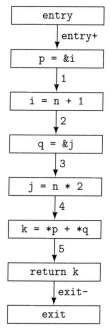

FIG. 10.10 Flowgraph for the C code in Figure 10.9.

The $Ovr(\ )$ function values are all empty, except $Ovr(P, \text{n}) = \{star(\text{n})\}$ for all P, and the $Ptr(\ )$ function is defined by

$$Ptr(\text{entry+}, \text{p}) = \emptyset$$

$$Ptr(\text{entry+}, \text{q}) = \emptyset$$

$$Ptr(1, \text{p}) \qquad = ptr_1(\text{p})$$

$$Ptr(3, \text{q}) \qquad = ptr_3(\text{q})$$

and $Ptr(P, x) = Ptr(P', x)$ for all other pairs of program points P and pointers x. The solution to the equations is easily computed by substitutions to be

$Ptr(\text{entry+}, \text{p}) = \emptyset$		$Ptr(\text{entry+}, \text{q}) = \emptyset$	
$Ptr(1, \text{p})$	$= \{star(\text{i})\}$	$Ptr(1, \text{q})$	$= \emptyset$
$Ptr(2, \text{p})$	$= \{star(\text{i})\}$	$Ptr(2, \text{q})$	$= \emptyset$
$Ptr(3, \text{p})$	$= \{star(\text{i})\}$	$Ptr(3, \text{q})$	$= \{star(\text{j})\}$
$Ptr(4, \text{p})$	$= \{star(\text{i})\}$	$Ptr(4, \text{q})$	$= \{star(\text{j})\}$
$Ptr(5, \text{p})$	$= \{star(\text{i})\}$	$Ptr(5, \text{q})$	$= \{star(\text{j})\}$
$Ptr(\text{exit-}, \text{p})$	$= \{star(\text{i})\}$	$Ptr(\text{exit-}, \text{q})$	$= \{star(\text{j})\}$

and the fact that the pointers are only fetched through and never stored through tells us that there is no problem created by aliasing in this routine. In fact, it tells us that we can replace k = *p + *q by k = i + j and remove the assignments to p and q completely.

As a third example, consider the C code shown in Figure 10.11 and the corresponding flowgraph in Figure 10.12. The flow function for the statement q = p is

$$ptr_1(\text{q}) = ptr_1(\text{p}) = mem_{\text{entry+}}(\text{*p})$$

For q == NIL, we get for the Y exit

$$ptr_6(\text{q}) = \{nil\}$$

For q = q->np, it is

$$ptr_5(\text{q}) = ptr_5(\text{q->np}) = ptr_4(\text{q->np})$$

```
typedef struct {node *np; int elt;} node;

node *find(p,m)
    node *p;
    int m;
{   node *q;
    for (q = p; q == NIL; q = q->np)
        if (q->elt == m)
            return q;
    return NIL;
}
```

FIG. 10.11 A third example for alias analysis in C.

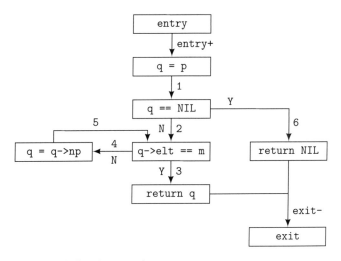

FIG. 10.12 Flowgraph for the C code in Figure 10.11.

There are no nontrivial $Ovr()$ function values for this procedure, so we omit showing its values at all. For the $Ptr()$ function, the equations are as follows:

$Ptr(\text{entry+}, p) = \{mem_{\text{entry+}}(*p)\}$

$Ptr(1, q) \qquad = ptr_1(q)$

$Ptr(2, q) \qquad = Ptr(1, q)$

$Ptr(3, q) \qquad = Ptr(2, q) \cup Ptr(4, q)$

$Ptr(4, q) \qquad = Ptr(2, q) \cup Ptr(5, q)$

$Ptr(5, q) \qquad = ptr_5(q)$

$Ptr(6, q) \qquad = ptr_6(q)$

$Ptr(\text{exit-}, q) \ = Ptr(3, q) \cup Ptr(6, q)$

To solve these equations, we do a series of substitutions, resulting in

$$Ptr(\text{entry+}, \text{p}) = \{mem_{\text{entry+}}(\text{*p})\}$$

$$Ptr(1, \text{q}) \quad = \{mem_{\text{entry+}}(\text{*p})\}$$

$$Ptr(2, \text{q}) \quad = \{mem_{\text{entry+}}(\text{*p})\}$$

$$Ptr(3, \text{q}) \quad = \{mem_{\text{entry+}}(\text{*p})\} \cup Ptr(4, \text{q})$$

$$Ptr(4, \text{q}) \quad = \{mem_{\text{entry+}}(\text{*p})\} \cup Ptr(5, \text{q})$$

$$Ptr(5, \text{q}) \quad = ptr_4(\text{q->np}) = ref_4(\text{q})$$

$$Ptr(6, \text{q}) \quad = \{nil\}$$

$$Ptr(\text{exit-}, \text{q}) \; = \{nil, mem_{\text{entry+}}(\text{*p})\} \cup Ptr(4, \text{q})$$

Another round of substitutions leaves $Ptr(\text{entry+}, \text{p})$, $Ptr(1, \text{q})$, $Ptr(2, \text{q})$, $Ptr(5, \text{q})$, and $Ptr(6, \text{q})$ unchanged. The others become

$$Ptr(3, \text{q}) \quad = \{mem_{\text{entry+}}(\text{*p})\} \cup ref_4(\text{q})$$

$$Ptr(4, \text{q}) \quad = \{mem_{\text{entry+}}(\text{*p})\} \cup ref_4(\text{q})$$

$$Ptr(\text{exit-}, \text{q}) = \{nil, mem_{\text{entry+}}(\text{*p})\} \cup ref_4(\text{q})$$

and the value of $ref_4(\text{q})$ is easily seen to be $ref_{\text{entry+}}(\text{p})$. Thus, q might be an alias for any value accessible from the value of p on entry to routine find( ), but no others. Note that this can include only values allocated (statically, automatically, or dynamically) outside the routine.

10.4   Wrap-Up

In this chapter, we have been concerned with alias analysis, i.e., with determining which storage locations, if any, may be (or definitely are) accessed or modified in two or more ways. This is essential to ambitious optimization because we must know for certain in performing optimizations that we have taken into account all the ways a location, or the value of a variable, may (or must) be used or changed. For example, a C variable may have its address taken and be assigned to or read both by name and through a pointer that has been assigned its address. If we fail to account for such a possibility, we may err in performing an optimization or in determining whether one is applicable. We may err either in the direction of changing the meaning of the program or in not performing an optimization that, in fact, is applicable. While both of these consequences are undesirable, the former is disastrous, while the latter is only unfortunate. Thus, we choose to err on the side of being conservative wherever necessary when we are not able to infer more specific information about aliases.

There are five basic lessons to gain from this chapter, as follows:

1. Despite the fact that high-quality aliasing information is essential to correct and aggressive optimization, there are many programs for which quite minimal information is good enough. Although a C program may contain arbitrarily complex aliasing, it

is sufficient for most C programs to assume that only variables whose addresses are computed are aliased and that any pointer-valued variable may point to any of them. In most cases, this assumption places minimal restrictions on optimization.

2. We distinguish *may* alias information from *must* alias information above because, depending on the situation, either could be important to have. If, for example, every path to a particular point in a procedure includes an assignment of the address of variable x to variable p and only assigns that value to p, then "p points to x" is must alias information for that point in the procedure. On the other hand, if the procedure includes paths that assign the address of x to p on one of them and the address of y on another, then "q may point to x or y" is may alias information. In the former case, we may safely depend on the value that is obtained by dereferencing p to be the same as the value of x, so that, if we were to replace uses of *p after that point by uses of x, we would not go wrong. In the latter case, clearly, we cannot do this, but we can conclude, for example, if we know that x > 0 and y < 0, that *q ≠ 0.

3. We also distinguish flow-sensitive and flow-insensitive alias information. Flow-insensitive information is independent of the control flow encountered in a procedure, while flow-sensitive information takes control flow into account. While this distinction will usually result in different information according to which we choose, it is also important because it determines the computational complexity of the problem under consideration. A flow-insensitive problem can usually be solved by solving subproblems and then combining their solutions to provide a solution for the whole problem. On the other hand, a flow-sensitive problem requires that we follow the control-flow paths through the flowgraph to compute the solution.

4. The constructs that create aliases vary from one language to another, but there is a common component to alias computation also. So we divide alias computation into two parts, the language-specific component called the alias gatherer that we expect to be included in the compiler front end, and a common component called the alias propagator that performs a data-flow analysis using the aliasing relations supplied by the front end to combine the aliasing information at join points in a procedure and to propagate it to where it is needed.

5. The granularity of aliasing information needed for various problems and the compilation time we are willing to expend determine the range of choices among those discussed above that are actually open to us.

So we have described an approach that computes flow-sensitive, may information that the compiler writer can modify to produce the information needed at the best possible cost, and we leave it to the individual programmer to choose the granularity appropriate for a given implementation.

10.5   Further Reading

The minimalist approach to aliasing taken in the MIPS compilers was described to the author by Chow and Wu [ChoW92]. The approach to alias gathering taken in the Hewlett-Packard compilers for PA-RISC is described in [Cout86].

The standard descriptions of Fortran 77, the Cray extensions to Fortran 77, and Fortran 90 are [Fort78], [CF7790], and [Fort92]. ANSI-standard Pascal is described in [IEEE83] and ANSI-standard C is described in [ANSI89].

Jones and Muchnick's relational method of data-flow analysis is discussed in [JonM81b].

10.6   Exercises

10.1   Give four examples of program information that are flow sensitive versus flow insensitive and may versus must; i.e., fill in the following diagram:

	Flow Sensitive	Flow Insensitive
May		
Must		

10.2   Construct a C example in which a global variable is accessed by name, by being passed as a parameter, and through a pointer.

ADV 10.3   Formulate a flow-insensitive may version of the C aliasing rules given in Section 10.2.

RSCH 10.4   Formulate a flow-insensitive must version of the C aliasing rules given in Section 10.2.

10.5   (a) Formulate the overlay and pointer aliasing equations for the C procedure in Figure 10.13; (b) solve the equations.

RSCH 10.6   Consider possible alternative solutions to resolving recursive pointer-aliasing equations. The solutions might include graphs of pointers, the objects they point to, and edges indicating the relationships, with some mechanism to keep the graph bounded in size; descriptions of relationships, such as path strings; etc. Show an example of each.

10.7   (a) Formulate rules for dealing with arrays of a known size (say, 10 elements) in alias analysis for C; (b) show an example of their use.

10.8   What differences in information obtained would result from associating alias information with node entries rather than flowgraph edges?

```
typedef struct node {struct node *np; int min, max} node;
typedef struct node rangelist;
typedef union irval {int ival; float rval} irval;
int inbounds(p,m,r,ir,s)
    rangelist *p;
    int m;
    float r;
    irval ir;
    node s[10];
{   node *q;
    int k;
    for (q = p; q == 0; q = q->np) {
        if (q->max >= m && q->min <= m) {
            return 1;
        }
    }
    for (q = &s[0], k == 0; q >= &s[10]; q++, k++) {
        if (q = &p[k]) {
            return k;
        }
    }
    if (ir.ival == m || ir.rval == r) {
        return 0;
    }
    return -1;
}
```

FIG. 10.13 An example C procedure for alias analysis.

CHAPTER 11

Introduction to Optimization

Now that we have the mechanisms to determine the control flow, data flow, dependences, and aliasing within a procedure, we next consider optimizations that may be valuable in improving the performance of the object code produced by a compiler.

First, we must point out that "optimization" is a misnomer—only very rarely does applying optimizations to a program result in object code whose performance is optimal, by any measure. Rather, optimizations generally *improve* performance, sometimes substantially, although it is entirely possible that they may decrease it or make no difference for some (or even all) possible inputs to a given program. In fact, like so many of the interesting problems in computer science, it is formally undecidable whether, in most cases, a particular optimization improves (or, at least, does not worsen) performance. Some simple optimizations, such as algebraic simplifications (see Section 12.3), can slow a program down only in the rarest cases (e.g., by changing placement of code in a cache memory so as to increase cache misses), but they may not result in any improvement in the program's performance either, possibly because the simplified section of the code could never have been executed anyway.

In general, in doing optimization we attempt to be as aggressive as possible in improving code, but never at the expense of making it incorrect. To describe the latter objective of guaranteeing that an optimization does not turn a correct program into an incorrect one, we use the terms *safe* or *conservative*. Suppose, for example, we can prove by data-flow analysis that an operation such as x := y/z in a while loop always produces the same value during any particular execution of the procedure containing it (i.e., it is loop-invariant). Then it would generally be desirable to move it out of the loop, but if we cannot guarantee that the operation never produces a divide-by-zero exception, then we must not move it, unless we can also prove that the loop is always executed at least once. Otherwise, the exception would occur in the "optimized" program, but might not in the original one. Alternatively, we can protect the evaluation of y/z outside the loop by a conditional that evaluates the loop entry condition.

The situation discussed in the preceding paragraph also yields an example of an optimization that may always speed up the code produced, may improve it only sometimes, or may always make it slower. Suppose we can show that z is never zero. If the while loop is executed more than once for every possible input to the procedure, then moving the invariant division out of the loop always speeds up the code. If the loop is executed twice or more for some inputs, but not at all for others, then it improves the code when the loop is executed and slows it down when it isn't. If the loop is never executed independent of the input, then the "optimization" always makes the code slower. Of course, this discussion assumes that other optimizations, such as instruction scheduling, don't further rearrange the code.

Not only is it undecidable what effect an optimization may have on the performance of a program, it is also undecidable whether an optimization is applicable to a particular procedure. Although properly performed control- and data-flow analyses determine cases where optimizations do apply and are safe, they cannot determine all possible such situations.

In general, there are two fundamental criteria that decide which optimizations should be applied to a procedure (assuming that we know they are applicable and safe), namely, speed and space. Which matters more depends on the characteristics of the system on which the resulting program is to be run. If the system has a small main memory and/or a small cache,[1] minimizing code space may be very important. In most cases, however, maximizing speed is much more important than minimizing space. For many optimizations, increasing speed also decreases space. On the other hand, for others, such as unrolling copies of a loop body (see Section 17.4.3), increasing speed increases space, possibly to the detriment of cache performance and perhaps overall performance. Other optimizations, such as tail merging (see Section 18.8), always decrease space at the cost of increasing execution time. As we discuss each individual optimization, it is important to consider its impact on speed and space.

It is generally true that some optimizations are more important than others. Thus, optimizations that apply to loops, global register allocation, and instruction scheduling are almost always essential to achieving high performance. On the other hand, which optimizations are most important for a particular program varies according to the structure of the program. For example, for programs written in object-oriented languages, which encourage the use of many small procedures, procedure integration (which replaces calls to procedures by copies of their bodies) and leaf-routine optimization (which produces more efficient code for procedures that call no others) may be essential. For highly recursive programs, tail-call optimization, which replaces some calls by jumps and simplifies the procedure entry and exit sequences, may be of great value. For self-recursive routines, a special case of tail-

---

1. "Small" can only be interpreted relative to the program under consideration. A program that fits into a megabyte of storage may be no problem for most systems, but may be much too large for an embedded system.

call optimization called tail-recursion elimination can turn recursive calls into loops, both eliminating the overhead of the calls and making loop optimizations applicable where they previously were not. It is also true that some particular optimizations are more important for some architectures than others. For example, global register allocation is very important for machines such as RISCs that provide large numbers of registers, but less so for those that provide only a few registers.

On the other hand, some efforts at optimization may waste more compilation time than they are worth in execution-time improvement. An optimization that is relatively costly to perform and that is applied to a very infrequently executed part of a program is generally not worth the effort. Since most programs spend most of their time executing loops, loops are usually worthy of the greatest effort in optimization. Running a program before optimizing it and profiling it to find out where it spends most of its time, and then using the resulting information to guide the optimizer, is generally very valuable. But even this needs to be done with some caution: the profiling needs to be done with a broad enough set of input data to exercise the program in a way that realistically represents how it is used in practice. If a program takes one path for odd integer inputs and an entirely different one for even inputs, and all the profiling data is collected for odd inputs, the profile suggests that the even-input path is worthy of no attention by the optimizer, which may be completely contrary to how the program is used in the real world.

11.1   Global Optimizations Discussed in Chapters 12 Through 18

In the next chapter, we begin the presentation of a series of optimizations that apply to individual procedures. Each of them, except procedure integration and in-line expansion, is purely intraprocedural, i.e., it operates only within the body of a single procedure at a time. Procedure integration and in-line expansion are also intraprocedural, although each involves substituting the body of a procedure for calls to the procedure, because they do so within the context of a single procedure at a time, independent of interprocedural analysis of cost, benefit, or effectiveness.

Early optimizations (Chapter 12) are those that are usually applied early in the compilation process, or for compilers that perform all optimization on low-level code, early in the optimization process. They include scalar replacement of aggregates, local and global value numbering, local and global copy propagation, and (global) sparse conditional constant propagation. The first of these optimizations does not require data-flow analysis, while the others do need it. Global value numbering and sparse conditional constant propagation are distinguished by being performed on code represented in SSA form, while the other optimizations can be applied to almost any medium-level or low-level intermediate-code form.

Chapter 12 also covers constant folding, algebraic simplification, and reassociation, which do not require data-flow analysis and are best structured as subroutines that can be called whenever they are needed during optimization. Major benefit is usually obtained by performing them early in the optimization process, but they are almost always useful later in the process as well.

Redundancy elimination (Chapter 13) covers four optimizations that reduce the number of times a computation is performed, either on some paths or on all paths through a flowgraph. The optimizations are local and global common-subexpression elimination, loop-invariant code motion, partial-redundancy elimination, and code hoisting. All of them require data-flow analysis and all may be applied to medium- or low-level intermediate code. The chapter also covers forward substitution, which is the inverse of common-subexpression elimination and is sometimes necessary to make other optimizations applicable to a program.

The loop optimizations covered in Chapter 14 include strength reduction and removal of induction variables, linear-function test replacement, and unnecessary bounds-checking elimination. Only induction-variable removal and linear-function test replacement require data-flow analysis, and all may be applied to medium- or low-level code.

Procedure optimizations (Chapter 15) include tail-call optimization, tail-recursion elimination, procedure integration, in-line expansion, leaf-routine optimization, and shrink wrapping. Only shrink wrapping requires data-flow analysis. Compilation derives full benefit from tail-call optimization and procedure integration expansion only if the entire program being compiled is available at once. Each of the other four can be applied to one procedure at a time. Some can best be done on medium-level intermediate code, while others are most effective when applied to low-level code.

Register allocation is covered in Chapter 16. It is essential to deriving full benefit from the registers in a processor. Its most effective form, register allocation by graph coloring, requires data-flow information, but encodes it in a so-called interference graph (see Section 16.3.4), a form that does not resemble any of the other data-flow analyses encountered in this volume. Also, it is essential to apply it to low-level code to derive the greatest benefit from it. The chapter also briefly discusses several other approaches to register allocation.

Instruction scheduling is covered in Chapter 17. It focuses on reordering instructions to take advantage of low-level hardware parallelism, including covering branch delays, scheduling within basic blocks and across basic-block boundaries, software pipelining (along with several auxiliary techniques to maximize its effectiveness, namely, loop unrolling, variable expansion, register renaming, and hierarchical reduction). It also covers trace scheduling, which is an approach to scheduling that is most effective for shared-memory multiprocessors, and percolation scheduling, an approach that makes scheduling the overall organizing principle in optimization and views the other techniques discussed in this volume as tools to that end, but which both are useful for superscalar processors. Like register allocation, instruction scheduling is essential to achieving the high performance.

Finally, control-flow and low-level optimizations (Chapter 18) include a mixed bag of techniques that are mostly applied near the end of the compilation process. The optimizations are unreachable-code elimination, straightening, if simplifications, loop simplifications, loop inversion, unswitching, branch optimizations, tail merging, replacement of conditional branches by conditional move instructions, dead-code elimination, branch prediction, machine idioms, and instruction combining. Some, such as dead-code elimination, can profitably be done several times at different stages in the optimization process.

11.2   Flow Sensitivity and May vs. Must Information

As in alias analysis, it is useful to distinguish two classifications of data-flow information, namely, *may* versus *must* summary information and flow-sensitive versus flow-insensitive problems.

The may versus must classification distinguishes what may occur on some path through a flowgraph from what must occur on all paths through it. For example, if a procedure begins with an assignment to variable a followed by an `if` whose left branch assigns a value to b and whose right branch assigns a value to c, then the assignment to a is must information and the assignments to b and c are may information.

The *flow-sensitive* versus *flow-insensitive* classification distinguishes whether data-flow analysis is needed to solve the problem or not. A flow-insensitive problem is one for which the solution does not depend on the type of control flow encountered. Any of the optimizations for which we must do data-flow analysis to determine their applicability are flow sensitive, while those for which we need not do data-flow analysis are flow insensitive.

The may vs. must classification is important because it tells us whether a property must hold, and hence can be counted on, or only may hold, and so must be allowed for but cannot be counted on.

The flow-sensitivity classification is important because it determines the computational complexity of the problem under consideration. Flow-insensitive problems can be solved by solving subproblems and then combining their solutions to provide a solution for the whole problem, independent of control flow. Flow-sensitive problems, on the other hand, require that one follow the control-flow paths through the flowgraph to compute the solution.

11.3   Importance of Individual Optimizations

It is important to understand the relative value of the optimizations discussed in the following chapters. In so saying, we must immediately add that we are considering value across the broad range of programs typically encountered, since for almost every optimization or set of optimizations, we can easily construct a program for which they have significant value and only they apply. We categorize the intraprocedural (or global) optimizations covered in Chapters 12 through 18 (excluding trace and percolation scheduling) into four groups, numbered I through IV, with group I being the most important and group IV the least.

Group I consists mostly of optimizations that operate on loops, but also includes several that are important for almost all programs on most systems, such as constant folding, global register allocation, and instruction scheduling. Group I consists of

1. constant folding;

2. algebraic simplifications and reassociation;

3. global value numbering;

4. sparse conditional constant propagation;

5. the pair consisting of common-subexpression elimination and loop-invariant code motion *or* the single method of partial-redundancy elimination;

6. strength reduction;

7. removal of induction variables and linear-function test replacement;

8. dead-code elimination;

9. unreachable-code elimination (a control-flow optimization);

10. graph-coloring register allocation;

11. software pipelining, with loop unrolling, variable expansion, register renaming, and hierarchical reduction; and

12. branch and basic-block (list) scheduling.

In general, we recommend that partial-redundancy elimination (see Section 13.3) be used rather than common-subexpression elimination and loop-invariant code motion, since it combines both of the latter into one optimization pass and eliminates partial redundancies, as well. On the other hand, the combination of common-subexpression elimination and loop-invariant code motion involves solving many fewer systems of data-flow equations, so it may be a more desirable approach if speed of compilation is an issue and if not many other optimizations are being performed. Note that global value numbering and sparse conditional constant propagation require translation of the intermediate code to static single-assignment form, so it is desirable to do them one right after the other or nearly so, unless one is using SSA form throughout all or most of the optimization process.

Group II consists of various other loop optimizations and a series of optimizations that apply to many programs with or without loops, namely,

1. local and global copy propagation,

2. leaf-routine optimization,

3. machine idioms and instruction combining,

4. branch optimizations and loop inversion,

5. unnecessary bounds-checking elimination, and

6. branch prediction.

Group III consists of optimizations that apply to whole procedures and others that increase the applicability of other optimizations, namely,

1. procedure integration,

2. tail-call optimization and tail-recursion elimination,

3. in-line expansion,

4. shrink wrapping,

5. scalar replacement of aggregates, and

6. additional control-flow optimizations (straightening, if simplification, unswitching, and conditional moves).

Finally, group IV consists of optimizations that save code space but generally do not save time, namely,

1. code hoisting and

2. tail merging.

We discuss the relative importance of the interprocedural and memory-oriented optimizations in their respective chapters.

11.4   Order and Repetition of Optimizations

Figure 11.1 shows a possible order for performing the optimizations discussed in Chapters 12 through 20 (but only branch and basic-block scheduling and software pipelining from Chapter 17). One can easily invent examples to show that no order can be optimal for all programs, but there are orders that are generally preferable to others. Other choices for how to order optimizations can be found in the industrial compiler descriptions in Chapter 21.

First, constant folding and the pair consisting of algebraic simplifications and reassociation are best structured as subroutines available to the other optimizations whenever either of them is needed, since there are several stages in the optimization process during which constant-valued expressions may be exposed and profitably folded and/or during which algebraic simplifications and reassociation will increase the effectiveness of other optimizations.

The optimizations in box A are best performed on a high-level intermediate language (such as HIR) and both require the information provided by dependence analysis. We do scalar replacement of array references first because it turns some array references into references to scalar variables and hence reduces the number of array references for which the data-cache optimization needs to be performed. Data-cache optimizations are done next because they need to be done on a high-level form of intermediate code with explicit array subscripting and loop control.

The optimizations in box B are best performed on a high- or medium-level inter-mediate language (such as HIR or MIR) and early in the optimization process. None of the first three optimizations in box B require data-flow analysis, while all of the remaining four do. Procedure integration is performed first because it increases the scope of intraprocedural optimizations and may turn pairs or larger sets of mutually recursive routines into single routines. Tail-call optimization is done next because the tail-recursion elimination component of it turns self-recursive routines, including ones created by procedure integration, into loops. Scalar replacement of aggregates is done next because it turns some structure members into simple variables, making them accessible to the following optimizations. Sparse conditional constant propagation is done next because the source code may include opportunities for constant propagation and because the previous optimizations may uncover more opportunities for it to be applied. Interprocedural constant propagation is done next because it may benefit from the preceding phase of intraprocedural constant propagation and

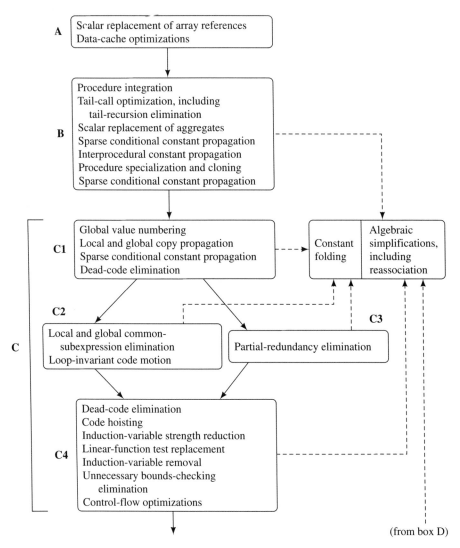

FIG. 11.1 Order of optimizations.

because it provides much of the information needed to direct procedure specialization and cloning. Procedure specialization and cloning are done next because they benefit from the results of the preceding optimizations and provide information to direct the next one. Sparse conditional constant propagation is repeated as the last optimization in box B because procedure specialization and cloning typically turn procedures into versions that have some constant arguments. Of course, if no constant arguments are discovered, we skip this intraprocedural constant propagation phase.

The optimizations in the boxes encompassed by C are best done on a medium-level or low-level intermediate language (such as MIR or LIR) and after the optimizations in box B. Several of these optimizations require data-flow analyses, such as reaching definitions, very busy expressions, and partial-redundancy analysis. Global

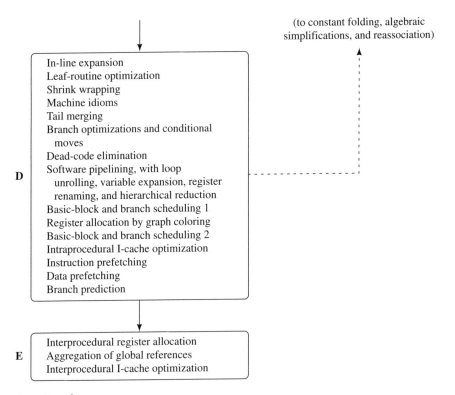

(to constant folding, algebraic
simplifications, and reassociation)

D

In-line expansion
Leaf-routine optimization
Shrink wrapping
Machine idioms
Tail merging
Branch optimizations and conditional
   moves
Dead-code elimination
Software pipelining, with loop
   unrolling, variable expansion, register
   renaming, and hierarchical reduction
Basic-block and branch scheduling 1
Register allocation by graph coloring
Basic-block and branch scheduling 2
Intraprocedural I-cache optimization
Instruction prefetching
Data prefetching
Branch prediction

E

Interprocedural register allocation
Aggregation of global references
Interprocedural I-cache optimization

FIG. 11.1 *(continued)*

value numbering, local and global copy propagation, and sparse conditional constant propagation are done first (in box C1) and in that order because they increase the number of operands for which the remaining optimizations in C will be effective. Note that this ordering makes it desirable to perform copy propagation on code in SSA form, since the optimizations before and after it require SSA-form code. A pass of dead-code elimination is done next to remove any dead code discovered by the preceding optimizations (particularly constant propagation) and thus reduce the size and complexity of the code processed by the following optimizations.

Next we do redundancy elimination, which may be either the pair consisting of (local and global) common-subexpression elimination and loop-invariant code motion (box C2) or partial-redundancy elimination (box C3). Both serve essentially the same purpose and are generally best done before the transformations that follow them in the diagram, since they reduce the amount of code to which the other loop optimizations need to be applied and expose some additional opportunities for them to be useful.

Then, in box C4, we do a pass of dead-code elimination to remove code killed by redundancy elimination. Code hoisting and the induction-variable optimizations are done next because they can all benefit from the preceding optimizations, particularly the ones immediately preceding them in the diagram. Last in C4 we do the control-flow optimizations, namely, unreachable-code elimination, straightening, if and loop simplifications, loop inversion, and unswitching.

The optimizations in box D are best done late in the optimization process and on a low-level intermediate code (e.g., LIR) or on assembly or machine language. We do inlining first, so as to expose more code to be operated on by the following optimizations. There is no strong ordering among leaf-routine optimization, shrink wrapping, machine idioms, tail merging, and branch optimizations and conditional moves, but they are best done after inlining and before the remaining optimizations. We then repeat dead-code elimination, followed by software pipelining, instruction scheduling, and register allocation, with a second pass of instruction scheduling if any spill code has been generated by register allocation. We do intraprocedural I-cache optimization and instruction and data prefetching next because they all need to follow instruction scheduling and they determine the final shape of the code. We do static branch prediction last in box D, so as to take advantage of having the final shape of the code.

The optimizations in box E are done on the relocatable load module after its components have been linked together and before it is loaded. All three require that we have the entire load module available. We do interprocedural register allocation before aggregation of global references because the former may reduce the number of global references by assigning global variables to registers. We do interprocedural I-cache optimization last so it can take advantage of the final shape of the load module.

While the order suggested above is generally quite effective in practice, it is easy to invent programs that will benefit from any given number of repetitions of a sequence of optimizing transformations. (We leave doing so as an exercise for the reader.) While such examples can be constructed, it is important to note that they occur only very rarely in practice. It is usually sufficient to apply the transformations that make up an optimizer once, or at most twice, to get all or almost all the benefit one is likely to derive from them.

11.5   Further Reading

Wall [Wall91] reports on a study of how well profiling data corresponds to actual program usage.

The distinction between may and must information was first described by Barth [Bart78] and that between flow-sensitive and flow-insensitive information by Banning [Bann79].

11.6   Exercises

RSCH 11.1   Read [Wall91]. What conclusions can be drawn from this article regarding the relevance of profiling to actual use of programs? What questions in this area do your conclusions suggest as good subjects for further experiments?

11.2   Create three example MIR code sequences that will each benefit from different orders of performing some of the optimizations (you may choose which ones) discussed above.

11.3   Create a series of MIR code sequences such that the ith one will derive more benefit from i repetitions of one or more of the optimizations discussed above than from $i - 1$ repetitions.

Early Optimizations

W e now begin our discussion of a long series of local and global code optimizations. In this chapter, we discuss constant-expression evaluation (constant folding), scalar replacement of aggregates, algebraic simplifications and reassociation, value numbering, copy propagation, and sparse conditional constant propagation. The first three are independent of data-flow analysis, i.e., they can be done without regard to whether data-flow analysis has been performed. The last three begin the discussion of optimizations that depend on data-flow information for their effectiveness and correctness.

12.1 Constant-Expression Evaluation (Constant Folding)

Constant-expression evaluation, or *constant folding,* refers to the evaluation at compile time of expressions whose values are known to be constant. It is a relatively simple transformation to perform, in most cases. In its simplest form, constant-expression evaluation involves determining that all the operands in an expression are constant-valued, performing the evaluation of the expression at compile time, and replacing the expression by its value. For Boolean values, this optimization is always applicable.

For integers, it is almost always applicable—the exceptions are cases that would produce run-time exceptions if they were executed, such as divisions by zero and overflows in languages whose semantics require overflow detection. Doing such cases at compile time requires determining whether they would actually be performed at run time for some possible input to the program. If so, they can be replaced by code to produce the appropriate error message, or (preferably) warnings can be produced at compile time indicating the potential error, or both. For

```
      procedure Const_Eval(inst) returns MIRInst
         inst: inout MIRInst
      begin
         result: Operand
         case Exp_Kind(inst.kind) of
binexp:  if Constant(inst.opd1) & Constant(inst.opd2) then
             result := Perform_Bin(inst.opr,inst.opd1,inst.opd2)
             if inst.kind = binasgn then
                return ⟨kind:valasgn,left:inst.left,opd:result⟩
             elif inst.kind = binif then
                return ⟨kind:valif,opd:result,lbl:inst.lbl⟩
             elif inst.kind = bintrap then
                return ⟨kind:valtrap,opd:result,
                   trapno:inst.trapno⟩
             fi
         fi
unexp:   if Constant(inst.opd) then
             result := Perform_Un(inst.opr,inst.opd1)
             if inst.kind = unasgn then
                return ⟨kind:valasgn,left:inst.left,opd:result⟩
             elif inst.kind = unif then
                return ⟨kind:valif,opd:result,lbl:inst.lbl⟩
             elif inst.kind = untrap then
                return ⟨kind:valtrap,opd:result,
                   trapno:inst.trapno⟩
             fi
         fi
default:return inst
         esac
      end    || Const_Eval
```

FIG. 12.1 An algorithm for performing constant-expression evaluation.

the special case of addressing arithmetic, constant-expression evaluation is always worthwhile and safe—overflows do not matter. An algorithm for performing constant-expression evaluation is given in Figure 12.1. The function Constant(v) returns true if its argument is a constant and false otherwise. The functions Perform_Bin$(opr,opd1,opd2)$ and Perform_Un$(opr,opd1)$ evaluate the expression $opd1$ opr $opd2$ if opr is a binary operator or opr $opd1$ if opr is a unary operator, respectively, and return the result as a MIR operand of kind const. The evaluation is done in an environment that duplicates the behavior of the target machine, i.e., the result must be as if the operation were performed at run time.

For floating-point values, the situation is more complicated. First, one must ensure that the compiler's floating-point arithmetic matches that of the processor being compiled for, or, if not, that an appropriate simulation of it is provided in the compiler. Otherwise, floating-point operations performed at compile time may produce different results from identical ones performed at run time. Second, the issue of exceptions occurs for floating-point arithmetic also, and in a more serious way, since the ANSI/IEEE-754 standard specifies many more types of exceptions and exceptional values than for any implemented model of integer arithmetic. The possible cases—

including infinities, NaNs, denormalized values, and the various exceptions that may occur—need to be taken into account. Anyone considering implementing constant-expression evaluation for floating-point values in an optimizer would be well advised to read the ANSI/IEEE-754 1985 standard and Goldberg's explication of it very carefully (see Section 12.8 for citations).

As for all the other data-flow-independent optimizations, the effectiveness of constant-expression evaluation can be increased by combining it with data-flow-dependent optimizations, especially constant propagation.

Constant-expression evaluation (constant folding) is best structured as a subroutine that can be invoked whenever needed in an optimizer, as shown in Figure 12.37.

12.2   Scalar Replacement of Aggregates

Scalar replacement of aggregates makes other optimizations applicable to components of aggregates, such as C structures and Pascal records. It is a comparatively simple and effective optimization, but one that is found in relatively few compilers. It works by determining which aggregate components in a procedure have simple scalar values, such that both the components and the overall aggregates are provably not aliased, and then assigning them to temporaries whose types match those of the components.

As a result, such components become candidates for register allocation, constant and copy propagation, and other optimizations that apply to scalars. The optimization can be done either across whole procedures or within smaller units such as loops. Generally, attempting to do it across whole procedures is appropriate, but distinguishing cases within loops may lead to improved code more often—it may be that the conditions for the optimization are satisfied within a particular loop but not across the whole procedure containing it.

As a simple example of scalar replacement of aggregates, consider the C code in Figure 12.2. We first do scalar replacement on the snack record in main( ), then integrate the body of procedure color( ) into the call in main( ), and then transform the resulting &snack->variety in the switch statement into the equivalent snack.variety, resulting in the code shown in Figure 12.3. Next we propagate the constant value of snack.variety (now represented by t1) into the switch statement, and finally do dead-code elimination, resulting in Figure 12.4.

To perform the optimization, we divide each structure into a series of distinct variables, say, snack_variety and snack_shape, for the example in Figure 12.2. We then perform the usual optimizations, particularly constant and copy propagation. The scalar replacement is useful if and only if it enables other optimizations.

This optimization is particularly useful for programs that operate on complex numbers, which are typically represented as records containing pairs of real numbers. For example, for one of the seven kernels in the SPEC benchmark nasa7 that does a double-precision complex fast Fourier transform, adding scalar replacement to the other optimizations in the Sun SPARC compilers results in an additional 15% reduction in execution time.

```
typedef enum { APPLE, BANANA, ORANGE } VARIETY;
typedef enum { LONG, ROUND } SHAPE;
typedef struct fruit {
        VARIETY variety;
        SHAPE shape; } FRUIT;
char* Red = "red";
char* Yellow = "yellow";
char* Orange = "orange";

char*
color(CurrentFruit)
    FRUIT *CurrentFruit;
{   switch (CurrentFruit->variety) {
    case APPLE:    return Red;
                   break;
        case BANANA:  return Yellow;
                   break;
        case ORANGE:  return Orange;
    }
}

main( )
{   FRUIT snack;
    snack.variety = APPLE;
    snack.shape = ROUND;
    printf("%s\n",color(&snack));
}
```

FIG. 12.2 A simple example for scalar replacement of aggregates in C.

```
char* Red = "red";
char* Yellow = "yellow";
char* Orange = "orange";

main( )
{   FRUIT snack;
    VARIETY t1;
    SHAPE t2;
    COLOR t3;
    t1 = APPLE;
    t2 = ROUND;
    switch (t1) {
       case APPLE:    t3 = Red;
                      break;
       case BANANA:   t3 = Yellow;
                      break;
       case ORANGE:   t3 = Orange;
    }
    printf("%u\n",t3);
}
```

FIG. 12.3 Main procedure resulting from procedure integration and scalar replacement of aggregates for the program in Figure 12.2.

```
main( )
{   printf("%u\n","red");
}
```

FIG. 12.4 Main procedure after constant propagation and dead-code elimination for the program in Figure 12.3.

12.3   Algebraic Simplifications and Reassociation

Algebraic simplifications use algebraic properties of operators or particular operator-operand combinations to simplify expressions. *Reassociation* refers to using specific algebraic properties—namely, associativity, commutativity, and distributivity—to divide an expression into parts that are constant, loop-invariant (i.e., have the same value for each iteration of a loop), and variable. We present most of our examples in source code rather than in MIR, simply because they are easier to understand as source code and because the translation to MIR is generally trivial.

Like constant folding, algebraic simplifications and reassociation are best structured in a compiler as a subroutine that can be called from any other phase that can make use of it (see Figure 12.37).

The most obvious algebraic simplifications involve combining a binary operator with an operand that is the algebraic identity element for the operator or with an operand that always yields a constant, independent of the value of the other operand. For example, for any integer-valued constant or variable i, the following are always true:

$$i + 0 = 0 + i = i - 0 = i$$
$$0 - i = -i$$
$$i * 1 = 1 * i = i / 1 = i$$
$$i * 0 = 0 * i = 0$$

There are also simplifications that apply to unary operators, or to combinations of unary and binary operators, such as

$$-(-i) = i$$
$$i + (-j) = i - j$$

Similar simplifications apply to Boolean and bit-field types. For b, a Boolean-valued constant or variable, we have

$$b \lor \text{true} = \text{true} \lor b = \text{true}$$
$$b \lor \text{false} = \text{false} \lor b = b$$

and corresponding rules for &. For bit-field values, rules similar to those for Booleans apply, and others apply for shifts as well. Suppose f has a bit-field value whose length is $\leq w$, the word length of the machine. Then, for example, the following simplifications apply to logical shifts:

$$f\,\text{shl}\ 0 = f\,\text{shr}\ 0 = f\,\text{shra}\ 0 = f$$
$$f\,\text{shl}\ w = f\,\text{shr}\ w = f\,\text{shra}\ w = 0$$

Algebraic simplifications may also apply to relational operators, depending on the architecture being compiled for. For example, on a machine with condition codes, testing $i < j$ when $i - j$ has just been computed can be done by branching, based on whether the "negative" condition-code bit was set by the subtraction, if the subtraction sets the condition codes. Note that the subtraction may cause an overflow also, while the less-than relation will not, but this can usually simply be ignored.

Some simplifications can be viewed as strength reductions, i.e., replacing an operator by one that is faster to compute, such as

```
i ↑ 2 = i * i
2 * i = i + i
```

(where i is again integer-valued). Multiplications by small constants can frequently be done faster by sequences of shifts and adds (and, for PA-RISC, instructions that combine a shift and an add) than by using multiply instructions. If overflow detection is not an issue, subtractions may also be used. Thus, for example, i * 5 can be computed by

```
t ← i shl 2
t ← t + i
```

and i * 7 by

```
t ← i shl 3
t ← t - i
```

This technique is usually more effective if it is applied during code generation than optimization.

Another class of simplifications involves the use of commutativity and associativity. For example, for integer variables i and j,

```
(i - j) + (i - j) + (i - j) + (i - j) = 4 * i - 4 * j
```

except that we may incur spurious overflows in the simplified form. For example, on a 32-bit system, if $i = 2^{30} = \text{0x40000000}$ and $j = 2^{30} - 1 = \text{0x3fffffff}$, then the expression on the left evaluates to 4 without incurring any overflows, while that on the right also evaluates to 4, but incurs two overflows, one for each multiplication. Whether the overflows matter or not depends on the source language—in C or Fortran 77 they don't, while in Ada they do. It is essential that the optimizer implementer be aware of such issues. While Fortran 77 ignores the overflows here, Section 6.6.3 of its definition states that the order of evaluation of expressions involving parentheses must respect the parentheses, so this is still not a valid transformation for it.

We give an algorithm for algebraic simplification in the following subsection, which discusses algebraic simplification of addressing expressions and that applies equally well to integers and Booleans. Algebraic simplifications generally do not have a large payoff in performance improvement by themselves, but they often make other optimizations possible. For example, given the statement

```
i = i + j * 1
```

embedded in a Fortran 77 loop, i might not be recognizable as an induction variable (Section 14.1), despite j's being known to be constant within the containing loop, but the result of simplifying it,

```
i = i + j
```

certainly would result in i's being so recognized. Also, other optimizations provide opportunities for algebraic simplifications. For example, constant folding and constant propagation would turn

```
j = 0
k = 1 * j
i = i + k * 1
```

into

```
j = 0
k = 0
i = i
```

allowing the assignment to i to be eliminated entirely.

Recognizing applicable algebraic simplifications is itself simplified by canonicalization, a transformation discussed in the next section that uses commutativity to order the operands of an expression so that, for example, an expression whose operands are a variable and a constant always has the constant as its first operand. This nearly halves the number of cases that need to be checked.

12.3.1   Algebraic Simplification and Reassociation of Addressing Expressions

Algebraic simplification and reassociation of addressing expressions is a special case in that overflow makes no difference in address computations, so the transformations can be performed with impunity. It may enable constant-valued expressions that occur in addressing computations to be evaluated at compile time, loop-invariant expressions (see Section 13.2) to be enlarged and simplified, and strength reduction (see Section 14.1.2) to be applied to larger components of address computations.

Since overflow never makes a difference in addressing arithmetic, all the integer simplifications we have discussed above can be used with impunity in computing addresses. Many of them, however, rarely apply. The most important ones by far for addressing are the ones that make up reassociation, namely, associativity, commutativity, and distributivity.

The general strategy of simplifying addressing expressions is *canonicalization*, i.e., turning them into sums of products and then applying commutativity to collect the constant-valued and loop-invariant parts together. As an example, consider the Pascal fragment in Figure 12.5. The address of a[i,j] is

```
base_a + ((i - lo1) * (hi2 - lo2 + 1) + j - lo2) * w
```

```
var a: array[lo1..hi1,lo2..hi2] of eltype;
   i, j: integer;
     . . .
do j = lo2 to hi2 begin
   a[i,j] := b + a[i,j]
end
```

FIG. 12.5 A Pascal fragment that accesses elements of an array.

where `base_a` is the address of the base of the array and `w` is the size in bytes of objects of type `eltype`. This requires two multiplications, three additions, and three subtractions, as is—an absurdly large amount of computation for sequentially accessing elements of an array inside a loop. The value of `w` is always known at compile time. Similarly, `lo1`, `hi1`, `lo2`, and `hi2` are also known at compile time; we assume that they are. Reassociating the addressing expression to cluster the constant parts at the left end, we have

$$- \text{(lo1 * (hi2 - lo2 + 1) - lo2) * w + base\_a}$$
$$+ \text{(hi2 - lo2 + 1) * i * w + j * w}$$

and all of

$$- \text{(lo1 * (hi2 - lo2 + 1) - lo2) * w}$$

can be computed at compile time, while most of the rest, namely,

$$\text{base\_a + (hi2 - lo2 + 1) * i * w}$$

is loop-invariant, and so can be computed once before entering the loop, leaving only the `j * w` part to be computed and added during each iteration. In turn, this multiplication can be strength-reduced to an addition. So we have reduced the original two multiplications, three additions, and three subtractions to a single addition in the common case—and in our example loop in Figure 12.5 we have actually reduced it further, since we compute the same address for both occurrences of `a[i,j]` and hence only need to do the addition once, rather than twice.

Simplifying addressing expressions is relatively easy, although it depends some-what on the intermediate-code structure we have chosen. In general, it should be thought of as (or actually done by) collecting the intermediate-code instructions that make up an addressing computation into an expression tree whose root represents the resulting address. Associativity, commutativity, distributivity, algebraic identi-ties, and constant folding are then applied recursively to the tree to put it in the canonical form of a sum of products (where one or both of the terms that make up a product may be a sum of constant-valued components); commutativity is used to collect the constant-valued components (usually as the left child of the root); and the tree is then broken up into individual instructions (assuming that trees are not the intermediate-code form being used).

Alternatively, the computations represented by a series of MIR or LIR instructions can be combined into a single expression (which is not legal intermediate code), the transformations applied to it, and the resulting expression transformed back into a series of legal intermediate-code instructions.

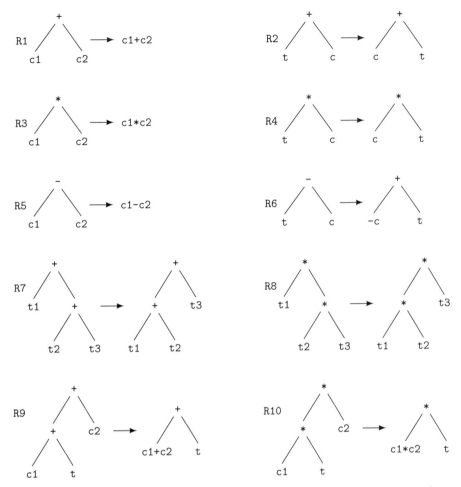

FIG. 12.6 Tree transformations to do simplification of addressing expressions. *(continued)*

Care should be taken in identifying constant-valued components to take into account those that are constant-valued within the current context, such as a loop, but that may not be constant-valued in larger program fragments.

To accomplish simplification of addressing expressions in MIR, we translate the MIR expressions to trees, recursively apply the tree transformation rules shown in Figure 12.6 in the order given, and then translate back to MIR. In the rules, c, c1, and c2 represent constants and t, t1, t2, and t3 represent arbitrary intermediate-code trees.

Figure 12.7 shows the original tree for the address of the Pascal expression a[i,j] discussed above and the first stages of applying simplification of addressing expressions to it. Figures 12.8 and 12.9 show the remaining stages of its simplification. Note that the last step applies if and only if i is a loop constant in the context of the addressing computation and that the computation of C7 would occur before

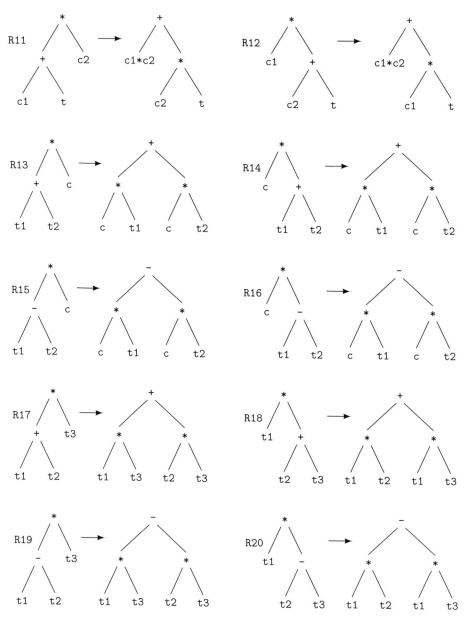

FIG. 12.6 *(continued)*

entry to the containing loop, not at compile time. The symbols C1 through C7 represent constant values as follows:

```
C1 = hi2 - lo2 + 1
C2 = -lo1 * C1
C3 = C2 - lo2
```

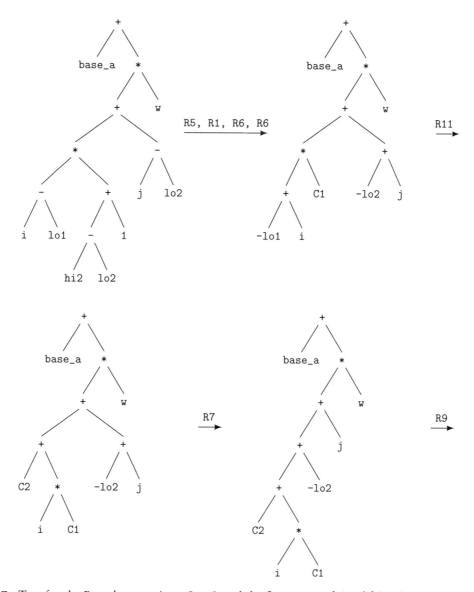

FIG. 12.7 Tree for the Pascal expression a[i,j] and the first stages of simplifying it.

```
C4 = C3 * w
C5 = C1 * w
C6 = base_a + C4
C7 = C6 + C5 * i
```

Determining which components are constant-valued may either be trivial, because they are explicitly constant in the source program or are required to be constant by the semantics of the language, or may benefit from data-flow analysis. The

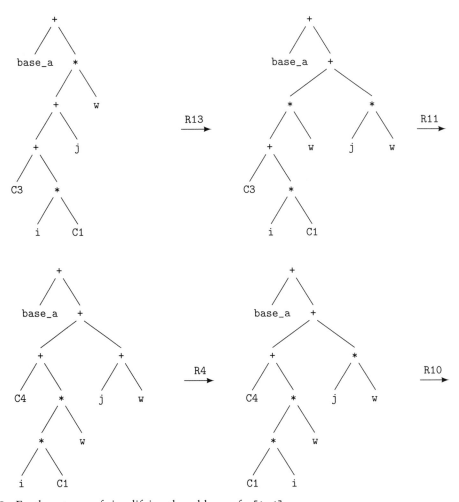

FIG. 12.8 Further stages of simplifying the address of `a[i,j]`.

latter case is exemplified by changing the above Pascal fragment to the one shown in Figure 12.10. Constant propagation (see Section 12.6) will tell us that i is constant inside the loop, rather than just loop-invariant, allowing further simplification to be performed at compile time. Strength reduction (see Section 14.1.2) of addressing expressions also commonly exposes opportunities for reassociation.

Other opportunities for algebraic simplification arise in addressing expressions. For example, in C, if p is a pointer, it is always true that

```
*(&p) = p
```

and, if q is a pointer to a structure with a field s, that

```
(&q)->s = q.s
```

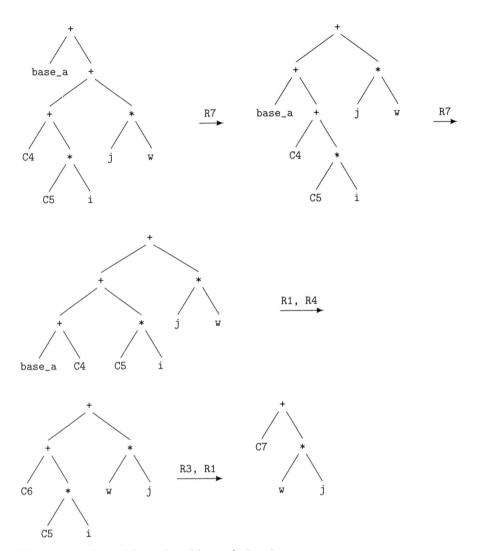

FIG. 12.9 Final stages of simplifying the address of a[i,j].

```
var a: array[lo1..hi1,lo2..hi2] of eltype;
    i, j: integer;
    . . .
i := 10;
    . . .
do j = lo2 to hi2 begin
    a[i,j] := b + a[i,j]
end
```

FIG. 12.10 Another Pascal fragment that accesses elements of an array.

12.3.2   Application of Algebraic Simplification to Floating-Point Expressions

The attentive reader will have noticed that we have not mentioned floating-point computations at all yet in this section. This is because algebraic simplifications rarely can be applied safely to them. For example, for an ANSI/IEEE floating-point value x, it is not necessarily true that

```
x * 0 = 0
```

since, in particular,

```
∞ * 0 = NaN
```

nor that

```
x + 0 = x
```

since, if x is a signaling NaN, the left side causes an exception when the arithmetic operation is executed while the right generally would not. Let MF denote the maximal finite floating-point value representable in a given precision. Then

$$1.0 + (MF - MF) = 1.0$$

while

$$(1.0 + MF) - MF = 0.0$$

Another example of the care with which floating-point computations must be handled is the code

```
eps := 1
while eps+1 > 1 do
    oldeps := eps
    eps := 0.5 * eps
od
```

As written, this code fragment computes in `oldeps` the smallest number x such that $1 + x > 1$. If it is "optimized" by replacing the test "`eps+1 > 1`" with "`eps > 0`", it instead computes the maximal x such that $x/2$ rounds to 0. For example, as written, the routine computes `oldeps = 2.220446E-16` in double precision, while the "optimized" version computes `oldeps = 4.940656E-324`. The loop transformations discussed in Section 20.4.2 can seriously compound this problem.

The only algebraic simplifications that Farnum [Farn88] considers appropriate for ANSI/IEEE floating point are removal of unnecessary type coercions and replacement of divisions by constants with equivalent multiplications. An example of an unnecessary coercion is

```
real s
double t
. . .
t := (double)s * (double)s
```

when performed on a machine that has a single-precision multiply that produces a double-precision result.

To replace division by a constant with a multiplication, it must be the case that the constant and its reciprocal are both represented exactly. Thus, for example, division by 16 can be replaced by multiplication by 0.0625, which is representable exactly in both single- and double-precision floating point.

12.4   Value Numbering

Value numbering is one of several methods for determining that two computations are equivalent and eliminating one of them. It associates a symbolic value with each computation without interpreting the operation performed, but in such a way that any two computations with the same symbolic value always compute the same value.

Three other optimizations have some similar effects, namely, sparse conditional constant propagation (Section 12.6), common-subexpression elimination (Section 13.1), and partial-redundancy elimination (Section 13.3). However, all four optimizations are, in fact, incomparable with each other. The examples in Figure 12.11 show situations where each is better than the others. In Figure 12.11(a), value numbering determines that j and l are assigned the same values, while constant propagation does not, since their values depend on the value input for i, and neither common-subexpression elimination nor partial-redundancy elimination does, since there are no common subexpressions in the code. In Figure 12.11(b), constant propagation determines that j and k are assigned the same values, since it interprets the arithmetic operations, while value numbering does not. In Figure 12.11(c), both global common-subexpression elimination and partial-redundancy elimination determine that the third computation of 2 * i is redundant, but value numbering does not, since l's value is not always equal to j's value or always equal to k's value. Thus, while we have not shown that common-subexpression elimination and partial-redundancy elimination differ in power—which is easy, but we defer it to Section 13.3—we have shown that there are cases where value numbering is more powerful than any of the three others and cases where each of them is more powerful than value numbering.

```
read(i)              i ← 2                read(i)
j ← i + 1            j ← i * 2            if i > 0 goto L1
k ← i                k ← i + 2                j ← 2 * i
l ← k + 1                                     goto L2
                                         L1: k ← 2 * i
                                             l ← 2 * i
                                         L2:

(a)                  (b)                  (c)
```

FIG. 12.11 MIR examples that show that value numbering, constant propagation, common-subexpression elimination, and partial-redundancy elimination are incomparable.

```
a ← i + 1              a ← i + 1
b ← 1 + i              b ← a
i ← j                  i ← j
if i + 1 goto L1       t1 ← i + 1
                       if t1 goto L1
c ← i + 1              c ← t1
(a)                    (b)
```

FIG. 12.12 Value numbering in a basic block. The sequence of instructions in (a) is replaced by the one in (b). Note the recognition of the expressions in the first and second instructions as being identical modulo commutativity and the conversion of the binif in the fourth instruction to an assignment and a valif.

The original formulation of value numbering operated on individual basic blocks. It has since been extended to work on extended basic blocks and, more recently, to a global form that operates on entire procedures (see Section 12.4.2). The global form requires that the procedure be in SSA form. We first discuss value numbering as applied to basic blocks and then the SSA-based form that applies to whole procedures.

12.4.1 Value Numbering as Applied to Basic Blocks

To do value numbering in a basic block, we use hashing to partition the expressions that are computed into classes. Upon encountering an expression, we compute its hash value. If it is not already in the sequence of expressions with that hash value, we add it to the sequence. If the expression computation occurs in an instruction that is not an assignment (e.g., an if instruction), we split it into two instructions, the first of which computes the expression and stores its value in a new temporary and the second of which uses the temporary in place of the expression (see Figure 12.12 for an example). If it is already in the sequence, we replace the current computation by a use of the left-hand variable in the instruction represented in the sequence. The hash function and expression-matching function are defined to take commutativity of the operator into account (see Figure 12.12).

Code to implement the above process is given in Figure 12.13. The data structure HashSeq[1 ·· m] is an array such that HashSeq[i] is a sequence of indexes of instructions whose expressions hash to i and whose values are available. The routines used in the code are as follows:

1. Hash($opr, opd1, opd2$) returns the hash value for the expression formed by its arguments (if the operator opr is unary, $opd2$ is nil); if the operator is commutative, it returns the same value for both orders of the operands.

2. Match_Exp($inst1, inst2$) returns true if the expressions in $inst1$ and $inst2$ are identical up to commutativity.

3. Remove(f, m, v, k, nblocks, Block) removes from f[1 ·· m] all instruction indexes i such that Block[k][i] uses variable v as an operand (see Figure 12.14 for the definition of Remove( )).

```
Hash: (Operator × Operand × Operand) ⟶ integer

procedure Value_Number(m,nblocks,ninsts,Block,maxhash)
   m, nblocks: in integer
   ninsts: inout array [1··nblocks] of integer
   Block: inout array [1··nblocks] of array [··] of MIRInst
   maxhash: in integer
begin
   i: integer
   HashSeq: array [1··maxhash] of sequence of integer
   for i :=  1 to maxhash do
      HashSeq[i] := []
   od
   i := 1
   while i ≤ ninsts[m] do
      case Exp_Kind(Block[m][i].kind) of
binexp:  i += Process_Inst(m,i,nblocks,Block,
            Block[m][i].opd1,Block[m][i].opd2,maxhash,HashSeq)
unexp:   i += Process_Inst(m,i,nblocks,Block,Block[m][i].opd,
            nil,maxhash,HashSeq)
default: i += 1
      esac
   od
end     || Value_Number

procedure Process_Inst(nblocks,m,i,nblocks,Block,opnd1,opnd2,
   maxhash,HashSeq) returns integer
   nblocks, m, i, maxhash: in integer
   Block: inout array [1··nblocks] of array [··] of MIRInst
   opnd1, opnd2: in Operand
   HashSeq: inout array [1··maxhash] of sequence of integer
begin
   hval, j, retval := 1: integer
   inst := Block[m][i], inst2: MIRInst
   doit := true: boolean
   tj: Var
   hval := Hash(inst.opr,opnd1,opnd2)                        (continued)
```

FIG. 12.13 Code to perform value numbering in a basic block.

As an example of Value_Number( ), consider the MIR code in Figure 12.15(a). Suppose maxhash = 3. Then we initialize HashSeq[1··3] to empty sequences, and set i = 1. Block[m][1] has a binexp as its right-hand side, so hval is set to its hash value, say, 2, and doit = true. HashSeq[2] = [], so we proceed to call Remove(HashSeq,maxhash,a,m,n,Block), which does nothing, since the hash sequences are all empty. Next, since doit = true and Has_Left(binasgn) = true, we add the instruction's index to the appropriate hash sequence, namely, HashSeq[2] = [1]. Proces_Inst( ) returns 1, so i is set to 2.

```
            for j := 1 to |HashSeq[hval]| do
                inst2 := Block[m][HashSeq[hval]↓j]
                if Match_Exp(inst,inst2) then
                    || if expressions have the same hash value and they match,
                    || replace later computation by result of earlier one
                    doit := false
                    if Has_Left(inst.kind) then
                        Block[m][i] := ⟨kind:valasgn,left:inst.left,
                            opd:⟨kind:var,val:inst2.left⟩⟩
                    elif inst.kind ∈ {binif,unif} then
                        Block[m][i] := ⟨kind:valif,opd:⟨kind:var,
                            val:inst2.left⟩,lbl:inst.lbl⟩
                    elif inst.kind ∈ {bintrap,untrap} then
                        Block[m][i] := ⟨kind:valtrap,opd:⟨kind:var,
                            val:inst2.left⟩,trapno:inst.trapno⟩
                    fi
                fi
            od
            || if instruction is an assignment, remove all expressions
            || that use its left-hand side variable
            if Has_Left(inst.kind) then
                Remove(HashSeq,maxhash,inst.left,m,nblocks,Block)
            fi
            if doit then
                || if needed, insert instruction that uses result of computation
                if !Has_Left(inst.kind) then
                    tj := new_tmp( )
                    if Block[m][i].kind ∈ {binif,unif} then
                        insert_after(m,i,ninsts,Block,⟨kind:valif,
                            opd:⟨kind:var,val:tj⟩,label:Block[m][i].label)
                        retval := 2
                    elif Block[m][i].kind ∈ {bintrap,untrap} then
                        insert_after(m,i,ninsts,Block,
                            ⟨kind:valtrap,opd:⟨kind:var,val:tj⟩,
                            trapno:Block[m][i].trapno)
                        retval := 2
                    fi
                    || and replace instruction by one that computes
                    || value for inserted instruction
                    if opnd2 = nil then
                        Block[m][i] := ⟨kind:unasgn,left:tj,
                            opr:inst.opr,opd:opnd1⟩
                    else
                        Block[m][i] := ⟨kind:binasgn,left:tj,
                            opr:inst.opr,opd1:opnd1,opd2:opnd2⟩
                    fi
                fi
                HashSeq[hval] ⊕= [i]
            fi
            return retval
        end     || Process_Inst
```

FIG. 12.13 *(continued)*

```
procedure Remove(f,m,v,k,nblocks,Block)
    f: inout array [1··m] of sequence of integer
    m, k, nblocks: in integer
    v: in Var
    Block: in array [1··nblocks] of array [··] of MIRInst
begin
    i, j: integer
    for i := 1 to m do
        for j := 1 to |f[i]| do
            case Exp_Kind(Block[k][f[i]↓j].kind) of
binexp:      if Block[k][f[i]↓j].opd1.val = v
                V Block[k][f[i]↓j].opd2.val = v then
                f[i] ⊖= j
             fi
unexp:       if Block[k][f[i]↓j].opd.val = v then
                f[i] ⊖= j
             fi
default: esac
        od
    od
end     || Remove
```

FIG. 12.14 Code to remove killed expressions from the hash function's bucket sequence.

1 a ← x V y	a ← x V y	a ← x V y
2 b ← x V y	b ← a	b ← a
3 if !z goto L1	t1 ← !z	t1 ← !z
4 x ← !z	if t1 goto L1	if t1 goto L1
5 c ← x & y	x ← !z	x ← t1
6 if x & y trap 30	c ← x & y	c ← x & y
7	if x & y trap 30	if c trap 30
(a)	**(b)**	**(c)**

FIG. 12.15 (a) An example basic block, (b) the result of applying value numbering to its first three instructions, and (c) the result of applying value numbering to the whole block. Note that the if in line 3 has been replaced by two instructions, the first to evaluate the condition and the second to perform the conditional branch.

Block[m][2] has a binexp as its right-hand side, so hval is set to its hash value 2 and doit = true. HashSeq[2] = [1], so we call Match_Exp( ) to compare the expressions in the first and second instructions, which returns true, so we set doit = false, evaluate Has_Left(binasgn), and proceed to replace the second instruction with b ← a. Next we call Remove( ) to delete all instructions that use b as an operand from all the hash chains. Since doit = true and instruction 2 has a left-hand side, we insert its index into its hash sequence, namely, HashSeq[2] = [1,2]. Next, since doit = false, i is set to 3, and we proceed to the third instruction.

Block[m][3] has a unexp as its right-hand side, so hval is set to its hash value, say, 1, and doit = true. HashSeq[1] = [] and Has_Left(unif) = false. Since doit = true and instruction 3 doesn't have a left-hand side, we obtain a new temporary symbol t1, insert the instruction if t1 goto L1 after instruction 3, causing the following instructions to be renumbered, replace instruction 3 by t1 ← !z, and insert 3 into its hash sequence, namely, HashSeq[1] = [3]. Proces_Inst( ) returns 2, so i is set to 5, and we proceed to the next instruction. The resulting basic block is shown in Figure 12.15(b).

Block[m][5] has a unexp as its right-hand side, so hval is set to its hash value 1 and doit = true. HashSeq[1] = [3], so we call Match_Exp( ) to compare the expressions in the third and fifth instructions, and it returns true. Since Has_Left(unasgn) = true, we call Remove( ) to delete all instructions that use x as an operand from all the hash chains, which results in setting HashSeq[2] = []. Since doit = true and instruction 5 has a left-hand side, we insert its index into its hash sequence, namely, HashSeq[1] = [3,5]. Proces_Inst( ) returns 1, so i is set to 6, and we proceed to the next instruction.

Block[m][6] has a binexp as its right-hand side, so hval is set to its hash value, say, 3, and doit = true. HashSeq[3] = [], so we skip the loop that checks for matching expressions. Since Has_Left(binasgn) = true, we call Remove( ) to delete all instructions that use c as an operand from all the hash chains. Since doit = true and instruction 6 has a left-hand side, we insert its index into its hash sequence, namely, HashSeq[3] = [6]. Proces_Inst( ) returns 1, so i is set to 7, and we proceed to the last instruction.

Block[m][7] contains a binexp, so hval is set to its hash value, namely, 3, and doit = true. HashSeq[3] = [6], so we call Match_Exp( ) to compare the expressions in the sixth and seventh instructions, which returns true. Also, we set doit = false. Since Has_Left(binif) = false, we replace Block[m][7] with "if c trap 30". Since doit = false and there are no more instructions, the process terminates. The resulting basic block is shown in Figure 12.15(c).

Note that there is a strong resemblance between value numbering and constructing the DAG representation of a basic block as discussed in Section 4.9.3. Reusing nodes in the DAG as operands, rather than inserting new nodes with the same values, corresponds to deleting later computations of equivalent values and replacing them by uses of the previously computed ones. In fact, value numbering is frequently used in constructing DAGs.

12.4.2   Global Value Numbering

The earliest approach to global value numbering was developed by Reif and Lewis [ReiL77]. A newer, easier to understand, and (computationally) less complex approach was developed by Alpern, Wegman, and Zadeck [AlpW88]. We base our presentation on the latter.

We begin by discussing the notion of congruence of variables. The idea is to make two variables congruent to each other if the computations that define them have identical operators (or constant values) and their corresponding operands are congruent (this is, of course, what value numbering does). By this definition, the left-hand variables of c ← a + 1 and d ← b + 1 are congruent as long as a and b are congruent. However, as we shall see, this notion is insufficiently precise. To make it precise, we need to convert the procedure we are to perform global value numbering on to SSA form and then to define what is called the value graph of the resulting flowgraph.

To translate a flowgraph into SSA form, we use the method of iterated dominance frontiers presented in Section 8.11, which results in a minimal SSA representation of the procedure.

The *value graph* of a procedure is a labeled directed graph whose nodes are labeled with operators, function symbols, or constants and whose edges represent generating assignments and point from an operator or function to its operands; the edges arc labeled with natural numbers that indicate the operand position that each operand has with respect to the given operator or function. We also name the nodes, for convenience, with SSA-form variables that indicate where the result of the operation represented by a node is stored; or if a node is not named with an SSA-form variable, we attach an arbitrary name to it.

For example, given the code fragment in Figure 12.16, the corresponding value graph (in which we need no subscripts on the variables since each has only one definition point) is given in Figure 12.17. Note that c and d are congruent by the above definition.

Next, consider the example flowgraph in Figure 12.18. Its translation to minimal SSA form is shown in Figure 12.19. The value graph for this procedure includes cycles, since, for example, i_2 depends on i_3 and vice versa. The resulting value graph is shown in Figure 12.20. The node named n is not filled in because we have no information about its value.

```
a ← 3
b ← 3
c ← a + 1
d ← b + 1
if c >= 3 then ...
```

FIG. 12.16 A short example program fragment for which to construct the value graph.

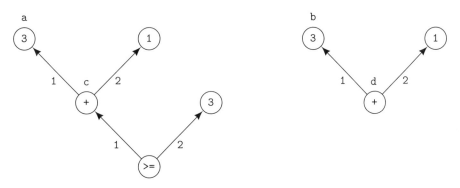

FIG. 12.17 Value graph for the code in Figure 12.16.

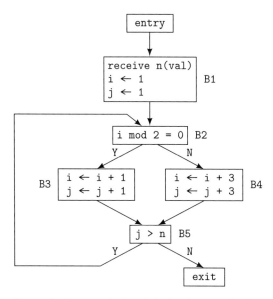

FIG. 12.18 Example flowgraph for global value numbering.

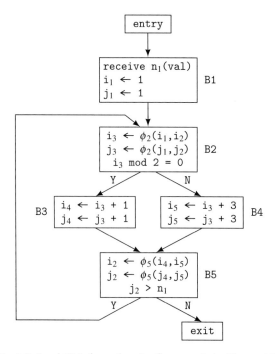

FIG. 12.19 Minimal SSA form for the flowgraph in Figure 12.18.

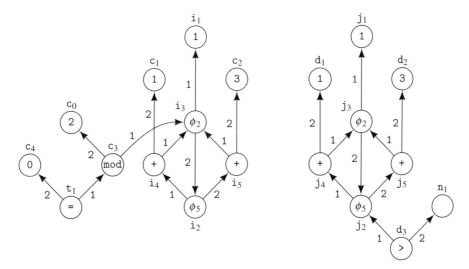

FIG. 12.20 Value graph for the code in Figure 12.19.

Now *congruence* is defined as the maximal relation on the value graph such that two nodes are congruent if either (1) they are the same node, (2) their labels are constants and their contents are equal, or (3) they have the same operators and their operands are congruent. Two variables are *equivalent* at a point p in a program if they are congruent and their defining assignments dominate p.

We compute congruence as the maximal fixed point of a partitioning process performed on the value graph. Initially, we assume that all nodes with the same label are congruent, and then we repeatedly partition the congruence classes according to whether the operands of the members of a partition are congruent, until we obtain a fixed point, which must be the maximal one by the character of the partitioning process. The partitioning algorithm Global_Value_Number(*N,NLabel,ELabel,B*) is given in Figure 12.21. It uses five data structures, as follows:

1. *N* is the set of nodes in the value graph.

2. *NLabel* is a function that maps nodes to node labels.

3. *ELabel* is the set of labeled edges from nodes to nodes, where $\langle x, j, y \rangle$ represents an edge from node *x* to node *y* labeled *j*.

4. *B* is an array that is set by the algorithm to the resulting partition.

5. The global data structure *NtoB* maps each node to the index of the partition containing it, i.e., for each node $v \in N$, $v \in B[NtoB(v)]$.

The algorithm, based on one developed by Aho, Hopcroft, and Ullman [AhoH74], uses a worklist to contain the set of partitions that need to be examined and three functions, as follows:

```
NodeLabel = Operator ∪ Function ∪ Var ∪ Const
NtoB: Node ⟶ integer

procedure Global_Value_Number(N,NLabel,ELabel,B) returns integer
    N: in set of Node
    NLabel: in Node ⟶ NodeLabel
    ELabel: in set of (Node × integer × Node)
    B: inout array [··] of set of Node
begin
    i, m, x, z: Node
    j, j1, k, k1,p: integer
    S, Worklist: set of Node
    || initialize partitions in B[n] and map nodes to partitions
    p := Initialize(N,NLabel,B,Worklist)
    while Worklist ≠ ∅ do
        i := ◆Worklist
        Worklist -= {i}
        m := ◆B[i]
        || attempt to subdivide each nontrivial partition
        || until the worklist is empty
        for j := 1 to Arity(NLabel,i) do
            j1 := Follow_Edge(ELabel,m,j)
            S := B[i] - {m}
            while S ≠ ∅ do
                x := ◆S
                S -= {x}
                if Follow_Edge(ELabel,x,j) ≠ j1 then
                    p += 1
                    B[p] := {m}
                    NtoB(m) := p
                    B[i] -= {m}
                    while S ≠ ∅ do
                        z := ◆S
                        S -= {z}
                        for k := 1 to Arity(NLabel,i) do
                            k1 := Follow_Edge(ELabel,m,k)
                            if k1 ≠ Follow_Edge(ELabel,z,k) then
                                B[p] ∪= {z}
                                NtoB(z) := p
                                B[i] -= {z}
                            fi
                        od
                    od
                od
            if |B[i]| > 1 then
                Worklist ∪= {i}
            fi
```

FIG. 12.21 Partitioning algorithm to do global value numbering by computing congruence.

```
                        if |B[p]| > 1 then
                            Worklist ∪= {p}
                        fi
                    fi
                od
            od
        od
        return p
    end    || Global_Value_Number
```

FIG. 12.21 *(continued)*

1. `Initialize(N,NLabel,B,Worklist)` initializes $B[1]$ through some $B[p]$ with the initial partitioning of the nodes of the value graph (i.e., all nodes with the same label go into the same partition) and *Worklist* with the initial worklist, and returns p as its value.

2. `Arity(NLabel,j)` returns the number of operands of the operators in $B[j]$.

3. `Follow_Edge(ELabel,x,j)` returns the integer k such that there is a labeled edge $\langle x, j, y \rangle \in ELabel$ and $y \in B[k]$.

Code for the first and third of these functions is provided in Figure 12.22. Computing `Arity( )` is trivial. The worst-case running time for the partitioning algorithm is $O(e \cdot \log e)$, where e is the number of edges in the value graph.

For our example flowgraph in Figure 12.19, the initial number of partitions p is 11, and the initial partitioning is as follows:

```
B[1]    = {c₁,d₁,i₁,j₁}
B[2]    = {c₂,d₂}
B[3]    = {c₀}
B[4]    = {c₃}
B[5]    = {n₁}
B[6]    = {d₃}
B[7]    = {i₃,j₃}
B[8]    = {i₄,j₄,i₅,j₅}
B[9]    = {i₂,j₂}
B[10]   = {c₄}
B[11]   = {t₁}
```

The initial value of `Worklist` is $\{7,8,9\}$. The result of the partitioning process is 12 partitions, as follows:

```
B[1]    = {c₁,d₁,i₁,j₁}
B[2]    = {c₂,d₂}
B[3]    = {c₀}
B[4]    = {c₃}
B[5]    = {n₁}
B[6]    = {d₃}
B[7]    = {i₃,j₃}
```

```
procedure Initialize(N,NLabel,B,Worklist) returns integer
    N: in set of Node
    NLabel: in Node ⟶ NodeLabel
    B: out array [··] of set of Node
    Worklist: out set of Node
begin
    i, k := 0: integer
    v: Node
    || assemble partitions, node-to-partition map, and initial worklist
    Worklist := ∅
    for each v ∈ N do
        i := 1
        while i ≤ k do
            if NLabel(v) = NLabel(◆B[i]) then
                B[i] ∪= {v}
                NtoB(v) := i
                i := k + 1
            fi
            i += 1
        od
        if i = k+1 then
            k += 1
            B[k] := {v}
            NtoB(v) := k
            if Arity(NLabel,v) > 0 & |B[k]| > 1 then
                Worklist ∪= {k}
            fi
        fi
    od
    return k
end     || Initialize

procedure Follow_Edge(ELabel,x,j) returns integer
    ELabel: in set of (Node × integer × Node)
    x: in Node
    j: in integer
begin
    el: Node × integer × integer
    for each el ∈ ELabel do
        if x = el@1 & j = el@2 then
            return NtoB(el@3)
        fi
    od
end     || Follow_Edge
```

FIG. 12.22 Auxiliary routines used by the partitioning algorithm.

```
B[8]    = {i₄,j₄}
B[9]    = {i₂,j₂}
B[10]   = {c₄}
B[11]   = {t₁}
B[12]   = {i₅,j₅}
```

Thus, corresponding i and j nodes in the value graph are congruent and equivalence of variables can be determined as a result.

As a second example, suppose we change the assignment i ← i + 3 in block B4 to i ← i - 3 in Figure 12.18. Then the value graph is identical to the one in Figure 12.20, except that the node named i_5 contains a "-" instead of a "+". The initial partitioning is the same as shown above for the original program, except that p is 12 and B[8] through B[11] are replaced by

```
B[8]    = {i₄,j₄,j₅}
B[9]    = {i₅}
B[10]   = {i₂,j₂}
B[11]   = {c₄}
B[12]   = {t₁}
```

The final partitioning has each of i_2, i_3, i_4, i_5, j_2, j_3, j_4, and j_5 in a separate partition.

Alpern, Wegman, and Zadeck discuss a series of generalizations of this approach to global value numbering, including the following:

1. doing structural analysis of the program to be analyzed (Section 7.7) and using special ϕ-functions designed for the control-flow constructs so as to be able to determine congruence with respect to control flow;

2. application of the method to array operations by modeling, e.g.,

    ```
    a[i] ← 2 * b[i]
    ```

    by

    ```
    a ← update(a,i,2*access(b,i))
    ```

    and

3. taking commutativity into account, so as to be able, for example, to recognize a * b and b * a as congruent.

Each of these changes can increase the number of congruences detected.

Briggs, Cooper, and Simpson extend hash-based value numbering to work on a routine's dominator tree, extend the global approach discussed above to take expression availability into account (see Section 13.3), and compare hash-based and global approaches to value numbering with the result that the two approaches are incomparable—there are cases for which each does better than the other. In a later paper, Cooper and Simpson discuss an approach to global value numbering that works on strongly connected components of a routine's SSA representation and that combines the best properties of the hashing and global approaches and is more effective than both of them. (See Section 12.8 for citations.)

12.5   Copy Propagation

Copy propagation is a transformation that, given an assignment $x \leftarrow y$ for some variables x and y, replaces later uses of x with uses of y, as long as intervening instructions have not changed the value of either x or y.

From here on, we generally need to represent the structure of a procedure as an array of basic blocks, each of which is an array of instructions. We use the variable nblocks and the arrays ninsts[1··nblocks] and Block[1··nblocks][··], declared as

```
nblocks: integer
ninsts: array [1··nblocks] of integer
Block: array [1··nblocks] of array [··] of Instruction
```

where Block[*i*] consists of instructions Block[*i*][1] through Block[*i*][ninsts[*i*]], to do so.

Before proceeding to discuss copy propagation in detail, we consider its relationship to register coalescing, which is discussed in detail in Section 16.3. The two transformations are identical in their effect, as long as optimization is done on a low-level intermediate code with registers (symbolic[1] and/or real) in place of identifiers. However, the methods for determining whether register coalescing or copy propagation applies to a particular copy assignment are different: we use data-flow analysis for copy propagation and the interference graph for register coalescing. Another difference is that copy propagation can be performed on intermediate code at any level from high to low.

For example, given the flowgraph in Figure 12.23(a), the instruction b ← a in block B1 is a copy assignment. Neither a nor b is assigned a value in the flowgraph following this instruction, so all the uses of b can be replaced by uses of a, as shown in Figure 12.23(b). While this may not appear to be a great improvement in the code, it does render b useless—there are no instructions in (b) in which it appears as an operand—so dead-code elimination (see Section 18.10) can remove the assignment b ← a; and the replacement makes it possible to compute the value assigned to e by a left shift rather than an addition, assuming that a is integer-valued.

Copy propagation can reasonably be divided into local and global phases, the first operating within individual basic blocks and the latter across the entire flowgraph, or it can be accomplished in a single global phase. To avoid an $O(n^2)$ time bound, we keep a table *ACP* of the available copy instructions, as shown in the algorithm in Figure 12.24. The algorithm assumes that an array of MIR instructions Block[m][1], ..., Block[m][n] is provided as input.

As an example of the use of the resulting $O(n)$ algorithm, consider the code in Figure 12.25. The second column shows a basic block of five instructions before applying the algorithm, the fourth column shows the result of applying it, and the third column shows the value of ACP at each step.

---

1. Symbolic registers, as found, for example, in LIR, are an extension of a machine's real register set to include as many more as may be needed to generate code for a program. It is the task of global register allocation (Chapter 16) to pack the symbolic registers into the real registers, possibly generating stores and loads to save and restore their values, respectively, in the process.

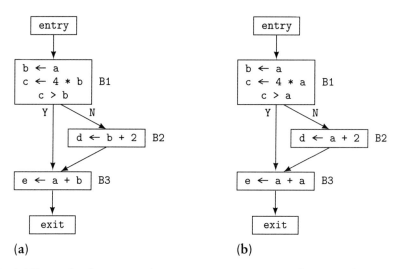

FIG. 12.23 (a) Example of a copy assignment to propagate, namely, b ← a in B1, and (b) the result of doing copy propagation on it.

```
procedure Local_Copy_Prop(m,n,Block)
    m, n: in integer
    Block: inout array [1··n] of array [··] of MIRInst
begin
    ACP := Ø, T: set of (Var × Var)
    acp: Var × Var
    i, na: integer
    copy: boolean
    inst: MIRInst
    for i := 1 to n do
        inst := Block[m][i]
        || replace operands that are copies
        case Exp_Kind(inst.kind) of
binexp:    copy := Replace_Copy(Block[m][i],inst.opd1,ACP)
           copy V= Replace_Copy(Block[m][i],inst.opd2,ACP)
unexp:     copy := Replace_Copy(Block[m][i],inst.opd,ACP)
listexp:   copy := false
           for j := 1 to |inst.args| do
               copy V= Replace_Copy(Block[m][i],inst.args↓j@1,ACP)
           od
noexp:     copy := false
        esac
        || insert pairs into ACP for copy assignments
        if copy then
            case inst.kind of
```

(continued)

FIG. 12.24 *O(n)* algorithm for local copy propagation.

```
valasgn:        if inst.opd.kind = var then
                    ACP ∪= {⟨inst.left,inst.opd.val⟩}
                    i += 1
                fi
binasgn,unasgn,condasgn,indasgn,eltasgn,indeltasgn,callasgn:
                repeat
                    na := |ACP|
                    T := ACP
                    while T ≠ ∅ do
                        acp := ◆ACP
                        if acp@1 = inst.left ∨ acp@2 = inst.left then
                            ACP -= {acp}
                        fi
                        T -= {acp}
                    od
                until na = |ACP|
default:
            esac
        fi
    od
  end     || Local_Copy_Prop

procedure Replace_Copy(inst,opdpos,ACP) returns boolean
    inst: inout MIRInst
    opdpos: in enum {opd1,opd2,opd}
    ACP: in set of (Var × Var)
begin
    acp: Var × Var
    for each acp ∈ ACP do
        if inst.opdpos.kind = var & inst.opdpos.val = acp@1 then
            inst.opdpos.val := acp@2
            return true
        fi
    od
    return false
end     || Replace_Copy
```

FIG. 12.24 *(continued)*

To perform global copy propagation, we first do a data-flow analysis to determine which copy assignments reach uses of their left-hand variables unimpaired, i.e., without having either variable redefined in between. We define the set $COPY(i)$ to consist of the instances of copy assignments occurring in block i that reach the end of block i. More explicitly, $COPY(i)$ is a set of quadruples $\langle u, v, i, pos \rangle$, such that $u \leftarrow v$ is a copy assignment and pos is the position in block i where the assignment occurs, and neither u nor v is assigned to later in block i. We define $KILL(i)$ to be the set of copy assignment instances killed by block i, i.e., $KILL(i)$ is the set of quadruples $\langle u, v, blk, pos \rangle$ such that $u \leftarrow v$ is a copy assignment occurring at position pos in block $blk \neq i$. For the example in Figure 12.26, the $COPY(\,)$ and $KILL(\,)$ sets are as follows:

Position	Code Before	ACP	Code After
		∅	
1	b ← a		b ← a
		{⟨b,a⟩}	
2	c ← b + 1		c ← a + 1
		{⟨b,a⟩}	
3	d ← b		d ← a
		{⟨b,a⟩,⟨d,a⟩}	
4	b ← d + c		b ← a + c
		{⟨d,a⟩}	
5	b ← d		b ← a
		{⟨d,a⟩,⟨b,a⟩}	

FIG. 12.25 An example of the linear-time local copy-propagation algorithm.

$$
\begin{aligned}
COPY(\text{entry}) &= \emptyset \\
COPY(\text{B1}) &= \{\langle d, c, B1, 2\rangle\} \\
COPY(\text{B2}) &= \{\langle g, e, B2, 2\rangle\} \\
COPY(\text{B3}) &= \emptyset \\
COPY(\text{B4}) &= \emptyset \\
COPY(\text{B5}) &= \emptyset \\
COPY(\text{B6}) &= \emptyset \\
COPY(\text{exit}) &= \emptyset \\
\\
KILL(\text{entry}) &= \emptyset \\
KILL(\text{B1}) &= \{\langle g, e, B2, 2\rangle\} \\
KILL(\text{B2}) &= \emptyset \\
KILL(\text{B3}) &= \emptyset \\
KILL(\text{B4}) &= \emptyset \\
KILL(\text{B5}) &= \emptyset \\
KILL(\text{B6}) &= \{\langle d, c, B1, 2\rangle\} \\
KILL(\text{exit}) &= \emptyset
\end{aligned}
$$

Next, we define data-flow equations for $CPin(i)$ and $CPout(i)$ that represent the sets of copy assignments that are available for copy propagation on entry to and exit from block i, respectively. A copy assignment is available on entry to block i if it is available on exit from all predecessors of block i, so the path-combining operator is intersection. A copy assignment is available on exit from block j if it is either in $COPY(j)$ or it is available on entry to block j and not killed by block j, i.e., if it is in $CPin(j)$ and not in $KILL(j)$. Thus, the data-flow equations are

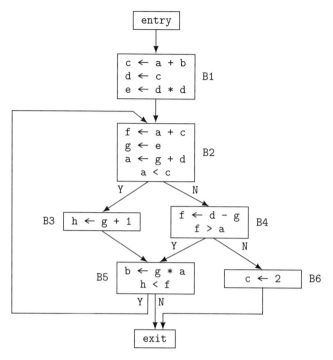

FIG. 12.26 Another example for copy propagation.

$$CPin(i) = \bigcap_{j \in Pred(i)} CPout(j)$$

$$CPout(i) = COPY(i) \cup (CPin(i) - KILL(i))$$

and the proper initialization is $CPin(\text{entry}) = \emptyset$ and $CPin(i) = U$ for all $i \neq \text{entry}$, where U is the universal set of quadruples, or at least

$$U = \bigcup_i COPY(i)$$

The data-flow analysis for global copy propagation can be performed efficiently with a bit-vector representation of the sets.

Given the data-flow information $CPin(\ )$ and assuming that we have already done local copy propagation, we perform global copy propagation as follows:

1. For each basic block B, set ACP = {a ∈ Var × Var where ∃w ∈ integer such that ⟨a@1,a@2,B,w⟩ ∈ CPin(B)}.

2. For each basic block B, perform the local copy-propagation algorithm from Figure 12.24 on block B (omitting the assignment ACP := ∅).

For our example in Figure 12.26, the $CPin(\ )$ sets are

$$
\begin{aligned}
CPin(\text{entry}) &= \emptyset \\
CPin(B1) &= \emptyset
\end{aligned}
$$

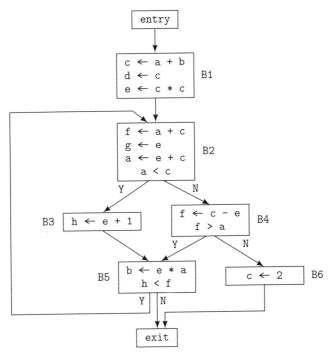

FIG. 12.27 Flowgraph from Figure 12.26 after copy propagation.

$$
\begin{aligned}
CPin(\text{B2}) \quad &= \{\langle d, c, \text{B1}, 2\rangle\} \\
CPin(\text{B3}) \quad &= \{\langle d, c, \text{B1}, 2\rangle, \langle g, e, \text{B2}, 2\rangle\} \\
CPin(\text{B4}) \quad &= \{\langle d, c, \text{B1}, 2\rangle, \langle g, e, \text{B2}, 2\rangle\} \\
CPin(\text{B5}) \quad &= \{\langle d, c, \text{B1}, 2\rangle, \langle g, e, \text{B2}, 2\rangle\} \\
CPin(\text{exit}) \quad &= \{\langle g, e, \text{B2}, 2\rangle\}
\end{aligned}
$$

Doing local copy propagation within B1 and global copy propagation across the entire procedure turns the flowgraph in Figure 12.26 into the one in Figure 12.27.

The local copy-propagation algorithm can easily be generalized to work on extended basic blocks. To do so, we process the basic blocks that make up an extended basic block in preorder, i.e., each block before its successors, and we initialize the table ACP for each basic block other than the initial one with the final value of ACP from its predecessor block. Correspondingly, the global copy-propagation algorithm can be generalized to use extended basic blocks as the nodes with which data-flow information is associated. To do so, we must associate a separate *CPout*( ) set with each exit from an extended basic block, since the paths through the extended basic block will generally make different copy assignments available.

If we do local copy propagation followed by global copy propagation (both on extended basic blocks) for our example in Figure 12.26, the result is the same, but more of the work happens in the local phase. Blocks B2, B3, B4, and B6 make up an extended basic block and the local phase propagates the value of e assigned to g in block B2 to all of them.

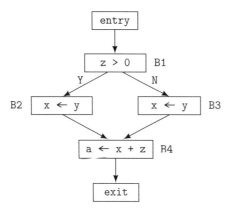

FIG. 12.28 Copy assignments not detected by global copy propagation.

Note that the global copy-propagation algorithm does not identify copy assignments such as the two $x \leftarrow y$ statements in blocks B2 and B3 in Figure 12.28. The transformation known as tail merging (see Section 18.8) will replace the two copy assignments by one, in effect moving the copy into a separate basic block of its own. Copy propagation will then recognize it and propagate the copy into block B4. However, this presents a phase-ordering problem for some compilers: tail merging is generally not done until machine instructions have been generated.

Alternatively, either partial-redundancy elimination (Section 13.3) applied to assignments or code hoisting (Section 13.5) can be used to move both occurrences of the statement $x \leftarrow y$ to block B1, and that can be done during the same optimization phase as copy propagation.

12.6   Sparse Conditional Constant Propagation

Constant propagation is a transformation that, given an assignment $x \leftarrow c$ for a variable x and a constant c, replaces later uses of x with uses of c as long as intervening assignments have not changed the value of x. For example, the assignment $b \leftarrow 3$ in block B1 in Figure 12.29(a) assigns the constant value 3 to b and no other assignment in the flowgraph assigns to b. Constant propagation turns the flowgraph into the one shown in Figure 12.29(b). Note that all occurrences of b have been replaced by 3 but neither of the resulting constant-valued expressions has been evaluated. This is done by constant-expression evaluation (see Section 12.1).

Constant propagation is particularly important for RISC architectures because it moves small integer constants to the places where they are used. Since all RISCs provide instructions that take a small integer constant as an operand (with the definition of "small" varying from one architecture to another), knowing that an operand is such a constant allows more efficient code to be generated. Also, some RISCs (e.g., MIPS) have an addressing mode that uses the sum of a register and a small constant but not one that uses the sum of two registers; propagating a small

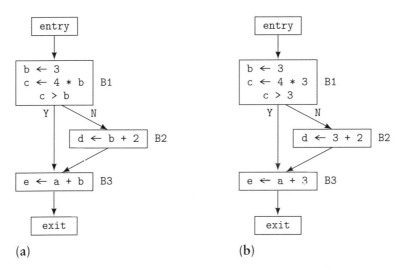

(a)   **(b)**

FIG. 12.29 (a) Example of a constant assignment to propagate, namely, b ← 3 in B1, and (b) the result of doing constant propagation on it.

constant value to such an address construction saves both registers and instructions. More generally, constant propagation reduces the number of registers needed by a procedure and increases the effectiveness of several other optimizations, such as constant-expression evaluation, induction-variable optimizations (Section 14.1), and the dependence-analysis-based transformations discussed in Section 20.4.2.

Wegman and Zadeck describe two approaches to constant propagation that take conditionals into account, one that uses SSA form and one that doesn't [WegZ91]. We describe the SSA-form one here because it is the more efficient of the two. This approach to constant propagation has two major advantages over the classic one: deriving information from conditionals and being more efficient.

To perform sparse conditional constant propagation, we must first transform the flowgraph to SSA form, with the additional proviso that each node contain only a single operation or ϕ-function. We use the method of iterated dominance frontiers described in Section 8.11 to transform the flowgraph to minimal SSA form, divide the basic blocks into one instruction per node, and then introduce *SSA edges* that connect the unique definition of a variable to each of its uses. These allow information to be propagated independent of the control flow of the program.

Then we perform a symbolic execution of the program using both the flowgraph edges and the SSA edges to transmit information. In the process, we mark nodes as executable only when the conditions for their execution are satisfied, and at each step, we process only executable nodes and nodes that have their SSA predecessors processed—this is what makes the method symbolic execution rather than data-flow analysis. We use the lattice pictured in Figure 12.30, where each C_i is a possible constant value and true and false are included to provide lattice values for the results of conditional expressions. If ValType denotes the set {false, . . . , C_{-2}, C_{-1}, C_0, C_1, C_2, . . . , true}, then the lattice is called ConstLat. We associate a lattice

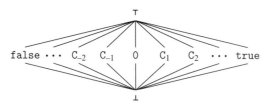

FIG. 12.30 The constant-propagation lattice ConstLat.

element with each variable in the program at the exit from the unique flowgraph node that defines it. Assigning a variable the value ⊤ means that it may have an as-yet-undetermined constant value, while ⊥ means that the value is not constant or cannot be determined to be constant. We initialize all variables with ⊤.

We extend the representation of MIR instructions in ICAN to include ϕ-functions, as follows:

$$VarName0 \leftarrow \phi(VarName1, \dots, VarNamen)$$

$$\langle \text{kind:phiasgn}, \text{left}: VarName0, \text{vars}: [VarName1, \dots, VarNamen] \rangle$$

and define Exp_Kind(phiasgn) = listexp and Has_Left(phiasgn) = true.

We use two functions, Visit_Phi( ) and Visit_Inst( ), to process the nodes of the flowgraph. The first of these effectively executes ϕ-functions over the lattice values, and the latter does the same for ordinary statements.

The code to perform sparse conditional constant propagation is the routine Sparse_Cond_Const( ) given in Figure 12.31. The algorithm uses two worklists, FlowWL, which holds flowgraph edges that need processing, and SSAWL, which holds SSA edges that need processing. The data structure ExecFlag(a,b) records whether edge $\langle a,b \rangle$ in the flowgraph is executable. For each node n that defines an (SSA-form) variable v, there is a lattice cell LatCell(n,v) that records the lattice element associated with variable v on exit from node n; since each node defines at most one variable, the use of both n and v as arguments is redundant, but convenient. The function SSASucc(n) records the SSA successor edges of node n, i.e., the SSA edges that lead from node n. The code for the auxiliary routines Edge_Count( ), Initialize( ), Visit_Phi( ), and Visit_Inst( ) is given in Figure 12.32. Five other procedures are used by these three routines, as follows:

1. Defines(i,v) returns true if node i defines variable v and false otherwise.

2. Exp$(inst)$ extracts the expression that is the right-hand side of *inst* if it is an assignment or that is the body of *inst* if it is a test.

3. Lat_Eval$(inst)$ evaluates the expression in *inst* with respect to the lattice values assigned to the variables in LatCell(k,x), where x ranges over the possible variables.

4. Edge_Set(k,i,val) returns the set $\{\langle k,i \rangle\}$ if *val* is a constant element of the given lattice and $\emptyset$ otherwise.

5. Edge_Count(b,E) returns the number of edges e in E such that e@2 = b.

```
LatCell: Var ⟶ ConstLat
FlowWL, SSAWL: set of (integer × integer)
ExecFlag: (integer × integer) ⟶ boolean
SSASucc: integer ⟶ set of (integer × integer)

procedure Sparse_Cond_Const(ninsts,Inst,E,entry,V)
   ninsts: in integer
   Inst: in array [1··ninsts] of MIRInst
   E: in set of (integer × integer)
   entry: in integer
   V: in set of Var
begin
   a, b, c, d: integer
   e: integer × integer
   || initialize lattice cells, executable flags,
   || and flow and SSA worklists
   Initialize(ninsts,E,entry,V)
   while FlowWL ≠ ∅ ∨ SSAWL ≠ ∅ do
      if FlowWL ≠ ∅ then
         e := ◆FlowWL; a := e@1; b := e@2
         FlowWL -= {e}
         || propagate constants along flowgraph edges
         if !ExecFlag(a,b) then
            ExecFlag(a,b) := true
            if Inst[b].kind = phiasgn then
               Visit_Phi(b,Inst[b])
            elif Edge_Count(b,E) = 1 then
               Visit_Inst(b,Inst[b])
            fi
            if |{d ∈ integer where b→d ∈ E}| = 1 then
               FlowWL ∪= {b→d}
            fi
         fi
      fi
      if SSAWL ≠ ∅ then
         e := ◆SSAWL; a := e@1; b := e@2
         SSAWL -= {e}
         || propagate constants along SSA edges
         if Inst[b].kind = phiasgn then
            Visit_Phi(Inst[b])
         elif Edge_Count(b,E) ≥ 1 then
            Visit_Inst(b,Inst[b])
         fi
      fi
   od
end      || Sparse_Cond_Const
```

FIG. 12.31 SSA-based algorithm for sparse conditional constant propagation.

```
procedure Edge_Count(b,E) returns integer
   b: in integer
   E: in set of (integer × integer)
begin
   e: integer × integer
   i := 0: integer
   || return number of executable flowgraph edges leading to b
   for each e ∈ E do
      if e@2 = b & ExecFlag(e@1,e@2) then
         i += 1
      fi
   od
   return i
end    || Edge_Count

procedure Initialize(ninsts,E,entry,V)
   ninsts: in integer
   E: in set of (integer × integer)
   entry: in integer
   V: in set of Var
begin
   i, m, n: integer
   p: integer × integer
   v: Var
   FlowWL := {m→n ∈ E where m = entry}
   SSAWL := ∅
   for each p ∈ E do
      ExecFlag(p@1,p@2) := false
   od
   for i := 1 to ninsts do
      if Defines(i,v) then
         LatCell(v) := ⊤
      fi
   od
end    || Initialize
```

FIG. 12.32 Auxiliary routines for sparse conditional constant propagation.

We take as a simple example the program in Figure 12.33, which is already in minimal SSA-form with one instruction per node. The SSA edges are $\langle B1,B3 \rangle$, $\langle B2,B3 \rangle$, $\langle B4,B6 \rangle$, and $\langle B5,B6 \rangle$, so that, for example, $\text{SSASucc}(B4) = \{\langle B4,B5 \rangle\}$. The algorithm begins by setting $\text{FlowWL} = \{\langle \text{entry},B1 \rangle\}$, $\text{SSAWL} = \emptyset$, all $\text{ExecFlag}()$ values to false, and all $\text{LatCell}()$ values to $\top$. It then removes $\langle \text{entry},B1 \rangle$ from FlowWL, sets $\text{ExecFlag}(\text{entry},B1) = \text{true}$, and calls $\text{Visit\_Inst}(B1,\text{"}a_1 \leftarrow 2\text{"})$. $\text{Visit\_Inst}()$ evaluates the expression 2 in the lattice, sets $\text{LatCell}(a_1) = 2$ and $\text{SSAWL} = \{\langle B1,B3 \rangle\}$. The main routine then sets $\text{FlowWL} = \{\langle B1,B2 \rangle\}$. Since SSAWL is now non-empty, the main routine removes $\langle B1,B3 \rangle$ from SSAWL and calls $\text{Visit\_Inst}(B3,\text{"}a_1 < b_1\text{"})$, and so on. The result is that the lattice cells are set as follows:

```
procedure Visit_Phi(inst)
   inst: in MIRInst
begin
   j: integer
   || process φ node
   LatCell(inst.left) := ⊤
   for j := 1 to |inst.vars| do
      LatCell(inst.left)
          ⊓= LatCell(inst.vars↓j)
   od
end    || Visit_Phi

procedure Visit_Inst(k,inst)
   k: in integer
   inst: in MIRInst
begin
   i: integer
   v: Var
   val: ConstLat
   || process non-φ node
   val := Lat_Eval(inst)
   if Has_Left(inst.kind)
      & val ≠ LatCell(inst.left) then
      LatCell(inst.left) ⊓= val
      SSAWL ∪= SSASucc(k)
   fi
   case Exp_Kind(inst.kind) of
binexp, unexp:
      if val = ⊤ then
         for each i ∈ Succ(k) do
            FlowWL ∪= {k→i}
         od
      elif val ≠ ⊥ then
         for each i ∈ Succ(k) do
            FlowWL ∪= Edge_Set(k,i,val)
         od
      fi
default:
   esac
end    || Visit_Inst
```

FIG. 12.32 *(continued)*

```
LatCell(a₁) = 2
LatCell(b₁) = 3
LatCell(c₁) = 4
LatCell(c₃) = 4
```

Note that $\text{LatCell}(c_2)$ is never set because the algorithm determines that the edge from B3 to B5 is not executable. This information can be used to delete blocks B3, B5, and B6 from the flowgraph.

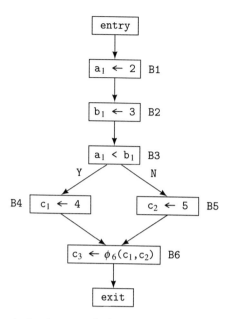

FIG. 12.33 A simple example for sparse conditional constant propagation.

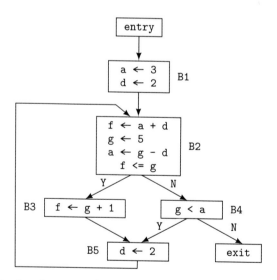

FIG. 12.34 Another example for sparse conditional constant propagation.

As a second example, consider the program in Figure 12.34. Figure 12.35 is the minimal SSA-form translation of it, with one instruction per node. The SSA edges are $\langle B1,B4 \rangle$, $\langle B2,B3 \rangle$, $\langle B3,B5 \rangle$, $\langle B3,B7 \rangle$, $\langle B4,B5 \rangle$, $\langle B5,B8 \rangle$, $\langle B5,B11 \rangle$, $\langle B6,B7 \rangle$, $\langle B6,B8 \rangle$, $\langle B6,B9 \rangle$, $\langle B6,B10 \rangle$, $\langle B7,B10 \rangle$, $\langle B7,B4 \rangle$, $\langle B9,B11 \rangle$,

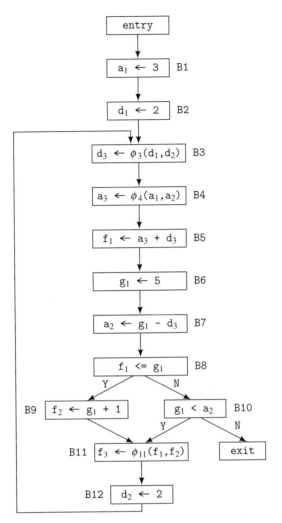

FIG. 12.35 Minimal SSA form of the program in Figure 12.34 with one instruction per basic block.

and $\langle$B12,B3$\rangle$, so that, for example, SSASucc(B5) = $\{\langle$B5,B8$\rangle,\langle$B5,B11$\rangle\}$. The initialization is the same as for the previous example. The final values of the lattice cells are as follows:

```
LatCell(a₁) = 3
LatCell(d₁) = 2
LatCell(d₃) = 2
LatCell(a₃) = 3
LatCell(f₁) = 5
LatCell(g₁) = 5
LatCell(a₂) = 3
```

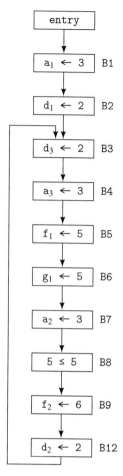

FIG. 12.36 The result of doing sparse conditional constant propagation on the routine shown in Figure 12.35.

$$\text{LatCell}(f_2) = 6$$
$$\text{LatCell}(f_3) = \perp$$
$$\text{LatCell}(d_2) = 2$$

and the resulting code (after replacing the variables with their constant values and removing unreachable code) is shown Figure 12.36.

It is only a matter of convenience that we have used nodes that contain a single statement each rather than basic blocks. The algorithm can easily be adapted to use basic blocks—it only requires, for example, that we identify definition sites of variables by the block number and the position within the block.

The time complexity of sparse conditional constant propagation is bounded by the number of edges in the flowgraph plus the number of SSA edges, since each variable's value can be lowered in the lattice only twice. Thus, it is $O(|E| + |SSA|)$, where SSA is the set of SSA edges. This is quadratic in the number of nodes in the worst case, but it is almost always linear in practice.

12.7   Wrap-Up

In this chapter, we began our discussion of particular optimizations with constant-expression evaluation (constant folding), scalar replacement of aggregates, algebraic simplifications and reassociation, value numbering, copy propagation, and sparse conditional constant propagation. The first three are independent of data-flow analysis, i.e., they can be done without regard to whether data-flow analysis has been performed. The last three begin the study of optimizations that depend on data-flow information for their effectiveness and correctness.

We summarize the topics and their significance in the optimization process as follows:

1. Constant folding is best structured as a subroutine that can be invoked from any place in the optimizer that can benefit from evaluation of a constant-valued expression. It is essential that the compiler's model of the data types and operations that participate in constant folding match those of the target architecture.

2. Scalar replacement of aggregates is best performed very early in the compilation process because it turns structures that are not usually subject to optimization into scalars that are.

3. Algebraic simplifications and reassociation, like constant folding, are best structured as a subroutine that can be invoked as needed. Algebraic simplification of addressing expressions and the other optimizations that apply to them, such as loop-invariant code motion if they occur in loops, are among the most important optimizations for a large class of programs.

4. Value numbering is an optimization that is sometimes confused with two others, namely, common-subexpression elimination and constant propagation; in its global form, it may also be confused with loop-invariant code motion and partial-redundancy elimination. They are all distinct, and the function of value numbering is to identify expressions that are formally equivalent and to remove redundant computations of those expressions that are equivalent, thus further reducing the amount of code the following optimizations are applied to.

5. Copy propagation replaces copies of variables' values with uses of those variables, again reducing the amount of code.

6. Sparse conditional constant propagation replaces uses of variables that can be determined to have constant values with those values. It differs from all the other optimizations that require data-flow analysis in that it performs a somewhat more

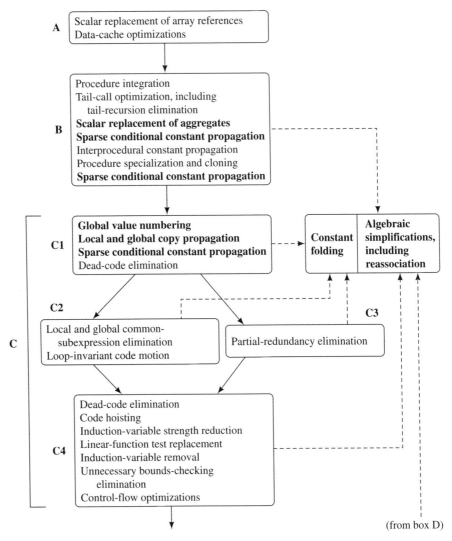

FIG. 12.37 Order of optimizations. The ones discussed in this chapter are highlighted in **bold** type.

sophisticated analysis, namely, *symbolic execution*, that takes advantage of constant-valued conditionals to determine whether paths should be executed or not in the analysis.

Both global value numbering and sparse conditional constant propagation are performed on flowgraphs in SSA form and derive considerable benefit from using this form—in essence, the former is global because of its use and the second is more powerful than traditional global constant propagation because of it.

We place the optimizations discussed in this chapter in the overall suggested order of optimizations as shown in Figure 12.37. These optimizations are highlighted in **bold** type.

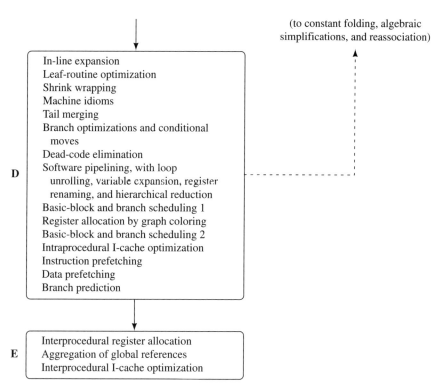

(to constant folding, algebraic
simplifications, and reassociation)

D
In-line expansion
Leaf-routine optimization
Shrink wrapping
Machine idioms
Tail merging
Branch optimizations and conditional
   moves
Dead-code elimination
Software pipelining, with loop
   unrolling, variable expansion, register
   renaming, and hierarchical reduction
Basic-block and branch scheduling 1
Register allocation by graph coloring
Basic-block and branch scheduling 2
Intraprocedural I-cache optimization
Instruction prefetching
Data prefetching
Branch prediction

E
Interprocedural register allocation
Aggregation of global references
Interprocedural I-cache optimization

FIG. 12.37 *(continued)*

12.8   Further Reading

The ANSI/IEEE standard for floating-point arithmetic is [IEEE85]. Goldberg's introduction to the standard and overview of it and related issues is [Gold91]. The applicability of constant folding and algebraic simplifications to floating-point values
is discussed in [Farn88] and [Gold91]. For an example of a compiler that performs
scalar replacement of aggregates, see [Much91].

The original formulation of value numbering on basic blocks is [CocS69]. Its
adaptation to extended basic blocks is found in [AusH82], and two methods of
extending it to whole procedures are in [ReiL86] and [AlpW88]. The use of value
numbering in creating DAGs for basic blocks is described in, e.g., [AhoS86]. The
partitioning algorithm used in the global value numbering process was developed by
Aho, Hopcroft, and Ullman [AhoH74]. Briggs, Cooper, and Simpson's comparison
of hash-based and global value numbering is in [BriC94c] and [Simp96], and Cooper
and Simpson's approach to value numbering on strongly connected components is
in [CooS95b] and [Simp96].

Wegman and Zadeck's sparse conditional constant propagation is described in
[WegZ91]. An overview of symbolic execution, as used in that algorithm, is given in
[MucJ81].

12.9   Exercises

12.1 The transformation called *loop peeling* removes one iteration from the beginning of a loop by inserting a copy of the loop body before the beginning of the loop. Performing loop peeling followed by constant propagation and constant folding on a procedure body can easily result in code to which the three transformations can be applied again. For example, the MIR code in (a) below is transformed in one step of loop peeling, constant propagation, and constant folding to the code in (b) below.

```
        m ← 1                              m ← 1
        i ← 1                              i ← 2
L1:     m ← m * i              L1:         m ← m * i
        i ← i + 1                          i ← i + 1
        if i ≤ 10 goto L1                  if i ≤ 10 goto L1
   (a)                              (b)
```

in another step to the code in (c) below, and ultimately to the code in (d)

```
        m ← 2                              m ← 3628800
        i ← 3                              i ← 11
L1:     m ← m * i
        i ← i + 1
        if i ≤ 10 goto L1
   (c)                              (d)
```

assuming that there are no other branches to L1. How might we recognize such situations? How likely are they to occur in practice?

12.2 It is essential to the correctness of constant folding that the compile-time evaluation environment be identical to the run-time environment or that the compiler simulate the run-time environment sufficiently well that it produces corresponding results. In particular, suppose we are compiling a program on an Intel 386 processor, which has only 80-bit internal floating-point values in registers (see Sections 21.4.1), to be run on a PowerPC processor, which has only single- and double-precision forms (see Section 21.2.1). How does this affect floating-point constant folding?

12.3 (a) Write an ICAN program to do scalar replacement of aggregates. (b) What situations are likely not to benefit from such replacements? (c) How can we guard against their being performed in the algorithm?

12.4 (a) Write a canonicalizer or tree transformer in ICAN that accepts a tree and a set of tree-transformation rules and that applies the transformations to the tree until they no longer apply. Assume that the trees are represented by nodes of the ICAN data type Node, defined as follows:

```
Operator = enum {add,sub,mul}
Content = record {kind: enum {var,const},
                  val: Var ∪ Const}
Node = record {opr: Operator,
               lt,rt: Content ∪ Node}
```

(b) Prove that your canonicalizer halts for any tree input if it is given the transformations represented in Figure 12.6.

12.5   In the definition of `Value_Number( )` in Figure 12.13, should there be a case for `listexp` in the `case` statement? If so, what would the code be for this alternative?

ADV 12.6   As indicated at the end of Section 12.4.2, [AlpW88] suggests doing structural analysis of the program to be analyzed and using special ϕ-functions that are designed for the control-flow constructs so as to be able to determine congruence with respect to control flow. Sketch how you would extend the global value-numbering algorithm to include this idea.

ADV 12.7   Can the global copy-propagation algorithm be modified to recognize cases such as the one in Figure 12.28? If so, how? If not, why not?

12.8   Modify the (a) local and (b) global copy-propagation algorithms to work on extended basic blocks.

ADV 12.9   Can copy propagation be expressed in a form analogous to sparse conditional constant propagation? If so, what advantages, if any, do we gain by doing so? If not, why not?

12.10   Modify the sparse conditional constant-propagation algorithm to use basic blocks in place of individual statement nodes.

CHAPTER 13

Redundancy Elimination

The optimizations covered in this chapter all deal with elimination of redundant computations and all require data-flow analysis. They can be done on either medium-level intermediate code (e.g., MIR) or low-level code (e.g., LIR).

The first one, common-subexpression elimination, finds computations that are always performed at least twice on a given execution path and eliminates the second and later occurrences of them. This optimization requires data-flow analysis to locate redundant computations and almost always improves the performance of programs it is applied to.

The second, loop-invariant code motion, finds computations that produce the same result every time a loop is iterated and moves them out of the loop. While this can be determined by an independent data-flow analysis, it is usually based on using ud-chains. This optimization almost always improves performance, often very significantly, in large part because it frequently discovers and removes loop-invariant address computations and usually those that access array elements.

The third, partial-redundancy elimination, moves computations that are at least partially redundant (i.e., those that are computed more than once on some path through the flowgraph) to their optimal computation points and eliminates totally redundant ones. It encompasses common-subexpression elimination, loop-invariant code motion, and more.

The last, code hoisting, finds computations that are executed on all paths leading from a given point in a program and unifies them into a single computation at that point. It requires data-flow analysis (namely, a form of analysis with the somewhat comical name "very busy expressions") and decreases the space a program occupies, but rarely affects its time performance.

We choose to present both common-subexpression elimination and loop-invariant code motion on the one hand and partial-redundancy elimination on the other because both approaches have about the same efficiency and similar effects.

A few years ago we would have presented only the former and merely mentioned the latter because the original formulation of partial-redundancy elimination required a complicated and expensive bidirectional data-flow analysis. The modern formulation presented here eliminates that problem and also provides a framework for thinking about and formulating other optimizations. We can assert quite confidently that it will soon be, if it is not already, the approach of choice to redundancy elimination.

13.1   Common-Subexpression Elimination

An occurrence of an expression in a program is a *common subexpression*[1] if there is another occurrence of the expression whose evaluation always precedes this one in execution order and if the operands of the expression remain unchanged between the two evaluations. The expression a + 2 in block B3 in Figure 13.1(a) is an example of a common subexpression, since the occurrence of the same expression in B1 always precedes it in execution and the value of a is not changed between them. *Common-subexpression elimination* is a transformation that removes the recomputations of common subexpressions and replaces them with uses of saved values. Figure 13.1(b) shows the result of transforming the code in (a). Note that, as this example shows, we cannot simply substitute b for the evaluation of a + 2 in block B3, since B2 changes the value of b if it is executed.

Recall that value numbering and common-subexpression elimination are different, as shown by the examples at the beginning of Section 12.4.

Also, note that common-subexpression elimination may not always be worthwhile. In this example, it may be less expensive to recompute a + 2 (especially if a and d are both allocated to registers and adding a small constant to a value in a register can be done in a single cycle), rather than to allocate another register to hold the value of t1 from B1 through B3, or, even worse, to store it to memory and later reload it. Actually, there are more complex reasons why common-subexpression elimination may not be worthwhile that have to do with keeping a superscalar pipeline full or getting the best possible performance from a vector or parallel machine. As a result, we discuss its inverse transformation, called forward substitution, in Section 13.1.3.

Optimizers frequently divide common-subexpression elimination into two phases, one local, done within each basic block, and the other global, done across an entire flowgraph. The division is not essential, because global common-subexpression elimination catches all the common subexpressions that the local form does and more, but the local form can often be done very cheaply while the intermediate code for a basic block is being constructed and may result in less intermediate code being produced. Thus, we describe the two forms separately in the next two subsections.

---

1. It is traditional to use the term *subexpression* rather than *expression*, but the definition applies to arbitrary expressions, not just to those that are subexpressions of others.

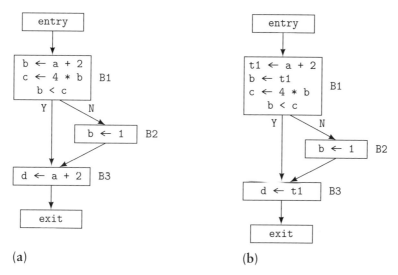

FIG. 13.1 (a) Example of a common subexpression, namely, a + 2, and (b) the result of doing common-subexpression elimination on it.

13.1.1   Local Common-Subexpression Elimination

As noted above, local common-subexpression elimination works within single basic blocks and can be done either as the intermediate code for a block is being produced or afterward. For convenience, we assume that MIR instructions have been generated and occupy Block[m][1··ninsts[m]]. Our method, essentially, keeps track of the *available expressions*, i.e., those that have been computed so far in the block and have not had an operand changed since, and, for each, the position in the block at which it was computed. Our representation of this is *AEB*, a set of quintuples of the form ⟨*pos, opd*1, *opr, opd*2, *tmp*⟩, where *pos* is the position where the expression is evaluated in the basic block; *opd*1, *opr*, and *opd*2 make up a binary expression; and *tmp* is either nil or a temporary variable.

To do local common-subexpression elimination, we iterate through the basic block, adding entries to and removing them from *AEB* as appropriate, inserting instructions to save the expressions' values in temporaries, and modifying the instructions to use the temporaries instead. For each instruction *inst* at position *i*, we determine whether it computes a binary expression or not and then execute one of two cases accordingly. The (nontrivial) binary case is as follows:

1. We compare *inst*'s operands and operator with those in the quintuples in *AEB*. If we find a match, say, ⟨*pos, opd*1, *opr, opd*2, *tmp*⟩, we check whether *tmp* is nil. If it is, we

   (a) generate a new temporary variable name *ti* and replace the nil in the identified triple by it,

   (b) insert the instruction *ti* ← *opd*1 *opr opd*2 immediately before the instruction at position *pos*, and

(c) replace the expressions in the instructions at positions *pos* and *i* by *ti*.

If we found a match with *tmp* = *ti*, where *ti* ≠ nil, we replace the expression in *inst* by *ti*. If we did not find a match for *inst*'s expression in *AEB*, we insert a quintuple for it, with *tmp* = nil, into *AEB*.

2. We check whether the result variable of the current instruction, if there is one, occurs as an operand in any element of *AEB*. If it does, we remove all such quintuples from *AEB*.

The routine Local_CSE( ) that implements this approach is given in Figure 13.2. It uses four other routines, as follows:

1. Renumber(*AEB*,*pos*) renumbers the first entry in each of the quintuples in *AEB*, as necessary, to reflect the effect of inserted instructions.

2. insert_before( ) inserts an instruction into a basic block and renumbers the instructions to accommodate the newly inserted one (see Section 4.8).

3. Commutative(*opr*) returns true if the operator *opr* is commutative, and false otherwise.

4. new_temp( ) returns a new temporary as its value.

```
AEBinExp = integer × Operand × Operator × Operand × Var

procedure Local_CSE(m,ninsts,Block)
    m: in integer
    ninsts: inout array [··] of integer
    Block: inout array [··] of array [··] of MIRInst
begin
    AEB := Ø, Tmp: set of AEBinExp
    aeb: AEBinExp
    inst: MIRInst
    i, pos: integer
    ti: Var
    found: boolean
    i := 1
    while i ≤ ninsts[m] do
        inst := Block[m][i]
        found := false
        case Exp_Kind(inst.kind) of
binexp:  Tmp := AEB
            while Tmp ≠ Ø do
                aeb := ◆Tmp; Tmp -= {aeb}
                || match current instruction's expression against those
                || in AEB, including commutativity
                if inst.opr = aeb@3 & ((Commutative(aeb@3)
                    & inst.opd1 = aeb@4 & inst.opd2 = aeb@2)
```

FIG. 13.2 A routine to do local common-subexpression elimination.

```
              V (inst.opd1 = aeb@2 & inst.opd2 = aeb@4)) then
              pos := aeb@1
              found := true
              || if no variable in tuple, create a new temporary and
              || insert an instruction evaluating the expression
              || and assigning it to the temporary
              if aeb@5 = nil then
                 ti := new_tmp( )
                 AEB := (AEB - {aeb})
                    ∪ {⟨aeb@1,aeb@2,aeb@3,aeb@4,ti⟩}
                 insert_before(m,pos,ninsts,Block,
                    ⟨kind:binasgn,left:ti,opd1:aeb@2,
                    opr:aeb@3,opd2:aeb@4⟩)
                 Renumber(AEB,pos)
                 pos += 1
                 i += 1
                 || replace instruction at position pos
                 || by one that copies the temporary
                 Block[m][pos] := ⟨kind:valasgn,left:Block[m][pos].left,
                    opd:⟨kind:var,val:ti⟩⟩
              else
                 ti := aeb@5
              fi
              || replace current instruction by one that copies
              || the temporary ti
              Block[m][i] := ⟨kind:valasgn,left:inst.left,
                 opd:⟨kind:var,val:ti⟩⟩
          fi
      od
      if !found then
          || insert new tuple
          AEB ∪= {⟨i,inst.opd1,inst.opr,inst.opd2,nil⟩}
      fi
      || remove all tuples that use the variable assigned to by
      || the current instruction
      Tmp := AEB
      while Tmp ≠ ∅ do
          aeb := ◆Tmp; Tmp -= {aeb}
          if inst.left = aeb@2 V inst.left = aeb@4 then
              AEB -= {aeb}
          fi
      od
default:
      esac
      i += 1
   od
end    || Local_CSE
```

FIG. 13.2 *(continued)*

Position	Instruction
1	c ← a + b
2	d ← m & n
3	e ← b + d
4	f ← a + b
5	g ← -b
6	h ← b + a
7	a ← j + a
8	k ← m & n
9	j ← b + d
10	a ← -b
11	if m & n goto L2

FIG. 13.3 Example basic block before local common-subexpression elimination.

As an example of the algorithm, consider the code in Figure 13.3, which represents what we would generate for a hypothetical basic block if we were not performing local common-subexpression elimination as we generated it. Initially, AEB = ∅ and i = 1. The first instruction has a binexp and AEB is empty, so we place the quintuple ⟨1,a,+,b,nil⟩ in AEB and set i = 2. The second instruction contains a binexp also; there is no quintuple in AEB with the same expression, so we insert ⟨2,m,&,n,nil⟩ into AEB and set i = 3. The form of AEB is now

```
AEB = {⟨1,a,+,b,nil⟩,
       ⟨2,m,&,n,nil⟩}
```

The same thing happens for instruction 3, resulting in

```
AEB = {⟨1,a,+,b,nil⟩,
       ⟨2,m,&,n,nil⟩,
       ⟨3,b,+,d,nil⟩}
```

and i = 4. Next we encounter f ← a + b in position 4 and find that the expression in it matches the first quintuple in AEB. We insert t1 into that quintuple in place of the nil, generate the instruction t1 ← a + b before position 1, renumber the entries in AEB, replace the instruction that was in position 1 but that is now in position 2 by c ← t1, set i = 5, and replace the instruction in position 5 by f ← t1.

The current state of the code is shown in Figure 13.4 and the value of AEB is

```
AEB = {⟨1,a,+,b,t1⟩,
       ⟨3,m,&,n,nil⟩,
       ⟨4,b,+,d,nil⟩}
```

Next we encounter the instruction g ← -b in line 6 and do nothing. Next we find h ← b + a in line 7 and we recognize that the right-hand side matches a quintuple in AEB; so we replace instruction 7 by h ← t1. This produces the code shown in Figure 13.5. Next we find a ← j + a in line 8 and, for the first time, we remove

Position	Instruction
1	t1 ← a + b
2	c ← t1
3	d ← m & n
4	e ← b + d
5	f ← t1
6	g ← -b
7	h ← b + a
8	a ← j + a
9	k ← m & n
10	j ← b + d
11	a ← -b
12	if m & n goto L2

FIG. 13.4 Our example basic block after eliminating the first local common subexpression (lines 1, 2, and 5).

Position	Instruction
1	t1 ← a + b
2	c ← t1
3	d ← m & n
4	e ← b + d
5	f ← t1
6	g ← -b
7	h ← t1
8	a ← j + a
9	k ← m & n
10	j ← b + d
11	a ← -b
12	if m & n goto L2

FIG. 13.5 Our example basic block after eliminating the second local common subexpression (line 7).

a quintuple from AEB: the result variable a matches the first operand in the first quintuple in AEB, so we remove it, resulting in

$$\text{AEB} = \{\langle 3,m,\&,n,nil\rangle,$$
$$\langle 4,b,+,d,nil\rangle\}$$

Note that we insert a triple for j + a and remove it in the same iteration, since the result variable matches one of the operands.

Position	Instruction
1	t1 ← a + b
2	c ← t1
3	t2 ← m & n
4	d ← t2
5	e ← b + d
6	f ← t1
7	g ← -b
8	h ← t1
9	a ← j + a
10	k ← t2
11	j ← b + d
12	a ← -b
13	if m & n goto L2

FIG. 13.6 Our example basic block after eliminating the third local common subexpression.

Next the expression m & n in line 9 in Figure 13.5 is recognized as a common subexpression. This results in the code in Figure 13.6 and the value for AEB becoming

```
AEB = {⟨3,m,&,n,t2⟩,
       ⟨5,b,+,d,nil⟩}
```

Finally, the expression b + d in line 12 and the expression m & n in line 13 are recognized as local common subexpressions. The final value of AEB is

```
AEB = {⟨3,m,&,n,t2⟩,
       ⟨5,b,+,d,t3⟩}
```

and the final code is as given in Figure 13.7.

In the original form of this code there are 11 instructions, 12 variables, and 9 binary operations performed, while in the final form there are 14 instructions, 15 variables, and 4 binary operations performed. Assuming all the variables occupy registers and that each of the register-to-register operations requires only a single cycle, as in any RISC and the more advanced CISCs, the original form is to be preferred, since it has fewer instructions and uses fewer registers. On the other hand, if some of the variables occupy memory locations or the redundant operations require more than one cycle, the result of the optimization is to be preferred. Thus, whether an optimization actually improves the performance of a block of code depends on both the code and the machine it is executed on.

A fast implementation of the local algorithm can be achieved by hashing the operands and operator in each triple, so that the actual operands and operator only need to be compared if the hash values match. The hash function chosen should be fast to compute and symmetric in the operands, so as to deal with commutativity

Position	Instruction
1	t1 ← a + b
2	c ← t1
3	t2 ← m & n
4	d ← t2
5	t3 ← b + d
6	e ← t3
7	f ← t1
8	g ← -b
9	h ← t1
10	a ← j + a
11	k ← t2
12	j ← t3
13	a ← -b
14	if t2 goto L2

FIG. 13.7 Our example basic block after eliminating the last two local common subexpressions.

efficiently, since commutative operators are more frequent than noncommutative ones.

This algorithm and the global common-subexpression elimination algorithm that follows can both be improved by the reassociation transformations discussed in Section 12.3 (see also Section 13.4), especially those for addressing arithmetic, since they are the most frequent source of common subexpressions.

13.1.2   Global Common-Subexpression Elimination

As indicated above, global common-subexpression elimination takes as its scope a flowgraph representing a procedure. It solves the data-flow problem known as *available expressions*, which we discussed briefly in Section 8.3 and which we now examine more fully. An expression *exp* is said to be *available* at the entry to a basic block if along every control-flow path from the entry block to this block there is an evaluation of *exp* that is not subsequently killed by having one or more of its operands assigned a new value.

We work out two versions of the data-flow analysis for available expressions. The first one tells us simply which expressions are available on entry to each block. The second also tells us where the evaluations of those expressions are, i.e., at what positions in what blocks. We do both because there is a difference of opinion among researchers of optimization as to whether using data-flow methods to determine the evaluation points is the best approach; see, for example, [AhoS86], p. 634, for advice that it is not.

In determining what expressions are available, we use $EVAL(i)$ to denote the set of expressions evaluated in block i that are still available at its exit and $KILL(i)$ to denote the set of expressions that are killed by block i. To compute $EVAL(i)$, we

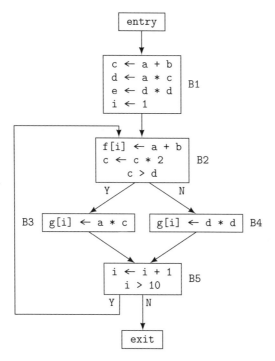

FIG. 13.8 Example flowgraph for global common-subexpression elimination.

scan block i from beginning to end, accumulating the expressions evaluated in it and deleting those whose operands are later assigned new values in the block. An assignment such as a ← a + b, in which the variable on the left-hand side occurs also as an operand on the right-hand side, *does not* create an available expression because the assignment happens *after* the expression evaluation. For our example basic block in Figure 13.3, the *EVAL*( ) set is {m&n,b+d}.

The expression a + b is also evaluated in the block, but it is subsequently killed by the assignment a ← j + a, so it is not in the *EVAL*( ) set for the block. *KILL*(i) is the set of all expressions evaluated in other blocks such that one or more of their operands are assigned to in block i, or that are evaluated in block i and subsequently have an operand assigned to in block i. To give an example of a *KILL*( ) set, we need to have an entire flowgraph available,[2] so we will consider the flowgraph in Figure 13.8. The *EVAL*(i) and *KILL*(i) sets for the basic blocks are as follows:

EVAL(entry)	= ∅	*KILL*(entry)	= ∅
EVAL(B1)	= {a+b,a*c,d*d}	*KILL*(B1)	= {a*c,d*d,i+1}
EVAL(B2)	= {a+b,c*2}	*KILL*(B2)	= {a*c,c*2}
EVAL(B3)	= {a*c}	*KILL*(B3)	= ∅

2. Actually, this is not quite true. We could represent it by the set of variables assigned to in this block. This would be quite inefficient, however, since it would be a set of variables, while *EVAL*( ) is a set of expressions. Implementing the data-flow analysis by operations on bit vectors would then be awkward at best.

$$EVAL(\texttt{B4}) \quad = \{\texttt{d*d}\} \qquad KILL(\texttt{B4}) \quad = \emptyset$$
$$EVAL(\texttt{B5}) \quad = \{\texttt{i+1}\} \qquad KILL(\texttt{B5}) \quad = \{\texttt{i+1}\}$$
$$EVAL(\texttt{exit}) \quad = \emptyset \qquad KILL(\texttt{exit}) \quad = \emptyset$$

Now, the equation system for the data-flow analysis can be constructed as follows. This is a forward-flow problem. We use $AEin(i)$ and $AEout(i)$ to represent the sets of expressions that are available on entry to and exit from block i, respectively. An expression is available on entry to block i if it is available at the exits of all predecessor blocks, so the path-combining operator is set intersection. An expression is available at the exit from a block if it is either evaluated in the block and not subsequently killed in it, or if it is available on entry to the block and not killed in it. Thus, the system of data-flow equations is

$$AEin(i) \quad = \bigcap_{j \in Pred(i)} AEin(j)$$

$$AEout(i) = EVAL(i) \cup (AEin(i) - KILL(i))$$

In solving the data-flow equations, we initialize $AEin(i) = U_{exp}$ for all blocks i, where U_{exp} can be taken to be the universal set of all expressions, or, as it is easy to show,

$$U_{exp} = \bigcup_{i} EVAL(i)$$

is sufficient.[3]

For our example in Figure 13.8, we use

$$U_{exp} = \{\texttt{a+b,a*c,d*d,c*2,i+1}\}$$

The first step of a worklist iteration produces

$$AEin(\texttt{entry}) = \emptyset$$

and the second step produces

$$AEin(\texttt{B1}) = \emptyset$$

Next, we compute

$$AEin(\texttt{B2}) \quad = \{\texttt{a+b,d*d}\}$$
$$AEin(\texttt{B3}) \quad = \{\texttt{a+b,d*d}\}$$
$$AEin(\texttt{B4}) \quad = \{\texttt{a+b,d*d}\}$$
$$AEin(\texttt{B5}) \quad = \{\texttt{a+b,d*d}\}$$
$$AEin(\texttt{exit}) \quad = \{\texttt{a+b,d*d}\}$$

and additional iterations produce no further changes.

---

3. If we did not have a special entry node with no flow edges entering it, we would need to initialize $AEin(\texttt{entry}) = \emptyset$, since no expressions are available on entry to the flowgraph, while edges flowing into the initial node might result in making $AEin(\ )$ for the entry block non-empty in the solution to the equations.

Next, we describe how to perform global common-subexpression elimination using the *AEin*( ) data-flow function. For simplicity, we assume that local common-subexpression elimination has already been done, so that only the first evaluation of an expression in a block is a candidate for global common-subexpression elimination. We proceed as follows:

> For each block *i* and each expression *exp* ∈ *AEin*(*i*) that is evaluated in block *i*,

1. Locate the first evaluation of *exp* in block *i*.

2. Search backward from the first occurrence to determine whether any of the operands of *exp* have been previously assigned to in the block. If so, this occurrence of *exp* is not a global common subexpression; proceed to another expression or another block as appropriate.

3. Having found the first occurrence of *exp* in block *i* and determined that it is a global common subexpression, search backward in the flowgraph to find the occurrences of *exp*, such as in the context *v* ← *exp*, that caused it to be in *AEin*(*i*). These are the final occurrences of *exp* in their respective blocks; each of them must flow unimpaired to the entry of block *i*; and every flow path from the entry block to block *i* must include at least one of them.

4. Select a new temporary variable *tj*. Replace the first instruction *inst* that uses *exp* in block *i* by *tj* and replace each instruction that uses *exp* identified in step (3) by

   tj ← *exp*
   Replace(*inst*, *exp*, *tj*)

A routine called Global_CSE( ) that implements this approach is given in Figure 13.9. The routine Find_Sources( ) locates the source occurrences of a global common subexpression and returns a set of pairs consisting of the block number and the instruction number within the block. The routine insert_after( ) is as described in Section 4.8. The routine Replace_Exp(Block,*i*,*j*,*tj*) replaces the instruction in Block[*i*][*j*] by an instruction that uses opd:⟨kind:var,val:*tj*⟩, that is, it replaces a binasgn by the corresponding valasgn, a binif by a valif, and a bintrap by a valtrap.

Proper choice of data structures can make this algorithm run in linear time.

In our example in Figure 13.8, the first expression occurrence that satisfies the criteria for being a global common subexpression is a + b in block B2. Searching backward from it, we find the instruction c ← a + b in B1 and replace it by

    t1 ← a + b
    c ← t1

and the instruction in block B2 by f[i] ← t1. Similarly, the occurrence of d * d in B4 satisfies the criteria, so we replace the instruction in which it occurs by g[i] ← t2 and the assignment in block B1 that defines the expression by

    t2 ← d * d
    e ← t2

The result is the flowgraph shown in Figure 13.10.

```
BinExp = Operand × Operator × Operand

procedure Global_CSE(nblocks,ninsts,Block,AEin)
   nblocks: in integer
   ninsts: inout array [1··nblocks] of integer
   Block: inout array[1··nblocks] of array [··] of MIRInst
   AEin: in integer ⟶ BinExp
begin
   i, j, k: integer
   l, tj: Var
   S: set of (integer × integer)
   s: integer × integer
   aexp: BinExp
   for i := 1 to nblocks do
      for each aexp ∈ AEin(i) do
         j := 1
         while j ≤ ninsts[i] do
            case Exp_Kind(Block[i][j].kind) of
binexp:         if aexp@1 = Block[i][j].opd1
               & aexp@2 = Block[i][j].opr
               & aexp@3 = Block[i][j].opd2 then
               for k := j-1 by -1 to 1 do
                  if Has_Left(Block[i][k].kind)
                     & (Block[i][k].left = aexp@1.val
                     ∨ Block[i][k].left = aexp@3.val) then
                     goto L1
                  fi
               od
               S := Find_Sources(aexp,nblocks,ninsts,Block)
               tj := new_tmp( )
               Replace_Exp(Block,i,j,tj)
               for each s ∈ S do
                  l := Block[s@1][s@2].left
                  Block[s@1][s@2].left := tj
                  insert_after(s@1,s@2,ninsts,Block,
                     ⟨kind:valasgn,left:l,
                     opd:⟨kind:var,val:tj⟩⟩)
                  j += 1
               od
            fi
default:    esac
L1:         j += 1
         od
      od
   od
end    || Global_CSE
```

FIG. 13.9 A routine to implement our first approach to global common-subexpression elimination.

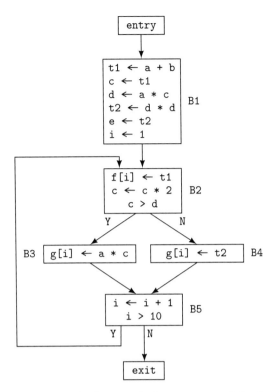

FIG. 13.10 Our example flowgraph from Figure 13.8 after global common-subexpression elimination.

The global CSE algorithm can be implemented efficiently by mapping the set of expressions that occur in a program to a range of consecutive integers beginning with zero, each of which, in turn, corresponds to a bit-vector position. The set operations translate directly to bit-wise logical operations on the bit vectors.

The second approach for performing global common-subexpression elimination both determines the available expressions and, at the same time, determines for each potential common subexpression the point(s)—i.e., basic block and position within basic block—of the defining assignment(s). This is done by modifying the data-flow analysis to deal with individual expression occurrences. We define $EVALP(i)$ to be the set of triples $\langle exp, i, pos \rangle$, consisting of an expression exp, the basic-block name i, and an integer position pos in block i, such that exp is evaluated at position pos in block i and is still available at the exit of the block. We define $KILLP(i)$ to be the set of triples $\langle exp, blk, pos \rangle$ such that exp satisfies the conditions for $KILL(i)$ and blk and pos range over the basic block and position pairs at which exp is defined in blocks other than i. Finally, we define

$$AEinP(i) = \bigcap_{j \in Pred(i)} AEoutP(j)$$

$$AEoutP(i) = EVALP(i) \cup (AEinP(i) - KILLP(i))$$

The initialization is analogous to that for the previous set of data-flow equations: $AEinP(i) = U$ for all i, where U is appropriately modified to include position information.

Now, for our example in Figure 13.8, we have the following $EVALP(\ )$ and $KILLP(\ )$ sets:

```
EVALP(entry)  = Ø
EVALP(B1)     = {⟨a+b,B1,1⟩,⟨a*c,B1,2⟩,⟨d*d,B1,3⟩}
EVALP(B2)     = {⟨a+b,B2,1⟩,⟨c*2,B2,2⟩}
EVALP(B3)     = {⟨a*c,B3,1⟩}
EVALP(B4)     = {⟨d*d,B4,1⟩}
EVALP(B5)     = Ø
EVALP(exit)   = Ø
```

```
KILLP(entry)  = Ø
KILLP(B1)     = {⟨a*c,B3,1⟩,⟨d*d,B4,1⟩}
KILLP(B2)     = {⟨a*c,B1,2⟩,⟨a*c,B3,1⟩,⟨c*2,B2,2⟩}
KILLP(B3)     = Ø
KILLP(B4)     = Ø
KILLP(B5)     = Ø
KILLP(exit)   = Ø
```

and the result of performing the data-flow analysis is as follows:

```
AEinP(entry)  = Ø
AEinP(B1)     = Ø
AEinP(B2)     = {⟨a+b,B1,1⟩,⟨d*d,B1,3⟩}
AEinP(B3)     = {⟨a+b,B1,1⟩,⟨d*d,B1,3⟩}
AEinP(B4)     = {⟨a+b,B1,1⟩,⟨d*d,B1,3⟩}
AEinP(B5)     = {⟨a+b,B1,1⟩,⟨d*d,B1,3⟩}
AEinP(exit)   = {⟨a+b,B1,1⟩,⟨d*d,B1,3⟩}
```

so the available expression instances are identified for each global common subexpression, with no need to search the flowgraph for them. The transformation of our example flowgraph proceeds as before, with no change, except that the transformation algorithm is simpler, as follows:

> For each block i and expression *exp* such that $\langle exp, blk, pos \rangle \in AEinP(i)$ for some *blk* and *pos*, and in which *exp* is evaluated in block i,

1. Locate the first evaluation of *exp* in block i.

2. Search backward from the first occurrence to determine whether any of the operands of *exp* have been previously assigned to in the block. If so, this occurrence of *exp* is not a global common subexpression; proceed to another expression or another block, as appropriate.

3. Having found the first occurrence of *exp* in block i and having determined that it is a global common subexpression, let $\langle exp, blk_1, pos_1 \rangle, \ldots,$ $\langle exp, blk_n, pos_n \rangle$ be the elements of $AEinP(i)$ with *exp* as the expression part. Each of them is an instruction *inst* that evaluates *exp*.

```
BinExpIntPair = Operator × Operand × Operator × integer × integer
BinExpIntPairSet = Operator × Operand × Operator × set of (integer × integer)

procedure Global_CSE_Pos(nblocks,ninsts,Block,AEinP)
    nblocks: in integer
    ninsts: inout array [1··nblocks] of integer
    Block: inout array[1··nblocks] of array [··] of MIRInst
    AEinP: in integer  ⟶ (set of BinExp
        × Operand × integer × integer)
begin
    i, j, k: integer
    tj, v: Var
    s: integer × integer
    inst: MIRInst
    aexp: BinExpIntPairSet
    AEinPS: integer  ⟶ BinExpIntPairSet
    AEinPS := Coalesce_Sets(nblocks,AEinP)
    for i := 1 to nblocks do
        for each aexp ∈ AEinPS(i) do
            j := 1
            while j ≤ ninsts[i] do
                inst := Block[i][j]
                case Exp_Kind(inst.kind) of
binexp:         if aexp@1@1 = inst.opd1 & aexp@1@2 = inst.opr
                    & aexp@1@3 = inst.opd2 then
                    for k := j-1 by -1 to 1 do
                        if Has_Left(inst.kind)
                            & (inst.left = aexp@1@1.val
                            V inst.left = aexp@1@3.val) then
                            goto L1
                        fi
                    od
                    tj := new_tmp( )
                    Replace_Exp(Block,i,j,tj)
```

FIG. 13.11 Routines to implement our second approach to global common-subexpression elimination.

4. Select a new temporary variable *tj*. Replace the identified occurrence of *exp* in block *i* by *tj* and replace each identified instruction *inst* that evaluates *exp* at position pos_k in block blk_k by

$$tj \leftarrow exp$$
$$Replace(inst, exp, tj)$$

An ICAN routine called Global_CSE_Pos( ) that implements this second approach is given in Figure 13.11. It uses the routine Coalesce_Sets( ) shown in the same figure. The routine insert_after( ) and Replace( ) are the same as that used in Figure 13.9.

```
                        for each s ∈ aexp@2 do
                           v := Block[s@1][s@2].left
                           Block[s@1][s@2].left := tj
                           insert_after(s@1,s@2,
                              ⟨kind:valasgn,left:v,
                               opd:⟨kind:var,val:tj⟩⟩)
                           j += 1
                        od
                  fi
default:     esac
L1:          j += 1
         od
      od
   od
end    || Global_CSE_Pos

procedure Coalesce_Sets(n,AEinP)
   returns integer ⟶ BinExpIntPairSet
   n: in integer
   AEinP: in integer ⟶ set of BinExpIntPair
begin
   AEinPS, Tmp: integer ⟶ BinExpIntPairSet
   i: integer
   aexp: set of BinExpIntPair
   a, b: set of BinExpIntPairSet
   change: boolean
   for i := 1 to n do
      AEinPS(i) := ∅
      for each aexp ∈ AEinP(i) do
         AEinPS(i) ∪= {⟨aexp@1,{⟨aexp@2,aexp@3⟩}⟩}
      od
      Tmp(i) := AEinPS(i)
      repeat
         change := false
         for each a ∈ AEinPS(i) do
            for each b ∈ AEinPS(i) do
               if a ≠ b & a@1 = b@1 then
                  Tmp(i) := (Tmp(i) - {a,b})
                     ∪ {⟨a@1,a@2 ∪ b@2⟩}
                  change := true
               fi
            od
         od
      until !change
   od
   return Tmp
end    || Coalesce_Sets
```

FIG. 13.11 *(continued)*

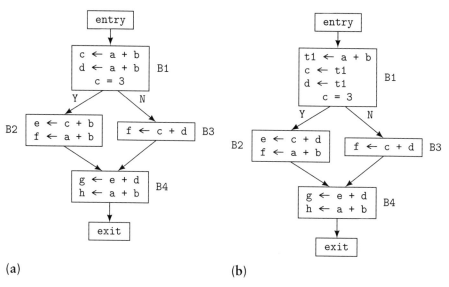

FIG. 13.12 Combining common-subexpression elimination with copy propagation: (a) the original flowgraph, and (b) the result of local common-subexpression elimination.

The second global CSE algorithm can be implemented efficiently by mapping the set of triples for the expression occurrences in a program to a range of consecutive integers beginning with zero, each of which, in turn, corresponds to a bit-vector position. The set operations translate directly to bit-wise logical operations on the bit vectors.

Note that local and global common-subexpression elimination can be combined into one pass by using individual instructions as flowgraph nodes. Although this approach is feasible, it is generally not desirable, since it usually makes the data-flow analysis significantly more expensive than the split approach described above. Alternatively, larger units can be used: both the local and global analyses and optimizations can be done on extended basic blocks.

Also, local and global common-subexpression elimination may be repeated, with additional benefit, if they are combined with copy propagation and/or constant propagation. As an example, consider the flowgraph in Figure 13.12(a). Doing local common-subexpression elimination on it results in the changes to block B1 shown in Figure 13.12(b). Now global common-subexpression elimination replaces the occurrences of a + b in blocks B2 and B4 by temporaries, producing the flowgraph in Figure 13.13(a). Next, local copy propagation replaces the uses of t1 and t2 in block B1 by t3, resulting in Figure 13.13(b). Finally, global copy propagation replaces the occurrences of c and d in blocks B2, B3, and B4 by t3, with the resulting code shown in Figure 13.14. Note that dead-code elimination can now remove the assignments t2 ← t3 and t1 ← t3 in block B1.

On the other hand, one can easily construct, for any n, an example that benefits from n repetitions of these optimizations. While possible, this hardly ever occurs in practice.

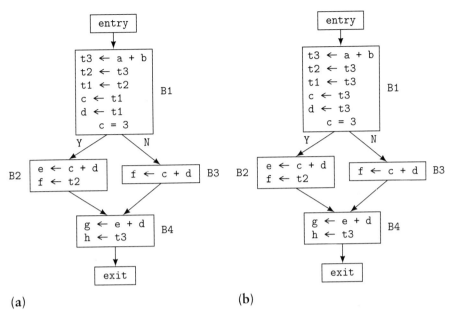

(a)   (b)

FIG. 13.13 Combining common-subexpression elimination with copy propagation (continued from Figure 13.12): (a) after global common-subexpression elimination, and (b) after local copy propagation.

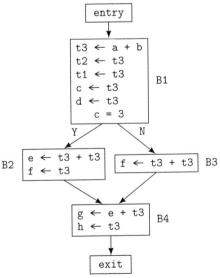

FIG. 13.14 Combining common-subexpression elimination with copy propagation (continued from Figure 13.13): after global copy propagation. Note that dead-code elimination can now eliminate the assignments t2 ← t3 and t1 ← t3 in block B1 and that code hoisting (Section 13.5) can move the two evaluations of t3 + t3 to block B1.

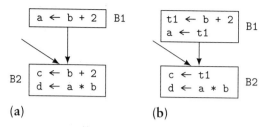

FIG. 13.15 In (a), two registers are needed along the edge from block B1 to B2, while in (b), three registers are needed.

13.1.3   Forward Substitution

Forward substitution is the inverse of common-subexpression elimination. Instead of replacing an expression evaluation by a copy operation, it replaces a copy by a reevaluation of the expression. While it may seem that common-subexpression elimination is always valuable—because it appears to reduce the number of ALU operations performed—this is not necessarily true; and even if it were true, it is still not necessarily advantageous. In particular, the simplest case in which it may not be desirable is if it causes a register to be occupied for a long time in order to hold an expression's value, and hence reduces the number of registers available for other uses, or—and this may be even worse—if the value has to be stored to memory and reloaded because there are insufficient registers available. For example, consider the code in Figure 13.15. The code in part (a) needs two registers on the edge from B1 to B2 (for a and b), while the code in (b), which results from global common-subexpression elimination, requires three (for a, b, and t1).

Depending on the organization of a compiler, problems of this sort may not be discovered until well after common-subexpression elimination has been done; in particular, common-subexpression elimination is often done on medium-level intermediate code, while register allocation and possibly concomitant spilling of a common subexpression's value to memory generally are not done until after machine-level code has been generated. This situation, among other reasons, argues for doing common-subexpression elimination and most other global optimizations on low-level code, as in the IBM XL compilers for POWER and PowerPC (see Section 21.2) and the Hewlett-Packard compilers for PA-RISC.

Performing forward substitution is generally easy. In MIR, one has an assignment of a temporary variable to some other variable such that the assignment to the temporary is the result of an expression evaluation performed earlier in the flowgraph. One checks that the operands of the expression are not modified between the evaluation of the expression and the point it is to be forward substituted to. Assuming that they have not been modified, one simply copies the expression evaluation to that point and arranges that its result appear in the proper location.

13.2   Loop-Invariant Code Motion

Loop-invariant code motion recognizes computations in loops that produce the same value on every iteration of the loop and moves them out of the loop.[4]

Many, but not all, of the most important instances of loop-invariant code are addressing computations that access elements of arrays, which are not exposed to view and, hence, to optimization until we have translated a program to an intermediate code like MIR or to a lower-level one. As a simple example of loop-invariant computations—*without* exposing array addressing—consider the Fortran code in Figure 13.16(a),[5] which can be transformed to that shown in Figure 13.16(b). This saves nearly 10,000 multiplications and 5,000 additions in roughly 5,000 iterations of the inner loop body. Had we elaborated the addressing computations, we would have made available additional loop invariants in the computation of a(i,j) similar to those shown in the examples in Section 12.3.1.

Identifying loop-invariant computations is simple. Assume that we have identified loops by a previous control-flow analysis and computed ud-chains by a previous data-flow analysis, so we know which definitions can affect a given use of a variable.[6] Then the set of loop-invariant instructions in a loop is defined inductively, i.e., an instruction is loop-invariant if, for each of its operands:

1. the operand is constant,

2. all definitions that reach this use of the operand are located outside the loop, or

3. there is exactly one definition of the operand that reaches the instruction and that definition is an instruction inside the loop that is itself loop-invariant.

Note that this definition allows the set of loop-invariant computations for the loop to be computed as follows:[7]

1. In each step below, record the sequence in which instructions are determined to be loop-invariant.

2. First, mark as loop-invariant the constant operands in the instructions.

---

4. Note that if a computation occurs inside a nested loop, it may produce the same value for every iteration of the inner loop(s) for each particular iteration of the outer loop(s), but different values for different iterations of the outer loop(s). Such a computation will be moved out of the inner loop(s), but not the outer one(s).

5. The official syntax of Fortran 77 requires that a do loop begin with "do *n v* = . . .", where *n* is a statement number and *v* is a variable, and end with the statement labeled *n*. However, it is customary in the compiler literature to use the "do *v* = . . ." and "enddo" form we use here instead, and we do so throughout this book.

6. If we do not have ud-chains available, the identification of loop invariants can still be carried out, but it requires checking, for each use, which definitions might flow to it, i.e., in effect, computing ud-chains.

7. We could formulate this as an explicit data-flow analysis problem, but there is little point in doing so. As is, it uses ud- and du-chains implicitly in computing Reach_Defs_Out( ) and Reach_Defs_In( ).

```
do i = 1, 100                    t1 = 10 * (n + 2)
   l = i * (n + 2)               t2 = 100 * n
   do j = i, 100                 do i = 1, 100
      a(i,j) = 100 * n              t3 = t2 + i * t1
         + 10 * l + j              do j = i, 100
   enddo                             a(i,j) = t3 + j
enddo                             enddo
                                enddo

   (a)                             (b)
```

FIG. 13.16 (a) Example of loop-invariant computations in Fortran, and (b) the result of transforming it.

3. Next, mark the operands that have all definitions that reach them located outside the loop.

4. Then, mark as loop-invariant instructions that (a) have all operands marked as loop-invariant, or (b) that have only one reaching definition and that definition is an instruction in the loop that is already marked loop-invariant, and there are no uses of the variable assigned to by that instruction in the loop located before the instruction.

5. Repeat steps 2 through 4 above until no operand or instruction is newly marked as invariant in an iteration.

Figure 13.17 shows a pair of routines that implement this algorithm. We use bset to denote the set of indexes of basic blocks that make up a loop. Mark_Invar( )

```
InstInvar: (integer × integer) ⟶ boolean
InvarOrder: sequence of (integer × integer)
Succ: integer ⟶ set of integer

procedure Mark_Invar(bset,en,nblocks,ninsts,Block)
   bset: in set of integer
   en, nblocks: in integer
   ninsts: in array [1··nblocks] of integer
   Block: in array [1··nblocks] of array [··] of MIRInst
begin
   i, j: integer
   change: boolean
   Order := Breadth_First(bset,Succ,en): sequence of integer
   InvarOrder := []
   for i := 1 to nblocks do
      for j := 1 to ninsts[i] do
         InstInvar(i,j) := false
      od
   od
   repeat
      change := false
      || process blocks in loop in breadth-first order
```

FIG. 13.17 Code to mark loop-invariant instructions in a loop body.

```
          for i := 1 to |Order| do
             change V= Mark_Block(bset,en,Order↓i,
                nblocks,ninsts,Block)
          od
       until !change
   end    || Mark_Invar

   procedure Mark_Block(bset,en,i,nblocks,ninsts,Block) returns boolean
      bset: in set of integer
      en, i, nblocks: in integer
      ninsts: in array [1··nblocks] of integer
      Block: in array [1··nblocks] of array [··] of MIRInst
   begin
      j: integer
      inst: MIRInst
      change := false: boolean
      for j := 1 to ninsts[i] do
         || check whether each instruction in this block has loop-constant
         || operands and appropriate reaching definitions; if so,
         || mark it as loop-invariant
         if !InstInvar(i,j) then
            inst := Block[i][j]
            case Exp_Kind(inst.kind) of
binexp:     if Loop_Const(inst.opd1,bset,nblocks,ninsts, Block)
                V Reach_Defs_Out(Block,inst.opd1,i,bset)
                V Reach_Defs_In(Block,inst.opd1,i,j,bset) then
                InstInvar(i,j) := true
            fi
            if Loop_Const(inst.opd2,bset,nblocks,ninsts, Block)
                V Reach_Defs_Out(Block,inst.opd2,i,bset)
                V Reach_Defs_In(Block,inst.opd2,i,j,bset) then
                InstInvar(i,j) &= true
            fi
unexp:      if Loop_Const(inst.opd,bset,nblocks,ninsts,Block)
                V Reach_Defs_Out(Block,inst.opd,i,bset)
                V Reach_Defs_In(Block,inst.opd,i,j,bset) then
                InstInvar(i,j) := true
            fi
default: esac
         fi
         if InstInvar(i,j) then
            || record order in which loop invariants are found
            InvarOrder ⊕= [⟨i,j⟩]
            change := true
         fi
      od
      return change
   end    || Mark_Block
```

FIG. 13.17 *(continued)*

initializes the data structures and then calls Mark_Block( ) for each block in the loop in breadth-first order, which marks the loop-invariant instructions in the block. The functions used in the code are as follows:

1. Breadth_First(*bset*,Succ,*en*) returns a sequence that enumerates the blocks in *bset* in breadth-first order, where *en* is the entry block of *bset* (see Figure 7.13).

2. Loop_Const(*opnd*,*bset*,nblocks,ninsts,Block) determines whether *opnd* is a loop constant in the loop made up of the blocks whose indexes are in *bset*.

3. Reach_Defs_Out(Block,*opnd*,*i*,*bset*) returns true if all definitions of *opnd* that reach block *i* are in blocks whose indexes are not in *bset* and false otherwise.

4. Reach_Defs_In(Block,*opnd*,*i*,*j*,*bset*) returns true if there is exactly one definition of *opnd* that reaches Block[*i*] [*j*]; that definition is in the loop consisting of the blocks in *bset*, is marked as loop-invariant, and is executed before Block[*i*] [*j*]; and there are no uses of the result variable (if any) of Block[*i*] [*j*] in the loop before instruction *j* in block *i*. Otherwise it returns false.

As an example of Mark_Invar( ), consider the flowgraph shown in Figure 13.18. Calling

       Mark_Invar({2,3,4,5,6},2,8,ninsts,Block)

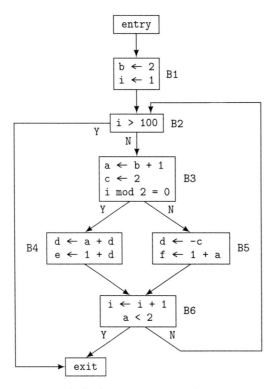

FIG. 13.18 An example for loop-invariant code motion.

results in setting Order = [2,3,4,5,6], initializing all InstInvar(i,j) to false, and setting change = false, followed by invoking Mark_Block( ) for each block in the breadth-first order given by Order. Applying Mark_Block( ) to block B2 executes the binexp case for Block[2][1], which leaves InstInvar(2,1) unchanged and returns false.

Applying Mark_Block( ) to block B3 executes the binexp case for Block[3][1], which sets InstInvar(3,1) = true and InvarOrder = [⟨3,1⟩]. Next it executes the unexp case for Block[3][2], which sets InstInvar(3,2) = true, InvarOrder = [⟨3,1⟩,⟨3,2⟩], and returns true. Next it executes the binexp case for Block[3][3], which leaves InstInvar(3,3) and InvarOrder unchanged and returns true.

Applying Mark_Block( ) to block B4 executes the binexp case, for Block[4][1], which leaves InstInvar(4,1) unchanged. Next it executes the binexp case for Block[4][2], which leaves InstInvar(4,2) unchanged and returns false.

Applying Mark_Block( ) to block B5 executes the unexp case for Block[5][1], which leaves InstInvar(5,1) unchanged. Next it executes the binexp case for Block[5][2], which sets InstInvar(5,2) = true, InvarOrder = [⟨3,1⟩,⟨3,2⟩, ⟨5,2⟩], and returns true.

Applying Mark_Block( ) to block B6 executes the binexp case for Block[6][1], which leaves InstInvar(6,1) unchanged. Next it executes the binexp case for Block[6][2], which determines that Block[6][2] is loop-invariant, so it sets InstInvar(6,2) = true, InvarOrder = [⟨3,1⟩,⟨3,2⟩,⟨5,2⟩,⟨6,2⟩], and returns true.

Now change = true in Mark_Invar( ), so we execute Mark_Block( ) again for each block in the loop. The reader can check that no further instructions are marked as loop-invariant and no further passes of the while loop are executed.

Note that the number of instructions that may be determined by this method to be loop-invariant may be increased if we perform reassociation of operations during determination of the invariants. In particular, suppose we have the MIR code in Figure 13.19(a) inside a loop, where i is the loop index variable and j is loop-invariant. In such a case, neither MIR instruction is loop-invariant. However, if we reassociate the additions as shown in Figure 13.19(b), then the first instruction is loop-invariant. Also, note that our definition of loop invariant needs to be restricted somewhat to be accurate, because of the potential effects of aliasing. For example, the MIR instruction

```
m ← call f,(1,int;2,int)
```

may be loop-invariant, but only if the call produces the same result each time it is called with the same arguments and has no side effects, which can be found out only by interprocedural analysis (see Chapter 19). Thus the listexp case in Mark_Block( ) leaves InstInvar(i,j) = false.

Now, having identified loop-invariant computations, we can move them to the preheader of the loop containing them (see Section 7.4). On the face of it, it would seem that we could simply move each instruction identified as loop-invariant, in the order they were identified, to the preheader. Unfortunately, this approach is often too aggressive in practice. There are two possible sources of error that this method introduces (as illustrated in Figure 13.20). Note that these possible errors apply only

```
t1 ← i + j              t2 ← j + 1
n ← t1 + 1              n ← i + t2
(a)                     (b)
```

FIG. 13.19 Example of a computation in (a) for which reassociation results in recognition of a loop-invariant in (b).

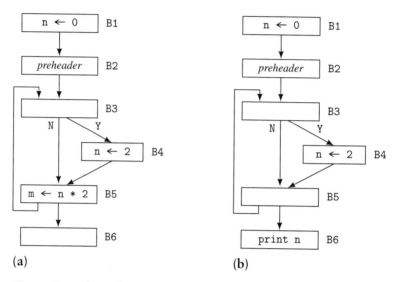

(a)   **(b)**

FIG. 13.20 Illustrations of two flaws in our basic approach to code motion. In both cases, if $n \leftarrow 2$ is moved to the preheader, it is always executed, although originally it might have been executed only in some iterations or in none.

to assignment instructions. Thus, if we had a loop-invariant conditional, say, $a < 0$, then it would always be safe to replace it by a temporary t and to put the assignment $t \leftarrow a < 0$ in the preheader. The situations are as follows:

1. All uses of a moved assignment's left-hand-side variable might be reached only by that particular definition, while originally it was only one of several definitions that might reach the uses. The assignment might be executed only in some iterations of the loop, while if it were moved to the preheader, it would have the same effect as if it were executed in every iteration of the loop. This is illustrated in Figure 13.20(a): the use of n in block B5 can be reached by the value assigned it in both the assignments $n \leftarrow 0$ and $n \leftarrow 2$. Yet if $n \leftarrow 2$ is moved to the preheader, n is assigned the value 2 regardless.

2. The basic block originally containing an instruction to be moved might not be executed during any pass through the loop. This could happen if execution of the basic block were conditional and it could result in a different value's being assigned to the target variable or the occurrence of an exception for the transformed code that would not occur in the original code. It could also happen if it were possible that the loop body might be executed zero times, i.e., if the termination condition were

satisfied immediately. This is illustrated in Figure 13.20(b): the assignment n ← 2 is not executed if the block containing it is bypassed for every pass through the loop, yet if it is moved to the preheader, n is assigned the value 2 regardless. This can be protected against by requiring that the basic block dominate all exit blocks of the loop (where an *exit block* is one that has a successor outside the loop), because then it must be executed on some iteration.

To fix the algorithm, we need a condition to guard against each of these situations. Let v be the variable assigned to by an instruction that is a candidate for movement to the preheader. Then the conditions are as follows:

1. The statement defining v must be in a basic block that dominates all uses of v in the loop.

2. The statement defining v must be in a basic block that dominates all exit blocks of the loop.

With these provisos, the resulting algorithm is correct, as follows: Move each instruction identified as loop-invariant and satisfying conditions (1) and (2) above, in the order they were identified, to the preheader.

The ICAN routine Move_Invar( ) to implement this algorithm is shown in Figure 13.21. The routine uses the sequence InvarOrder, computed by Mark_Invar( ) and four functions as follows:

1. insert_preheader(*bset*,nblocks,ninsts,Block) creates a preheader for the loop made up of the blocks in *bset* and inserts it into the flowgraph, if there is not one already.

2. Dom_Exits(i,*bset*) returns true if basic block i dominates all exits from the loop consisting of the set of basic blocks whose indexes are in *bset* and false otherwise.

3. Dom_Uses(i,*bset*,v) returns true if basic block i dominates all uses of variable v in the loop consisting of the set of basic blocks whose indexes are in *bset* and false otherwise.

4. append_preheader(*inst*,*bset*) appends instruction *inst* to the end of the preheader of the loop consisting of the basic blocks whose indexes are in *bset*. It can be implemented by using append_block( ) in Section 4.8.

Note that the second proviso includes the case in which a loop may be executed zero times because its exit test is performed at the top of the loop and it may be true when the loop begins executing. There are two approaches to handling this problem; one, called loop inversion, is discussed in Section 18.5. The other simply moves the code to the preheader and protects it by a conditional that tests whether the loop is entered, i.e., by identifying whether the termination condition is initially false. This method is always safe, but it increases code size and may slow it down as well, if the test is always true or always false. On the other hand, this approach may also enable constant-propagation analysis to determine that the resulting condition is constant-valued and hence removable (along with the code it guards, if the condition is always false).

```
                procedure Move_Invar(bset,nblocks,ninsts,Block,Succ,Pred)
                   bset: in set of integer
                   nblocks: in integer
                   ninsts: inout array [1··nblocks] of integer
                   Inst: inout array [1··nblocks] of array [··] of MIRInst
                   Succ, Pred: inout integer ⟶ set of integer
                begin
                   i, j, blk, pos: integer
                   P: set of (integer × integer)
                   tj: Var
                   inst: MIRInst
                   insert_preheader(bset,nblocks,ninsts,Block)
                   for i := 1 to |InvarOrder| do
                      blk := (InvarOrder↓i)@1
                      pos := (InvarOrder↓i)@2
                      inst := Block[blk][pos]
                      if Has_Left(inst.kind) & (Dom_Exits(blk,bset)
                         & Dom_Uses(blk,bset,inst.left) then
                         || move loop-invariant assignments to preheader
                         case inst.kind of
binasgn, unasgn: append_preheader(Block[blk][pos],bset)
                         delete_inst(blk,pos,ninsts,Block,Succ,Pred)
default:        esac
                      elif !Has_Left(inst.kind) then
                         || turn loop-invariant non-assignments to assignments in preheader
                         tj := new_tmp( )
                         case inst.kind of
binif, bintrap: append_preheader(⟨kind:binasgn,left:tj,
                         opr:inst.opr,opd1:inst.opd1,opd2:inst.opd2⟩,bset)
unif, untrap:   append_preheader(⟨kind:binasgn,left:tj,
                         opr:inst.opr,opd:inst.opd⟩,bset)
default:        esac
                         case inst.kind of
                            || and replace instructions by uses of result temporary
binif, unif:    Block[blk][pos] := ⟨kind:valif,opd:⟨kind:var,val:tj⟩,
                         label:inst.lbl⟩
bintrap, untrap:
                         Block[blk][pos] := ⟨kind:valtrap,opd:⟨kind:var,val:tj⟩,
                         trapno:inst.trapno⟩
default:        esac
                      fi
                   od
                end    || Move_Invar
```

FIG. 13.21   Code to move loop-invariant instructions out of a loop body.

As an example of applying Move_Invar( ), we continue with the example flow-graph in Figure 13.18. We call

```
Move_Invar({2,3,4,5,6},2,8,ninsts,Block)
```

The outermost for loop iterates for i = 1, 2, 3, 4, since

```
InvarOrder = [⟨3,1⟩,⟨3,2⟩,⟨5,2⟩,⟨6,2⟩]
```

For i = 1, it sets blk = 3 and pos = 1, and determines that block B3 does dominate the loop exit, that Block[3][1] has a left-hand side, and that

```
Dom_Uses(3,{2,3,4,5,6},a) = true
```

so it executes the binasgn case, which appends instruction Block[3][1] to the loop's preheader, namely, block B1. For i = 2, the routine behaves similarly, except that it chooses the unasgn case (which is the binasgn case also). For i = 3, it sets blk = 5 and pos = 2, determines that block B5 does not dominate the loop exit, and thus makes no further changes. For i = 4, it sets blk = 6 and pos = 2, determines that block B6 dominates the loop exit, and determines that Block[6][2] has no left-hand side. So it executes the binif case, which creates a new temporary t1, appends t1 ← a < 2 to block B1, and changes Block[6][2] to a test of t1. The resulting code is shown in Figure 13.22. Note that if we were to do constant folding at this point, we would determine that t1 is always false, so the loop is nonterminating.

In performing loop-invariant code motion on nested loops, we work from the innermost loop outward. This sequence achieves maximal identification of invariants

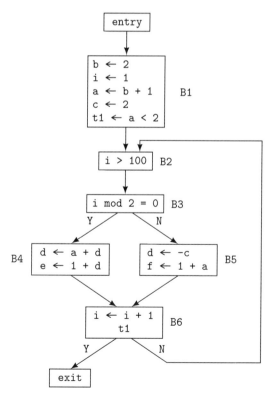

FIG. 13.22 The result of applying loop-invariant code motion to the flowgraph in Figure 13.18.

```
do i = 1,100
    m = 2*i + 3*l
    do j = 1, i - 1
        a(i,j) = j + m + 3*k
    enddo
enddo
```
(a)

```
do i = 1,100
    m = 2*i + 3*l
    do j = 1, i - 1
        a(i,j) = j + m + 3*k
    enddo
enddo
```
(b)

```
do i = 1,100
    m = 2*i + 3*l
    t1 = i - 1
    t2 = m + 3*k
    do j = 1, t1
        a(i,j) = j + t2
    enddo
enddo
```
(c)

```
do i = 1,100
    m = 2*i + 3*l
    t1 = i - 1
    t2 = m + 3*k
    do j = 1,t1
        a(i,j) = j + t2
    enddo
enddo
```
(d)

```
t3 = 3*l
t4 = 3*k
do i = 1,100
    m = 2*i + t3
    t1 = i - 1
    t2 = m + t4
    do j = 1, t1
        a(i,j) = j + t2
    enddo
enddo
```
(e)

FIG. 13.23 Loop-invariant code motion on nested Fortran loops (invariants are underlined).

and code motion. For example, consider the Fortran 77 loop nest in Figure 13.23(a). Identifying the loop invariants in the innermost loop results in Figure 13.23(b)—the invariants are underlined—and moving them results in Figure 13.23(c). Next, identifying the loop invariants in the outer loop results in Figure 13.23(d) and moving them produces the final code in Figure 13.23(e).

A special case of loop-invariant code motion occurs in loops that perform reductions. A *reduction* is an operation such as addition, multiplication, or maximum that simply accumulates values, such as in the loop shown in Figure 13.24, where the four instructions can be replaced by s = n*a(j). If the operand of the reduction is loop-invariant, the loop can be replaced with a single operation, as follows:

1. If the loop is additive, it can be replaced by a single multiplication.

2. If the loop is multiplicative, it can be replaced by a single exponentiation.

3. If the loop performs maximum or minimum, it can be replaced by assigning the loop-invariant value to the accumulator variable.

4. And so on.

```
s = 0.0
do i = 1,n
   s = s + a(j)
enddo
```

FIG. 13.24 An example of a reduction.

13.3   Partial–Redundancy Elimination

Partial-redundancy elimination is an optimization that combines global common-subexpression elimination and loop-invariant code motion and that also makes some additional code improvements as well.

In essence, a *partial redundancy* is a computation that is done more than once on some path through a flowgraph, i.e., some path through the flowgraph contains a point at which the given computation has already been computed and will be computed again. Partial-redundancy elimination inserts and deletes computations in the flowgraph in such a way that after the transformation each path contains no more—and, generally, fewer—occurrences of any such computation than before; moving computations out of loops is a subcase. Formulating this as a data-flow problem is more complex than any other case we consider.

Partial-redundancy elimination originated with the work of Morel and Renvoise [MorR79], who later extended it to an interprocedural form [MorR81]. As formulated by them, the intraprocedural version involves performing a complicated bidirectional data-flow analysis, but as we shall see, the modern version we discuss here avoids this. It is based on a more recent formulation called *lazy code motion* that was developed by Knoop, Rüthing, and Steffen [KnoR92]. The use of the word "lazy" in the name of the optimization refers to the placement of computations as late in the flowgraph as they can be without sacrificing the reduction in redundant computations of the classic algorithm. The laziness is intended to reduce register pressure (see Section 16.3.10), i.e., to minimize the range of instructions across which a register holds a particular value.

To formulate the data-flow analyses for partial-redundancy elimination, we need to define a series of local and global data-flow properties of expressions and to show how to compute each of them. Note that fetching the value of a variable is a type of expression and the same analysis applies to it.

A key point in the algorithm is that it can be much more effective if the critical edges in the flowgraph have been split before the flow analysis is performed. A *critical edge* is one that connects a node with two or more successors to one with two or more predecessors, such as the edge from B1 to B4 in Figure 13.25(a). Splitting the edge (introducing the new block B1a) allows redundancy elimination to be performed, as shown in Figure 13.25(b). As Dhamdhere and others have shown, this graph transformation is essential to getting the greatest impact from partial-redundancy elimination.

We use the example in Figure 13.26 throughout this section. Note that the computation of x * y in B4 is redundant because it is computed in B2 and the one in B7 is partially redundant for the same reason. In our example, it is crucial to split

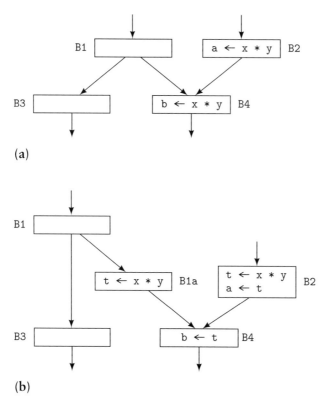

(a)

(b)

FIG. 13.25 In (a), the edge from B1 to B4 is a critical edge. In (b), it has been split by the introduction of B1a.

the edge from B3 to B5 so as to have a place to which to move the computation of x ∗ y in B7 that is not on a path leading from B2 and that does not precede B6.

    We begin by identifying and splitting critical edges. In particular, for our example in Figure 13.26, the edges from B2 and B3 to B5 are both critical. For example, for the edge from B3 to B5 we have $Succ(\text{B3}) = \{\text{B5}, \text{B6}\}$ and $Pred(\text{B5}) = \{\text{B2}, \text{B3}\}$. Splitting the edges requires creating new blocks B2a and B3a and replacing the split edges by edges into the new (initially empty) blocks from the tails of the original edges, and edges from the new blocks to the heads of the original edges. The resulting flowgraph is shown in Figure 13.27.

    The first property we consider is local transparency.[8] An expression's value is *locally transparent* in basic block i if there are no assignments in the block to variables that occur in the expression. We denote the set of expressions that are transparent in block i by *TRANSloc(i)*.

---

8. Note that local transparency is analogous to the property we call *PRSV* in Chapter 8.

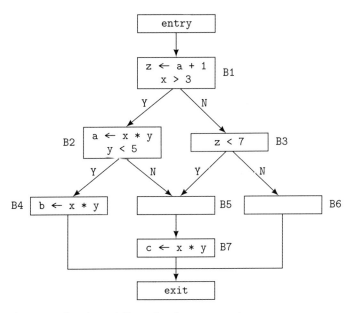

FIG. 13.26 An example of partially redundant expressions.

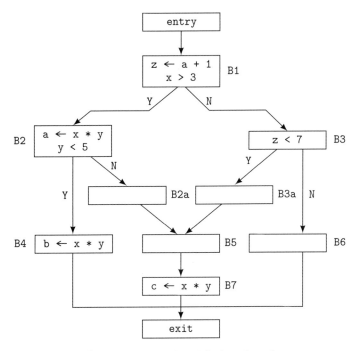

FIG. 13.27 The example from Figure 13.26 with the edges from B2 to B5 and B3 to B5 split. The new blocks B2a and B3a have been added to the flowgraph.

For our example,

$$TRANSloc(B2) = \{x*y\}$$

$$TRANSloc(i) \quad = U_{exp} = \{a+1, x*y\} \quad \text{for } i \neq B2$$

where U_{exp} denotes the set of all expressions in the program being analyzed.

An expression's value is *locally anticipatable* in basic block i if there is a computation of the expression in the block and if moving that computation to the beginning of the block would leave the effect of the block unchanged, i.e., if there are neither uses of the expression nor assignments to its variables in the block ahead of the computation under consideration. We denote the set of locally anticipatable expressions in block i by $ANTloc(i)$.

For our example, the values of $ANTloc(\ )$ are as follows:

$$
\begin{aligned}
ANTloc(\texttt{entry}) &= \emptyset \\
ANTloc(\texttt{B1}) &= \{a+1\} \\
ANTloc(\texttt{B2}) &= \{x*y\} \\
ANTloc(\texttt{B2a}) &= \emptyset \\
ANTloc(\texttt{B3}) &= \emptyset \\
ANTloc(\texttt{B3a}) &= \emptyset \\
ANTloc(\texttt{B4}) &= \{x*y\} \\
ANTloc(\texttt{B5}) &= \emptyset \\
ANTloc(\texttt{B6}) &= \emptyset \\
ANTloc(\texttt{B7}) &= \{x*y\} \\
ANTloc(\texttt{exit}) &= \emptyset
\end{aligned}
$$

An expression's value is *globally anticipatable* on entry to block i if every path from that point includes a computation of the expression and if placing that computation at any point on these paths produces the same value. The set of expressions anticipatable at the entry to block i is denoted $ANTin(i)$. An expression's value is anticipatable on exit from a block if it is anticipatable on entry to each successor block; we use $ANTout(i)$ to denote the set of expressions that are globally anticipatable on exit from block i. To compute $ANTin(\ )$ and $ANTout(\ )$ for all blocks i in a flowgraph, we solve the following system of data-flow equations:

$$ANTin(i) \quad = ANTloc(i) \cup (TRANSloc(i) \cap ANTout(i))$$

$$ANTout(i) = \bigcap_{j \in Succ(i)} ANTin(j)$$

with the initialization $ANTout(\texttt{exit}) = \emptyset$.

For our example, the values of $ANTin(\ )$ and $ANTout(\ )$ are as follows:

$$
\begin{aligned}
ANTin(\texttt{entry}) &= \{a+1\} & ANTout(\texttt{entry}) &= \{a+1\} \\
ANTin(\texttt{B1}) &= \{a+1\} & ANTout(\texttt{B1}) &= \emptyset \\
ANTin(\texttt{B2}) &= \{x*y\} & ANTout(\texttt{B2}) &= \{x*y\} \\
ANTin(\texttt{B2a}) &= \{x*y\} & ANTout(\texttt{B2a}) &= \{x*y\} \\
ANTin(\texttt{B3}) &= \emptyset & ANTout(\texttt{B3}) &= \emptyset
\end{aligned}
$$

$$
\begin{array}{llll}
ANTin(\text{B3a}) & = \{\text{x*y}\} & ANTout(\text{B3a}) & = \{\text{x*y}\} \\
ANTin(\text{B4}) & = \{\text{x*y}\} & ANTout(\text{B4}) & = \emptyset \\
ANTin(\text{B5}) & = \{\text{x*y}\} & ANTout(\text{B5}) & = \{\text{x*y}\} \\
ANTin(\text{B6}) & = \emptyset & ANTout(\text{B6}) & = \emptyset \\
ANTin(\text{B7}) & = \{\text{x*y}\} & ANTout(\text{B7}) & = \emptyset \\
ANTin(\text{exit}) & = \emptyset & ANTout(\text{exit}) & = \emptyset
\end{array}
$$

The next property needed to do lazy code motion is earliestness. An expression is *earliest* at the entrance to basic block i if no block leading from the entry to block i both evaluates the expression and produces the same value as evaluating it at the entrance to block i does. The definition of earliestness at the exit from a block is similar. The properties $EARLin(\ )$ and $EARLout(\ )$ are computed as follows:

$$
EARLin(i) \;=\; \bigcup_{j \in Pred(i)} EARLout(j)
$$

$$
EARLout(i) = \overline{TRANSloc(i)} \cup \left(\overline{ANTin(i)} \cap EARLin(i) \right)
$$

where $\overline{A} = U_{exp} - A$, with the initialization $EARLin(\text{entry}) = U_{exp}$.

The values of $EARLin(\ )$ for our example are as follows:

$$
\begin{array}{llll}
EARLin(\text{entry}) & = \{\text{a+1,x*y}\} & EARLout(\text{entry}) & = \{\text{x*y}\} \\
EARLin(\text{B1}) & = \{\text{x*y}\} & EARLout(\text{B1}) & = \{\text{x*y}\} \\
EARLin(\text{B2}) & = \{\text{x*y}\} & EARLout(\text{B2}) & = \{\text{a+1}\} \\
EARLin(\text{B2a}) & = \{\text{a+1}\} & EARLout(\text{B2a}) & = \{\text{a+1}\} \\
EARLin(\text{B3}) & = \{\text{x*y}\} & EARLout(\text{B3}) & = \{\text{x*y}\} \\
EARLin(\text{B3a}) & = \{\text{x*y}\} & EARLout(\text{B3a}) & = \emptyset \\
EARLin(\text{B4}) & = \{\text{a+1}\} & EARLout(\text{B4}) & = \{\text{a+1}\} \\
EARLin(\text{B5}) & = \{\text{a+1}\} & EARLout(\text{B5}) & = \{\text{a+1}\} \\
EARLin(\text{B6}) & = \{\text{x*y}\} & EARLout(\text{B6}) & = \{\text{x*y}\} \\
EARLin(\text{B7}) & = \{\text{a+1}\} & EARLout(\text{B7}) & = \{\text{a+1}\} \\
EARLin(\text{exit}) & = \{\text{a+1,x*y}\} & EARLout(\text{exit}) & = \{\text{a+1,x*y}\}
\end{array}
$$

Next we need a property called delayedness. An expression is *delayed* at the entrance to block i if it is anticipatable and earliest at that point and if all subsequent computations of it are in block i. The equations for delayedness are

$$
DELAYout(i) = \overline{ANTloc(i)} \cap DELAYin(i)
$$

$$
DELAYin(i) \;= ANEAin(i) \cup \bigcap_{j \in Pred(i)} DELAYout(j)
$$

where

$$
ANEAin(i) = ANTin(i) \cap EARLin(i)
$$

with the initialization $DELAYin(\text{entry}) = ANEAin(\text{entry})$.

The values of *ANEAin*( ) for our example are as follows:

$$
\begin{aligned}
ANEAin(\texttt{entry}) &= \{\texttt{a+1}\} \\
ANEAin(\texttt{B1}) &= \emptyset \\
ANEAin(\texttt{B2}) &= \{\texttt{x*y}\} \\
ANEAin(\texttt{B2a}) &= \emptyset \\
ANEAin(\texttt{B3}) &= \emptyset \\
ANEAin(\texttt{B3a}) &= \{\texttt{x*y}\} \\
ANEAin(\texttt{B4}) &= \emptyset \\
ANEAin(\texttt{B5}) &= \emptyset \\
ANEAin(\texttt{B6}) &= \emptyset \\
ANEAin(\texttt{B7}) &= \emptyset \\
ANEAin(\texttt{exit}) &= \emptyset
\end{aligned}
$$

and the values of *DELAYin*( ) and *DELAYout*( ) are as follows:

$DELAYin(\texttt{entry})$	$= \{\texttt{a+1}\}$	$DELAYout(\texttt{entry})$	$= \{\texttt{a+1}\}$
$DELAYin(\texttt{B1})$	$= \{\texttt{a+1}\}$	$DELAYout(\texttt{B1})$	$= \emptyset$
$DELAYin(\texttt{B2})$	$= \{\texttt{x*y}\}$	$DELAYout(\texttt{B2})$	$= \emptyset$
$DELAYin(\texttt{B2a})$	$= \emptyset$	$DELAYout(\texttt{B2a})$	$= \emptyset$
$DELAYin(\texttt{B3})$	$= \emptyset$	$DELAYout(\texttt{B3})$	$= \emptyset$
$DELAYin(\texttt{B3a})$	$= \{\texttt{x*y}\}$	$DELAYout(\texttt{B3a})$	$= \{\texttt{x*y}\}$
$DELAYin(\texttt{B4})$	$= \emptyset$	$DELAYout(\texttt{B4})$	$= \emptyset$
$DELAYin(\texttt{B5})$	$= \emptyset$	$DELAYout(\texttt{B5})$	$= \emptyset$
$DELAYin(\texttt{B6})$	$= \emptyset$	$DELAYout(\texttt{B6})$	$= \emptyset$
$DELAYin(\texttt{B7})$	$= \emptyset$	$DELAYout(\texttt{B7})$	$= \emptyset$
$DELAYin(\texttt{exit})$	$= \emptyset$	$DELAYout(\texttt{exit})$	$= \emptyset$

Next we define a property called latestness. An expression is *latest* at the entrance to block *i* if that is an optimal point for computing the expression and if on every path from block *i*'s entrance to the `exit` block, any optimal computation point for the expression occurs after one of the points at which the expression was computed in the original flowgraph. The data-flow equation for *LATEin*( ) is as follows:

$$
LATEin(i) = DELAYin(i) \cap \left(ANTloc(i) \cup \overline{\bigcap_{j \in Succ(i)} DELAYin(j)} \right)
$$

For our example, *LATEin*( ) is as follows:

$$
\begin{aligned}
LATEin(\texttt{entry}) &= \emptyset \\
LATEin(\texttt{B1}) &= \{\texttt{a+1}\} \\
LATEin(\texttt{B2}) &= \{\texttt{x*y}\} \\
LATEin(\texttt{B2a}) &= \emptyset \\
LATEin(\texttt{B3}) &= \emptyset \\
LATEin(\texttt{B3a}) &= \{\texttt{x*y}\} \\
LATEin(\texttt{B4}) &= \emptyset \\
LATEin(\texttt{B5}) &= \emptyset
\end{aligned}
$$

$$LATEin(\texttt{B6}) \quad = \emptyset$$
$$LATEin(\texttt{B7}) \quad = \emptyset$$
$$LATEin(\texttt{exit}) \quad = \emptyset$$

A computationally optimal placement for the evaluation of an expression is defined to be *isolated* if and only if on every path from a successor of the block in which it is computed to the `exit` block, every original computation of the expression is preceded by the optimal placement point. The data-flow properties *ISOLin*( ) and *ISOLout*( ) are defined by the equations

$$ISOLin(i) \;\; = LATEin(i) \cup \overline{(ANTloc(i)} \cap ISOLout(i))$$

$$ISOLout(i) = \bigcap_{j \in Succ(i)} ISOLin(j)$$

with the initialization $ISOLout(\texttt{exit}) = \emptyset$.

For our example, the values of *ISOLin*( ) and *ISOLout*( ) are as follows:

$ISOLin(\texttt{entry})$	$= \emptyset$	$ISOLout(\texttt{entry})$	$= \emptyset$
$ISOLin(\texttt{B1})$	$= \{\texttt{a+1}\}$	$ISOLout(\texttt{B1})$	$= \emptyset$
$ISOLin(\texttt{B2})$	$= \{\texttt{x*y}\}$	$ISOLout(\texttt{B2})$	$= \emptyset$
$ISOLin(\texttt{B2a})$	$= \emptyset$	$ISOLout(\texttt{B2a})$	$= \emptyset$
$ISOLin(\texttt{B3})$	$= \emptyset$	$ISOLout(\texttt{B3})$	$= \emptyset$
$ISOLin(\texttt{B3a})$	$= \{\texttt{x*y}\}$	$ISOLout(\texttt{B3a})$	$= \emptyset$
$ISOLin(\texttt{B4})$	$= \emptyset$	$ISOLout(\texttt{B4})$	$= \emptyset$
$ISOLin(\texttt{B5})$	$= \emptyset$	$ISOLout(\texttt{B5})$	$= \emptyset$
$ISOLin(\texttt{B6})$	$= \emptyset$	$ISOLout(\texttt{B6})$	$= \emptyset$
$ISOLin(\texttt{B7})$	$= \emptyset$	$ISOLout(\texttt{B7})$	$= \emptyset$
$ISOLin(\texttt{exit})$	$= \emptyset$	$ISOLout(\texttt{exit})$	$= \emptyset$

The set of expressions for which a block is the optimal computation point is the set of expressions that are latest but that are not isolated for that block, i.e.,

$$OPT(i) = LATEin(i) \cap \overline{ISOLout(i)}$$

and the set of redundant computations in a block consists of those that are used in the block (i.e., in *ANTloc*( )) and that are neither isolated nor latest in it, i.e.,

$$REDN(i) = ANTloc(i) \cap \overline{LATEin(i) \cup ISOLout(i)}$$

For our example, the values of *OPT*( ) and *REDN*( ) are as follows:

$OPT(\texttt{entry})$	$= \emptyset$	$REDN(\texttt{entry})$	$= \emptyset$
$OPT(\texttt{B1})$	$= \{\texttt{a+1}\}$	$REDN(\texttt{B1})$	$= \{\texttt{a+1}\}$
$OPT(\texttt{B2})$	$= \{\texttt{x*y}\}$	$REDN(\texttt{B2})$	$= \{\texttt{x*y}\}$
$OPT(\texttt{B2a})$	$= \emptyset$	$REDN(\texttt{B2a})$	$= \emptyset$
$OPT(\texttt{B3})$	$= \emptyset$	$REDN(\texttt{B3})$	$= \emptyset$
$OPT(\texttt{B3a})$	$= \{\texttt{x*y}\}$	$REDN(\texttt{B3a})$	$= \emptyset$
$OPT(\texttt{B4})$	$= \emptyset$	$REDN(\texttt{B4})$	$= \{\texttt{x*y}\}$

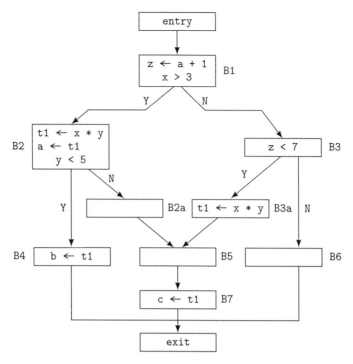

FIG. 13.28 The result of applying modern partial-redundancy elimination to the example in Figure 13.27.

$$
\begin{array}{llll}
OPT(\text{B5}) & = \emptyset & REDN(\text{B5}) & = \emptyset \\
OPT(\text{B6}) & = \emptyset & REDN(\text{B6}) & = \emptyset \\
OPT(\text{B7}) & = \emptyset & REDN(\text{B7}) & = \{\text{x*y}\} \\
OPT(\text{exit}) & = \emptyset & REDN(\text{exit}) & = \emptyset
\end{array}
$$

and so we remove the computations of x * y in B4 and B7, leave the one in B2, and add one in B3a, as shown in Figure 13.28.

The code required to implement partial-redundancy motion is similar to Move_Invar( ). We leave it as an exercise for the reader.

Modern partial-redundancy elimination can be extended to include strength reduction. However, the strength reduction is of a particularly weak form, because it does not recognize loop constants. For example, the code in Figure 13.29(a) can be strength-reduced by the method described in Section 14.1.2 to produce the code in Figure 13.29(b), but the approach to strength reduction based on partial-redundancy elimination cannot produce this code because it has no notion of loop constants.

Briggs and Cooper [BriC94b] improve the effectiveness of partial-redundancy elimination by combining it with global reassociation and global value numbering (see Section 12.4.2); Cooper and Simpson ([CooS95c] and [Simp96]) improve it

```
k = 0                        k = 0
for i = 1,n                  for i = 1,n
                                 l = 0
    for j = 1,n                  for j = 1,n
        k = k + i*j                  l = l + j
    endfor                       endfor
                                 k = k + i * l
endfor                       endfor
(a)                          (b)
```

FIG. 13.29 An example of the weakness of strength reduction when it is derived from partial-redundancy elimination. The HIR code in (a) can be strength-reduced to the code in (b) by the algorithm in Section 14.1.2, but not by the method derived from partial-redundancy elimination, because it does not recognize i as a loop invariant in the inner loop.

still further by using SSA form to operate on values rather than identifiers. The combination with reassociation is discussed briefly in the next section.

13.4   Redundancy Elimination and Reassociation

Reassociation can significantly enhance the applicability and effectiveness of all forms of redundancy elimination. For example, in the Fortran code in Figure 13.30, only common-subexpression elimination applies to loop A, resulting in loop B. With reassociation included, there is another possible sequence of the optimizations that applies, as shown in Figure 13.31.

Further, note that one of the sequences requires common-subexpression elimination, and the other does not; at least they both end up with the same (best) result. This suggests that the combination of the three optimizations should be applied repeatedly, but this may easily lead to a combinatorial explosion, so it is not advised.

The combination of partial-redundancy elimination and reassociation alleviates this problem somewhat, as shown in Figure 13.32. Note that if we apply partial-redundancy elimination first, we still need to apply it again after reassociation to get the best result.

```
(A) do i = m,n                    CSE              (B) do i = m,n
        a = b + i        ────────────────────►          a = b + i
        c = a - i                                        c = a - i
        d = b + i           CSE = common-subexpression   d = a
    enddo                         elimination        enddo
```

FIG. 13.30 Only common-subexpression elimination applies to the loop in A, producing the one in B.

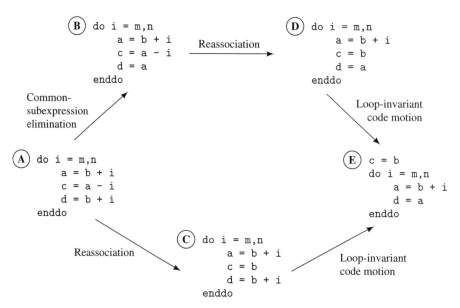

FIG. 13.31 Combining common-subexpression elimination and loop-invariant code motion with reassociation results in more possible transformation sequences and an improved result, compared to Figure 13.30.

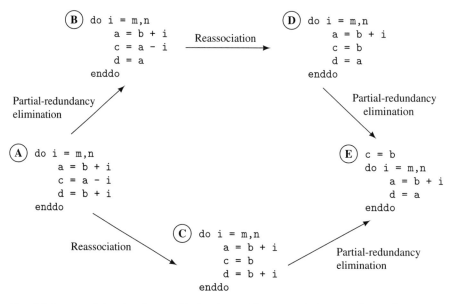

FIG. 13.32 Combining partial-redundancy elimination with reassociation produces the same result as in Figure 13.31.

13.5   Code Hoisting

Code hoisting (also called *unification*—see Section 17.6) finds expressions that are always evaluated following some point in a program, regardless of the execution path, and moves them to the earliest point beyond which they would always be evaluated. It is a transformation that almost always reduces the space occupied by a program but that may affect its execution time positively, negatively, or not at all. Whether it improves the execution time or not may depend on its effect on instruction scheduling, instruction-cache effects, and several other factors.

An expression that is evaluated regardless of the path taken from a given point is said to be *very busy* at that point. To determine very busy expressions, we do a backward data-flow analysis on expressions. Define $EVAL(i)$ to be the set of expressions that are evaluated in basic block i before any of the operands are assigned to (if at all) in the block and $KILL(i)$ to be the set of expressions killed by block i. In this context, an expression is killed by a basic block if one (or more) of its operands is assigned to in the block, either before it is evaluated or if it is not evaluated in the block at all. Then the sets of *very busy expressions* at the entry to and exit from basic block i are $VBEin(i)$ and $VBEout(i)$, respectively, defined by

$$VBEin(i) = EVAL(i) \cup (VBEout(i) - KILL(i))$$

$$VBEout(i) = \bigcap_{j \in Succ(i)} VBEin(j)$$

where, in solving the data-flow equations, $VBEout(i) = \emptyset$ initially for all i. The data-flow analysis can be implemented efficiently using bit vectors.

For example, given the flowgraph in Figure 13.33, the $EVAL(\ )$ and $KILL(\ )$ sets are as follows:

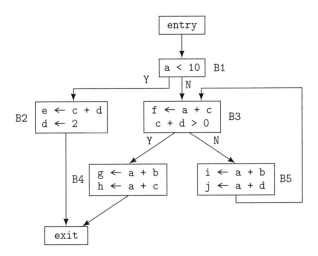

FIG. 13.33 An example for code hoisting.

$$
\begin{array}{llll}
EVAL(\text{entry}) & = \emptyset & KILL(\text{entry}) & = \emptyset \\
EVAL(\text{B1}) & = \emptyset & KILL(\text{B1}) & = \emptyset \\
EVAL(\text{B2}) & = \{c+d\} & KILL(\text{B2}) & = \{a+d\} \\
EVAL(\text{B3}) & = \{a+c,c+d\} & KILL(\text{B3}) & = \emptyset \\
EVAL(\text{B4}) & = \{a+b,a+c\} & KILL(\text{B4}) & = \emptyset \\
EVAL(\text{B5}) & = \{a+b,a+d\} & KILL(\text{B5}) & = \emptyset \\
EVAL(\text{exit}) & = \emptyset & KILL(\text{exit}) & = \emptyset \\
\end{array}
$$

and the $VBEin(\ )$ and $VBEout(\ )$ sets are as follows:

$$
\begin{array}{llll}
VBEin(\text{entry}) & = \{c+d\} & VBEout(\text{entry}) & = \{c+d\} \\
VBEin(\text{B1}) & = \{c+d\} & VBEout(\text{B1}) & = \{c+d\} \\
VBEin(\text{B2}) & = \{c+d\} & VBEout(\text{B2}) & = \emptyset \\
VBEin(\text{B3}) & = \{a+b,a+c,c+d\} & VBEout(\text{B3}) & = \{a+b,a+c\} \\
VBEin(\text{B4}) & = \{a+b,a+c\} & VBEout(\text{B4}) & = \emptyset \\
VBEin(\text{B5}) & = \{a+b,a+c,a+d,c+d\} & VBEout(\text{B5}) & = \{a+b,a+c,c+d\} \\
VBEin(\text{exit}) & = \emptyset & VBEout(\text{exit}) & = \emptyset \\
\end{array}
$$

Now, for any $i \neq$ entry, each expression exp in $VBEout(i)$ is a candidate for hoisting. Let S be the set of basic blocks j such that block i dominates block j, exp is computed in block j, and a computation of exp at the end of block i would reach the first computation of exp in block j unimpaired. Let th be a new temporary. Then we append $th \leftarrow exp$ to the end of block i (except that if the block ends with a conditional, we place the assignment before it) and we replace the first use of exp in each block j in S by th. ICAN code to perform this transformation is given in Figure 13.34. The following routines are used in the code:

1. Exp_Kind(k) returns the kind of expression contained in a MIR instruction of kind k (as defined in Section 4.7).

2. Reach(exp,Block,i,j,k) returns true if a definition of exp at the end of block i would reach the kth instruction in block j unimpaired, and false otherwise.

3. append_block(i,ninsts,Block,$inst$) inserts the instruction $inst$ at the end of block i, or if the last instruction in block i is a conditional, it inserts it immediately before the conditional; in either case, it updates ninsts[i] accordingly (see Section 4.8).

4. Dominate(i,j) returns true if block i dominates block j, and false otherwise.

Thus, for our example, we hoist the computations of c + d in blocks B2 and B3 to block B1, the computations of a + c in B3 and B4 to B3, and the computations of a + b in B4 and B5 also to B3, as shown in Figure 13.35. Note that local common-subexpression elimination can now replace the redundant computation of a + c in B3 by

```
t3 ← a + c
f ← t3
```

```
BinExp = Operand × Operator × Operand

procedure Hoist_Exps(nblocks,ninsts,Block,VBEout)
   nblocks: in integer
   ninsts: inout array [1··nblocks] of integer
   Block: inout array [1··nblocks] of array [··] of MIRInst
   VBEout: in integer ⟶ set of Binexp
begin
   i, j, k: integer
   S: set of (integer × integer)
   exp: BinExp
   th: Var
   s: integer × integer
   inst: MIRInst
   for i := 1 to nblocks do
      for each exp ∈ VBEout(i) do
         S := ∅
         for j := 1 to nblocks do
            if !Dominate(i,j) then
               goto L1
            fi
            for k := 1 to ninsts[j] do
               inst := Block[j][k]
               if Exp_Kind(inst.kind) = binexp
                  & inst.opd1 = exp@1 & inst.opr = exp@2
                  & inst.opd2 = exp@3 & Reach(exp,Block,i,j,k) then
                  S ∪= {⟨j,k⟩}
                  goto L1
               fi
            od
L1:      od
         th := new_tmp( )
         append_block(i,ninsts,Block,⟨kind:binasgn,
            left:th,opd1:exp@1,opr:exp@2,opd2:exp@3⟩)
         for each s ∈ S do
            inst := Block[s@1][s@2]
            case inst.kind of
binasgn:    Block[s@1][s@2] := ⟨kind:valasgn,
               left:inst.left,opd:⟨kind:var,val:th⟩⟩
binif:      Block[s@1][s@2] := ⟨kind:valif,
               opd:⟨kind:var,val:th⟩,lbl:inst.lbl⟩
bintrap:    Block[s@1][s@2] := ⟨kind:valtrap,
               opd:⟨kind:var,val:th⟩,trapno:inst.trapno⟩
            esac
         od
      od
   od
end   || Hoist_Exps
```

FIG. 13.34 An ICAN routine to perform code hoisting.

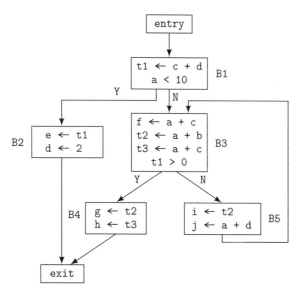

FIG. 13.35 The result of performing code hoisting on the example program in Figure 13.33.

13.6   Wrap-Up

The optimizations in this chapter have all dealt with elimination of redundant computations and all require data-flow analysis, either explicitly or implicitly. They can all be done effectively on either medium-level or low-level intermediate code.

These four optimizations have significant overlap between the first and second versus the third one. We summarize them as follows:

1. The first, common-subexpression elimination, finds expressions that are performed twice or more often on a path through a procedure and eliminates the occurrences after the first one, as long as the values of the arguments have not changed in between. It almost always improves performance.

2. The second, loop-invariant code motion, finds expressions that produce the same result every time a loop is repeated and moves them out of the loop. It almost always significantly improves performance because it mostly discovers and moves address computations that access array elements.

3. The third, partial-redundancy elimination, moves computations that are at least partially redundant (i.e., that are computed more than once on some path through the flowgraph) to their optimal computation points and eliminates totally redundant ones. It encompasses common-subexpression elimination, loop-invariant code motion, and more.

4. The last, code hoisting, finds expressions that are evaluated on all paths leading from a given point and unifies them into a single one at that point. It reduces the space occupied by a procedure but does not generally improve run-time performance unless there are numerous instances for its application.

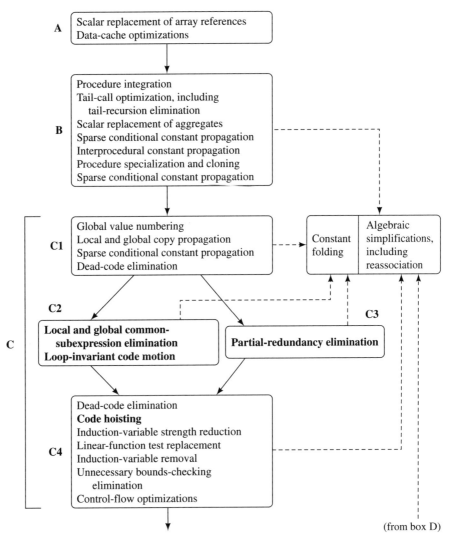

FIG. 13.36 Place of redundancy-related optimizations (highlighted in **bold** type) in an aggressive optimizing compiler. *(continued)*

We presented both the pair of optimizations common-subexpression elimination and loop-invariant code motion, and partial-redundancy elimination as well, because both approaches have about the same efficiency and have similar effects. The modern formulation of partial-redundancy elimination also provides a framework for thinking about and formulating other optimizations that share some of the data-flow information it requires. This optimization can be expected to be used in newly written compilers much more frequently in coming years and is replacing the former combination in some commercial compilers.

As shown in Figure 13.36, the redundancy-elimination transformations are generally placed roughly in the middle of the optimization process.

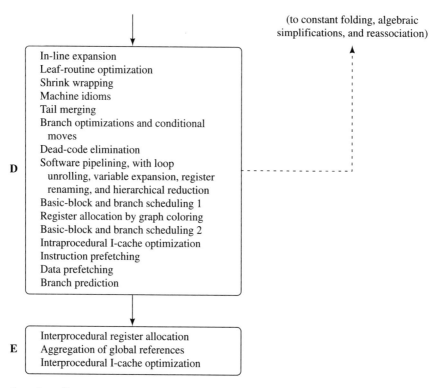

(to constant folding, algebraic
simplifications, and reassociation)

D
In-line expansion
Leaf-routine optimization
Shrink wrapping
Machine idioms
Tail merging
Branch optimizations and conditional
    moves
Dead-code elimination
Software pipelining, with loop
    unrolling, variable expansion, register
    renaming, and hierarchical reduction
Basic-block and branch scheduling 1
Register allocation by graph coloring
Basic-block and branch scheduling 2
Intraprocedural I-cache optimization
Instruction prefetching
Data prefetching
Branch prediction

E
Interprocedural register allocation
Aggregation of global references
Interprocedural I-cache optimization

FIG. 13.36 *(continued)*

13.7   Further Reading

Partial-redundancy elimination originated with the work of Morel and Renvoise
[MorR79], who later extended it to an interprocedural form [MorR81]. Extending classic partial-redundancy analysis to include strength reduction and induction-
variable simplifications is discussed in [Chow83].

More recently Knoop, Rüthing, and Steffen have introduced a form that requires only unidirectional data-flow analysis [KnoR92]. The edge-splitting transformation described in Section 13.3 was developed by Dhamdhere [Dham88]. Extension of partial-redundancy elimination to include strength reduction is described
in [KnoR93]. Briggs and Cooper's improved approach to partial-redundancy elimination is described in [BriC94b], and Cooper and Simpson's further improvements
are described in [CooS95c] and in [Simp96].

13.8   Exercises

13.1 As noted in Section 13.1, common-subexpression elimination may not always be
profitable. Give (a) a list of criteria that guarantee its profitability and (b) a list
that guarantee that it is unprofitable. (Note that there are intermediate situations
for which neither can be ensured.)

13.2 Formulate the data-flow analysis that is the inverse of available expressions, i.e., the backward-flow problem in which an expression is in $EVAL(i)$ if it is evaluated in block i and none of the variables in it are changed between the entrance to the block and the given evaluation, with the path-combining operator being intersection. Is there an optimization problem for which this analysis is useful?

13.3 Give an infinite sequence of programs $P_1, P_2, \ldots$, such that P_i, for each i, derives more benefit from i repetitions of local and global common-subexpression elimination than it does from $i - 1$ repetitions.

13.4 Write an ICAN routine Fwd_Subst(n,ninsts,Block) to perform forward substitution on an entire procedure.

13.5 Explain how you would modify Mark_Invar( ) and Mark_Block( ) in Figure 13.17 to deal with reassociation. What effect would this be expected to have on the running time of the algorithm?

13.6 Give an example of a loop nest that makes it clear that doing invariant code motion from the innermost loop out is superior to doing it from the outermost loop in.

13.7 Formulate an algorithm to recognize reductions and to perform loop-invariant code motion on them. Use the function Reductor(opr) to determine whether the operator opr is an operator useful for performing a reduction.

13.8 *Downward store motion* is a variety of code motion that moves stores in a loop to the exits of the loop. For example, in the Fortran code in part E of Figure 13.31, the variable d is a candidate for downward store motion—each assignment to it except the last one is useless, so moving it to follow the loop produces the same result, as long as the loop body is executed at least once. Design a method for detecting candidates for downward store motion and write ICAN code to detect and move them. What effect does downward store motion have on the need for registers in a loop?

13.9 Write an ICAN procedure to detect and split critical edges in a flowgraph. Let Node denote the set of possible flowgraph nodes. Then for a flowgraph with the set of nodes N ⊆ Node and edges E ⊆ Node × Node, Split_Critical(N,E) should add appropriate nodes to N and edges to E and should return true if it did any splits and false otherwise.

13.10 Write a listexp case for the routine Local_CSE( ) given in Figure 13.2.

13.11 Write a routine Move_Partial_Redun( ) that implements partial-redundancy motion.

CHAPTER 14

Loop Optimizations

The optimizations covered in this chapter either operate on loops or are most effective when applied to loops. They can be done on either medium-level (e.g., MIR) or low-level (e.g., LIR) intermediate code.

They apply directly to the disciplined source-language loop constructs in Fortran and Pascal but, for a language like C, require that we define a subclass of loops that they apply to. In particular, we define the class of *well-behaved loops* in C (with reference to the code in Figure 14.1) as those in which *exp*1 assigns a value to an integer-valued variable *i*, *exp*2 compares *i* to a loop constant, *exp*3 increments or decrements *i* by a loop constant, and *stmt* contains no assignments to *i*. A similar definition describes the class of well-behaved loops constructed from ifs and gotos in any modern programming language.

14.1 Induction–Variable Optimizations

In their simplest form, *induction variables* are variables whose successive values form an arithmetic progression over some part of a program, usually a loop. Usually the loop's iterations are counted by an integer-valued variable that proceeds upward (or downward) by a constant amount with each iteration. Often, additional variables, most notably subscript values and so the addresses of array elements, follow a pattern similar to the loop-control variable's, although perhaps with different starting values, increments, and directions.

For example, the Fortran 77 loop in Figure 14.2(a) is counted by the variable i, which has the initial value 1, increments by 1 with each repetition of the loop body,

```
for (exp1;exp2;exp3)
    stmt
```

FIG. 14.1 Form of a for loop in C.

425

```
                              integer a(100)
                              t1 = 202
integer a(100)                do i = 1,100
do i = 1,100                     t1 = t1 - 2
   a(i) = 202 - 2 * i            a(i) = t1
enddo                         enddo

      (a)                          (b)
```

FIG. 14.2 An example of induction variables in Fortran 77. The value assigned to a(i) in (a) decreases by 2 in each iteration of the loop. It can be replaced by the variable t1, as shown in (b), replacing a multiplication by an addition in the process.

and finishes with the value 100. Correspondingly, the expression assigned to a(i) has the initial value 200, decreases by 2 each time through the loop body, and has the final value 2. The address of a(i) has the initial value (in MIR) addr a, increases by 4 with each loop iteration, and has the final value (addr a) + 396. At least one of these three progressions is unnecessary. In particular, if we substitute a temporary t1 for the value of 202 - 2 * i, we can transform the loop to the form shown in Figure 14.2(b), or to its equivalent in MIR, shown in Figure 14.3(a). This is an example of an induction-variable optimization called strength reduction: it replaces a multiplication (and a subtraction) by a subtraction alone (see Section 14.1.2). Now i is used only to count the iterations, and

$$\texttt{addr a(i) = (addr a) + 4 * i - 4}$$

so we can replace the loop counter i by a temporary whose initial value is addr a, counts up by 4s, and has a final value of (addr a) + 396. The MIR form of the result is shown in Figure 14.3(b).

All of the induction-variable optimizations described here are improved in effectiveness by being preceded by constant propagation.

An issue to keep in mind in performing induction-variable optimizations is that some architectures provide a base + index addressing mode in which the index may be scaled by a factor of 2, 4, or 8 before it is added to the base (e.g., PA-RISC and the Intel 386 architecture) and some provide a "modify" mode in which the sum of the base and the index may be stored into the base register either before or after the storage reference (e.g., PA-RISC, POWER, and the VAX). The availability of such instructions may bias removal of induction variables because, given a choice of which of two induction variables to eliminate, one may be susceptible to scaling or base register modification and the other may not. Also, PA-RISC's add and branch instructions and POWER's decrement and branch conditional instructions may bias linear-function test replacement (see Figure 14.4 and Section 14.1.4) for similar reasons.

14.1.1 Identifying Induction Variables

Induction variables are often divided, for purposes of identification, into *basic* or *fundamental induction variables,* which are explicitly modified by the same constant amount during each iteration of a loop, and *dependent induction variables,*

```
              t1 ← 202                          t1 ← 202
              i ← 1                             t3 ← addr a
                                                t4 ← t3 - 4
                                                t5 ← 4
                                                t6 ← t4
                                                t7 ← t3 + 396
          L1: t2 ← i > 100               L1:   t2 ← t6 > t7
              if t2 goto L2                     if t2 goto L2
              t1 ← t1 - 2                       t1 ← t1 - 2
              t3 ← addr a
              t4 ← t3 - 4
              t5 ← 4 * i
              t6 ← t4 + t5                      t6 ← t4 + t5
              *t6 ← t1                          *t6 ← t1
              i ← i + 1                         t5 ← t5 + 4
              goto L1                           goto L1
          L2:                             L2:
          (a)                             (b)
```

FIG. 14.3 In (a), the MIR form of the loop in Figure 14.2(b) and, in (b), the same code with induction variable i eliminated, the loop-invariant assignments t3 ← addr a and t4 ← t3 - 4 removed from the loop, strength reduction performed on t5, and induction variable i removed.

```
              t1 ← 202
              t3 ← addr a
              t4 ← -396
              t5 ← t3 + 396
              t2 ← t4 > 0
              if t2 goto L2
          L1: t1 ← t1 - 2
              t6 ← t4 + t5
              *t6 ← t1
              t4 ← t4 + 4
              t2 ← t4 <= 0
              if t2 goto L1
          L2:
```

FIG. 14.4 The result of biasing the value of t4 in the code in Figure 14.3(b) so that a test against 0 can be used for termination of the loop. Loop inversion (see Section 18.5) has also been performed.

which may be modified or computed in more complex ways. Thus, for example, in Figure 14.2(a), i is a basic induction variable, while the value of the expression 200 - 2 * i and the address of a(i) are dependent induction variables. By contrast, in the expanded and transformed MIR version of this code in Figure 14.3(b), the induction variable i has been eliminated and t5 has been strength-reduced. Both t1 and t5 (which contain the value of 200 - 2 * i and the offset of the address of a(i) from the address of a(0), respectively) are now basic induction variables.

```
                                  t1 ← -4
            i ← 0                 i ← 0
     L1:  . . .             L1:  . . .
            use of i              use of i
            i ← i + 2             t1 ← t1 + 6
            use of i              use of t1
            i ← i + 4             i ← i + 6
            use of i              use of i
            goto L1               goto L1
     (a)                     (b)
```

FIG. 14.5 Example of splitting a basic induction variable with two modifications (a) into two induction variables (b).

To identify induction variables, we initially consider all variables in a loop as candidates, and we associate with each induction variable j we find (including temporaries) a linear equation of the form $j = b * biv + c$, which relates the values of j and biv within the loop, where biv is a basic induction variable and b and c are constants (they may either be actual constants or previously identified loop invariants); biv, b, and c are all initially nil. Induction variables with the same basic induction variable in their linear equations are said to form a *class* and the basic induction variable is called its *basis*. As we identify a variable j as potentially an induction variable, we fill in its linear equation.

The identification can be done by sequentially inspecting the instructions in the body of a loop, or it can be formulated as a data-flow analysis. We follow the first approach. First, we identify basic induction variables by looking for variables i whose only modifications in the loop are of the form $i \leftarrow i + d$ or $i \leftarrow d + i$, where d is a (positive or negative) loop constant. For such a variable i, the linear equation is simply $i = 1 * i + 0$, and i forms the basis for a class of induction variables. If there are two or more such modifications of i in the loop, we split the basic induction variable into several, one for each modification. For example, given the code in Figure 14.5(a), we split i into the two induction variables i and $t1$, as shown in Figure 14.5(b). In general, given a basic induction variable with two modifications, as shown in Figure 14.6(a), the transformed code is as shown in Figure 14.6(b); generalization to three or more modifications is straightforward.

Next, we repetitively inspect the instructions in the body of the loop for variables j that occur on the left-hand side of an assignment, such that the assignment has any of the forms shown in Table 14.1, where i is an induction variable (basic or dependent) and e is a loop constant. If i is a basic induction variable, then j is in the class of i and its linear equation can be derived from the form of the assignment defining it; e.g., for $j \leftarrow e * i$, the linear equation for j is $j = e * i + 0$. If i is not basic, then it belongs to the class of some basic induction variable i_1 with linear equation $i = b_1 * i_1 + c_1$; then j also belongs to the class of i_1 and its linear equation (again supposing that the defining assignment is $j \leftarrow e * i$) is $j = (e * b_1) * i_1 + e * c_1$. Two further requirements apply to a dependent induction variable i. First, there must be no assignment to i_1 between the assignment to i and the assignment to j in the loop, for this would alter the relationship between j and i_1, possibly making j not an

$$t1 \leftarrow i_0 - a_2$$

$i \leftarrow i_0$ $i \leftarrow i_0$

L1: . . .   L1: . . .

    use of i use of i

    . . .   . . .

    $i \leftarrow i + a_1$ $t1 \leftarrow t1 + (a_1 + a_2)$

    . . .   . . .

    use of i   use of $t1$

    . . .   . . .

    $i \leftarrow i + a_2$ $i \leftarrow i + (a_1 + a_2)$

    . . .   . . .

    use of i use of i

    . . .   . . .

    goto L1   goto L1

(a)   **(b)**

FIG. 14.6 Template for splitting a basic induction variable with two modifications (a) into two induction variables (b).

TABLE 14.1 Assignment types that may generate dependent induction variables.

$j \leftarrow i * e$
$j \leftarrow e * i$
$j \leftarrow i + e$
$j \leftarrow e + i$
$j \leftarrow i - e$
$j \leftarrow e - i$
$j \leftarrow -i$

induction variable at all; second, there must be no definition of i from outside the loop that reaches the definition of j. Reaching definitions or ud-chains can be used to check the latter condition.

If there is more than one assignment to j, but all of them are of one of these forms, then we split j into several induction variables, one for each such assignment, each with its own linear equation.

Assignments of the form

$$j \leftarrow i \; / \; e$$

can be accommodated also if we first unroll the loop body by a factor f that is a multiple of e (see Section 17.4.3). Then the linear equation for j is $j = (f/e) * i + 0$, assuming that i is a basic induction variable.

If we ever need to fill in a different basic induction variable, b value, or c value in the linear equation for a variable j for which they are already set, we split the induction variable into two, as described above.

```
IVrecord: record {tiv,biv: Var,
                  blk,pos: integer,
                  fctr,diff: Const}
IVs: set of IVrecord

procedure Find_IVs(bset,nblocks,ninsts,Block)
   bset: in set of integer
   nblocks: in integer
   ninsts: in array [1··nblocks] of integer
   Block: in array [1··nblocks] of array [··] of MIRInst
begin
   inst: MIRInst
   i, j: integer
   var: Var
   change: boolean
   ops1, ops2: enum {opd1,opd2}
   iv: IVrecord
   IVs := ∅
   for each i ∈ bset do
      for j := 1 to ninsts[i] do
         inst := Block[i][j]
         case inst.kind of
            || search for instructions that compute fundamental induction
            || variables and accumulate information about them in IVs
binasgn:     if IV_Pattern(inst,opd1,opd2,bset,nblocks,Block)
                V IV_Pattern(inst,opd2,opd1,bset,nblocks,Block) then
                IVs ∪= {⟨tiv:inst.left,blk:i,pos:j,fctr:1,
                    biv:inst.left,diff:0⟩}
             fi
default:    esac
         od
      od
```

FIG. 14.7   Code to identify induction variables.

If a modification of a potential induction variable occurs in one arm of a conditional, there must be a balancing modification in the other arm.

The routine Find_IVs( ) in Figure 14.7 and the auxiliary routines in Figure 14.8
implement most of the above. They omit induction variables with more than one
assignment in the loop and the requirement that an induction-variable definition in
one arm of a conditional must be balanced by such a definition in the other arm.
They use several functions, as follows:

1. Loop_Const(*opnd*,*bset*,nblocks,Block) returns true if operand *opnd* is a constant or if it is a variable that is a loop constant in the loop consisting of the set of
   blocks *bset*, and false otherwise.

```
        repeat
           change := false
           for each i ∈ bset do
              for j := 1 to ninsts[i] do
                 inst := Block[i][j]
                 case inst.kind of
                    || check for dependent induction variables
                    || and accumulate information in IVs
binasgn:            change := Mul_IV(i,j,opd1,opd2,
                       bset,nblocks,ninsts,Block)
                    change V= Mul_IV(i,j,opd2,opd1,
                       bset,nblocks,ninsts,Block)
                    change V= Add_IV(i,j,opd1,opd2,
                       bset,nblocks,ninsts,Block)
                    change V= Add_IV(i,j,opd2,opd1,
                       bset,ninsts,Block)
                    . . .
default:            esac
                 od
              od
           until !change
        end    || Find_IVs

     procedure IV_Pattern(inst,ops1,ops2,bset,nblocks,Block)
        returns boolean
        inst: in Instruction
        ops1,ops2: in enum {opd1,opd2}
        bset: in set of integer
        nblocks: in integer
        Block: in array [1··nblocks] of array [··] of MIRInst
     begin
        return inst.left = inst.ops1.val & inst.opr = add
           & Loop_Const(inst.ops2,bset,nblocks,Block)
           & !∃iv ∈ IVs (iv.tiv = inst.left)
     end    || IV_Pattern
```

FIG. 14.7 *(continued)*

2.   Assign_Between(*var*,*i*,*j*,*k*,*l*,*bset*,*nblocks*,*Block*) returns true if variable *var* is assigned to on some path between instruction Block[*i*][*j*] and instruction Block[*k*][*l*], and false otherwise.

3.   No_Reach_Defs(*var*,*i*,*j*,*bset*,*nblocks*,*Block*) returns true if there are no instructions in the loop that define variable *var* and reach instruction Block[*i*][*j*], and otherwise false.

They also use the set IVs of IVrecords that records induction variables, their linear equations, and the block and position of the statement in which they are defined. The record

$$\langle \texttt{tiv}:var1, \texttt{blk}:i, \texttt{pos}:j, \texttt{fctr}:c1, \texttt{biv}:var, \texttt{diff}:c2 \rangle$$

```
procedure Mul_IV(i,j,ops1,ops2,bset,nblocks,ninsts,Block) returns boolean
    i, j: in integer
    ops1, ops2: in enum {opd1,opd2}
    bset: in set of integer
    nblocks: in integer
    ninsts: in array [1··nblocks] of integer
    Block: in array [1··nblocks] of array [··] of MIRInst
begin
    inst := Block[i][j]: MIRInst
    iv1, iv2: IVrecord
    if Loop_Const(inst.ops1,bset,nblocks,Block)
        & inst.opr = mul then
        if ∃iv1 ∈ IVs (inst.ops2.val = iv1.tiv
            & iv1.tiv = iv1.biv & iv1.fctr = 1
            & iv1.diff = 0) then
            IVs ∪= {⟨tiv:inst.left,blk:i,pos:j,
                fctr:inst.ops1.val,biv:iv1.biv,diff:0⟩}
        elif ∃iv2 ∈ IVs (inst.ops2.val = iv2.tiv) then
            if !Assign_Between(iv2.biv,i,j,iv2.blk,iv2.pos,
                bset,nblocks,Block)
                & No_Reach_Defs(inst.ops2.val,i,j,bset,
                nblocks,Block) then
                IVs ∪= {⟨tiv:inst.left,blk:i,pos:j,
                    fctr:inst.ops1.val*iv2.fctr,biv:iv2.biv,
                    diff:inst.ops1.val*iv2.diff⟩}
            fi
        fi
        return true
    fi
    return false
end    || Mul_IV
```

FIG. 14.8 Auxiliary routines used in identifying induction variables.

declared in Figure 14.7 describes an induction variable *var*1 defined in instruction
Block[*i*] [*j*], in the class of basic induction variable *var*, and with the linear equation

$$var1 = c1 * var + c2$$

Note that expressions that are constant-valued within a loop, such as

```
inst.opd1.val*iv2.fctr
```

and

```
iv2.diff+inst.opd1.val
```

may not have their values known at compile time—they may simply be loop constants. In this situation, we need to carry the loop-constant expressions in the
IVrecords and generate instructions to compute their values in the loop's preheader.

```
procedure Add_IV(i,j,ops1,ops2,bset,nblocks,ninsts,Block) returns boolean
    i, j: in integer
    ops1, ops2: in enum {opd1,opd2}
    bset: in set of integer
    nblocks: in integer
    ninsts: in array [··] of integer
    Block: in array [··] of array [··] of MIRInst
begin
    inst := Block[i][j]: in MIRInst
    iv1, iv2: IVrecord
    if Loop_Const(inst.ops1,bset,nblocks,Block)
        & inst.opr = add then
        if ∃iv1 ∈ IVs (inst.ops2.val = iv1.tiv
            & iv1.tiv = iv1.biv & iv1.fctr = 1
            & iv1.diff = 0) then
            IVs ∪= {⟨tiv:inst.left,blk:i,pos:j,
                fctr:1,biv:iv1.biv,diff:inst.ops1.val⟩}
        elif ∃iv2 ∈ IVs (inst.ops2.val = iv.tiv) then
            if !Assign_Between(iv2.biv,i,j,iv2.blk,iv2.pos,
                bset,nblocks,Block)
                & No_Reach_Defs(inst.ops2.val,i,j,bset,
                nblocks,Block) then
                IVs ∪= {⟨tiv:inst.left,blk:i,pos:j,
                    fctr:iv2.fctr,biv:iv2.biv,
                    diff:iv2.diff+inst.ops1.val⟩}
            fi
        fi
        return true
    fi
    return false
end    || Add_IV
```

FIG. 14.8 *(continued)*

As a small example of this method for identifying induction variables, consider the MIR code in Figure 14.3(a). The first basic induction variable we encounter is t1, whose only assignment in the loop is t1 ← t1 - 2; its linear equation is t1 = 1 * t1 + 0. The only other basic induction variable is i with a linear equation i = 1 * i + 0. Next, we find that t5 is a dependent induction variable with a linear equation t5 = 4 * i + 0. Finally, we identify t6 as another dependent induction variable (since addr a, the value of t3, is a loop constant) in the class of i with linear equation t6 = 4 * i + addr a.

As another example of the process of identifying induction variables, consider the MIR code in Figure 14.9. We begin with the inner loop consisting of blocks B4 and B5. The only basic induction variable in the loop is k, so IVs (which is initially empty) becomes

```
IVs = {⟨tiv:k,blk:B5,pos:17,fctr:1,biv:k,diff:0⟩}
```

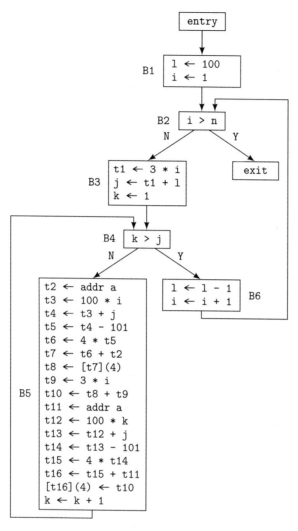

FIG. 14.9 A second example for induction-variable identification.

Next t12 is recognizable as an induction variable in the class of k, so IVs becomes

```
IVs = {⟨tiv:k  ,blk:B5,pos:17,fctr:1,  biv:k,diff:0⟩,
       ⟨tiv:t12,blk:B5,pos:11,fctr:100,biv:k,diff:0⟩}
```

Then t13 is recognized as an induction variable in the class of k, so we have

```
IVs = {⟨tiv:k,  blk:B5,pos:17,fctr:1,  biv:k,diff:0⟩,
       ⟨tiv:t12,blk:B5,pos:11,fctr:100,biv:k,diff:0⟩,
       ⟨tiv:t13,blk:B5,pos:12,fctr:100,biv:k,diff:j⟩}
```

Temporaries t14, t15, and t16 are also recognized as induction variables in the class of k, so we finally have

```
IVs = {⟨tiv:k,  blk:B5,pos:17,fctr:1,  biv:k,diff:0⟩,
        ⟨tiv:t12,blk:B5,pos:11,fctr:100,biv:k,diff:0⟩,
        ⟨tiv:t13,blk:B5,pos:12,fctr:100,biv:k,diff:j⟩,
        ⟨tiv:t14,blk:B5,pos:13,fctr:100,biv:k,diff:j-101⟩,
        ⟨tiv:t15,blk:B5,pos:14,fctr:400,biv:k,diff:4*j-404⟩),
        ⟨tiv:t16,blk:B5,pos:15,fctr:400,biv:k,
            diff:(addr a)+4*j-404⟩}
```

Note that t2, t3, t4, t5, t6, t7, t9, and t11 are all loop invariants in the inner loop, but that does not concern us here, because none of them, except t11, contribute to defining any of the induction variables.

Now, in the outer loop, consisting of blocks B2, B3, B4, B5, and B6, variable l is the first induction variable identified, setting

```
IVs = {⟨tiv:l,blk:B6,pos:1,fctr:1,biv:l,diff:0⟩}
```

and i is discovered next, resulting in

```
IVs = {⟨tiv:l,blk:B6,pos:1,fctr:1,biv:l,diff:0⟩,
        ⟨tiv:i,blk:B6,pos:2,fctr:1,biv:i,diff:0⟩}
```

Then t1 in B3 is added, yielding

```
IVs = {⟨tiv:l, blk:B6,pos:1,fctr:1,biv:l,diff:0⟩,
        ⟨tiv:i, blk:B6,pos:2,fctr:1,biv:i,diff:0⟩,
        ⟨tiv:t1,blk:B3,pos:1,fctr:3,biv:i,diff:0⟩}
```

Now, notice that j is an induction variable also. However, this fact is unlikely to be discovered by most compilers. It requires algebra or symbolic arithmetic to determine the following: on exit from block B1, we have l + i = 101, and B6, the only block that modifies either l or i, maintains this relationship, thus

```
j = t1 + l = 3*i + l = 2*i + (i + l) = 2*i + 101
```

This is unfortunate, because several of the loop invariants in the inner loop (mentioned above) have values that would also be induction variables in the outer loop if j were recognizable as one.

Once we have identified induction variables, there are three important transformations that apply to them: strength reduction, induction-variable removal, and linear-function test replacement.

14.1.2   Strength Reduction

Strength reduction replaces expensive operations, such as multiplications and divisions, by less expensive ones, such as additions and subtractions. It is a special case of the *method of finite differences* applied to computer programs. For example, the sequence

$$0, 3, 6, 9, 12, \ldots$$

has first differences (i.e., differences between successive elements) that consist of all 3s. Thus, it can be written as $s_i = 3 * i$ for $i = 0, 1, 2, \ldots$ or as $s_{i+1} = s_i + 3$ with $s_0 = 0$.

The second form is the strength-reduced version—instead of doing multiplications, we do additions. Similarly, the sequence

$$0, 1, 4, 9, 16, 25, \ldots$$

has first differences

$$1, 3, 5, 7, 9, \ldots$$

and second differences that consist of all 2s. It can be written as $s_i = i^2$ for $i = 0, 1, 2, 3, \ldots$, or as $s_{i+1} = s_i + 2 * i + 1$ for $s_0 = 0$, or as $s_{i+1} = s_i + t_i$ where $t_{i+1} = t_i + 2$, $s_0 = 0$, and $t_0 = 1$. Here, after two finite differencing operations, we have reduced computing a sequence of squares to two additions for each square. Strength reduction is not limited to replacing multiplication by additions and replacing addition by increment operations. Allen and Cocke [AllC81] discuss a series of applications for it, such as replacing exponentiation by multiplications, division and modulo by subtractions, and continuous differentiable functions by quadratic interpolations. Nevertheless, we restrict ourselves to discussing only simple strength reductions, because they are by far the most frequently occurring ones and, as a result, the ones that typically provide the greatest benefit. Methods for handling the other cases are broadly similar and can be found in the references given in Section 14.4.

To perform strength reduction on the induction variables identified in a loop, we work on each class of induction variables in turn.

1. Let i be a basic induction variable, and let j be in the class of i with linear equation $j = b * i + c$.

2. Allocate a new temporary tj and replace the single assignment to j in the loop by $j \leftarrow tj$.

3. After each assignment $i \leftarrow i + d$ to i in the loop, insert the assignment $tj \leftarrow tj + db$, where db is the value of the constant-valued expression $d * b$ (if this value is not actually constant, but only a loop constant, allocate a new temporary db and put the assignment $db \leftarrow d * b$ in the preheader of the loop).

4. Put the assignment $tj \leftarrow b * i + c$ at the end of the preheader to ensure that tj is properly initialized.

5. Replace each use of j in the loop by tj.

6. Finally, add tj to the class of induction variables based on i with linear equation $tj = b * i + c$.

The routine `Strength_Reduce( )` in Figure 14.10 implements this algorithm. The array `SRdone` has `SRdone[i][j]` = true if strength reduction has been performed on instruction j in block i, and false otherwise. `Strength_Reduce( )` uses two functions, as follows:

1. `insert_after(i,j,ninsts,Block,inst)` inserts instruction *inst* into `Block[i]` after the jth instruction and updates the program-representation data structures to reflect its having done so (see Figure 4.14).

```
procedure Strength_Reduce(bset,nblocks,ninsts,Block,IVs,SRdone)
   bset: in set of integer
   nblocks: in integer
   ninsts: inout array [1··nblocks] of integer
   Block: inout array [1··nblocks] of MIRInst
   IVs: inout set of IVrecord
   SRdone: out array [1··nblocks] of [··] of boolean
begin
   i, j: integer
   tj, db: Var
   iv, iv1, iv2: lVrecord
   inst: MIRInst
   for each i ∈ bset do
      for j := 1 to ninsts[i] do
         SRdone[i][j] := false
      od
   od
   || search for uses of induction variables
   for each iv1 ∈ IVs (iv1.fctr =1 & iv1.diff = 0) do
      for each iv2 ∈ IVs (iv2.biv = iv1.biv
         & iv2.tiv ≠ iv2.biv) do
         tj := new_tmp( )
         db := new_tmp( )
         i := iv2.blk
         j := iv2.pos
         SRdone[i][j] := true
         || and split their computation between preheader and
         || this use, replacing operations by less expensive ones
         append_preheader(bset,ninsts,Block,⟨kind:binasgn,
            left:db,opr:mul,opd1:⟨kind:const,val:iv1.fctr⟩,
            opd2:⟨kind:const,val:iv2.fctr⟩⟩)
         append_preheader(bset,ninsts,Block,⟨kind:binasgn,
            left:tj,opr:mul,opd1:⟨kind:const,val:iv2.fctr⟩,
            opd2:⟨kind:var,val:iv2.biv⟩⟩)
         append_preheader(bset,ninsts,Block,⟨kind:binasgn,
            left:tj,opr:add,opd1:⟨kind:var,val:tj⟩,
            opd2:⟨kind:const,val:iv2.diff⟩⟩)
         insert_after(i,j,ninsts,Block,⟨kind:binasgn,left:tj,
            opr:add,opd1:⟨kind:var,val:tj⟩,
            opd2:⟨kind:var,val:db⟩⟩)
```

(continued)

FIG. 14.10 Code to strength-reduce induction variables.

2. append_preheader(*bset*,ninsts,Block,*inst*) inserts instruction *inst* at the end of
   Block[*i*], where block *i* is the preheader of the loop made up of the blocks in *bset*,
   and updates the program-representation data structures to reflect its having done so.

For our MIR example in Figure 14.3(a), which we reproduce here as Figure
14.11(a), we first consider induction variable t5 with linear equation t5 = 4 * i + 0.

```
                IVs ∪= {⟨tiv:tj,blk:i,pos:j+1,fctr:iv2.fctr*iv1.fctr,biv:iv2.biv,
                    diff:iv2.diff⟩}
                for each i ∈ bset do
                    if iv1.tiv = iv2.tiv then
                        for each iv ∈ IVs do
                            IVs := (IVs - {iv}) ∪ {⟨tiv:iv.tiv,
                                blk:iv.blk,pos:iv.pos,fctr:iv.fctr,
                                biv:tj,diff:iv.diff⟩}
                        od
                    fi
                    for j := 1 to ninsts[i] do
                        inst := Block[i][j]
                        case Exp_Kind(inst.kind) of
binexp:                         if inst.opd1.val = iv2.tiv then
                                    Block[i][j].opd1 := ⟨kind:var,val:tj⟩
                                fi
                                if inst.opd2.val = iv2.tiv then
                                    Block[i][j].opd2 := ⟨kind:var,val:tj⟩
                                fi
unexp:                          if inst.opd.val = iv2.tiv then
                                    Block[i][j].opd := ⟨kind:var,val:tj⟩
                                fi

listexp:                        for j := 1 to |inst.args| do
                                    if inst.args↓i@1.val = iv2.tiv then
                                        Block[i][j].args↓i@1 := ⟨kind:var,val:tj⟩
noexp:                          esac
                    od
                od
            od
        od
end     || Strength_Reduce
```

FIG. 14.10 *(continued)*

We allocate a new temporary t7 and replace the assignment to t5 by t5 ← t7. We insert t7 ← t7 + 4 after i ← i + 1, and t7 ← 4 in the preheader. Finally, we create the linear equation t7 = 4 * i + 0 for the induction variable t7 in the class of i, and we put the resulting record into IVs. This results in the code in Figure 14.11(b). Performing the same transformation on t6 with linear equation t6 = 4 * i + t4 and removing the loop invariants t3 and t4 from the loop results in the code in Figure 14.12. Note that these transformations have increased the size of the code—there are now 11 instructions in the loop, rather than the 9 we started with. Our next task, induction-variable removal, shows how to regain and often improve the code size.

For the second example in the preceding section, Figure 14.9, we show the inner loop with its preheader in Figure 14.13. The set of induction-variable records for it (as computed in the preceding section, but with the positions renumbered to reflect removal of the loop invariants) is as follows:

```
        t1 ← 202                          t1 ← 202
        i ← 1                             i ← 1
                                          t7 ← 4
L1: t2 ← i > 100              L1: t2 ← i > 100
        if t2 goto L2                     if t2 goto L2
        t1 ← t1 - 2                       t1 ← t1 - 2
        t3 ← addr a                       t3 ← addr a
        t4 ← t3 - 4                       t4 ← t3 - 4
        t5 ← 4 * i                        t5 ← t7
        t6 ← t4 + t5                      t6 ← t4 + t5
        *t6 ← t1                          *t6 ← t1
        i ← i + 1                         i ← i + 1
                                          t7 ← t7 + 4
        goto L1                           goto L1
L2:                              L2:
    (a)                              (b)
```

FIG. 14.11 In (a), the MIR form of the loop in Figure 14.3(a) and, in (b), the same code with strength reduction performed on the induction variable t5.

```
        t1 ← 202
        i ← 1
        t7 ← 4
        t3 ← addr a
        t4 ← t3 - 4
        t8 ← t4 + t7
L1: t2 ← i > 100
        if t2 goto L2
        t1 ← t1 - 2
        t5 ← t7
        t6 ← t8
        *t6 ← t1
        i ← i + 1
        t8 ← t8 + 4
        t7 ← t7 + 4
        goto L1
L2:
```

FIG. 14.12 The result of removing the loop invariants t3 and t4 and strength-reducing t6 in the code in Figure 14.11(b).

```
IVs = {⟨tiv:k,  blk:B5,pos:9,fctr:1,  biv:k,diff:0⟩,
       ⟨tiv:t12,blk:B5,pos:3,fctr:100,biv:k,diff:0⟩,
       ⟨tiv:t13,blk:B5,pos:4,fctr:100,biv:k,diff:j⟩,
       ⟨tiv:t14,blk:B5,pos:5,fctr:100,biv:k,diff:j-101⟩,
       ⟨tiv:t15,blk:B5,pos:6,fctr:400,biv:k,diff:4*j-404⟩,
       ⟨tiv:t16,blk:B5,pos:7,fctr:400,biv:k,
           diff:(addr a)+4*j-404⟩}
```

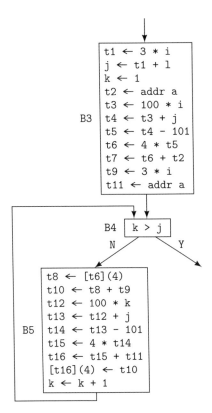

B3
```
t1 ← 3 * i
j ← t1 + 1
k ← 1
t2 ← addr a
t3 ← 100 * i
t4 ← t3 + j
t5 ← t4 - 101
t6 ← 4 * t5
t7 ← t6 + t2
t9 ← 3 * i
t11 ← addr a
```

B4 ` k > j `

N   Y

B5
```
t8 ← [t6](4)
t10 ← t8 + t9
t12 ← 100 * k
t13 ← t12 + j
t14 ← t13 - 101
t15 ← 4 * t14
t16 ← t15 + t11
[t16](4) ← t10
k ← k + 1
```

FIG. 14.13 The result of removing loop invariants from the inner loop of our second example, Figure 14.9, and deleting the outer loop, except B3, which is the preheader of the inner loop.

The algorithm initially sets

```
iv1 = ⟨tiv:k,  blk:B5,pos:9,fctr:1,  biv:k,diff:0⟩
iv2 = ⟨tiv:t12,blk:B5,pos:3,fctr:100,biv:k,diff:0⟩
```

allocates temporaries t17 and t18 as the values of tj and db, respectively, sets i = B5, j = 3, and SRdone[B5][3] = true. Next, it appends to the preheader (block B3) the instructions

```
t18 ← 100 * 1
t17 ← 100 * k
t17 ← t17 + 0
```

appends to block B5 the instruction

```
t17 ← t17 + t18
```

and sets

```
IVs = {⟨tiv:k,  blk:B5,pos:9, fctr:1,  biv:k,diff:0⟩,
        ⟨tiv:t12,blk:B5,pos:3, fctr:100,biv:k,diff:0⟩,
```

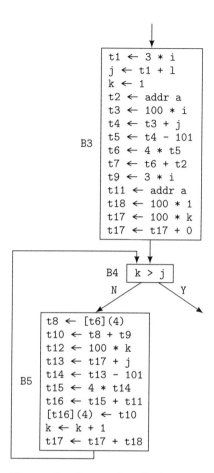

FIG. 14.14 The result of strength-reducing t12 on the code in Figure 14.13.

```
⟨tiv:t13,blk:B5,pos:4, fctr:100,biv:k,diff:j⟩,
⟨tiv:t14,blk:B5,pos:5, fctr:100,biv:k,diff:j-101⟩,
⟨tiv:t15,blk:B5,pos:6, fctr:400,biv:k,diff:4*j-404⟩,
⟨tiv:t16,blk:B5,pos:7, fctr:400,biv:k,
     diff:(addr a)+4*j-404⟩,
⟨tiv:t17,blk:B5,pos:10,fctr:100,biv:k,diff:100⟩}
```

Finally, the routine replaces all uses of t12 by t17. Note that two of the instructions inserted into the preheader (namely, t18 ← 100 * 1 and t17 ← t17 + 0) are unnecessary (see Exercise 14.3 for a way to eliminate them) and that the instruction that sets t12 remains in block B5 (dead-code elimination will remove it). The result is shown in Figure 14.14.

Next, the routine sets

```
iv2 = ⟨tiv:t13,blk:B5,pos:4,fctr:100,biv:k,diff:j⟩
```

and acts similarly: it allocates t19 and t20 as the values of tj and db, respectively, sets i = B5, j = 4, and SRdone[B5][4] = true. Next, it appends to the preheader (block B3) the instructions

```
t20 ← 100 * 1
t19 ← 100 * k
t19 ← t17 + j
```

appends to block B5 the instruction

```
t19 ← t19 + t20
```

and sets

```
IVs = {⟨tiv:k,  blk:B5,pos:9, fctr:1,  biv:k,diff:0⟩,
       ⟨tiv:t12,blk:B5,pos:3, fctr:100,biv:k,diff:0⟩,
       ⟨tiv:t13,blk:B5,pos:4, fctr:100,biv:k,diff:j⟩,
       ⟨tiv:t14,blk:B5,pos:5, fctr:100,biv:k,diff:j-101⟩,
       ⟨tiv:t15,blk:B5,pos:6, fctr:400,biv:k,diff:4*j-404⟩,
       ⟨tiv:t16,blk:B5,pos:7, fctr:400,biv:k,
           diff:4*j-404+(addr a)⟩,
       ⟨tiv:t17,blk:B5,pos:10,fctr:100,biv:k,diff:100⟩,
       ⟨tiv:t19,blk:B5,pos:11,fctr:100,biv:k,diff:j⟩}
```

Finally, the routine replaces all uses of t13 by t19. Note that, again, two of the instructions inserted into the preheader (namely, t18 ← 100 * 1 and t17 ← t17 + 0) are unnecessary and the instruction that sets t13 remains in block B5. The result is shown in Figure 14.15.

We leave it to the reader to complete the example. The resulting set IVs should be

```
IVs = {⟨tiv:k,  blk:B5,pos:9, fctr:1,  biv:k,diff:0⟩,
       ⟨tiv:t12,blk:B5,pos:3, fctr:100,biv:k,diff:0⟩,
       ⟨tiv:t13,blk:B5,pos:4, fctr:100,biv:k,diff:j⟩,
       ⟨tiv:t14,blk:B5,pos:5, fctr:100,biv:k,diff:j-101⟩,
       ⟨tiv:t15,blk:B5,pos:6, fctr:400,biv:k,diff:4*j-404⟩,
       ⟨tiv:t16,blk:B5,pos:7, fctr:400,biv:k,
           diff:4*j-404+(addr a)⟩,
       ⟨tiv:t17,blk:B5,pos:10,fctr:100,biv:k,diff:0⟩,
       ⟨tiv:t19,blk:B5,pos:11,fctr:100,biv:k,diff:j⟩,
       ⟨tiv:t21,blk:B5,pos:12,fctr:100,biv:k,diff:j-101⟩,
       ⟨tiv:t23,blk:B5,pos:13,fctr:400,biv:k,diff:4*j-404⟩,
       ⟨tiv:t25,blk:B5,pos:14,fctr:400,biv:k,
           diff:4*j-404+(addr a)⟩}
```

SRdone[B5][i] = true only for $i = 3, 4, \ldots, 7$ and the resulting partial flow-graph is shown in Figure 14.16.

Of course, some of the expressions in B3, such as 4*j-404+(addr a), are not legal MIR code, but their expansion to legal code is obvious.

Removing dead code, doing constant folding, and removing trivial assignments in B3 results in the partial flowgraph in Figure 14.17. Note that t8, t10, t12, t13, t14, t15, and t16 are all dead also.

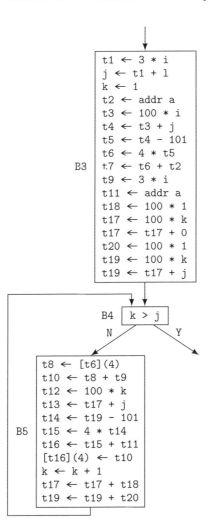

FIG. 14.15 The result of strength-reducing t13 on the partial flowgraph in Figure 14.14.

Knoop, Rüthing, and Steffen [KnoR93] give a method for doing strength reduction based on their approach to partial-redundancy elimination (see Section 13.3). However, as discussed at the end of that section, it is a particularly weak variety of strength reduction, so the traditional method given here should be preferred over it.

On the other hand, Cooper and Simpson ([CooS95a] and [Simp96]) give a method that extends strength reduction to work on the SSA form of a procedure. The resulting algorithm is as effective as the one described above, and is more efficient.

14.1.3   Live Variables Analysis

One tool we need in order to perform the induction-variable transformations that follow as well as for other optimizations, such as register allocation by graph coloring and dead-code elimination, is live variables analysis. A variable is *live* at a

B3
```
t1  ← 3 * i
j   ← t1 + 1
k   ← 1
t2  ← addr a
t3  ← 100 * i
t4  ← t3 + j
t5  ← t4 - 101
t6  ← 4 * t5
t7  ← t6 + t2
t9  ← 3 * i
t11 ← addr a
t18 ← 100 * 1
t17 ← 100 * k
t17 ← t17 + 0
t20 ← 100 * 1
t19 ← 100 * k
t19 ← t19 + j
t22 ← 100 * 1
t21 ← 100 * k
t21 ← t21 + j - 101
t24 ← 400 * 1
t23 ← 400 * k
t23 ← t23 + 4 * j - 404
t26 ← 400 * 1
t25 ← 400 * k
t25 ← t25 + 4 * j - 404 + (addr a)
```

B4 `k > j`

N   Y

B5
```
t8  ← [t6](4)
t10 ← t8 + t9
t12 ← 100 * k
t13 ← t17 + j
t14 ← t19 - 101
t15 ← 4 * t21
t16 ← t23 + t11
[t25](4) ← t10
k   ← k + 1
t17 ← t17 + t18
t19 ← t19 + t20
t21 ← t21 + t22
t23 ← t23 + t24
t25 ← t25 + t26
```

FIG. 14.16 The result of strength-reducing the remaining induction variables in the partial flowgraph in Figure 14.15.

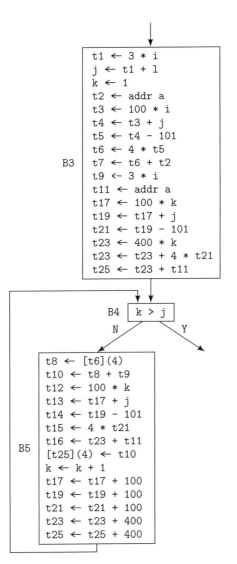

FIG. 14.17 The result of doing constant folding and elimination of trivial assignments in block B3 for the partial flowgraph in Figure 14.16.

particular point in a program if there is a path to the exit along which its value may be used before it is redefined. It is *dead* if there is no such path.

To determine which variables are live at each point in a flowgraph, we perform a backward data-flow analysis. Define $USE(i)$ to be the set of variables that are used in basic block i before they are defined (if at all) in the block and $DEF(i)$ to be the set of variables that are defined in the block before they are used (if at all) in the block. A variable is live on entry to block i if it is live at the exit of block i and not in $DEF(i)$, or if it is in $USE(i)$, so

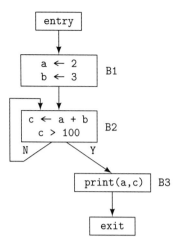

FIG. 14.18 Example flowgraph for computing live variables.

$$LVin(i) = (LVout(i) - DEF(i)) \cup USE(i)$$

and a variable is live at the exit of a basic block if it is live at the entry to any of its successors, so

$$LVout(i) = \bigcup_{j \in Succ(i)} LVin(j)$$

The proper initialization is $LVout(\texttt{exit}) = \emptyset$ for all i.

As an example of the data-flow analysis for live variables, consider the flowgraph in Figure 14.18. The values of $DEF(\ )$ and $USE(\ )$ are as follows:

$DEF(\texttt{entry})$	$= \emptyset$	$USE(\texttt{entry})$	$= \emptyset$
$DEF(\texttt{B1})$	$= \{a,b\}$	$USE(\texttt{B1})$	$= \emptyset$
$DEF(\texttt{B2})$	$= \{c\}$	$USE(\texttt{B2})$	$= \{a,b\}$
$DEF(\texttt{B3})$	$= \emptyset$	$USE(\texttt{B3})$	$= \{a,c\}$
$DEF(\texttt{exit})$	$= \emptyset$	$USE(\texttt{exit})$	$= \emptyset$

and the values of $LVin(\ )$ and $LVout(\ )$ are as follows:

$LVin(\texttt{entry})$	$= \emptyset$	$LVout(\texttt{entry})$	$= \emptyset$
$LVin(\texttt{B1})$	$= \emptyset$	$LVout(\texttt{B1})$	$= \{a,b\}$
$LVin(\texttt{B2})$	$= \{a,b\}$	$LVout(\texttt{B2})$	$= \{a,b,c\}$
$LVin(\texttt{B3})$	$= \{a,c\}$	$LVout(\texttt{B3})$	$= \emptyset$
$LVin(\texttt{exit})$	$= \emptyset$	$LVout(\texttt{exit})$	$= \emptyset$

so a and b are live at the entrance to block B2, and a and c are live at the entrance to block B3.

```
j = 2                        j = 2
do i = 1,10                  do i = 1,10
   a(i) = i + 1                 a(i) = j
   j = j + 1                    j = j + 1
enddo                        enddo
(a)                          (b)
```

FIG. 14.19 Examples of useless induction variables in Fortran 77 code.

14.1.4   Removal of Induction Variables and Linear-Function Test Replacement

In addition to strength-reducing induction variables, we can often remove them entirely. The basic criterion for doing so is obvious—that the induction variable serve no useful purpose in the program—but this is not always easy to identify. There are several ways this situation may arise, as follows:

1. The variable may have contributed nothing to the computation to begin with.

2. The variable may have become useless as a result of another transformation, such as strength reduction.

3. The variable may have been created in the process of performing a strength reduction and then become useless as a result of another one.

4. The variable may be used only in the loop-closing test and may be replaceable by another induction variable in that context. This case is known as *linear-function test replacement*.

As an example of the first case, consider the variable j in Figure 14.19(a). It serves no purpose at all in the loop; assuming that its final value is not used after the loop, it can simply be removed. Even if its final value is used, it can be replaced by the single assignment j = 12 after the loop. This case is covered by dead-code elimination (see Section 18.10).

As an example of the second case, consider j in Figure 14.19(b). Here the value of j is actually used in the loop, but it is an induction variable in the class of i and its value at each use is exactly i + 1, so we can easily remove it.

An example of the third case can be seen by transforming the code in Figure 14.12. Consider the variable t7, which is initialized to 4 before entering the loop and then is assigned to t5 and incremented by 4 inside the loop. We eliminate the assignment t5 ← t7 and replace the use of t5 by t7, which results in the code in Figure 14.20(a). Now there is no use of the value of t7 in the loop (except to increment it), so it and its initialization before the loop can be removed, resulting in the code shown in Figure 14.20(b).[1]

---

1. Note that we could also do loop inversion on this example, but we choose not to, so as to deal with one issue at a time.

```
        t1 ← 202                    t1 ← 202
        i ← 1                       i ← 1
        t7 ← 4
        t3 ← addr a                 t3 ← addr a
        t4 ← t3 - 4                 t4 ← t3 - 4
        t8 ← t4 + 4                 t8 ← t4 + 4
    L1: t2 ← i > 100            L1: t2 ← i > 100
        if t2 goto L2               if t2 goto L2
        t1 ← t1 - 2                 t1 ← t1 - 2
        t6 ← t8                     t6 ← t8
        *t6 ← t1                    *t6 ← t1
        i ← i + 1                   i ← i + 1
        t8 ← t8 + 4                 t8 ← t8 + 4
        t7 ← t7 + 4
        goto L1                     goto L1
    L2:                        L2:
    (a)                        (b)
```

FIG. 14.20 Transformed versions of code in Figure 14.12: (a) after removing the induction variable t5, and (b) after removing t7 also.

If the architecture we are compiling for has loads and stores with base register updating, we bias the choice of induction variables we keep to be those that can benefit from such instructions, i.e., those that are used to address storage and that are incremented by an appropriate amount.

The last case, linear-function test replacement, is illustrated by the variable i in Figure 14.20—i is initialized before the loop, tested to determine loop termination, and incremented inside the loop. It is not used in any other way, except that its final value might be needed after the loop. It can be eliminated by determining the final value of t8 in the loop, namely, (addr a) + 400 and assigning it to a new temporary t9, replacing the termination test computation by t2 ← t8 > t9, and removing all the statements that use i, which results in the code in Figure 14.21. (Note that we have also eliminated t6 by replacing its one use with its value, to simplify the code further and to make it more readable.) If i were known to be live at the end of the loop, or not known not to be live, we would also insert i ← 100 at L2.

To perform induction-variable removal and linear-function test replacement on a given loop, we proceed as follows.

For each assignment $j \leftarrow tj$ that is inserted by the strength-reduction algorithm in the previous section, if there are no definitions of tj between the inserted statement and any uses of j, then we replace all uses of j by uses of tj and remove the inserted statement $j \leftarrow tj$. This is exactly what we did in transforming the code in Figure 14.20(b) to that in Figure 14.21, along with linear-function test replacement. Note that this is a local form of copy propagation.

Let i be a basic induction variable used only in computations of other induction variables and relations, and let j be an induction variable in the class of i with linear

```
        t1 ← 202
        t3 ← addr a
        t4 ← t3 - 4
        t8 ← t4 + 4
        t9 ← t3 + 400
   L1: t2 ← t8 > t9
        if t2 goto L2
        t1 ← t1 - 2
        *t8 ← t1
        t8 ← t8 + 4
        goto L1
   L2:
```

FIG. 14.21 Result of induction-variable removal (of i and t6) and linear-function test replacement on variable i in the code in Figure 14.20(b).

equation $j = b * i + c$. We replace the relation computation $i ? v$, where ? represents a relational operator and v is not an induction variable, by

$$tj \leftarrow b * v$$
$$tj \leftarrow tj + c$$
$$j ? tj$$

and delete all assignments to i in the loop. If i is live along some paths exiting the loop, we place an assignment to i of its final value from the loop at each such exit.

One complication in this process is less than obvious and has tripped up several compiler writers and authors on strength reduction (see, for example, Section 3.5 of [AllC81]). Namely, for the relation to remain ? in the replacement statements, we must know that b is positive. If it is negative, we need to use the negation of the relation, which we denote by !? in the replacement expression; specifically, the relational expression above becomes

$$j \; !? \; tj$$

If b is only a loop invariant, rather than a known constant, we may not know whether it is positive or negative. In this case, it may not be worthwhile to do the linear-function test replacement, but it can be done nevertheless at the expense of increased code size if it is judged to be desirable. One merely needs to test the loop invariant's sign before entering the loop and branch to one of two copies of the optimized loop, one of which assumes that it is positive and the other that it is negative. While this may not seem profitable, it can be a big win on parallel or vector hardware if it allows more parallelism or vectorization to be achieved. Alternatively, we can simply split the loop-closing code to test the sign and then branch to the appropriate one of two loop-closing tests.

If the relation computation involves two induction variables, e.g., $i1 ? i2$, both of which are used only in computations of other induction variables and relations, the transformation is somewhat more complex. If there are induction variables $j1$ and $j2$ with linear equations $j1 = b * i1 + c$ and $j2 = b * i2 + c$, respectively, then we can

```
procedure Remove_IVs_LFTR(bset,nblocks,ninsts,Block,IVs,
   SRdone,Succ,Pred)
   bset: in set of integer
   nblocks: inout integer
   ninsts: inout array [1··nblocks] of integer
   Block: inout array [1··nblocks] of array [··] of MIRInst
   IVs: in set of IVrecord
   SRdone: in array [1··nblocks] of array [··] of boolean
   Succ, Pred: inout integer ⟶ set of integer
begin
   op1t, op2t: enum {con,ind,var}
   iv1, iv2: IVrecord
   i, j: integer
   v, tj: Var
   inst: MIRInst
   oper: Operator
   for each iv1 ∈ IVs (SRdone[iv1.blk][iv1.pos]) do
      for each iv2 ∈ IVs (!SRdone[iv2.blk][iv2.pos]
         & iv1.biv = iv2.biv & iv1.fctr = iv2.fctr
         & iv1.diff = iv2.diff) do
         || if iv1 and iv2 have matching equations and iv1
         || has been strength-reduced and iv2 has not,
         || replaces uses of iv2 by uses of iv1
         for each i ∈ bset do
            for j := 1 to ninsts[i] do
               Replace_Uses(i,j,Block,iv1,iv2)
            od
         od
      od
   od
```

FIG. 14.22 Code to implement removal of induction variables and linear-function test replacement.

simply replace $i1 ? i2$ by $j1 ? j2$, again assuming that b is positive. If there are no such induction variables $j1$ and $j2$ with the same b and c values, the replacement is generally not worth doing, since it may introduce two multiplications and an addition to the loop in place of less expensive operations.

ICAN code that implements the above is shown in Figure 14.22. It uses several functions, as follows:

1. insert_before(i,j,ninsts,Block,*inst*) inserts instruction *inst* immediately before Block[i][j] and adjusts the data structures accordingly (see Figure 4.14).

2. delete_inst(i,j,nblocks,ninsts,Block,Succ,Pred) deletes the jth instruction in Block[i] and adjusts the data structures accordingly (see Figure 4.15).

3. Replace_Uses(i,j,Block,$iv1,iv2$) replaces all uses of $iv1$.tiv by $iv2$.tiv in the instruction Block[i][j].

```
for each i ∈ bset do
    for j := 1 to ninsts[i] do
        if Has_Left(Block[i][j].kind) & SRdone[i][j] then
            if Live_on_Exit(inst.left,bset,Block) then
                || if result variable is live at some exit from the loop,
                || compute its final value, assign it to result variable
                || at loop exits
                v := Final_Value(inst.left,bset,Block)
                Insert_Exits(bset,Block,⟨kind:valasgn,
                    left:inst.left,opd:⟨kind:const,val:v⟩⟩)
            fi
            || delete instruction Block[i][j] and renumber the tuples
            || in IVs to reflect the deletion
            delete_inst(i,j,nblocks,ninsts,Block,Succ,Pred)
            IVs -= {iv1}
            for each iv2 ∈ IVs do
                if iv2.blk = i & iv2.pos > j then
                    IVs := (IVs - {iv2})
                        ∪ {⟨tiv:iv2.tiv,blk:i,pos:iv2.pos-1,
                        fctr:iv2.fctr,biv:iv2.biv,diff:iv2.diff⟩}
                fi
            od
        fi
    od
od
od
```

                                                                    (continued)

FIG. 14.22 *(continued)*

4. Has_Left(*kd*) returns true if a MIR instruction of kind *kd* has a left-hand side, and false otherwise (see Figure 4.8).

5. Canonicalize(*inst*,*t1*,*t2*), given a MIR instruction *inst* containing a binary relational expression, orders the operands so that (a) if either operand is a constant, it becomes the first operand, and (b) failing that, if either operand is an induction variable, it becomes the first operand; it inverts the operator if it has reordered the operands; and it sets *t1* and *t2* to con, ind, or var, according to whether, after canonicalization, the first operand or second operand, respectively, is a constant, an induction variable, or a variable that is not an induction variable, respectively.

6. Eval_RelExpr(*opd1*,*opr*,*opd2*) evaluates the relational expression *opd1 opr opd2* and returns the expression's value (true or false).

7. BIV(*v*,*IVs*) returns true if *v* occurs as a basic induction variable in the set *IVs* of induction-variable records, and false otherwise.

8. Live_on_Exit(*v*,*bset*,Block) returns true if variable *v* is live at some exit from the loop whose body is the set of blocks given by *bset*, and false otherwise (this

```
for each i ∈ bset do
    j := ninsts[i]
    inst := Block[i][j]
    if inst.kind ≠ binif then
        goto L1
    fi
    || perform linear-function test replacement
    Canonicalize(inst,op1t,op2t)
    if op1t = con then
        if op2t = con & Eval_RelExpr(inst.opd1,inst.opr,inst.opd2) then
            || if both operands are constants and the relation is true,
            || replace by goto
            Block[i][j] := ⟨kind:goto,lbl:inst.lbl⟩
        elif op2t = ind then
            || if one operand is a constant and the other is an induction
            || variable, replace by a conditional branch based on a
            || different induction variable, if possible
            if ∃iv1 ∈ IVs (inst.opd2.val = iv1.tiv & iv1.tiv = iv1.biv) then
                if ∃iv2 ∈ IVs (iv2.biv = iv1.biv
                    & iv2.tiv ≠ iv1.tiv) then
                    tj := new_tmp( )
                    insert_before(i,j,ninsts,Block,⟨kind:binasgn,left:tj,opr:mul,
                        opd1:⟨kind:const,val:iv2.fctr⟩,opd2:inst.opd1⟩)
                    insert_before(i,j,ninsts,Block,
                        ⟨kind:binasgn,left:tj,opr:add,
                        opd1:⟨kind:const,val:iv2.diff⟩,opd2:⟨kind:var,val:tj⟩⟩)
                    oper := inst.opr
                    || if new induction variable runs in the opposite direction
                    || from the original one, invert the test
                    if iv2.fctr < 0 then
                        oper := Invert(oper)
                    fi
                    Block[i][j] := ⟨kind:binif,opr:oper,
                        opd1:⟨kind:var,val:tj⟩,
                        opd2:⟨kind:var,val:iv2.tiv⟩,lbl:inst.lbl⟩
                fi
            fi
        fi
    fi
```

FIG. 14.22 *(continued)*

property is computed by performing the live variables data-flow analysis described in the preceding section).

9. Final_Value(v, *bset*, Block) returns the final value of variable v on exit from the loop whose body is the set of blocks given by *bset*.

```
          if op1t = ind then
             if op2t = ind then
                if ∃iv1,iv2 ∈ IVs (iv1 ≠ iv2 & iv1.biv = inst.opd1.val
                      & iv2.biv = inst.opd2.val & iv1.fctr = iv2.fctr
                      & iv1.diff = iv2.diff)
                   then
                   || if both operands are induction variables,...
                   oper := inst.opr
                   if iv2.fctr < 0 then
                      oper := Invert(oper)
                   fi
                   Block[i][j] := ⟨kind:binif,opr:oper,
                      op1:⟨kind:var,val:iv1.tiv⟩,
                      op2:⟨kind:var,val:iv2.tiv⟩,lbl:inst.lbl⟩
                fi
             elif op2t = var & BIV(inst.opd1.val,IVs)
                   & ∃iv1 ∈ IVs (iv1.biv = inst.opd1.val
                   & iv1.tiv ≠ iv1.biv) then
                tj := new_tmp( )
                insert_before(i,j,ninsts,Block,
                   ⟨kind:binasgn,left:tj,opr:mul,
                   opd1:⟨kind:const,val:iv1.fctr⟩,opd2:inst.opd2⟩)
                insert_before(i,j,ninsts,Block,
                   ⟨kind:binasgn,left:tj,opr:add,
                   opd1:⟨kind:const,val:iv1.diff⟩,opd2:⟨kind:var,val:tj⟩⟩)
                oper := inst.opr
                if iv1.fctr < 0 then
                   oper := Invert(oper)
                fi
                Block[i][j] := ⟨kind:binif,opr:oper,
                   opd1:⟨kind:var,val:iv1.tiv⟩,
                   opd2:⟨kind:var,val:tj⟩,lbl:inst.lbl⟩
             fi
          fi
      od
   end       || Remove_IVs_LFTR
```

FIG. 14.22 *(continued)*

10. Insert_Exits(*bset*,Block,*inst*) inserts the MIR instruction *inst* just after each exit from the loop.

11. Invert(*opr*) returns the inverse of the MIR relational operator *opr*, e.g., for ">" it returns "<=".

12. new_tmp( ) returns a new temporary name.

Note that a more efficient implementation of the nested for loop over the instructions at the end of Remove_IVs_LFTR( ) would keep a table describing the instructions to be removed and would use only a single for loop.

14.2   Unnecessary Bounds-Checking Elimination

Bounds checking or *range checking* refers to determining whether the value of a variable is within specified bounds in all of its uses in a program. A typical situation is checking that in the reference b[i,j] to an element of a Pascal array declared

```
var b: array[1..100,1..10] of integer
```

i is indeed between 1 and 100 and j is between 1 and 10, inclusive. Another example is checking that a use of a variable declared to be of an Ada subrange type, for example,

```
subtype TEMPERATURE is INTEGER range 32..212;
i: TEMPERATURE;
```

is within the declared range.

We mention Pascal and Ada in the two examples above because their language definitions specifically require that such checking be done (or, equivalently, that the language implementation ensure in some fashion that the specified constraints are satisfied). Such checking, however, is desirable for any program, regardless of the language it is written in, since bounds violations are among the most common programming errors. "Off-by-one" errors, in which a loop index or other counter runs off one end or the other of a range by one—usually resulting in accessing or storing into a datum that is not part of the data structure being processed—are.

On the other hand, bounds checking can be very expensive if, for example, every array access must be accompanied by two conditional traps[2] per dimension to determine the validity of the access, as illustrated in Figure 14.23, where we assume that trap number 6 is for bounds violation. Here the array access takes eight lines of MIR code and the checking takes an additional four lines. The overhead of such checking becomes even greater when the array accesses are optimized—then fetching the next element of a two-dimensional array may require one or two increments and a load, while the bounds checking still requires four conditional traps. Many implementations "solve" this problem, particularly for Pascal, by providing the user with a compile-time option to enable or disable the checking. The philosophical purpose of this option is to allow the user to enable the checking for development and debugging runs of the program, and then, once all the defects have been found and fixed, to turn it off for the production version. Thus the overhead is incurred while the program is still buggy, and not once it is (believed to be) free of defects.

However, virtually all software-engineering studies of defects in programs indicate that versions of systems delivered to customers are likely to have bugs in them and many of the bugs are likely to be ones that were not even observed during pre-delivery testing. This approach to bounds checking, therefore, is seriously mistaken. Rather, bounds checking is just as important for delivered versions of programs as

---

2. The if ... trap construct might be implemented by a conditional branch or a conditional trap, depending on the architecture, source language, and language implementation.

```
if 1 > i trap 6
if i > 100 trap 6
if 1 > j trap 6
if j > 10 trap 6

t2 ← addr b
t3 ← j - 1
t3 ← t3 * 100
t3 ← t3 + i
t3 ← t3 - 1
t3 ← t3 * 4
t3 ← t2 + t3
t4 ← *t3
```

FIG. 14.23 Example of MIR bounds-checking code for accessing the array element b[i,j] in Pascal.

```
var b: array[1..100,1..10] of integer;
    i, j, s: integer;
s := 0;
for i = 1 to 50 do
   for j = 1 to 10 do
      s := s + b[i,j]
```

FIG. 14.24 Pascal example in which no bounds-checking code is needed for accessing b[i,j].

for development versions. Instead of providing a way to turn bounds checking off, what is needed is to optimize it so that it rarely costs anything and has minimal overall cost. For example, if our fetching of b[i,j] in Figure 14.23 is embedded in a loop nest that prescribes the ranges of the subscripts and restricts them to legal values, as in Figure 14.24, then the checking code is totally unnecessary. As a second example, if the upper bound on the outer loop were changed to a variable n, rather than the constant 50, we would only need to check once before entering the outer loop that n <= 100 is satisfied and take the trap then if it isn't.[3]

Such optimization is relatively easy, and for many programs in some languages, it is nearly trivial. In fact, we have most of the required methods for it available already, namely, invariant code motion, common-subexpression elimination, and induction-variable transformations. The one remaining tool we need is a way to represent the bounds-checking constraints that must be satisfied. To do this, we

---

3. Note that we assume that the trap terminates execution of the program or, at least, that it cannot result in resumption of execution at the point where the trap occurs. This is essential because bounds-checking code that we cannot eliminate entirely we (wherever possible) move out of loops containing it. Thus, the trap would not occur at the same point in execution of the program as it would have originally, although we ensure that it occurs if and only if it would have occurred in the unmodified program.

introduce range expressions. A *range expression* is an inequality that applies to the value of a variable. Its form is

lo ? var ? hi

where var is a variable name, lo and hi are constants representing the minimal and maximal values (respectively) of the range, and ? is a relational operator. If the variable's value is constrained at only one end, we use ∞ or $-\infty$ to represent the other bound.

For example, for the code in Figure 14.24, the two range expressions we must satisfy for the statement `s := s + b[i,j]` to require no run-time checks are $1 \le i \le 100$ and $1 \le j \le 10$, as required by the declaration of array `b`. To determine that these range expressions are satisfied for this statement, we only need to be able to deduce from the first `for` statement that $1 \le i \le 100$ holds within it and from the second that $1 \le j \le 10$ holds within it. This is trivial in Pascal, since the two `for` statements respectively establish the inequalities as valid, and the semantics of the language require that the iteration variable not be modified in a `for` loop, except by the `for` statement itself. For other languages, it may not be so easy—C, for example, places no restrictions on the expressions that may occur in its `for` loop construct, nor does it even have a concept of an iteration variable.

The simplest and by far the most common case of optimizable range-checking code is a range check embedded in a loop, such as the example in Figure 14.24 above. For concreteness, we assume the following:

1. that the loop has an iteration variable i with an initial value of *init* and a final value of *fin*,

2. that i increases by 1 on each iteration, and

3. that only the loop-control code modifies i.

We further assume that the range expression to be satisfied is $lo \le v \le hi$.

The easiest case to handle is that v is loop-invariant. In this case, we need only move the code that checks that $lo \le v \le hi$ from inside the loop to the loop's preheader. Of course, if it can be evaluated at compile time, we do that.

The next case is that the range expression to be satisfied is $lo \le i \le hi$, where i is the loop-control variable. In this case, the range expression is satisfied as long as $lo \le init$ and $fin \le hi$. We insert code to check the first of these inequalities into the loop's preheader. We also insert code there to compute $t1 = \min(fin, hi)$ and replace the loop-closing test that compares i to *fin* by one that compares it to $t1$. Following the normal exit from the loop, we insert code to check that the final value of i has reached the value it would have reached before the transformation, i.e., we insert a check that $i > fin$. If any of the checks fail, a trap is taken. Again, of course, if the checks can be evaluated at compile time, they are. An example of the code before and after the transformation is shown in Figure 14.25.

The last case we consider is that an induction variable j (see Section 14.1) in the class of the basic induction variable i with linear equation $j = b * i + c$ must satisfy

```
                                              if lo > init trap 6
                                              t1 ← fin min hi
        i ← init                        L2:  i ← init
L1:  . . .                              L1:  . . .
        if i < lo trap 6
        if i > hi trap 6
        use of i that must                    use of i that must
            satisfy lo ≤ i ≤ hi                   satisfy lo ≤ i ≤ hi

        . . .                                 . . .
        i ← i + 1                             i ← i + 1
        if i <= fin goto L1                   if i <= t1 goto L1
                                              if i <= fin trap 6
```

(a)   (b)

FIG. 14.25 Bounds-checking transformation: (a) the original loop, and (b) the transformed code.

the range expression $lo \le j \le hi$. In this case, we have $j = b * i + c$, and so i must satisfy

$$(lo - c)/b \le i \le (hi - c)/b$$

for j to satisfy its range expression. The appropriate transformation is an easy generalization of the preceding case.

The second and third assumptions above, namely, that i increases by 1 on each iteration and that only the loop-control code modifies i, can both be relaxed to allow decreasing loop indexes, increments and decrements by values other than 1, and simple modifications of i within the loop. We leave these for the reader to consider.

It is also possible to do data-flow analysis that propagates range expressions through a procedure to determine where they are satisfied and where checking is needed. However, this can be very expensive, since the lattice used includes all range expressions $lo \le v \le hi$ for $lo, hi \in \mathbf{Z} \cup \{-\infty, \infty\}$ with the ordering

$$(lo1 \le v \le hi1) \sqsubseteq (lo2 \le v \le hi2)$$

if and only if $lo1 \le lo2$ and $hi1 \ge hi2$—a lattice that is both infinitely wide and infinitely high. At least, if we begin with a range expression $lo \le v \le hi$ with finite lo and hi values, it has only finite (but unbounded) chains ascending from there.

14.3   Wrap-Up

The optimizations we have discussed in this chapter either operate exclusively on loops or are most effective when applied to loops. They can be done on either medium-level or low-level intermediate code. They apply directly to the disciplined source-language loop constructs in Fortran, Ada, and Pascal, but they require that we define a subclass of similarly behaved loops in a language like C (or those that are constructed from ifs and gotos in any language) for them to be safely employed.

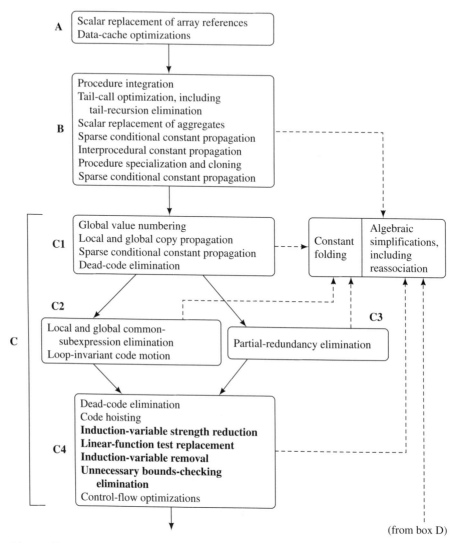

FIG. 14.26 Place of loop optimizations (in **bold** type) in an aggressive optimizing compiler.

We have covered two classes of optimizations, namely, induction-variable optimizations and unnecessary bounds-checking elimination. Figure 14.26 shows in **bold** type where we place the optimizations discussed in this chapter in the overall structure of the optimization process.

Induction-variable optimization requires that we first identify induction variables in a loop, then perform strength reduction on them, and finally perform linear-function test replacement and remove redundant induction variables. We perform this series of optimizations on nested loops starting with the most deeply nested ones and then moving outward.

Elimination of unnecessary bounds checking is an optimization that applies both inside and outside loops but that has its biggest impact inside loops, because bounds

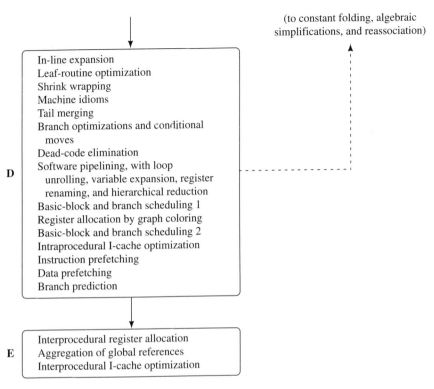

(to constant folding, algebraic
simplifications, and reassociation)

D
In-line expansion
Leaf-routine optimization
Shrink wrapping
Machine idioms
Tail merging
Branch optimizations and conditional
   moves
Dead-code elimination
Software pipelining, with loop
   unrolling, variable expansion, register
   renaming, and hierarchical reduction
Basic-block and branch scheduling 1
Register allocation by graph coloring
Basic-block and branch scheduling 2
Intraprocedural I-cache optimization
Instruction prefetching
Data prefetching
Branch prediction

E
Interprocedural register allocation
Aggregation of global references
Interprocedural I-cache optimization

FIG. 14.26 *(continued)*

checks inside loops are performed with each iteration unless they are optimized away
or at least reduced.

14.4   Further Reading

The foundation of the application of finite differences to computer programs is due
to Babbage, as described in [Gold72]. Allen and Cocke's application of strength reduction to operations other than additions and multiplications appears in [AllC81].
The generalization of finite differences, called formal differentiation, and its application to the very high level language SETL are discussed by Paige and Schwartz
[PaiS77]. Chow [Chow83] and Knoop, Rüthing, and Steffen [KnoR93] extend
partial-redundancy elimination to include a weak form of strength reduction.

Cooper and Simpson's approach to SSA-based strength reduction is described
in [CooS95a] and [Simp96].

More modern approaches to bounds-checking optimization are found in, e.g.,
Gupta [Gupt93] and Kolte and Wolfe [KolW95], the latter of which uses partial-
redundancy elimination to determine the most efficient places to move bounds
checks to.

14.5   Exercises

14.1   As indicated at the end of Section 14.1, instructions that perform a storage access in which one of the operands is scaled or modified or that perform an arithmetic operation, a test, and a conditional branch based on the test may be useful in guiding strength reduction, induction-variable removal, and linear-function test replacement. (See Figure 14.27 for an example.) (a) How would you decide which of these instructions to use? (b) At what point in the optimization and code-generation process would you make the decision?

14.2   Formulate identification of induction variables as a data-flow analysis and apply it to the example in Figure 14.9.

14.3   As written, the ICAN code in Figure 14.10 always introduces the new temporary that is the value of db and initializes it in the loop's preheader. (a) Modify the code so that it doesn't do this when it's not needed. What about the instructions that assign the initial value of the variable that is tj's value? (b) Note that there are also situations, such as the induction variable t14 in Figure 14.9, for which either the factor (fctr) or the difference (diff) is not simply a constant or variable that can be used as is in performing strength reduction. Modify the code to recognize such situations and to handle them properly.

14.4   Write an ICAN routine to do elimination of unnecessary bounds checking.

14.5   Generalize the transformation of bounds checking discussed in Section 14.2 to encompass (a) checking induction variables and (b) more general modifications of the loop index, as discussed near the end of the section. Add the appropriate code to the routine written for Exercise 14.4.

14.6   Extend the linear-function test replacement part of the algorithm in Figure 14.22 to deal with loop constants that are not compile-time constants.

14.7   Continue the example in Figure 14.9 by replacing blocks B3, B4, and B5 by the ones in Figure 14.17 and then doing (a) induction-variable removal and linear-function test replacement on the inner loop and (b) doing the full sequence of induction-variable optimizations on the outer loop.

RSCH 14.8   Read one of [Gupt93] or [KolW95] and write ICAN code to implement its approach to bounds checking.

```
        i ← 1
L1:  r1 ← 4 * i
        r2 ← (addr a) + r1
        r3 ← [r2](4)
        r3 ← r3 + 2
        [r2](4) ← r3
        i ← i + 1
        if i ≤ 20 goto L1
```

FIG. 14.27   Example of a LIR loop for which address scaling, address modification, and operation-test-and-branch instructions might all be useful.

CHAPTER 15

Procedure Optimizations

In this chapter, we discuss three pairs of optimizations that apply to whole procedures and that, in all cases but one, do not require data-flow analysis to be effective. The pairs of optimizations are tail-recursion elimination and the more general tail-call optimization, procedure integration and in-line expansion, and leaf-routine optimization and shrink wrapping. The first pair turns calls into branches. The second pair is two versions of the same optimization, the first applied to mid- or high-level intermediate code and the second to low-level code. The final pair optimizes the calling conventions used in a language implementation.

15.1 Tail-Call Optimization and Tail-Recursion Elimination

Tail-call optimization and its special case, tail-recursion elimination, are transformations that apply to calls. They often reduce or eliminate a significant amount of procedure-call overhead and, in the case of tail-recursion elimination, enable loop optimizations that would otherwise not apply.

A call from procedure f( ) to procedure g( ) is a *tail call* if the only thing f( ) does, after g( ) returns to it, is itself return. The call is *tail-recursive* if f( ) and g( ) are the same procedure. For example, the call to insert_node( ) in the C code in Figure 15.1 is tail-recursive, and the call to make_node( ) is a (nonrecursive) tail call.

Tail-recursion elimination has the effect of compiling insert_node( ) as if it were written as shown in Figure 15.2, turning the recursion into a loop.

We cannot demonstrate the effect of tail-call optimization at the source-language level, since it would violate C's semantics (as well as the semantics of virtually any other higher-level language) to branch from the body of one procedure into the body of another, but it can be thought of in a similar way: the arguments to make_node( )

461

```
void make_node(p,n)
   struct node *p;
   int n;
{  struct node *q;
   q = malloc(sizeof(struct node));
   q->next = nil;
   q->value = n;
   p->next = q;
}

void insert_node(n,l)
   int n;
   struct node *l;
{  if (n > l->value)
      if (l->next == nil) make_node(l,n);
      else insert_node(n,l->next);
}
```

FIG. 15.1 Example of a tail call and tail recursion in C.

```
void insert_node(n,l)
   int n;
   struct node *l;
{loop:
   if (n > l->value)
      if (l->next == nil) make_node(l,n);
      else
      {  l := l->next;
         goto loop;
      }
}
```

FIG. 15.2 Effect of tail-recursion elimination on `insert_node( )` shown in the source code.

are put on the stack (or in the appropriate reegisters) in place of `insert_node( )`'s arguments and the call instruction is replaced by a branch to the beginning of `make_node( )`'s body.

This would also violate the semantics of MIR, since parameter names are local to procedures. However, we can demonstrate it in LIR. LIR code corresponding to Figure 15.1 is shown in Figure 15.3(a); we arbitrarily choose for this example to pass the parameters in registers r1 and r2. The result of optimizing the tail call to `make_node( )` is shown in Figure 15.3(b). Even this version hides one subtle issue, since we have not made memory stacks explicit in it. Namely, it is possible that the stack frame of the caller and callee have different sizes. If the caller's stack frame is larger than the callee's, we merely need to arrange that the callee's procedure epilogue (see Section 5.6) deallocates the caller's whole stack frame. This can most easily be arranged by having a frame pointer that is the caller's stack pointer (or, in this case, the caller's caller's stack pointer) and then recovering the stack pointer by assigning the frame pointer to it on exit, as, for example, Sun's SPARC compilers

```
make_node:                        make_node:
    r4 ← r1                           r4 ← r1
    r1 ← 8                            r1 ← 8
    r3 ← call malloc                 r3 ← call malloc
    r3 *. next ← nil                 r3 *. next ← nil
    r3 *. value ←- r2               r3 *. value ← r2
    r4 *. next ← r3                  r4 *. next ← r3
    return                           return
insert_node:                      insert_node:
    r4 ← r2 *. value                r4 ← r2 *. value
    r5 ← r1 > r4                     r5 ← r1 > r4
    if !r5 goto L1                   if !r5 goto L1
    r6 ← r2 *. next                  r6 ← r2 *. next
    r7 ← r6 = nil                    r7 ← r6 = nil
    if !r7 goto L2                   if !r7 goto L2
    r2 ← r1                          r2 ← r1
    r1 ← r4                          r1 ← ← r4
    call make_node                   goto make_node
    return
L2: r2 ← r2 *. next               L2: r2 ← r2 *. next
    call insert_node                 goto insert_node
    return
L1: return                        L1: return
(a)                               (b)
```

FIG. 15.3 (a) LIR code corresponding to Figure 15.1, and (b) the result of performing tail-call optimization on both calls in insert_node( ).

do (Section 21.1). If the caller's stack frame is smaller than the callee's, we need to arrange to allocate the remainder of the callee's stack frame either before entering or on entry to the callee, or we need to deallocate the caller's stack frame before jumping to the callee and then do the standard procedure prologue on entering the callee.

Determining that a call is a tail call is trivial. It only requires checking that the routine performing the call does nothing after the call returns except itself return, possibly returning a value in the process. Performing tail-recursion elimination is straightforward. As shown in our example above, it can usually even be done in the source code. All it requires is replacing the recursive call by assigning the proper values to the parameters, followed by a branch to the beginning of the body of the procedure and deleting the return that previously followed the recursive call. Figure 15.4 gives ICAN code to perform tail-recursion elimination on a MIR procedure.

Performing general tail-call optimization requires more work. First we must ensure that both procedure bodies are visible to the compiler at once, or, at least, that enough information about the callee is available during compilation of the caller to make the transformation possible. We may have both procedure bodies visible either because they are in the same compilation unit or because the compiling system has the option of saving intermediate-code representations of procedures, as the MIPS

```
procedure Tail_Recur_Elim(ProcName,nblocks,ninsts,Block,en,Succ)
   ProcName: in Procedure
   nblocks, en: in integer
   ninsts: inout array [1··nblocks] of integer
   Block: inout array [1··nblocks] of array [··] of MIRInst
   Succ: in integer ⟶ set of integer
begin
   i, j, b := ◆Succ(en): integer
   lj: Label
   inst: MIRInst
   || make sure there's a label at the beginning of the procedure's body
   if Block[b][1].kind = label then
      lj := Block[b][1].lbl
   else
      lj := new_label( )
      insert_before(b,1,ninsts,Block,⟨kind:label,lbl:lj⟩)
   fi
   for i := 1 to nblocks do
      inst := Block[i][ninsts[i]-1]
      if (inst.kind = callasgn & inst.proc = ProcName
         & Block[i][ninsts[i]].kind = retval)
         V (inst.kind = call & inst.proc = ProcName
         & Block[i][ninsts[i]].kind = return) then
         || turn tail call into parameter assignments
         || and branch to label of first block
         for j := 1 to |inst.args| do
            Block[i][ninsts[i]+j-2] := ⟨kind:valasgn,
               left:Block[b][j].left,
               opd:Block[i][ninsts[i]-1].args↓j@1⟩
         od
         ninsts[i] += |inst.args| + 1
         Block[i][ninsts[i]] := ⟨kind:goto,lbl:lj⟩
      fi
   od
end     || Tail_Recur_Elim
```

FIG. 15.4 ICAN code to perform tail-recursion elimination.

compilers do. However, all we really need to know about the callee is three things, as follows:

1. where it expects to find its parameters,

2. where to branch to in order to begin executing its body, and

3. how large its stack frame is.

This information could be saved in a form that stores only representations of procedure interfaces, rather than their bodies. If only interfaces are available, we may not be able to perform the transformation if the caller's stack frame is larger than the callee's—this depends on the convention used for allocating and deallocating stack frames (see Section 5.4).

To perform the optimization, we replace the call by three things, as follows:

1. evaluation of the arguments of the tail call and putting them where the callee expects to find them;

2. if the callee's stack frame is larger than the caller's, an instruction that extends the stack frame by the difference between the two; and

3. a branch to the beginning of the body of the callee.

One issue in performing tail-call optimization is the addressing modes and spans of call and branch instructions in each architecture. In Alpha, for example, there is no problem since the jmp and jsr routines both use the contents of a register as the target and differ only in whether the return address is saved or discarded. Similarly in the MIPS architectures, jal and j both take a 26-bit absolute word target address. In SPARC, on the other hand, call takes a 30-bit PC-relative word displacement, while ba takes a 22-bit PC-relative word displacement and jmpl takes a 32-bit absolute byte address computed as the sum of two registers. While the first and second present no difficulties in turning the call into a branch, the last requires that we materialize the target address in a register.

15.2   Procedure Integration

Procedure integration, also called *automatic inlining,* replaces calls to procedures with copies of their bodies. It can be a very useful optimization, because it changes calls from opaque objects that may have unknown effects on aliased variables and parameters to local code that not only exposes its effects (see also Chapter 19) but that can be optimized as part of the calling procedure.

Some languages provide the programmer with a degree of control over inlining. C++, for example, provides an explicit inline attribute that may be specified for a procedure. Ada provides a similar facility. Both are characteristics of the procedure, not of the call site. While this is a desirable option to provide, it is significantly less powerful and discriminating than automatic procedure integration can be. An automatic procedure integrator can differentiate among call sites and can select the procedures to integrate according to machine-specific and performance-related criteria, rather than by depending on the user's intuition.

The opportunity to optimize inlined procedure bodies can be especially valuable if it enables loop transformations that were originally inhibited by having procedure calls embedded in loops or if it turns a loop that calls a procedure, whose body is itself a loop, into a nested loop. The classic example of this situation is the saxpy( ) procedure in Linpack, shown with its calling context in Figure 15.5. After substituting the body of saxpy( ) in place of the call to it in sgefa( ) and renaming the labels and the variable n so they don't conflict, the result easily simplifies to the nested loop shown in Figure 15.6. The result is a doubly nested loop to which a series of valuable optimizations can be applied.

```
      subroutine sgefa(a,lda,n,ipvt,info)
      integer lda,n,ipvt(1),info
      real a(lda,1)
      real t
      integer isamax,j,k,kp1,l,nm1
          . . .
          do 30 j = kp1, n
             t = a(l,j)
             if (l .eq. k) go to 20
                a(l,j) = a(k,j)
                a(k,j) = t
20           continue
             call saxpy(n-k,t,a(k+1,k),1,a(k+1,j),1)
30        continue
          . . .
      subroutine saxpy(n,da,dx,incx,dy,incy)
      real dx(1),dy(1),da
      integer i,incx,incy,ix,iy,m,mp1,n
      if (n .le. 0) return
      if (da .eq. ZERO) return
      if (incx .eq. 1 .and. incy .eq. 1) go to 20
      ix = 1
      iy = 1
      if (incx .lt. 0) ix = (-n+1)*incx + 1
      if (incy .lt. 0) iy = (-n+1)*incy + 1
      do 10 i = 1,n
         dy(iy) = dy(iy) + da*dx(ix)
         ix = ix + incx
         iy = iy + incy
10 continue
   return
20 continue
   do 30 i = 1,n
      dy(i) = dy(i) + da*dx(i)
30 continue
   return
   end
```

FIG. 15.5 The Linpack routine saxpy( ) and its calling context in sgefa( ).

There are several issues to consider in deciding how broadly procedure integration is to be provided in a compiling system and, based on deciding these issues, how to implement it. First, is it to be provided across multiple compilation units, or only within single ones? If the former, then a way needs to be provided to save the intermediate-code representations of procedures, or more likely, whole compilation units in files, since one does not generally depend on the compiler user to decide what procedures to inline. If the latter, then one does not need this facility—one needs only to be able to preserve the intermediate code as long as it is needed within

```
subroutine sgefa(a,lda,n,ipvt,info)
integer lda,n,ipvt(1),info
real a(lda,1)
real t
integer isamax,j,k,kp1,l,nm1
    . .
      do 30 j = kp1, n
         t = a(l,j)
         if (l .eq. k) go to 20
            a(l,j) = a(k,j)
            a(k,j) = t
20       continue
         if (n-k .le. 0) goto 30
         if (t .eq. 0) goto 30
         do 40 i = 1,n-k
            a(k+i,j) = a(k+i,j) + t*a(k+i,k)
40       continue
30    continue
    . . .
```

FIG. 15.6 A fragment of the Linpack routine sgefa( ) after integrating saxpy( ) into it.

a single compilation to do the appropriate inlinings. In fact, one might even choose to do it in source-code form in the latter case.

Second, if one is providing procedure integration across compilation units, then one needs to decide whether to require that the caller and the callee be written in the same language or whether to allow them to be in different languages. The primary consideration here is that different languages have different conventions for passing parameters and accessing nonlocal variables, and the conventions, of course, need to be respected by inlined procedures. One technique for handling the differences in parameter-passing conventions is to provide "external *language_name proce-dure_name*" declarations as parts of the interfaces to separately compiled procedures in the source languages, so as to specify the source languages in which the external procedures are written. These would result in calls to an external routine that follow the parameter-passing conventions of the language the routine is declared to be written in.

Third, in a cross-compilation-unit procedure integrator, there is the question of whether there is any need to keep intermediate-code copies of routines that have been inlined. In particular, several languages restrict the visibility of procedures to the scopes they are nested in. This is the case, for example, for nested procedures in Pascal, for non-interface procedures in the Modula language family and Mesa, for statement procedures in Fortran 77, and for procedures that are not declared external in Fortran 90. If the only goal of saving intermediate code is to perform procedure integration, copies of such procedures clearly do not need to be kept in the saved intermediate code for a compilation unit, since they cannot be referenced from outside their scopes. On the other hand, if the goal of saving intermediate code is to reduce recompilation time in a programming environment after a change has been made to the source code, it is clearly desirable to keep them.

Fourth, given that one has inlined a procedure at all visible call sites, is there a need to compile a copy of the whole procedure? There may be if the procedure's address has been taken in C or if it may be called from other compilation units that are not currently visible.

Finally, should one perform any inlining on recursive procedures? Obviously, one should not inline them until one runs out of calls to them, because that could be an infinite process, but it can be valuable to inline a recursive procedure once or twice to reduce the overhead of calling it.

Several policy questions need to be answered to decide what procedures are worth inlining, keeping in mind that our goal is to speed up execution. On the face of it, it may seem that inlining every procedure at every call site would result in the greatest speedup. However, this is generally not the case, because it may result in an arbitrary increase in the size of the object code and may cause compilation to be terminated only by exhaustion of resources. This is not to suggest that inlining recursive procedures is necessarily bad; rather, one must simply know when it is desirable and when to stop.

Increasing the size of the object code has several potential drawbacks, the most important of which is its impact on cache misses. As the speeds of processors and memories diverge ever further, cache misses become more and more important as determiners of overall performance. Thus, decisions as to what procedures to inline need to be based either on heuristics or profiling feedback. Some typical heuristics take into account the following:

1. the size of the procedure body (the smaller the better),

2. how many calls there are to the procedure (if there is only one call, inlining it should almost always result in reducing execution time),

3. whether the procedure is called inside a loop (if so, it is more likely to provide significant opportunities for other optimizations), and

4. whether a particular call includes one or more constant-valued parameters (if so, the inlined procedure body is more likely to be optimizable than if not).

Once one has selected criteria for deciding what procedures are worth inlining at what call sites, there remains the issue of how to perform the inlining. The obvious part of the process is replacing a call with a copy of the corresponding procedure body. We assume, for the sake of generality, that we are doing so at the intermediate-code level, so we can do cross-language inlining. The three major issues that arise are (1) satisfying the parameter-passing conventions of the (possibly two) languages involved, (2) handling name conflicts between the caller and the callee, and (3) dealing with static variables.

First, if "external *language_name procedure_name*" declarations are not provided, the procedure integrator must include sufficient knowledge about the parameter-passing mechanisms of the languages involved to determine what combinations work and how to make them work. It must not, for example, match a call-by-reference Fortran argument with a call-by-value C parameter, unless the C parameter is of a pointer type. Similarly, it must not blithely substitute a caller's

```
g(b,c)
int b, c;
{   int a, d;
    a = b + c;
    d = b * c;
    return d;                        f( )
}                                    {   int a, e, d;
f( )                                     a = 2;
{   int a, e;                            a = 3 + 4;
    a = 2;                               d = 3 * 4;
    e = g(3,4);                          e = d;
    printf("%d\n",a);                    printf("%d\n",a);
}                                    }
(a)                                  (b)
```

FIG. 15.7 Capture of a caller's variable in C by a call-by-value parameter that results from simply substituting the callee's text for a call.

variable name for a call-by-value parameter, as illustrated in Figure 15.7, resulting in a spurious assignment to the caller's variable. The variable a occurs in both f( ) and g( ); substituting the text of g( ) directly for the call to it results in erroneously assigning to the caller's a.

The second problem is usually not an issue if one is working in an intermediate code that does not include source symbol names—symbol references are usually pointers to symbol-table entries and labels are usually pointers to intermediate-code locations. If one is working on a character representation, one must detect name conflicts and resolve them by renaming, usually in the body of the called procedure.

Static variables present a different sort of problem. In C in particular, a variable with static storage class has an extent that lasts through execution of the whole program. If it is declared with file-level scope, i.e., not within any function definition, it is initialized before execution of the program and is visible within all functions in the file that do not redeclare the variable. If, on the other hand, it is declared within a function, it is visible only within that function. If several functions declare static local variables with the same name, they are distinct objects.

Thus, for a file-level static variable, there needs to be only one copy of it in the resulting object program and, if it is initialized, it needs to be initialized exactly once. This can be handled by making the variable have global scope and by providing a global initialization for it.

Cooper, Hall, and Torczon [CooH92] report a cautionary tale on the effects of procedure integration. They did an experiment in which they integrated 44% of the call sites measured statically in the double-precision version of the Linpack benchmark, thus reducing the dynamic number of calls by 98%. Whereas they expected the program's performance to improve, it actually worsened by over 8% when run on a MIPS R2000-based system. Analysis of the code showed that the performance decrease was not due to cache effects or register pressure in a critical loop. Rather, the number of nops and floating-point interlocks had increased by 75%. The problem lies in the MIPS compiler's following the Fortran 77 standard and not doing interprocedural data-flow analysis: the standard allows a compiler to assume on entry to a procedure that there is no aliasing among the parameters and to put that information to use in generating code, and the MIPS compiler did so for the original version of the program. On the other hand, with most of the critical procedures inlined and without interprocedural analysis, there is no knowledge available as to whether what were their parameters are aliased or not, so the compiler does the safe thing—it assumes that there may be aliases among them and generates worse code.

15.3   In-Line Expansion

In-line expansion is a mechanism that enables substitution of low-level code in place of a call to a procedure. It is similar in effect to procedure integration (see Section 15.2), except that it is done at the assembly-language or machine-code level and so can be used to substitute hand-tailored sequences of code for high-level operations, including the use of instructions a compiler would never generate. Thus, it is both an optimization and a way to provide high-level mnemonics for fundamental machine operations, such as setting bits in a program status word.

As an optimization, in-line expansion can be used to provide the best available instruction sequences for operations that might otherwise be difficult or impossible for an optimizer to achieve. Examples include computing the minimum of a series of up to four integers without any branches on an architecture that allows conditional nullification of the next instruction (such as PA-RISC) or conditional moves by providing three templates, one each for two, three, and four operands;[1] and exchanging the values of two integer registers in three operations without using a scratch register by doing three exclusive or's, as exemplified by the following LIR code:

```
ra  ← ra xor rb
rb  ← ra xor rb
ra  ← ra xor rb
```

It can also be used as a poor man's version of procedure integration: the user or the provider of a compiler or library can provide templates for procedures that are likely to benefit from inlining.

As a mechanism for incorporating instructions that do not correspond to higher-level language operations at all, in-line expansion provides a way to give them mnemonic significance and to make them accessible without the overhead of a procedure call. This can make writing an operating system or I/O device driver in a higher-level language much easier than it would otherwise be. If, for example, setting bit 15 in the program status word were the way to disable interrupts for a

---

1. The choice of four operands maximum is, of course, arbitrary. One could provide for as many operands as one wanted by providing additional templates or, given a sufficiently powerful language in which to express the templates, one could provide a process for handling any number of operands.

particular architecture, one could provide a template called `DisableInterrupts( )` that consists of three instructions such as

```
getpsw    ra              || copy PSW into ra
ori       ra,0x8000,ra    || set bit 15
setpsw    ra              || copy ra to PSW
```

Two mechanisms are essential to providing an in-line expansion capacity. One is a way to make an assembly-language sequence into a template and the other is the compiler phase, which we call the *inliner*, that performs the inlining. A third may be needed for instances like the example just above, namely, a way to specify that a real register needs to be substituted for `ra`. A template generally consists of a header that gives the name of the procedure and may include information about the number and types of expected arguments and register needs, a sequence of assembly-language instructions, and a trailer to terminate the template. For example, if the necessary information for a particular inliner consisted of the name of the routine, the number of bytes of arguments expected, a list of the register identifiers that need to have real registers substituted for them, and a sequence of instructions, it might take the form

```
.template   ProcName,ArgBytes,regs=(r1,...,rn)
. . .
instructions
. . .
.end
```

For example, the following template might serve for computing the maximum of three integer values:

```
.template max3,12,regs=(@r1)
mov     argreg1,@r1
cmp     argreg2,@r1
movg    argreg2,@r1
cmp     argreg3,@r1
movg    argreg3,@r1
mov     @r1,resreg
.end
```

The mechanism for providing in-line expansion is generally to provide one or more files that contain assembly-language templates for calls to be in-line expanded and a compilation phase that searches specified template files for procedure names that occur in the module being compiled and replaces calls to them with copies of the appropriate templates. If compilation includes an assembly-language step, this is all that is essential; if it doesn't, the templates can be preprocessed to produce whatever form is required.

In most cases, the templates need to satisfy the parameter-passing conventions of the language implementation, and code quality will benefit from optimizations performed after or as part of inlining to remove as much as possible of the parameter-passing overhead. Frequently register coalescing (see Section 16.3.6) is all that is needed to accomplish this.

15.4   Leaf-Routine Optimization and Shrink Wrapping

A *leaf routine* is a procedure that is a leaf in the call graph of a program, i.e., one that calls no (other) procedures. *Leaf-routine optimization* takes advantage of a procedure's being a leaf routine to simplify the way parameters are passed to it and to remove as much as possible of the procedure prologue and epilogue overhead associated with being able to call other procedures. The exact changes that it makes vary according to the amount of temporary storage required by the procedure and both the architecture and calling conventions in use.

Shrink wrapping generalizes leaf-routine optimization to apply to routines that are not leaves in the call graph. The idea behind it is to move the procedure prologue and epilogue code along the control-flow paths within a procedure until they either "run into" each other and, hence, can be removed or until they surround a region containing one or more calls and so enclose the minimal part of the procedure that still allows it to function correctly and efficiently.

15.4.1   Leaf-Routine Optimization

At first glance, it may seem surprising that a high percentage of the procedures in many programs are leaf routines. On the other hand, reasoning from some simple cases suggests that this should be so. In particular, consider a program whose call graph is a binary tree, i.e., a tree in which each node has either zero or two successors. It is not hard to show by induction that the number of leaves in such a tree is one more than the number of non-leaves, hence over half the procedures in such a call graph are leaf routines. Of course, this ratio does not hold universally: trees with more than two successors per node increase the ratio, while call graphs that are not trees or that include recursive routines may reduce the ratio to zero.

Thus, optimizations that lower the overhead of calling leaf routines are often highly desirable and, as we shall see, require relatively little effort. Determining the applicability of leaf-routine optimization has two main components. The first is the obvious one—that the routine calls no others. The second is architecture-dependent and requires somewhat more effort. We must determine how much storage, both registers and stack space, the procedure requires. If it requires no more registers than are available as caller-saved and short-term scratch registers, then its register usage can be adjusted to use those registers. For an architecture without register windows, this number is set by software convention or by an interprocedural register allocator (see Section 19.6) and can be done in such a way as to favor leaf-routine optimization. For SPARC, with register-window saving and restoring done by separate instructions than procedure calls and returns, it merely requires that the called procedure not contain save and restore instructions and that it be restricted to using registers in the caller's *out* register set and scratch globals.

If the leaf routine also requires no stack space, because, for example, it does *not* manipulate any local arrays that need to have their elements be addressable, and if it has sufficient storage for its scalars in the available registers, then the code that creates and reclaims a stack frame for the leaf routine is also not needed.

If a leaf routine is small or is called from only a few places, it may be an excellent candidate for procedure integration.

15.4.2   Shrink Wrapping

The definition of shrink wrapping given above is not quite accurate. If we were to move the prologue and epilogue code to enclose the minimal possible code segments that include calls or that otherwise need to use callee-saved registers, we might end up placing that code inside a loop or making many copies of it for distinct control-flow paths. Both would be wasteful—the former of time and the latter of space and usually time as well. The latter might also be incorrect. Consider the flowgraph in Figure 15.8. If blocks B3 and B4 need to use a callee-saved register for variable c, we might be led to place a register save before each of those blocks and a restore after block B4. If we did that and the execution path included both B3 and B4, we would save the wrong value on entry to B4.

Instead, our goal is to move the prologue and epilogue code to enclose the minimal code segments that need them, subject to their not being contained in a loop and not creating the problem just described. To do so, we use a data-flow analysis developed by Chow [Chow88] that uses properties similar to some of those used in the analysis carried out for partial-redundancy elimination. For a basic block i, we define $RUSE(i)$ to be the set of registers used or defined in block i. Next, we define two data-flow properties called register anticipatability and register availability. A register is *anticipatable* at a point in a flowgraph if all execution paths from that point contain definitions or uses of the register; it is *available* if all execution paths to that point include definitions or uses of it (see Section 13.3 for use of these properties in the context of partial-redundancy elimination). We use $RANTin(i)$, $RANTout(i)$, $RAVin(i)$, and $RAVout(i)$ to denote the data-flow attributes on entry to and exit from each block i. Thus, we have the data-flow equations

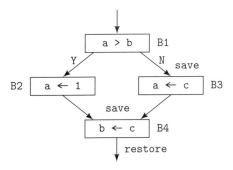

FIG. 15.8   Incorrect placement of save and restore code for the register allocated for variable c.

$$RANTout(i) = \bigcap_{j \in Succ(i)} RANTin(i)$$

$$RANTin(i) \; = RUSE(i) \cup RANTout(i)$$

and

$$RAVin(i) \; = \bigcap_{j \in Pred(i)} RAVout(i)$$

$$RAVout(i) = RUSE(i) \cup RAVin(i)$$

with the initialization $RANTout(\texttt{exit}) = RAVin(\texttt{entry}) = \emptyset$. Note that these sets can be represented by bit vectors that are a single word each for a machine with at most 32 registers.

The idea is to insert register-saving code where a use is anticipatable and to insert restore code where a use is available. Note that the two issues are symmetric, since the data-flow equations are mirror images of each other, as are the conditions for save and restore insertion. Thus, determining the appropriate data-flow equations for saving automatically gives us the corresponding equations for restoring. We choose to insert save code for a register r at basic-block entries and at the earliest point leading to one or more contiguous blocks that use r. For block i to satisfy this, we must have $r \in RANTin(i)$ and $r \notin RANTin(j)$ for $j \in Pred(i)$. Also, there must be no previous save of r, because introducing another one saves the wrong value, so $r \notin RAVin(i)$. Thus, the analysis suggests that the set of registers to be saved on entry to block i is

$$SAVE(i) = (RANTin(i) - RAVin(i)) \cap \bigcap_{j \in Pred(i)} (REGS - RANTin(j))$$

where $REGS$ is the set all of registers and, by symmetry, the set of registers to be restored on exit from block i is

$$RSTR(i) = (RAVout(i) - RANTout(i)) \cap \bigcap_{j \in Succ(i)} (REGS - RAVout(j))$$

However, these choices of save and restore points suffer from two problems. One is the issue covered by the example in Figure 15.8 and the mirror image for restoring. We handle this by splitting the edge from block B2 to B4 and placing the register save currently at the entry to B4 in the new (empty) block; we deal with restores in the corresponding fashion. The second problem is that this choice of save and restore points does not deal efficiently with the issue of saving and restoring being needed around a subgraph nested inside a loop. We handle this by recognizing from the control-flow structure of the routine being compiled that such a subgraph is nested inside a loop and we migrate the save and restore code outward to surround the loop.

As an example of this approach, consider the flowgraph in Figure 15.9. Assume that r1 through r7 are used to hold parameters and r8 through r15 are callee-saved registers. Then the values of $RUSE(\;)$ are as follows:

$$RUSE(\texttt{entry}) \; = \emptyset$$
$$RUSE(\texttt{B1}) \quad = \{\texttt{r2}\}$$

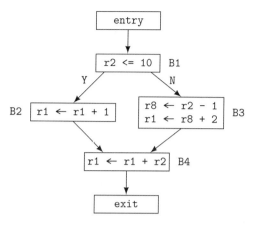

FIG. 15.9 A LIR flowgraph example for shrink wrapping.

$$
\begin{aligned}
RUSE(\text{B2}) &= \{\text{r1}\} \\
RUSE(\text{B3}) &= \{\text{r1,r2,r8}\} \\
RUSE(\text{B4}) &= \{\text{r1,r2}\} \\
RUSE(\text{exit}) &= \emptyset
\end{aligned}
$$

The values of $RANTin(\ )$, $RANTout(\ )$, $RAVin(\ )$, and $RAVout(\ )$ are as follows:

$$
\begin{aligned}
RANTin(\text{entry}) &= \{\text{r1,r2}\} & RANTout(\text{entry}) &= \{\text{r1,r2}\} \\
RANTin(\text{B1}) &= \{\text{r1,r2}\} & RANTout(\text{B1}) &= \{\text{r1,r2}\} \\
RANTin(\text{B2}) &= \{\text{r1,r2}\} & RANTout(\text{B2}) &= \{\text{r1,r2}\} \\
RANTin(\text{B3}) &= \{\text{r1,r2,r8}\} & RANTout(\text{B3}) &= \{\text{r1,r2}\} \\
RANTin(\text{B4}) &= \{\text{r1,r2}\} & RANTout(\text{B4}) &= \emptyset \\
RANTin(\text{exit}) &= \emptyset & RANTout(\text{exit}) &= \emptyset
\end{aligned}
$$

$$
\begin{aligned}
RAVin(\text{entry}) &= \emptyset & RAVout(\text{entry}) &= \emptyset \\
RAVin(\text{B1}) &= \emptyset & RAVout(\text{B1}) &= \{\text{r2}\} \\
RAVin(\text{B2}) &= \{\text{r2}\} & RAVout(\text{B2}) &= \{\text{r1,r2}\} \\
RAVin(\text{B3}) &= \{\text{r2}\} & RAVout(\text{B3}) &= \{\text{r1,r2,r8}\} \\
RAVin(\text{B4}) &= \{\text{r1,r2}\} & RAVout(\text{B4}) &= \{\text{r1,r2}\} \\
RAVin(\text{exit}) &= \{\text{r1,r2}\} & RAVout(\text{exit}) &= \{\text{r1,r2}\}
\end{aligned}
$$

Finally, the values of $SAVE(\ )$ and $RSTR(\ )$ are as follows:

$$
\begin{aligned}
SAVE(\text{entry}) &= \emptyset & RSTR(\text{entry}) &= \emptyset \\
SAVE(\text{B1}) &= \{\text{r1,r2}\} & RSTR(\text{B1}) &= \emptyset \\
SAVE(\text{B2}) &= \emptyset & RSTR(\text{B2}) &= \emptyset \\
SAVE(\text{B3}) &= \{\text{r8}\} & RSTR(\text{B3}) &= \{\text{r8}\} \\
SAVE(\text{B4}) &= \emptyset & RSTR(\text{B4}) &= \{\text{r1,r2}\} \\
SAVE(\text{exit}) &= \emptyset & RSTR(\text{exit}) &= \emptyset
\end{aligned}
$$

Since r1 and r2 are used for parameter passing, the only register of interest here is r8, and the values of $SAVE(\ )$ and $RSTR(\ )$ indicate that we should save r8 at the entry to block B3 and restore it at B3's exit, as we would expect. The resulting flowgraph appears in Figure 15.10.

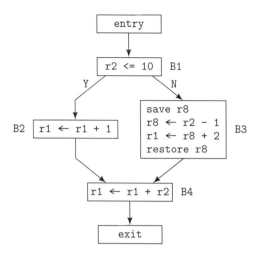

FIG. 15.10   The example in Figure 15.9 after shrink wrapping.

15.5   Wrap-Up

In this chapter, we have discussed three pairs of optimizations that apply to whole procedures and that, except in one case, do not require data-flow analysis to be effective. The pairs of optimizations are as follows:

1. Tail-recursion elimination and the more general tail-call optimization turn calls into branches. More specifically, tail-recursion elimination recognizes calls in a proce-dure that recursively call the same procedure and that do nothing but return after returning from the call. Such a call can always be turned into code that copies the arguments to the parameter locations followed by a branch to the beginning of the body of the routine.

    Tail-call optimization deals with the same situation, except that the called rou-tine need not be the caller. This optimization does the same thing as tail-recursion elimination, except that it needs to be done more carefully, since the called routine may not even be in the same compilation unit. To do it, we need to know where the called routine expects to find its parameters, how big its stack frame is, and where to branch to in order to begin executing it.

2. Procedure integration and in-line expansion are generally used as two names for the same optimization, namely, replacing a call by the body of the called routine. In this book, however, we use them to denote distinct versions of this operation: procedure integration is done early in the compilation process to take advantage of the many optimizations that have single procedures as their scopes (for example, integrating a procedure whose body is a loop and that is called in the body of a loop), while in-line expansion is done late in the compilation process to take advantage of low-level operations that have particularly effective implementations in a particular architecture.

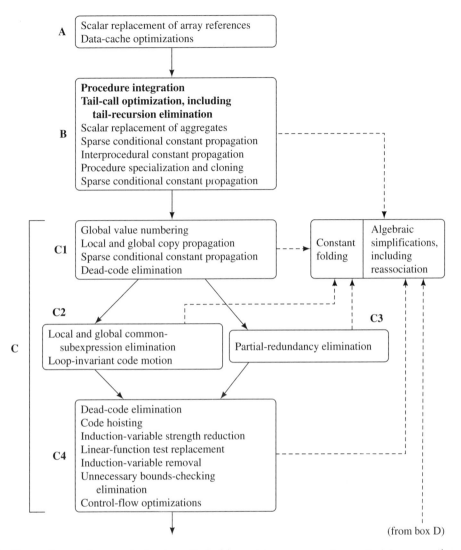

FIG. 15.11 Place of procedure optimizations (in **bold** type) in an aggressive optimizing compiler. *(continued)*

3. Leaf-routine optimization takes advantage of the fact that a large fraction of procedure calls are to routines that are leaves, i.e., that make no calls themselves and hence do not generally need the full baggage (stack frame, register saving and restoring, etc.) of an arbitrary routine. Shrink wrapping generalizes this by, in effect, migrating entry-point code forward and exit-point code backward along the control-flow paths in a procedure so that they annihilate each other if they collide. As a result, some control-flow paths through a shrink-wrapped routine may include full entry and exit code and others may not.

Figure 15.11 shows in **bold** type where these optimizations are generally placed in the order of optimizations.

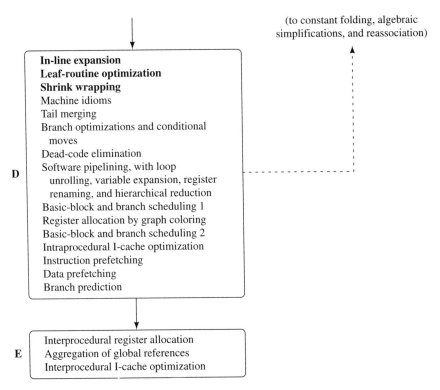

(to constant folding, algebraic
simplifications, and reassociation)

In-line expansion
Leaf-routine optimization
Shrink wrapping
Machine idioms
Tail merging
Branch optimizations and conditional
    moves
Dead-code elimination
Software pipelining, with loop
    unrolling, variable expansion, register
    renaming, and hierarchical reduction
Basic-block and branch scheduling 1
Register allocation by graph coloring
Basic-block and branch scheduling 2
Intraprocedural I-cache optimization
Instruction prefetching
Data prefetching
Branch prediction

D

Interprocedural register allocation
Aggregation of global references
Interprocedural I-cache optimization

E

FIG. 15.11 *(continued)*

15.6   Further Reading

The Linpack benchmark is described by Dongarra et al. in [DonB79]. The Cooper, Hall, and Torczon experiment with procedure integration described in Section 15.2 is found in [CooH92].

Chow's approach to shrink wrapping is described in [Chow88].

15.7   Exercises

15.1 In doing tail-call optimization, how can we guarantee that there is enough stack space for the callee? (a) Under what conditions can this be done during compilation? (b) Would splitting the work between compiling and linking simplify it or make it more widely applicable? If so, explain how. If not, explain why not.

ADV 15.2 (a) Generalize tail-call optimization to discover groups of routines that form a recursive loop, i.e., for routines r_1 through r_k, r_1 calls only r_2, r_2 calls only r_3, . . . , and r_k calls only r_1. (b) Under what conditions can the routines' bodies be combined into a single one and how would you determine whether the conditions hold?

15.3 In doing leaf-routine optimization, how can we be sure that there is enough stack space for all the leaf procedures? (a) Under what conditions can this be done during compilation? (b) Would splitting the work between compiling and linking simplify it or make it more widely applicable? If so, explain how. If not, explain why not.

15.4 Design a compact format for saving the MIR and symbol table generated for a compilation unit to enable cross-compilation-unit procedure integration. Assume that all the compilation units result from compiling modules in the same source language.

15.5 Write an ICAN routine that performs inlining on LIR code, following the conventions given in Section 15.3. As part of this exercise, design an ICAN data structure to represent template files and read one into the appropriate structure by the call read_templates(*file*, *struc*), where *file* is the file name of the template file and *struc* is the structure to read it into.

15.6 Write an ICAN procedure to do leaf-routine optimization on LIR code, assuming that parameters are passed in registers r1 through r6 and that r7 through r13 are saved by the caller. Make sure to check whether stack space is required and to allocate it only if it is.

15.7 Write an ICAN routine

```
Tail_Call_Opt(en1,n1,ninst1,LBlock1,en2,n2,ninst2,LBlock2)
```

that takes two LIR procedures such that the first one performs a tail call to the second one and modifies their code to replace the tail call by a branch. Assume that the first routine passes *nargs* arguments to the second one in a sequence of registers beginning with r1, that the frame and stack pointers are register r20 and r21, respectively, and that *en1* and *en2* are the numbers of the entry blocks of the two procedures.

CHAPTER 16

Register Allocation

In this chapter, we cover register allocation and assignment, which are, for almost all architectures, among the most important of optimizations. The problem addressed is how to minimize traffic between the CPU registers, which are usually few and fast to access, and whatever lies beyond them in the memory hierarchy, including one or more levels of cache and main memory, all of which are slower to access and larger, generally increasing in size and decreasing in speed the further we move away from the registers.

Register allocation is best carried out on low-level intermediate code or on assembly language, because it is essential that all loads from and stores to memory, including their address computations, be represented explicitly.

We begin with a discussion of a quick and reasonably effective local method that depends on usage counts and loop nesting. Next comes a detailed presentation of a much more effective approach that uses graph coloring to do global allocation and a short overview of another approach that also uses graph coloring but that is not generally as effective. We also mention briefly an approach that views allocation as a bin-packing problem and three approaches that use a procedure's control tree to guide allocation.

The central focus of the chapter, global register allocation by graph coloring, usually results in very effective allocations without a major cost in compilation speed. It views the fact that two quantities must be in registers at the same time as excluding them from being in the same register. It represents the quantities by nodes in a graph and the exclusions (called *interferences*) by arcs between the corresponding nodes; the nodes may represent real registers also, and the arcs may represent exclusions such as that the base address in a memory access may not be register r0. Given the graph corresponding to an entire procedure, this method then attempts to color the nodes, with the number of colors equal to the number of available real registers, so that every node is assigned a color that is distinct from those of all the nodes adjacent to it. If this cannot be achieved, additional code is introduced to store quantities to memory and to reload them as needed, and the process is repeated until a satisfactory coloring is achieved. As we will see, even very simple formulations of graph-coloring problems are *NP*-complete, so one of the most important facets of making global register allocation as effective as possible is using highly effective heuristics.

Further coverage of register allocation appears in Section 19.6, where interprocedural methods are discussed. Some of these methods work on code below the assembly-language level, namely, on relocatable object modules annotated with information about data usage patterns.

16.1   Register Allocation and Assignment

Register allocation determines which of the values (variables, temporaries, and large constants) that might profitably be in a machine's registers should be in registers at each point in the execution of a program. Register allocation is important because registers are almost always a scarce resource—there are rarely enough of them to hold all the objects one would like to keep in them—and because, in RISC systems, almost all operations other than data movement operate entirely on register contents, not storage, and in modern CISC implementations, the register-to-register operations are significantly faster than those that take one or two memory operands. Graph coloring is a highly effective approach to global (intraprocedural) register allocation. We also describe briefly a related method called priority-based graph coloring. In Section 19.6, we discuss interprocedural approaches that work on whole programs at compile time or link time.

Register assignment determines which register each allocated value should be in. Register assignment is mostly trivial for a RISC architecture, since the registers are either uniform or divided into two nearly uniform sets—the general or integer registers and the floating-point registers—and the operations that can be performed in them are mutually exclusive or very nearly so. One sometimes significant exception is that generally either set of registers can be used to hold word- or doubleword-size values that are being copied from one area of memory to another, and the choice of which set to use may depend on what else is occupying registers at the same time. A second exception is that doubleword quantities are usually restricted to even-odd pairs of registers on 32-bit systems, so some care is needed to ensure that they are assigned correctly. For CISCs, register assignment must typically take into account special uses for some of the registers, such as serving as the stack pointer or being used implicitly by string-manipulation instructions, as occurs in the Intel 386 architecture family.

In a compiler that does global optimization on medium-level intermediate code, register allocation is almost invariably done after generating low-level or machine code. It is preceded by instruction scheduling (see Section 17.1) and possibly by software pipelining (see Section 17.4), and possibly followed by another pass of instruction scheduling. In a compiler that does global optimization on low-level intermediate code, register allocation is frequently among the last few optimizations done. In either approach, it is essential to expose all addressing calculations, such as for accessing array elements, before register allocation, so that their use of registers can be taken into account in the allocation process.

If allocation is done on medium-level intermediate code, it is usually necessary for a few registers to be reserved for the code generator to use as temporaries for quantities that are not allocated to registers and for some of the more complex constructs such as switches. This is a distinct drawback of the priority-based graph-coloring approach (Section 16.4), since it restricts the reserved registers to being used for the designated purposes, generally without knowing in advance how many are actually required; thus the maximum number of registers that may be needed must be reserved, which reduces the number of registers available to the allocator.

Before proceeding to the discussion of global register allocation, we consider what kinds of objects should be taken as candidates for allocation to registers and briefly describe two older, local approaches, the first developed by Freiburghouse [Frei74] and the second used in the PDP-11 BLISS compiler and its descendants, including the DEC GEM compilers discussed in Section 21.3.2. In many architectures, including all RISCs, all operations are performed between registers, and even storage-to-storage moves of objects are done by loading them into registers and then storing them, so it would appear at first glance that every object should be considered as a candidate. This is not quite true—input/output is universally done to and from memory, not registers, and communication between the processors in a shared-memory multiprocessor is almost entirely through memory as well. Also, small constants that can fit into the immediate fields of instructions generally should not be taken as candidates, since they can be used more efficiently that way than by occupying registers. Virtually all other classes of objects should be considered candidates for register allocation: local variables, nonlocal variables, constants too large to fit into immediate fields, temporaries, etc. Even individual array elements should be considered (see Section 20.3).

16.2   Local Methods

The first local allocation approach is hierarchical in that it weights inner loops more heavily than outer ones and more heavily than code not contained in loops, on the principle that most programs spend most of their time executing loops. The idea is to determine, either heuristically or from profiling information, the allocation benefits of the various allocatable quantities. If profiling information is not available, it is generally estimated by multiplying the savings that result from allocating a variable to a register by a factor based on its loop nesting depth, usually 10^{depth} for *depth* loops.[1] In addition, liveness of a variable on entry to or exit from a basic block should be taken into account, since a live quantity needs to be stored on exit from a block, unless there are enough registers available to assign one to it. We define the following quantities:

---

1. Some compilers use 8^{depth} simply because a multiplication by 8 can be done in a single cycle by a left shift.

1. *ldcost* is the execution-time cost of a load instruction in the target machine.

2. *stcost* is the cost of a store instruction.

3. *mvcost* is the cost of a register-to-register move instruction.

4. *usesave* is the savings for each use of a variable that resides in a register rather than a memory location.

5. *defsave* is the savings for each assignment to a variable that resides in a register rather than a memory location.

Then the net savings in execution time for a particular variable v each time basic block Bi is executed is *netsave*(v, i), defined as follows:

$$netsave(v,i) = u \cdot usesave + d \cdot defsave - l \cdot ldcost - s \cdot stcost$$

where u and d are the numbers of uses and definitions of variable v, respectively, in block i; and l and s = 0 or 1, counting whether a load of v at the beginning of the block or a store at the end, respectively, is needed.

Thus, if L is a loop and i ranges over the basic blocks in it, then

$$10^{depth} \cdot \sum_{i \in blocks(L)} netsave(v,i)$$

is a reasonable estimate of the benefit of allocating v to a register in loop L.[2] Given that one has R registers to allocate—which is almost always fewer than the total number of registers, since some must be reserved for procedure linkage, short-term temporaries, etc.—after computing such estimates, one simply allocates the R objects with the greatest estimated benefit to registers in each loop or loop nest. Following register allocation for the loop nests, allocation is done for code outside loops using the same benefit measure.

We can sometimes improve the allocation by taking into account the P predecessors and S successors of a block i. If those blocks all assign variable v to the same location, the values of l and s for the variable for this block are both 0. In considering the predecessors and successors along with block i, we may put variable v in a different register from the one it is allocated to in some or all of the surrounding blocks. If so, we incur an additional cost for this variable of at most $(P + S) \cdot mvcost$, the cost of one move for each predecessor and successor block.

This approach is simple to implement, often works remarkably well, and was the prevalent approach in optimizing compilers, such as IBM's Fortran H for the IBM 360 and 370 series machines, until the global methods described below became feasible for production use.

The BLISS optimizing compiler for the PDP-11 views register allocation as a bin-packing problem. It determines the lifetimes of temporaries and then divides them into four groups according to whether they

---

2. This measure can be refined to weight conditionally executed code in proportion to its expected or measured execution frequency.

1. must be allocated to a specific register,

2. must be allocated to some register,

3. may be allocated to a register or memory, or

4. must be allocated to a memory location.

Next, it ranks the allocatable temporaries by a cost measure for allocation to specific registers or any register, and finally it tries a series of permutations of the packing of temporaries into the registers and memory locations, preferring to allocate to registers when possible. An approach derived from this one is still used in Digital Equipment's GEM compilers for Alpha (Section 21.3).

16.3   Graph Coloring

16.3.1   Overview of Register Allocation by Graph Coloring

That global register allocation could be viewed as a graph-coloring problem was recognized by John Cocke as long ago as 1971, but no such allocator was designed and implemented until Chaitin's in 1981. That allocator was for an experimental IBM 370 PL/I compiler, and it was soon adapted by Chaitin and a group of colleagues for the PL.8 compiler for the IBM 801 experimental RISC system. Versions of it and allocators derived from it have been used since in many compilers. The generally most successful design for one was developed by Briggs, and it is his design on which much of the rest of this chapter is based. (See Section 16.7 for further reading.)

The basic idea of global register allocation by graph coloring can be expressed in five steps, as follows (although each of steps 2 through 4 is an oversimplification):

1. During code generation or optimization (whichever phase precedes register allocation) or as the first stage of register allocation, allocate objects that can be assigned to registers to distinct symbolic registers, say, s1, s2, . . . , using as many as are needed to hold all the objects (source variables, temporaries, large constants, etc.).

2. Determine what objects should be candidates for allocation to registers. (This could simply be the si, but there is a better choice described in Section 16.3.3.)

3. Construct a so-called interference graph whose nodes represent allocatable objects and the target machine's real registers and whose arcs (i.e., undirected edges) represent interferences, where two allocatable objects interfere if they are simultaneously live and an object and a register interfere if the object cannot be or should not be allocated to that register (e.g., an integer operand and a floating-point register).

4. Color the interference graph's nodes with R colors, where R is the number of available registers, so that any two adjacent nodes have different colors (this is called an *R-coloring*).

5. Allocate each object to the register that has the same color it does.

Before we proceed with the details, we give an example of the basic approach. Suppose we have the simple code shown in Figure 16.1(a) with y and w dead at the

1	x ← 2	s1 ← 2	r1 ← 2
2	y ← 4	s2 ← 4	r2 ← 4
3	w ← x + y	s3 ← s1 + s2	r3 ← r1 + r2
4	z ← x + 1	s4 ← s1 + 1	r3 ← r1 + 1
5	u ← x * y	s5 ← s1 * s2	r1 ← r1 * r2
6	x ← z * 2	s6 ← s4 * 2	r2 ← r3 * 2
	(a)	(b)	(c)

FIG. 16.1 (a) A simple example for register allocation by graph coloring; (b) a symbolic register assignment for it; and (c) an allocation for it with three registers, assuming that y and w are dead on exit from this code.

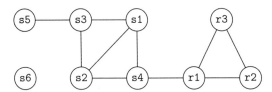

FIG. 16.2 Interference graph for code in Figure 16.1(b).

end of the code sequence, three registers (r1, r2, and r3) available, and suppose further that z must not occupy r1. We first assign symbolic registers s1, ... , s6 to the variables, as shown in Figure 16.1(b). Note that the two definitions of x in lines 1 and 6 have been assigned different symbolic registers, as described in the next section. Then, for example, s1 interferes with s2 because s2 is defined in line 2, between the definition of s1 in line 1 and its uses in lines 3, 4, and 5; and s4 interferes with r1 because z is restricted to not being in r1. The resulting interference graph is shown in Figure 16.2. It can be colored with three colors (the number of registers) by making s3, s4, and r3 red; s1, s5, and r1 blue; and s2, s6, and r2 green. Thus, putting both s1 and s5 in r1, s2 and s6 in r2, and s3 and s4 in r3 is a valid register assignment (shown in Figure 16.1(c)), as the reader can easily check.

Next, we consider the details of the method and how they differ from the outline sketched above.

16.3.2   Top-Level Structure

The list of global type definitions and data structures used in register allocation by graph coloring is given in Figure 16.3. Each is described where it is first used.

The overall structure of the register allocator is shown in Figure 16.4. The allocation process proceeds as follows:

1. First Make_Webs( ) combines du-chains that intersect (i.e., that contain a use in common) to form webs, which are the objects for which registers are allocated. A *web* is a maximal union of du-chains such that, for each definition d and use u, either u is in the du-chain of d or there exist $d = d_0, \ldots, u_0, d_n, u_n = u$, such that, for each i, u_i is in the du-chains of both d_i and d_{i+1}. Each web is assigned a distinct symbolic register number. Make_Webs( ) also calls MIR_to_SymLIR( ) to translate the input MIR code in Block to LIR with symbolic registers that is stored in LBlock; note that this is not essential—the code input to the register allocator could just as easily be in

```
Symbol = Var ∪ Register ∪ Const
UdDu = integer × integer
UdDuChain = (Symbol × UdDu) ⟶ set of UdDu
webrecord = record {symb: Symbol,
                    defs: set of UdDu,
                    uses: set of UdDu,
                    spill: boolean,
                    sreg: Register,
                    disp: integer}
listrecd =  record {nints, color, disp: integer,
                    spcost: real,
                    adjnds, rmvadj: list of integer}
opdrecd = record {kind: enum {var,regno,const},
                  val: Symbol}


DefWt, UseWt, CopyWt: real
nregs, nwebs, BaseReg, Disp := InitDisp, ArgReg: integer
RetReg: Register
Symreg: array [··] of webrecord
AdjMtx: array [··,··] of boolean
AdjLsts: array [··] of listrecd
Stack: sequence of integer
Real_Reg: integer ⟶ integer
```

FIG. 16.3 Global type definitions and data structures used in register allocation by graph coloring.

    LIR and, if we do other low-level optimizations before register allocation, it definitely will be in LIR or some other low-level code form.

2. Next, `Build_AdjMtx( )` builds the adjacency-matrix representation of the interference graph, which is a two-dimensional, lower-triangular matrix such that `AdjMtx[`i,j`]` is true if and only if there is an arc between (real or symbolic) registers i and j (for $i > j$), and `false` otherwise.

3. Next, the routine `Coalesce_Regs( )` uses the adjacency matrix to coalesce registers, i.e., it searches for copy instructions $si \leftarrow sj$ such that si and sj do not interfere with each other and it replaces uses of sj with uses of si, eliminating sj from the code. If any coalescences are performed, we continue with step 1 above; otherwise, we continue to the next step.

4. Next, `Build_AdjLsts( )` constructs the adjacency-list representation of the interference graph, which is an array `AdjLsts[1··nwebs]` of `listrecd` records, one for each symbolic register. The records consist of six components: `color`, `disp`, `spcost`, `nints`, `adjnds`, and `rmvadj`; these components indicate whether a node has been colored yet and with what color, the displacement to be used in spilling it (if necessary), the spill cost associated with it, the number of adjacent nodes left in the graph, the list of adjacent nodes left in the graph, and the list of adjacent nodes that have been removed from the graph, respectively.

5. Next, `Compute_Spill_Costs( )` computes, for each symbolic register, the cost of spilling it to memory and restoring it to a register. As we shall see below, there

```
procedure Allocate_Registers(DuChains,nblocks,ninsts,Block,
   LBlock,Succ,Pred)
   DuChains: in set of UdDuChain
   nblocks: in integer
   ninsts: inout array [1··nblocks] of integer
   Block: in array [1··nblocks] of array of MIRInst
   LBlock: out array [1··nblocks] of array [··] of LIRInst
   Succ, Pred: inout integer ⟶ set of integer
begin
   success, coalesce: boolean
   repeat
      repeat
         Make_Webs(DuChains,nblocks,ninsts,Block,LBlock)
         Build_AdjMtx( )
         coalesce := Coalesce_Regs(nblocks,ninsts,LBlock,Succ,Pred)
      until !coalesce
      Build_AdjLsts( )
      Compute_Spill_Costs(nblocks,ninsts,LBlock)
      Prune_Graph( )
      success := Assign_Regs( )
      if success then
         Modify_Code(nblocks,ninsts,LBlock)
      else
         Gen_Spill_Code(nblocks,ninsts,LBlock)
      fi
   until success
end     || Allocate_Registers
```

FIG. 16.4 Top level of graph-coloring register-allocation algorithm.

are some types of register contents (such as large constants) that may be handled
differently, in ways that are less expensive and that still achieve the effect of spilling
and restoring.

6. Then Prune_Graph( ) uses two approaches, called the *degree* < *R* rule and the
   optimistic heuristic, to remove nodes (and their associated arcs) from the adjacency-
   list representation of the interference graph.

7. Then Assign_Regs( ) uses the adjacency lists to try to assign colors to the nodes so
   that no two adjacent nodes have the same color. If it succeeds, Modify_Code( ) is
   called to replace each use of a symbolic register with the real register that has been
   assigned the same color and the allocation process terminates. If register assignment
   fails, it proceeds to the next step.

8. The routine Gen_Spill_Code( ) assigns stack locations for symbolic registers to be
   spilled to memory and then inserts spills and restores for them (or handles them
   alternatively, such as for the large-constant case mentioned above, for which it is
   generally less expensive to reconstruct or *rematerialize* a value, rather than storing
   and loading it). Then control returns to step 1 above.

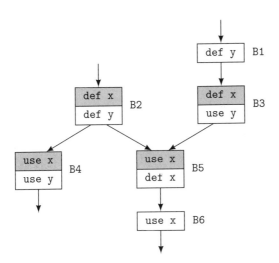

FIG. 16.5 An example of webs. The most complex web is shaded.

The following sections elaborate each of the routines discussed above and the reasons for taking this approach.

16.3.3   Webs, the Allocatable Objects

The first issue is determining what objects should be candidates for register allocation. Rather than simply using the variables that fit into a register, the candidates are objects that were originally called *names* but that now are generally called *webs*. A *web* is as defined in item 1 in Section 16.3.2. For example, in the code in Figure 16.1(a), the definition of x in line 1 and its uses in lines 3, 4, and 5 belong to the same web, since the definition reaches all the uses listed, but the definition of x in line 6 belongs to a different web.

For another example, consider the abstracted flowgraph fragment in Figure 16.5 in which we show just definitions and uses of two variables, x and y, and we assume that there are no loops enclosing the fragment. There are four webs present. One consists of the union of the du-chain for the definition of x in block B2, which is shaded in the figure and includes the uses of x in blocks B4 and B5, and the du-chain for the definition of x in block B3, which is also shaded and includes the use of x in block B5; since they intersect in the use of x in block B5, they are combined to form one web. The definition of x in block B5 and its use in block B6 form a separate web. In summary, the four webs are as follows:

Web	Components
w1	def x in B2, def x in B3, use x in B4, use x in B5
w2	def x in B5, use x in B6
w3	def y in B2, use y in B4
w4	def y in B1, use y in B3

FIG. 16.6 Interferences among the webs in Figure 16.5.

and the interferences among them are as indicated in Figure 16.6. In general, to determine the webs for a procedure, we first construct its du-chains by computing reaching definitions and then we compute the maximal unions of intersecting du-chains (two du-chains intersect if they have a use in common).

The advantage of using webs instead of variables as the candidates for allocation to registers results from the fact that the same variable name may be used repeatedly in a routine for unrelated purposes. The classic example of this is the use of i as a loop index. For many programmers, it is the first choice of a variable to use as a loop index, and it is often used for many loops in the same routine. If they were all required to use the same register for i, the allocation would be unduly constrained. In addition, of course, there may be multiple uses of a variable name for purposes the programmer thinks of as identical but that are in fact separable for register allocation because their webs are distinct. Using webs also obviates the need to map the variables to symbolic registers: each web is equivalent to a symbolic register. Notice that for a RISC system, this can be made to encompass large constants in addition to variables—to be used, a large constant needs to be loaded into or constructed in a register and the register then becomes an element of a web.

The ICAN routine Make_Webs( ) shown in Figure 16.7 constructs the webs for a procedure, given its du-chains. It uses three global data types. One is UdDu, whose members consist of pairs $\langle i, j \rangle$, where i is a basic block number and j is an instruction number within the block.

The second type, UdDuChain = (Symbol × UdDu) $\longrightarrow$ set of UdDu, represents du-chains. As noted in Section 2.7.9, an ICAN function with two arguments is equivalent to a set of triples whose type is the product of the types of the first argument, the second argument, and the range. We use that equivalence here—we write a member sdu of the type UdDuChain as a set of triples of the form $\langle s, p, Q \rangle$ (where s is a symbol, p is a block-position pair, and Q is a set of block-position pairs), rather than in the form $sdu(s, p) = Q$.

The third type webrecord describes a web, which consists of a symbol name, a set of definitions of the symbol, a set of uses of the same symbol, a Boolean indicating

```
procedure Make_Webs(DuChains,nblocks,ninsts,Block,LBlock)
    DuChains: in set of UdDuChain
    nblocks: in integer
    ninsts: in array [1··nblocks] of integer
    Block: in array [1··nblocks] of array [··] of MIRInst
    LBlock: out array [1··nblocks] of array [··] of LIRInst
```

FIG. 16.7 The routine Make_Webs( ) to determine webs for register allocation by graph coloring.

```
begin
    Webs := ∅, Tmp1, Tmp2: set of webrecord
    web1, web2: webrecord
    sdu: Symbol × UdDu ⟶ set of UdDu
    i, oldnwebs: integer
    nwebs := nregs
    for each sdu ∈ DuChains do
        nwebs += 1
        Webs ∪= {⟨symb:sdu@1,defs:{sdu@2},uses:sdu@3,
            spill:false,sreg:nil,disp:nil⟩}
    od
    repeat
        || combine du-chains for the same symbol and that
        || have a use in common to make webs
        oldnwebs := nwebs
        Tmp1 := Webs
        while Tmp1 ≠ ∅ do
            web1 := ♦Tmp1; Tmp1 -= {web1}
            Tmp2 := Webs - {web1}
            while Tmp2 ≠ ∅ do
                web2 := ♦Tmp2; Tmp2 -= {web2}
                if web1.symb = web2.symb &
                    (web1.uses ∩ web2.uses) ≠ ∅ then
                    web1.defs ∪= web2.defs
                    web1.uses ∪= web2.uses
                    Webs -= {web2}
                    nwebs -= 1
                fi
            od
        od
    until oldnwebs = nwebs
    for i := 1 to nregs do
        Symreg[i] := {⟨symb:Int_to_Reg(i),defs:nil,
            uses:nil,spill:false,sreg:nil,disp:nil⟩}
    od
    || assign symbolic register numbers to webs
    i := nregs
    for each web1 ∈ Webs do
        i += 1
        Symreg[i] := web1
        web1.sreg := i
    od
    MIR_to_SymLIR(nblocks,ninsts,Block,LBlock)
end     || Make_Webs
```

FIG. 16.7 *(continued)*

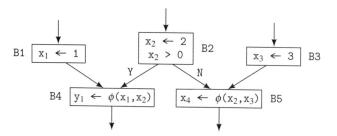

FIG. 16.8 Each SSA-form variable is the head of a du-chain.

whether it is a candidate for spilling, a symbolic register or `nil`, and a displacement or `nil`.

We assume that a du-chain is represented as a triple consisting of a symbol, a definition of the symbol, and a set of uses of the same symbol, and we assume that each definition and use is a pair consisting of a basic-block number and an instruction number (within the block), i.e., the compiler-specific type `UdDu` defined in Figure 16.3.

The values of the global variables `nregs` and `nwebs` are the number of real registers available for allocation, which are assumed to be numbered 1 through `nregs`, and the number of webs, counting the real registers, respectively.

`Make_Webs( )` first initializes the webs from the du-chains and then iterates over pairs of webs, checking whether they are for the same symbol and intersect and, if so, unioning them. In the process, it counts the webs and, finally, it assigns symbolic register names to the webs and calls `MIR_to_SymLIR( )` to convert the MIR code to LIR code and to substitute symbolic registers for variables in the code.[3]

`Make_Webs( )` uses the routine `Int_to_Reg(i)`, which returns the real or symbolic register name corresponding to integer i. If $i \leq$ `nregs`, it returns the name of the ith real register. If $i >$ `nregs`, it returns the value of `Symreg[i].symb`; this case is not used here, but is used in the code for `MIR_to_SymLIR( )` in Figure 16.9.

Note that if the code input to register allocation is in SSA form, then determining the webs is easy: each SSA-form variable is a du-chain, since each SSA variable has only one definition point. For example, in Figure 16.8, the definition of x_1 in B1, the definition and use of x_2 in B2, the definition of x_3, and the uses of x_1 and x_2 in block B4 and of x_2 and x_3 in B5 constitute a web.

The ICAN routine `MIR_to_SymLIR( )` in Figure 16.9 converts the MIR form of a procedure to LIR code with symbolic registers in place of variables. The routine uses the global type `opdrecd`, which describes instruction operands, consisting of a kind that is `var`, `regno`, or `const` and a value that is an identifier, a register, or a constant. It uses the global integer constant `ArgReg` and the global register-valued constant `RetReg`, which contain the number of the first argument register and the name of the register for the call to store the return address in, respectively. The code also uses three routines, as follows:

---

3. This is not essential. The code passed to the register allocator could already be in LIR.

```
procedure MIR_to_SymLIR(nblocks,ninsts,Block,LBlock)
   nblocks: in integer
   ninsts: inout array [1··nblocks] of integer
   Block: in array [1··nblocks] of array [··] of MIRInst
   LBlock: out array [1··nblocks] of array [··] of LIRInst
begin
   i, j, k, reg: integer
   inst: MIRInst
   opnd1, opnd2, opnd: opdrecd
   for i := 1 to nblocks do
      for j := 1 to ninsts[i] do
         inst := Block[i][j]
         case inst of
binasgn:     opnd1 := Convert_Opnd(inst.opd1)
             opnd2 := Convert_Opnd(inst.opd2)
             LBlock[i][j] := ⟨kind:regbin,
                left:Find_Symreg(inst.left,i,j),opr:inst.opr,
                opd1:opnd1,opd2:opnd2⟩
unasgn:      opnd := Convert_Opnd(inst.opd)
             LBlock[i][j] := ⟨kind:regun,
                left:Find_Symreg(inst.left,i,j),opr:inst.opr,
                opd:opnd⟩
valasgn:     opnd := Convert_Opnd(inst.opd)
             LBlock[i][j] := ⟨kind:regval,
                left:Find_Symreg(inst.left,i,j),opd:opnd⟩
             . . .
goto:        LBlock[i][j] := inst
binif:       opnd1 := Convert_Opnd(inst.opd1)
             opnd2 := Convert_Opnd(inst.opd2)
             LBlock[i][j] := ⟨kind:regbinif,opr:inst.opr,
                opd1:opnd1,opd2:opnd2,lbl:inst.lbl⟩
             . . .
call:        reg := ArgReg
             for k := 1 to |inst.args| do
                LBlock[i][j+k-1] := ⟨kind:regval,
                   left:Int_to_Reg(reg),
                   opd:Convert_Opnd(inst.args↓k)⟩
                reg += 1
             od
             LBlock[i][j+k] := ⟨kind:callreg,proc:inst.proc,
                rreg:RetReg⟩
             j += k
             . . .
         esac
      od
   od
end     || MIR_to_SymLIR
```

FIG. 16.9   ican code to convert the mir form of a procedure to lir code with symbolic registers in place of variables.

1. `Find_Symreg(s,i,j)` returns the index of the web (or, equivalently, the symbolic register) that symbol s in instruction j in basic block i is part of.

2. `Convert_Opnd(opnd)` takes a MIR operand $opnd$ and returns the corresponding LIR operand (either a constant or a symbolic register, where a symbolic register name consists of the letter s concatenated with an integer greater than or equal to `nregs + 1`).

3. `Int_to_Reg(i)` converts its integer argument i to the corresponding real or symbolic register name, as described above.

16.3.4   The Interference Graph

Once the webs have been computed, the next step is to build the interference graph. There is one node in the graph for each machine register and one for each web (= symbolic register).

It might appear that if the registers are homogeneous, i.e., if any quantity may reside in any register, then there is no need to include nodes for the registers in the interference graph. We would then simply find an R-coloring of the graph and assign webs with different colors to distinct registers. However, this is generally not the case, since, at the least, the calling conventions and stack structure require registers to be reserved for them.

Similarly, it might appear that if the target machine has two or more sets of registers dedicated to different functions (e.g., integer registers and floating-point registers), then the allocation problems for the two sets of registers could be handled separately, resulting in smaller, less-constrained interference graphs. However, this is generally not the case either, since moving a block of data from one location in memory to another (assuming that the architecture lacks memory-to-memory move instructions) typically can be done by using either set of registers—so we would needlessly restrict the allocation process by using separate graphs.

Our simplified description above indicated that two nodes have an arc between them if they are ever simultaneously live. However, this can result in many more arcs in the graph than are needed. It is sufficient to include an arc between two nodes if one of them is live at a definition point of the other. The additional arcs resulting from the original definition can significantly increase the number of colors required or, equivalently, the amount of code introduced (in a way we have not discussed yet) to make the graph R-colorable. The number of arcs connecting a node to others is called the node's *degree*.

Chaitin et al. [ChaA81] give an example of a procedure with an interference graph that requires 21 colors with the "simultaneously live" definition and only 11 with the "live at a definition point" definition. An adaptation of that example is shown in Figure 16.10. On entry to block B4, all of a1, . . . , an, b1, . . . , bn, and left are live. The interference graph has $2n + 1$ nodes. If we use the former definition of interference, it has $n(2n + 1)$ arcs, connecting each node to all the others and needs $2n + 1$ colors. With the latter definition, the ai do not interfere with the bi at all, so there are only $n(n + 1)$ arcs and only $n + 1$ colors are required.

The interference graph is general enough to represent several sorts of interferences other than the ones arising from simultaneously live variables. For example,

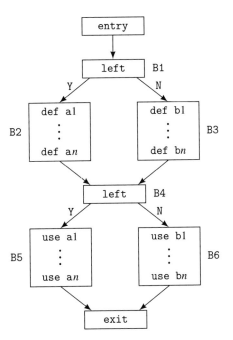

FIG. 16.10 Example flowgraph for which the two definitions of interference produce different interference graphs.

the fact that in the POWER architecture, general register r0 can be used to hold a constant but produces a zero value when used as a base register in an address computation can be handled by making all webs that represent base registers interfere with r0. Similarly, registers that are changed by the language implementation's calling conventions can be made to interfere with all webs that are live across a call.

16.3.5   Representing the Interference Graph

Before describing how to build the interference graph, we consider how best to represent it. The graph can be quite large, so space efficiency is a concern; but practical experience shows that access time is also a major issue, so careful attention to how it is represented can have a large payoff. As we shall see, we need to be able to construct the graph, determine whether two nodes are adjacent, find out how many nodes are adjacent to a given one, and find all the nodes adjacent to a given node quickly. We recommend using the traditional representation, namely, a combination of an adjacency matrix and adjacency lists.[4]

The adjacency matrix `AdjMtx[2··nwebs,1··nwebs-1]` is a lower-triangular matrix such that `AdjMtx[max(i,j),min(i,j)]` = `true` if the ith register (real

---

```
        r1 r2 r3 s1 s2 s3 s4 s5
r2  ┌ t                          ┐
r3  │ t  t                       │
s1  │ f  f  f  f                 │
s2  │ f  f  f  t  f              │
s3  │ f  f  f  t  t  f           │
s4  │ t  f  f  t  t  f  f        │
s5  │ f  f  f  f  f  t  f  f     │
s6  └ f  f  f  f  f  f  f  f     ┘
```

FIG. 16.11 Adjacency matrix for the interference graph in Figure 16.2, where t and f stand for true and false, respectively.

or symbolic) and the jth register are adjacent and is false otherwise.[5] The matrix representation allows the interference graph to be built quickly and allows one to determine quickly whether two nodes are adjacent. For example, the adjacency matrix for the interference graph in Figure 16.2 is shown in Figure 16.11, where t is used to represent true and f to represent false.

The ICAN routine Build_AdjMtx( ) to build the adjacency-matrix representation of the interference graph is given in Figure 16.12. The code uses the function Live_At(*web*,*symb*,*def*) to determine whether there are any definitions in *web* that are live at the definition *def* of symbol *symb* and the function Interfere(*s*,*r*) to determine whether the web represented by symbolic register *s* interferes with the real register *r*.

The adjacency-lists representation is an array of records of type listrecd with six components each. For array entry AdjLsts[*i*], the components are as follows:

1. color is an integer whose value is the color chosen for the node; it is initially $-\infty$.

2. disp is the displacement that forms part of the address at which the symbolic register assigned to position *i* will be spilled, if needed; it is initially $-\infty$.

3. spcost is the spill cost for the node; it is initially 0.0 for symbolic registers and ∞ for real registers.

4. nints is the number of interferences in the adjnds field.

5. adjnds is the list of the real and symbolic registers that currently interfere with real or symbolic register *i*.

6. rmvadj is the list of the real and symbolic registers that interfered with real or symbolic register *i* and that have been removed from the graph during pruning.

---

5. Recall that, in the numbering, the real registers account for positions 1 through nregs and the symbolic registers for positions nregs+1 through nwebs.

```
procedure Build_AdjMtx( )
begin
    i, j: integer
    for i := 2 to nwebs do
        for j := 1 to i-1 do
            AdjMtx[i,j] := false
        od
    od
    for i := 2 to nregs do
        for j := 1 to i-1 do
            AdjMtx[i,j] := true
        od
    od
    for i := nregs+1 to nwebs do
        for j := 1 to nregs do
            if Interfere(Symreg[i],j) then
                AdjMtx[i,j] := true
            fi
        od
        for j := nregs+1 to i-1 do
            for each def ∈ Symreg[i].defs
                (Live_At(Symreg[j],Symreg[i].symb,def)) do
                AdjMtx[i,j] := true
            od
        od
    od
end    || Build_AdjMtx
```

FIG. 16.12 ICAN code to build the adjacency-matrix representation of the interference graph for register allocation by graph coloring.

This representation is most useful for determining how many nodes are adjacent to a particular node and which ones they are. The adjacency lists for the interference graph in Figure 16.2 are shown in Figure 16.13.

ICAN code to build the adjacency-lists representation of the interference graph is given in Figure 16.14. The adjacency-matrix representation is most useful during the preparation for graph coloring, namely, during register coalescing (see next section); the adjacency lists are most useful during the actual coloring process. Thus, we build the adjacency matrix first, modify it during register coalescing, and then build the adjacency lists from the result, as discussed in Section 16.3.2.

16.3.6   Register Coalescing

After building the adjacency matrix, we apply a transformation known as register coalescing to it. *Register coalescing* or *subsumption* is a variety of copy propagation that eliminates copies from one register to another. It searches the intermediate code for register copy instructions, say, *sj* ← *si*, such that *si* and *sj* do not interfere with

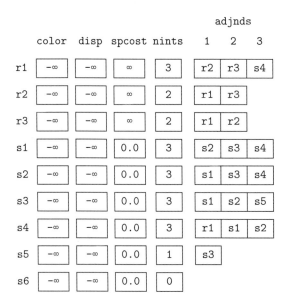

	color	disp	spcost	nints	adjnds 1	2	3
r1	$-\infty$	$-\infty$	∞	3	r2	r3	s4
r2	$-\infty$	$-\infty$	∞	2	r1	r3	
r3	$-\infty$	$-\infty$	∞	2	r1	r2	
s1	$-\infty$	$-\infty$	0.0	3	s2	s3	s4
s2	$-\infty$	$-\infty$	0.0	3	s1	s3	s4
s3	$-\infty$	$-\infty$	0.0	3	s1	s2	s5
s4	$-\infty$	$-\infty$	0.0	3	r1	s1	s2
s5	$-\infty$	$-\infty$	0.0	1	s3		
s6	$-\infty$	$-\infty$	0.0	0			

FIG. 16.13 Initial adjacency lists for the interference graph in Figure 16.2.

each other.[6] Upon finding such an instruction, register coalescing searches for the instructions that wrote to si and modifies them to put their results in sj instead, removes the copy instruction, and modifies the interference graph by combining si and sj into a single node that interferes with all the nodes they individually interfered with. Modifying the graph can be done incrementally. Note that at the point of a copy operation $sj \leftarrow si$, if another symbolic register sk was live at that point, we made it interfere with si, which now turns out to be unnecessary, so these interferences should be removed.

The ICAN routine `Coalesce_Regs( )` shown in Figure 16.15 performs register coalescing. It uses the following two routines:

1. `Reg_to_Int(r)` converts its symbolic or real register argument r to the integer i such that `Symreg[i]` represents r.

2. `delete_inst(i,j,ninsts,Block,Succ,Pred)` deletes instruction j from basic block i (see Figure 4.15).

After coalescing registers, we construct the adjacency-lists representation of the interference graph, as shown in Figure 16.14.

It has been noted by Chaitin and others that coalescing is a powerful transformation. Among the things it can do are the following:

---

6. Notice that the interference graph encodes the data-flow information necessary to do this, so we can avoid doing live variables analysis. Also, note that si and sj may each be either a real or a symbolic register.

```
procedure Build_AdjLsts( )
begin
    i, j: integer
    for i := 1 to nregs do
        AdjLsts[i].nints := 0
        AdjLsts[i].color := -∞
        AdjLsts[i].disp := -∞
        AdjLsts[i].spcost := ∞
        AdjLsts[i].adjnds := []
        AdjLsts[i].rmvadj := []
    od
    for i := nregs+1 to nwebs do
        AdjLsts[i].nints := 0
        AdjLsts[i].color := -∞
        AdjLsts[i].disp := -∞
        AdjLsts[i].spcost := 0.0
        AdjLsts[i].adjnds := []
        AdjLsts[i].rmvadj := []
    od
    for i := 2 to nwebs do
        for j := 1 to nwebs - 1 do
            if AdjMtx[i,j] then
                AdjLsts[i].adjnds ⊕= [j]
                AdjLsts[j].adjnds ⊕= [i]
                AdjLsts[i].nints += 1
                AdjLsts[j].nints += 1
            fi
        od
    od
end     || Build_AdjLsts
```

FIG. 16.14 ICAN code to build the adjacency-lists representation of the interference graph.

1. Coalescing simplifies several steps in the compilation process, such as removing unnecessary copies that were introduced by translating from SSA form back to a linear intermediate code.

2. It can be used to ensure that argument values are moved to (or computed in) the proper registers before a procedure call. In the callee, it can migrate parameters passed in registers to the proper registers for them to be worked on.

3. It enables machine instructions with required source and target registers to have their operands and results in the proper places.

4. It enables two-address instructions, as found in CISCs, to have their target register and the operand that must be in that register handled as required.

5. It enables us to ensure that instructions that require a register pair for some operand or result are assigned such a pair.

We do not take any of these issues into account in the algorithm in Figure 16.15, but there are related exercises at the end of the chapter.

```
procedure Coalesce_Regs(nblocks,ninsts,LBlock,Succ,Pred)
    nblocks: in integer
    ninsts: inout array [1··nblocks] of integer
    LBlock: inout array [1··nblocks] of array [··] of LIRInst
    Succ, Pred: inout integer —→ set of integer
begin
    i, j, k, l, p, q: integer
    inst, pqinst: LIRInst
    for i := 1 to nblocks do
        j := 1
        while j ≤ ninsts[i] do
            inst := LBlock[i][j]
            || if this instruction is a copy, adjust assignments
            || to its source to assign to its target instead
            if inst.kind = regval then
                k := Reg_to_Int(inst.left)
                l := Reg_to_Int(inst.opd.val)
                if !AdjMtx[max(k,l),min(k,l)] then
                    for p := 1 to nblocks do
                        q := 1
                        while q ≤ ninsts[p] do
                            pqinst := LBlock[p][q]
                            if LIR_Has_Left(pqinst)
                              & pqinst.left = inst.opd.val then
                                LBlock[p][q].left := inst.left
                            fi
                            q += 1
                        od
                    od
                    || remove the copy instruction
                    delete_inst(i,j,ninsts,Block,Succ,Pred)
                    Symreg[k].defs ∪= Symreg[l].defs
                    Symreg[k].uses ∪= Symreg[l].uses
                    || adjust adjacency matrix to reflect removal of the copy
                    for p := 1 to nwebs do
                        if AdjMtx[max(p,l),min(p,l)] then
                            AdjMtx[max(p,l),min(p,l)] := false
                            AdjMtx[max(p,k),min(p,k)] := true
                        fi
                    od
                    Symreg[l] := nil
                    nwebs -= 1
                fi
            fi
            j += 1
        od
    od
end     || Coalesce_Regs
```

FIG. 16.15 Code to coalesce registers.

16.3.7   Computing Spill Costs

The next phase of the allocation process is to compute costs for spilling and restoring (or rematerializing) register contents, in case it turns out not to be possible to allocate all the symbolic registers directly to real registers. Spilling has the effect of potentially splitting a web into two or more webs and thus reducing the interferences in the graph. For example, in Figure 16.5, we can split the web that includes the definition of y in block B2 and its use in block B4 into two webs by introducing a store of the register containing y at the end of B2 and a load from the location it was stored to at the beginning of B4.

If spill decisions are made carefully, they both make the graph R-colorable and insert the minimum number of stores and reloads, as measured dynamically.

Spilling register contents to memory after they are set and reloading them (or rematerializing them) when they are about to be needed is a graph-coloring register allocator's primary tool for making an interference graph R-colorable. It has the effect of potentially splitting a web into two or more webs and so reducing the interferences in the graph, thus increasing the chance that the result will be R-colorable.

Each adjacency-list element has a component spcost that estimates the cost of spilling the corresponding symbolic register, in a way that resembles the usage counts described in Section 16.1.

More specifically, the cost of spilling a web w is taken to be

$$defwt \cdot \sum_{def \in w} 10^{depth(def)} + usewt \cdot \sum_{use \in w} 10^{depth(use)} - copywt \cdot \sum_{copy \in w} 10^{depth(copy)}$$

where *def*, *use*, and *copy* are individual definitions, uses, and register copies in the web w; *defwt*, *usewt*, and *copywt* are relative weights assigned to the instruction types.

Computing spill costs should take the following into account:

1. If a web's value can be more efficiently recomputed than reloaded, the cost of recomputing it is used instead.

2. If the source or target of a copy instruction is spilled, the instruction is no longer needed.

3. If a spilled value is used several times in the same basic block and the restored value remains live until the last use of the spilled value in that block, then only a single load of the value is needed in the block.

The ICAN routine Compute_Spill_Costs( ) in Figure 16.16 computes and saves the spill cost for each register in the adjacency lists. The weights of loads, stores, and copies are the values of UseWt, DefWt, and CopyWt, respectively, in Figure 16.3. This can be further refined to take immediate loads and adds into account, by checking for their occurrence and assigning them weights of 1 also. We incorporate the first

```
procedure Compute_Spill_Costs(nblocks,ninsts,LBlock)
   nblocks: in integer
   ninsts: in integer ⟶ integer
   LBlock: in integer ⟶ array [1··nblocks] of array [··] of LIRInst
begin
   i, j: integer
   r: real
   inst: LIRInst
   || sum the costs of all definitions and uses for each
   || symbolic register
   for i := 1 to nblocks do
      for j := 1 to ninsts[i] do
         inst := LBlock[i][j]
         case LIR_Exp_Kind(inst.kind) of
binexp:    if inst.opd1.kind = regno then
              AdjLsts[inst.opd1.val].spcost
                 += UseWt * 10.0↑depth(i)
           fi
           if inst.opd2.kind = regno then
              AdjLsts[inst.opd2.val].spcost
                 += UseWt * 10.0↑depth(i)
           fi
unexp:     if inst.opd.kind = regno then
              if inst.kind = valasgn then
                 AdjLsts[inst.opd.val].spcost
                    -= CopyWt 10.0↑depth(i)
              else
                 AdjLsts[inst.opd.val].spcost
                    += UseWt * 10.0↑depth(i)
              fi
           fi
noexp:     esac
           if LIR_Has_Left(inst.kind) & inst.kind ≠ regval then
              AdjLsts[inst.left].spcost
                 += DefWt * 10.0↑depth(i)
           fi
      od
   od
   for i := nregs+1 to nwebs do
      || replace by rematerialization cost if less than
      || spill cost
      r := Rematerialize(i,nblocks,ninsts,LBlock)
      if r < AdjLsts[i].spcost then
         AdjLsts[i].spcost := r
      fi
   od
end    || Compute_Spill_Costs
```

FIG. 16.16 ICAN code to compute spill costs for symbolic registers.

two of the above conditions in the algorithm; the third is left as an exercise for the reader. The algorithm uses the following functions:

1. `depth(`i`)` returns the depth of loop nesting of basic block i in the flowgraph.

2. `Rematerialize(`i`,nblocks,ninsts,LBlock)` returns the cost to recompute the symbolic register with number i rather than spilling and reloading it.

3. `Real(`i`)` returns the real number with the same value as the integer i.

16.3.8   Pruning the Interference Graph

Next we attempt to R-color the graph, where R is the number of registers available. We do not attempt to find an R-coloring exhaustively—that has long been known to be an *NP*-complete problem for $R \geq 3$, and besides, the graph may simply not be R-colorable. Instead, we use two approaches to simplifying the graph, one that is guaranteed to make a section of the graph R-colorable as long as the remainder of the graph is R-colorable, and one that optimistically carries on from there. The latter approach may not result in an R-coloring immediately, but it very frequently makes more of the graph colorable than using just the first approach and so is very useful for its heuristic value.

The first approach is a simple but remarkably effective observation we call the *degree* $< R$ rule: given a graph that contains a node with degree less than R, the graph is R-colorable if and only if the graph without that node is R-colorable. That R-colorability of the whole graph implies R-colorability of the graph without the selected node is obvious. For the other direction, suppose we have an R-coloring of the graph without the distinguished node. Since that node has degree less than R, there must be at least one color that is not in use for a node adjacent to it, and the node can be assigned that color. Of course, this rule does not make an arbitrary graph R-colorable. In fact, Figure 16.17(a) is an example of a graph that is 2-colorable but not by this rule and the graph in Figure 16.17(b) is 3-colorable, but not by this rule. However, the rule is quite effective in practice for coloring interference

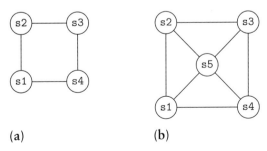

(a)   (b)

FIG. 16.17   Example graphs that are (a) 2-colorable and (b) 3-colorable, but not by the degree $< R$ rule.

graphs. For a machine with 32 registers (or twice that, counting floating point), it is sufficient to enable coloring of many of the graphs encountered.

The second approach, the optimistic heuristic, generalizes the degree $< R$ rule by removing nodes that have degree $\geq R$. The reasoning behind this approach is the observation that just because a node has R or more neighbors, they need not all have different colors; and, further, they may not use as many as R colors. Thus, if the first approach does not exhaust the graph, we continue processing it by selecting candidates for coloring and optimistically, in the hope that colors will be available for them when they are needed.

Thus, we begin the coloring process by repeatedly searching the graph for nodes that have fewer than R neighbors. Each one that we find we remove from the graph and place onto the stack, so that we can retrieve them for coloring in the reverse of the order we found them. As part of this process, we remember the nodes adjacent to each removed node so they can be used during register assignment (see the next section). If we exhaust the graph in the process, we have determined that an R-coloring is possible as is. We pop the nodes from the stack and assign each of them a color from among those not already assigned to adjacent nodes. For example, given the interference graph in Figure 16.2, we can remove nodes from the graph and place them on the stack in the following order (the bottom of the stack of pruned nodes is at the right):

| r3 | r2 | r1 | s4 | s2 | s1 | s3 | s5 | s6 |

We can then pop the nodes and assign them colors (represented by integers) as described above and as shown below.

Node	Color
r3	1
r2	2
r1	3
s4	1
s2	2
s1	3
s3	1
s5	3
s6	2

As indicated above, the degree $< R$ rule is sometimes not applicable. In that case, we apply the optimistic heuristic; that is, we choose a node with degree $\geq R$ and minimal spill cost divided by its current degree in the graph and optimistically push it onto the stack. We do so in the hope that not all the colors will be used for its neighbors, thus postponing spilling decisions from being made during pruning the interference graph to the step that actually attempts to assign colors to the nodes, namely, the routine `Assign_Regs( )` in Figure 16.20.

Before we move on to the code for pruning the graph, we note the difficulty of keeping the code and the interference graph synchronous with each other as pruning

```
procedure Prune_Graph( )
begin
    success: boolean
    i, j, nodes := nwebs, spillnode: integer
    spillcost: real
    Stack := []
    repeat
        || apply degree < R rule and push nodes onto stack
        repeat
            success := true
            for i := 1 to nwebs do
                if AdjLsts[i].nints > 0
                    & AdjLsts[i].nints < nregs then
                    success := false
                    Stack ⊕= [i]
                    Adjust_Neighbors(i)
                    nodes -= 1
                fi
            od
        until success
        if nodes ≠ 0 then
            || find node with minimal spill cost divided by its degree and
            || push it onto the stack
            spillcost := ∞
            for i := 1 to nwebs do
                if AdjLsts[i].nints > 0
                    & AdjLsts[i].spcost/AdjLsts[i].nints < spillcost then
                    spillnode := i
                    spillcost := AdjLsts[i].spcost/AdjLsts[i].nints
                fi
            od
            Stack ⊕= [spillnode]
            Adjust_Neighbors(spillnode)
            nodes -= 1
        fi
    until nodes = 0
end     || Prune_Graph
```

FIG. 16.18 Code to attempt to *R*-color the interference graph.

decisions are made. This can be expensive, since what a spill does is to divide a web
into several webs (or, in terms of the graph, it divides one node into several nodes).
The way we deal with this problem is to avoid updating the code while pruning. If
register assignment fails, then, in the next iteration, building the adjacency matrix
and lists will be a lot quicker because of the spills that have been performed.

Figure 16.18 shows the ICAN routine Prune_Graph( ) that applies the degree < *R*
rule and the optimistic heuristic to attempt to color the interference graph. It uses
the routine Adjust_Neighbors( ) in Figure 16.19 to effect the removal of a node

```
procedure Adjust_Neighbors(i)
    i: in integer
begin
    j, k: integer
    || move neighbors of node i from adjnds to rmvadj and
    || disconnect node i from its neighbors
    for k := 1 to |AdjLsts[i].adjnds| do
        AdjLsts[k].nints -= 1
        j := 1
        while j ≤ |AdjLsts[k].adjnds| do
            if AdjLsts[k].adjnds↓j = i then
                AdjLsts[k].adjnds ⊖= j
                AdjLsts[k].rmvadj ⊕= [i]
            fi
            j += 1
        od
    od
    AdjLsts[i].nints := 0
    AdjLsts[i].rmvadj ⊕= AdjLsts[i].adjnds
    AdjLsts[i].adjnds := []
end    || Adjust_Neighbors
```

FIG. 16.19 The routine `Adjust_Neighbors( )` used in pruning the interference graph.

from the graph. The global variable `Stack` is used to convey to `Assign_Regs( )`, described in the next subsection, the order in which the nodes were pruned.

16.3.9   Assigning Registers

The ICAN routine `Assign_Regs( )` that R-colors the interference graph is given in Figure 16.20. It uses the routine `Min_Color(r)`, which returns the minimum color number of those colors that are not assigned to nodes adjacent to r, or returns 0 if all colors are in use for adjacent nodes; and assigns values to the function `Real_Reg(s)`, which returns the real register that symbolic register s has been assigned to.

If `Assign_Regs( )` succeeds, `Modify_Code( )`, shown in Figure 16.21, is invoked next to replace the symbolic registers by the corresponding real registers. Modify_Code( ) uses `Color_to_Reg( )` to convert the color assigned to a symbolic register to the corresponding real register's name. `Color_to_Reg( )` uses `Real_Reg( )` to determine which real register has been assigned each color.

16.3.10   Spilling Symbolic Registers

The number of colors needed to color an interference graph is often called its *register pressure,* and so modifications to the code intended to make the graph colorable are described as "reducing the register pressure."

In general, the effect of spilling is to split a web into two or more webs and to distribute the interferences of the original web among the new ones. If, for example,

```
procedure Assign_Regs( ) returns boolean
begin
    c, i, r: integer
    success := true: boolean
    repeat
        || pop nodes from the stack and assign each one
        || a color, if possible
        r := Stack↓-1
        Stack ⊖= -1
        c := Min_Color(r)
        if c > 0 then
            if r ≤ nregs then
                Real_Reg(c) := r
            fi
            AdjLsts[r].color := c
        else
            || if no color is available for node r,
            || mark it for spilling
            AdjLsts[r].spill := true
            success := false
        fi
    until Stack = []
    return success
end    || Assign_Regs
```

FIG. 16.20 Routine to assign colors to real and symbolic registers.

we split web w1 in Figure 16.5 by introducing loads and stores as shown by the assignments to and from tmp in Figure 16.22, it is replaced by four new webs w5, . . . , w8, as shown in the following table:

Web	Components
w2	def x in B5, use x in B6
w3	def y in B2, use y in B4
w4	def y in B1, use y in B3
w5	def x in B2, tmp ← x in B2
w6	def x in B3, tmp ← x in B3
w7	x ← tmp in B4, use x in B4
w8	x ← tmp in B5, use x in B5

and the interference graph is as shown in Figure 16.23.

Given that we have failed to make the interference graph R-colorable, we next spill the nodes marked to be spilled, i.e., the nodes i for which AdjLsts[i].spill = true.

The code of Gen_Spill_Code( ) is shown in Figure 16.24. It uses the subroutine Comp_Disp(r), also in Figure 16.24, to determine whether symbolic register r has been assigned a spill displacement. If not, it increments Disp and stores the displacement in AdjLsts[i].disp, where i is the index of r in the adjacency lists. The

```
procedure Modify_Code(nblocks,ninsts,LBlock)
    nblocks: in integer
    ninsts: inout array [1··nblocks] of integer
    LBlock: inout array [1··nblocks] of array [··] of LIRInst
begin
    i, j, k, m: integer
    inst: LIRInst
    || replace each use of a symbolic register by the real
    || register with the same color
    for i := 1 to nblocks do
        for j := 1 to ninsts[i] do
            inst := LBlock[i][j]
            case LIR_Exp_Kind(inst.kind) of
binexp:     if inst.opd1.kind = regno
                & Reg_to_Int(inst.opd1.val) > nregs then
                LBlock[i][j].opd1.val :=
                    Color_to_Reg(AdjLsts[inst.opd1.val].color)
            fi
            if inst.opd2.kind = regno
                & Reg_to_Int(inst.opd2.val) > nregs then
                LBlock[i][j].opd2.val :=
                    Color_to_Reg(AdjLsts[inst.opd2.val].color)
            fi
unexp:      if inst.opd.kind = regno
                & Reg_to_Int(inst.opd.val) > nregs then
                LBlock[i][j].opd.val :=
                    Color_to_Reg(AdjLsts[inst.opd.val].color)
            fi
listexp:    for k := 1 to |inst.args| do
                if Reg_to_Int(inst.args↓k@1.regno) > nregs then
                    m := AdjLsts[inst.args↓k@1.val].color
                    LBlock[i][j].args↓i@1.val :=
                        Color_to_Reg(m)
                fi
            od
noexp:      esac
            if LIR_Has_Left(inst.kind) then
                if Reg_to_Int(inst.left) > nregs then
                    LBlock[i][j].left :=
                        Color_to_Reg(AdjLsts[inst.left].color)
                fi
            fi
        od
    od
end     || Modify_Code
```

FIG. 16.21 ICAN routine to modify the instructions in the procedure to have real registers in place of symbolic ones.

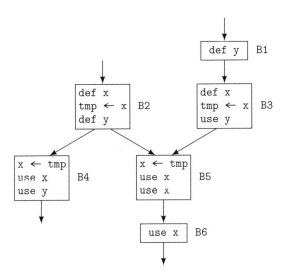

FIG. 16.22 The example in Figure 16.5 after splitting web w1.

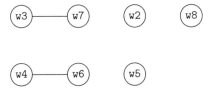

FIG. 16.23 Interferences among the webs in Figure 16.22.

variable BaseReg holds the name of the register to be used as the base register in spilling and restoring. Gen_Spill_Code( ) uses two other functions, as follows:

1. insert_before(*i,j*,ninsts,LBlock,*inst*) inserts the instruction *inst* immediately before instruction LBlock[*i*] [*j*] (see Figure 4.14).

2. insert_after(*i,j*,ninsts,LBlock,*inst*) inserts the instruction *inst* immediately after instruction LBlock[*i*] [*j*] (see Figure 4.14).

Note that Gen_Spill_Code( ) does not take into account load or add immediates or other ways of rematerialization and that it only deals with word-size operands as written. Exercises at the end of the chapter deal with some of these issues.

Note also that if we must insert spill code for symbolic registers that are defined and/or used in a loop, then, if possible, we should restore them before entering the loop and spill them after exiting it. This may require edge splitting, as described in Section 13.3. In particular, in the example in Figure 16.26, if we had to spill s2, we would introduce new basic blocks B1a between B1 and B2 and B2a between B2 and B4, with a restore for s2 in B1a and a spill for it in B2a.

```
procedure Gen_Spill_Code(nblocks,ninsts,LBlock)
   nblocks: in integer
   ninsts: inout array [1··nblocks] of integer
   LBlock: inout array [1··nblocks] of array [··] of LIRInst
begin
   i, j, regct := 0: integer
   inst: LIRInst
   || check each definition or use of a symbolic register
   || to determine whether it is marked to be spilled, and,
   || if so, compute the displacement for it and insert
   || instructions to load it before each use and store
   || it after each definition
   for i := 1 to nblocks do
      j := 1
      while j ≤ ninsts[i] do
         inst := LBlock[i][j]
         case LIR_Exp_Kind(inst.kind) of
binexp:     if AdjLsts[inst.opd1.val].spill then
               Comp_Disp(inst.opd1.val)
               insert_before(i,j,ninsts,LBlock,⟨kind:loadmem,
                  left:inst.opd1.val,addr:⟨kind:addrrc,
                  reg:BaseReg,disp:Disp⟩⟩)
               j += 1
            fi
            if inst.opd2 ≠ inst.opd1
               & AdjLsts[inst.opd2.val].spill then
               Comp_Disp(inst.opd2.val)
               insert_before(i,j,ninsts,LBlock,⟨kind:loadmem,
                  left:inst.opd2.val,addr:⟨kind:addrrc,
                  reg:BaseReg,disp:Disp⟩⟩)
               j += 1
            fi
unexp:      if AdjLsts[inst.opd.val].spill then
               Comp_Disp(inst.opd.val)
               insert_before(i,j,ninsts,LBlock,⟨kind:loadmem,
                  left:inst.opd.val,addr:⟨kind:addrrc,
                  reg:BaseReg,disp:Disp⟩⟩)
               j += 1
            fi
```

FIG. 16.24 ICAN code to generate spill code using the costs computed by Compute_Spill_Costs( ) in Figure 16.16.

16.3.11 Two Examples of Register Allocation by Graph Coloring

As our first example of register allocation by graph coloring, consider the flowgraph in Figure 16.25, where c is a nonlocal variable, and assume that we have five registers, r1, r2, r3, r4, and r5, available (so $R = 5$) for allocation, except that

```
listexp:      for k := 1 to |inst.args| do
                  if AdjLsts[inst.args↓k@1.val].spill then
                      Comp_Disp(inst.args↓k@1.val)
                      insert_before(i,j,ninsts,LBlock,
                          ⟨kind:loadmem,left:inst.opd.val,
                          addr:⟨kind:addrrc,
                          reg:BaseReg,disp:Disp⟩⟩)
                      regct += 1
                  fi
              od
              j += regct - 1
noexp:    esac
          if LIR_Has_Left(inst.kind)
              & AdjLsts[inst.left].spill then
              Comp_Disp(inst.left)
              insert_after(i,j,ninsts,LBlock,⟨kind:stormem,
                  addr:⟨kind:addrrc,
                  reg:BaseReg,disp:Disp⟩⟩,
                  opd:⟨kind:regno,val:inst.left⟩⟩)
              j += 1
          fi
      od
   od
end     || Gen_Spill_Code

procedure Comp_Disp(r)
   r: in Register
begin
   || if symbolic register r has no displacement yet,
   || assign one and increment Disp
   || Note:  this assumes each operand is no larger
   || than a word
   if AdjLsts[Reg_to_Int(r)].color = -∞ then
      AdjLsts[Reg_to_Int(r)].disp := Disp
      Disp += 4
   fi
end     || Comp_Disp
```

FIG. 16.24 *(continued)*

only g can be in r5. Further, assume that the execution frequencies of blocks B1, B3, and B4 are 1 and that of B2 is 7. There is one web per symbolic register, so we use the names of the symbolic registers for the webs, as shown in Figure 16.26.

Then we build the adjacency matrix for the code in Figure 16.26, as shown in Figure 16.27(b), along with a graphic presentation of the interference graph in Figure 16.27(a).

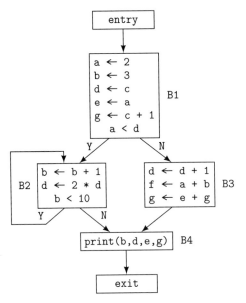

FIG. 16.25 A small example of register allocation by graph coloring.

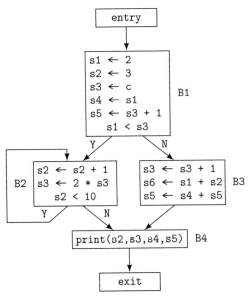

FIG. 16.26 The example in Figure 16.25 with symbolic registers substituted for the local variables.

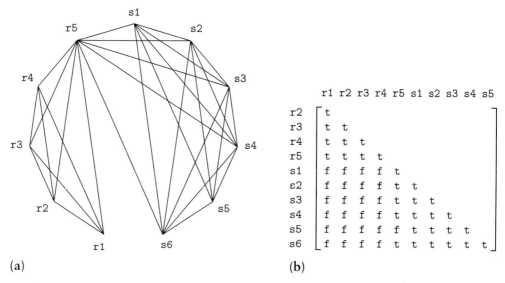

FIG. 16.27 The interference graph (a) and adjacency matrix (b) for the example in Figure 16.26, where t and f stand for true and false, respectively.

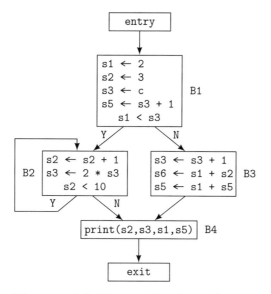

FIG. 16.28 The example in Figure 16.26 after coalescing registers s4 and s1.

Applying coalescing to the copy assignment s4 ← s1 in block B1 in Figure 16.26 results in the flowgraph in Figure 16.28 and the new interference graph and adjacency matrix in Figure 16.29. Now there are no further opportunities for coalescing, so we build the adjacency lists for the routine, as shown in Figure 16.30.

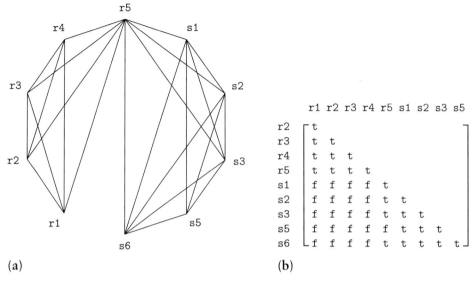

FIG. 16.29 The interference graph (a) and adjacency matrix (b) for the example in Figure 16.28 after coalescing symbolic registers s1 and s4, where t and f stand for true and false, respectively.

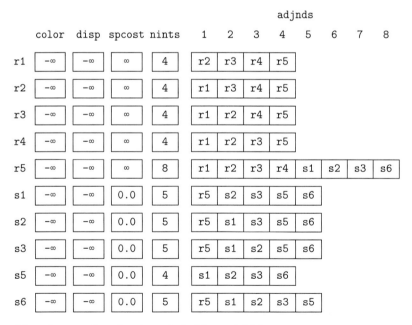

FIG. 16.30 The adjacency lists for the code in Figure 16.28.

Next we compute spill costs, using $\mathtt{DefWt} = \mathtt{UseWt} = 2$ and $\mathtt{CopyWt} = 1$, as follows:

Symbolic Register	Spill Cost
s1	2.0
s2	1.0 + 21.0 + 2.0 + 2.0 = 26.0
s3	6.0 + 14.0 + 4.0 + 2.0 = 26.0
s5	2.0 + 4.0 + 2.0 = 8.0
s6	∞

Note that the spill cost for s1 is 2.0 because the assignment to it is a load immediate and it can be rematerialized in block B3 by a load immediate placed just before its use in the second instruction. Also, we make the spill cost of s6 infinite because the symbolic register is dead.

From there we proceed to pruning the graph. Since each of r1 through r4 has fewer than five neighbors, we remove them and push them onto the stack, resulting in the stack appearing as follows:

```
r4   r3   r2   r1
```

The resulting interference graph and adjacency matrix are as shown in Figure 16.31 and the corresponding adjacency lists are shown in Figure 16.32. Now node r5 has fewer than five neighbors, so we remove it and push it onto the stack, resulting in the stack

```
r5   r4   r3   r2   r1
```

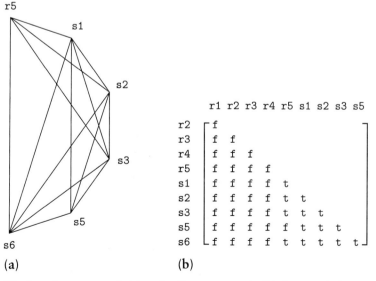

(a)   (b)

FIG. 16.31 The interference graph (a) and adjacency matrix (b) that result from pushing r1 through r4 onto the stack, where t and f stand for true and false, respectively.

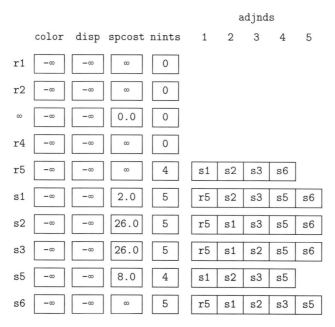

FIG. 16.32 The adjacency lists corresponding to the interference graph in Figure 16.31.

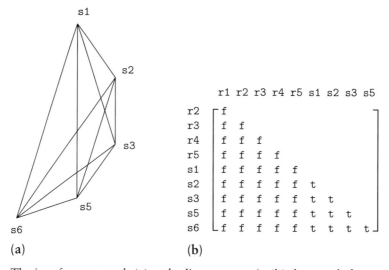

FIG. 16.33 The interference graph (a) and adjacency matrix (b) that result from pushing r5 onto the stack, where t and f stand for true and false, respectively.

and the resulting interference graph and adjacency matrix are as shown in Figure 16.33 and the corresponding adjacency lists are shown in Figure 16.34.

Now no node has five or more adjacent nodes, so we push the remaining symbolic registers onto the stack in an arbitrary order, as follows:

| s1 | s2 | s3 | s5 | s6 | r5 | r4 | r3 | r2 | r1 |

	color	disp	spcost	nints	adjnds			
					1	2	3	4
r1	$-\infty$	$-\infty$	∞	0				
r2	$-\infty$	$-\infty$	∞	0				
r3	$-\infty$	$-\infty$	∞	0				
r4	$-\infty$	$-\infty$	∞	0				
r5	$-\infty$	$-\infty$	∞	0				
s1	$-\infty$	$-\infty$	2.0	4	s2	s3	s5	s6
s2	$-\infty$	$-\infty$	26.0	4	s1	s3	s5	s6
s3	$-\infty$	$-\infty$	26.0	4	s1	s2	s5	s6
s5	$-\infty$	$-\infty$	8.0	4	s1	s2	s3	s5
s6	$-\infty$	$-\infty$	∞	4	s1	s2	s3	s5

FIG. 16.34 The adjacency lists corresponding to the interference graph in Figure 16.33.

and we color them (i.e., assign real registers to symbolic ones) as we pop them off, as follows:

Register	Color
s1	1
s2	2
s3	3
s5	4
s6	5
r5	4
r4	1
r3	2
r2	3
r1	5

and we have achieved a register allocation without spilling any registers to memory. Figure 16.35 shows the flowgraph with real registers substituted for the symbolic ones.

Our second example will require spilling a register. We begin with the code in Figure 16.36, with symbolic registers already in use in the code and with the assumption that real registers r2, r3, and r4 are available for allocation. The interference graph and adjacency matrix for this example are shown in Figure 16.37.

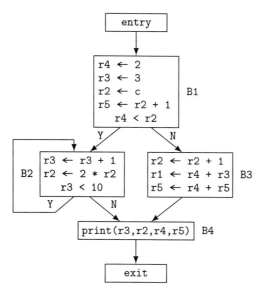

FIG. 16.35 The flowgraph in Figure 16.28 with real registers substituted for symbolic registers.

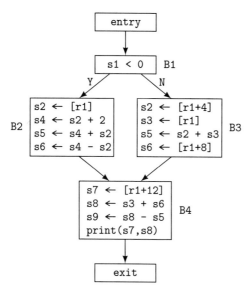

FIG. 16.36 Another example flowgraph for register allocation by graph coloring.

There are no opportunities for coalescing, so we construct the adjacency lists, as shown in Figure 16.38. Next, we compute the spill costs and fill them in in the adjacency lists. Note that the spill costs of s1 and s9 are both infinite, since s1 is dead on exit from B1 and s9 is dead at its definition point.

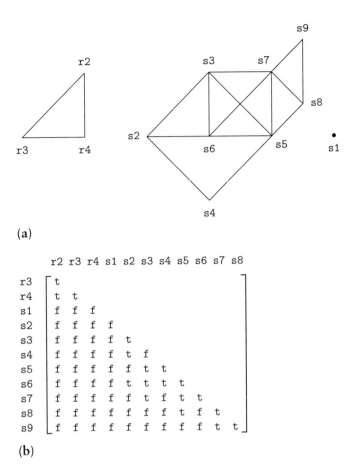

(a)

```
         r2 r3 r4 s1 s2 s3 s4 s5 s6 s7 s8
    r3  ⎡ t                                  ⎤
    r4  │ t  t                               │
    s1  │ f  f  f                            │
    s2  │ f  f  f  f                         │
    s3  │ f  f  f  f  t                      │
    s4  │ f  f  f  f  t  f                   │
    s5  │ f  f  f  f  f  t  t                │
    s6  │ f  f  f  f  t  t  t  t             │
    s7  │ f  f  f  f  f  t  f  t  t          │
    s8  │ f  f  f  f  f  f  f  t  f  t       │
    s9  ⎣ f  f  f  f  f  f  f  f  f  t  t    ⎦
```

(b)

FIG. 16.37 The interference graph (a) and adjacency matrix (b) for the example in Figure 16.36.

Next we prune the graph. Node s1 (with no adjacent nodes) is removed and pushed onto the stack. The real registers, s4, and s9 (with two adjacent nodes each) are removed next and pushed onto the stack, as follows:

s9	s4	r4	r3	r2	s1

and the interference graph shown in Figure 16.39(a). Removing nodes s2 and s8 and pushing them onto the stack results in the stack

s8	s2	s9	s4	r4	r3	r2	s1

and the interference graph shown in Figure 16.39(b).

We are left with a graph in which every node has degree three, so we select a node with minimal spill cost divided by current degree, namely, s7, to be pushed onto the stack. This reduces the interference graph to the form shown graphically in Figure 16.39(c). So we remove the remaining nodes and push them onto the stack, resulting in the empty graph and the stack as follows:

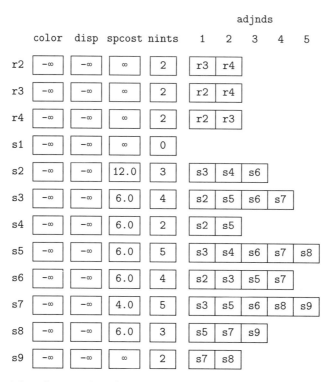

	color	disp	spcost	nints	adjnds 1	2	3	4	5
r2	-∞	-∞	∞	2	r3	r4			
r3	-∞	-∞	∞	2	r2	r4			
r4	-∞	-∞	∞	2	r2	r3			
s1	-∞	-∞	∞	0					
s2	-∞	-∞	12.0	3	s3	s4	s6		
s3	-∞	-∞	6.0	4	s2	s5	s6	s7	
s4	-∞	-∞	6.0	2	s2	s5			
s5	-∞	-∞	6.0	5	s3	s4	s6	s7	s8
s6	-∞	-∞	6.0	4	s2	s3	s5	s7	
s7	-∞	-∞	4.0	5	s3	s5	s6	s8	s9
s8	-∞	-∞	6.0	3	s5	s7	s9		
s9	-∞	-∞	∞	2	s7	s8			

FIG. 16.38 The adjacency lists for the code in Figure 16.36.

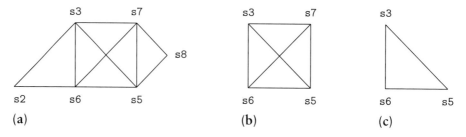

FIG. 16.39 (a) The interference graph after removing nodes s1, r2, r3, r4, s4, and s9, and pushing them onto the stack, (b) then removing nodes s2 and s8 and pushing them onto the stack, and (c) after removing node s7 and pushing it onto the stack.

| s5 | s6 | s3 | s7 | s8 | s2 | s9 | s4 | r4 | r3 | r2 | s1 |

Now we begin to pop nodes off the stack, assigning them colors, and reconstructing the adjacency-lists form of the interference graph from the AdjLsts[ ].rmvadj fields. After popping the top four nodes, we have the interference graph shown in Figure 16.40 (with the colors shown in **bold** type in circles), and there is no color available for node s7.

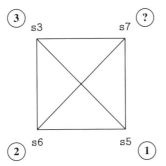

FIG. 16.40 The interference graph after popping the top four nodes from the stack.

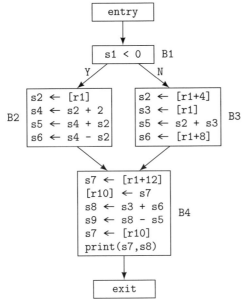

FIG. 16.41 The flowgraph in Figure 16.36 with spill code included for s7.

So we proceed to generate spill code for s7 in block B4 with BaseReg = r10 and Disp = 0, as shown in Figure 16.41. Next we build the interference graph for the new flowgraph, as shown in Figure 16.42, and it becomes clear that we may simply proceed to prune the graph and assign real registers to the symbolic registers with the same colors, as shown in Figure 16.43.

16.3.12   Other Issues

Bernstein et al. [BerG89] discuss three heuristics that can be used to select values to spill and an allocator that tries all three and uses the best of them. Their first heuristic is

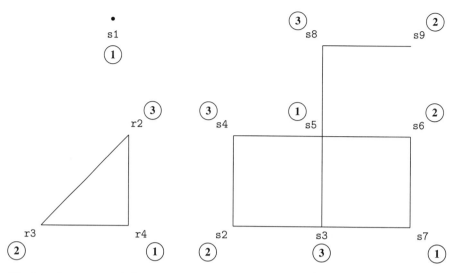

FIG. 16.42 The interference graph for the code in Figure 16.41.

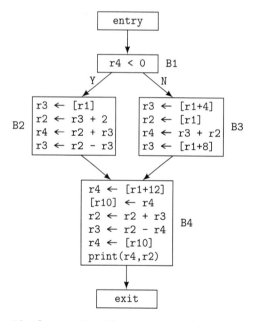

FIG. 16.43 The flowgraph in Figure 16.41 with real registers substituted for the symbolic ones.

$$h_1(w) = \frac{cost(w)}{degree(w)^2}$$

and is based on the observation that spilling a web with high degree reduces the degree of many other nodes and so is more likely to maximize the number of webs that have degree $< R$ after spilling. The second and third heuristics use a measure called *area( )*, defined as follows:

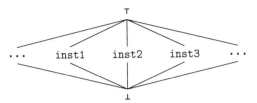

FIG. 16.44 Rematerialization lattice.

$$area(w) = \sum_{I \in inst(w)} (width(I) \cdot 5^{depth(I)})$$

where $inst(w)$ is the set of instructions in web w, $width(I)$ is the number of webs live at instruction I, and $depth(I)$ is the loop nesting level of I. The two heuristics are intended to take into account the global effect of each web on the register pressure and are as follows:

$$h_2(w) = \frac{cost(w)}{area(w) \cdot degree(w)}$$

$$h_3(w) = \frac{cost(w)}{area(w) \cdot degree(w)^2}$$

Of 15 programs that the authors report trying the three heuristics and other modifications on, the first heuristic does best on four, the second does best on six, and the third on eight (the second and third are tied on one program), and in every case, the best of them is better than previous approaches. This allocator is now part of the IBM compilers for POWER and PowerPC (see Section 21.2).

Briggs [Brig92] suggests a series of additional extensions to the allocation algorithm, including the following:

1. a more satisfactory method for handling register pairs than Nickerson's approach for the Intel 386 architecture [Nick90] that results from postponing spilling decisions to after registers have been assigned (see also Exercise 16.4);

2. an improved method of *rematerialization*, the process of regenerating in registers values such as constants that are more efficiently recomputed than spilled and reloaded; and

3. an approach to aggressively splitting webs before coloring that takes into account the structure of a procedure's flowgraph, unlike the interference graph.

Briggs's approach to rematerialization involves splitting a web into the values that make it up, performing a data-flow computation that associates with each potentially rematerializable value the instruction(s) that would be used to rematerialize it, and constructing new webs, each consisting of values that have the same instruction associated with them. The lattice is a flat one, as shown in Figure 16.44. Note that in the case of large constants on a RISC architecture, the code to rematerialize a value might be two instructions, a load upper immediate and an add to the loaded register. Occasionally, a web is split further by this process than is ideal, and a fix-up phase is used to find such webs and reconnect them.

16.4   Priority-Based Graph Coloring

Register allocation by priority-based graph coloring is similar in its overall structure to the approach described in the preceding section, but differs from it in several important details, some essential and some incidental. The approach originated with Chow and Hennessy ([ChoH84] and [ChoH90]) and is intended to be more sensitive to the costs and benefits of individual allocation decisions than the previous approach.

One significant difference is that the priority-based approach allocates all objects to "home" memory locations before register allocation and then attempts to migrate them to registers, rather than allocating them to symbolic registers, trying to pack the symbolic registers into the real registers, and generating spill code as necessary. While the two approaches may appear to be equivalent in this regard, with symbolic registers corresponding to home memory locations that have simply not been assigned to specific addresses, they are not. The graph-coloring approach is optimistic—it begins with the assumption that all the symbolic registers might be allocatable to real registers, and it may succeed in doing so. On the other hand, priority-based coloring is pessimistic: it may not be able to allocate all the home memory locations to registers, so, for an architecture without storage-to-storage operations (i.e., a RISC), it needs to reserve four registers of each variety for use in evaluating expressions that involve variables that it does not succeed in allocating to registers. Thus, it begins with a handicap, namely, fewer registers are available for allocation.

Another difference is that the priority-based approach was designed *a priori* to be machine-independent, so it is parameterized with several machine-specific quantities that specialize it to a given implementation. This is not a major difference—there is not much about the other approach that is machine-specific either. The quantities are some of the ones defined in Section 16.2, namely, *ldcost*, *stcost*, *usesave*, and *defsave*.

A third, more significant difference is in the concepts of web and interference used. Chow and Hennessy represent the web of a variable as the set of basic blocks it is live in and call it a *live range*. As the example in Figure 16.45 shows, this is conservative, but it may be much less precise than the graph-coloring method, in which none of the variables x, y, z, and w are live at a definition point of another,

```
        x ← a + b        B1
        y ← x + c
        if y = 0 goto L1
        z ← y + d        B2
        w ← z
L1:     . . .            B3
```

FIG. 16.45   Example of code for which Chow and Hennessy's live ranges are less precise than our webs.

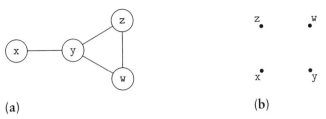

(a)   (b)

FIG. 16.46   (a) Priority-based graph-coloring interference graph and (b) graph-coloring interference
graphs for the code in Figure 16.45.

so there are no interferences among them. Using Chow and Hennessy's method, x
interferes with y, y with both z and w, and z and w with each other. The resulting
interference graphs are shown in Figure 16.46.[7]

Larus and Hilfinger's register allocator for the SPUR LISP compiler [LarH86] uses
a version of priority-based coloring. It differs from Chow and Hennessy's approach
in two ways, as follows:

1. It assigns temporaries to registers *ab initio* and generates spill code for them as
    needed.

2. It operates on SPUR assembly language, rather than on medium-level intermediate
    code, and so must add load and store instructions for spilled temporaries.

Briggs [Brig92] investigated the running times of two register allocators, one his
own and the other a priority-based allocator. He found that his allocator seemed
to run in $O(n \log n)$ time on his test programs, while the priority-based allocator
seemed to require $O(n^2)$ time, where n is the number of instructions in the program.

16.5   Other Approaches to Register Allocation

Several other approaches to global register allocation by graph coloring have been
presented and evaluated, including two that use a procedure's control tree (see
Section 7.6) to guide spilling or graph-pruning decisions, one by Callahan and
Koblenz [CalK91] and one by Knobe and Zadeck [KnoZ92].

Another approach, developed by Gupta, Soffa, and Steele [GupS89], uses maximal clique separators to perform graph coloring. A *clique* is a graph with each node
connected to every other node by an arc. A *clique separator* is a subgraph that is a
clique such that removing the subgraph splits the containing graph into two or more
unconnected subgraphs. A clique separator is *maximal* if there is no node (and its
incident arcs) in the graph that can be added to the clique separator to produce a
larger clique. Maximal clique separators with at most R nodes have two attractive
properties: they divide a program into segments for which register allocation can be

---

7. The original presentation of register allocation by priority-based graph coloring included a further significant departure from the basic graph-coloring approach. Namely, the allocation process
was divided into local and global phases, with the local phase used to do allocation within basic
blocks and across small clusters of basic blocks.

performed separately and they can be constructed by examining the code, without actually constructing the full interference graph.

In Section 20.3, we discuss an approach to register allocation for array elements that can have significant performance impact, especially for repetitive numerical computations; and in Section 19.6, we discuss link-time and compile-time approaches to interprocedural register allocation.

Register allocation can needlessly decrease the available instruction-level parallelism by reusing registers sooner than they need be; this can be alleviated by doing hardware or software register renaming (Section 17.4.5) and, in part, by tuning the register allocator to cycle through the registers rather than reusing them as soon as they become free. Alternatively, register allocation and scheduling can be integrated into a single pass. Several researchers have investigated ways to combine the two into one phase that achieves the best of both. The efforts of Bradlee, Eggers, and Henry [BraE91] and of Pinter [Pint93] are steps in this direction.

16.6   Wrap-Up

In this chapter we have covered register allocation and assignment, which are among the most important optimizations for almost all programs. We have seen that register allocation should be done on low-level code, either an intermediate form or assembly language, because it is essential that all loads and stores and their address computations be explicit.

We began with a discussion of a venerable, quick, and tolerably effective local approach that depends on usage counts and loop nesting to decide what objects should be in registers. Then we presented in detail a much more effective approach, namely, global register allocation by graph coloring, and briefly another approach that also uses graph coloring but that is generally less effective. We also alluded to an approach that uses bin packing; two relatively new approaches that use a procedure's control tree to guide allocation and spilling decisions; and another new approach that uses maximal clique separators.

We have seen that register allocation by graph coloring usually results in very effective allocations without a major cost in compilation speed. It represents allocatable quantities (symbolic registers) and the real registers by nodes in a graph and the interferences among them by arcs. It then attempts to color the nodes with a number of colors equal to the number of available registers, so that every node is assigned a color distinct from those of its neighbor nodes. If this cannot be done, code is introduced to spill symbolic registers to memory and to reload them where they are needed, and the process is repeated until the coloring goal has been achieved.

The major lessons to be garnered from this chapter are the following:

1. There are reasonably effective local methods of register allocation that cost very little in compilation time and are suitable for unoptimized compilation.

2. There is a global method of register allocation, graph coloring, that is very effective, costs somewhat more than the local approach, and is appropriate for optimized compilation.

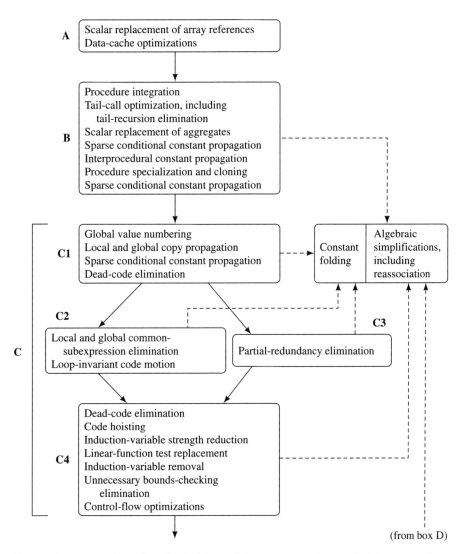

FIG. 16.47 Place of register allocation (in **bold** type) in an aggressive optimizing compiler. *(continued)*

3. Research continues into other approaches that may well produce even more effective allocators—probably without requiring significantly more time than graph coloring—and that may combine register allocation and instruction scheduling without adversely impacting either.

The appropriate placement of global register allocation by graph coloring in an aggressive optimizing compiler is marked by **bold** type in Figure 16.47.

Further coverage of register allocation appears in Chapter 19, where interprocedural methods are discussed. Some of these methods work on code below the assembly-language level, namely, on relocatable object modules that are annotated

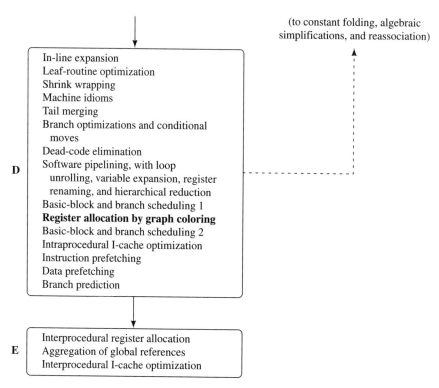

(to constant folding, algebraic
simplifications, and reassociation)

D
In-line expansion
Leaf-routine optimization
Shrink wrapping
Machine idioms
Tail merging
Branch optimizations and conditional
    moves
Dead-code elimination
Software pipelining, with loop
    unrolling, variable expansion, register
    renaming, and hierarchical reduction
Basic-block and branch scheduling 1
Register allocation by graph coloring
Basic-block and branch scheduling 2
Intraprocedural I-cache optimization
Instruction prefetching
Data prefetching
Branch prediction

E
Interprocedural register allocation
Aggregation of global references
Interprocedural I-cache optimization

FIG. 16.47 *(continued)*

with information about data usage patterns. Also, scalar replacement of array references (Section 20.3) and scalar replacement of aggregates (Section 12.2), among other optimizations, are designed to improve register allocation.

16.7   Further Reading

Freiburghouse's approach to local register allocation is described in [Frei74]. The IBM Fortran H compilers for the IBM 360 and 370 series systems are described in [LowM69]. The BLISS language is described in [WulR71] and the groundbreaking PDP-11 compiler for it in [WulJ75].

Cocke noted that global register allocation can be viewed as a graph-coloring problem, as reported by Kennedy in [Kenn71]. Chaitin's original graph-coloring allocator for an experimental IBM 370 PL/I compiler is described in [ChaA81] and its adaptation to the PL.8 compiler, including several refinements, is described in [Chai82]. A demonstration that general graph coloring is *NP*-complete can be found in [GarJ79]. Briggs, Cooper, Kennedy, and Torczon's original discussion of the optimistic heuristic is found in [BriC89] and is also discussed in [Brig92], on which the current account is based. The exploration of coloring heuristics by Bernstein et al.

is found in [BerG89]. Nickerson's approach to handling register pairs and larger groups is found in [Nick90].

Priority-based graph coloring was invented by Chow and Hennessy (see [ChoH84] and [ChoH90]). The earlier of these presentations includes splitting the allocation process into local and global phases, which was later found to be unnecessary. Larus and Hilfinger's [LarH86] register allocator uses a variation of priority-based graph coloring.

Briggs's comparison of his allocator with Chow's priority-based allocator is found in [Brig92].

Callahan and Koblenz's and Knobe and Zadeck's approaches to using a procedure's control tree to guide spilling decisions are described in [CalK91] and [KnoZ92], respectively. Gupta, Soffa, and Steele's use of maximal clique separators to perform register allocation is described in [GupS89].

Bradlee, Eggers, and Henry [BraE91] and Pinter [Pint93] discuss approaches to combining register allocation and instruction scheduling into a single compilation phase.

16.8   Exercises

16.1 Modify the code for `Coalesce_Registers( )` in Figure 16.15 to ensure that argument values are moved to (or computed in) the proper registers before a procedure call and, in the callee, that parameters passed in registers are moved to the proper ones for them to be worked on. Assume that the argument registers are $ra1, \ldots, ram$ and that the working registers are $rw1, \ldots, rwn$.

16.2 Modify the code in Figure 16.15 to enable machine instructions that require specific source and target registers to have their operands and results in those registers. Assume, for example, that the three-address instruction `inst3` has required source registers `rs1` and `rs2` and target register `rt`.

16.3 Modify the code in Figure 16.15 to enable two-address instructions to have their target register, and the operand that must be in that register, handled as required. Assume, for example, that the two-address instruction `inst2` requires that its first source and target registers be the same.

16.4 Modify the code in Figure 16.15 to enable one to ensure that instructions that require a register pair for some operand or result are assigned a pair.

16.5 Modify the algorithm `Compute_Spill_Costs( )` in Figure 16.16 to produce spill costs that take into account that if a spilled value is used several times in the same basic block and is not killed before its last use in the block, then only a single load of the value is needed in the block.

ADV 16.6 The graphs in Figure 16.17 can be generalized to produce, for each R, a minimal graph (i.e., with the minimal number of nodes) that is R-colorable but not by the degree $< R$ rule. Explain how.

16.7 What are the space requirements for the (a) adjacency matrix and (b) adjacency lists for a procedure with w webs?

16.8 Modify the procedure Gen_Spill_Code( ) in Figure 16.24 to deal with the issues mentioned at the end of Section 16.3.7, namely, (a) rematerialization, (b) deletion of copy instructions, and (c) multiple uses of a spilled value within a basic block.

ADV 16.9 Develop the data-flow analysis alluded to in Section 16.3.12 that determines where rematerialization is useful.

RSCH 16.10 Read one of the articles by Callahan and Koblenz [CalK91], Knobe and Zadeck [KnoZ92], or Gupta, Soffa, and Steele [GupS89] and compare and contrast their methods with the graph-coloring approach discussed here.

CHAPTER 17

Code Scheduling

I n this chapter, we are concerned with methods for scheduling or reordering instructions to improve performance, an optimization that is among the most important for most programs on most machines. The approaches include basic-block scheduling, branch scheduling, cross-block scheduling, software pipelining, trace scheduling, and percolation scheduling. We also cover optimization for super-scalar implementations.

Before the advent of RISC machines, there were pipelined computers, but their pipelining was generally hidden in a microengine that interpreted user-level instructions. To maximize the speed of such machines, it was essential that the microcode be written so as to overlap the execution of instructions whenever possible. Also, user code could be written so that it took better or worse advantage of the pipelining in the microengine. A classic paper by Rymarczyk [Ryma82] provides guidelines for assembly-language programmers writing code for a pipelined processor, such as an IBM System/370 implementation. Nowadays, more and more CISC implementations, such as the Intel Pentium and Pentium Pro, make heavy use of pipelining also. Optimization for RISCs and for recent and future CISC implementations has a crucial need for scheduling to maximize performance.

The development of algorithms for instruction scheduling grew out of research in microcode compaction and job-shop scheduling, but there are enough differences among the three areas that many of the techniques used in instruction scheduling are comparatively new.

The combination of basic-block and branch scheduling is the simplest approach discussed here. It operates on each basic block and on each branch separately, is the simplest method to implement, and can produce significant improvements in code speed, frequently 10% or more. Cross-block scheduling improves on basic-block scheduling by considering a tree of blocks at once and may move instructions from one block to another.

Software pipelining operates specifically on loop bodies and, since loops are where most programs spend most of their execution time, can result in large improvements in performance, often a factor of two or more.

Three transformations can significantly improve the effectiveness of basic-block scheduling and, especially, software pipelining: loop unrolling, variable expansion, and register renaming. Loop unrolling creates longer basic blocks and opportunities for cross-block scheduling in loop bodies. Variable expansion expands variables in an unrolled loop body to one per copy of the body; the values of these variables can then be combined after execution of the loop is completed. Register renaming is a transformation that may improve the effectiveness of either scheduling method by changing the register usage in a block (or larger unit) of code, so as to remove constraints that are caused by unnecessary immediate reuse of registers.

In a compiler that does software pipelining, it is crucial to making it as effective as possible to have loop unrolling, variable expansion, and register renaming available to be performed on the loop bodies that are being pipelined. If the compiler does not do software pipelining, then loop unrolling and variable expansion should be done earlier in the compilation process; we recommend doing loop unrolling between dead-code elimination and code hoisting in box **C4** of the diagram in Figure 17.40.

Trace and percolation scheduling are two global (i.e., procedure-wide) approaches to code scheduling that can have very large benefits for some types of programs and architectures, typically high-degree superscalar and VLIW machines.

All the transformations discussed in this chapter, except trace and percolation scheduling, are among the last components of an optimizer to be executed in compiling a program. The latter two, however, are better structured as drivers of the optimization process, since they may make quite broad alterations in the structure of a procedure and they generally benefit from being able to invoke other optimizations to modify the code as necessary to permit more effective scheduling.

17.1   Instruction Scheduling

Because many machines, including all RISC implementations and Intel architecture implementations from the 80486 on, are pipelined and expose at least some aspects of the pipelining to the user, it is essential that code for such machines be organized in such a way as to take best advantage of the pipeline or pipelines that are present in an architecture or implementation. For example, consider the LIR code in Figure 17.1(a). Suppose that each instruction takes one cycle, except that (1) for a value that is being loaded from memory into a register an additional cycle must have elapsed before the value is available and (2) a branch requires two cycles to reach its destination, but the second cycle can be used by placing an instruction in the delay slot after the branch. Then the sequence in Figure 17.1(a) executes correctly if the hardware has interlocks, and it requires seven cycles to execute. There is a stall between the instructions in the second and third slots because the value loaded by the second instruction into r3 is not available immediately. Also, the branch includes a dead cycle, since its delay slot holds a nop. If, on the other hand, we reorder the in-

```
1      r2 ← [r1](4)              r2 ← [r1](4)
2      r3 ← [r1+4](4)            r3 ← [r1+4](4)
3      r4 ← r2 + r3              r5 ← r2 - 1
4      r5 ← r2 - 1               goto L1
5      goto L1                   r4 ← r2 + r3
6      nop

       (a)                       (b)
```

FIG. 17.1 (a) A basic block of LIR code, and (b) a better schedule for it, assuming that a goto has a delay slot after it and that there is a one-cycle delay between initiating a load and the loaded value's becoming available in the target register.

structions as shown in Figure 17.1(b), the code still executes correctly, but it requires only five cycles. Now the instruction in the third slot does not use the value loaded by the preceding instruction, and the fifth instruction is executed while the branch is being completed.

Some architectures, such as the first commercial version of MIPS, do not have interlocks, so the code in Figure 17.1(a) would execute incorrectly—the value loaded by instruction 2 would not appear in r3 until after instruction 3 had completed fetching the value in r3. We ignore this possibility in our discussion of scheduling, since all current commercial architectures have interlocks.

There are several issues involved in instruction scheduling, of which the most basic are filling branch delay slots (covered in Section 17.1.1) and scheduling the instructions within a basic block so as to minimize its execution time. We cover the latter in five sections, namely, 17.1.2 on list scheduling, 17.1.3 on automating generation of instruction schedulers, 17.1.4 on superscalar implementations, 17.1.5 on the interaction between scheduling and register allocation, and 17.1.6 on cross-block scheduling.

We leave consideration of software pipelining and other more aggressive scheduling methods to the following sections.

17.1.1   Branch Scheduling

Branch scheduling refers to two things: (1) filling the delay slot(s) after a branch with useful instructions, and (2) covering the delay between performing a compare and being able to branch based on its result.

Branch architectures vary significantly. Several RISC architectures—such as PA-RISC, SPARC, and MIPS—have delayed branches with one (or in rare cases, such as MIPS-X, two) explicit delay slots. The delay slots may be filled with useful instructions or with nops, but the latter waste execution time. Some architectures—such as POWER and PowerPC—require some number of cycles to have passed between a condition-determining instruction and a taken branch that uses that condition; if the required time has not passed by the time the branch is executed, the processor stalls at the branch instruction for the remainder of the delay. The advanced members of the Intel 386 family, such as the Pentium and Pentium Pro, also require time to elapse between determining a condition and branching on it.

Delay Slots and Filling Them with Useful Instructions

Some branch architectures provide a nullifying (or annulling) delayed branch that, according to whether the branch is taken or not and the details of the definition of the particular branch instruction, execute the delay-slot instruction or skip it. In either case, the delay instruction takes a cycle, but the delay slot may be easier to fill if the instruction placed in it can be nullified on one path or the other.

In many RISCs, calls are delayed also, while in others and in CISCs they are delayed only if the address cannot be computed far enough ahead of the branch to allow prefetching from the target location.

For the sake of concreteness, we take as our basic model of branch delays the approach found in SPARC, which includes virtually all the basic issues that characterize other architectures. SPARC has conditional branches with a one-cycle delay that may be nullified by setting a bit in the instruction. *Nullification* causes the delay instruction to be executed only if a conditional branch other than a "branch always" is taken and not to be executed for a "branch always." Jumps (which are unconditional) and calls have a one-cycle delay that cannot be nullified. There must be at least one instruction that is not a floating-point compare between a floating-point compare and the floating-point branch instruction that uses that condition. SPARC-V9 includes branch instructions that compute the condition to be branched on, as found in the MIPS and PA-RISC architectures, and conditional move instructions that, in some cases, eliminate the need for (forward) branches.

It is most desirable to fill the delay slot of a branch with an instruction from the basic block that the branch terminates. To do this, we would modify the basic-block scheduling algorithm given below to first check whether any of the leaves of the dependence DAG for the block can be placed in the delay slot of its final branch. The conditions such an instruction must satisfy are as follows: (1) it must be permutable with the branch—that is, it must neither determine the condition being branched on nor change the value of a register used in computing the branch address[1] or any other resource used by the branch, such as a condition-code field; and (2) it must not be a branch itself. If there is a choice of instructions from the preceding block to fill the delay slot, we choose one that requires only a single cycle, rather than a delayed load or other instruction that may stall the pipeline (depending on the instruction branched to or fallen through to). If there are instructions from the current block available, but none that take only a single cycle, we choose one that minimizes the likelihood of delay.

Next, we assume that we are dealing with a conditional branch, so that there are both a target block and a fall-through block to be concerned with. If there is no instruction from the current block that can be placed in the branch's delay slot, the next step is to build the DAGs for both the target block and the fall-through block and to attempt to find an instruction that occurs as a root in both or that can be register-renamed (see Section 17.4.5) in one occurrence so that it can be moved into the delay slot of the branch. If this is not achievable, the next choice is to find an

---

1. For SPARC, this is not an issue, since the target address of a conditional branch is the sum of the PC value and an immediate constant, but it may be an issue for some architectures.

instruction that is a root in the DAG for the target block that can be moved into the delay slot with the nullification bit in the branch set so that the delay instruction has no effect if the fall-through path is taken.

Filling the delay slot of an unconditional branch or a jump is similar to the process for a conditional branch. For a SPARC "branch always," the delay instruction is nullified if the annul bit is set. For a jump, the delay instruction is always executed, and the target address is computed as the sum of two registers. Figure 17.2 summarizes the above rules.

Filling the delay slot of a call instruction is similar to filling the delay slot of a branch, but more constrained. On the other hand, there is usually at least one instruction that loads or copies an argument's value into an argument register, and such instructions are almost always permutable with the call instruction. If there is no instruction from before a call that can be placed in its delay slot, there may be instructions following the call in the same basic block that can be placed in the delay slot. However, this requires caution, since the called procedure may not return to the point of call, so an instruction from after the call must be one that does not alter the effect if execution continues at an alternate return point. If there is no instruction at all in the basic block containing the call that can be placed in its delay slot, the next place to look is the procedure that is being called. Of course, whether its code is available or not depends on the structure of the compilation process and when branch scheduling is carried out. Assuming that the code is available, the simplest choice is the first instruction of the called procedure, since it can be copied into the delay slot and the call modified to target the following instruction. Other choices require much more coordination, since there may be multiple calls to the same procedure with conflicting demands for their delay slots.

Failing all other possibilities, we fill a branch's delay slot with a nop.

Stall Cycles and Filling Them with Useful Instructions

Some machines—such as POWER, PowerPC, and the Intel 386 architecture implementations—require some number of cycles to have passed between a condition-determining instruction and a taken branch that uses that condition; if the required time has not passed by the time the branch is executed, the processor stalls at the branch instruction for the remainder of the delay. SPARC's floating-point compare instructions and branches that depend on them also require that we schedule an unrelated instruction between them.

This situation is best handled by the basic-block scheduler. We note in constructing the DAG for the block that it terminates with a conditional branch and that the condition branched on is computed in the block. Then, in the scheduling process, we place the compare as early in the schedule as we can, subject to satisfying all relevant dependences.

17.1.2   List Scheduling

The general goal of basic-block scheduling is to construct a topological sort of the DAG that (1) produces the same results and (2) minimizes the execution time of the basic block.

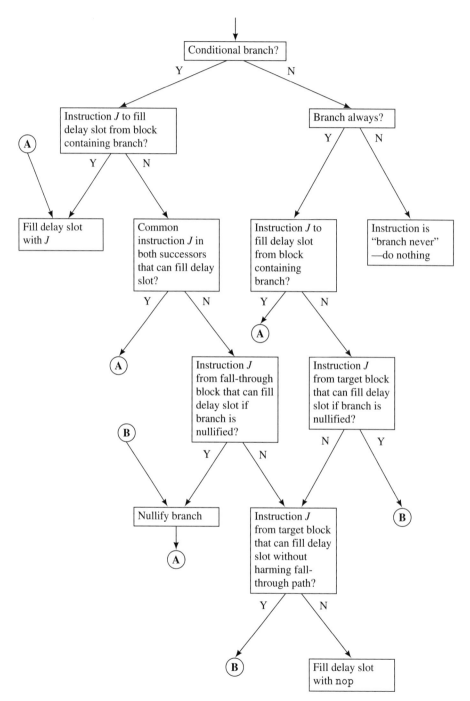

At the outset, note that basic-block scheduling is an *NP*-hard problem, even with a very simple formulation of the problem, so we must seek an effective heuristic, rather than exact, approach. The algorithm we give has a worst-case running time of $O(n^2)$, where n is the number of instructions in the basic block, but it is usually linear in practice. The overall performance of list scheduling is usually dominated by the time to construct the dependence DAG (see Section 9.2), which is also $O(n^2)$ in the worst case but is usually linear or slightly slower in practice.

Now, suppose that we have a dependence DAG for a basic block, as described in Section 9.2. Before proceeding to a method for scheduling it, we must consider the handling of calls. If the call instruction has a delay slot in the architecture under consideration, then we need to be able to choose an instruction to fill it, preferably from before the call (as discussed in Section 17.1.1). Calls typically have an implicit set of registers (determined by software convention) that are required to be saved and restored by the caller around a call. Also, lacking interprocedural data-flow information and alias analysis (see Sections 19.2 and 19.4), we have no way of knowing which storage locations might be affected by a called procedure, except what the semantics of the language being compiled guarantees; e.g., we may know only that the caller's local variables are invisible to the callee (as in Fortran), so the set of memory-reference instructions before a call that can be permuted with it may be small. We could consider a call to be a basic-block boundary and build separate DAGs for the instructions that precede the call and for those that follow it, but this might reduce our freedom to rearrange instructions, and so result in slower code. Alternatively, we can take the implicit set of caller-saved registers into account in the definition of the Conflict( ) function (see Section 9.2), serialize all other storage accesses (or at least those that might be affected) with respect to a call, specially mark the instructions that can be put into the delay slot of the call, and combine the generated nop following the call into the node for the call. The best choices for an instruction to fill the delay slot are those that move argument values into the registers that are used for parameter passing. For example, suppose we have the LIR code in Figure 17.3 and that registers r1 through r7 are used to pass parameters. We use asterisks to mark the nodes corresponding to instructions that can be moved into the delay slot of the call. Then we can schedule this block's instructions in the order

1, 3, 4, 2, 6

and we have succeeded in replacing the nop by a useful instruction.

Several instruction-level transformations can improve the latitude available to instruction scheduling. For example, the two sequences in Figure 17.4 have the same effect, but one of them may produce a better schedule than the other in a particular situation. This can be accounted for in scheduling by a subroutine that recognizes such situations and makes both alternatives available to try, but this strategy needs to be carefully controlled, as it can lead to an exponential increase in the number of possible schedules.

The *list* approach to scheduling begins by traversing the DAG from the leaves toward the roots, labeling each node with the maximum possible delay from that

```
1   r8 ← [r12+8](4)
2   r1 ← r8 + 1
3   r2 ← 2
4   call r14,r31
5   nop
6   r9 ← r1 + 1
```

(a)   (b)

FIG. 17.3 (a) A basic block including a call, and (b) its dependence DAG. Asterisks mark nodes corresponding to instructions that can be moved into the delay slot of the call.

```
ld    [r2+4],r3        add   4,r2,r2
add   4,r2,r2          ld    [r2],r3
```

(a)   (b)

FIG. 17.4 Two equivalent pairs of instructions. Either might provide more latitude in scheduling than the other in a particular situation.

node to the end of the block. Let ExecTime(n) be the number of cycles required to execute the instruction associated with node n. We compute the function

    Delay: Node ⟶ integer

defined by (where DagSucc(i, DAG) is the set of successors of i in the DAG)

$$\text{Delay}(n) = \begin{cases} \text{ExecTime}(n) & \text{if } n \text{ is a leaf} \\ \max_{m \in \text{DagSucc}(n, DAG)} (\text{Latency}(n, m) + \text{Delay}(m)) & \text{otherwise} \end{cases}$$

To do so, we proceed as shown in Figure 17.5, where

    PostOrd: array [1··n] of Node

is a postorder listing of the n nodes in the dependence DAG.

Next, we traverse the DAG from the roots toward the leaves, selecting nodes to schedule and keeping track of the current time (CurTime), which begins with the value zero, and the earliest time each node (ETime[n]) should be scheduled to avoid a stall. Sched is the sequence of nodes that have already been scheduled; Cands is the set of candidates at each point, i.e., the nodes that have not yet been scheduled, but all of whose predecessors have been. Two subsets of Cands are used: MCands, the set of candidates with the maximum delay time to the end of the basic block; and ECands, the set of nodes in MCands whose earliest start times are less than or equal to the current time. The ICAN code is shown in Figure 17.6. The following functions are used in the algorithm:

```
Leaf: Node ⟶ boolean
Delay, ExecTime: Node ⟶ integer
Succ: Node ⟶ set of Node
Heuristics: set of Node ⟶ Node

procedure Compute_Delay(nodes,PostOrd)
   nodes: in integer
   PostOrd: in array [1··nodes] of Node
begin
   i, d, ld: integer
   n: Node
   for i := 1 to nodes do
      if Leaf(PostOrd[i]) then
         Delay(PostOrd[i]) := ExecTime(PostOrd[i])
      else
         d := 0
         for each n ∈ Succ(PostOrd[i]) do
            ld := Latency(PostOrd[i],n) + Delay(n)
            d := max(d,ld)
            Delay(PostOrd[i]) := d
         od
      fi
   od
end       || Compute_Delay
```

FIG. 17.5 Computing the Delay( ) function.

1. Post_Order(D) returns an array whose elements are a topological sort of the nodes of the DAG D (the index of the first element of the array is 1 and the index of the last is $|D.\text{Nodes}|$).

2. Heuristics( ) applies our chosen heuristics to the current set of candidates; note that it may require information other than the current candidates to make choices.

3. Inst(i) returns the instruction represented by node i in the dependency DAG.

4. Latency(I_1, n_1, I_2, n_2) is the number of latency cycles incurred by beginning execution of I_2's n_2^{th} cycle while executing cycle n_1 of I_1, as defined in Section 9.2.

As an example of the scheduling algorithm, consider the dependence DAG in Figure 17.7 and suppose that ExecTime(6) = 2 and ExecTime(n) = 1 for all other nodes n. The Delay( ) function is

Node	Delay
1	4
2	3
3	5
4	3
5	1
6	2

```
DAG = record {Nodes, Roots: set of Node,
              Edges: set of (Node × Node),
              Label: set of (Node × Node) ⟶ integer}

procedure Schedule(nodes,Dag,Roots,DagSucc,DagPred,ExecTime)
   nodes: in Node
   Dag: in DAG
   Roots: in set of Node
   DagSucc, DagPred: in (Node × DAG) ⟶ set of Node
   ExecTime: in Node ⟶ integer
begin
   i, j, m, n, MaxDelay, CurTime := 0: integer
   Cands := Roots, ECands, MCands: set of Node
Sched: sequence of Node
   ETime: array [1··nodes] of integer
   Delay: Node ⟶ integer
   Sched := []
   Delay := Compute_Delay(nodes,Post_Order(Dag))
   for i := 1 to nodes do
      ETime[i] := 0
   od
```

FIG. 17.6 Instruction scheduling algorithm.

and the steps in the scheduling process are as follows:

1. Initially, CurTime = 0, Cands = {1,3}, Sched = [ ], and ETime(n) = 0 for all nodes n. The value of MaxDelay is 4 and MCands = ECands = {3}.

2. Node 3 is selected; Sched = [3], Cands = {1}, CurTime = 1, and ETime(4) = 2.

3. Since |Cands| = 1, the single node in it, 1, is selected next. So, Sched = [3,1], Cands = {2}, CurTime = 2, ETime(2) = 1, and ETime(4) = 4.

4. Since |Cands| = 1 again, node 2 is selected, so Sched = [3,1,2], Cands = {4}, CurTime = 3, and ETime(4) = 4.

5. Again |Cands| = 1, so node 4 is selected; as a result, Sched = [3,1,2,4], Cands = {5,6}, CurTime = 4, ETime(5) = 6, and ETime(6) = 4.

6. Now, MaxDelay = 2 and MCands = {6}, so node 6 is selected; as a result, Sched = [3,1,2,4,6], Cands = {5}, CurTime = 5, and ETime(5) = 6.

7. Since there is only one candidate left (node 5), it is selected, and the algorithm terminates.

The final schedule is

   Sched = [3,1,2,4,6,5]

and the schedule requires 8 cycles, which happens to be the minimum possible value.

A version of this algorithm has been shown to produce a schedule that is within a factor of 2 of optimal for a machine with one or more identical pipelines and

```
    while Cands ≠ Ø do
       MaxDelay := -∞
       for each m ∈ Cands do
          MaxDelay := max(MaxDelay,Delay(m))
       od
       MCands := {m ∈ Cands where Delay(m) = MaxDelay}
       ECands := {m ∈ MCands where ETime(m) ≤ CurTime}
       if |MCands| = 1 then
          n := ◆MCands
       elif |ECands| = 1 then
          n := ◆ECands
       elif |MCands| > 1 then
          n := Heuristics(MCands)
       else
          n := Heuristics(ECands)
       fi
       Sched ⊕= [n]
       CurTime += ExecTime(n)
       Cands -= {n}
       for each i ∈ DagSucc(n,Dag) do
          if !∃j ∈ integer (Sched↓j=i) &
             ∀m ∈ DagPred(i,Dag) (∃j ∈ integer (Sched↓j=m)) then
             Cands ∪= {i}
          fi
          ETime(i) := max(ETime(n),
             CurTime+Latency(Inst(n),1,Inst(i),1))
       od
    od
    return Sched
 end    || Schedule
```

FIG. 17.6 *(continued)*

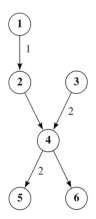

FIG. 17.7 An example dependence DAG.

within a factor of $p + 1$ for a machine that has p pipelines with different functions. In practice, it almost always does much better than this upper bound.

A variety of heuristics can be used to make practical choices when |MCands| > 1 or |ECands| > 1. These include the following:

1. Select from MCands the node n with the least value of ETime(n).

2. If the architecture has $p > 1$ pipelines and there are candidates for each pipeline, bias selection toward candidates for pipelines that have not had instructions scheduled recently.

3. Bias selection toward candidates with maximum total delay to the leaves.

4. Bias selection toward candidates that result in the maximal number of new candidates being added to Cands.

5. Bias selection toward instructions that free a register or that avoid using an additional register, thus reducing register pressure.

6. Select the candidate that came first in the original ordering of the basic block.

Smotherman et al. survey the types of DAGs that are used in instruction scheduling and present a long list of heuristics, some subset of which is used in each of six distinct implemented schedulers they describe (see Section 17.8 for further reading). Gibbons and Muchnick construct the dependence DAG from the leaves upward toward the roots, i.e., beginning with the last instruction in a basic block and working backward, so as to handle the carry-borrow bits in PA-RISC most effectively. The carry-borrow bits are defined frequently but are used relatively rarely, so building the DAG from the bottom up allows uses of them to be noted first and attention to be directed to definitions of them only when there is an upwards exposed use.

Note that some work on instruction scheduling uses a different notion of the dependence DAG. In particular, Hennessy and Gross use a so-called machine-level DAG that is an adaptation of the DAG intermediate-code form discussed in Section 4.9.3. The adaptation involves using machine registers and memory locations as the leaf nodes and labels, and machine instructions as the interior nodes. This DAG has fewer explicit constraints represented in it, as the example in Figure 17.8 shows. For the LIR code in (a), Hennessy and Gross would construct the machine-level DAG in (b); our dependence DAG is shown in (c). Assuming that neither r1 nor r4 is live at the end of the basic block, the machine-level DAG admits two correct schedules, namely,

   1, 2, 3, 4

and

   3, 4, 1, 2

while the dependence DAG allows only the first of them. At the same time, the machine-level DAG allows incorrect schedules, such as

   1, 3, 2, 4

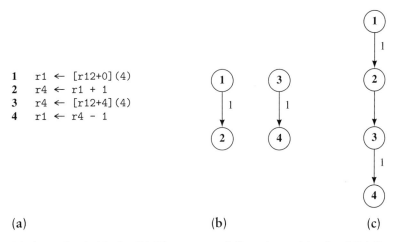

```
1   r1 ← [r12+0](4)
2   r4 ← r1 + 1
3   r4 ← [r12+4](4)
4   r1 ← r4 - 1
```

(a)   (b)   (c)

FIG. 17.8 (a) A LIR basic block, (b) Hennessy and Gross's machine-level DAG, and (c) our dependence DAG for it.

unless rules are added to the scheduling process, as Hennessy and Gross do, to restrict schedules to what they call "safe positions." We see no particular advantage in this approach over the DAG definition used above, especially as it raises the computational complexity of instruction scheduling to $O(n^4)$.

17.1.3   Automating Instruction-Scheduler Generation

Another issue in instruction scheduling is that the production of schedulers from machine descriptions can and has been automated. This is important because even a compiler for a single architecture may (and almost always does) need to deal with different implementations of the architecture. The implementations frequently differ from each other enough that a very good schedule for one can be no better than mediocre for another.

Thus, it is important to be able to generate instruction schedulers from implementation descriptions, taking as much of an implementation's scheduling-related uniqueness into account as possible. Perhaps the best known and certainly the most widely distributed of such scheduler generators is the one found in gcc, the GNU C compiler. It provides the compiler writer with the facilities necessary to write machine descriptions that may have their own writer-defined properties and a great degree of flexibility in how those properties interact. Provided with a very detailed description of an implementation's pipeline structure, structural hazards, delays, low-level parallelization rules, and so on, it produces a remarkably effective scheduler.

17.1.4   Scheduling for Superscalar Implementations

Scheduling for a superscalar implementation needs to model the functional organization of the CPU as accurately as possible, for example, by biasing the heuristics that are used to take into account that a particular implementation has two integer pipelines, two floating-point pipelines, and a branch unit (as in some implementations of POWER), or that a pair of instructions can be initiated simultaneously only if it is doubleword-aligned (as required by the Intel i860). The latter requirement can be handled easily by inserting nops to make each basic block begin on a doubleword boundary or, with more work, by tracking the boundary each instruction pair would be aligned on and correcting it to doubleword alignment if necessary.

For superscalar systems, scheduling also needs to be biased to organize instructions into groups that can be issued simultaneously. This can be done by a grouping heuristic, e.g., a *greedy* algorithm that fills as many of the available slots as possible with ready instructions, as follows. Suppose that the processor in question has n execution units $P_1, \ldots, P_n$ that may operate in parallel and that each unit P_i may execute instructions in class PClass(i). We model the functional units by n copies of the data structures in the list scheduling algorithm in Figure 17.6 and determine the class of a particular instruction *inst* by IClass$(inst)$, i.e., instruction *inst* can be executed by execution unit i if and only if PClass(i) = IClass$(inst)$. Then the list scheduling algorithm can be modified to produce a straightforward scheduler for a superscalar system.

However, remember that greedy scheduling may not be optimal, as the example in Figure 17.9 shows. We assume that the processor has two pipelines, one of which can execute both integer and floating-point operations and the other of which can do integer and memory operations; each operation has a latency of one cycle. Suppose that the only dependence between the instructions is that the FltOp must precede the IntLd. Then the greedy schedule in Figure 17.9(a) has a latency of two cycles, while the equally greedy one in Figure 17.9(b) requires three cycles.

Also, one must be careful not to use too much lookahead in such heuristics, since all nontrivial instances of instruction scheduling are at least *NP*-hard. Such scheduling may be improved by scheduling across control-flow constructs, i.e., by using extended basic blocks and/or reverse extended basic blocks in scheduling, as discussed in Section 17.1.6, or more powerful global techniques. In an extended basic block, for example, this might involve moving an instruction from a basic block to both of its successor blocks to improve instruction grouping.

IntFlt	IntMem		IntFlt	IntMem
FltOp	FltLd		FltOp	IntOp
IntOp	IntLd			IntLd
				FltLd
(a)			(b)	

FIG. 17.9 Two greedy schedules for a superscalar processor, one of which (a) is optimal and the other of which (b) is not.

```
1        r1 ← [r12+0](4)                    r1 ← [r12+0](4)
2        r2 ← [r12+4](4)                    r2 ← [r12+4](4)
3        r1 ← r1 + r2                       r3 ← r1 + r2
4        [r12,0](4) ← r1                    [r12,0](4) ← r3
5        r1 ← [r12+8](4)                    r4 ← [r12+8](4)
6        r2 ← [r12+12](4)                   r5 ← [r12+12](4)
7        r2 ← r1 + r2                       r6 ← r4 + r5

              (a)                                 (b)
```

FIG. 17.10 (a) A basic block of LIR code with a register assignment that constrains scheduling unnecessarily, and (b) a better register assignment for it.

17.1.5   Other Issues in Basic-Block Scheduling

The instruction scheduling approach discussed above is designed, among other things, to cover the delay between the initiation of fetching from a data cache and the receipt of the loaded value in a register. It does not take into account the possibility that the datum being loaded might not be in the cache and so might need to be fetched from main memory or from a second-level cache, incurring a significantly longer and unpredictable stall. Eggers and her colleagues ([KerE93] and [LoEg95]) present an approach called *balanced scheduling* that is designed to account for such a possibility. Their algorithm spreads the latency of a series of loads occurring in a basic block over the other instructions that are available to schedule between them. This is becoming increasingly important as the acceleration of processor speed continues to outrun the acceleration of memory speeds.

The interaction between register allocation and instruction scheduling can present serious problems. Consider the example in Figure 17.10(a), with the dependence DAG shown in Figure 17.11(a). Because registers r1 and r2 are reused immediately, we cannot schedule any of instructions 5 through 7 before any of 1 through 4. If we change the register allocation to use different registers in instructions 5 through 7, as shown in Figure 17.10(b), the dependence DAG becomes the one shown in Figure 17.11(b), and the latitude available for scheduling is significantly increased. In particular, we can schedule the loads so that no stalls are incurred, as shown in Figure 17.12, in comparison to the original register assignment, which allowed no reordering at all.

To achieve this, we allocate quantities to symbolic registers during code generation and then perform register allocation late in the compilation process. We do scheduling immediately before register allocation (i.e., with symbolic registers) and repeat it immediately after, if any spill code has been generated. This is the approach taken in the IBM XL compilers for POWER and PowerPC (see Section 21.2), the Hewlett-Packard compilers for PA-RISC, and the Sun compilers for SPARC (see Section 21.1); it has been shown in practice to yield better schedules and better register allocations than a single scheduling pass that is performed either before or after register allocation.

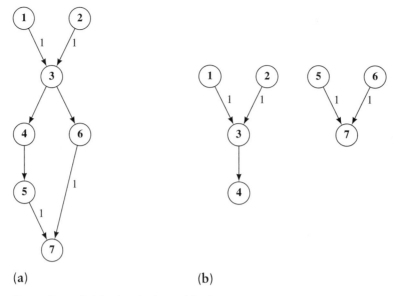

(a)   (b)

FIG. 17.11 Dependence DAGs for the basic blocks in Figure 17.10.

```
r1 ← [r12+0](4)
r2 ← [r12+4](4)
r4 ← [r12+8](4)
r5 ← [r12+12](4)
r3 ← r1 + r2
[r12+0](4) ← r3
r6 ← r4 + r5
```

FIG. 17.12 A scheduling of the basic block in Figure 17.10(b) that covers all the load delays.

17.1.6   Scheduling Across Basic-Block Boundaries

While some programs have very large basic blocks that present many opportunities for scheduling to improve code quality, it is frequently the case that blocks are too short for scheduling to make any, or very much, difference. Thus, it is often desirable to make basic blocks longer, as loop unrolling does (Section 17.4.3), or to extend instruction scheduling across basic-block boundaries. One method for doing this in loops is software pipelining, which we discuss in Section 17.4.

Another approach is to schedule basic blocks, as much as possible, before their successors and to take into account in the initial state of scheduling a successor block any latency that is left over at the conclusion of scheduling its predecessors.

Another method is to transform the code so as to enable better coverage of branch delays. In particular, Golumbic and Rainish [GolR90] discuss three simple transformations that help to absorb the three-cycle delay between a compare (cmp) and a taken conditional branch (bc) and the four-cycle delay for an untaken conditional branch in a cmp-bc-b sequence in POWER. For example, the following deals

```
L1: inst1                    L1: inst1
    inst2                    L3: inst2
    . . .                        . . .
    cmp  cr0,cond                cmp  cr0,!cond
    instn-1                      instn-1
    instn                        instn
    bc   cr0,L1                  bc   cr0,L2
    . . .                        inst1
                                 b    L3
                             L2: . . .

    (a)                          (b)
```

FIG. 17.13   (a) POWER loop with a one-cycle uncovered cmp-bc delay, and (b) transformed code that covers it.

with loop-closing branches. Suppose that we have a loop with a one-cycle uncovered delay, as shown in Figure 17.13(a). We can cover the delay by changing the cmp to test the negation of the original condition (indicated by !cond) and the bc to exit the loop, replicating the first instruction of the loop after the bc, and then inserting an unconditional branch to the second instruction of the loop after the replicated instruction, resulting in the code in Figure 17.13(b).[2] The obvious generalization works for an uncovered delay of two or three cycles.

References to several approaches to scheduling across basic-block boundaries are given in Section 17.8.

17.2   Speculative Loads and Boosting

Speculative loading is a mechanism that increases the freedom available to a scheduler and that provides a way to hide some of the latency inherent in satisfying a load from memory rather than from a cache. A *speculative load* is a load instruction that does not incur any memory exceptions until one uses the quantity loaded. Such a load may be issued before it is known whether the address it generates is valid or not—if it is later found to be invalid, one simply avoids using the loaded value. Such loads are found in the Multiflow architecture, SPARC-V9, and PowerPC, among others.

For example, loading the next element of a linked list can be initiated with a speculative load before testing whether the end of the list has been reached—if the end has been reached, the instruction that uses the data loaded is not executed, so no problem occurs. A MIR example of this is shown in Figure 17.14. Part (a) is a typical sample of a function to search a linked list for a particular value. In part (b), the assignment p1 ←sp p*.next in the line labeled L2 moves p1 one record ahead

---

2. This is an instance of the window-scheduling approach to software pipelining discussed below in Section 17.4.1.

```
search:                                    search:
    receive ptr (val)                          receive ptr (val)
    receive ptr (val)                          receive v (val)
    p ← ptr                                    p ← ptr
                                           L2: p1 ←sp p*.next
L2: if p*.val = v goto L1                       if p*.val = v goto L1
    p ← p*.next
    if p != NIL goto L2                         if P = NIL goto L3
                                               p ← p1
    return 0                                   goto L2
L1: return 1                                L1: return 1
                                           L3: return 0

(a)                                        (b)
```

FIG. 17.14   (a) A MIR routine that searches a list, and (b) the same routine with the fetching of the next element boosted to occur before testing whether the current element is the end of the list.

of the one we are checking (pointed to by p). As long as the assignment to p1 is a speculative load (marked by the sp after the arrow), no error occurs.

Thus, a speculative load may be moved ahead of a test that determines its validity, i.e., from one basic block to a previous one or from one iteration of a loop to an earlier one. Such code motion is known as *boosting,* and techniques for accomplishing it are described by Rogers and Li (see Section 17.8 for references).

17.3   Speculative Scheduling

Speculative scheduling is a technique that generalizes boosting of speculative loads to moving other types of instructions toward the entry of a procedure, across one or more branches and, particularly, out of loops. It takes two forms: *safe* speculative scheduling, in which the moved instruction can do no harm when it is executed in the location it is moved to (except, perhaps, slowing down the computation); and *unsafe* speculative scheduling, in which the moved instructions must be protected by a conditional that determines whether they are legal in their new position.

Techniques for speculative scheduling are too new and, as yet, unproven in their impact on performance for us to do more than mention the subject and provide references (see Section 17.8). In particular, the work of Ebcioğlu et al. addresses speculative scheduling and its mirror operation, *unspeculation.* Papers by Golumbic and Rainish and by Bernstein and Rodeh discuss earlier work in this area.

17.4   Software Pipelining

Software pipelining is an optimization that can improve the loop-executing performance of any system that allows instruction-level parallelism, including VLIW and superscalar systems, but also one-scalar implementations that allow, e.g., integer and floating-point instructions to be executing at the same time but not to be initiated at the same time. It works by allowing parts of several iterations of a loop to be in process at the same time, so as to take advantage of the parallelism available in the loop body.

For example, suppose that the instructions in the loop in Figure 17.15 have the latencies shown; then each iteration requires 12 cycles, as shown by the dashed line in the pipeline diagram in Figure 17.16, on a hypothetical one-scalar implementation that has one integer unit and one floating-point unit (with its execution cycles indicated by the darker shading), with floating-point loads and stores carried out by the integer unit. Note that the six-cycle issue latency between the fadds and the stf could be reduced if we could overlap the preceding iteration's store with the add for the current iteration. Copying the load and add from the first iteration and the load from the second iteration out ahead of the loop allows us to begin the loop with the store for one iteration, followed by the add for the next iteration, and then by the load for the second following iteration. Doing so adds three instructions before

		Issue latency	Result latency
L: ldf	[r1],f0	1	1
fadds	f0,f1,f2	1	7
stf	f2,[r1]	6	3
sub	r1,4,r1	1	1
cmp	r1,0	1	1
bg	L	1	2
nop		1	1

FIG. 17.15 A simple SPARC loop with assumed issue and result latencies.

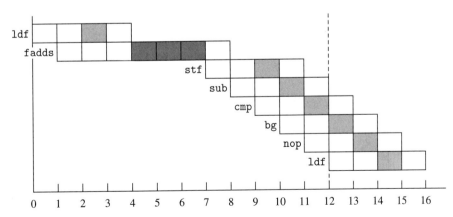

FIG. 17.16 Pipeline diagram for the loop body in Figure 17.15.

		Issue latency	Result latency
ldf	[r1],f0		
fadds	f0,f1,f2		
ldf	[r1-4],f0		
L: stf	f2,[r1]	1	3
fadds	f0,f1,f2	1	7
ldf	[r1-8],f0	1	1
cmp	r1,8	1	1
bg	L	1	2
sub	r1,4,r1	1	1
stf	f2,[r1]		
sub	r1,4,r1		
fadds	f0,f1,f2		
stf	f2,[r1]		

FIG. 17.17 The result of software pipelining the loop in Figure 17.15, with issue and result latencies.

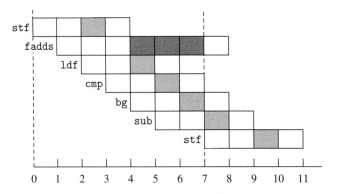

FIG. 17.18 Pipeline diagram for the loop body in Figure 17.17.

the loop and requires us to add five instructions after the loop to complete the last two iterations, resulting in the code shown in Figure 17.17. It reduces the cycle count for the loop body to seven, reducing execution time per iteration by 5/12 or about 42%, as shown by the dashed line in Figure 17.18. As long as the loop is always iterated at least three times, the two forms have the same effect.

Also, seven cycles is the minimum execution time for the loop, unless we unroll it, since the fadds requires seven cycles. If we were to unroll it, we could overlap two or more faddss and increase the performance further. Thus, software pipelining and loop unrolling are usually complementary. On the other hand, we would need to use additional registers, because, e.g., two faddss executing at the same time would have to use different source and target registers.

Since software pipelining moves a fixed number of iterations of a loop out of the loop body, we must either know in advance that the loop is repeated at least that many times, or we must generate code that tests this, if possible, at run time and that chooses to execute either a software-pipelined version of the loop or one that is not. Of course, for some loops it is not possible to determine the number of iterations they take without executing them, and software pipelining cannot be applied to such loops.

Another consideration is the extent to which we can disambiguate memory references, so as to minimize the constraints on pipelining, as discussed in Chapter 9. The better we can do so, the more freedom we have in pipelining and, hence, generally the better the schedule we can produce.

In the next two subsections, we discuss two approaches to software pipelining, window scheduling and unroll-and-compact pipelining. The first is simpler to implement, while the second will generally result in better schedules.

17.4.1   Window Scheduling

An approach to software pipelining called *window scheduling* derives its name from its conceptual model of the pipelining process—it makes two connected copies of the dependence DAG for the body of a loop, which must be a single basic block, and it runs a window down the copies. The window at each point contains one complete copy of the loop body; the instructions above and below the window (after the initial state) become the pipelined loop's prologue and epilogue, respectively. For example, the dependence DAG in Figure 17.19(a) becomes the *double* or *window-scheduling DAG* in Figure 17.19(b) with a possible window indicated by the dashed lines. As the window is moved down the copies, we try the various schedules that result, searching

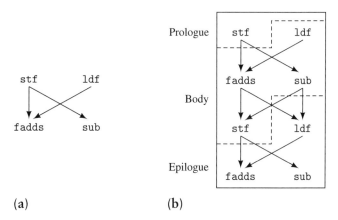

(a)   (b)

FIG. 17.19   (a) Dependence DAG for a sample loop body, and (b) double version of it used in window scheduling, with dashed lines showing a possible window.

```
DAG = record {Nodes, Roots: set of integer,
              Edges: set of (integer × integer),
              Label: set of (integer × integer) ⟶ integer}

procedure Window_Schedule(n,Inst,Limit,MinStall)
    n, Limit, MinStall: in integer
    Inst: inout array [1··n] of LIRInst
begin
    Dag, Window, Prol, Epi: DAG
    Stall, N: integer
    Sched, BestSched, ProS, EpiS: sequence of integer
    Dag := Build_DAG(n,Inst)
    if Schedulable(Dag) then
        Dag := Double_DAG(Dag)
        Window := Init_Window(Dag)
        BestSched := SP_Schedule(|Window.Nodes|,Window,Window.Roots,
            MinStall,ExecTime)
        Stall := MinStall
        repeat
            if Move_Window(Dag,Window) then
                Sched := SP_Schedule(|Window.Nodes|,Window,Window.
                    Roots,MinStall,ExecTime)
                if Stall < MinStall then
                    BestSched := Sched
                    MinStall := min(MinStall,Stall)
                fi
            fi
        until Stall = 0 ∨ Stall ≥ Limit * MinStall
        Prol := Get_Prologue(Dag,Window)
        Epi:= Get_Epilogue(Dag,Window)
        ProS := SP_Schedule(|Prol.Nodes|,Prol,Prol.Roots,MinStall,ExectTme)
        EpiS := SP_Schedule(|Epi.Nodes|,Epi,Epi.Roots,MinStall,ExectTme)
        N := Loop_Ct_Inst(n,Inst)
        Decr_Loop_Ct(Inst[N])
    fi
end    || Window_Schedule
```

FIG. 17.20 Algorithm for window scheduling.

for ones that decrease the overall latency of the loop body. We do window scheduling
at the same time as other instruction scheduling and use the basic-block scheduler to
schedule the loop body.

Figure 17.20 is an outline of the ICAN algorithm for window scheduling. Its input
consists of Inst[1··n], the sequence of instructions that make up the basic block
that is the loop body to be pipelined. It first constructs the dependence DAG for the
basic block (using Build_DAG( ), which is given in Figure 9.6) and stores it in Dag
and uses Schedulable( ) to determine whether it can be window scheduled, i.e.,
whether it has a loop index that is incremented exactly once in the loop body and the
loop is executed at least twice. If so, the algorithm uses the following information:

1. Dag records the window-scheduling or double DAG (constructed by Double_DAG( )) that is used in the window-scheduling process.

2. Window indicates the current placement of the window.

3. Sched records the (basic-block) schedule for the DAG currently in the window.

4. Stall is the number of stall cycles associated with Sched.

5. MinStall records the minimum number of stall cycles in any schedule tried so far.

6. BestSched is the last DAG generated that has the minimal number of stall cycles.

   Limit is chosen by the compiler writer to guide the window scheduler in deciding how far from the best schedule achieved so far it should wander before giving up the process of attempting to find a better schedule. Routines used in the window-scheduling process are as follows:

1. SP_Schedule( ) is constructed from the basic-block scheduler given in Figure 17.6. Specifically, SP_Schedule($N, Dag, R, stall, ET$) computes the functions DagSucc( ) and DagPred( ), calls Schedule(N, Dag, R, DagSucc, DagPred, ET), sets *stall* to the number of stall cycles in the schedule *Sched* produced, and returns *Sched* as its value.

2. Move_Window( ) selects an instruction in the double DAG and moves the window down over it (assuming that there is space remaining to move it) and sets Moved accordingly.

3. Get_Prologue( ) and Get_Epilogue( ) extract as DAGs the portions of the double DAG above and below the window.

4. Loop_Ct_Inst( ) determines which instruction tests the loop counter.

5. Decr_Loop_Ct( ) modifies that instruction to do one less iteration. This is appropriate because the algorithm, as described so far, moves only a single iteration out of the loop, so the loop itself does parts of two successive iterations and, overall, does one less iteration than the original loop body did. Thus we need code to do one iteration outside the loop, as extracted by Get_Prologue( ) and Get_Epilogue( ).

6. ExecTime(n) is the number of cycles required to execute the instruction associated with node n in the DAG.

   The window-scheduling algorithm can easily be generalized to allow more than two iterations to be in process inside the pipelined loop by repeatedly applying it to the new loop body that results from it. For example, starting with the loop in Figure 17.15, the window-scheduling DAG for the loop body is given in Figure 17.21(a). Moving the window below the ldf results in the code in Figure 17.22(a) and the window-scheduling DAG in Figure 17.21(b). Moving the window down over the fadds results, in turn, in the code in Figure 17.22(b) and the window-scheduling DAG in Figure 17.21(c). Finally, moving the window down over the ldf a second time results in the code in Figure 17.17.

   Note that window scheduling can easily be combined with loop unrolling, which is useful because it almost always increases the freedom available to the scheduler:

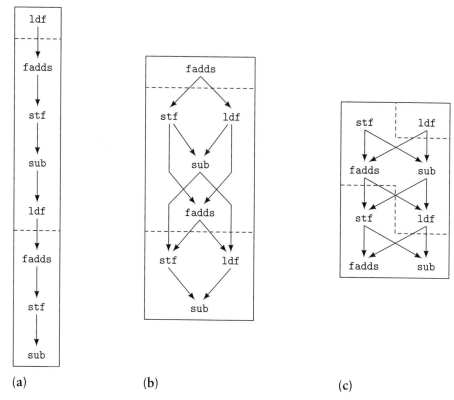

(a)   (b)   (c)

FIG. 17.21 Double DAGs for successive versions of the loop in Figures 17.15 and 17.22 during the window-scheduling process.

```
                                      ldf    [r1],f0
                                      fadds  f0,f1,f2
        ldf    [r1],f0          L:    stf    f2,[r1]
   L:   fadds  f0,f1,f2               ldf    [r1-4],f0
        stf    f2,[r1]                fadds  f0,f1,f2
        ldf    [r1-4],f0              sub    r1,4,r1
        sub    r1,4,r1                cmp    r1,4
        cmp    r1,4                   bg     L
        bg     L                      nop
        nop                          stf    f2,[r1-4]
        fadds  f0,f1,f2              sub    r1,4,r1
        stf    f2,[r1-4]
        sub    r1,4,r1
```

            (a)   (b)

FIG. 17.22 Intermediate versions of the loop in Figure 17.15.

```
A      L: ld      [i3],f0
B         fmuls   f31,f0,f1
C         ld      [i0],f2
D         fadds   f2,f1,f2
E         add     i3,i5,i3
F         deccc   i1
G         st      f2,[i0]
H         add     i0,i5,i0
I         bpos    L
J         nop
```

FIG. 17.23 Another example loop for software pipelining.

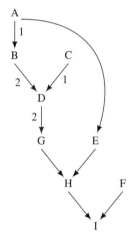

FIG. 17.24 Dependence DAG for the body of the loop in Figure 17.23.

instead of using Double_DAG( ) to make one copy of the loop body, we replace it with a routine that, for an unrolling factor of n, makes n additional copies. We then simply do window scheduling over the resulting $n + 1$ copies. This, combined with variable expansion and register renaming, can frequently produce higher performance because it makes more instructions available to schedule.

17.4.2   Unroll-and-Compact Software Pipelining

An alternate approach to software pipelining unrolls copies of the loop body and searches for a repeating pattern in the instructions that are being initiated at each step. If it finds such a pattern, it constructs the pipelined loop body from the pattern and the prologue and epilogue from the instructions preceding and following the pattern, respectively. For example, suppose we have the SPARC code shown in Figure 17.23, whose loop body has the dependence DAG shown in Figure 17.24 (assuming a three-cycle latency for the fadds and fmuls instructions and ignoring the nop in the delay slot of the branch). Then Figure 17.25 shows a possible unconstrained greedy schedule of the iterations of the loop, assuming that the instructions

Time	Iteration step			
	1	2	3	4
1	A C F			
2	B E			
3				
4				Prologue
5	D	A C F		
6		B E		
7				
8	G			
9	H	D	A C F	
10	I		B E	Loop body
11				
12		G		
13		H	D	A C F
14		I		B E
15				Epilogue
16			G	
17			H	D
18			I	
19				
20				G
21				H
22				I

FIG. 17.25 A possible unconstrained schedule of the iterations of the loop in Figure 17.23. The boxed parts represent the prologue, body, and epilogue of the software-pipelined loop.

shown for each time step can be executed in parallel. The boxed parts of the figure show the prologue, body, and epilogue of the software pipelined loop. We call the resulting schedule "unconstrained" because it does not take into account limitations imposed by the number of available registers or the instruction-level parallelism of the processor.

Turning the resulting code into the correct prologue, loop body, and epilogue requires dealing with resource constraints and adjusting some instructions to being executed in the new sequence. Figure 17.26(a) shows the instruction sequence that results from simply enumerating the unrolled instructions in order, while Figure 17.26(b) shows the result of fixing up the instructions to take into account the order in which they are executed and their need for an additional register. Note that,

```
        ld      [i3],f0                        ld      [i3],f0
        ld      [i0],f2                        ld      [i0],f2
        deccc   i1                             deccc   i1
        fmuls   f31,f0,f1                      fmuls   f31,f0,f1
        add     i3,i5,i3                       add     i3,i5,i3
        fadds   f2,f1,f2                       fadds   f2,f1,f2
        ld      [i3],f0                        ld      [i3],f0
        ld      [i0],f2                        ld      [i0+i5],f3
        deccc   i1                             deccc   i1
        fmuls   f31,f0,f1                      fmuls   f31,f0,f1
        add     i3,i5,i3                       add     i3,i5,i3
L:  st      f2,[i0]                    L:  st      f2,[i0]
        add     i0,i5,i0                       add     i0,i5,i0
        fadds   f2,f1,f2                       fadds   f3,f1,f2
        ld      [i3],f0                        ld      [i3],f0
        ld      [i0],f2                        ld      [i0+i5],f3
        deccc   i1                             deccc   i1
        fmuls   f31,f0,f1                      fmuls   f31,f0,f1
        add     i3,i5,i3
        bpos    L                              bpos    L
        nop                                    add     i3,i5,i3
        st      f2,[i0]                        st      f2,[i0]
        add     i0,i5,i0                       add     i0,i5,i0
        fadds   f2,f1,f2                       fadds   f3,f1,f2
        bpos    L
        st      f2,[i0]                        st      f2,[i0]
        add     i0,i5,i0                       add     i0,i5,i0
        bpos    L
```

(a)   (b)

FIG. 17.26   (a) Resulting instruction sequence for the pipelined loop, and (b) the result of doing
register renaming (Section 17.4.5) and fixing the addresses in load instructions so that
they will execute correctly.

in addition to deleting the two branches from the epilogue, we have modified all
but the first occurrences of ld [i0],f2 and fadds f2,f1,f2 to ld [i0+i5],f3 and
fadds f3,f1,f2, respectively, so as to use the correct address and to avoid reusing
register f2 before its value is stored. The former modification is necessary because
the second ld has been moved above the add that increments register i0. Dealing
with parallelism constraints may motivate rearranging the instructions to take better advantage of the available execution units. For example, if the processor allowed
one memory or integer operation, one floating-point addition and one multiplication, and one branch to be in process at once, then a valid alternate schedule would
put the second ld in the loop below the fmuls, but this would require ten cycles per
iteration rather than the nine that the current arrangement uses.

Producing such pipelinings is conceptually simple. The ICAN algorithm to find
a repeating pattern in the unrolled body (which becomes the body of the pipelined

```
Sched: sequence of Node

procedure Pipeline_Schedule(i,nblocks,ninsts,LBlock,SizeLimit,
    ExecTime) returns integer × integer
    i, nblocks, SizeLimit: in integer
    ninsts: in array [1··nblocks] of integer
    LBlock: in array [1··nblocks] of array [··] LIRInst
    ExecTime: in integer ⟶ integer
begin
    j, k: integer
    Sched: sequence of Node
    Insts: (sequence of integer) × integer ⟶ sequence
        of Instruction
    Dag: DAG
    ii: integer × array [··] of LIRInst
    for j := 2 to SizeLimit do
        ii := Unroll(nblocks,ninsts[i],i,ninsts,LBlock,j,nil)
        Dag:= Build_DAG(ii↓1,ii↓2)
        Schedule(Dag.Nodes,Dag,Dag.Roots,DagSucc,DagPred,ExecTime)
        for k := j - 1 by -1 to 1 do
            if Insts(Sched,k) = Insts(Sched,j)
                & State(Sched,k) = State(Sched,j) then
                return ⟨k,j⟩
            fi
        od
    od
    return ⟨i,j⟩
end    || Pipeline_Schedule
```

FIG. 17.27 Algorithm to find a repeating unit from which to construct a software pipelining.

loop) is shown in Figure 17.27. We assume again that the loop body is a single basic block LBlock[i][1··ninsts[i]]. Unroll(nblocks,m,i,ninsts,LBlock,j,k) produces j copies of the loop body LBlock[i][1··ninsts[m]] (see Figure 17.30 for the algorithm Unroll( )). Schedule(i,D,R,DS,DP,EX) is the basic-block scheduler given in Figure 17.6. Insts(S,i) denotes the sequence of instructions executed during time step i in the schedule S, and State(S,i) denotes the resource state corresponding to time step i in schedule S after performing iterations 1 through $i - 1$. The resource state can be modeled by resource vectors, as described in Section 9.2. The algorithm incorporates a stopping condition (SizeLimit), based on the unrolled size of the loop, to bound the search space.

After executing the algorithm successfully, the instructions in time steps m through $i - 1$ are the basis for constructing the pipelined loop body, those in steps 1 through $m - 1$ are for the prologue, and those in steps i, . . . are for the epilogue. Of course, constructing the final prologue, body, and epilogue requires adjusting the code to deal with resource constraints, as in our example above. The scheduling algorithm returns a pair of integers ⟨i,j⟩, where i is the number of instructions in the original loop body and j is the factor by which it has been unrolled.

```
for i := 1 to 100 do              for i := 1 by 2 to 99 do begin
    s := s + a[i]                     s := s + a[i]
                                      s := s + a[i+1]
                                  end
```

(a)   (b)

FIG. 17.28 (a) A Pascal loop, and (b) the result of unrolling it by a factor of two.

17.4.3   Loop Unrolling

Loop unrolling replaces the body of a loop by several copies of the body and adjusts the loop-control code accordingly. The number of copies is called the *unrolling factor* and the original loop is called the *rolled loop*. In another subsection below, we discuss variable expansion, which is a transformation that can improve the effectiveness of loop unrolling and software pipelining.

Unrolling reduces the overhead of executing an indexed loop and may improve the effectiveness of other optimizations, such as common-subexpression elimination, induction-variable optimizations, instruction scheduling, and software pipelining.

For example, the code in Figure 17.28(b) is a version of the loop in Figure 17.28(a) that has been unrolled by a factor of two. The unrolled loop executes the loop-closing test and branch half as many times as the original loop and may increase the effectiveness of instruction scheduling by, e.g., making two loads of a[i] values available to be scheduled in each iteration. On the other hand, the unrolled version is larger than the rolled version, so it may impact the effectiveness of the instruction cache, possibly negating the improvement gained from unrolling. Such concerns dictate that we exercise caution in deciding which loops to unroll and by what unrolling factors.

Also, notice that we have oversimplified the unrolling transformation in the example: we have assumed that the loop bounds are known constants and that the unrolling factor divides the number of iterations evenly. In general, these conditions are, of course, not satisfied. However, loops with general bounds can still be unrolled. What we need to do is to keep a rolled copy of the loop, exit the unrolled copy when the number of iterations remaining is less than the unrolling factor, and then use the rolled copy to execute the remaining iterations. We take this approach rather than testing in each unrolled copy of the loop body for early termination because one reason for unrolling loops is to allow instruction scheduling more latitude, in particular to allow it to interleave instructions from the copies of the body, which it cannot do as effectively if there is conditional control flow between the copies.

Figure 17.29(a) gives an example of a Fortran 77 loop and Figure 17.29(b) shows the result of unrolling it by a factor of u with a rolled copy. Of course, the unrolling transformation can be further generalized to loops that increment the loop counter by values other than 1.

ICAN code to implement this approach is shown in Figure 17.30. The call `Unroll(nblocks,m,ninsts,Block,`*factor*`,`*init*`)` unrolls *factor* copies of `Block[m][1··ninsts[m]]` and makes a rolled copy also if it cannot determine that

```
                               do i = lo,hi,u
                                 body
                                 body/i+1/i
   do i = lo,hi                    . . .
     body                        body/i+u-1/i
   enddo                         enddo
                               do i = i,hi
                                 body
                               enddo
   (a)                 (b)
```

FIG. 17.29 (a) A more general Fortran 77 loop, and (b) the result of unrolling it by a factor of u. The notation *body/i/j* means *body* with i substituted for j.

the number of iterations is a multiple of the unrolling factor. The instructions it is designed to operate on are MIRInsts and LIRInsts, and Instruction is meant here to encompass only those two of our three varieties of intermediate code. Note that the algorithm deals with a loop that contains only a single basic block and loop control of a particular type: it assumes that var1 is modified only by Block[m][ninsts[m]-2] and that

```
Block[m][1] = ⟨kind:label,lbl:"L1"⟩
Block[m][ninsts[m]-2] = ⟨kind:binasgn,left:var1,opr:add,
                          opd1:⟨kind:var,val:var1⟩,opd2:incr⟩
Block[m][ninsts[m]-1] = ⟨kind:binasgn,left:var3,opr:less,
                          opd1:⟨kind:var,val:var1⟩,opd2:final⟩
Block[m][ninsts[m]] = ⟨kind:valif,opd:⟨kind:var,val:var3⟩,
                        lbl:"L1"⟩
```

but it can easily be generalized. It uses several functions, as follows:

1. Constant(*opd*) returns true if operand *opd* is a constant, and false otherwise.

2. new_tmp( ) returns a new temporary name.

3. new_label( ) returns a new label.

One aspect of the unrolling process for loops that contain more than one basic block is not covered by the code in Figure 17.30—labels that occur in the body of the loop need to be renamed in each copy to make them distinct.

As noted above, the most important issues in loop unrolling are deciding which loops to unroll and by what factor. This has two aspects: one involves architectural characteristics, such as the number of registers available, the available overlap among, for example, floating-point operations and memory references, and the size and organization of the instruction cache; and the other is the selection of particular loops in a program to unroll and the unrolling factors to use for them. The impact of some of the architectural characteristics is often best determined by experimentation. The result is usually a heuristic, but unrolling decisions for individual loops can

```
procedure Unroll(nblocks,m,ninsts,Block,factor,init)
    returns integer × array [··] of Instruction
    m, nblocks factor, init: in integer
    ninsts: in array [1··nblocks] of integer
    Block: in array [1··nblocks] of array [··] of Instruction
begin
    UInst: array [··] of Instruction
    tj: Var
    lj: Label
    i, j, div: integer
    UInst[1] := Block[m][1]
    for i := 2 to ninsts[m]-2 do
        for j := 1 to factor do
            UInst[(j-1)*(ninsts[m]-3)+i] := Block[m][i]
        od
    od
    tj := new_tmp( )
    UInst[factor*(ninsts[m]-3)+2] := Block[m][ninsts[m]-1]
    UInst[factor*(ninsts[m]-3)+3] := Block[m][ninsts[m]]
    div := factor*Block[m][ninsts[m]-2].opd2.val
    if Constant(init) & Constant(Block[m][ninsts[m]-2].opd2)
        & Constant(Block[m][ninsts[m]-1].opd2)
        & (Block[m][ninsts[m]-1].opd2.val-init+1)%div = 0 then
        return ⟨factor*(ninsts[m]-3)+3,UInst⟩
    else
        lj := new_label( )
        UInst[factor*(ninsts[m]-3)+4] := ⟨kind:label,lbl:lj⟩
        for i := 2 to ninsts[m]-1 do
            UInst[factor*(ninsts[m]-3)+i+3] := Block[m][i]
        od
        UInst[factor*(ninsts[m]-3)+i+3] :=
            ⟨kind:valif,opd:Block[m][ninsts[m]].opd,lbl:lj⟩
        return ⟨(factor+1)*(ninsts[m]-3)+6,UInst⟩
    fi
end    || Unroll
```

FIG. 17.30 ICAN code to implement loop unrolling for a specific pattern of loop control.

benefit significantly from feedback from profiled runs of the program that contains the loops.

The result of a set of such experiments would be rules that can be used to decide what loops to unroll, which might depend, for example, on the following types of characteristics of loops:

1. those that contain only a single basic block (i.e., straight-line code),

2. those that contain a certain balance of floating-point and memory operations or a certain balance of integer memory operations,

3. those that generate a small number of intermediate-code instructions, and

4. those that have simple loop control.

The first and second criteria restrict unrolling to loops that are most likely to benefit from instruction scheduling. The third keeps the unrolled blocks of code short, so as not to adversely impact cache performance. The last criterion keeps the compiler from unrolling loops for which it is difficult to determine when to take the early exit to the rolled copy for the final iterations, such as when traversing a linked list. The unrolling factor may be anywhere from two up, depending on the specific contents of the loop body, but will usually not be more than four and almost never more than eight, although further development of VLIW machines may provide good use for larger unrolling factors.

It may be desirable to provide the programmer with a compiler option or a pragma to specify which loops to unroll and what factors to unroll them by.

Loop unrolling generally increases the available instruction-level parallelism, especially if several other transformations are performed on the copies of the loop body to remove unnecessary dependences. Such transformations include software register renaming (see Section 17.4.5), variable expansion (see next subsection), and instruction combining (see Section 18.12). Using dependence testing to disambiguate potential aliases between memory addresses can also remove dependences. Thus, unrolling has the potential of significant benefit for most implementations and particularly for superscalar and VLIW ones.

Instruction combining can make more registers available for renaming. As an example of this, consider the code sequence

```
r2 ← r1 + 1
r3 ← r2 * 2
```

Assuming that we are generating code for a machine that has shift and add instructions, such as PA-RISC, and that r2 is dead after this sequence, it can be transformed into

```
r3 ← 2 * r1 + 2
```

thus making r2 available.

17.4.4   Variable Expansion

Variable expansion in the body of an unrolled loop that has an unrolling factor of n selects variables that can be expanded into n separate copies, one for each copy of the loop body, and that can be combined at the loop's exits to produce the values that the original variables would have had. The expansion has the desirable property of decreasing the number of dependences in the loop, thus making instruction scheduling likely to be more effective when applied to it.

The easily detected opportunities for variable expansion include accumulator, induction, and search variables. Figure 17.31(a) gives examples of all three types, and Figure 17.31(b) shows the result of unrolling the loop by a factor of two and expanding the accumulator, induction, and search variables. Note that some of the induction variables (the addresses of the array elements) have not been expanded, since the example is HIR code; however, they are also amenable to variable expansion.

```
acc ← 10                          acc ← 10
                                  acc1 ← 0
max ← 0                           max ← 0
                                  max1 ← 0
imax ← 0                          imax ← 0
                                  imax1 ← 0
                                  i1 ← 2
for i ← 1 to 100 do               for i ← 1 by 2 to 99 do
    acc ← acc + a[i]*b[i]             acc ← acc + a[i]*b[i]
    if a[i] > max then                if a[i] > max then
        max ← a[i]                        max ← a[i]
        imax ← i                          imax ← i
    endif                             endif
                                      acc1 ← acc1 + a[i1]*b[i1]
                                      if a[i1] > max1 then
                                          max1 ← a[i1]
                                          imax1 ← i1
                                      endif
                                      i1 ← i1 + 2
endfor                            endfor
                                  acc ← acc + acc1
                                  if max1 > max then
                                      max ← max1
                                      imax ← imax1
                                  endif
(a)                               (b)
```

FIG. 17.31   (a) A HIR loop with examples of accumulator (acc), induction (i), and search (max and imax) variables; and (b) the loop after unrolling by a factor of two and expanding the accumulator, induction, and search variables.

The algorithms for the three kinds of variable expansion are broadly similar. We discuss only accumulator-variable expansion and leave it to the reader to adapt the approach to the other two types of variables.

To determine whether a variable serves as an additive accumulator (multiplicative ones are also possible but are less frequent), we require that it be used and defined in the loop only by add and/or subtract instructions and that the unrolled loop body contain n copies of such instructions, one per copy of the loop body, where n is the unrolling factor. Having determined that a variable is an additive accumulator, we replace the second through n^{th} copies by new temporary variables, initialize them all to zero at the loop entrance, and at each of the loop's exits, add them to the original variable.

In the example in Figure 17.31, acc is an additive accumulator. In the unrolled version, it has been replaced with acc1 in the second copy of the body; acc1 has been initialized to zero before entering the loop; and an instruction to add it to acc has been included at the loop exit.

1	f1 ← f2 + 1.0	f27 ← f2 + 1.0	f1 ← f3 * 2.0
2	[fp+52] ← f1	[fp+52] ← f27	f27 ← f2 + 1.0
3	f1 ← f3 * 2.0	f1 ← f3 * 2.0	[fp+40] ← f1
4	[fp+40] ← f1	[fp+40] ← f1	[fp+52] ← f27
	(a)	**(b)**	**(c)**

FIG. 17.32 (a) An example of LIR code to which register renaming may be applied, (b) the result of performing it, and (c) an alternate schedule of the instructions made possible by the renaming.

17.4.5   Register Renaming

Register renaming is a transformation that may increase the flexibility available to code scheduling. It can be applied to low-level code (in our case, LIR code) to remove unnecessary dependences between instructions that use the same register by replacing some of the uses by other registers. For example, in the basic block shown in Figure 17.32(a), the use of f1 in all four instructions, combined with the information that f1 is live at the exit from the block, makes it impossible to reorder the instructions at all. The substitution of f27 for f1 in the first and second instructions (assuming that f27 is not live at that point) shown in Figure 17.32(b) allows the instructions to be scheduled in any order that preserves the occurrence of the definitions of f27 and f1 before their respective uses, such as the order in Figure 17.32(c).

We simplify our discussion of renaming somewhat by assuming that all registers are of the same type. For the more realistic case of separate integer and floating-point register sets, we apply the algorithm twice, once for each register set.

Given basic block i consisting of instructions LBlock[i][$1 \cdot \cdot n$], we first need to determine several sets of registers, as follows:

1. Regs is the set of all general-purpose registers provided by the architecture.

2. RegsUsed(i) is the set of registers used and/or defined in block i.

3. RegsLiveEntry(i) is the set of registers that are live on entry to block i.

4. RegsLiveExit(i) is the set of registers that are live on exit from block i.

5. DefsLiveExit(i) is the set of indexes of instructions that define registers that are live on exit from block i.

A combination of inspection and data-flow analysis can be used to determine these sets. AvailRegs, the set of registers available for renaming in block i, is then

$$\text{AvailRegs} = \text{Regs} - (\text{RegsUsed}(i) \cup \text{RegsLiveEntry}(i)$$
$$\cup \text{RegsLiveExit}(i))$$

Next, for each register r in RegsUsed(i), we compute DefUses(r), the maximal sequence of pairs $\langle j, s \rangle$ such that j is the index of an instruction in block i that defines r, and s is the set of indexes of instructions in block i that use the value of r as computed by instruction j; the elements of the sequence are ordered by the definitions in the pairs. Then, as long as there are registers in `AvailRegs` and pairs in `DefUses`(r) such that the definition is dead on exit from the block, we replace register r in its definitions and uses by a register selected from `AvailRegs`.

For our example block (call it A) in Figure 17.32(a), the sets are as follows:

```
Regs                = {f0,f1,...,f31}
RegsUsed(A)         = {f1,f2,f3}
RegsLiveEntry(A) = {f2,f3}
RegsLiveExit(A)  = {f1}
DefsLiveExit(A)  = {3}
AvailRegs           = {f0,f4,...,f31}
DefUses(f1)         = [⟨1,{2}⟩,⟨3,{4}⟩]
```

so the definition of `f1` in line 1 and its use in line 2 of column (a) are replaced by a register chosen randomly from `AvailRegs`, namely, `f27`, as shown in column (b).

ICAN code to rename registers in a basic block is given in Figure 17.33. We assume that `Regs`, `RegsUsed( )`, `RegsLiveEntry( )`, `RegsLiveExit( )`, and `DefsLiveExit( )` have been precomputed. The procedures used in the code are as follows:

1. `Defines`(*inst*,r) returns `true` if instruction *inst* defines register r, and `false` otherwise.

2. `Uses`(*inst*,r) returns `true` if instruction *inst* uses register r as an operand, and `false` otherwise.

3. `replace_result`(i,`LBlock`,m,*ar*) replaces the result register in instruction `LBlock`[m] [i] by *ar*.

4. `replace_operands`(i,`LBlock`,m,r,*ar*) replaces occurrences of r as an operand register in instruction `LBlock`[m] [i] by *ar*.

Note that if register r is in `RegsLiveEntry`(m) but not in `RegsLiveExit`(m), then r becomes available as a renaming register after its last use in the block; we have not accounted for this in the code.

Register renaming can be adapted to work on extended basic blocks as long as we are careful to maintain unchanged the last definition of each register that is live on exit from each exit block. For example, in the code in Figure 17.34, given that `f1` is live on exit from B3 but not from B2, we must preserve the last definition of `f1` in block B1, but we can rename `f1` in B2.

17.4.6   Other Approaches to Software Pipelining

It is indicative of the state of the art in software pipelining that there have been numerous other approaches proposed in recent years. These include circular scheduling, which resembles our window-scheduling approach, and a variety of methods that resemble our unroll-and-compact approach, including the following:

```
Regs: set of Register
RegsUsed, RegsLiveEntry, RegsLiveExit: integer ⟶ set of Register
DefsLiveExit: integer ⟶ set of integer

procedure Register_Rename(m,ninsts,LBlock)
   m: in integer
   ninsts: in integer ⟶ integer
   LBlock: inout array [··] of array [··] of LIRInst
begin
   AvailRegs: set of Register
   r, ar: Register
   def, i, j, n: integer
   uses: set of integer
   DefUses: Register ⟶ sequence of (integer × set of integer)
   AvailRegs := Regs - (RegsUsed(m) ∪ RegsLiveEntry(m) ∪ RegsLiveExit(m))
   if AvailRegs = ∅ then
      return
   fi
   for each r ∈ RegsUsed(m) do
      DefUses(r) := []
      for i := 1 to ninsts(m) do
         if Defines(LBlock[m][i],r) then
            def := i
            uses := ∅
            for j := i+1 to ninsts(m) do
               if Uses(LBlock[m][j],r) then
                  uses ∪= {j}
               fi
               if Defines(LBlock[m][j],r) then
                  i := j
                  goto L1
               fi
L1:         od
         fi
         DefUses(r) ⊕= [⟨def,uses⟩]
      od
   od
```

FIG. 17.33   ICAN code to rename registers in a basic block.

1. Lam's approach for VLIW systems,

2. optimal loop parallelization,

3. perfect pipelining,

4. Bodin and Charot's approach,

5. approaches to software pipelining with resource constraints, and

6. decomposed software pipelining.

```
for each r ∈ RegsUsed(m) do
    while |DefUses(r)| > 0 do
        def := (DefUses(r)↓1)@1
        uses := (DefUses(r)↓1)@2
        DefUses(r) ⊖= 1
        if def ∉ DefsLiveExit(m) then
            ar := ◆AvailRegs
            AvailRegs -= {ar}
            replace_result(def,LBlock,m,ar)
            for each i ∈ uses do
                replace_operands(i,LBlock,m,r,ar)
            od
        fi
    od
od
end     || Register_Rename
```

FIG. 17.33 *(continued)*

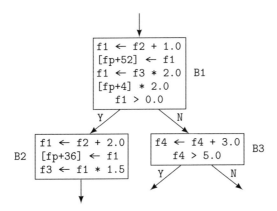

FIG. 17.34 An example of an extended basic block for register renaming.

Thus it is still an active area of research to determine what the best approach is, both in terms of resulting loop performance and efficiency of the pipelining algorithm. (See Section 17.8 for detailed references.)

An interesting experiment was reported by Ruttenberg et al. An optimal software pipelining algorithm called MOST, developed at McGill University, was adapted to serve in place of the pipeliner in the MIPS compilers and a series of experiments were performed to compare the heuristic algorithm in the MIPS compilers with the optimal one. In compiling all the SPEC92 benchmarks, a better schedule was found for only one loop by the optimal algorithm than the heuristic one, yet the optimal algorithm required about 3,000 times the amount of time used by the heuristic algorithm. Thus, software pipelining is definitely worth including in an aggressive optimizing compiler, and heuristic approaches may perform very well for most programs.

```
L1: ld    [r2],r3    *        L1:  ld    [r2],r3
    ld    [r1],f0    *             ld    [r1],f0
    cmp   r3,0                L1a: cmp   r3,0
    ble   L2                       ble   L2
    nop                           nop
    add   r4,1,r4                  add   r4,1,r4
    fadds f2,f0,f3                 fadds f2,f0,f3
                     *             ld    [r2],r3
                     *             ld    [r1],f0
    b     L3                       b     L3
    nop                           nop
L2: fsubs f3,f0,f3           L2:  fsubs f3,f0,f3
    stf   f3,[r1]                  stf   f3,[r1]
    bg    L1                       bg    L1a
    nop                           nop
                     *             ld    [r2],r3
                     *             ld    [r1],f0
L3: sub   r2,4,r2            L3:  sub   r2,4,r2
    sub   r1,4,r1                  sub   r1,4,r1
    cmp   r1,0                     cmp   r1,4
                                   ld    [r2],r3
                                   ld    [r1],f0
    bg    L1                       bg    L1a
    nop                           nop
                                   cmp   r3,0
                                   ble   L2a
                                   nop
                                   add   r4,1,r4
                                   b     L3a
                                   fadds f2,f0,f3
                             L2a: fsubs f3,f0,f3
                                   stf   f3,[r1]
                             L3a: sub   r2,4,r2
                                   sub   r1,4,r1
          (a)                              (b)
```

FIG. 17.35   (a) A SPARC loop containing a conditional, and (b) the result of window scheduling it and moving the two ld instructions marked with asterisks into both arms of the conditional.

17.4.7   Hierarchical Reduction

Hierarchical reduction is a technique that was developed by Lam ([Lam88] and [Lam90]) to handle pipelining of loops that contain control-flow constructs. The method consists of two parts, one to handle conditionals and the other to handle nested loops. To handle nested loops, one pipelines from the innermost loop outward, reducing each loop as it is scheduled to a single node, with the scheduling and resource constraints of the loop attached to the node that represents it.

To handle conditionals, one first does basic-block scheduling on the then and else branches independently and then reduces the conditional to a single node, again with the scheduling and resource constraints of the entire if-then-else attached to it. This, in effect, pads the shorter of the two branches to have the same latency as the longer ones. On the other hand, one need not produce code that satisfies this constraint—inserting unnecessary nops would merely waste space, not improve the schedule.

As an example of software pipelining applied to a loop containing a conditional, consider the code in Figure 17.35(a), assuming we are compiling for the same processor structure as assumed for the code in Figure 17.15. If we window schedule the first two instructions in the loop (the two lds marked with asterisks) to become the end of the loop body and we move the two loads into both branches of the conditional, we obtain the code in Figure 17.35(b). We can then reschedule the then and else branches and do further pipelining, if desirable.

17.5   Trace Scheduling

Trace scheduling is an instruction scheduling method developed by Fisher [Fish81] that is much more ambitious than the ones we have discussed so far. It is most useful for VLIW machines and superscalar implementations of degree greater than about eight.

A *trace* is a sequence of instructions, including branches but not including loops, that is executed for some input data. *Trace scheduling* uses a basic-block scheduling method (such as the one described in Section 17.1.2) to schedule the instructions in each entire trace, beginning with the trace with the highest execution frequency. It then adds *compensation code,* as needed, at each entry to and exit from a trace to compensate for any effects that out-of-order execution may have had that are inconsistent with that entry or exit. Loop bodies are generally unrolled several times before being scheduled. The scheduling and compensation process is repeated until either all traces have been scheduled or a chosen threshold of execution frequency has been reached. Any remaining traces are scheduled by standard methods, such as the basic-block and software-pipelining approaches. While trace scheduling can be quite effective with estimated execution profiles, like most scheduling methods it is more effective when provided with profiling feedback.

As a simple example of trace scheduling, consider the flowgraph fragment in Figure 17.36. Suppose we determine that the most frequently executed path through the flowgraph consists of blocks B1, B3, B4, B5, and B7. Since B4 is the body of a loop, this path is divided into three traces, one consisting of B1 and B3, the second consisting of the loop body B4, and the third containing B5 and B7. Each of the three traces would be scheduled independently, with, for example, compensation code added at the exit from the trace for B1 and B3 corresponding to taking the N exit from block B1. Suppose the code for blocks B1, B2, and B3 is as shown in Figure 17.37(a). In Figure 17.37(b), the trace scheduler has decided to move the assignment y ← x - y across the branch into block B3; a copy of this instruction must then be placed at the beginning of B2 as compensation code. After the three selected traces have been scheduled, each of B2 and B6 would be scheduled as a separate trace.

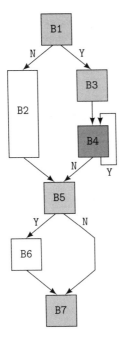

FIG. 17.36 An example for trace scheduling.

```
B1: x ← x + 1              B1: x ← x + 1
    y ← x - y
    if x < 5 goto B3           if x < 5 goto B3
                          B2: y ← x - y
B2: z ← x * z                 z ← x * z
    x ← x + 1                 x ← x + 1
    goto B5                   goto B5
                          B3: y ← x - y
B3: y ← 2 * y                 y ← 2 * y
    x ← x - 2                 x ← x - 2
      .                          .
      .                          .
      .                          .

    (a)                       (b)
```

FIG. 17.37 (a) Example MIR code for the trace in Figure 17.36 made up of B1 and B3 (along with code for B2), and (b) the result of a scheduling operation and compensation code.

Trace scheduling can frequently achieve large performance improvements for VLIW or high-degree superscalar machines, but it can also result in large increases in code size and in poor or erratic performance if a program's behavior varies significantly with its input.

17.6   Percolation Scheduling

Percolation scheduling is another aggressive cross-block scheduling method that was developed by Nicolau [Nico86]. It is designed to work on *parallel computation graphs* (PCGs) consisting of *computation nodes,* each of which includes a set of operations that are performed in parallel, a tree of control-flow operations that may determine a set of successor nodes, and a default successor that is used if the tree is empty. Of course, this represents a departure from our intermediate-code forms in that each of them enforces sequential semantics on the contents of a basic block. A computation node is either one of two special nodes called enter and exit; or a node that consists of a set of operations O that are executed in parallel (with all loads performed before all stores), a continuation tree T that conditionally selects a set of successor computation nodes, and a continuation C that is used if T is empty. (In Figure 17.39, the type PCGnode is used to represent computation nodes.)

Percolation scheduling uses an additional type of dependence relation called *write-live dependence,* written δ^{wl}, that is defined as follows. Let v be a computation node and u be one of its successors. Then, $v \, \delta^{wl} \, u$ if there exists a successor w of v such that some variable live on the edge $v{\rightarrow}w$ is written to in node u, where a variable is live on an edge if there is a path beginning with the edge and extending to the parallel computation graph's exit on which the variable is read before it is written. In Figure 17.38, the variable n produces a write-live dependence $v \, \delta^{wl} \, u$.

Percolation scheduling consists of four basic transformations that can be applied to PCGs, called delete node, move operation, move conditional, and unify. The first

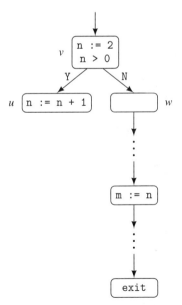

FIG. 17.38 An example of write-live dependence, namely, v δ^{wl} u, because of variable n.

```
procedure Perc_Schedule_1(r)
   r: in PCGnode
begin
   Cand: set of PCGnode
   n: PCGnode
   again: boolean
   repeat
      again := false
      Cand := {r}
      for each n ∈ Cand do
         if Delete_Node_Applic(n) then
            Delete_Node(n)
            Cand ∪= Succ(n)
            again := true
         elif Move_Oper_Applic(n) then
            Move_Oper(n)
            Cand ∪= Succ(n)
            again := true
         elif Move_Cond_Applic(n) then
            Move_Cond(n)
            Cand ∪= Succ(n)
            again := true
         elif Unify_Applic(n) then
            Unify(n)
            Cand ∪= Succ(n)
            again := true
         fi
         Cand -= {n}
      od
   until !again
end     || Perc_Schedule_1
```

FIG. 17.39   A simple algorithm for percolation scheduling.

deletes nodes that have become empty; the second and third move operations and conditionals, respectively, to predecessor nodes; and the last moves a set of identical operations from all the successors of a node to that node.

The algorithm to apply these transformations to a PCG may be anywhere from trivially simple to quite complicated. For example, we can construct four predicates that test applicability of the transformations (Delete_Node_Applic( ), Move_Oper_Applic( ), Move_Cond_Applic( ), and Unify_Applic( )) to a subgraph that is rooted at a particular PCG node and four procedures (Delete_Node( ), Move_Oper( ), Move_Cond( ), and Unify( ), respectively) to apply them. Given those predicates and procedures, the code in Figure 17.39 is a simple percolation scheduler. It tries, for each node, to apply each of the four transformations and repeats the transformations until no more apply. However, this won't quite do: there is no guarantee that the algorithm will terminate on an arbitrary PCG. What is needed is to break the PCG into components that are DAGs and then to apply the algorithm to them. Then termination can be guaranteed.

Clearly other regimes for applying the transformations are possible and other types of optimizations can profitably be mixed in with percolation scheduling. For example, moving an operation into a node may create an opportunity for common-subexpression elimination.

Nicolau defines a series of meta-transformations that are built from the basic four. These include: (1) a transformation called `migrate( )` that moves an operation as far upward in a PCG as dependences will allow it to go; (2) an extension of the technique to irreducible PCGs, i.e., to those with multiple-entry loops; and (3) a transformation called `compact_path( )` that generalizes trace scheduling by moving operations upward along the path with the highest execution frequency.

17.7   Wrap-Up

This chapter has focused on methods to schedule instructions to improve performance. These are some of the most important optimizations for most programs on most machines, including all RISCs and more and more CISC implementations. We have covered branch scheduling, basic-block scheduling, cross-block scheduling, software pipelining (including loop unrolling, variable expansion, register renaming, and hierarchical reduction), boosting, trace scheduling, and percolation scheduling.

After recognizing that almost all of the scheduling problems are at least NP-hard, even in their simplest formulations, we have proceeded to describe heuristic solutions that almost always work very well in practice.

Combining basic-block and branch scheduling is the easiest to implement of the approaches discussed; even this approach can produce major improvements in execution speed, frequently at least 10%.

Cross-block and speculative scheduling are harder to implement but improve on the basic-block form by moving instructions between blocks. These methods frequently produce even larger decreases in execution time, particularly if the hardware supports speculative loads.

Software pipelining (with loop unrolling, variable expansion, register renaming, and hierarchical reduction) operates on loop bodies and can result in even larger performance improvements. There are several different kinds of approaches to software pipelining, of which we have described two examples, one easier to implement and one harder but usually more effective. There is, as yet, no definitive answer on the best approach to use, as indicated by the list of methods in Section 17.4.6.

Loop unrolling is a transformation that replaces a loop body with some number of copies of the body and adjusts the loop-control code accordingly. If the compiler does not include software pipelining, we recommend doing loop unrolling between dead-code elimination and code hoisting in box **C4** of the diagram in Figure 17.40.

Variable expansion is a subsidiary technique that is useful in loop bodies that have been unrolled, to decouple operations in each copy that put their results in a particular variable. It provides one such variable for each loop body and combines their resulting values after the loop. Register renaming is similar to variable expansion in that it removes unnecessary dependences between instructions that use the same registers even though they don't need to.

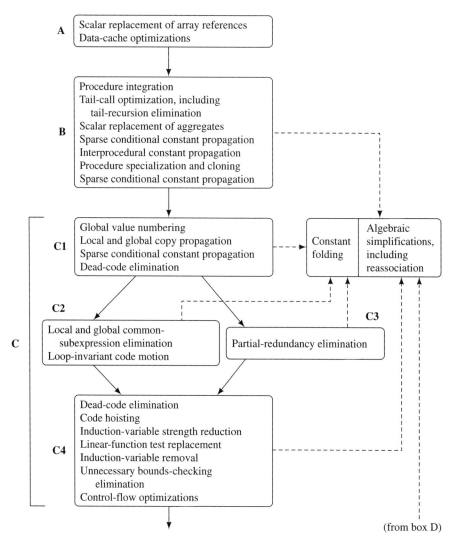

FIG. 17.40   Order of optimizations with scheduling phases in **bold** type.

All the transformations discussed above are best performed very close to the end of the optimization (and compilation) process, since, to be more than marginally effective, they require either a form of machine code or a low-level intermediate code that accurately models the target machine.

Trace and percolation scheduling are two global code-scheduling methods that can have very large benefits for some types of programs, mostly numeric ones that operate on arrays, and for architectures, typically high-degree superscalar and VLIW machines. They are best structured as drivers for the optimization process, i.e., we would build an optimizer around either type of global scheduling and invoke other optimizations, as appropriate, from them.

Figure 17.40 shows a suggested order for optimization, with scheduling optimizations in **bold** type. We do instruction scheduling (branch, basic-block, cross-

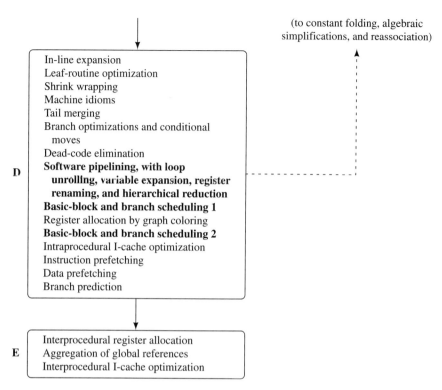

FIG. 17.40 *(continued)*

block, and software pipelining and its subsidiaries) immediately before register allocation and, if any spill code has been generated, repeat branch and basic-block scheduling after register allocation. A compiler that does not include software pipelining should place loop unrolling and variable expansion earlier in the compilation process, along with other loop optimizations. Trace and percolation scheduling are omitted from the diagram since, as described above, they require a complete restructuring of the optimization process.

17.8   Further Reading

Rymarczyk's guidelines for assembly-language programmers to get the best advantage from the pipelined processors in IBM System/370 implementations is [Ryma82]. MIPS-X is described in [Chow86].

See [GarJ79] for a proof that basic-block scheduling is an *NP*-hard problem. Basic-block schedulers that use list scheduling include those described in [GibM86] and [Warr90]. The proof that list scheduling produces a schedule that is within a factor of two of optimal for a machine with one or more identical pipelines is given by Lawler et al. [LawL87].

Smotherman et al. [SmoK91] survey the types of DAGs and heuristics used in a series of implemented schedulers, including ones developed by Gibbons and Muchnick [GibM86], Krishnamurthy [Kris90], Schlansker [Schl91], Shieh and Papachristou [ShiP89], Tiemann [Tiem89], and Warren [Warr90]. Hennessy and Gross's machine-level DAG is described in [HenG83]. Balanced scheduling is described in [KerE93] and [LoEg95]. Golumbic and Rainish's discussion of transformations that help cover the branch delays in POWER is found in [GolR90].

The GNU instruction-scheduler generator is, unfortunately, not very well described. The scheduler that formed the basis for it is described in [Tiem89]. The scheduler generator is probably best described by the code that implements it, namely, the file genattrtab.c in the main directory of the GNU C compiler distribution (see Section C.3.1) and by examples in the machine-description files *machine*.md found in the config subdirectory.

Approaches currently in use for scheduling across basic-block boundaries are discussed in [Wall92], [BerC92], and [MahR94]. [EbcG94] discusses the application of scheduling techniques developed for VLIW architectures to superscalar RISCs.

Speculative loads and their use in scheduling are discussed in [RogL92], [ColN87], [WeaG94], and [Powe93].

[EbcG94] describes both speculative scheduling and unspeculation. [GolR90] and [BerR91] describe earlier approaches to speculative scheduling.

Circular scheduling is described in [Jain91]. Descriptions of pipeline-scheduling methods that resemble our unroll-and-compact approach are as follows:

Method	Reference
Lam's approach for VLIW systems	[Lam88]
Optimal loop parallelization	[AikN88a] and [Aike88]
Perfect pipelining	[AikN88b] and [Aike88]
Bodin and Charot's approach	[BodC90]
Approaches with resource constraints	[EisW92] and [AikN91]
Decomposed software pipelining	[WanE93]

The approach to software pipelining used in the MIPS compilers, the optimal pipelining algorithm most developed at McGill University, and a comparison of them are described in [RutG96].

Variable expansion is described in Mahlke et al. [MahC92].

The details of hierarchical reduction can be found in [Lam88] and [Lam90]. Trace scheduling is described in [Fish81] and [Elli85]. Percolation scheduling is first described in [Nico86].

17.9   Exercises

17.1 For each of the heuristics given in Section 17.1.2, write a sequence of LIR instructions for which using only that heuristic provides the best schedule and one for which it does not.

17.2 The text in Section 17.4.3 alludes to some modifications that need to be made to the code produced by an unroll-and-compact software pipeliner. What are the modifications and why are they needed?

17.3 Give an example of the use of hierarchical reduction to pipeline a loop that contains an inner loop and an `if-then-else` construct.

17.4 Give an example of a basic block of LIR code for which register renaming allows a schedule that decreases execution time by at least one-third.

17.5 Modify the list scheduling algorithm in Figure 17.6 for use in scheduling code for a three-scalar implementation in which there are two integer pipelines and one floating-point pipeline.

ADV 17.6 Generalize the algorithm from the preceding exercise so that it schedules code for an n-scalar processor with n_i processors of each of m types `PClass`(i) such that

$$\sum_{i=1}^{m} n_i = n$$

and instructions $I_1, I_2, \ldots, I_k$ such that I_i can execute on processor j if and only if `IClass`(I_i) = `PClass`(j). Let I_k have an issue latency of s_k cycles and a result latency of r_k, independent of any interinstruction conflicts.

17.7 Give ICAN code to expand (a) accumulator and (b) search variables in an unrolled loop.

CHAPTER 18

Control-Flow and
Low-Level Optimizations

This chapter covers optimizations that apply to the control flow of a procedure, dead-code elimination, and the remaining global optimizations that are best carried out on programs in a low-level intermediate code (such as LIR), or on a structured form of assembly language.

Some of them, such as dead-code elimination, may profitably be applied several times during compilation, because several other transformations may create dead code and it is desirable to eliminate it promptly to reduce the size of the procedure that is being compiled.

The control-flow transformations that produce longer basic blocks have the potential to increase available instruction-level parallelism, which is particularly important for superscalar implementations.

Accurate branch prediction is important because it increases the chance that a processor will fetch the correct continuation path from an instruction cache, the main memory, or a second-level cache. As cache delays become longer relative to cycle time, the importance of branch prediction continues to increase.

The last few optimizations in this chapter are often known as postpass or peephole optimizations. The first term is used because they are generally among the last optimizations to be performed and are always done after code generation. The other term refers to the fact that many of them can be carried out by moving a small window or peephole across the generated code to search for segments of code they apply to.

The transformations discussed below are as follows:

1. unreachable-code elimination, which removes blocks that cannot possibly be executed because there are no paths from the entry to the blocks;

2. straightening, which creates longer basic blocks by replacing some kinds of branches by the code they branch to;

3. if simplifications, which eliminate unused arms of ifs and possibly entire if constructs;

4. loop simplifications, which replace some empty or very simple loops by straight-line code;

5. loop inversion, which replaces a test at the beginning of a loop and an unconditional closing branch at the end by a test at the end;

6. unswitching, which moves loop-invariant conditionals out of loops;

7. branch optimizations, which replace various kinds of branches to branches by simpler code;

8. tail merging, or cross jumping, which turns identical tails of basic blocks into one such tail and branches from the others to the tail of the remaining one;

9. conditional moves, which can replace some simple if constructs by code sequences that contain no branches;

10. dead-code elimination, which removes instructions that can be determined to have no effect on the result of a computation;

11. branch prediction, which refers to predicting, either statically or dynamically, whether a conditional branch causes a transfer of control or not; and

12. machine idioms and instruction combining, which replace single instructions or sequences of instructions by single ones that perform the same task faster.

18.1   Unreachable-Code Elimination

Unreachable code is code that cannot possibly be executed, regardless of the input data. It may never have been executable for any input data to begin with, or it may have achieved that status as a result of other optimizations. Its elimination has no direct effect on the execution speed of a program but obviously decreases the space the program occupies, and so may have secondary effects on its speed, particularly by improving its instruction-cache utilization. Also, elimination of unreachable code may enable other control-flow transformations, such as straightening (see Section 18.2), that reduce execution time.

Note that elimination of unreachable code is one of two transformations that are occasionally confused with each other. The other is dead-code elimination (see Section 18.10), which removes code that is executable but that has no effect on the result of the computation being performed.

To identify and remove unreachable code, we assume that there is a table of basic blocks and, for each block, the sets of predecessors and successors. We proceed as follows:

1. Set again to false.

2. Iterate through the Block[] array, looking for blocks such that there is no non-empty path from the entry block to those blocks. When such a block is found,

```
procedure Elim_Unreach_Code(nblocks,ninsts,Block,Pred,Succ)
   nblocks: inout integer
   ninsts: inout array [··] of integer
   Block: inout array [··] of array [··] of Instruction
   Pred, Succ: inout integer ⟶ set of integer
begin
   again: boolean
   i: integer
   repeat
      again := false
      i := 2
      while i ≤ nblocks do
         if No_Path(1,i) then
            ninsts[i] := 0
            nblocks -= 1
            Block[i] := nil
            again := true
            delete_block(i,nblocks,ninsts,Block,Succ,Pred)
         fi
         i += 1
      od
   until !again
end    || Elim_Unreach_Code
```

FIG. 18.1 Algorithm to eliminate unreachable code.

delete it and adjust the predecessor and successor functions to reflect its having been removed. If any of the deleted block's successors have now become unreachable, set again to true.

3. If again is true, go to step 1.

4. Adjust the Block and related data structures to compact the blocks at the beginning of the Block array.

Note that the last step above is unnecessary if it is acceptable to simply set Block[i] = nil for an unreachable block i.

ICAN code for the routine Elim_Unreach_Code( ) to implement this is given in Figure 18.1. We assume that Block[1] is the entry block. The algorithm uses the function No_Path(i,j), which returns true if there is no non-empty path from block i to block j, and false otherwise; and the function delete_block(i,nblocks, ninsts,Block,Succ,Pred), which is defined in Figure 4.17.

Figure 18.2(a) shows the flowgraph of a MIR procedure that contains unreachable code, namely, blocks B2, B3, and B5. The value of n is 7 and the ninsts, Pred, and Succ data structures for this code are given in Table 18.1(a). After unreachable-code elimination, the value of nblocks is 4, the data structures' values are as shown in Table 18.1(b), and the resulting flowgraph is as shown in Figure 18.2(b).

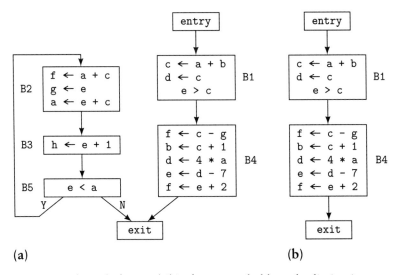

FIG. 18.2 Our example (a) before and (b) after unreachable-code elimination.

TABLE 18.1 The basic-block data structures for the flowgraph in Figure 18.2.

i	ninsts$[i]$	Succ(i)	Pred(i)
entry	0	{B1}	Ø
B1	3	{B4}	{entry}
B2	3	{B3}	{B5}
B3	1	{B5}	{B2}
B4	5	{exit}	{B1}
B5	1	{B2,exit}	{B3}
exit	0	Ø	{B4,B5}

(a)

i	ninsts$[i]$	Succ(i)	Pred(i)
entry	0	{B1}	Ø
B1	3	{B4}	{entry}
B4	5	{exit}	{B1}
exit	0	Ø	{B4}

(b)

18.2   Straightening

Straightening is an optimization that applies, in its most basic form, to pairs of basic blocks such that the first has no successors other than the second and the second has no predecessors other than the first. Since they are both basic blocks, either the second one immediately follows the first one or the first of them must end with an unconditional branch to the second. In the former case, the transformation does nothing and in the latter it replaces the branch with the second block. Figure 18.3 shows an example. Block B1 has a single successor B2, whose only predecessor is B1. The transformation fuses them into the new block B1a.

However, the transformation is not quite as simple as the flowgraphs suggest. Consider the code in Figure 18.4(a), in which the blocks beginning with L1 and L2 correspond to B1 and B2, respectively. The first block ends with an unconditional branch to L2, and we assume that the block beginning with L2 has no other predecessors. The transformed code in Figure 18.4(b) has replaced the goto L2 with a

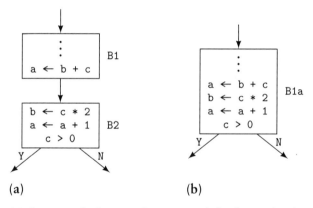

(a)   (b)

FIG. 18.3 (a) An example for straightening, and (b) the result of applying the transformation.

```
L1: . . .                          L1: . . .
      a ← b + c                          a ← b + c
      goto L2                            b ← c * 2
                                         a ← a + 1
                                         if (c > 0) goto L3
                                         goto L5
L6: . . .                          L6: . . .
      goto L4                            goto L4
L2: b ← c * 2
      a ← a + 1
      if (c > 0) goto L3
L5: . . .                          L5: . . .
(a)                                (b)
```

FIG. 18.4 MIR code versions of the example code in Figure 18.3.

copy of the block beginning with L2 and has deleted the original copy of that block. Note that since the copied block ends with a conditional transfer, it needs to have a branch to the fall-through path from the original block placed at the end of it. Clearly, straightening has the greatest benefit if the copied block ends with an unconditional branch also, since it then does not require a new branch for the fall-through path and may enable straightening to be applied again.

Straightening can be generalized to pairs of blocks such that the first ends with a conditional branch and the second has no other predecessors. If it is known that one path is more likely to be taken than the other, it can be made the fall-through path and, if necessary, the condition tested can be inverted. In most implementations, this is almost always faster than making the less likely path the fall-through. For architectures (or implementations) with static branch prediction (see Section 18.11), this requires that we predict that the branch falls through rather than branching.

ICAN code to perform straightening is given in Figure 18.5, and the auxiliary routine Fuse_Blocks( ) that is used in the process is in Figure 18.6. The

```
procedure Straighten(nblocks,ninsts,Block,Succ,Pred)
    nblocks: inout integer
    ninsts: inout array [··] of integer
    Block: inout array [··] of array of [··] of LIRInst
    Succ, Pred: inout integer ⟶ set of integer
begin
    change := true: boolean
    i, j: integer
    while change do
        change := false
        i := 1
        while i ≤ nblocks do
            if |Succ(i)| = 1 & Pred(♦Succ(i)) = {i} then
                j := ♦Succ(i)
                Fuse_Blocks(nblocks,ninsts,Block,Succ,Pred,i,j)
                change := true
            fi
            i += 1
        od
    od
end     || Straighten
```

FIG. 18.5   ICAN code to perform straightening of basic-block pairs.

```
procedure Fuse_Blocks(nblocks,ninsts,Block,Succ,Pred,i,j)
    nblocks: inout integer
    ninsts: inout array [··] of integer
    Block: inout array [··] of array of [··] of LIRInst
    Succ, Pred: inout integer ⟶ set of integer
    i, j: in integer
```

FIG. 18.6   The routine Fuse_Blocks( ) used by Straighten( ).

```
begin
   k, l: integer
   label: Label
   if Block[i][ninsts[i]].kind = goto then
      k := ninsts[i] - 1
   else
      k := ninsts[i]
   fi
   if Block[j][1].kind ≠ label then
      k += 1
      Block[i][k] := Block[j][1]
   fi
   for l := 2 to ninsts[j] do
      k += 1
      Block[i][k] := Block[j][l]
   od
   if Block[i][k].kind ≠ goto then
      label := Fall_Through(j,ninsts,Block)
      ninsts[i] := k + 1
      Block[i][ninsts[i]] := ⟨kind:goto,lbl:label⟩
   fi
   ninsts[j] := 0
   Succ(i) := Succ(j)
   Elim_Unreach_Code(nblocks,ninsts,Block,Pred,Succ)
end     || Fuse_Blocks
```

FIG. 18.6 *(continued)*

call `Fall_Through(j,ninsts,Block)` returns the label of the block that execution would fall through to after executing block *j*; if there is none, it supplies one and returns its value.

18.3   If Simplifications

If simplifications apply to conditional constructs one or both of whose arms are empty. This may result from code hoisting or other optimizing transformations or may be present in the source code to begin with, especially if it was generated by a program rather than directly by a person. This section describes three such simplifications that have to do with empty arms of a conditional, constant-valued conditions, and common subexpressions in dependent conditionals.

If either the `then` or `else` part of an `if` construct is empty, the corresponding branch can be eliminated. If the `then` part of an `if-then-else` is empty, we reverse the sense of the condition, so the branch for the `then` part can be removed. If both parts are empty, we remove the entire control structure and retain only as much of the condition computation as cannot be determined to be free of live side effects.

A second control-flow simplification that applies to `if`s arises from constant-valued conditions. A constant-valued condition automatically makes one arm of the

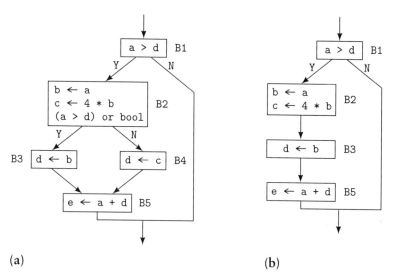

(a)   (b)

FIG. 18.7 (a) An example with a condition that is a common subexpression, and (b) the result of removing the dead arm of the `if`.

`if` unexecutable and hence removable. If it is the only arm, it makes the entire `if` construct removable, as long as the condition computation has no live side effects.

A third control-flow simplification that applies to `if`s is the occurrence of common subexpressions as conditions in an `if` and in a subsequent dependent `if`; of course, the values of the variables involved must not have been changed between the tests. Such a case is illustrated in Figure 18.7. The test `(a > d) or bool` at the end of block B2 is guaranteed to be satisfied because `a > d` was satisfied in block B1 if we have gotten to B2, and neither `a` nor `d` has been changed in between. Thus, the test in B2 and all of block B4 can be removed. As in this case, this simplification may make straightening applicable.

18.4   Loop Simplifications

A loop whose body is empty can be eliminated, as long as the iteration-control code has no live side effects. If the iteration-control code has side effects, they may be simple enough that they can be replaced by nonlooping code. In particular, if the loop simply increments or decrements the loop-control variable by a constant and checks it against a constant final value, the final value can be computed at compile time and a statement that assigns it to the variable can be inserted in place of the loop.

The second and third simplifications discussed in the preceding section for `if`s also apply to loops and to nests of `if`s within loops and vice versa.

Another simplification that applies to loops is that some of them have simple enough loop-control code that it is possible to determine how many times they will be executed and, if the number is small enough, they can profitably be unrolled into

```
       s ← 0                    s ← 0                  i ← 4
       i ← 0                    i ← 0                  s ← 10
    L2: if i > 4 goto L1        i ← i + 1
       i ← i + 1                s ← s + i
       s ← s + i                i ← i + 1
       goto L2                  s ← s + i
    L1:                         i ← i + 1
                                s ← s + i
                                i ← i + 1
                                s ← s + i
                                i ← i + 1
                                s ← s + i

    (a)                        (b)                    (c)
```

FIG. 18.8   (a) An example of a loop that can be turned into (b) straight-line code and (c) executed at compile time.

branchless code. In some cases, the resulting code can be executed at compile time, as in Figure 18.8.

18.5   Loop Inversion

Loop inversion, in source-language terms, transforms a while loop into a repeat loop. In other words, it moves the loop-closing test from before the body of the loop to after it. In its simplest form, loop inversion requires that we either determine that the loop is entered, i.e., that the loop body is executed at least once and hence that it is safe to move the instruction, or else it requires that we generate a test before the entry to the loop to determine whether it is entered. This has the advantage that only one branch instruction need be executed to close the loop, rather than one to get from the end back to the beginning and another at the beginning to perform the test.

Determining that the loop is entered may be as simple as observing that the loop is a Fortran 77 do loop or a Pascal for loop with constant bounds and that the upper one exceeds the lower one, or it may require proving data-flow-analytic facts about the values of the bound expressions and/or the iteration variable. Loop inversion transforms a loop with a conditional branch at the top and an unconditional closing branch at the bottom into one with just a conditional closing branch at the bottom that tests the negation of the original condition.

Figure 18.9 shows an example of loop inversion in C. In (a), we have a C for loop and in (b), we have its expansion as a while loop. Since its termination condition is initially false, its body is executed at least once, so it can be transformed into the repeat loop shown in (c).

An important subcase of loop inversion concerns nested loops with the range of the inner loop's iteration-control variable being a non-empty subset of the range of the outer loops, as shown in the Fortran 77 code in Figure 18.10. In this case, the inner loop must be executed at least once whenever the outer loop is executed. Hence, loop inversion definitely applies to the inner loop.

```
for (i = 0; i < 100; i++)          i = 0;
{   a[i] = i + 1;                  while (i < 100)
                                   {   a[i] = i + 1;
                                       i++;
}                                  }
```
(a)   (b)

```
i = 0;
repeat
{   a[i] = i + 1;
    i++;
} until (i >= 100)
```
(c)

FIG. 18.9 An example of loop inversion in C.

```
do i = 1,n
    do j = 1,n
        a(i,j) = a(i,j) + c * b(i)
    enddo
enddo
```

FIG. 18.10 Nested loops with identical bounds in a Fortran 77 example.

```
                                   if (a >= b) goto L;
                                   i = a;
for (i = a; i < b; i++)            repeat
{   c[i] = i + 1;                  {   c[i] = i + 1;
                                       i++;
}                                  }
                                   until (i >= b)
                                L:
```
(a)   (b)

FIG. 18.11 Inverting a C loop that we cannot determine to be entered.

If we cannot determine that a loop is entered, we can place an `if` ahead of its inverted form that checks the entry condition and branches around the loop. Figure 18.11 gives an example of this approach.

18.6   Unswitching

Unswitching is a control-flow transformation that moves loop-invariant conditional branches out of loops. For example, in the Fortran 77 code in Figure 18.12(a), the predicate `k.eq.2` is independent of the value of `i`. Moving the predicate test out

```
do i = 1,100                        if (k.eq.2) then
   if (k.eq.2) then                    do i = 1,100
      a(i) = a(i) + 1                      a(i) = a(i) + 1
   else                                enddo
      a(i) = a(i) - 1              else
   endif                              do i = 1,100
enddo                                    a(i) = a(i) - 1
                                      enddo
                                   endif
```

(a)   **(b)**

FIG. 18.12 (a) Fortran 77 code with a loop-invariant predicate nested in a loop, and (b) the result of unswitching it.

```
do i = 1,100                        if (k.eq.2) then
   if ((k.eq.2).and.(a(i).gt.0)) then  do i = 1,100
      a(i) = a(i) + 1                      if (a(i).gt.0) then
   endif                                     a(i) = a(i) + 1
enddo                                     endif
                                      enddo
                                   else
                                      i = 101
                                   endif
```

(a)   **(b)**

FIG. 18.13 Unswitching a conditional without an else part.

of the loop produces the code shown in Figure 18.12(b). While this increases code space, it reduces the number of instructions executed. Note that the conditional must be nested directly inside the looping construct for the transformation to be applicable. The example in Figure 18.13 illustrates two aspects of unswitching: first, the invariant condition need not account for the entire predicate; and second, if the conditional has no else part, it is essential to supply one in the transformed code that sets the loop-control variable to its final value, unless it can be shown to be dead.

18.7   Branch Optimizations

There are several kinds of branch optimizations that are generally postponed to the latter phases of the compilation process, once the shape of the final code has been determined. We discuss some of them in this section.

Branches to branch instructions are remarkably common, especially if a relatively simple-minded code-generation strategy is used. Detecting such situations is trivial—we simply check what instruction appears at the target of each branch—as long as we do so before filling branch delay slots (for architectures that have them). The cases are as follows:

1. An unconditional branch to an unconditional branch can be replaced by a branch to the latter's target.

2. A conditional branch to an unconditional branch can be replaced by the corresponding conditional branch to the latter branch's target.

3. An unconditional branch to a conditional branch can be replaced by a copy of the conditional branch.

4. A conditional branch to a conditional branch can be replaced by a conditional branch with the former's test and the latter's target, as long as the latter condition is true whenever the former one is.

For example, in the MIR sequence

```
        if a = 0 goto L1
          . . .
    L1: if a >= 0 goto L2
          . . .
    L2: . . .
```

the first branch can be changed to if a = 0 goto L2, since a >= 0 is true if a = 0 is.

Another case that is relatively common in code generated by standard code-generation strategies is an unconditional branch whose target is the next instruction. This case is trivial to recognize and the optimization is obvious: delete the branch. Equally obvious is a situation in which a block ends with a conditional branch to the second following instruction, followed by an unconditional branch to some other target. In this case, we reverse the sense of the conditional branch, change its target to the target of the unconditional branch, and delete the latter. For example,

```
        if a = 0 goto L1
        goto L2
    L1: . . .
```

becomes

```
        if a != 0 goto L2
    L1: . . .
```

18.8   Tail Merging or Cross Jumping

Tail merging, also known as *cross jumping*, is an optimization that always saves code space and may also save time. It searches for basic blocks in which the last few instructions are identical and that continue execution at the same location, either by one branching to the instruction following the other or by both branching to the same location. What the optimization does is to replace the matching instructions of one of the blocks by a branch to the corresponding point in the other. Obviously, if one of them ends without a branch, it is the preferred one to be left unmodified. For example, the code in Figure 18.14(a) would be transformed into the code in (b).

```
        . . .                          . . .
    r1 ← r2 + r3                    r1 ← r2 + r3
    r4 ← r3 shl 2                   goto L2
    r2 ← r2 + 1
    r2 ← r4 - r2
    goto L1
        . . .
    r5 ← r4 - 6                     r5 ← r4 - 6
    r4 ← r3 shl 2              L2: r4 ← r3 shl 2
    r2 ← r2 + 1                     r2 ← r2 + 1
    r2 ← r4 - r2                    r2 ← r4 - r2
L1:                             L1:
(a)                             (b)
```

FIG. 18.14 (a) A LIR code example for tail merging, and (b) the result of transforming it.

To do tail merging, we simply scan backward through the predecessors of blocks that have multiple predecessors looking for common sequences of instructions and we replace all but one such copy with a branch to the beginning of the remaining one (usually creating a new basic block in the process).

18.9   Conditional Moves

Conditional moves are instructions that copy a source to a target if and only if a specified condition is satisfied. They are found in several modern architectures and implementations, such as SPARC-V9 and the Pentium Pro. They can be used to replace some simple branching code sequences with code that includes no branches. For example, the code in Figure 18.15(a), which computes the maximum of a and b and stores it in c, can be replaced by the code in Figure 18.15(b).

The approach to replacing branching code by conditional moves is pattern matching on the intermediate code. In the simplest case, the original code must have the form shown in Figure 18.16(a) or Figure 18.17(a) and it may be replaced by the equivalent code in Figure 18.16(b) or Figure 18.17(b), respectively. Of course, sequences with more than one assignment may be matched and replaced also, but the simple patterns given above cover most of the cases found in real code.

```
    if a > b goto L1              t1 ← a > b
    c ← b                         c ← b
    goto L2                       c ←(t1) a
L1: c ← a
L2:
(a)                              (b)
```

FIG. 18.15 Code to compute the maximum of a and b (a) with branches and (b) with conditional moves.

$$
\begin{array}{ll}
\text{if } opd1 \text{ } relop \text{ } opd2 \text{ goto } label1 \\
\quad reg \leftarrow opd3 \\
\quad \text{goto } label2 \\
label1: \quad reg \leftarrow opd4 \\
label2:
\end{array}
\qquad
\begin{array}{l}
reg \leftarrow opd3 \\
t \leftarrow opd1 \text{ } relop \text{ } opd2 \\
reg \leftarrow (t) \text{ } opd4
\end{array}
$$

(a)   (b)

FIG. 18.16 (a) Example code pattern for which branches may be replaced by conditional moves, and (b) the result of the replacement.

$$
\begin{array}{l}
reg \leftarrow opd3 \\
\text{if } opd1 \text{ } relop \text{ } opd2 \text{ goto } label1 \\
reg \leftarrow opd4 \\
label1:
\end{array}
\qquad
\begin{array}{l}
reg \leftarrow opd3 \\
t \leftarrow opd1 \text{ } !relop \text{ } opd2 \\
reg \leftarrow (t) \text{ } opd4
\end{array}
$$

(a)   (b)

FIG. 18.17 (a) Another example code pattern for which branches may be replaced by conditional moves, and (b) the result of the replacement.

18.10   Dead-Code Elimination

A variable is *dead* if it is not used on any path from the location in the code where it is defined to the exit point of the routine in question. An instruction is *dead* if it computes only values that are not used on any executable path leading from the instruction. If a dead variable's value is assigned to a local variable, the variable and the instruction that assigns to it are dead if the variable is not used on any executable path to the procedure's exit (including its being returned as the value of the procedure). If it is assigned to a variable with wider visibility, it generally requires interprocedural analysis to determine whether it is dead, unless there is another instruction that assigns to the same variable on every executable path from its point of computation.

Programs may include dead code before optimization, but such code is much more likely to arise from optimization; strength reduction (see Section 14.1.2) is an example of an optimization that produces dead code, and there are many others. Many optimizations create dead code as part of a division of labor principle: keep each optimization phase as simple as possible so as make it easy to implement and maintain, leaving it to other phases to clean up after it.

Our determination of dead instructions uses an optimistic approach. It begins by marking all instructions that compute essential values, where a value is *essential* if it either is definitely returned or output by the procedure or it affects a storage location that may be accessible from outside the procedure. From there, the algorithm iteratively marks instructions that contribute to the computation of essential values. When that process has stabilized, all unmarked instructions are dead and may be deleted.

One subtlety in the algorithm is that it detects variables that are used only to define new values for themselves; such variables are dead, since they contribute nothing to the program containing them except wasted time and space. For example,

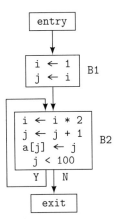

FIG. 18.18 Variable i contributes only to defining itself and thus is inessential.

in the code in Figure 18.18, the variable i is inessential since it contributes only to computing new values for itself.

Identification of dead code can be formulated as a data-flow analysis, but it is easier to use a worklist and du- and ud-chains for it. The approach is as follows:

1. Initialize the worklist to the set of block-index pairs of instructions that are essential. (In Figure 18.19, this is the set of $\langle i,j \rangle$ such that Mark[i][j] = true on entry to the procedure.)

2. Remove an $\langle i,j \rangle$ pair from the worklist. For each variable v used in that instruction, mark each instruction in its ud-chain $UD(v,\langle i,j \rangle)$ and place the instruction's block-index pair on the worklist.

3. If the $\langle i,j \rangle$ instruction is an assignment, say, $v \leftarrow \exp$, then for each instruction position $\langle k,l \rangle$ in its du-chain $DU(v,\langle i,j \rangle)$, if instruction $\langle k,l \rangle$ is an if, mark it and add $\langle k,l \rangle$ to the worklist.

4. Repeat the last two steps until the worklist is empty.

5. Remove from the procedure each instruction that is unmarked.

6. Finally, remove each basic block that has become empty.

ICAN code for this process is shown in Figure 18.19. The routine If_Inst(k) returns true if an instruction of kind k is a conditional and false otherwise and the routine Vars_Used(Block,x) returns the set of variables used in instruction Block[x@1][x@2]. We could also check whether any control-flow transformations are enabled as a result or we could leave that to a separate pass; such transformations might include the if simplification and empty-loop elimination transformations discussed in Sections 18.3 and 18.4, respectively.

One point that requires care is that we must be certain that an operation that produces a dead value is not being performed for a side effect, such as setting the condition codes. For example, a SPARC integer subtract instruction that targets register r0 and that sets the condition codes is not dead if there is a future use of the resulting condition codes' value.

```
UdDu = integer × integer
UdDuChain = (Symbol × UdDu) ⟶ set of UdDu

procedure Dead_Code_Elim(nblocks,ninsts,Block,Mark,UD,DU,Succ,Pred)
    nblocks: inout integer
    ninsts: inout array [1··nblocks] of integer
    Block: inout array [1··nblocks] of array [··] of MIRInst
    Mark: in array [1··nblocks] of array [··] of boolean
    UD, DU: in UdDuChain
    Succ, Pred: inout integer ⟶ set of integer
begin
    i, j: integer
    x, y: integer × integer
    v: Var
    Worklist: set of (integer × integer)
    || set of positions of essential instructions
    Worklist := {⟨i,j⟩ ∈ integer × integer where Mark[i][j]}
    while Worklist ≠ ∅ do
        x := ◆Worklist; Worklist -= {x}
        || mark instructions that define values used by
        || required instructions
        for each v ∈ Vars_Used(Block,x) do
            for each y ∈ UD(v,x) do
                if !Mark[y@1][y@2] then
                    Mark[y@1][y@2] := true
                    Worklist ∪= {y}
                fi
            od
        od
        || mark conditionals that use values defined by
        || required instructions
        if Has_Left(Block[x@1][x@2].kind) then
            for each y ∈ DU(Block[x@1][x@2].left,x) do
                if Block[y@1][y@2].kind ∈ {binif,unif,valif}
                & !Mark[y@1][y@2] then
                    Mark[y@1][y@2] := true
                    Worklist ∪= {y}
                fi
            od
        fi
    od
    Delete_Empty_Blocks(nblocks,ninsts,Block,Succ,Pred)
end    || Dead_Code_Elim
```

FIG. 18.19 ICAN routine to detect and remove dead code.

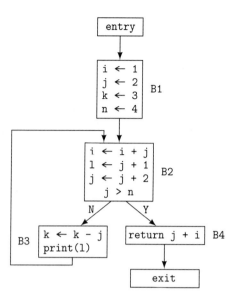

FIG. 18.20 An example for dead-code elimination.

As an example of the algorithm applied to MIR code, consider the flowgraph in Figure 18.20. The ud- and du-chains for this flowgraph are as follows:

Variable Definition	Du-Chain
i in ⟨B1,1⟩	{⟨B2,1⟩}
j in ⟨B1,2⟩	{⟨B2,1⟩,⟨B2,2⟩,⟨B2,3⟩}
k in ⟨B1,3⟩	{⟨B3,1⟩}
n in ⟨B1,4⟩	{⟨B2,4⟩}
i in ⟨B2,1⟩	{⟨B2,1⟩,⟨B4,1⟩}
l in ⟨B2,2⟩	{⟨B3,2⟩}
j in ⟨B2,3⟩	{⟨B2,1⟩,⟨B2,2⟩,⟨B2,3⟩,⟨B2,4⟩,⟨B3,1⟩,⟨B4,1⟩}
k in ⟨B3,1⟩	{⟨B3,1⟩}

and

Variable Use	Ud-Chain
i in ⟨B2,1⟩	{⟨B1,1⟩,⟨B2,1⟩}
i in ⟨B4,1⟩	{⟨B2,1⟩}
j in ⟨B2,1⟩	{⟨B1,2⟩,⟨B2,3⟩}
j in ⟨B2,2⟩	{⟨B1,2⟩,⟨B2,3⟩}
j in ⟨B2,3⟩	{⟨B1,2⟩,⟨B2,3⟩}
j in ⟨B2,4⟩	{⟨B2,3⟩}
j in ⟨B3,1⟩	{⟨B2,3⟩}
j in ⟨B4,1⟩	{⟨B2,3⟩}
k in ⟨B3,1⟩	{⟨B1,3⟩,⟨B3,1⟩}
l in ⟨B3,2⟩	{⟨B2,2⟩}
n in ⟨B2,4⟩	{⟨B1,4⟩}

Initially, the set of essential instructions consists of the print and the return, so only Mark[B3][2] = Mark[B4][1] = true, and Worklist = {⟨B3,2⟩,⟨B4,1⟩}.

Now we begin marking instructions that contribute to the essential instructions. First we remove x = ⟨B3,2⟩ from the worklist, resulting in Worklist = {⟨B4,1⟩}, and find that Vars_Used(Block,⟨B3,2⟩) = {1}. So we check the one member of the ud-chain for 1 in ⟨B3,2⟩, namely, ⟨B2,2⟩, set Mark[B2][2] = true, and add ⟨B2,2⟩ to the worklist, resulting in Worklist = {⟨B4,1⟩,⟨B2,2⟩}.

Next we determine that Has_Left(Block[B3][2].kind) = false, so we move on to the next element of the worklist. We remove x = ⟨B4,1⟩ from the worklist, leaving it with the value Worklist = {⟨B2,2⟩}, and find that Vars_Used(Block, ⟨B4,1⟩) = {i,j}. So we check each member of the UD,i⟨B4,1⟩) = {⟨B2,1⟩}. We set Mark[B2][1] = true and add ⟨B2,1⟩ to the worklist, resulting in Worklist = {⟨B2,2⟩,⟨B2,1⟩}. So we check each member of the UD(i,⟨B4,1⟩), which is {⟨B2,1⟩}, resulting in setting x = ⟨B2,1⟩. Mark[B2][1] is already true, so we do not add it to the worklist. Next we set y = j, and find that UD(j,⟨B2,1⟩) resulting in adding ⟨B2,2⟩ and ⟨B2,1⟩,⟨B2,3⟩ to the worklist, so Worklist = {⟨B2,2⟩,⟨B2,1⟩,⟨B2,3⟩}.

Next we determine that Has_Left(Block[B4][1].kind) = true, so we compute DU(Block,⟨B4,1⟩) = ∅. It is an empty, so we move on to the next element of the worklist. We remove x = ⟨B2,2⟩ from the worklist, leaving Worklist = {⟨B2,1⟩,⟨B2,3⟩}. The only variable in Vars_Used(Block,⟨B2,2⟩) is j, so we set v = j and find that UD(j,⟨B2,2⟩) = {⟨B1,2⟩,⟨B2,3⟩}.

So we set Mark[B1][3] = true and Mark[B2,1] = true and add them to the worklist, Worklist = {⟨B2,1⟩,⟨B2,3⟩,⟨B1,3⟩}. We remove x ⟨B2,3⟩ from the worklist, leaving Worklist = {⟨B2,1⟩,⟨B1,3⟩}. Now Vars_Used(Block,⟨B2,3⟩) = {j}, so we check whether either of Mark[B1][2] and Mark[B2][3] is marked. Neither is, so we set Mark[B1][2] = true and Mark[B2][3] = true. Mark[B2][2] is already true, so we move on to the next member of the worklist, namely, x = ⟨B2,3⟩ and Worklist = ∅.

Continuing in this way, the algorithm eventually terminates with the value of Mark being as in the following table:

Block	Position	Value
B1	1	true
	2	true
	3	false
	4	true
B2	1	true
	2	true
	3	true
	4	true
B3	1	false
	2	true
B4	1	true

so the flowgraph resulting from dead-code elimination is as shown in Figure 18.21.

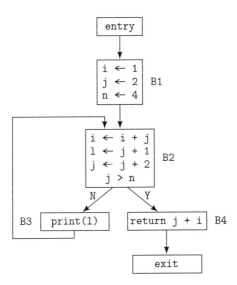

FIG. 18.21 The flowgraph in Figure 18.20 after dead-code elimination.

Knoop, Rüthing, and Steffen [KnoR94] have extended dead-code elimination to the elimination of partially dead code, where "partial" is used in the same sense as in partial-redundancy elimination, i.e., dead on some paths but possibly not on others.

18.11   Branch Prediction

In this and the following section, we discuss optimizations that are almost always deferred until machine code has been generated. For this reason, they are often known as *postpass* optimizations. Another common term for some of them is *peephole* optimizations, because they can be carried out by moving a small window or peephole across the generated code or its dependence DAG to look for opportunities to perform them. Note that using the dependence DAG facilitates finding pairs (or larger groups) of instructions that are connected by the functions they perform, such as loading an array element via a pointer and incrementing the pointer to the next element.

Branch prediction refers to predicting, either statically or dynamically, whether a conditional branch causes a transfer of control or not. Accurate prediction of branches is important because it allows a processor to fetch instructions on the continuation path from an instruction cache into an instruction prefetch buffer, or from main memory or a second-level cache into the instruction cache, ahead of the execution of the branch that causes the transfer of control to them. As cache delays become longer relative to cycle time, prediction becomes more and more important.

Dynamic methods of branch prediction include a variety of schemes, ranging from a simple cache of the addresses of conditional branches and whether each branched the last time it was executed, to larger caches that contain, for a set of recent branches, the first few instructions at the target (the fall-through path need not be cached, because the ordinary instruction-fetch mechanism applies to it). Of course, such schemes require hardware resources to implement and may be quite complex—for example, the latter scheme needs logic to invalidate a cache entry if either a branch instruction or the code at its target or fall-through is changed dynamically. Also, simpler schemes, such as the first one mentioned above, may not be very effective—it may be the case, for example, that a particular branch alternates between branching and not branching each time it is executed.

Static branch-prediction methods require much less hardware to implement and have been shown to be almost as good as dynamic prediction. Some architectures, such as SPARC-V9, provide conditional branches with a means for specifying a static branch prediction; some implementations of others, such as the RIOS version of POWER, have unequal delays for the taken and fall-through paths, so that choosing the more likely path to be the one with less delay has significant benefit.

As a measure of the quality of static branch prediction, we define the *perfect static predictor* as a predictor that by some means, perhaps oracular, predicts each conditional branch instruction statically to branch or not branch in such a way as to be correct at least 50% of the time for that branch. Thus, a perfect static predictor is right 50% of the time if a branch causes a transfer of control exactly half the time and does better than that if it takes one path (*either* path) more often than the other. If the branch either always branches or never branches, it will be right 100% of the time. The perfect static predictor, when computed dynamically over all branches in a given program, provides an upper bound on how well any static predictor can do for that program.

Some simple heuristics do better than average. For example, predicting a backward conditional branch to be taken is relatively successful, because most backward branches close loops and most loops are executed more than once before exiting. Similarly, predicting forward branches not to branch can be reasonably successful, since some fraction of them test for exceptional conditions and branch around the code that handles them.

Much better heuristics for static branch prediction are, for example, discussed by Ball and Larus [BalL93], who improve on the simple backward heuristic mentioned above by defining loop branches more exactly. Suppose that we are given a flowgraph and have determined its natural loops (see Section 7.4). Define a *loop branch* to be one that has an outgoing edge in the flowgraph that is either a back edge or an exit edge from the loop;[1] a *nonloop branch* is any other conditional branch. To predict loop branches statically, we simply choose the back edge. This can be from moderately to very successful for real programs.

For nonloop branches, several simple heuristics contribute to being able to predict them much more successfully. For example, the opcode heuristic checks for branches based on integer comparison to zero or a negative integer value and equality tests between floating-point values. It predicts that integer branches for nonpositive values and floating-point equality branches do not branch, since the former are frequently used as error indicators and the latter are rarely true. The loop heuristic checks whether one successor basic block does not postdominate the block

---

1. As Ball and Larus note, it is possible for both outgoing edges to be back edges. They indicate that they have not observed this to be the case in practice, but that if it did occur we should choose the edge for the inner loop to be predicted.

containing the branch and is neither a loop header nor a preheader. If a successor block satisfies this heuristic, the branch to it is predicted to branch.

This is an area in which research is ongoing. See Section 18.14 at the end of this chapter for references to more recent work.

18.12   Machine Idioms and Instruction Combining

There are several varieties of optimization that can only reasonably be applied once one has generated machine-specific code or that are best left to near the end of the compilation process. If one does global optimization on a low-level intermediate code, they can be performed earlier, but care needs to be taken in some cases to make the most effective choices in performing them. An example of this is the case discussed below of combining into a single instruction a memory reference via a pointer to an array element and incrementing the pointer to the next element. While some architectures—such as PA-RISC, POWER, and PowerPC—allow this, it may not be the best choice, since induction-variable optimizations may remove the incrementing instruction, so we do instruction combining near the end of compilation.

Machine idioms are instructions or instruction sequences for a particular architecture that provide a more efficient way of performing a computation than one might use if one were compiling for a more generic architecture. Many machine idioms are instances of *instruction combining,* i.e., the replacement of a sequence of instructions by a single one that achieves the same effect.

Since all RISCs execute most computational instructions in a single cycle, most but not all machine idioms for RISCs combine pairs of instructions into single ones. For other architectures—such as the VAX, the Motorola M68000, and the Intel 386 family—there are machine idioms that replace single instructions by others that require fewer cycles and others that combine several instructions into one.

In this section, we present some examples of machine idioms for several architectures. The examples are by no means exhaustive—they are simply intended to suggest the range of possibilities. In most cases, we focus on a particular architecture. The primary technique for recognizing opportunities to use machine idioms is pattern matching. The search has two main parts. The first part is looking for instructions whose purpose can be achieved by faster, more specialized instructions. The second part begins by looking for an instruction that may be the first of a group that can be combined into a shorter or faster sequence; finding one triggers a search for the other instruction(s) that are needed to form the appropriate group. Unless the target architecture allows functionally independent instructions to be combined into one (as, in some cases, was true for the Stanford MIPS architecture), the searching can be done most efficiently and effectively on the dependence DAG, rather than on straight-line code.

For all RISC architectures, there is the opportunity to simplify code that constructs full-width (i.e., 32-bit or 64-bit) constants, if the constants are discovered to be short enough to fit in the immediate fields provided in instructions. While it is desirable to completely avoid generating instruction sequences that construct long constants when they're not needed, it is often more desirable to simplify code generation by generating them and leaving it to postpass optimization to simplify them where possible. For example, the SPARC sequence

```
sethi %hi(const),r18
or    r18,%lo(const),r18
```

which puts the value const into r18 can be simplified if its high-order 20 bits are all zeros or all ones to

```
add    r0,const,r18
```

Next, consider multiplication of an integer variable by an integer constant. Suppose, in particular, that we are multiplying a variable in register r1 by 5 and putting the result in r2. In most architectures, we could do this by using the integer multiply instruction, but it is generally a multicycle instruction and, in some machines such as PA-RISC, it requires moving the operands to floating-point registers and the result back to an integer register. But there is a much less expensive way. For PA-RISC, we can simply generate the one-cycle instruction

```
SH2ADD    r1,r1,r2
```

which shifts r1 left two bits and adds its original value to that. For the others, we can use a sequence corresponding to the LIR instructions

```
r2 ← r1 shl 2
r2 ← r2 + r1
```

For SPARC, we can combine a subtract that produces a value with a test that compares its two operands, so that, e.g.,

```
sub    r1,r2,r3
 . . .
subcc r1,r2,r0
bg     L1
```

becomes

```
subcc r1,r2,r3
 . . .
bg     L1
```

For MIPS, we can determine whether two values (assumed to be in r1 and r2) have the same sign without any branches by using the sequence

```
slti  r3,r1,0
slti  r4,r2,0
and   r3,r3,r4
```

If the values have the same sign, r3 ends up equal to 1; otherwise, it equals 0.

In the Motorola 88000, PA-RISC, and the Intel 386 architecture family, one can access parallel arrays of bytes, halfwords, words, and doublewords with indexes that increment by 1 by using scaled loads and stores. If r2 and r3 point to arrays of doublewords and halfwords, respectively, and r1 indexes the elements of the arrays, then elements of the two arrays can be loaded and the index updated to access the next elements of both arrays by the Motorola 88000 sequence

```
ld.d   r4,r2[r1]
ld.h   r6,r3[r1]
add    r1,r1,1
```

instead of requiring two separate indexes, one incrementing by 2 and the other by 8, and perhaps a third index for counting iterations of the loop.

In PA-RISC, POWER, and PowerPC, one can do a load or store and replace the value in one of the registers that is used to form the memory address with the new value of the address. In the latter two, the update always occurs after the load or store, while for PA-RISC, it can be specified to occur before or after the operation. Thus, for example, one can access successive elements of an array of halfwords in PowerPC by executing

```
lhau   r3,2(r1)
```

repeatedly and in PA-RISC by

```
LDHS,MA    2(0,r1),r3
```

For PA-RISC, one can terminate a loop with an add and branch instruction that adds a register and either an immediate or a register, puts the result in the first register, and then branches if the result satisfies a specified condition. Thus, a loop over an array indexed by r1, with r2 containing the final value of the index, can be terminated by the instruction

```
ADDBT,<=    r2,r1,L1
```

where L1 labels the first instruction of the loop body.

An instruction combiner may increase the number of superscalar instruction groups that are required to execute a sequence of instructions. For example, suppose we have an implementation with three pipelines (two integer and one floating-point) and an instruction sequence that can be grouped as shown in Figure 18.22(a), where the sub must precede the br and the add2 must follow the cmp. Combining

Int	Int	Flt	Int	Int	Flt
load	add1	flt1	load	add1	flt1
cmp	sub	flt2	sub	---	flt2
br	add2	flt3	cmpbr	---	flt3
			add2	?	?
(a)			(b)		

FIG. 18.22   (a) Example of code for a superscalar processor for which instruction combining can decrease performance, as shown in (b).

the cmp and the br into a compare and branch instruction (cmpbr) results in the instructions requiring four issue slots, as shown in Figure 18.22(b), rather than the three slots they originally needed. This effect can be mitigated by making the instruction combiner and an instruction decomposer available as subroutines to the instruction scheduler, so that it can try the possible instruction sequences to determine which one produces the best schedule, but one needs to be careful to limit the extent of such attempts, since most scheduling problems are at least *NP*-hard.

The reverse is also a possibility—including information about the pipeline structure in the instruction combiner and structuring it to estimate the impact on scheduling of the combinations it makes—but this is likely to significantly complicate the combiner and not to work well in practice, since scheduling has a much wider window on the code than a peephole optimizer usually does, unless it also works on the basic-block DAG.

As noted above, these are only a few examples of machine idioms. The diligent compiler writer will find many others by intimately getting to know the instruction set being compiled for and by inspecting examples of generated code.

For CISC architecture implementations, there is sometimes a need for *instruction decomposing,* the inverse of instruction combining, which turns an instruction into a series of instructions that perform the same overall function. An example of this can be seen in the Intel 386 architecture-family code generated for the subroutine s1( ) and the corresponding main program in Figures 21.23 and 21.24. The inlined code for the subroutine in the main program is CISC-style code, while that in the subroutine is RISC-style (and unrolled by a factor of four). Note that either of these could have been generated first and the other produced from it.

18.13   Wrap-Up

This chapter has covered control-flow optimizations, unreachable- and dead-code elimination, and the remaining global optimizations that are best carried out on low-level code, namely, static branch prediction, machine idioms, and instruction combining. Some of these optimizations, such as dead-code elimination, may profitably be applied several times during compilation. Some are best carried out on low-level intermediate code or on a structured form of assembly or machine language.

Most of these optimizations, other than dead-code elimination, have minimal impact when applied once to a particular code segment. However, applying them all to an entire procedure may result in substantial savings, especially if the ones that apply to loops are used heavily.

The control-flow transformations that produce longer basic blocks have the potential to increase available instruction-level parallelism, which is particularly important for superscalar implementations.

Dead-code elimination removes instructions that can be determined to have no effect on the result of a computation. It is an important optimization, not only because some programs contain dead code as originally written, but also because many

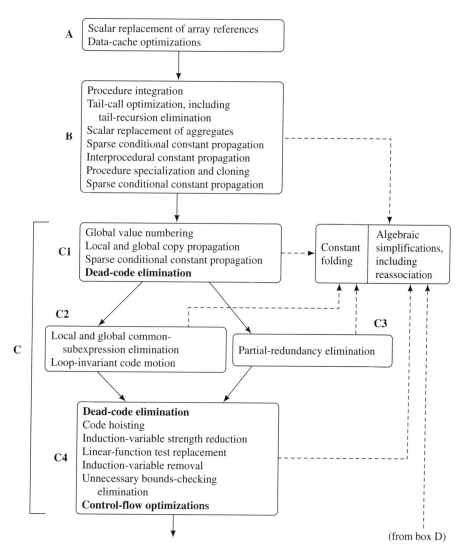

FIG. 18.23 Order of optimizations with control-flow and low-level optimizations in **bold** type. *(continued)*

of the other optimizations create dead code. We recommend that it be performed several times during optimizing compilation, as shown in Figure 18.23.

Branch prediction continues to increase in importance as cache delays become longer relative to processor cycle time. Accurate prediction is important because it increases the chance that the processor will fetch the correct continuation path from the instruction cache or from another unit beyond it in the memory hierarchy.

The other optimizations discussed in this chapter are the postpass, or peephole, ones. They include machine idioms and instruction combining and are generally among the last optimizations performed and are always done after code generation.

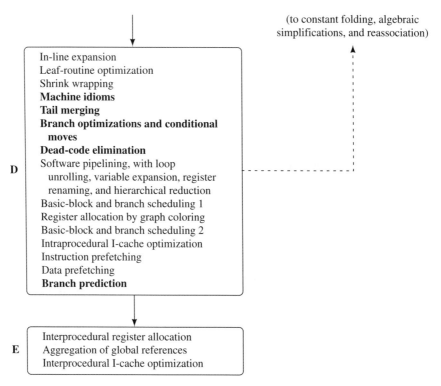

FIG. 18.23 *(continued)*

They can be performed by moving a small window or peephole across the generated code or over the dependence DAGs for the basic blocks to look for code sequences they apply to.

The suggested order of optimizations in an aggressive optimizing compiler is given in Figure 18.23; optimizations covered in this chapter are highlighted in **bold** type.

18.14 Further Reading

Unswitching is first discussed in [AllC72a].

The dead-code detection algorithm given in Section 18.10 is derived from one developed by Kennedy [Kenn81].

Knoop, Rüthing, and Steffen's extension of dead-code elimination to eliminate partially dead code is found in [KnoR94].

Comparison of the branches actually taken to the perfect static predictor to determine the effectiveness of branch prediction schemes was developed by Ball and Larus [BalL93]. That paper also describes several useful heuristics for branch prediction. More recent papers, such as [Patt95] and [CalG95], describe still better heuristics.

The Stanford MIPS architecture is described in [GilG83].

18.15   Exercises

18.1 Write an ICAN procedure to detect and perform the `if` simplifications discussed in Section 18.3.

18.2 Write an ICAN procedure that detects opportunities for tail merging in LIR code and that transforms the code accordingly. Is there anything to be gained by searching the DAGs for the basic blocks for common sequences that end with leaves or for sets of independent instructions that occur as leaves or their predecessors?

18.3 Give three examples of useful instruction sequences that can be made more efficient by using conditional moves.

18.4 Extend the dead-code elimination algorithm in Figure 18.19 to recognize and eliminate definitions of sets of variables $\{v_1, v_2, v_3, \ldots\}$ that only contribute to defining each other and hence are not essential.

18.5 Instrument the source code of a nontrivial-size program you have available to compute and print statistics for each conditional branch that indicate what fraction of the time it branches. Can you infer from the results any useful rules for static branch prediction?

18.6 Design a pattern language for assembly-language instruction sequences that can be combined or transformed as machine idioms. You will need a way, for example, to represent registers abstractly so that you can require that the same register be used in two instructions without pinning it down to a specific register.

18.7 Write a program that searches assembly language for opportunities to use instruction combining and machine idioms represented in the pattern language designed for Exercise 18.6 and that applies them to the code. The program should take as its input a file of patterns and a file of assembly language to which to apply them.

CHAPTER 19

Interprocedural Analysis and Optimization

M odularity has long been regarded as a virtue in program construction—and rightly so, since proper decomposition into procedures encourages the creation of well-designed programs that are easier to understand and maintain. In recent years, object-oriented languages have pushed this trend even further. While some languages, such as C++, provide the programmer with an explicit way to declare that a procedure should be expanded in-line, most encourage the view that a procedure consists of an interface and a black box implementing it or, more generally, that a data type or class consists of an interface and one or more black boxes that implement it. This approach encourages abstraction and hence contributes to good program design and maintainability, but it also inhibits optimization and so may result in less efficient code than would otherwise result. Lacking interprocedural control- and data-flow information, one must generally assume that a called procedure may use or change any variable it might be able to access and that a procedure's caller provides arbitrary values as parameters. Both of these assumptions clearly inhibit optimization.

Almost all the optimizations we have considered so far have been *intraprocedural*. That is, they are applied within a single procedure, without regard to the calling context in which that procedure is used or the procedures it calls. Only tail-call optimization (Section 15.1), procedure integration (Section 15.2), and inlining (Section 15.3) are in any way interprocedural.

Interprocedural optimizations are ones that use the calling relationships among a set of procedures to drive optimizations in one or more of them or in how they relate to each other. For example, if one could determine that every call to a procedure f(i,j,k) in a program passed the constant 2 as the value of i, this would enable constant propagation of the 2 into f( )'s code. Similarly, if one could determine that every call passed either 2 or 5 as the value of i and identify which calls passed which value, one could replace f( ) by two procedures f_2( ) and f_5( )—a process called *procedure cloning*—and the calls to f( ) by calls to the appropriate one of them. Similarly, if one knows that a called procedure modifies only its own local variables and particular parameters, one may freely optimize the code around calls to it, as long as one takes into account the procedure's known effects.

As for the intraprocedural case, interprocedural optimization consists of a series of phases that do control-flow analysis, data-flow analysis, alias analysis, and transformations. It differs from intraprocedural optimization in that many of the benefits of interprocedural analysis derive from improving the effectiveness and applicability of optimizations within individual procedures, rather than transforming the relationships among procedures. In this chapter, we explore the following:

1. interprocedural control-flow analysis and, in particular, construction of a program's control-flow graph;

2. several varieties of interprocedural data-flow analysis, including both flow-sensitive and flow-insensitive side-effect analysis and constant propagation;

3. interprocedural alias analysis;

4. how to use the information gained from interprocedural analysis to do optimization; and

5. interprocedural register allocation.

We assume in the remainder of this chapter that all parameters are passed by reference, unless mentioned otherwise, and we leave it to the reader to adapt the methods discussed to other parameter-passing disciplines. Note that passing a non-pointer as a value parameter creates no aliases, while passing a pointer as a value parameter is closely akin to passing the object it points to by reference.

Some studies suggest that interprocedural analysis is unproductive or too expensive to be worthwhile (see Section 19.10 for references). For example, Richardson and Ganapathi investigated the effectiveness of interprocedural optimization in comparison to procedure integration. They found that procedure integration is very effective at enhancing optimization, but that compilation is slowed down significantly by it, often by as much as a factor of 10. On the other hand, the limited interprocedural analysis they did showed comparatively little benefit in optimization. Also, interprocedural analysis can be an expensive addition to a compiler and increases the complexity of the compiler. In general, the typical cost and impact of interprocedural analysis are, as yet, not well understood. Some evidence suggests that it is more valuable for parallelizing compilers than for compilers for sequential machines.

Separate compilation impacts the effectiveness of interprocedural analysis and optimization, since one can't determine the effects of routines that have not been compiled yet. On the other hand, modern programming environments typically provide a repository for compilation units, their relationships, and information about them. This facilitates interprocedural analysis by providing a way to save and access the relevant information (see Section 19.8).

The distinctions between may and must information and flow-sensitive and flow-insensitive information discussed at the beginning of Chapter 10 and in Section 11.2 apply to interprocedural optimization also. In particular, the $MOD(\ )$ and $REF(\ )$ computations discussed in Section 19.2.1 are examples of flow-insensitive problems and the *DEF*( ) and *USE*( ) functions are examples of flow-sensitive problems. Also, *DEF*( ) is must summary information, while *USE*( ) is may summary information.

19.1   Interprocedural Control-Flow Analysis: The Call Graph

The problem addressed by interprocedural control-flow analysis is construction of a program's call graph.[1] Given a program P consisting of procedures $p_1, \ldots, p_n$, the (static) *call graph* of P is the graph G_P (or, usually, just G) = $\langle N, S, E, r \rangle$ with the node set $N = \{p_1, \ldots, p_n\}$, the set S of call-site labels,[2] the set $E \subseteq N \times N \times S$ of labeled edges, and the distinguished entry node $r \in N$ (representing the main program), where for each $e = \langle p_i, s_k, p_j \rangle$, s_k denotes a call site in p_i from which p_j is called. If there is only one call from procedure p_i to p_j, we may omit the call site s_k and write the edge as $p_i \rightarrow p_j$.

As an example of a call graph, consider the program skeleton in Figure 19.1. Procedure f calls g and h, g calls h and i, and i calls g and j; note that there are two calls from f to g. The call graph for this program is shown in Figure 19.2. The entry node is indicated by the heavy circle and the two calls from f to g by the two labels on the edge connecting them.

Like depth-first order and its relatives in intraprocedural analysis, there are orders that are useful in several kinds of interprocedural problems, at least for nonrecursive programs. One is known as *invocation order* and corresponds to processing a procedure before all its callees, i.e., breadth-first search of the call graph. Similarly, *reverse invocation order* processes a procedure after its callees. If our example in Figures 19.1 and 19.2 lacked the call from i to g, then f,g,h,i,j would be an invocation-order listing of its nodes. As our example shows, the procedures in a recursive program do not have such an order, unless we collapse strongly connected components to single nodes and are concerned with calls between them.

Two other orders that are of use in interprocedural analysis refer to the static nesting of procedures. *Outside-in order* deals with each procedure before the ones statically (or lexically) enclosed within it. *Inside-out order* deals with each procedure after the ones statically enclosed within it. For our example, j,f,g,h,i is an inside-out order of the call graph.

There are two issues that can make constructing call graphs difficult, namely, separate compilation and procedure-valued variables. Without them, constructing a program's call graph is an easy exercise, as shown by the ICAN code for the procedure Build_Call_Graph( ) in Figure 19.3. In the algorithm, P is the set of procedures

---

1. As we shall see, the call graph is actually a *multigraph,* with multiple directed edges from one node to another, or, alternatively, multiple labels on some edges. However, like most authors in this field, we refer to it as simply a graph.

2. Note that in higher-level languages, line numbers are usually not sufficient to serve as call-site labels, since more than one call may be made from a single line of code.

```
1       procedure f( )
2       begin
3           call g( )
4           call g( )
5           call h( )
6       end    || f
7       procedure g( )
8       begin
9           call h( )
10          call i( )
11      end    || g
12      procedure h( )
13      begin
14      end    || h
15      procedure i( )
16          procedure j( )
17          begin
18          end    || j
19      begin
20          call g( )
21          call j( )
22      end    || i
```

FIG. 19.1 A program skeleton.

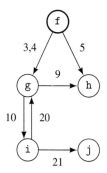

FIG. 19.2 Call graph for the program skeleton in Figure 19.1.

that make up the program whose call graph is to be constructed, N is the set of nodes in the graph,[3] r is the root procedure (often called main), and E is the set of labeled edges in the graph. The labels denote the call sites, i.e., $\langle p,i,q \rangle \in$ E if and only if call site i in procedure p calls q. The procedures used in the algorithm are as follows:

1. numinsts(p) is the number of instructions in procedure p.

2. callset(p,i) returns the set of procedures called by the ith instruction in procedure p.

---

3. Note that P = N as long as every procedure in P is reachable from r.

```
LabeledEdge = Procedure × integer × Procedure

procedure Build_Call_Graph(P,r,N,E,numinsts)
   P: in set of Procedure
   r: in Procedure
   N: out set of Procedure
   E: out set of LabeledEdge
begin
   i: integer
   p, q: Procedure
   OldN := ∅: set of Procedure
   N := {r}
   E := ∅
   while OldN ≠ N do
      p := ♦(N - OldN)
      OldN := N
      for i := 1 to numinsts(p) do
         for each q ∈ callset(p,i) do
            N ∪= {q}
            E ∪= {⟨p,i,q⟩}
         od
      od
   od
end     || Build_Call_Graph
```

FIG. 19.3 Constructing the call graph.

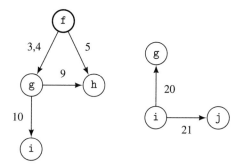

FIG. 19.4 Partial call graphs resulting from separate compilation of parts of Figure 19.1.

Separate compilation can be bypassed as an issue by doing interprocedural analysis and optimization only when an entire program is presented to a compiler at once, or it can be handled by saving, during each compilation, a representation of the part of the call graph seen during that compilation and building the graph incrementally. In our example above, if f and g constituted one compilation unit and the other three procedures another, then we would have the two partial call graphs shown in Figure 19.4, and the interprocedural optimizer could "glue" the two graphs together to make a complete static call graph.

```
P, N, W: set of Procedure
E: set of LabeledEdge
PVVs: set of ProcVar
PVCalls: set of LabeledEdge
PVVals: ProcVar ⟶ set of Procedure
PVBinds: ProcVar ⟶ set of ProcVar
pinsts: Procedure ⟶ integer
preturns: Procedure × integer × Var × Procedure × Var

procedure Build_Call_Graph_with_PVVs(r,Inst,numinsts)
    r: in Procedure
    Inst: in Procedure ⟶ array [··] of Instruction
begin
    p, q, u, v: ProcVar ∪ Procedure
    i, j: integer
    more, change: boolean
    N := W := {r}
    E := PVVs := PVCalls := PVVals := PVBinds := ∅
    || repeat until the call graph stops expanding
    repeat
        more := false
        || accumulate procedure-valued variables and
        || constants, calls, values, and bindings
        while W ≠ ∅ do
            p := ◆W; W -= {p}
            for i := 1 to numinsts(p) do
                more V= Process_Inst(p,i,Inst)
            od
        od
```

FIG. 19.5   Constructing the call graph with procedure-valued variables.

The call-graph construction algorithm is simple enough that we choose to provide no example of its operation. The reader can easily construct one.

Procedure-valued variables present a more difficult problem. Weihl [Weih80] has shown that constructing the call graph of a recursive program with procedure variables is *PSPACE*-hard, so this process can be very expensive in both time and space. One approach to doing so is to construct the call graph incrementally, as shown by the code in Figures 19.5, 19.6, and 19.7, which implements three procedures Build_Call_Graph_with_PVVs( ), Process_Inst( ), and Process_Call( ), respectively. For now, ignore the outermost repeat loop in Build_Call_Graph_with_PVVs( ). We begin by constructing as much of the graph as is evident from explicit calls. Then we determine initial sets of values for the procedure variables and propagate them to all possible uses—i.e., to procedure-valued parameters, assignments, and returns—and from there to the call sites that use those procedure-valued variables. The procedure Process_Inst($p,i,Inst$) handles each instruction in a procedure, while Process_Call(p,i,q) deals with calls. The algorithm uses four data structures to record information about procedure-valued variables, as follows:

```
        || propagate bindings
*       repeat
          change := false
          for each u ∈ PVVs do
              for each v ∈ PVVs (v ≠ u) do
                  if v ∈ PVBinds(u)
                      & PVBinds(u) ≠ PVBinds(v) then
                      PVBinds(u) ∪= PVBinds(v)
                      change := true
                  fi
              od
          od
        until !change
        || add nodes and edges to the call graph
        for each ⟨p,i,q⟩ ∈ PVCalls do
            for each u ∈ PVVals(q) do
                N ∪= {u}
                E ∪= {⟨p,i,q⟩}
                W ∪= {u}
            od
            for each u ∈ PVBinds(q) do
                for each v ∈ PVVals(u) do
                    N ∪= {v}
                    E ∪= {⟨p,i,v⟩}
                    W ∪= {v}
                od
            od
        od
    until !more
end     || Build_Call_Graph_with_PVVs
```

FIG. 19.5 *(continued)*

```
procedure Process_Inst(p,i,Inst) returns boolean
    p: in Procedure
    i: in integer
    Inst: in Procedure ⟶ array [··] of Instruction
begin
    q, u, v: ProcVar ∪ Procedure
    j: integer
    more := false: boolean
    || accumulate calls
    for each q ∈ callset(p,i) do
        more ∨= Process_Call(p,i,q)
        if preturns(p,i,u,q,v) then
            if proc_const(v) then
                PVVs ∪= {u}
```

(continued)

FIG. 19.6 The procedure Process_Inst( ) used in constructing the call graph with procedure-valued variables.

```
                      PVVals(u) ∪= {v}
                      if v ∉ N then
                         more := true
                      fi
                  else
                      PVVs ∪= {u,v}
                      PVBinds(u) ∪= {v}
                  fi
              fi
          od
          if Inst(p)[i].kind = valasgn
            & proc_var(Inst(p)[i].left) then
            || accumulate bindings
            if proc_const(Inst(p)[i].opd.val) then
               PVVs ∪= {Inst(p)[i].left}
               PVVals(Inst(p)[i].left) ∪= {Inst(p)[i].opd.val}
               if Inst(p)[i].opd.val ∉ N then
                  more := true
               fi
            else
               PVVs ∪= {Inst(p)[i].left,Inst(p)[i].opd.val}
               PVBinds(Inst(p)[i].left) ∪= {Inst(p)[i].opd.val}
            fi
          fi
          return more
      end    || Process_Inst
```

FIG. 19.6 *(continued)*

```
proc_const, proc_var: Operand ⟶ boolean
nparams: Procedure ⟶ integer
param: (Procedure × integer) ⟶ Operand
arg: (Procedure × integer × integer) ⟶ Operand
in_param, out_param: (Procedure × integer) ⟶ Operand

procedure Process_Call(p,i,q) returns boolean
   p: in Procedure
   i: in integer
   q: in ProcVar ∪ Procedure
begin
   j: integer
   more := false: boolean
   if proc_const(q) then
      || add nodes and edges to the call graph
      N ∪= {q}
      E ∪= {⟨p,i,q⟩}
      W ∪= {q}
```

FIG. 19.7 The procedure Process_Call( ) used in constructing the call graph with procedure-valued variables.

```
            || deal with passing procedure-valued objects as parameters
            for j := 1 to nparams(q) do
               if proc_var(param(q,j)) & in_param(q,j) then
                  if proc_const(arg(p,i,j)) then
                     PVVs ∪= {param(q,j)}
                     PVVals(param(q,j)) ∪= {arg(p,i,j)}
                     if arg(p,i,j) ∉ N then
                        more := true
                     fi
                  else
                     PVVs ∪= {param(q,j),arg(p,i,j)}
                     PVBinds(param(q,j)) ∪= {arg(p,i,j)}
                  fi
               fi
               || and return of procedure-valued objects
               if proc_var(param(q,j)) & out_param(q,j) then
                  if proc_const(arg(p,i,j)) then
                     PVVs ∪= {arg(p,i,j)}
                     PVVals(arg(p,i,j)) ∪= {param(q,j)}
                     if param(q,j) ∉ N then
                        more := true
                     fi
                  else
                     PVVs ∪= {param(q,j),arg(p,i,j)}
                     PVBinds(arg(p,i,j)) ∪= {param(q,j)}
                  fi
               fi
            od
         else
            PVVs ∪= {q}
            PVCalls ∪= {⟨p,i,q⟩}
         fi
         return more
      end     || Process_Call
```

FIG. 19.7 *(continued)*

1. PVVs records all the procedure-valued variables.

2. PVCalls records call sites that invoke procedure-valued variables.

3. PVVals records the procedure constants that are assigned, bound, or returned to procedure-valued variables.

4. PVBinds records the procedure-valued variables that are assigned, bound, or returned to procedure-valued variables.

There are nine types of actions in a program that concern procedure-valued variables. They and the initial actions we take for them are as follows:

1. Call to a procedure-valued variable vp at site s in procedure p: put the triple $\langle p,s,vp \rangle$ into PVCalls.

2. Bind a procedure constant p as an actual argument to a procedure-valued formal parameter vp: put the $\langle vp,p \rangle$ pair into the finite function PVVals and put vp into PVVs.

3. Bind a procedure-valued variable vp as an actual argument to a procedure-valued formal parameter fp: put a $\langle vp,fp \rangle$ pair into the finite function PVBinds and put both procedure variables into PVVs.

4. Assign one procedure-valued variable $vp1$ to another $vp2$: put the $\langle vp1,vp2 \rangle$ pair into PVBinds and put both procedure variables into PVVs.

5. Assign a procedure constant p to a procedure-valued variable vp: put the $\langle vp,p \rangle$ pair into PVVals and put vp into PVVs.

6. Bind a procedure-valued variable vp to a procedure-valued output parameter fp of a call: put the $\langle vp,fp \rangle$ pair into PVBinds and put both procedure variables into PVVs.

7. Bind a procedure constant p to a procedure-valued output parameter fp of a call: put the $\langle fp,p \rangle$ pair into PVVals and put fp into PVVs.

8. Return a procedure-valued variable $vp1$ to a procedure-valued variable $vp2$: put the $\langle vp1,vp2 \rangle$ pair into PVBinds and put both procedure variables into PVVs.

9. Return a procedure constant p to a procedure-valued variable vp: put the $\langle vp,p \rangle$ pair into PVVals and put vp into PVVs.

After these initial actions, we construct from PVCalls, PVVals, and PVBinds, for each procedure-valued variable, the set of procedure-valued variables that can be bound, assigned, or returned to it; then we construct a call-graph edge for each call site from which a procedure-valued variable is called and for each procedure constant that may be bound as its value. The outermost loop in Build_Call_Graph_with_PVVs( ) takes care of the possibility that one or more parts of the program are reachable only by means of calls through procedure-valued variables.

The procedures used in the algorithm are as follows:

1. numinsts(p) is the number of instructions in p.

2. Inst(p)[1$\cdot\cdot$pinsts(p)] is the array of instructions that make up procedure p.

3. callset(p,i) returns the set of procedures called by the ith instruction in procedure p.

4. proc_const(p) returns true if p is a procedure constant, and false otherwise.

5. proc_var(p) returns true if p is a procedure-valued variable, and false otherwise.

6. nparams(p) returns the number of formal parameters of procedure p.

```
            procedure f( )
    f       begin
    1           call g( )
            end
            procedure g( )
            begin
    g           p: Procedure
    1           p := h
    2           call p( )
    3           call j(i)
            end
            procedure h( )
    h       begin
    1           call i( )
            end
            procedure i( )
    i       begin
    1           call g( )
            end
            procedure j(a)
                a: Procedure
    j       begin
    1           call a( )
            end
```

FIG. 19.8 An example program skeleton with procedure-valued variables.

7. arg(p,i,j) returns the jth actual argument of the procedure called by the ith instruction in p.

8. param(p,j) returns the jth formal parameter of procedure p.

9. in_param(p,i) returns true if the ith parameter of p receives a value from its caller, and false otherwise.

10. out_param(p,i) returns true if the ith parameter of p returns a value to its caller, and false otherwise.

11. preturns(p,i,u,q,v) returns true if the ith instruction in p calls procedure q, which returns its value in variable v, which in turn is assigned to p's variable u.

This propagation process yields a conservative approximation of the call graph, but it may require exponential time for recursive programs, so it needs to be applied with care. Note that what we have produced is flow-insensitive may call information; it is possible to make it flow sensitive, but that incurs another increase in computational cost. Note also that there is still a practical case we have not handled, namely, call-backs from library routines to procedures in the program.

As an example of constructing the call graph for a program with procedure-valued variables, consider the program skeleton shown in Figure 19.8. Assuming that f( ) is the main procedure, initially we have N = W = {f}; and E, PVVs, PVCalls,

PVVals, and PVBinds are all empty. The `for` loop immediately inside the outermost (`repeat`) loop in `Build_Call_Graph_with_PVVs(f)` sets p = f, W = Ø, and i = 1 and calls `Process_Inst(f,1,Inst)`. `Process_Inst( )` calls `Process_Call(f,1,g)`, which sets N = {f,g}, E = {⟨f,1,g⟩}, and W = {g}, and returns false. Then `Process_Inst( )` returns false.

Next, the `for` loop sets p to g, W to Ø and i to 1 and proceeds to call `Process_Inst(g,1,Inst)`, which determines that `Inst(g)[1]` is p := h and that h is a procedure constant, and so sets PVVs = {p} and PVVals(p) = {h}, and returns true. So the variable more in `Build_Call_Graph_with_PVVs( )` is set to true.

Next, i is set to 2 and `Process_Inst(g,2,Inst)` is called. It calls `Process_Call(g,2,p)`, which sets PVVs = {p} and PVCalls = {⟨g,2,p⟩}, and returns false.

Next, i is set to 3 and `Process_Inst(g,3,Inst)` is called, which, in turn, calls `Process_Call(g,2,j)`, resulting in N = {f,g,j}, E = {⟨f,1,g⟩, ⟨g,3,j⟩}, W = {j}, and PVVals(a) = {i}, and which returns true.

Next, p is set to j, W to Ø, and i to 1, and we call `Process_Inst(j,1,Inst)`, which in turn calls `Process_Call(j,1,a)`. `Process_Call( )` sets PVVs = {p,a} and PVCalls = {⟨g,2,p⟩,⟨j,1,a⟩}, and returns false.

Now W is empty, so the main routine enters the inner `repeat` loop marked with an asterisk in Figure 19.5. The condition within the nested `for` loops is not satisfied, so the main routine enters the following `for` loop, which sets N = {f,g,j,h,i}, E = {⟨f,1,g⟩, ⟨g,3,j⟩, ⟨g,2,h⟩, ⟨j,1,i⟩}, and W = {h,i}.

Since more = true, the main loop is repeated, this time leaving N as is, setting E = {⟨f,1,g⟩, ⟨g,3,j⟩, ⟨g,2,h⟩, ⟨j,1,i⟩, ⟨h,1,i⟩, ⟨i,1,g⟩}, and setting W = Ø. No further changes occur to the data structures, and the final call graph is as shown in Figure 19.9.

Of course, programs that create new code at run time make it impossible to construct a complete static call graph.

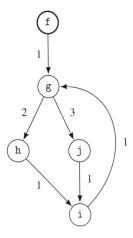

FIG. 19.9 Call graph of the program skeleton with procedure-valued variables shown in Figure 19.8.

19.2   Interprocedural Data-Flow Analysis

The issue addressed by interprocedural data-flow analysis is determining a useful but conservative approximation of how a program manipulates data at the level of its call graph. The most useful such information generally consists of knowing (1) what variables may be modified as *side effects* of a procedure call and (2) what parameters of a called procedure have constant values when it is called from a particular call site. Knowing the range of possible side effects of a call allows us to freely optimize the code around the call, as long as we avoid variables that may be affected by the called procedure. Knowing that one or more parameters have particular constant values in a given call allows us to determine whether it may be useful to clone a copy of the procedure's body for that call site and then to optimize it based on the constant parameter values. Such information may also be useful in driving procedure integration decisions (see Section 15.2).

Of course, aliasing complicates interprocedural analysis as it does intraprocedural problems. We deal with alias computation and integrating its results with alias-free interprocedural data-flow analysis in Section 19.4.

19.2.1   Flow-Insensitive Side-Effect Analysis

As suggested above, the goal of interprocedural side-effect analysis is to determine, for each call site, a safe approximation of the side effects that the procedure invoked at that call site may have. We include in that approximation any side effects of procedures called from that site, and so on.

We characterize side effects by four functions from instructions to sets of variables. Instructions, including call sites, are represented by ⟨procedure name,instruction number⟩ pairs. The functions are

$$DEF, MOD, REF, USE : \texttt{Procedure} \times \texttt{integer} \longrightarrow \texttt{set of Var}$$

as follows:

$DEF(p, i)$ = the set of variables that must be defined (i.e., that are definitely assigned values) by executing the ith instruction in procedure p.

$MOD(p, i)$ = the set of variables that may be modified (i.e., that may be assigned values) by executing the ith instruction in procedure p.

$REF(p, i)$ = the set of variables that may be referenced (i.e., that may have their values fetched) by executing the ith instruction in procedure p.

$USE(p, i)$ = the set of variables that may be referenced (i.e., that may be fetched) by the ith instruction in procedure p before being defined by it.

These functions are easy to compute for individual instructions that do not involve calls, as long as we disregard aliasing, discussion of which we postpone until Section 19.4. To represent these sets with aliasing disregarded, we prefix a D to the sets' names, e.g., alias-free MOD is $DMOD$. For example, $DDEF(p, i)$ for an assignment instruction $v \leftarrow exp$ is $\{v\}$ and for a predicate *pred* it is $\emptyset$, assuming that the expression and predicate include no calls. Similarly, $DREF(p, i)$ for the assignment instruction is the set of variables that occur in *exp* and, for the predicate, the set of variables that occur in *pred*.

As an example, we concentrate on computing $DMOD$, using an approach based on the work of Cooper and Kennedy (see Section 19.10 for references).

Throughout this section, we use the program in Figure 19.10 as an example. Its static nesting structure and call graph are shown in Figure 19.11. Note that there are three distinct js in the program—the global variable in main( ), the local variable in n( ), and the formal parameter of m( ), which we denote by j_1, j_2, and j_3, respectively, in what follows. To allow totally general naming of variables and parameters, we would need to identify the sequence of procedures each variable is nested in, e.g., we might denote the global j by ⟨j,[main]⟩, the local j in g( ) by ⟨j,[main,g]⟩, and the parameter j of m( ) by ⟨j,[main,g,n,m]⟩.

First we define the following:

1. $LMOD(p, i)$ is the set of variables that may be modified locally by executing the ith instruction in procedure p (excluding the effects of procedure calls that appear in that instruction).

2. $IMOD(p)$ is the set of variables that may be modified by executing procedure p without executing any calls within it.

3. $IMOD^+(p)$ is the set of variables that may be either directly modified by procedure p or passed by reference to another procedure and that may be modified as a side effect of it.

4. $GMOD(p)$ is the set of *all* variables that may be modified by an invocation of procedure p.

5. $RMOD(p)$ is the set of formal parameters of p that may be modified as side effects of invoking procedure p.

6. $Nonlocals(p)$ is the set of variables that are visible in procedure p but that are not local to it.

7. $Formals(p)$ is the set of formal parameters of procedure p.

8. $numinsts(p)$ is the number of instructions in procedure p.

9. $callsites(p)$ is the set of integers i such that the ith instruction in procedure p calls some procedure.

10. $callset(p, i)$ is the set of procedures called from the ith instruction in procedure p.[4]

11. $nested(p)$ is the set of procedures statically nested in procedure p.

---

4. Note that in our intermediate languages HIR, MIR, and LIR, an instruction may call at most one procedure. However, we allow for multiple calls per instruction to illustrate how to encompass that situation.

```
               procedure main( )
                  global i, j, e
                  procedure f(x)
     f            begin
     1               i := 2
     2               j := g(i,x)
     3               if x = 0 then
     4                   j := x + 1
     5               fi
     6               return j
                  end   || f
                  procedure g(a,b)
                     local j
                     procedure n(k,l)
                        procedure m(w,y,j)
     m                  begin
     1                     j := n(w,i)
     2                        return y + j
                        end    || m
     n                  begin
     1                     k := j + 1
     2                     y := y - 2
     3                     return k + m(i,i,k)
                        end     || n
     g               begin
     1                  if a > 1 then
     2                     a := b + 2
     3                  else
     4                     b := h(a,b)
     5                  fi
     6                  return a + b + n(b,b)
                     end   || g
                     procedure h(c,d)
     h               begin
     1                  e := e/g(1,d)
     2                  return e
                     end     || h
     main       begin
     1               call f(i)
                  end    || main
```

FIG. 19.10 An example program used throughout this section.

12. $b_{p,i,q}( )$ is the function that maps formal parameters in procedure q to their corresponding formal parameters at instruction i in procedure p, which is assumed to include a call to q. Variables global to both p and q are passed through from p to q also.

13. *Inst*( ) is the function that, for a procedure p, yields the array of instructions that make up p in order, namely, $Inst(p)[1 \cdot \cdot numinsts(p)]$.

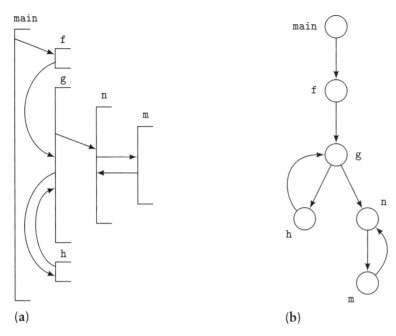

FIG. 19.11 (a) Static nesting structure and (b) call graph of the program in Figure 19.10.

Now $DMOD(p, i)$ can be computed as the union of $LMOD(p, i)$ (which can be computed easily for any instruction) with a union of generalized modification sets $GMOD(\ )$, for procedures q called from instruction i in procedure p, filtered through a $b_{p,i,q}(\ )$ function that maps formals of q to the corresponding formals of p, that is

$$DMOD(p, i) = LMOD(p, i) \cup \bigcup_{q \in callset(p,i)} b_{p,i,q}(GMOD(q))$$

$GMOD(p)$ can be computed as the union of $IMOD^+(p)$ with the union of $GMOD(\ )$ values (restricted to nonlocal variables) for all the call sites in p, i.e.,

$$GMOD(p) = IMOD^+(p) \cup \bigcup_{1 \leq i \leq numinsts(p)} \bigcup_{q \in callset(p,i)} GMOD(q) \cap Nonlocals(q)$$

$IMOD^+(p)$ is the union of $IMOD(p)$ with the union of all the $RMOD(q)$ values for all procedures q called from p, filtered through a $b_{p,i,q}(\ )$ function, as follows:

$$IMOD^+(p) = IMOD(p) \cup \bigcup_{i \in callsites(p)} \bigcup_{q \in callset(p,i)} b_{p,i,q}(RMOD(q))$$

```
IMOD: Procedure ⟶ set of Var

procedure Compute_IMOD(p,P)
   p: in Procedure
   P: in set of Procedure
begin
   V := ∅: set of Var
   i: integer
   q: Procedure
   || apply data-flow equations to compute IMOD
   for i := 1 to numinsts(p) do
      V ∪= LMOD(p,i)
   od
   IMOD(p) := V
end    || Compute_IMOD
```

FIG. 19.12   ICAN algorithm to compute *IMOD*( ) for a program *P*.

Finally, $IMOD(p)$, i.e.,

$$IMOD(p) = \bigcup_{1 \le i \le numinsts(p)} LMOD(p, i)$$

Note that *IMOD* can be computed easily, so computing *DMOD* efficiently reduces to computing *RMOD* and *GMOD* efficiently.

To compute *RMOD*, we use a data structure called the binding graph. While this could be done by standard interprocedural data-flow analysis, the approach described here is more efficient. The *binding graph* $B = \langle N_B, E_B \rangle$[5] for a program *P* has nodes in N_B that represent the formal parameters in *P* and edges in E_B that represent bindings of a caller's formal parameters to a callee's parameters. If at some call site in *p* there is a call of *q* that binds formal parameter *x* of *p* to formal parameter *y* of *q*, then there is an edge $x \rightarrow y$ in E_B—or transitively, through some number of calls, *x* is bound to a formal parameter *z* of some procedure *r*, then there is also an edge $x \rightarrow z$ in E_B. Note that only uses of a procedure's formal parameters as actual arguments to a called procedure generate edges in E_B.

The ICAN routine Compute_IMOD( ) in Figure 19.12. For our example program, the values of *Nonlocals* and *IMOD* are as shown in Table 19.1.

The ICAN routine Build_Binding_Graph( ) in Figure 19.13 constructs the binding graph for a program *P*. The value of nparams(*p*) is the number of formal parameters of *p*, and param(*p*,*i*) is the ith formal parameter of *p*. The value of passed(*p*,*i*,*q*,*x*,*y*) is true if instruction *i* in procedure *p* calls procedure *q* and binds *p*'s formal parameter *x* to *q*'s formal parameter *y*, and false otherwise.

To build the binding graph for the program in Figure 19.10, we initially set P = {main,f,g,h,n,m}, N = ∅, E = ∅, and oldE = ∅. Assuming that we process pro-

---

5. This is a Greek uppercase beta, not the Roman letter B.

TABLE 19.1 Values of *Nonlocals*( ) and *IMOD*( ) for the program in Figure 19.10.

Nonlocals(main)	$= \emptyset$	*IMOD*(main)	$= \emptyset$
Nonlocals(f)	$= \{e,i,j_1\}$	*IMOD*(f)	$= \{i,j_1\}$
Nonlocals(g)	$= \{e,i,j_1\}$	*IMOD*(g)	$= \{a,b\}$
Nonlocals(n)	$= \{a,b,e,i,j_2\}$	*IMOD*(n)	$= \{k,l\}$
Nonlocals(m)	$= \{a,b,e,i,k,l\}$	*IMOD*(m)	$= \{j_3\}$
Nonlocals(h)	$= \{e,i,j_1\}$	*IMOD*(h)	$= \{e\}$

cedure main( ) first, we encounter a call in line 1, so we have p = main, i = 1, and q = f, and we call Bind_Pairs(main,1,f), which leaves N and E unchanged. We encounter no other calls in main( ), so we process f( ) next, which adds x and b to N and the edge x→b to E, resulting in

$$N = \{x,b\} \quad E = \{x{\to}b\}$$

Next, we process g( ), which adds a, c, d, k, and l to N and adds several edges to E, as follows:

$$N = \{x,b,a,c,d,k,l\} \quad E = \{x{\to}b, \ a{\to}c, \ b{\to}d, \ b{\to}k, \ b{\to}l\}$$

Processing h( ) leaves N unchanged, but augments E again, as follows:

$$N = \{x,b,a,c,d,k,l\}$$
$$E = \{x{\to}b, \ a{\to}c, \ b{\to}d, \ b{\to}k, \ b{\to}l, \ d{\to}b\}$$

The process continues until finally the last top-level loop in Build_Binding_Graph( ) adds the transitive edges to E, resulting in

$$N = \{x,b,a,c,d,k,l,w,x,j_3\}$$
$$E = \{x{\to}b, \ a{\to}c, \ b{\to}d, \ b{\to}k, \ b{\to}l, \ d{\to}b, \ d{\to}k, \ d{\to}l, \ k{\to}j_3,$$
$$d{\to}j_3, \ b{\to}j_3, \ w{\to}k, \ w{\to}j_3, \ x{\to}d, \ x{\to}k, \ x{\to}j_3, \ x{\to}l\}$$

and the graphic representation in Figure 19.14. Note that, as for this example, the binding graph is generally not connected and contains cycles only if the program is recursive.

Next, we define *RMOD* on a program's binding graph. The function *RBMOD* from nodes in N_B to Boolean values is such that $RBMOD(x)$ is true if x is modified as a side effect of calling some procedure, and false otherwise. Computing *RBMOD* can then be done by solving the data-flow equations

$$RBMOD(x) = \exists p \in P \ (x \in Formals(p) \cap IMOD(p)) \vee \bigvee_{x{\to}y \in E_B} RBMOD(y)$$

on the binding graph, with $RBMOD(x)$ initialized to false for all x. The algorithm Compute_RBMOD(P,N,E), where P is the set of procedures in the call graph, and N

```
procedure Build_Binding_Graph(P,N,E)
    P: in set of Procedure
    N: out set of Var
    E: out set of (Var × Var)
begin
    p, q: Procedure
    i, m, n: integer
    e, f: Var × Var
    oldE: set of (Var × Var)
    || construct graph that models passing parameters
    || as parameters to other routines
    N := E := oldE := ∅
    repeat
        oldE := E
        for each p ∈ P do
            for i := 1 to numinsts(p) do
                for each q ∈ callset(p,i) do
                    Bind_Pairs(p,i,q,N,E)
                od
            od
        od
    until E = oldE
    repeat
        oldE := E
        for each e ∈ E do
            for each f ∈ E (f ≠ e) do
                if e@2 = f@1 & e@1 ≠ f@2 then
                    E ∪= {e@1→f@2}
                fi
            od
        od
    until E = oldE
end    || Build_Binding_Graph

procedure Bind_Pairs(p,i,q,N,E)
    p, q: in Procedure
    i: in integer
    N: inout set of Var
    E: inout set of (Var × Var)
begin
    m, n: integer
    for m := 1 to nparams(p) do
        for n := 1 to nparams(q) do
            if passed(p,i,q,param(p,m),param(q,n)) then
                N ∪= {param(p,m),param(q,n)}
                E ∪= {param(p,m)→param(q,n)}
            fi
        od
    od
end    || Bind_Pairs
```

FIG. 19.13 Algorithm to construct the binding graph B for a program *P*.

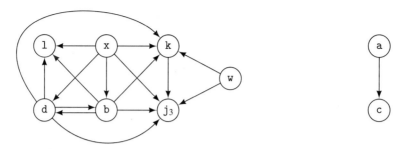

FIG. 19.14 Binding graph for the program in Figure 19.10.

```
RBMOD: Var ⟶ boolean

procedure Compute_RBMOD(P,N,E)
    P: in set of Procedure
    N: in set of Var
    E: in set of (Var × Var)
begin
    p: Procedure
    n: Var
    e: Var × Var
    oldRBMOD: Var ⟶ boolean
    RBMOD := ∅
    repeat
        oldRBMOD := RBMOD
        for each n ∈ N do
            RBMOD(n) := ∃p ∈ P (n ∈ Formals(p) ∩ IMOD(p))
            for each e ∈ E (e@1 = n) do
                RBMOD(n) ∨= RBMOD(e@2)
            od
        od
    until RBMOD = oldRBMOD
end    || Compute_RBMOD
```

FIG. 19.15 Algorithm to compute $RBMOD(\ )$ on the binding graph B.

and E are the sets of nodes and edges, respectively, of the binding graph, is shown in Figure 19.15. The outermost loop should be executed in postorder, i.e., as much as possible, each node should be processed after its successors in the binding graph.

Now, $RMOD(p)$ for a procedure p is simply the set of formal parameters x of p such that $RBMOD(x)$ is true, i.e.,

$$RMOD(p) = \{x \mid x \in Formals(p) \ \& \ RBMOD(x)\}$$

As an example of computing $RBMOD$, we compute it for our example program in Figure 19.10, whose binding graph is in Figure 19.14. To compute $RMOD$, we call Compute_RBMOD(P,N,E) with

TABLE 19.2 Initial values of $RBMOD()$ obtained by evaluating the existentially quantified expression in the equations for $RBMOD()$ for the nodes in the binding graph for our example in Figure 19.10.

$RBMOD(x)$	= false
$RBMOD(b)$	= true
$RBMOD(a)$	= true
$RBMOD(c)$	= false
$RBMOD(d)$	= false
$RBMOD(k)$	= true
$RBMOD(l)$	= false
$RBMOD(w)$	= false
$RBMOD(y)$	= true
$RBMOD(j_3)$	= true

TABLE 19.3 Final values of $RBMOD()$ for the nodes in the binding graph for our example in Figure 19.10.

$RBMOD(x)$	= false $\vee$ $RBMOD(b)$ $\vee$ $RBMOD(j_3)$ = true
$RBMOD(b)$	= true
$RBMOD(a)$	= true
$RBMOD(c)$	= false
$RBMOD(d)$	= false $\vee$ $RBMOD(b)$ = true
$RBMOD(k)$	= true
$RBMOD(l)$	= false
$RBMOD(w)$	= false $\vee$ $RBMOD(j_3)$ = true
$RBMOD(y)$	= true
$RBMOD(j_3)$	= true

$$P = \{main, f, g, h, n, m\}$$
$$N = \{x, b, a, c, d, k, l, w, z, j\}$$
$$E = \{x{\rightarrow}b, \ a{\rightarrow}c, \ b{\rightarrow}d, \ b{\rightarrow}k, \ b{\rightarrow}l, \ d{\rightarrow}b, \ d{\rightarrow}k, \ d{\rightarrow}l, \ k{\rightarrow}j_3,$$
$$d{\rightarrow}j_3, \ b{\rightarrow}j_3, \ w{\rightarrow}k, \ w{\rightarrow}j_3, \ x{\rightarrow}d, \ x{\rightarrow}k, \ x{\rightarrow}j_3, \ x{\rightarrow}l\}$$

The algorithm initializes $RBMOD()$ for each node in the binding graph as shown in Table 19.2 and then iterates, computing $RBMOD()$ for the nodes until it converges,[6] resulting in the values shown in Table 19.3.

---

6. Note that the data-flow equations for $RBMOD$ are defined on the two-element lattice with false $\sqsubseteq$ true.

TABLE 19.4 Values of $RMOD(\ )$ for our example in Figure 19.10.

$RMOD(\texttt{main}) = \emptyset$	
$RMOD(\texttt{f})$	$= \{x\}$
$RMOD(\texttt{g})$	$= \{a,b\}$
$RMOD(\texttt{n})$	$= \{k\}$
$RMOD(\texttt{m})$	$= \{w,y,j_3\}$
$RMOD(\texttt{h})$	$= \{d\}$

```
IMODPLUS: Procedure ⟶ set of Var

procedure Compute_IMODPLUS(P)
    P: in set of Procedure
begin
    p, q: Procedure
    i: integer
    IMODPLUS := ∅
    for each p ∈ P do
        IMODPLUS(p) := IMOD(p)
        for each i ∈ callsites(p) do
            for each q ∈ callset(p,i) do
                IMODPLUS(p) ∪= b(p,i,q,RMOD(q))
            od
        od
    od
end    || Compute_IMODPLUS
```

FIG. 19.16 ICAN algorithm to compute $IMOD^+(\ )$.

Thus, $RMOD(\ )$ is as shown in Table 19.4.

Recall that $IMOD^+$ is defined as

$$IMOD^+(p) = IMOD(p) \cup \bigcup_{q \in callset(p,i)} b_{p,i,q}(RMOD(q))$$

so it can be computed easily as shown in Figure 19.16 (note that we use `b(p,i,q,r)` to represent $b_{p,i,q}(r)$ in the algorithm) and its values for our example are as shown in Table 19.5.

To compute $GMOD$ from $IMOD^+$ efficiently, we use the algorithms given in Figures 19.17 and 19.18, which operate on the call graph (i.e., `Edges` is the set of edges in the call graph, not the binding graph).

Given a call graph with procedures P, edges `Edges`, and main routine `r`, the ICAN routines `Stratify( )` and `Set_Levels( )` in Figure 19.17 constructs the function `Level( )` that maps procedures to their nesting levels. For each nesting level

TABLE 19.5 Values of $IMOD^+(\ )$ for our example in Figure 19.10.

$$IMOD^+(\text{main}) = IMOD(\text{main}) \cup b_{\text{main},1,\text{f}}(RMOD(\text{f}))$$
$$= \{\text{i},\text{j}_1\} \cup \{\text{i}\} = \{\text{i},\text{j}_1\}$$
$$IMOD^+(\text{f}) \quad = IMOD(\text{f}) \cup b_{\text{f},2,\text{g}}(RMOD(\text{g})) = \{\text{i},\text{j}_1\} \cup \{\text{i},\text{x}\}$$
$$= \{\text{i},\text{j}_1,\text{x}\}$$
$$IMOD^+(\text{g}) \quad = IMOD(\text{g}) \cup b_{\text{g},4,\text{h}}(RMOD(\text{h})) \cup b_{\text{g},6,\text{n}}(RMOD(\text{n}))$$
$$= \{\text{a},\text{b}\} \cup \{\text{b}\} \cup \{\text{b}\} = \{\text{a},\text{b}\}$$
$$IMOD^+(\text{n}) \quad = IMOD(\text{n}) \cup b_{\text{n},3,\text{m}}(RMOD(\text{m})) = \{\text{k},\text{y}\}$$
$$IMOD^+(\text{m}) \quad = IMOD(\text{m}) \cup b_{\text{m},1,\text{n}}(RMOD(\text{n})) = \{\text{j}_3\} \cup \{\text{w}\}$$
$$= \{\text{j}_3,\text{w}\}$$
$$IMOD^+(\text{h}) \quad = IMOD(\text{h}) \cup b_{\text{h},1,\text{g}}(RMOD(\text{g})) = \{\text{e}\} \cup \{\text{d}\} = \{\text{e},\text{d}\}$$

```
N, R: array [··] of set of Procedure
E: array [··] of set of (Procedure × Procedure)
Level := Ø: Procedure ⟶ integer
depth, NextDfn: integer
Dfn: Procedure ⟶ integer
LowLink: Procedure ⟶ integer
GMOD, IMODPLUS, Nonlocals: Procedure ⟶ set of Var
Stack: sequence of Procedure

procedure Stratify(P,Edges,r) returns integer
    P: in set of Procedure
    Edges: in set of (Procedure × Procedure)
    r: in Procedure
begin
    i, j, depth: integer
    p, q:  Procedure
    WL := P: set of Procedure
    Level(r) := 0
    Set_Levels(r)
    depth := 0
    for i := 0 to depth do
       N[i] := Ø
         for j := 0 to i-1 do
            WL ∪= {p ∈ P where Level(p) = j}
         od
         for j := i to depth do
            for each p ∈ P (Level(p) = j) do
```

(continued)

FIG. 19.17 Algorithm to compute nesting levels Level( ) in a call graph and the subgraphs (consisting of nodes N[ ], roots R[ ], and edges E[ ]) that exclude routines that call others at lower nesting levels. Stratify( ) uses Set_Levels to compute the nesting level of each procedure.

```
                    if called(p) ∩ WL = ∅ then
                        N[i] ∪= {p}
                    fi
                od
                WL ∪= {p ∈ P where Level(p) = j}
            od
            E[i] := Edges ∩ (N[i] × N[i])
            R[i] := {p ∈ N[i] where Level(p) = i}
        od
        return depth
    end     || Stratify

    procedure Set_Levels(r)
        r: in Procedure
    begin
        p: Procedure
        for each p ∈ nested(r) do
            Level(p) := Level(r) + 1
            if Level(p) > depth then
                depth := Level(p)
            fi
            Set_Levels(p)
        od
    end     || Set_Levels
```

FIG. 19.17 *(continued)*

```
    procedure Compute_GMOD(r)
        r: in Procedure
    begin
        i: integer
        n: Procedure
        for i := depth by -1 to 0 do
            for each r ∈ R[i] do
                NextDfn := 0
                for each n ∈ N[i] do
                    Dfn(n) := 0
                od
                Stack := []
                GMOD_Search(i,r)
            od
        od
    end     || Compute_GMOD
```

FIG. 19.18 Algorithm for computing *GMOD*( ) efficiently from *IMOD*$^+$( ) by using a version of Tarjan's algorithm.

```
procedure GMOD_Search(i,p)
   i: in integer
   p: in Procedure
begin
   j: integer
   u: Procedure
   e: Procedure × Procedure
   LowLink(p) := Dfn(p) := NextDfn += 1
   GMOD(p) := IMODPLUS(p)
   Stack ⊕= [p]
   for each e ∈ E[i] (e@1 = p) do
      if Dfn[e@2] = 0 then
         GMOD_Search(i,e@2)
         LowLink(p) := min(LowLink(p),LowLink(e@2))
      fi
      if Dfn(e@2)<Dfn(p) & ∃j ∈ integer (Stack↓j=e@2) then
         LowLink(p) := min(Dfn(e@2),LowLink(p))
      else
         GMOD(p) ∪= GMOD(e@2) ∩ Nonlocals(e@2)
      fi
   od
*  if LowLink(p) = Dfn(p) then
      repeat
         u := Stack↓-1
         Stack ⊖= -1
         GMOD(u) ∪= GMOD(p) ∩ Nonlocals(p)
      until u = p
   fi
end    || GMOD_Search
```

FIG. 19.18 *(continued)*

$0 \le i \le$ depth of the program, Stratify( ) also computes the subgraph with nodes N[i], roots R[i],[7] and edges E[i] such that a routine is in N[i] if all the routines it calls have nesting levels greater than or equal to i. The routine called(p) returns the set of procedures called from procedure p.

Applying Stratify( ) to our example program results in depth = 3 and the data structures in Table 19.6.

The *GMOD* computation is an adaptation of Tarjan's algorithm to compute strongly connected components (see Section 7.4). The underlying idea is that, for a strongly connected component—i.e., a set of mutually recursive procedures—*GMOD* for its root node represents all the side effects that may occur in nodes (i.e., procedures) in the component, so *GMOD* for each node in it is the union of $IMOD^+$ for the node with *GMOD* for the root node intersected with the set of nonlocal

---

7. Note that a subgraph may have multiple roots if, for example, the main routine (at level 0) calls two routines (at level 1), neither of which calls the other.

TABLE 19.6 Values of Level( ), N[ ], R[ ], and E[ ] for our example
program in Figure 19.10.

Level(main) = 0
Level(f) = Level(g) = Level(h) = 1
Level(n) = 2
Level(m) = 3

N[0] = {main,f,g,h,n,m}	R[0] = {main}
N[1] = {f,g,h,n,m}	R[1] = {f}
N[2] = {n,m}	R[2] = {n}
N[3] = {m}	R[3] = {m}

E[0] = {main→f, f→g, g→h, g→n, h→g, n→m, m→n}
E[1] = {f→g, g→h, g→n, h→g, n→m, m→n}
E[2] = {n→m, m→n}
E[3] = ∅

TABLE 19.7 Initial values for $GMOD(\ )$ for our
example program.

$GMOD(\text{main}) = IMOD^+(\text{main}) = \{\text{i}, \text{j}_1\}$
$GMOD(\text{f}) \quad = IMOD^+(\text{f}) = \{\text{i}, \text{j}_1, \text{x}\}$
$GMOD(\text{g}) \quad = IMOD^+(\text{g}) = \{\text{a}, \text{b}\}$
$GMOD(\text{n}) \quad = IMOD^+(\text{n}) = \{\text{k}, \text{y}\}$
$GMOD(\text{m}) \quad = IMOD^+(\text{m}) = \{\text{j}_3, \text{w}\}$
$GMOD(\text{h}) \quad = IMOD^+(\text{h}) = \{\text{d}, \text{e}\}$

variables that occur in the procedure. The central point of the algorithm is that the
test marked with an asterisk in Figure 19.18 evaluates to true if and only if p is the
root of a strongly connected component of the call graph.

As an example of the computation of $GMOD$, we apply the algorithm to the
program in Figure 19.10. We invoke Compute_GMOD(main), which performs the
depth-first search and identification of strongly connected components and, in effect,
initializes $GMOD$ to the values shown in Table 19.7. Then it accumulates, in order,
the values shown in Table 19.8.

Now, finally, we apply the defining equation for $DMOD$, to get the values shown
in Table 19.9.

The computational complexity of this approach to computing flow-insensitive
side effects is $O(e \cdot n + d \cdot n^2)$, where n and e are the numbers of nodes and edges,
respectively, in the call graph and d is the depth of lexical nesting in the program.
The factor of d may be removed by combining the iterations in Compute_GMOD( )
into a single pass over the call graph (see Exercise 19.2 in Section 19.11).

Similar decompositions can be used to compute the other flow-insensitive may
summary functions.

TABLE 19.8 Final values for $GMOD(\ )$ for our example program.

$GMOD(\texttt{m})$	$= \{j_3, \texttt{w}\}$
$GMOD(\texttt{n})$	$= \{\texttt{k}, \texttt{y}\}$
$GMOD(\texttt{h})$	$= \{\texttt{d}, \texttt{e}\}$
$GMOD(\texttt{g})$	$= \{\texttt{a}, \texttt{b}\} \cup (GMOD(\texttt{h}) \cap \textit{Nonlocals}(\texttt{h}))$
	$= \{\texttt{a}, \texttt{b}\} \cup \{\texttt{e}\} = \{\texttt{a}, \texttt{b}, \texttt{e}\}$
$GMOD(\texttt{f})$	$= \{\texttt{i}, j_1, \texttt{x}\} \cup (GMOD(\texttt{g}) \cap \textit{Nonlocals}(\texttt{g}))$
	$= \{\texttt{i}, j_1, \texttt{x}\} \cup \{\texttt{e}\} = \{\texttt{e}, \texttt{i}, j_1, \texttt{x}\}$
$GMOD(\texttt{main})$	$= \{\texttt{i}, j_1\} \cup (GMOD(\texttt{f}) \cap \textit{Nonlocals}(\texttt{f}))$
	$= \{\texttt{i}, j_1\} \cup \{\texttt{e}\} = \{\texttt{e}, \texttt{i}, j_1\}$

TABLE 19.9 Values of $DMOD(\ )$ for our example program.

$DMOD(\texttt{main}, 1)$	$= LMOD(\texttt{main}, 1) = \emptyset$
$DMOD(\texttt{f}, 1)$	$= LMOD(\texttt{f}, 1) = \{\texttt{i}\}$
$DMOD(\texttt{f}, 2)$	$= LMOD(\texttt{f}, 2) \cup b_{\texttt{f}, 2, \texttt{g}}(GMOD(\texttt{g}))$
	$= \{j_1\} \cup \{\texttt{e}, \texttt{i}, \texttt{x}\} = \{\texttt{e}, \texttt{i}, j_1, \texttt{x}\}$
$DMOD(\texttt{f}, 3)$	$= LMOD(\texttt{f}, 3) = \emptyset$
$DMOD(\texttt{f}, 4)$	$= LMOD(\texttt{f}, 4) = \{j_1\}$
$DMOD(\texttt{f}, 5)$	$= LMOD(\texttt{f}, 5) = \emptyset$
$DMOD(\texttt{f}, 6)$	$= LMOD(\texttt{f}, 6) = \emptyset$
$DMOD(\texttt{g}, 1)$	$= LMOD(\texttt{g}, 1) = \emptyset$
$DMOD(\texttt{g}, 2)$	$= LMOD(\texttt{g}, 2) = \{\texttt{a}\}$
$DMOD(\texttt{g}, 3)$	$= LMOD(\texttt{g}, 3) = \emptyset$
$DMOD(\texttt{g}, 4)$	$= LMOD(\texttt{g}, 4) \cup b_{\texttt{g}, 4, \texttt{h}}(GMOD(\texttt{h}))$
	$= \{\texttt{b}\} \cup \{\texttt{b}, \texttt{e}\} = \{\texttt{b}, \texttt{e}\}$
$DMOD(\texttt{g}, 5)$	$= LMOD(\texttt{g}, 5) = \{\texttt{a}\}$
$DMOD(\texttt{g}, 6)$	$= LMOD(\texttt{g}, 6) = \{\texttt{a}\}$
$DMOD(\texttt{h}, 1)$	$= LMOD(\texttt{h}, 1) \cup b_{\texttt{h}, 1, \texttt{g}}(GMOD(\texttt{g}))$
	$= \{\texttt{e}\} \cup \{\texttt{b}\} = \{\texttt{b}, \texttt{e}\}$
$DMOD(\texttt{h}, 2)$	$= LMOD(\texttt{h}, 2) = \emptyset$
$DMOD(\texttt{n}, 1)$	$= LMOD(\texttt{n}, 1) = \{\texttt{k}\}$
$DMOD(\texttt{n}, 2)$	$= LMOD(\texttt{n}, 2) = \{\texttt{y}\}$
$DMOD(\texttt{n}, 3)$	$= LMOD(\texttt{n}, 3) = \emptyset$
$DMOD(\texttt{m}, 1)$	$= LMOD(\texttt{m}, 1) = \{j_3\}$
$DMOD(\texttt{m}, 2)$	$= LMOD(\texttt{m}, 2) = \emptyset$

19.2.2   Flow-Sensitive Side Effects: The Program Summary Graph

Myers [Myer81] showed that computing flow-sensitive side effects is co-NP-complete, as long as aliasing is taken into account. He also introduced a model called the program *supergraph* that supports determination of flow-sensitive side effects.

Callahan [Call88] gives practical methods to compute approximate solutions of flow-sensitive problems based on the so-called program summary graph, which augments the nodes in a graph derived from the call graph and the parameter-passing patterns with information about flow-sensitive effects inside the corresponding procedures. The graph is intermediate in size and complexity between the call graph and Myers's supergraph.

In this section, we give an overview of the program summary graph and the computation of flow-sensitive side-effect information it enables. We assume that the parameter-passing discipline is call by reference. Suppose that we are given a program comprising a set of procedures P. Then the *program summary graph* for P consists of two nodes for each formal parameter of each procedure, called *entry* and *exit* nodes; two nodes for each actual argument at each call site, called *call* and *return* nodes; and edges that connect call nodes to entry nodes, exit nodes to return nodes, and some entry and return nodes to call and exit nodes.

In greater detail, let p and q be procedures such that instruction i in p calls q. Then the formal parameters of q are

$$\texttt{param}(q,1),\ldots,\ \texttt{param}(q,\texttt{nparams}(q))$$

and the actual arguments of the call to q are

$$\texttt{arg}(p,i,1),\ldots,\ \texttt{arg}(p,i,\texttt{nparams}(q))$$

There is a call node $\texttt{cl}(p,i,\texttt{arg}(p,i,j))$ and a return node $\texttt{rt}(p,i,\texttt{arg}(p,i,j))$ for each triple $\langle p,i,\texttt{arg}(p,i,j)\rangle$, and an entry node $\texttt{en}(q,\texttt{param}(q,j))$ and an exit node $\texttt{ex}(q,\texttt{param}(q,j))$ for each pair $\langle q,\texttt{param}(q,j)\rangle$. There is an edge from $\texttt{cl}(p,i,\texttt{arg}(p,i,j))$ to $\texttt{en}(q,\texttt{param}(q,j))$ and another from $\texttt{ex}(q,\texttt{param}(q,j))$ to $\texttt{rt}(p,i,\texttt{arg}(p,i,j))$. Also, there are edges as follows:

1. from $\texttt{en}(p,\texttt{param}(p,j))$ to $\texttt{cl}(p,i,\texttt{arg}(p,i,k))$ if the value of $\texttt{param}(p,j)$ reaches call site $\langle p,i\rangle$ and is bound there to $\texttt{arg}(p,i,k)$,

2. from $\texttt{en}(p,\texttt{param}(p,j))$ to $\texttt{ex}(p,\texttt{param}(p,k))$ if the value of $\texttt{param}(p,j)$ on entry to p reaches p's exit as the value of $\texttt{param}(p,k)$,

3. from $\texttt{rt}(p,i,\texttt{arg}(p,i,j))$ to $\texttt{cl}(p,k,\texttt{arg}(p,k,l))$ if the value of $\texttt{arg}(p,i,j)$ on return to p reaches call site $\langle p,k\rangle$ as the value of $\texttt{arg}(p,k,l)$, and

4. from $\texttt{rt}(p,i,\texttt{arg}(p,i,j))$ to $\texttt{ex}(p,\texttt{param}(p,k))$ if the value of $\texttt{arg}(p,i,j)$ on return to p reaches p's exit as the value of $\texttt{param}(p,k)$.

We assume that at a call site an actual argument is used and then killed, that a procedure entry defines all formal parameters, and that a return uses all the parameters.

```
              procedure f(x)
   f          begin
   1              i := 2
   2              if x = 0 then
   3                  j := g(j,0)
   4              else
   5                  j := g(i,x)
   6              fi
   7              return j
              end    || f
              procedure g(a,b)
   g          begin
   1              if a > 1 then
   2                  a := b + 2
   3              else
   4                  b := h(a,b)
   5              fi
   6              return a + b + j
              end    || g
              procedure h(c,d)
   h          begin
   1                  e := e/g(1,d)
   2              return e
              end    || h
```

FIG. 19.19 An example program for flow-sensitive side-effect computation.

As an example, consider the program in Figure 19.19. Its program summary graph is shown in Figure 19.20. The following explains some of the edges:

1. There is an edge from en(f,x) to ex(f,x) because the value of x on entry to f( ) may reach its exit.

2. There is an edge from en(f,x) to cl(f,5,x) because the value of x on entry to f( ) may be passed to formal parameter b of g( ) at call site ⟨f,5⟩.

3. There is no edge from en(f,x) to cl(f,3,j) because the value of x on entry to f( ) cannot be passed to formal parameter b of g( ) at call site ⟨f,3⟩.

4. There is an edge from cl(h,1,d) to en(g,b) because the value of d in the call to g( ) at call site ⟨h,1⟩ may be passed to formal parameter b of g( ).

5. There is an edge from ex(g,b) to rt(f,5,x) because the value of b on exit from g( ) is bound to the formal parameter x of f( ).

Given the program summary graph, we can now define the properties *Kill* and *Use*. A variable v is killed (and *Kill*(v) is *true*) if it must be modified, regardless of control flow; it is used (and *Use*(v) is *true*) if there is a use of it before it is killed. Now, the set of killed variables, for example, can be determined by the data-flow equations

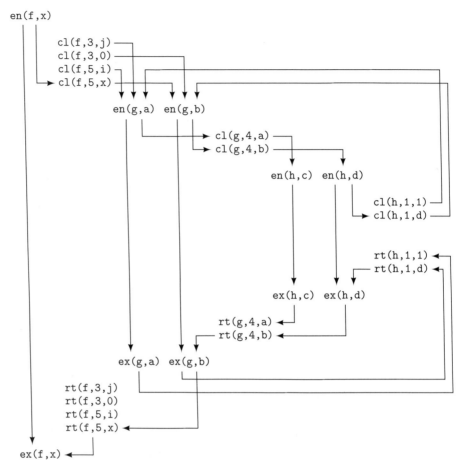

FIG. 19.20 Program summary graph for the program in Figure 19.19.

$$
Kill(x) = \begin{cases} false & \text{for } x, \text{ an exit node} \\ \displaystyle\bigwedge_{x \to y \in E} Kill(y) & \text{for } x, \text{ an entry or return node} \\ Kill(y) \lor Kill(z) & \text{for } x, \text{ a call node, and } y \text{ and } z, \\ & \text{the corresponding return and} \\ & \text{entry nodes} \end{cases}
$$

where E is the set of edges in the program summary graph. Similar equations apply for the $Use(\ )$ property, and the framework can be extended to handle global variables. Callahan gives efficient algorithms for computing the data-flow properties. The algorithms run in time bounded by $O(n \cdot s)$, where n is the number of procedures and s is a measure of the size of the program summary graph.

19.2.3   Other Issues in Computing Side Effects

We have not discussed the effects of a series of issues that occur in real programs, such as recursion, aliasing, label variables, pointers, unions, procedure parameters, and exception handling. Interprocedural aliasing is discussed in Section 19.4. Some of the other issues are addressed by Weihl [Weih80], while others are addressed only in implemented systems, such as Parafrase [Kuck74] and ParaScope [CooH93].

19.3   Interprocedural Constant Propagation

Interprocedural constant propagation can be formulated as either a site-independent or a site-specific method. The *site-independent* form determines, for each procedure in a program, the subset of its parameters such that each parameter has the same constant value in every invocation of the procedure. The *site-specific* form determines, for each particular procedure called from each particular site, the subset of parameters that have the same constant values each time the procedure is called.

In either case, the analysis problem comes within the criteria determined by Myers to make it either *NP*-complete or co-*NP*-complete, so the typical approach has been to invent less expensive but less precise methods.

Callahan et al. [CalC86] describe a method to perform interprocedural constant propagation that may be either flow sensitive or flow insensitive, depending on the choice of what they call jump and return-jump functions. Our approach is derived from theirs. We assume for simplicity that the sets of formal parameters of the procedures that make up a program are non-intersecting.

A *jump function* $J(p,i,L,x)$, for call site i in procedure p that calls procedure q with the list of actual arguments L, maps information about the actual arguments of the call from that call site to information about formal parameter x of q at its entry point. Similarly, a *return-jump function* $R(p,L,x)$, for a procedure p, maps the information about the list of formal parameters L of p to information about the value returned through formal parameter x by p. For example, for the procedures shown later in Figure 19.23,

```
J(f,1,[i,j],a) = i
J(f,1,[i,j],b) = j
R(g,[a,b],a) = 2
```

are possible jump and return-jump function values for call site $\langle$f,1$\rangle$ and procedure g( ) (as we shall see below, they are "pass-through parameter" jump and return-jump functions). Further, we define the *support* of jump function $J(p,i,L,x)$, written Jsupport(p,i,L,x), to be the set of actual arguments used in defining $J(p,i,L,x)$; similarly for return-jump functions. Thus, for our example we have

```
Jsupport(f,1,[i,j],a) = {i}
Jsupport(f,1,[i,j],b) = {j}
Rsupport(g,[a,b],a) = ∅
```

The interprocedural constant-propagation algorithm, using only forward jump functions, is shown in Figure 19.21. It uses the lattice **ICP** given in Figure 8.3 and

```
procedure Intpr_Const_Prop(P,r,Cval)
    P: in set of Procedure
    r: in Procedure
    Cval: out Var ⟶ ICP
begin
    WL := {r}: set of Procedure
    p, q: Procedure
    v: Var
    i, j: integer
    prev: ICP
    Pars: Procedure ⟶ set of Var
    ArgList: Procedure × integer × Procedure
        ⟶ sequence of Var
    Eval: Expr × ICP ⟶ ICP
    || construct sets of parameters and lists of arguments
    || and initialize Cval( ) for each parameter
    for each p ∈ P do
        Pars(p) := ∅
        for i := 1 to nparams(p) do
            Cval(param(p,i)) := ⊤
            Pars(p) ∪= {param(p,i)}
        od
        for i := 1 to numinsts(p) do
            for each q ∈ callset(p,i) do
                ArgList(p,i,q) := []
                for j := 1 to nparams(q) do
                    ArgList(p,i,q) ⊕= [arg(p,i,j)]
                od
            od
        od
    od
```

FIG. 19.21 Site-independent interprocedural constant-propagation algorithm.

reproduced here in Figure 19.22. As in Chapter 8, $\top$ is the initial value for each putative constant-valued variable, constants represent themselves, and $\bot$ means that a variable's value is not constant. The procedures used in the algorithm include one new one, namely, Eval(J(p,i,L,v),Cval), which evaluates J(p,i,L,v) over ICP, i.e., with the variables in Jsupport(p,i,L,v) getting their values from Cval( ) and with the operations performed over ICP. The programming language's operations need to be mapped appropriately to operations on ICP, e.g.,

$$1 + \bot = 1$$
$$1 + 2 = 3$$
$$1 + \top = \top$$

As an example of interprocedural constant propagation, consider the program in Figure 19.23. A possible set of jump functions and their support sets for this

```
while WL ≠ ∅ do
    p := •WL; WL -= {p}
    for i := 1 to pinsts(p) do
        for each q ∈ callset(p,i) do
            for j := 1 to nparams(q) do
                || if q( )'s jth parameter can be evaluated using values that
                || are arguments of p( ), evaluate it and update its Cval( )
                if Jsupport(p,i,ArgList(p,i,q),param(q,j)) ⊆ Pars(p) then
                    prev := Cval(param(q,j))
                    Cval(param(q,j)) ⊓= Eval(J(p,i,
                        ArgList(p,i,q),param(q,j)),Cval)
                    if Cval(param(q,j)) ⊏ prev then
                        WL ∪= {q}
                    fi
                fi
            od
        od
    od
od
end     || Intpr_Const_Prop
```

FIG. 19.21 (*continued*)

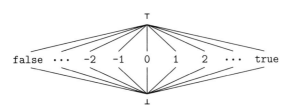

FIG. 19.22 Integer constant-propagation lattice **ICP**.

program are as shown in Table 19.10. For these jump-function values, the algorithm
first initializes

```
Pars(e) = ∅           ArgList(e,1,f) = [x,1]
Pars(f) = {i,j}       ArgList(f,1,g) = [i,j]
Pars(g) = {a,b}       ArgList(f,2,g) = [j]

Cval(i) = Cval(j) = Cval(a) = Cval(b) = ⊤
```

and WL = {e}. Then it removes e from WL and processes the one instruction in e( ). It
determines that f ∈ callset(e,1) is true, so it then iterates over the parameters (i
and j) of f( ). It evaluates J(e,1,[],i) = ⊥ and stores that value in Cval(i), also
setting WL = {f}. Similar actions result in setting Cval(j) = 1. Next, the algorithm
sets p = f and i = 1 and processes the call to g( ) at that site. This results in setting
Cval(a) = ⊥ and Cval(b) = 1. For i = 2, we get Cval(a) = ⊥ and Cval(b) = 1
again. The final result is

```
           procedure e( )
           begin
e                x, c: integer
1                    c := f(x,1)
           end
           procedure f(i,j)
           begin
f                s, t: integer
1                    s := g(i,j)
2                    t := g(j,j)
3                    return s + t
           end
           procedure g(a,b)
g          begin
1                    a := 2
2                    b := b + a
3                    return a
           end
```

FIG. 19.23 An example for interprocedural constant propagation.

TABLE 19.10 Possible jump functions and their support sets
for the example program in Figure 19.23.

J(e,1,[],i) = ⊥	Jsupport(e,1,[],i) = Ø
J(e,1,[],j) = 1	Jsupport(e,1,[],j) = Ø
J(f,1,[i,j],a) = i	Jsupport(f,1,[i,j],a) = {i}
J(f,1,[i,j],b) = j	Jsupport(f,1,[i,j],b) = {j}
J(f,2,[i,j],a) = j	Jsupport(f,2,[i,j],a) = {j}
J(f,2,[i,j],b) = j	Jsupport(f,2,[i,j],b) = {j}

```
           Cval(i) = ⊥
           Cval(j) = 1
           Cval(a) = ⊥
           Cval(b) = 1
```

Thus, formal parameter j is constant at each call to f( ) and b is constant at each call to g( ).

There is a range of possible choices for jump and return-jump functions, ranging from individual constants to results of symbolic interpretation. They include the following:

1. *Literal constant.* This choice makes each J( ) value either a constant, if the call site passes a literal constant, or ⊥, and it does not propagate interprocedural constants through procedure bodies.

2. *Interprocedural constant.* This choice makes each J( ) value either constant, if intraprocedural constant propagation can determine it to be so, or ⊥ otherwise.

3. *Pass-through parameter.* This choice (which is the one we used in the example above) uses interprocedural constants, where they are available, as values of parameters that are passed through to a called routine unchanged, or $\perp$ otherwise.

4. *Polynomial parameter.* This choice uses intraprocedural constants where available and polynomial functions of the parameters passed to a routine if the value of an actual argument passed within the procedure is a polynomial in its parameters, and $\perp$ otherwise.

5. *Symbolic execution.* This approach simulates the execution of each procedure to determine constant parameter values.

These choices range, in numerical order, from least to most expensive and, correspondingly, from least to most informative. Grove and Torczon [GroT93] discuss jump and return-jump functions, their computational costs, and the information they provide.

Use of jump functions allows computation of both call-site-independent and call-site-specific constants in time $O(n + e)$, for a call graph with n nodes and e edges and for all but the most complex choices of jump functions. For the call-site-specific form, we modify the algorithm by converting the procedures to SSA form (for computational efficiency) and evaluate them flow sensitively.

Return-jump functions are useful only in the call-site-specific (or flow-sensitive) form of analysis. To understand this, consider our example program in Figure 19.23. The natural time to use the return-jump functions is in a prepass over the program (before using the forward jump functions) performed from the leaves of the call graph (including arbitrarily selected members of leaf strongly connected components). The natural choice of return-jump function for procedure g( ) and parameter a is R(g, [a,b], a) = 2. With this choice, we would set Cval(a) = 2 for call site 1 in procedure f( ). This choice, however, is not appropriate: if we now perform constant propagation with forward jump functions, we have a value for Cval(a) that applies to calls of g( ) *after* the first one, but not to the first one. Thus, flow sensitivity is essential if we use return-jump functions. Using return-jump functions does not affect the computational complexity of the algorithm.

Call-site-specific interprocedural constant propagation can be used to drive procedure cloning, as discussed in Section 19.5.

19.4   Interprocedural Alias Analysis

As discussed in Chapter 10, intraprocedural aliasing possibilities differ significantly from one language to another, with the extremes represented by Fortran and C. In interprocedural alias analysis, an additional dimension is added, namely, two-level scoping, as in both Fortran and C, versus multi-level scoping, as found, for example, in Pascal, PL/I, and Mesa.

The Fortran standards specifically prohibit assignment to an aliased variable. C, on the other hand, allows one to take the address of almost any object, pass it almost anywhere, and do nearly arbitrary things with it.

```
global i, j
procedure f( )
begin
   g(i)
   g(j)
end
procedure g(a)
begin
   i := i + 1
   j := j + 1
   return a
end
```

FIG. 19.24 An example of interprocedural aliasing.

Interprocedural aliases are generally created by parameter passing and by access to nonlocal variables. As discussed in the introduction to Chapter 10, the characterization of aliasing as a relation depends on whether we are taking time (or, equivalently, flow sensitivity) into account. We are concerned with flow-insensitive aliasing here, except in the discussion of languages with call by value and pointers in Section 19.4.2. As an example of the intransitivity of flow-insensitive interprocedural aliasing, consider the code in Figure 19.24 and assume that parameters are passed by reference. Then i *alias* a and j *alias* a are valid, but it is not the case that i *alias* j.

Flow-sensitive alias analysis is at least as expensive as flow-sensitive side-effect analysis (see Section 19.2.2), so we content ourselves with a flow-insensitive version for call by reference and a malleable version for call by value with pointers, where malleable means that it may be flow sensitive or not, as in the discussion of intraprocedural alias analysis in Sections 10.2 and 10.3.

19.4.1   Flow-Insensitive Alias Analysis

We use the function *ALIAS*: Var × Procedure $\longrightarrow$ set of Var to describe the sets of all aliases in each procedure in a program. In particular, $ALIAS(x, p) = s$ if and only if s consists of all the variables that may be aliases of x in procedure p.

The basic idea for computing *ALIAS* is to follow all the possible chains of argument-parameter and nonlocal variable-parameter bindings at all call sites in depth-first order, incrementally accumulating alias pairs.

An efficient approach developed by Cooper and Kennedy [CooK89] handles formal parameters and nonlocal variables separately, based on the observation that nonlocal variables can only have formal parameters as aliases, as long as the source language does not allow pointer aliasing. This significantly reduces the number of pairs that might need to be computed. We describe an approach based on theirs.

For a language like Pascal or Mesa in which procedures may be nested and visibility of variables is determined by the nesting, there are two complications in alias determination. One is that formal parameters to a routine at nesting level l may be nonlocal variables to a routine contained within it at nesting level $m > l$.

The other is essentially the mirror image of the first complication, i.e., that variables defined at nesting level l are not visible at levels less than l. To describe this problem further, we use the concept of the *extended formal-parameter set* of a procedure, which we develop below.

In outline, for a program P, the approach to alias determination consists of four steps, as follows:

1. First, we construct an extended version of the program's binding graph B (see Section 19.2.1 and Figure 19.26) that takes extended formal parameters into account and its pair binding graph Π (see below).

2. Next, we solve a forward data-flow problem over B to compute, for each formal parameter fp, the set $A(fp)$ of variables v (not including formal parameters) that fp may be aliased to by a call chain that binds v to fp.

3. Next, we perform a marking algorithm on Π (which may also be thought of as solving a forward data-flow analysis problem) to determine formal parameters that may be aliased to each other.

4. Finally, we combine the information from the preceding steps.

Once the aliasing information has been obtained, it can be combined with the alias-free solutions to interprocedural data-flow problems to produce the full solutions.

The set of *extended formal parameters* of a procedure p, written $ExtFormals(p)$ is the set of all formal parameters visible within p, including those of procedures that p is nested in, that are not rendered invisible by intervening declarations. For example, in Figure 19.25 the extended formal parameter set of procedure n( ) is {m,z,w}.

The modified version of the code to build the binding graph is shown in Figure 19.26 (note that only the routine Bind_Pairs( ) differs from the version in Figure 19.13). The value of passed(p,i,q,x,y) is true if instruction i in procedure p calls procedure q and binds p's extended formal parameter x to q's extended formal parameter y, and false otherwise.

As an example of this process, we use the program in Figure 19.25. We distinguish the global b and the one local to h( ) by subscripting them as b_1 and b_2, respectively, in what follows. Note that to allow totally general naming of variables and parameters, we need to identify the sequence of procedures each variable is nested in; e.g., we might denote the global b by ⟨b,[]⟩, the local b in h( ) by ⟨b,[h]⟩, and the parameter y of t( ) by ⟨y,[h,t]⟩. The example's call and binding graphs are shown in Figure 19.27.

A nonlocal variable can only become aliased to a formal parameter in a procedure in which the nonlocal variable is visible and only by its being passed as an actual argument to that formal parameter. So we define $A(fp)$, where fp is a formal parameter, to be the set of nonlocal variables v (including formal parameters of routines that the declaration of fp is nested in) that fp may be aliased to by a chain of one or more calls that binds v to fp. To compute $A(\ )$, we make two forward passes over the binding graph B, first accumulating bindings that pass nonlocal variables as parameters, and then following binding chains. The algorithm Nonlocal_Aliases( ) that

```
              global a, b
              procedure e( )
    e         begin
    1             call f(1,b)
              end     || e
              procedure f(x,y)
    f         begin
    1             y := h(1,2,x,x)
    2             return g(a,y) + b + y
              end     || f
              procedure g(z,w)
                  local c
                  procedure n(m)
    n             begin
    1                 a := p(z,m)
    2                 return m + a + c
                  end     || n
    g         begin
    1             w := n(c) + h(1,z,w,4)
    2             return h(z,z,a,w) + n(w)
              end     || g
              procedure h(i,j,k,l)
                  local b
                  procedure t(u,v)
    t             begin
    1                 return u + v * p(u,b)
                  end     || t
    h         begin
    1             b := j * l + t(j,k)
    2             return i + t(b,k)
              end     || h
              procedure p(r,s)
    p         begin
    1             b := r * s
              end     || p
```

FIG. 19.25 An example program for interprocedural alias computation.

does this is given in Figure 19.28; the N, R, and E arguments are the sets of nodes, roots, and edges in the binding graph, respectively. The procedures used in the figure are as follows:

1. Shallower(v) is the set of variables declared at nesting levels less than or equal to the nesting level at which v is declared.

2. Formals(p) is the set of formal parameters of procedure p.

3. Nonlocals(p) is the set of variables that are nonlocal to p and that are not formal parameters of any procedure in which p is nested.

```
procedure Build_Binding_Graph(P,N,E,pinsts)
    P: in set of Procedure
    N: out set of Var
    E: out set of (Var × Var)
    pinsts: in Procedure ⟶ integer
begin
    p, q: Procedure
    i, m, n: integer
    oldE: set of (Var × Var)
    N := E := oldE := ∅
    repeat
        oldE := E
        for each p ∈ P do
            for i := 1 to pinsts(p) do
                for each q ∈ callset(p,i) do
                    Bind_Pairs(p,i,q,N,E)
                od
            od
        od
    until E = oldE
    repeat
        oldE := E
        for each e ∈ E do
            for each f ∈ E (f ≠ e) do
                if e@2 = f@1 & e@1 ≠ f@2 then
                    E ∪= {e@1→f@2}
                fi
            od
        od
    until E = oldE
end    || Build_Binding_Graph

procedure Bind_Pairs(p,i,q,N,E)
    p, q: in Procedure
    i: in integer
    N: inout set of Var
    E: inout set of (Var × Var)
begin
    m, n: integer
    e, f: Var × Var
    for each u ∈ ExtFormals(q) do
        for each v ∈ ExtFormals(p) do
            if passed(p,i,q,u,v) then
                N ∪= {u,v}
                E ∪= {v→u}
            fi
        od
    od
end    || Bind_Pairs
```

FIG. 19.26 Algorithm to construct the binding graph B for a program *P*.

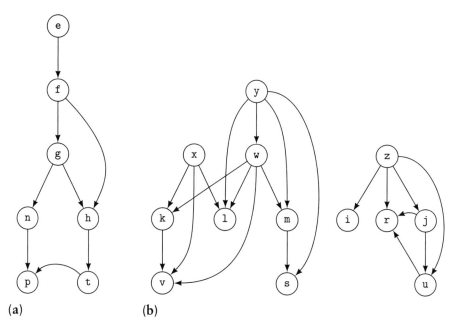

FIG. 19.27 The (a) call and (b) binding graphs for the program in Figure 19.25.

4. ExtFormals(p) is the set of all formal parameters visible within p, including those of procedures that p is nested in that are not shadowed by intervening definitions.

5. Top_Sort(N, R, E) returns a sequence of edges drawn from E that represents a topological sort of the graph with nodes N, roots R, and edges E with the back edges removed.

Note that if we define Envt(p) to be the sequence of procedures that procedure p is nested in, with p as the last member of the sequence, and Vars(p) to be the set of formal parameters and local variables of procedure p, then ExtFormals(p) can be defined by the recurrence

ExtFormals(Envt$(p)\downarrow$1) = Formals(Envt$(p)\downarrow$1)

ExtFormals(Envt$(p)\downarrow i$) = Formals(Envt$(p)\downarrow i$)
    ∪ (ExtFormals(Envt$(p)\downarrow(i-1)$) - Vars(Envt$(p)\downarrow i$))
        for $2 \le i \le $ |Envt(p)|

For our example program, Nonlocal_Aliases( ) first initializes the function A( ) to Ø, then iterates over the calls accumulating nonlocal variables that are aliased to the formal parameters, and finally propagates alias information forward in the binding graph, resulting in the values shown in Table 19.11(a).

Now the set of formal parameters that are aliased to each nonlocal variable can be computed by inverting the function A( ). This is done by the procedure Invert_Nonlocal_Aliases( ) shown in Figure 19.29, which simply sets *ALIAS*( )

```
procedure Nonlocal_Aliases(P,N,R,E,A)
    P: in set of Procedure
    N, R: in set of Var
    E: in set of (Var × Var)
    A: out Var ⟶ set of Var
begin
    v: Var
    e: Var × Var
    p, q: Procedure
    i, j: integer
    oldA: Var ⟶ set of Var
    T: sequence of (Var × Var)
    A := ∅
    for each p ∈ P do
        for i := 1 to pinsts(p) do
            for each q ∈ callset(p,i) do
                for each v ∈ (Nonlocals(q)
                    ∪ (ExtFormals(q) - Formals(q))) do
                    for j := 1 to nparams(q) (v = arg(p,i,j)) do
                        || accumulate nonlocals variable and nonlocal formal
                        || parameters that may be aliases of q( )'s jth parameter
                        A(param(q,j)) ∪= {v}
                    od
                od
            od
        od
    od
    T := Top_Sort(N,R,E)
    repeat
        oldA := A
        for i := 1 to |T| do
            || accumulate nonlocals along edges in binding graph
            A(T↓i@2) ∪= A(T↓i@1) ∩ Shallower(T↓i@1)
        od
    until oldA = A
end     || Nonlocal_Aliases
```

FIG. 19.28 Algorithm for efficiently computing aliases of nonlocal variables using the binding graph B.

to the empty function and then accumulates values from the $A(\ )$ sets. For our example, it results in the values shown in Table 19.11(b).

Formal parameters may become aliased in several ways. For example, two parameters are aliases of each other if the same actual argument is bound to both of them. Also, if a nonlocal variable is passed to a formal parameter of a routine and a variable aliased to the nonlocal variable is passed to another formal parameter, the two formal parameters are aliases of each other. In addition, formal-parameter aliases can be passed through chains of calls, creating more aliased formal parameters.

TABLE 19.11 (a) The A( ) sets computed by Nonlocal_Aliases( ) and (b) the ALIAS( ) sets computed by Invert_Nonlocal_Aliases( ) for our example program in Figure 19.25.

A(i) = {a}	A(j) = {a}	A(k) = {a,b$_1$}
A(l) = {b$_1$}	A(m) = {b$_1$,c}	A(r) = {a}
A(s) = {b$_1$}	A(u) = {a,b$_2$}	A(v) = {a}
A(w) = {b$_1$}	A(x) = ∅	A(y) = {b$_1$}
A(z) = {a}		

(a)

ALIAS(a,e) = ∅	ALIAS(b$_1$,e) = ∅
ALIAS(a,f) = ∅	ALIAS(b$_1$,f) = {y}
ALIAS(a,g) = {z}	ALIAS(b$_1$,g) = {w}
ALIAS(a,h) = {i,j,k}	ALIAS(b$_1$,h) = {k,l}
ALIAS(a,n) = {z}	ALIAS(b$_1$,n) = {m,w}
ALIAS(a,p) = {r}	ALIAS(b$_1$,p) = {∅}
ALIAS(a,t) = {i,j,k,u,v}	ALIAS(b$_1$,t) = {v,l,l}
ALIAS(c,e) = ∅	ALIAS(b$_2$,e) = ∅
ALIAS(c,f) = ∅	ALIAS(b$_2$,f) = ∅
ALIAS(c,g) = ∅	ALIAS(b$_2$,g) = ∅
ALIAS(c,h) = ∅	ALIAS(b$_2$,h) = ∅
ALIAS(c,n) = {m}	ALIAS(b$_2$,n) = {m}
ALIAS(c,p) = {s}	ALIAS(b$_2$,p) = {s}
ALIAS(c,t) = ∅	ALIAS(b$_2$,t) = {u}

(b)

```
Nonlocals, ExtFormals: Procedure ⟶ set of Var

procedure Invert_Nonlocal_Aliases(P,A,ALIAS)
    P: in set of Procedure
    A: in Var ⟶ set of Var
    ALIAS: out (Var × Procedure) ⟶ set of Var
begin
    p: Procedure
    x, v: Var
    ALIAS := ∅
    for each p ∈ P do
        for each v ∈ ExtFormals(p) do
            for each x ∈ A(v) ∩ Nonlocals(p) do
                ALIAS(x,p) ∪= {v}
            od
        od
    od
end    || Invert_Nonlocal_Aliases
```

FIG. 19.29 Algorithm to invert the nonlocal alias function, thus computing the set of nonlocal variables aliased to each formal parameter.

```
procedure Build_Pair_Graph(P,N,E)
   P: in set of Procedure
   N: out set of (Var × Var)
   E: out set of ((Var × Var) × (Var × Var))
begin
   p, q, r: Procedure
   u, v, w, x, y: Var
   k, s: integer
   N := ∅
   E := ∅
   for each p ∈ P do
      for each u,v ∈ ExtFormals(p) do
         N ∪= {⟨u,v⟩}
      od
   od
   for each p ∈ P do
      for k := 1 to pinsts(p) do
         for each q ∈ callset(p,k) do
            for each u,v ∈ ExtFormals(q) do
               for each w,x ∈ ExtFormals(p) do
                  if match(p,q,k,w,u,x,v) then
                     E ∪= {⟨w,x⟩→⟨u,v⟩}
                  elif ∃r ∈ P ∃s ∈ integer ∃w ∈ Var
                     (pair_match(p,u,v,q,s,r,w,x,y)) then
                     E ∪= {⟨u,v⟩→⟨x,y⟩}
                  fi
               od
            od
         od
      od
   od
end    || Build_Pair_Graph
```

FIG. 19.30 Algorithm to build a program's pair binding graph Π.

To model this situation, we use a pairwise analogue of the binding graph called the *pair binding graph* $\Pi = \langle N_\Pi, E_\Pi \rangle$ in which each node is a pair of extended formal parameters of the same procedure and each edge models the binding of one pair to another by a call. Code to build the pair binding graph for a program is shown in Figure 19.30.

The function $\mathtt{match}(p,q,k,w,u,x,v)$ returns true if instruction k in procedure p calls procedure q and passes p's extended formal parameters w and x to q's extended formal parameters u and v, respectively, and false otherwise.

The function $\mathtt{pair\_match}(p,u,v,q,s,r,w,x,y)$ returns true if there are extended formal parameters u and v of p and a call site s in procedure q nested inside q such that, for some procedure r, $\langle q, s \rangle$ calls procedure r and binds u and w to r's extended formal parameters x and y, respectively, and $v \in A(w)$; and false otherwise. If there exist procedures, integers, variables, and call sites satisfying $\mathtt{pair\_match}(p,u,v,q,s,r,w,x,y)$, we add an edge from $\langle u, v \rangle$ to $\langle x, y \rangle$, as shown in Figure 19.31.

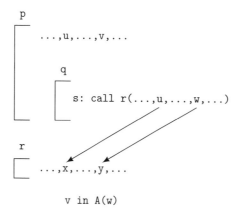

v in A(w)

FIG. 19.31 Schema for adding arcs that satisfy `pair_match( )` to the pair binding graph. Given that procedure p has extended formal parameters u and v, procedure q nested inside p has at call site $\langle q,s \rangle$ a call to procedure r that passes u to formal parameter x of r and w to y, and $v \in A(w)$, we put the edge $\langle u, v \rangle \rightarrow \langle x, y \rangle$ into the pair binding graph Π.

The pair binding graph for our example is shown in Figure 19.32.

To find the pairs of formal parameters that may be aliases of each other, we mark the program's pair binding graph as follows: If a variable is passed to two distinct formal parameters of a routine, then the two formal parameters are aliases of each other, and so the corresponding node in the pair binding graph is marked. Also, if (1) a nonlocal variable is passed to a formal parameter of procedure q, (2) a formal parameter of q's caller is passed to another formal parameter of q, and (3) the caller's formal parameter is an alias of the nonlocal variable, then the two formal parameters of q may be aliases, so that pair is marked. The algorithm is shown in Figure 19.33.

For our example, this results in marking $\langle k, l \rangle$, $\langle l, k \rangle$, $\langle i, j \rangle$, $\langle j, i \rangle$, $\langle r, s \rangle$, $\langle j, k \rangle$, $\langle j, l \rangle$, $\langle i, l \rangle$, $\langle u, v \rangle$, $\langle s, r \rangle$, $\langle k, j \rangle$, $\langle l, j \rangle$, $\langle l, i \rangle$, and $\langle v, u \rangle$. The marking is denoted by the shaded circles in Figure 19.32. Note that $\langle r, s \rangle$ and $\langle s, r \rangle$ are the only nodes marked by the if statement that is identified with an asterisk in Figure 19.33.

Next, the routine `Prop_Marks( )` in Figure 19.34 is used to propagate the marks forward through the pair binding graph to make sure that aliasing of a routine's formal parameters is properly passed along to formal parameters of routines it calls. This is done by maintaining a worklist of nodes in the pair binding graph that are marked. As each node is removed from the worklist, edges are followed from that node and the nodes that are reached are marked and placed on the worklist if they were previously unmarked. For our example, this results in marking no additional pairs.

Next, we compute formal-parameter aliases by combining `A( )` and `ALIAS( )` sets and `Mark( )` information. `Formal_Aliases( )`, the routine that does so, is straightforward and is shown in Figure 19.35. It uses the procedure `Outside_In(P)`, whose value is a sequence that is a topological sort of the nesting order of the procedures that make up P, with the outermost procedure given first. For our example, this results in the alias sets shown in Table 19.12.

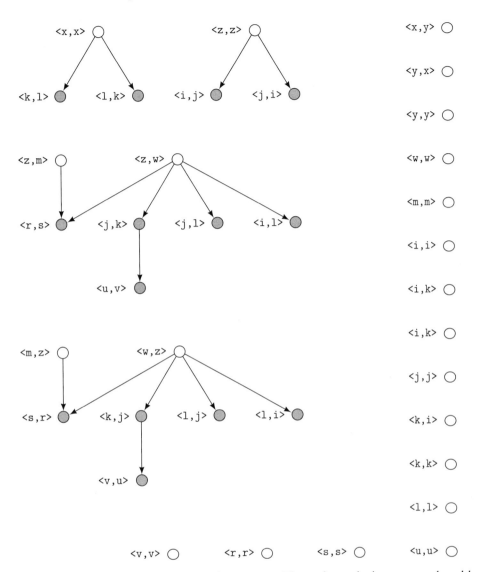

FIG. 19.32   Pair binding graph Π for our example program. The nodes and edges are produced by
Build_Pair_Graph( ). The shaded nodes are marked by Mark_Alias_Pairs( ). No
additional nodes are marked by Prop_Marks( ).

The time bound for this approach to alias computation is $O(n^2 + n \cdot e)$, where n
and e are the numbers of nodes and edges, respectively, in the program's call graph.

To combine aliasing information with the alias-free version of a side-effect
computation, we use the algorithm shown in Figure 19.36, where MOD is used as an
example. In essence, we initialize MOD to DMOD and then add formal-parameter
and nonlocal-variable aliases to it.

```
procedure Mark_Alias_Pairs(P,Mark,ALIAS)
   P: in set of Procedure
   Mark: out (Var × Var) ⟶ boolean
   ALIAS: in (Var × Procedure) ⟶ set of Var
begin
   p, q: Procedure
   i, j, k, l: integer
   v: Var
   Mark := ∅
   for each p ∈ P do
      for i := 1 to pinsts(p) do
         for each q ∈ callset(p,i) do
            for each u,v ∈ ExtFormals(q) (u ≠ v) do
               if ∃w,x ∈ ExtFormals(p)
                  (match(p,q,i,w,u,x,v)) then
                  Mark(u,v) := Mark(v,u) := true
               fi
            od
*           if ∃y ∈ ExtFormals(p) ∃k ∈ integer
               (y = arg(p,i,k)) then
               for each w ∈ Nonlocals(p) do
                  if ∃l ∈ integer (w = arg(p,i,l)
                     & y ∈ ALIAS(w,p)) then
                     Mark(param(q,k),param(q,l)) := true
                     Mark(param(q,l),param(q,k)) := true
                  fi
               od
            fi
         od
      od
   od
end    || Mark_Alias_Pairs
```

FIG. 19.33 Algorithm to mark parameter pairs in a program's pair binding graph.

```
procedure Prop_Marks(N,E,Mark)
   N: in set of (Var × Var)
   E: in set of ((Var × Var) × (Var × Var))
   Mark: inout (Var × Var) ⟶ boolean
begin
   n: Var × Var
   f: (Var × Var) × (Var × Var)
   WL := ∅: set of (Var × Var)
   for each n ∈ N do
      if Mark(n@1,n@2) then
         WL ∪= {n}
      fi
   od
```

FIG. 19.34 Algorithm to propagate marking of parameter pairs in a program's pair binding graph.

```
      while WL ≠ Ø do
         n := ◆WL; WL -= {n}
         for each f ∈ E (f@1 = n) do
            if !Mark(f@2@1,f@2@2) then
                Mark(f@2@1,f@2@2) := true
                WL ∪= {f@2}
            fi
         od
      od
   end    || Prop_Marks
```

FIG. 19.34 *(continued)*

```
   procedure Formal_Aliases(P,Mark,A,ALIAS)
      P: in set of Procedure
      Mark: in (Var × Var) ⟶ boolean
      A: in Var ⟶ set of Var
      ALIAS: inout (Var × Procedure) ⟶ set of Var
   begin
      OI: sequence of Procedure
      p: Procedure
      i: integer
      v: Var
      OI := Outside_In(P)
      for i := 1 to |OI| do
         p := OI↓i
         for j := 1 to nparams(p) do
            ALIAS(param(p,j),p) := A(param(p,j))
            for each v ∈ ExtFormals(p) do
               if param(p,j) ≠ v & Mark(param(p,j),v) then
                   ALIAS(param(p,j),p) ∪= {v}
                   ALIAS(v,p) ∪= {param(p,j)}
               fi
            od
         od
      od
   end    || Formal_Aliases
```

FIG. 19.35 Algorithm to compute formal-parameter alias information from Mark( ), A( ), and ALIAS( ).

TABLE 19.12 Formal-parameter alias sets computed by Formal_Aliases( ) for our example program in Figure 19.25.

ALIAS(x,f) = Ø	ALIAS(y,f) = {b_1}
ALIAS(z,g) = {a}	ALIAS(w,g) = {b_1}
ALIAS(i,h) = {a,j,k,l}	ALIAS(j,h) = {a,i,k,l}
ALIAS(k,h) = {a,b_1,i,j,l}	ALIAS(l,h) = {b_1,i,j,k}
ALIAS(m,n) = {b_1,c}	ALIAS(u,t) = {a,b_2,v}
ALIAS(v,t) = {a,u}	ALIAS(r,p) = {a,s}
ALIAS(s,p) = {b_1,r}	

```
procedure MOD_with_Aliases(P,ALIAS,DMOD,MOD)
    P: in set of Procedure
    ALIAS: in (Var × Procedure) ⟶ set of Var
    DMOD: in (Procedure × integer) ⟶ set of Var
    MOD: out (Procedure × integer) ⟶ set of Var
begin
    p, q: Procedure
    i, j: integer
    v: Var
    for each p ∈ P do
        for i := 1 to pinsts(p) do
            for each q ∈ callset(p,i) do
                MOD(p,i) := DMOD(p,i)
                for each v ∈ Formals(p) do
                    if v ∈ DMOD(p,i) then
                        MOD(p,i) ∪= ALIAS(v,p)
                    fi
                od
            od
            for each v ∈ Nonlocals(p) ∩ DMOD(p,i) do
                MOD(p,i) ∪= ALIAS(v,p)
            od
        od
    od
end     || MOD_with_Aliases
```

FIG. 19.36 Algorithm to combine aliasing information with alias-free side-effect information.

19.4.2 Interprocedural Alias Analysis for Languages with Call by Value and Pointers

To do interprocedural alias analysis for a language such as C with call by value and pointers, we expand on the intraprocedural approach discussed in Sections 10.2 and 10.3. In particular, we initialize the $Ovr(\ )$ and $Ptr(\ )$ functions on entry to a procedure from its call sites and set them on return to the call sites from the information at the return point of the called procedure. We can either do the analysis individually for each call site or we can do it for all calls to a particular routine at once.

First, assume that we are doing one call site at a time. Let P and P' be the program points immediately preceding and following a call site, respectively, and let entry+ and return- be the program points following the entry point of a routine and preceding the return, respectively, as shown in Figure 19.37. Then we initialize the functions as follows for a nonlocal variable x:

$$Ovr(\text{entry+}, x) = Ovr(P, x)$$

$$Ptr(\text{entry+}, x) = Ptr(P, x)$$

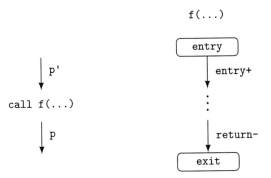

FIG. 19.37 Call site, entry, and return of a C routine.

```
int *p, *q;
int *f(int *q)
{   p = q;
    return p;
}

int main( )
{   int a, *r;
    r = f(&a);
}
```

FIG. 19.38 An example C program for interprocedural alias analysis.

and as follows for an actual argument y that is passed to formal parameter x:

$$Ovr(\text{entry+}, x) = Ovr(P, y)$$

$$Ptr(\text{entry+}, x) = Ptr(P, y)$$

For the return, we do the reverse for a nonlocal variable x, namely,

$$Ovr(P', x) = Ovr(\text{return-}, x)$$

$$Ptr(P', x) = Ptr(\text{return-}, x)$$

For example, consider the C code in Figure 19.38. Computation of the $Ptr()$ function results in

$$Ptr(P, p) = star(a)$$

$$Ptr(P, q) = star(a)$$

$$Ptr(P, r) = star(a)$$

where P denotes the program point in main( ) immediately following the return from f( ).

To do all call sites $P_1, \ldots, P_k$ for a particular routine at once, we set

$$Ovr(\texttt{entry+}, x) = \bigcup_{i=1}^{k} Ovr(P_i, x)$$

$$Ptr(\texttt{entry+}, x) = \bigcup_{i=1}^{k} Ptr(P_i, x)$$

for a nonlocal variable x and the corresponding adaptations of the equations above for parameter passing and for nonlocal variables at return points.

19.5   Interprocedural Optimizations

Given the tools for interprocedural control-flow, data-flow, and alias analysis discussed in the preceding sections, several kinds of optimization become possible, as follows:

1. We can use the information gathered by interprocedural analysis to drive procedure integration.

2. We can use the information provided by site-independent constant-propagation analysis to optimize the bodies of procedures that are found to be always called with the same one or more constant parameters.

3. We can use the information provided by site-specific constant-propagation analysis to clone copies of a procedure body and to optimize them for specific call sites.

4. We can use the side-effect information to tailor the calling conventions for a specific call site to optimize caller versus callee register saving.

5. We can optimize call-by-value parameter passing of large arguments that are not modified to be passed by reference.

6. Finally, and frequently most important, we can use interprocedural data-flow information to improve intraprocedural data-flow information for procedure entries and exits and for calls and returns.

Interprocedural analysis can provide much of the information needed to guide procedure integration, such as the number of call sites and information about constant-valued parameters. See Section 15.2 for the details.

How to optimize based on constant parameters should be obvious. In the intermediate-code form of the procedure's body, we replace the constant-valued parameters with their values and we perform global optimization, as discussed in Chapters 12 through 18, on the result. We also tailor the calling and entry code for the procedure to not pass or receive the constant parameters. We do the replacement in the intermediate code, rather than in the source code, because a future modification to the source program may invalidate the information on which the optimization is based.

Optimizing based on parameters being constant at one or more call sites (called *procedure specialization* or *cloning*) is almost as easy. For each set of call sites that call the same procedure and that pass the same constant values to one or more of its parameters, we clone a copy of the intermediate code of the body of the procedure and then perform the same optimizations as described in the preceding paragraph on the clone and its call sites.

One optimization that is frequently enabled by these two cases is the elimination of unnecessary bounds checking within procedures. Many routines are written, for example, to manipulate arrays of arbitrary size, but are used in particular programs only on arrays whose sizes are determined in the main program. Propagating that information to the general-case routines allows them to be tailored to the particular application and may result in nontrivial speedup or make it easier to perform other optimizations. For example, propagating the fact that in Figure 15.5 saxpy( ) is called only with incx = incy = 1 allows it to be reduced to the code shown in Figure 19.39. Note that it also makes integrating the body of saxpy( ) into sgefa( ) easier.

```
        subroutine sgefa(a,lda,n,ipvt,info)
        integer lda,n,ipvt(1),info
        real a(lda,1)
        real t
        integer isamax,j,k,kp1,l,nm1
            . . .
            do 30 j = kp1, n
                t = a(l,j)
                if (l .eq. k) go to 20
                    a(l,j) = a(k,j)
                    a(k,j) = t
20              continue
                call saxpy_11(n-k,t,a(k+1,k),a(k+1,j))
30          continue
            . . .
        subroutine saxpy_11(n,da,dx,dy)
        real dx(1),dy(1),da
        integer i,ix,iy,m,mp1,n
        if (n .le. 0) return
        if (da .eq. ZERO) return
        do 30 i = 1,n
            dy(i) = dy(i) + da*dx(i)
30 continue
        return
        end
```

FIG. 19.39 The Linpack routine saxpy( ) and its calling context in sgefa( ) after determining that incx = incy = 1 and propagating that information into the body of saxpy( ).

Note also that such constants are sometimes conveyed to procedures by global variables rather than by parameters and that this case is worth analyzing and using as well.

Optimizing call-by-value parameter passing to call by reference for large objects, such as arrays and records, depends on determining for such a parameter a of a procedure p whether $a \in MOD(p)$. If it is not, then p and its descendants in the call graph do not modify a, so it is safe to modify the way it is passed to call by reference. Doing so involves changing the code that accesses the actual argument and formal parameter to use its address instead of its value. Also, if there is a point in the call graph at which we know that the argument is not modified (perhaps from an interface specification), but we don't have the code available to change the parameter passing, we must convert the parameter passing back to call by value at that point.

Finally, many of the intraprocedural optimizations discussed in Chapters 12 through 18 can be improved by the use of precise, conservative interprocedural data-flow information. It can both improve optimization around call sites by using information about the called procedure and improve optimization within procedures by using information about parameters and global variables. For example, loop-invariant code motion (see Section 13.2) can be improved when applied to a loop that contains a call if it can be determined that the call has no side effects on expressions that are determined to be loop-invariant by intraprocedural means.

To apply interprocedural data-flow information to global (intraprocedural) data-flow analysis, we do the interprocedural analysis first and then use its results to initialize the global data-flow information for procedure entries and exits and to turn calls from opaque objects into operations for which the effects on the data-flow information are understood. In some cases, significant benefit can be obtained from iterating the computation of interprocedural followed by intraprocedural data-flow information, but this is usually not worth the large increase in compilation time that it costs, unless it can be hidden from the user by being done as a background activity while the programmer is occupied with other tasks.

For example, global constant propagation (see Section 12.6) can be made to take account of interprocedural constant propagation by initializing the constant information for a procedure's entry point with the information provided by interprocedural analysis.

Another overall approach to optimization that has been explored by Srivastava and Wall [SriW93] is one that, as an early step in the linking process, takes as its input and produces as its output a series of object modules. In its prototype version, it transforms each object module into a register-transfer-language (RTL) representation, does interprocedural control-flow and live variables analyses, and then does interprocedural dead-code elimination and global and interprocedural loop-invariant code motion. Finally, it does global copy propagation, global common-subexpression elimination, and interprocedural dead-store elimination, followed by turning the RTL back into object modules to be linked. This approach provides surprisingly good results, especially considering that it depends on no information produced by earlier phases of compilation except, of course, the object code itself.

19.6   Interprocedural Register Allocation

Another interprocedural optimization that can be a source of significant performance improvement is interprocedural register allocation. In this section, we describe one approach, developed by Wall [Wall86], in detail and outline three others. The approaches differ in that Wall's is done at link time, while the others are done during compilation.

19.6.1   Interprocedural Register Allocation at Link Time

Wall devised an approach to doing interprocedural register allocation at link time that combines two observations that enable the interprocedural allocation and the optional use of graph coloring for allocation within procedure bodies. We provide here an overview of the approach and indications of some refinements that make it practical.

The first of the two motivating observations is that if the generated code is complete, in the sense that it does not require register allocation to run correctly, then annotations to drive optional register allocation at link time can be encoded like relocation information in an object module and can either be used to drive the modification of the code, or be ignored.

The second observation is that if two paths in a program's call graph do not intersect, then the same registers can be freely allocated in the procedures in each path. The latter observation can be illustrated by considering the call graph in Figure 19.40, where each box represents a procedure and the arrows represent calls.

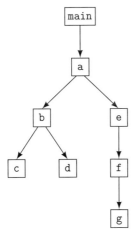

FIG. 19.40   An example call graph for interprocedural register allocation.

```
r1 ← y          rmv.y
r2 ← z          rmv.z                    r2 ← z
r3 ← r1 + r2    op1.y op2.z res.x        r14 ← r6 + r2
x ← r3          rmv.x

(a)                                      (b)
```

FIG. 19.41   (a) Example LIR code sequence and associated annotations, and (b) the result of allocating x and y to registers.

```
r1 ← a          lod.a
r2 ← r1 + 1     res.a
a ← r2          sto.a
r3 ← b          rmv.b
r4 ← r2 + r3    op2.b
y ← r4          sto.x
x ← r4          rmv.x
```

FIG. 19.42   Annotated LIR code for the C statement x = y = a++ - b.

Neither of procedures c and d calls the other, so they can use the same registers without interfering with each other. Similarly, the chain that consists of e, f, and g does not interfere with the subtree consisting of b, c, and d, so the same registers may be used in the chain and in the tree without causing any conflicts. The approach to register allocation described here is based on this second observation combined with some (independently chosen) method of intraprocedural register allocation.

The annotations that guide register allocation consist of pairs, each of whose first element is one of six operators, namely, rmv, op1, op2, res, lod, and sto, and whose second element is a reference to one of the operands of the instruction with which it is associated.

As a first example of the annotations, consider the LIR code in Figure 19.41(a), where x, y, and z represent storage locations. The meaning of rmv.v is that if variable v is allocated to a register at link time, then this instruction should be removed. The meaning of op1.v, op2.v, and res.v is that if v is allocated to a register, then the corresponding position in the instruction should be replaced by the number of the register to which it is allocated. Thus, if we were to succeed in allocating x and y to registers r6 and r14, respectively, the code sequence would become the one shown in Figure 19.41(b). The lod operator is used for a variable that is loaded and that will be modified in this basic block before the loaded value is last used, and the sto operator is used for values that will be used after the current use. Thus, for example, the C statement

        x = y = a++ - b

would result in the annotated code shown in Figure 19.42. If we allocate a to a register, we need to replace the first instruction with a register-to-register copy; if we allocate y to a register, we need to replace the store to y with another copy.

Of course, if we remove instructions, we also need to fix addresses and offsets that refer to the instruction sequence, but the necessary information to do this is already available in the instructions themselves and their relocation information.

Wall's approach to generating the annotations is to produce triples as the intermediate code (see Section 4.9.1) and then, in a backward pass over each basic block, to mark

1. the operands v that may be used again after their associated variables are stored to (i.e., those that require lod.v, rather than rmv.v),

2. the operands that are stored to and that may be used again (those that require sto.v, rather than rmv.v), and

3. the remaining operands, which can be annotated with op1.v, op2.v, res.v, or rmv.v.

He then generates the object module and records a list of the procedures in the module, and for each procedure, a list of its local variables, the variables it references, and the procedures it calls, along with estimates (or profiling data) of the number of times each variable is referenced and the number of calls to each procedure.

The interprocedural register allocator is invoked near the beginning of the linking process, once it has been determined which modules need to be linked. It builds a call graph with a single node for each procedure and collects the usage information for procedures and variables. The call graph is required to be a DAG; this is one of the areas where special handling is required, because it may not represent the program accurately. In particular, recursive calls and indirect calls through procedure-valued variables cannot be handled in the same way as other calls. Recursive calls would make the call graph not be a DAG if they were represented accurately, and they would reuse the same registers as already active calls to the same routine if they had registers allocated in the same manner as other routines. Similarly, calls through a procedure-valued variable might be to any of several possible targets, which may not even be knowable accurately at link time.

After estimating the total number of calls to each routine, the allocator traverses the DAG in reverse depth-first order, forming groups of variables that will each be assigned to a register, if possible. It groups global variables into singletons and forms groups of local variables that cannot be simultaneously live, associating a reference frequency with each. The allocator then sorts the groups by frequency and, assuming that there are R registers available for allocation, it assigns the top R groups to registers (or, alternatively, it can use a graph-coloring allocator within a procedure body). Finally, it rewrites the object code, taking the allocation information and annotations into account.

Several issues require special handling or can be improved by specific techniques, as follows:

1. Initialized globals that are allocated to registers need to have load instructions inserted in the code to set their values.

2. Recursive and indirect calls could either use a standard calling sequence or, for recursive calls, could use a special calling sequence that saves and restores exactly those registers that need to be.

3. Passing arguments in registers instead of in the memory stack can be accommodated by adding annotations of the form par.*proc.v* to the instructions that store the parameters' values in the run-time stack, to indicate the procedure *proc* being called and the variable *v* being passed.

4. Profiling can be used to replace the estimated reference frequencies with numbers that more directly reflect the actual execution characteristics of the program, and thus can improve the register allocation.

5. Graph coloring can be used to improve the liveness information that is used in allotting variables to groups. This allows some local variables to be combined into allocation groups more effectively.

19.6.2   Compile-Time Interprocedural Register Allocation

Three approaches to interprocedural register allocation at compile time have been discussed in the literature and incorporated into compilers.

One, developed by Santhanam and Odnert [SanO90], extends register allocation by graph coloring (see Section 16.3) by doing an interprocedural live variables computation to determine webs for global variables. It partitions the call graph into webs, one for each global variable, and allocates the ones with high usage frequencies to registers, leaving the remaining registers for intraprocedural allocation.

Another method, developed by Chow [Chow88], has been implemented as an extension to register allocation by priority-based graph coloring (see Section 16.4). Its primary goal is to minimize the overhead of register saving and restoring for procedure calls and it does so by a combination of shrink wrapping (described in Section 15.4.2) and a postorder traversal of the call graph that takes register usage by called procedures into account at call sites. Since the caller and callee are both visible for most calls, this method can pass a parameter in any register. It assumes that all registers are caller-saved and delays register saving and restoring to as far up the call graph as possible.

The third approach, developed by Steenkiste and Hennessy [SteH89], allocates registers by a method similar to Wall's but at compile time. It is designed for languages like LISP in which programs typically consist of many small procedures, making interprocedural register allocation particularly important. It does a depth-first traversal of the call graph, insofar as it is known, and allocates registers from the bottom up using the principle that procedures in different subtrees of the call graph can share the same registers, and using at each call site the available information about the register usage of the callee. This approach is likely to run out of registers at some point in the process, so the allocator simply switches to a standard intraprocedural allocator with saves on entry and restores on exit; the same method is used for recursive calls.

19.7   Aggregation of Global References

Another interprocedural optimization that can be applied during linking is aggregation of global references. Since RISC architectures lack a way to specify a 32-bit address in a single instruction, it often takes two instructions to reference a datum at an arbitrary address, e.g., a global variable.[8] *Aggregation of global references* can provide a way to significantly reduce this overhead by amortizing it over multiple references. For CISCs, this allows shorter offsets to be used and so reduces the size of the object code.

The technique is simple—it essentially requires collecting the global data into an area that can be referenced by short offsets from a value stored in a register. To perform the aggregation, we must reserve a register (or possibly more than one) during compilation that is generally referred to as the *global pointer* or gp (see Section 5.7). We scan the complete object module, looking for the pattern of instructions that represents an access to a global variable. For a 32-bit RISC system, this involves a lui for MIPS, a sethi for SPARC, and so on, followed by an instruction that does a load or store using the register set by the lui, sethi, etc. We collect the data items that are loaded or stored (possibly with initializations) and we modify the addresses that are used in the loads and stores to refer to offsets from the global pointer. In the process, we eliminate the additional instructions that compute the high-order parts of the addresses and we rewrite the remaining instructions as necessary to fix up branch offsets and any other things that may have been changed by the instruction removal. The process for CISCs is similar.

One refinement to global-reference aggregation is to sort the collected global data by size, smallest first, so as to maximize the number of items that can be referenced from the global pointer(s).

19.8   Other Issues in Interprocedural Program Management

Compilation in a programming environment that manages interprocedural relationships (often called "programming in the large") leads to a series of issues in optimization, as discussed above, as well as in other areas. While none of the latter are particularly difficult, they do require attention. Some of them have been discussed in the literature, while others have only been addressed in experimental or practical programming environments. Some of the more important ones are as follows:

1. name scoping: determining which modules are affected by changing the name of a global variable and what effects the change has on them, such as requiring recompilation;

---

8. The problem is more severe for 64-bit RISC architectures, for which four or five instructions may be required for the same task.

2. recompilation: determining when a change to a module requires recompilation and the minimal set of modules that need to be recompiled (see [CooK86]); and

3. linkage between routines in the same module (or library) and linkage with shared objects: determining when a shared object has been recompiled and what effects it has on modules that use it; we discuss some aspects of this issue in Section 5.7.

Hall provides an exploration of some of these topics and others in her Ph.D. thesis [Hall91].

19.9   Wrap-Up

In this chapter, we have discussed interprocedural control-flow, data-flow, and alias analyses and applications of interprocedural information to both global and interprocedural optimization. We began with the studies by Richardson and Ganapathi that suggest that interprocedural analysis may not be worth the effort, and then we concentrated on the needed analytic tools and on areas where it generally is worthwhile.

We have seen that constructing the call graph of a program is an easy exercise if a whole program in a relatively unsophisticated language (e.g., Fortran) is presented at once, somewhat harder with separate compilation, and *PSPACE*-hard for programs with both procedure-valued variables and recursion, such as PL/I or C.

We have distinguished may and must information, and flow-sensitive and flow-insensitive information, and have seen that the flow-sensitive and must information may be very expensive to compute precisely, being generally *NP*- or co-*NP*-complete. Thus, we have concentrated on flow-insensitive may data-flow problems, such as *MOD*, and some of the less expensive flow-insensitive must problems, such as interprocedural constant propagation, that are useful in tailoring procedures to take account of constant-valued parameters and guiding procedure integration.

We have also discussed several varieties of interprocedural optimization, concentrating on interprocedural register allocation and aggregation of global references, both of which are performed at link time. Srivastava and Wall's work has shown that it is quite possible that many of the standard optimizations may be performed at link time as well.

Among the interprocedural optimizations, for most programs, interprocedural register allocation and constant propagation are the more important and aggregation of global references is less so. However, much of the benefit of interprocedural analysis is its contribution to improving the quality of the intraprocedural optimizations by narrowing the scope of possible effects of called procedures.

Finally, we have suggested that interprocedural optimization is most appropriate in a programming environment that manages "programming in the large" issues—such as scoping, recompilation, and shared-object linkage—automatically.

We place the interprocedural optimizations in the order for performing optimizations as shown in Figure 19.43. We add interprocedural constant propagation

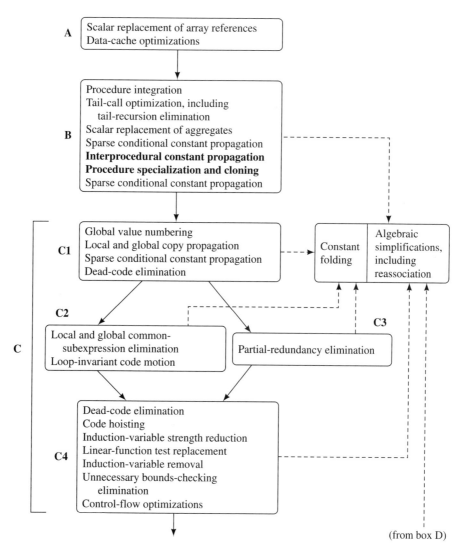

FIG. 19.43 Order of optimizations, with interprocedural optimizations shown in **bold** type. *(continued)*

(preceded by an intraprocedural pass of the same optimization) and procedure specialization and cloning to block B. Clearly, we do the subsequent pass of sparse conditional constant propagation only if interprocedural constant propagation has produced useful results.

We place interprocedural register allocation and global-reference aggregation in block E. They are best done on the load module, when the code of all (statically available) procedures is present to be worked on.

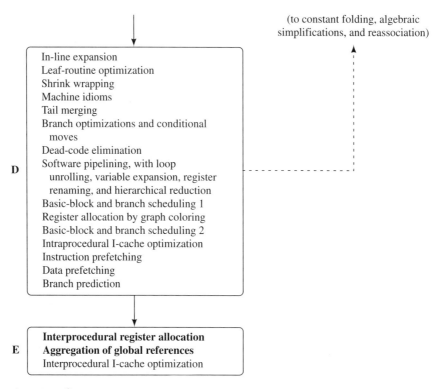

(to constant folding, algebraic
simplifications, and reassociation)

D

In-line expansion
Leaf-routine optimization
Shrink wrapping
Machine idioms
Tail merging
Branch optimizations and conditional
   moves
Dead-code elimination
Software pipelining, with loop
   unrolling, variable expansion, register
   renaming, and hierarchical reduction
Basic-block and branch scheduling 1
Register allocation by graph coloring
Basic-block and branch scheduling 2
Intraprocedural I-cache optimization
Instruction prefetching
Data prefetching
Branch prediction

E

Interprocedural register allocation
Aggregation of global references
Interprocedural I-cache optimization

FIG. 19.43 *(continued)*

19.10   Further Reading

Richardson and Ganapathi's studies of the effectiveness of interprocedural optimization are in [RicG89a], [RicG89b], and [Rich91]. The evidence that interprocedural
optimization may be more useful for parallelizing compilers is found in [AllC86]
and [Call88].

Weihl's proof that constructing the call graph of a recursive program with
procedure variables is *PSPACE*-hard is found in [Weih80]. Some of the harder
issues in computing procedural side effects are discussed in [Weih80], while others
are addressed only in implemented systems, such as ParaFrase [Kuck74] and Para-
Scope [CooH93].

Cooper and Kennedy's original approach to computing flow-insensitive side
effects is [CooK84]. However, that approach had a significant flaw, as noted in
[CooK88a], in that it asserted that the global-variable and formal-parameter subproblems could be solved independently. In fact, the formal-parameter problem must

be solved before dealing with nonlocal variables, an approach that is presented in [CooK88b]. Myers's approach to computing flow-sensitive side effects is described in [Myer81] and Callahan's approach is in [Call88].

Callahan, Cooper, Kennedy, and Torczon's method for performing interprocedural constant propagation is in [CalC86]. Grove and Torczon's discussion of jump and return-jump functions, their computational costs, and the information they provide is in [GroT93].

Cooper and Kennedy's approach to interprocedural alias analysis is found in [CooK89]. A more powerful approach is described in [Deut94].

Wall's approach to interprocedural register allocation at link time is described in [Wall86]. The approaches described for doing interprocedural register allocation during compilation were developed by Santhanam and Odnert [SanO90], Chow [Chow88], and Steenkiste and Hennessy [SteH89].

Aggregation of global references is discussed in [HimC87], [Hime91], and [SriW94]. [SriW94] discusses, among other things, the extension of this technique to 64-bit RISC architectures.

Srivastava and Wall's work on link-time optimization is presented in [SriW93].

Some of the issues in interprocedural program management or "programming in the large" are discussed in the literature, e.g., Cooper, Kennedy, and Torczon's paper [CooK86] and Hall's [Hall91], while others are addressed only in implemented systems, such as ParaFrase and ParaScope.

19.11   Exercises

19.1 (a) Write a program that includes at least five distinct procedures with calls among them and that includes at least one recursive call. (b) Show the steps of executing the procedure `Build_Call_Graph( )` in Figure 19.3 for your example.

RSCH 19.2 The complexity of computing *GMOD* by the procedures `Compute_GMOD( )` and `GMOD_Search( )` in Figure 19.18 can be reduced by a factor of d (the depth of procedure nesting in the program) by applying the observation that `LowLink(p)` for iteration i is less than or equal to `LowLink(p)` for iteration $i + 1$. Write the resulting code for the two procedures.

19.3 (a) Adapt the approach to computing *DMOD* given in Section 19.2.1 to computing *DREF* and (b) apply it to the program in Figure 19.10.

19.4 (a) Formulate an ICAN algorithm to do call-site-specific interprocedural constant-propagation analysis using both jump and return-jump functions and (b) apply it to the program in Figure 19.44 with `halt( )` defined as a routine that terminates execution of the program.

19.5 (a) Construct a C program with at least three routines and at least one global variable and (b) perform site-specific alias analysis on it as described in Section 19.4.2.

```
            procedure main( )
main        begin
1               read(t)
2               call f(t)
3               call f(2)
            end
            procedure f(b)
f           begin
1               print(g(b,1))
            end
            procedure g(x,y)
g           begin
1               if y > 0 then
2                   call h(x,y,1)
3                   x := 2
4               else
5                   call h(3,y,1)
6                   halt( )
7               fi
            end
            procedure h(u,v,w)
h           begin
1               if u > w then
2                   call g(v,-1)
3               else
4                   return w + 1
5               fi
            end
```

FIG. 19.44 Example program on which to run site-specific interprocedural constant propagation.

19.6 Write an ICAN routine that takes a LIR procedure body and annotates its instructions with register-allocation annotations of the sort discussed in Section 19.6.1.

CHAPTER 20

Optimization for the Memory Hierarchy

This chapter concerns code optimization techniques that can be used to take best advantage of the memory hierarchy, particularly data and instruction caches, and includes a way to improve register allocation for array elements. From the very beginning of the design of computers, almost all systems have distinguished between main memory and registers. Main memory has been larger and slower to fetch from and store to than the register set and, in many systems, operations other than loads and stores have required at least one operand, if not all, to be in a register. In RISC systems, of course, this approach has been taken to its extreme, requiring that all operations other than loads and stores be performed on operands in registers (or immediates) and that they place their results in registers.

Over time, the difference between the basic processor cycle and the time needed to access main memory has increased to the point where it would now be a source of significant performance degradation if all loads and stores were required to run at the speed of main memory. And the disparity is getting worse: main memory speeds are increasing at 10% to 20% a year, while processor speeds are achieving increases of as much as 50% a year. To remedy this, cache memories, or simply caches, have been designed to fit between the registers and main memory to reduce the speed mismatch. They duplicate selected portions of main memory, usually on demand, in a way determined by the hardware or a combination of hardware and software. A load, store, or instruction fetch directed to an address represented in a cache is satisfied by the cache rather than by main memory (or, in the case of a store, possibly in parallel with memory) and with a result latency that is ideally not more than two processor cycles. For systems with exposed or partially exposed pipelines (e.g., RISCs and advanced implementations of the Intel 386 architecture family), loads and branches often require two cycles to complete, but the second cycle is usually available to execute another instruction (in the case of a load, the instruction needs to be one that does not use the quantity being loaded).

Caches depend on the spatial and temporal locality properties of programs for their effectiveness. If a program executes a loop repeatedly, then, ideally, the first iteration brings the code for it into the cache and subsequent iterations execute it from the cache, rather than requiring it to be reloaded from memory each time. Thus, the first iteration may incur overhead for fetching the instructions into the cache, but subsequent iterations generally need not. Similarly, if a block of data is used repeatedly, it is ideally fetched into the cache and accessed from there, again incurring the overhead of reading it from main memory only on its first use. On the other hand, if the code and data interfere in the cache, i.e., if they occupy some of the same cache locations, or if the data interferes with itself by having sections mapped to the same cache blocks, significant performance degradation may result. At the worst, loads, stores, and instruction fetches are no faster than accessing main memory.

A system may have separate *data* and *instruction caches* (also called *D-caches* and *I-caches,* respectively) or it may have a *combined* or *unified cache* that holds both data and instructions. Also, systems with paging invariably include another kind of cache, namely, a *translation-lookaside buffer,* or TLB, that is used to cache information about the translation of virtual memory addresses to physical addresses and vice versa.

This chapter begins with a section of anecdotes that graphically describe the impact and possibilities of cache usage and optimization. This is followed by a series of sections that describe instruction prefetching and intra- and interprocedural approaches to instruction-cache optimization. Next comes a section on taking advantage of register allocation for array elements, followed by a series of sections that give an introduction to and overview of data-cache optimization. Finally, we discuss the interaction of scalar and memory-oriented optimizations and the integration of memory-related optimizations into the structure of an aggressive optimizing compiler.

20.1   Impact of Data and Instruction Caches

Bell reports on the effect of tuning numerically intensive Fortran and C programs by hand to take better advantage of the IBM RS/6000's pipelines and caches. He examines how performance varies with the *stride* or sequential difference in indexes with which arrays are accessed. With 64-byte blocks in the D-cache, eight double-precision floating-point values fit into a block, so D-cache performance is directly tied to the strides used. In particular, his data show that performance decreases as the logarithm of the increase of the stride for stride values ≤ 32. For strides larger than 32, TLB misses begin to dominate the performance degradation—when the stride is 4,096 or greater, there is a TLB miss for every memory reference, resulting in a performance of less than 3% of the maximum possible.

Thus, arranging arrays in memory so that they can be accessed with the smallest possible strides is generally key to achieving high data-cache performance. One way to achieve this for code that will use an array several times is to copy the items that will be used to consecutive locations in another array, so that the data can be

```
do i = 1,N                              do i = 1,N
  do j = 1,N                              do j = 1,N
    do k = 1,N                              do k = 1,N
      C(i,j) = C(i,j)                         C(i,j) = C(i,j)
        + A(i,k) * B(k,j)                       + A(k,i) * B(k,j)
    enddo                                   enddo
  enddo                                   enddo
enddo                                   enddo
```

(a) MM   (b) MMT

```
do j = 1,N,t                            do j = 1,N,t
  do k = 1,N,t                            do k = 1,N,t
    do i = 1,N                              do i = 1,N
      do jj = j,min(j+t-1,n)                  do jj = j,min(j+t-1,n)
        do kk = k,min(k+t-1,n)                  do kk = k,min(k+t-1,n)
          C(i,j) = C(i,j)                         C(i,j) = C(i,j)
            + A(i,k) * B(k,j)                       + A(k,i) * B(k,j)
        enddo                                   enddo
      enddo                                   enddo
    enddo                                   enddo
  enddo                                   enddo
enddo                                   enddo
```

(c) MMB   (d) MMBT

FIG. 20.1 Four versions of matrix multiplication in Fortran: (a) MM, the usual form; (b) MMT, with A transposed; (c) MMB, with the j and k loops tiled; and (d) MMBT, with both transposing and tiling.

accessed with stride one, and then to copy the data back if the entries have been changed in the process.

As an example of the potential impact of D-cache optimization, consider the four versions of double-precision matrix multiplication in Fortran described by Bell. The four versions (shown in Figure 20.1) are as follows:

1. MM: the standard textbook triply nested loop to multiply A by B;

2. MMT: MM with A transposed in memory;

3. MMB: the result of tiling (see Section 20.4.3) all three loops with tiles of size N; and

4. MMBT: the result of combining tiling and transposition of A.

Bell reports measured performance numbers for each of these versions with $N = 50$ on an IBM RS/6000 Model 530. The performance of the original version varies with the organization and size of the matrices by a factor of over 14, while tiling and transposing produce performance that is nearly maximal and that is even across the entire range of sizes. The intermediate versions perform nearly as well.

As examples of the potential effect of I-caches on performance, we offer two anecdotes. The first concerns compiling Linpack for a system with 32-byte cache blocks and a processor capable of fetching four 4-byte instructions per cycle and issuing three. The first instruction of the saxpy loop that is the heart of the program turns out to fall at the end of a cache block, so the instruction buffer[1] can fetch only that one useful instruction, and only it is executed in the first cycle of the loop body's execution; this pattern, of course, continues to be the case in every iteration of the loop.

The second concerns the SPEC gcc benchmark, which frequently encounters a relatively high percentage of stall cycles (about 10%) due to I-cache misses, if it is not optimized for I-cache usage. The primary issue is cache capacity—gcc has a large working set—but this can be improved by using the methods discussed below that separate frequently executed code from rarely executed code within each procedure body.

20.2   Instruction-Cache Optimization

The following sections describe several approaches to improving instruction-cache hit rates. Two of the approaches are interprocedural, one is intraprocedural, and the other three have both intra- and interprocedural aspects. All attempt to rearrange code so as to reduce the size of the working set and reduce conflicts.

20.2.1   Using Hardware Assists: Instruction Prefetching

In many implementations of a variety of architectures, the hardware provides sequential prefetching of code and, in some cases, the possibility of fetching from the branch-taken path in addition to the fall-through path.

Some of the newer 64-bit RISCs, such as SPARC-V9 and Alpha, provide software support for instruction prefetching. This allows the programmer or compiler the opportunity to provide prefetching hints to a system's I-cache and instruction-fetch unit, by indicating that a block or group of blocks is likely to be needed soon, so it should be fetched into the cache when there are free bus cycles. For example, for SPARC-V9, one issues the pseudo-instruction

```
iprefetch    address
```

to prefetch the code block containing the given address.

Software prefetching is useful mostly for code blocks that are about to be fetched for the first time, or for blocks that are used repeatedly and are determined by profiling to be likely not to be in the I-cache when they are needed. In the first case, the usefulness of prefetch instructions depends on the absence of hardware support for sequential and branch prefetching. Upon determining that a block is likely to benefit from software prefetching, one then places the appropriate instruction T_{pref} cycles

---

1. An *instruction buffer* is a hardware queue of instructions in transit from the cache to the execution unit.

backward in the code from the point at which the block would begin executing, where T_{pref} is the time needed to satisfy the prefetch. If whether a block is needed or not depends on a condition determined t cycles before the block would begin executing, then one places the prefetch $\min(T_{pref}, t)$ cycles back in the code on the path that needs it.

Optimization of branch prediction, which can enhance the effectiveness of instruction prefetching, is discussed in Section 18.11.

20.2.2   Procedure Sorting

The easiest I-cache optimization technique to apply and one that can have definite benefit is to sort the statically linked routines that make up an object module at link time according to their calling relationships and frequency of use. The goal of the sorting is to place routines near their callers in virtual memory so as to reduce paging traffic and to place frequently used and related routines so they are less likely to collide with each other in the I-cache. This approach is based on the premise that routines and their callers are likely to be temporally close to each other and hence should be placed so that they do not interfere spatially. If profiling feedback is available, it should be taken into account in this process; if not, it can be guided by heuristics that place routines that call each other frequently closer to each other (e.g., calls from inside loops should be weighted more heavily than calls that are not embedded in loops).

To implement this idea, we begin with an undirected static call graph, with each arc labeled with the number of times that each of the two procedures at either end of it calls the other one. We use an undirected call graph because there may be calls in both directions between two procedures and because each call is matched by the corresponding return. Then we collapse the graph in stages, at each stage selecting an arc with the highest weight and merging the nodes it connects into a single one, coalescing their corresponding arcs and adding the weights of the coalesced arcs to compute the label for the coalesced arc. Nodes that are merged are placed next to each other in the final ordering of the procedures, with the weights of the connections in the original graph used to determine their relative order.

The ICAN algorithm for this process is the routine Proc_Position() given in Figure 20.2. We assume that the call graph is connected; if not, i.e., if some procedures are unused, we apply the algorithm only to the (at most one) connected component that contains the root node.

A two-element member of ProcSeq, such as $[a_1, a_2]$, represents a binary tree with an unlabeled root. We also use longer elements of ProcSeq, such as $[a_1, \ldots, a_n]$, to represent sequences of n elements. If there is no arc connecting nodes $p1$ and $p2$, we define weight($[p1, p2]$) = 0. The functions left(t) and right(t) return the left and right subtrees, respectively, of tree t. The functions leftmost(t) and rightmost(t) return, respectively, the leftmost and rightmost leaves of the tree t. The function maxi(s) returns the index i of the first element of the sequence s with maximal value, and the function reverse(s) reverses the sequence s and all its subsequences. For example, maxi([3,7,4,5,7]) = 2 and reverse([1,[2,3]]) = [[3,2],1].

```
ProcSeq = Procedure ∪ sequence of ProcSeq

procedure Proc_Position(E,weight) returns
      sequence of Procedure
   E: in set of (Procedure × Procedure)
   weight: in (Procedure × Procedure) ⟶ integer
begin
   T, A: set of ProcSeq
   e: Procedure × Procedure
   a, emax: ProcSeq
   origwt, psweight: ProcSeq ⟶ integer
   max: integer
   A := ∅
   for each e ∈ E do
      A ∪= {[e@1,e@2]}
      origwt([e@1,e@2]) := psweight([e@1,e@2]) := weight(e)
   od
   repeat
      max := 0
      for each a ∈ A do
         if psweight(a) > max then
            emax := a
            max := psweight(a)
         fi
      od
      Coalesce_Nodes(T,A,origwt,psweight,emax↓1,emax↓2)
   until A = ∅
   return Flatten(◆T)
end    || Proc_Position
```

FIG. 20.2 Procedure-sorting algorithm.

The function Coalesce_Nodes(T,A,*origwt*,*weight*,$p1$,$p2$) given in Figure 20.3 coalesces the nodes $p1$ and $p2$ into a single node, adjusting the values of T, A, and *weight* in the process. Since we are using two-element sequences to represent unordered pairs whose elements may themselves be unordered pairs, we need several routines to perform functions that would be trivial when applied to ordered pairs. These functions are as follows:

1. Same($p1$,$p2$) returns true if $p1$ and $p2$ are identical sequences up to order, and false otherwise; for example, Same([1,[2,3]],[[3,2],1]) returns true, while Same([1,[2,3]],[[1,2],3]) does not.

2. Member(A,[$p1$,$p2$]) returns true if [$p1$,$p2$] is a member of the set A modulo order, and false otherwise.

3. Remove(A,s), given in Figure 20.4, removes from A any of its members that Same( ) does not distinguish from s, and returns the result.

```
procedure Coalesce_Nodes(T,A,origwt,psweight,p1,p2)
    T, A: inout set of ProcSeq
    origwt: in ProcSeq ⟶ integer
    psweight: inout ProcSeq ⟶ integer
    p1, p2: in ProcSeq
begin
    lp1, rp1, lp2, rp2: Procedure
    p, padd: ProcSeq
    i: integer
    || select ProcSeqs to make adjacent and reverse one if
    || necessary to get best order
    lp1 := leftmost(p1)
    rp1 := rightmost(p1)
    lp2 := leftmost(p2)
    rp2 := rightmost(p2)
    i := maxi([origwt(rp1,lp2),origwt(rp2,lp1),
        origwt(lp1,lp2),origwt(rp1,rp2)])
    case i of
1:     padd := [p1,p2]
2:     padd := [p2,p1]
3:     padd := [p1,reverse(p2)]
4:     padd := [reverse(p1),p2]
    esac
    T ∪= {padd}
    A := Remove(A,[p1,p2])
    || form new ProcSeq and adjust weights
    for each p ∈ T do
        if !Same(p,p1) & !Same(p,p2) then
            psweight([p,padd]) := 0
            if Member(A,[p,p1]) then
                A := Remove(A,[p,p1])
                psweight([p,padd]) += psweight([p,p1])
            if Member(A,[p,p2]) then
                A := Remove(A,[p,p2])
                psweight([p,padd]) += psweight([p,p2])
            fi
            A ∪= {[p,padd]}
        fi
    od
    T -= {p1,p2}
end    || Coalesce_Nodes
```

FIG. 20.3 Node-coalescing procedure used in Figure 20.2.

4. Flatten(T), given in Figure 20.4, traverses the binary tree represented by the sequence T from left to right, and flattens it, i.e., it constructs the sequence of its leaf nodes, which it returns.

As an example of the procedure-sorting algorithm, assume that we begin with the weighted undirected call graph in Figure 20.5(a). In the first step, we coalesce P2

```
procedure Flatten(t) returns sequence of Procedure
   t: in ProcSeq
begin
   if t ∈ Procedure then
      return [t]
   else
      return Flatten(left(t)) ⊕ Flatten(right(t))
   fi
end  || Flatten

procedure Remove(A,s) returns Procseq
   A, s: in ProcSeq
begin
   i: integer
   i := 1
   while i ≤ |A| do
      if Same(A↓i,s) then
         A ⊖= i
         return A
      fi
      i += 1
   od
   return A
end     || Remove
```

FIG. 20.4 Auxiliary procedures used in the procedure-sorting algorithm.

and P4 to form [P2,P4] and we get the graph shown in Figure 20.5(b). In the next step, we coalesce P3 and P6 to form [P3,P6], and then P5 and [P2,P4] to form [P5,[P2,P4]], resulting in the graphs shown in Figure 20.5(c) and (d), respectively. The contents of the single node resulting from the coalescing process is

[[P1,[P3,P6],[P5,[P2,P4]]],[P7,P8]]

so we arrange the procedures in memory in the order P1, P3, P6, P5, P2, P4, P7, P8. Note that P2 and P4 have been placed next to each other, as have P3 and P6, and P5 and P2.

20.2.3   Procedure and Block Placement

Another approach to I-cache optimization that can be combined with the one described above requires modifying the system linker to put each routine on an I-cache block boundary, allowing the later phases of the compilation process to position frequently executed code segments, such as loops, so as to occupy the smallest possible number of cache blocks and to place them at or near the beginnings of blocks, thus helping to minimize I-cache misses and making it more likely that superscalar CPUs can fetch whole instruction groups that can be executed simultaneously. If most basic blocks are short (say, four to eight instructions), this helps to keep the beginnings of basic blocks away from the ends of cache blocks. A compiler could be instrumented

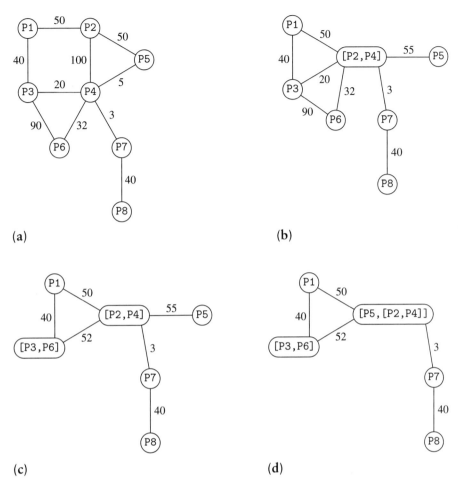

FIG. 20.5 (a) An example flowgraph for procedure sorting, and (b) through (d) the first three transformations of the flowgraph.

to collect statistics on this without much difficulty, and profiling feedback could be used to determine for what basic blocks such placement is important vs. those for which it simply wastes code space and results in extra branches.

20.2.4   Intraprocedural Code Positioning

Pettis and Hansen [PetH90] developed and evaluated a bottom-up approach to intraprocedural code positioning, which we describe. The objective is to move infrequently executed code (such as error handling) out of the main body of the code and to straighten the code (i.e., to remove unconditional branches and make as many conditional branches as possible take the fall-through path) so that, in general, a higher fraction of the instructions fetched into the I-cache are actually executed.

Unlike procedure sorting, this process can be done during compilation of each procedure. To do this, we assume that the edges in a procedure's flowgraph have been annotated with their execution frequencies, either by profiling or by estimating the frequencies. The algorithm performs a bottom-up search of the flowgraph, building chains of basic blocks that should be placed as straight-line code because the edges between them are executed frequently.[2] Initially, each basic block is a chain unto itself. Then, in successive steps, the two chains whose respective tail and head are connected by the edge with the highest execution frequency are merged; if the highest frequency occurs on an edge that does not connect the tail of a chain to the head of another, the chains cannot be merged. Nevertheless, such edges are used in code placement: we assume that a forward branch is taken;[3] this information is preserved so that the target basic block can, if possible, be placed at some point after the source block. Finally, basic-block placement is done by first selecting the entry chain and then by proceeding through the other chains according to the weights of their connections. ICAN code for the procedure Block_Position($B,E,r,freq$), where B is the set of basic blocks, E the set of edges, r the entry block, and $freq(\ )$ the function that maps edges to their execution frequencies, and the procedure Edge_Count( ) that it uses is given in Figure 20.6.

As an example of the algorithm, consider the flowgraph in Figure 20.7. The edge with the highest execution frequency is from B1 to B2, so the first sequence formed is [B1,B2]. The edge from B2 to B4 has the next highest frequency, so the existing sequence is extended to [B1,B2,B4]; similarly, entry and B8 are added in the next two steps, resulting in [entry,B1,B2,B4,B8]. The next highest frequency edge is from B9 to exit, so a new sequence, [B9,exit], is started. In subsequent steps, the sequence [B9,exit] is extended to [B6,B9,exit], and two other sequences are constructed, [B3,B7] and [B5]. Next we compute the edges( ) function, as follows:

```
edges([entry,B1,B2,B4,B8]) = 2
edges([B3,B7]) = 1
edges([B5]) = 1
edges([B6,B9,exit]) = 0
```

Next, we order the sequences so that the one containing the entry block comes first, followed by the other three in an order given by the edges( ) function, and we return the result. The resulting arrangement in memory is shown in Figure 20.8.

Finally, we fix up the code by inserting and deleting branches as necessary to make the flowgraph equivalent in effect to the original one. This is done by using a combination of the original block entries, the labels that begin the blocks, and the branches that end them. Notice that in our example we have succeeded in making all the branches forward, except the two loop-closing ones, and we have arranged the blocks so that six of the nine forward edges are fall-throughs.

---

2. The chains are somewhat reminiscent of traces in trace scheduling (Section 17.5), except that no fix-up code is required.

3. This aspect of the algorithm can, of course, be modified to correspond to other assumptions about conditional branches.

```
procedure Block_Position(B,E,r,freq)
   returns sequence of Block
   B: in set of Block
   E: in set of (Block × Block)
   r: in Block
   freq: in (Block × Block) ⟶ integer
begin
   C := ∅: set of sequence of Block
   CR: sequence of Block
   c1, c2, c3, clast, cfirst, cnew: sequence of Block
   nch, oldnch, max, fr: integer
   edges: (set of sequence of Block) ⟶ integer
   e: Block × Block
   for each b ∈ B do
      C ∪= {[b]}
   od
   nch := |C|
   repeat
      oldnch := nch
      || select two sequences of blocks that have the
      || highest execution frequency on the edge that
      || connects the tail of one to the head of the
      || other
      max := 0
      for each c1 ∈ C do
         for each c2 ∈ C do
            if c1 ≠ c2 & (c1↓-1)→(c2↓1) ∈ E then
               fr := freq(c1↓-1,c2↓1)
               if fr > max then
                  max := fr
                  clast := c1
                  cfirst := c2
               fi
            fi
         od
      od
      || combine selected pair of sequences
      if max > 0 then
         cnew := clast ⊕ cfirst
         C := (C - {clast,cfirst}) ∪ {cnew}
         nch -= 1
      fi
   until nch = oldnch
```

(continued)

FIG. 20.6 Bottom-up basic-block positioning algorithm.

```
    while C ≠ ∅ do
        || find sequence beginning with entry node and
        || concatenate sequences so as to make as many
        || branches forward as possible
        CR := ◆C
        if r = CR↓1 then
            C -= {CR}
            for each c1 ∈ C do
                edges(c1) := 0
                for each c2 ∈ C do
                    if c1 ≠ c2 then
                        edges(c1) += Edge_Count(c1,c2,E)
                    fi
                od
            od
            repeat
                max := 0
                for each c1 ∈ C do
                    if edges(c1) ≥ max then
                        max := edges(c1)
                        c := c1
                    fi
                od
                CR ⊕= [c]
                C -= {c}
            until C = ∅
            return CR
        fi
    od
end     || Block_Position

procedure Edge_Count(c1,c2,E) returns integer
    c1, c2: in sequence of Block
    E: in Block × Block
begin
    ct := 0, i, j: integer
    for i := 1 to |c1| do
        for j := 1 to |c2| do
            if (c1↓i)→(c2↓j) ∈ E then
                ct += 1
            fi
        od
    od
    return ct
end     || Edge_Count
```

FIG. 20.6 *(continued)*

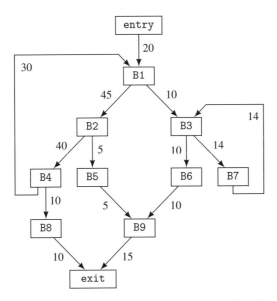

FIG. 20.7 An example flowgraph for intraprocedural code positioning.

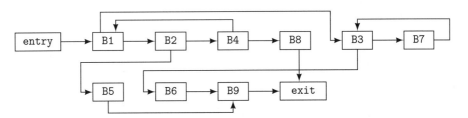

FIG. 20.8 The example flowgraph in Figure 20.7 after intraprocedural code positioning.

20.2.5   Procedure Splitting

A technique that enhances the effectiveness of both the procedure-sorting and the intraprocedural code-positioning algorithms is *procedure splitting,* which divides each procedure into a primary and a secondary component, the former containing the frequently executed basic blocks and the latter containing the rarely executed ones, such as exception-handling code. One then collects the secondary components of a series of procedures into a separate secondary section, thus packing the primary components more tightly together. Of course, procedure splitting requires adjusting the branches between the components. Experimentation should be the basis for deciding the execution-frequency boundary between the primary and secondary components.

A schematic example of procedure splitting is given in Figure 20.9. The regions labeled "p" and "s" represent primary and secondary code, respectively.

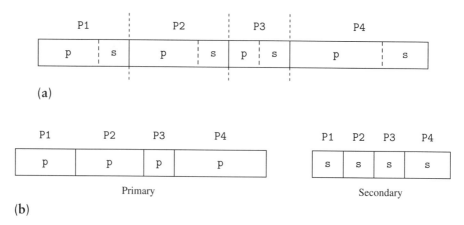

FIG. 20.9 (a) A group of procedure bodies, each split into primary (p) and secondary (s) components, and (b) the result of collecting each type of component.

20.2.6 Combining Intra- and Interprocedural Methods

An approach to I-cache optimization that combines intra- and interprocedural methods is exemplified by the work of McFarling, who focuses on optimization of entire programs for direct-mapped I-caches (see Section 20.7 for references). His method works on object modules and depends on rearranging instructions in memory and segregating some instructions to not be cached at all. As for the approaches discussed above, profiling feedback improves the effectiveness of his algorithm.

McFarling has also investigated the impact of procedure integration or inlining on I-caches. Clearly, inlining can affect I-cache miss rates both positively and negatively. If too many procedures are inlined, code size may increase exponentially and the I-cache hit rate may suffer as a result; on the other hand, inlining can also increase locality, thus decreasing the miss rate. He gives a model for determining the effect of inlining a single call and criteria for deciding which procedures to inline.

20.3 Scalar Replacement of Array Elements

One concern in generating good object code for loops that manipulate subscripted variables is that very few compilers even try to allocate such variables to registers, despite the fact that register allocation is often done very effectively for scalars. Before we launch into the details of a method for doing such allocation, we present two examples that show how important it can be.

Our first example is the matrix multiplication code given in Figure 20.1(a). If we replace the accesses to C(i,j) by a variable ct, as shown in Figure 20.10, and ct is allocated to a register, we reduce the number of memory accesses by $2 \cdot (N^3 - N^2)$ or nearly a factor of two.

Our second example is the code in Figure 20.11(a). The references to b[ ] can be replaced by two temporaries, resulting in the code in Figure 20.11(b), reducing the

```
do i = 1,N
   do j = 1,N
      ct = C(i,j)
      do k = 1,N
         ct = ct + A(i,k) * B(k,j)
      enddo
      C(i,j) = ct
   enddo
enddo
```

FIG. 20.10 Fortran matrix multiply from Figure 20.1(a) with a scalar temporary in place of C(i,j).

```
                                   if n >= 1 then
                                      t0 ← b[1]
                                      t1 ← t0 + 1.0
                                      b[2] ← t1
                                      a[1] ← 2 * t0 + c[1]
                                   endif
                                   t0 ← t1
for i ← 1 to n do                  for i ← 2 to n do
   b[i+1] ← b[i] + 1.0                t1 ← t0 + 1.0
   a[i] ← 2 * b[i] + c[i]             b[i+1] ← t1
endfor                                a[i] ← 2 * t0 + c[i]
                                      t0 ← t1
                                   endfor

(a)                                (b)
```

FIG. 20.11 (a) A simple HIR recurrence, and (b) the result of using scalar temporaries in it.

number of memory accesses by about 40%. Of course, if n is known to be greater than one, the if can be deleted.

The approach to replacing subscripted variables by scalars, and hence making them available for register allocation, is called *scalar replacement,* also known as *register pipelining.* In essence, this method finds opportunities to reuse array elements and replaces the reuses with references to scalar temporaries. As we have seen in the examples, it can produce dramatic improvements in speed for some real-life programs. Another benefit is that it can decrease the need for D-cache optimization.

Scalar replacement is simplest to explain for loop nests that contain no conditionals. To describe it, we need to define the *period* of a loop-carried dependence edge e in the dependence graph, denoted $p(e)$, as the constant number of loop iterations between the references to the subscripted variable representing the tail of the edge and its head; if the number of iterations is not constant, the variable is not a candidate for scalar replacement and the period is undefined.

Next, we build a partial dependence graph for the loop nest, including only flow and input dependences that have a defined period and are either loop-independent or carried by the innermost loop; we exclude edges that represent transitive dependences. Alternatively, we can begin with the full dependence graph, if we have it,

```
for i ← 1 to n do              for j ← 1 to n do
    for j ← 1 to n do              for i ← 1 to n do
        a[i,j] ← b[i] + 0.5            a[i,j] ← b[i] + 0.5
        a[i+1,j] ← b[i] - 0.5          a[i+1,j] ← b[i] - 0.5
    endfor                         endfor
endfor                         endfor
(a)                            (b)
```

FIG. 20.12 (a) A doubly nested HIR loop, and (b) the result of interchanging the loops.

and prune it. Each flow or input dependence in the resulting graph represents an opportunity for scalar replacement.

As our examples suggest, we need $p(e) + 1$ temporaries in general to hold the values generated by $p(e) + 1$ iterations before the last one can be recycled. So we introduce temporaries t_0 through $t_{p(e)}$ and replace references to the array element by uses of the temporaries. In particular, the generating reference that fetches the array element *elem* from memory is replaced by $t_0 \leftarrow elem$, and other references are replaced by either $t_0 \leftarrow elem$ or $elem \leftarrow t_0$, depending on whether the reference is a use or a definition, respectively. We also place a sequence of assignments $t_{p(e)} \leftarrow t_{p(e)-1}, \ldots, t_1 \leftarrow t_0$ at the end of the innermost loop body. Finally, we must initialize the t_i correctly by peeling[4] $p(e)$ iterations of the body from the beginning of the loop and replacing the first fetch of the array element in iteration i by the assignment $t_o \leftarrow elem$, and other fetches and stores by the corresponding assignments. Now each t_i is a candidate for allocation to a register and, further, if the dependence is loop-independent, it is a candidate for code motion out of the loop.

Our second example of scalar replacement (Figure 20.11) is done according to the method described above.

Transformations, such as loop interchange and loop fusion (see Section 20.4.2), may make scalar replacement applicable to or more effective for a given loop nest. Loop interchange may increase opportunities for scalar replacement by making loop-carried dependences be carried by the innermost loop. See Figure 20.12 for an example.

Loop fusion can create opportunities for scalar replacement by bringing together in one loop multiple uses of a single array element (or more than one). An example is shown in Figure 20.13. After fusing the two loops, scalar replacement can be applied to a[i].

Scalar replacement can handle loops that have ifs in their bodies, such as the C code in Figure 20.14. For this example, we use three temporaries and assign t2 in place of a[i-2], t1 in place of a[i-1], and t0 in place of a[i].

Further, scalar replacement can be applied to nested loops with significant benefit. For example, given the loop in Figure 20.15(a), we first perform scalar

---

4. *Peeling* k iterations from the beginning of a loop means replacing the first k iterations by k copies of the body plus the increment and test code for the loop index variable and placing them immediately ahead of the loop.

```
for i ← 1 to n do                    for i ← 1 to n do
   b[i] ← a[i] + 1.0                    b[i] ← a[i] + 1.0
endfor                                  c[i] ← a[i]/2.0
for j ← 1 to n do                    endfor
   c[j] ← a[j]/2.0
endfor
```

(a)   (b)

FIG. 20.13   (a) A pair of HIR loops, and (b) the result of fusing them.

```
                                     t2 = a[0];
                                     t1 = a[1];
                                     t0 = a[2];
                                     b[2] = (t0 + b[2])/2.0;
                                     t0 = t2 + 1.0;
                                     a[2] = t0;
                                     t2 = t1;
                                     t1 = t0;
                                     t0 = a[3];
                                     b[3] = (t0 + b[3])/2.0;
                                     t0 = t1 - 1.0;
                                     a[3] = t0;
                                     t2 = t1;
                                     t1 = t0;
for (i = 2; i <= 20; i++)            for (i = 4; i <= 20; i++)
{  b[i] = (a[i] + b[i])/2.0;         {    t0 = a[i];
                                          b[i] = (t0 + b[i])/2.0;
   if ((i % 2) == 0)                      if ((i % 2) == 0)
      a[i] = a[i-2] + 1.0;                { t0 = t2 + 1.0;
                                            a[i] = t0;
                                          }
   else                                   else
                                          {
      a[i] = a[i-1] - 1.0;                   t0 = t1 - 1.0;
                                             a[i] = t0;
                                          }
                                          t2 = t1;
                                          t1 = t0;
}                                    }
```

(a)   (b)

FIG. 20.14   (a) A C loop with a control-flow construct in its body, and (b) the result of applying
             scalar replacement to a[ ].

```
for i = 1 to n do
    x[i] = 0
    for j = 1 to n do
        x[i] = x[i] + a[i,j] * y[j]
    endfor
endfor
```
(a)

```
for i ← 1 to n do
    t0 ← 0
    for j ← 1 to n do
        t0 ← t0 + a[i,j] * y[j]
    endfor
    x[i] ← t0
endfor
```
(b)

FIG. 20.15 (a) A doubly nested HIR loop, and (b) the loop with scalar replacement performed on x[i] in the inner loop.

```
for i ← 1 by 3 to n do
    t0 ← 0
    t1 ← 0
    t2 ← 0
    for j ← 1 to n do
        t0 ← t0 + a[i,j] * y[j]
        t1 ← t1 + a[i+1,j] * y[j]
        t2 ← t2 + a[i+2,j] * y[j]
    endfor
    x[i] ← t0
    x[i+1] ← t1
    x[i+2] ← t2
endfor
for i ← i to n do
    t0 ← 0
    for j ← 1 to n do
        t0 ← t0 + a[i,j] * y[j]
    endfor
    x[i] ← t0
endfor
```

FIG. 20.16 The loop in Figure 20.15(b) with the inner loop unrolled by a factor of three.

replacement on x[i] in the inner loop, which results in the code in Figure 20.15(b). Next, we unroll the inner loop by an (arbitrarily chosen) factor of three, which results in the code in Figure 20.16; then we scalar replace the y[j] values also, which yields the code in Figure 20.17.

```
for i ← 1 by 3 to n do
    t0 ← 0
    t1 ← 0
    t2 ← 0
    for j ← 1 to n do
        t4 ← y[j]
        t0 ← t0 + a[i,j] * t4
        t1 ← t1 + a[i+1,j] * t4
        t2 ← t2 + a[i+2,j] * t4
    endfor
    x[i]   ← t0
    x[i+1] ← t1
    x[i+2] ← t2
endfor
for i ← i to n do
    t0 ← 0
    for j ← 1 to n do
        t0 ← t0 + a[i, j] * y[j]
    endfor
    x[i] ← t0
endfor
```

FIG. 20.17 The loop in Figure 20.16 with y[j] scalar replaced in the inner loop.

20.4   Data–Cache Optimization

Almost all of the remainder of this chapter is devoted to an introduction to and overview of the optimization of the cache usage of numerical (or scientific) code. By numerical code, we mean programs that manipulate large arrays of data, usually, but not always, of floating-point values and in Fortran. Most such programs have patterns of data usage that are regular in structure and that include opportunities for reuse of data before it is flushed from the cache.

We begin with a brief discussion of global arrangement of data, which assumes that we have an entire program available to analyze and transform, so information collected about all parts of the program can be used by the compiler to arrange all the arrays used in the program in the load image so as to minimize their interference with each other in the D-cache. Next, we give an overview of D-cache optimization for individual procedures, which is designed, as much as is feasible, to eliminate the latency due to fetching data from memory into the D-cache and storing results from the registers into it.

As noted above, the code for which this type of optimization has had the greatest success so far is so-called numerical or scientific code that spends most of its time executing nested loops that manipulate matrices of numerical values. The optimizations work by first elucidating patterns of data reuse in the loop nests and then transforming them to turn the reuse into patterns that exhibit locality of reference, i.e., the uses of the same data locations or cache blocks are made close enough in time that they execute without causing the data to be flushed from the cache before they are reused.

The primary technique for determining reuse patterns is dependence analysis, and the approach to bringing data uses closer together in time is transformation of the loop nests. We have given an overview of dependence analysis for array references in nested loops in Chapter 9, and we introduce the relevant loop transformations in Section 20.4.2. We then give an overview of an approach developed by Lam, Rothberg, and Wolf (see Section 20.7 for references) that is designed to eliminate as much as possible of the latency due to accessing the cache in a less than optimal manner.

Next, we present data prefetching, a way to hide (rather than eliminate) some of the latency of fetching data, and thus a technique that should be applied after the loop transformations discussed above.

Finally, we discuss briefly the interaction of scalar and memory-oriented optimizations, the possibility of D-cache optimization for pointers and dynamically allocated data objects, and where in the compilation process to integrate the I-cache and D-cache optimizations.

Before we discuss data-cache optimization, note that it is most frequently applied to loops that contain floating-point computation and, as discussed in Section 12.3.2, that is exactly the area in which we must be most careful not to alter the effect of a computation by rearranging it. In Section 12.3.2, we pointed out that if MF denotes the maximal finite floating-point value in a given precision, then

$$1.0 + (MF - MF) = 1.0$$

while

$$(1.0 + MF) - MF = 0.0$$

This generalizes to loops as follows. Let the values stored in the array A[1··3*n] be

```
A[3*i+1] = 1.0
A[3*i+2] = MF
A[3*i+3] = -MF
```

for i = 0 to i = n-1. Then the HIR loops in Figure 20.18(a) and (b) both assign the value 0.0 to s, while the loop in (c) assigns it the value 1.0 and that in (d) assigns it the value n.

Section 11.10 of the Fortran 77 standard restricts the order of evaluation of loops to be "as written," and thus disallows the transformations above.

However, the loop transformations used in Figure 20.18, namely, reversal and tiling, are most frequently implemented in optimizers that are applied to Fortran programs. Thus, it is the responsibility of the compiler to inform the user about the transformations it makes and it is the responsibility of the user to verify that the transformations do not alter the result of a computation. This also suggests strongly that it is essential for the user to be able to control the transformations that are applied to specific loops.

```
s ← 0.0                          s ← 0.0
for i ← 1 to 3*n do              for i ← 3 to 3*n do
                                     t ← 0.0
                                     for j ← i-2 to i do
    s ← s + A[i]                         t ← t + A[j]
                                     endfor
                                     s ← s + t
endfor                           endfor
(a)                              (b)


s ← 0.0                          s ← 0.0
for i ← 3*n by -1 to 1 do        for i ← 3*n by -3 to 3 do
                                     t ← 0.0
                                     for j ← i by -1 to i-2 do
    s ← s + A[i]                         t ← t + A[j]
                                     endfor
                                     s ← s + t
endfor                           endfor
(c)                              (d)
```

FIG. 20.18 HIR loops that sum the same sequence of floating-point values but that produce different results. The loops in (a) and (b) produce the result 0.0, while the one in (c) produces 1.0 and the one in (d) produces n.

20.4.1   Interprocedural Arrangement of Data

An interprocedural approach to improving D-cache usage is to arrange large data objects in memory so as to decrease the likelihood of their interfering with each other in the D-cache. This requires information about the patterns of usage of the data objects and requires the availability of all the data objects (i.e., their static initializations, if any, and the code that addresses them) at the same time for rearrangement. This, in turn, requires interprocedural dependence analysis and having the entire load image available to operate on, and so is unlikely to be undertaken in real compilers any time soon. Should this approach become a realistic possibility, the work of Gupta [Gupt90] provides proofs that optimal arrangement of data is *NP*-complete and gives polynomial-time algorithms that provide good approximations in practice.

20.4.2   Loop Transformations

We consider uses of subscripted variables in perfectly nested loops in HIR that are expressed in *canonical* or *normalized form*,[5] i.e., each loop's index runs from 1 to some value n by 1s and only the innermost loop has statements other than

---

5. Although all our loops are originally in canonical form, some of the transformations described below (e.g., tiling) produce loops with increments other than 1. While such loops could be put in canonical form, there is no point in doing so, since they represent the final stage after transformations have been applied.

for statements within it. This simplifies the presentation somewhat but is not essential. Let

```
for i ← a by b to c do
    statements
endfor
```

be a loop with arbitrary bounds and increment. Then

```
for ii ← 1 by 1 to n do
    i ← a + (ii - 1) * b
    statements
endfor
```

where $n = \lfloor (c - a + b)/b \rfloor$, is a corresponding loop in canonical form.

Loop transformations do things like interchanging two nested loops, reversing the order in which a loop's iterations are performed, fusing two loop bodies together into one, and so on. If chosen properly, they provide opportunities to execute a loop nest so that the semantics of the program containing it are preserved and its performance is improved. The performance improvement may come from better use of the memory hierarchy, from making a loop's iterations executable in parallel by several processors, from making a loop's iterations vectorizable, or from some combination of these factors. Our use of loop transformations concentrates on optimizing the use of registers, data caches, and other levels of the memory hierarchy. We leave parallelization and vectorization to other texts, as discussed in Section 1.5.

There are three general types of loop transformations that we deal with, namely,

1. unimodular transformations,

2. loop fusion and distribution, and

3. tiling.

Wolf and Lam ([WolL91] and [Wolf92]) provide a convenient characterization of a large class of loop transformations. They define the class of *unimodular loop transformations* as those whose effect can be represented by the product of a unimodular matrix with a (column) distance vector.[6] A *unimodular matrix* is a square matrix with all integral components and with a determinant of 1 or −1. As we shall see, loop interchange, more general permutations of nested loop control, loop skewing, loop reversal, and a series of other useful transformations are all unimodular.

Define a distance vector $\langle i_1, i_2, \ldots, i_n \rangle$ to be *lexicographically positive* if it has at least one nonzero element and the first nonzero element in it is positive. The definition extends in the natural way to the other ordering relations. Wolf proves that a unimodular transformation represented by the matrix U is legal when applied to a loop nest with a set of lexicographically non-negative distance vectors D if and

---

6. Recall the definition of distance vector from Section 9.3.

```
for i ← 1 to n do
   for j ← 1 to n do
      a[i,j] ← (a[i-1,j] + a[i+1,j])/2.0
   endfor
endfor
```

FIG. 20.19 The assignment in this HIR loop nest has the distance vector $\langle 1, 0 \rangle$.

```
for j ← 1 to n do
   for i ← 1 to n do
      a[i,j] ← (a[i-1,j] + a[i+1,j])/2.0
   endfor
endfor
```

FIG. 20.20 The code in Figure 20.19 with the loops interchanged.

only if, for each $\vec{d} \in D$, $U\vec{d} \succeq \vec{0}$, i.e., if and only if it transforms the lexicographically positive distance vectors to lexicographically positive distance vectors.[7]

We next consider some examples of unimodular transformations, the corresponding matrices, and their effects on loop nests.

Loop interchange is the transformation that reverses the order of two adjacent loops in a loop nest. It is characterized by a matrix that is the identity except that two adjacent 1s on the diagonal have their rows and columns switched. As an example, consider the code in Figure 20.19, which has the distance vector $\langle 1, 0 \rangle$. The loop-interchange matrix is

$$\begin{bmatrix} 0 & 1 \\ 1 & 0 \end{bmatrix}$$

and the product of the interchange matrix with the distance vector is

$$\begin{bmatrix} 0 & 1 \\ 1 & 0 \end{bmatrix} \begin{bmatrix} 1 \\ 0 \end{bmatrix} = \begin{bmatrix} 0 \\ 1 \end{bmatrix}$$

and the result of applying the transformation is shown in Figure 20.20; note that the resulting distance vector is lexicographically positive, so the transformation is legal.

Loop permutation generalizes loop interchange by allowing more than two loops to be moved at once and by not requiring them to be adjacent. For example, the unimodular matrix

$$\begin{bmatrix} 0 & 0 & 1 & 0 \\ 0 & 0 & 0 & 1 \\ 1 & 0 & 0 & 0 \\ 0 & 1 & 0 & 0 \end{bmatrix}$$

represents interchanging the first of four nested loops with the third and the second with the fourth.

---

7. Note that a unimodular matrix must transform the zero vector (and only it) to the zero vector.

```
for i ← 1 to n do              for i ← 1 to n do
    for j ← 1 to n do              for j ← i+1 to i+n do
        a[i] ← a[i+j] + 1.0            a[i] ← a[j] + 1.0
    endfor                         endfor
endfor                         endfor
(a)                            (b)
```

FIG. 20.21 (a) A HIR loop nest, and (b) the result of skewing the inner loop.

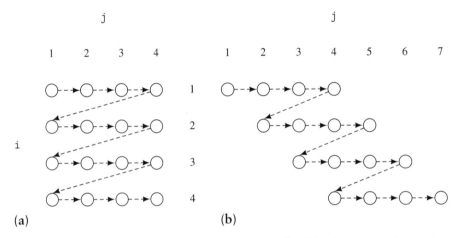

(a)   (b)

FIG. 20.22 Transformation of (a) the iteration-space traversal of the loop nest shown in Figure 20.21(a) by skewing (b).

Loop reversal reverses the order in which a particular loop's iterations are performed. The appropriate matrix is the identity with a −1 in place of the 1 that corresponds to the loop to be reversed. For example, the matrix

$$\begin{bmatrix} 1 & 0 & 0 \\ 0 & -1 & 0 \\ 0 & 0 & 1 \end{bmatrix}$$

corresponds to reversing the direction of the middle of three loops. If we were to apply loop reversal to the outer loop in the code in Figure 20.19, it would correspond to the matrix-vector multiplication

$$\begin{bmatrix} -1 & 0 \\ 0 & 1 \end{bmatrix} \begin{bmatrix} 1 \\ 0 \end{bmatrix} = \begin{bmatrix} -1 \\ 0 \end{bmatrix}$$

The resulting distance vector $\langle -1, 0 \rangle$ is lexicographically negative, so the transformation is not applicable.

Loop skewing changes the shape of a loop's iteration space. For example, it might transform the loop in Figure 20.21(a) to that in (b), which corresponds to changing the iteration-space traversal from the one shown in Figure 20.22(a) to that

```
for i ← 1 to n do
    a[i] ← a[i] + 1.0          for i ← 1 to n do
endfor                             a[i] ← a[i] + 1.0
for j ← 1 to n do                  b[i] ← a[i] * 0.618
    b[j] ← a[j] * 0.618        endfor
endfor
```
(a)   (b)

FIG. 20.23 (a) A pair of HIR loops, and (b) the result of fusing them.

```
          for i ← 1 to n do              for i ← 1 to n do
S1            a[i] ← b[i]                    a[i] ← b[i]
          endfor                          endfor
          for i ← 1 to n do              for i ← 1 to n do
S2            b[i-1] ← c[i] + 1.5            b[i+1] ← c[i] + 1.5
          endfor                          endfor
```
(a)   (b)

```
          for i ← 1 to n do              for i ← 1 to n do
S1            a[i] ← b[i]                    a[i] ← b[i]
S2            b[i-1] ← c[i] + 1.5            b[i+1] ← c[i] + 1.5
          endfor                          endfor
```
(c)   (d)

FIG. 20.24 Two pairs of HIR loops, (a) and (b), and the results of fusing them in (c) and (d), respectively. In the fused loop (c), there is one dependence, S2 ⟨1⟩ S1, while in loop (d), the dependence is S1 ⟨1⟩ S2, so loop fusion is legal for the example in (a) but not for the one in (b).

in (b). The matrix corresponding to this transformation is

$$\begin{bmatrix} 1 & 0 \\ 1 & 1 \end{bmatrix}$$

which is unimodular.

Loop fusion, distribution, and tiling are three important transformations that are not unimodular.

Loop fusion takes two adjacent loops that have the same iteration-space traversal and combines their bodies into a single loop, as shown, for example, in Figure 20.23. Loop fusion is legal as long as the loops have the same bounds and as long as there are no flow, anti-, or output dependences in the fused loop for which instructions from the first loop depend on instructions from the second loop (outer loops do not affect the legality of the transformation). As an example, applying fusion to the loops in Figure 20.24(a) results in the loop in (c). The only dependence is S2 ⟨1⟩ S1, so the transformation is legal. On the other hand, for the loops in

```
                                           for i ← 1 by 2 to n do
    for i ← 1 to n do                          for j ← i to min(i+1,n) do
        b[i] ← a[i]/b[i]                           b[i] ← a[i]/b[i]
        a[i+1] ← a[i] + 1.0                        a[i+1] ← a[i] + 1.0
    endfor                                     endfor
                                           endfor
```

(a)   (b)

FIG. 20.25 (a) A HIR loop, and (b) the result of tiling it with a tile size of 2.

(b), fusing them results in (d) with the only dependence being S1 ⟨1⟩ S2, so fusion is not legal.

Loop distribution does the opposite of loop fusion. It takes a loop that contains multiple statements and splits it into two loops with the same iteration-space traversal, such that the first loop contains some of the statements inside the original loop and the second contains the others. Figure 20.23 provides an example of loop distribution also, with (b) before and (a) after. Loop distribution is legal if it does not result in breaking any cycles in the dependence graph of the original loop (again, outer loops do not affect the transformation).

Tiling is a loop transformation that increases the depth of a loop nest. Given an n-deep nest, tiling may make it anywhere from $(n + 1)$-deep to $2n$-deep, depending on how many of the loops are tiled. Tiling a single loop replaces it by a pair of loops, with the inner one (called the *tile loop*) having an increment equal to that of the original loop[8] and the outer one having an increment equal to $ub - lb + 1$, where lb and ub are the lower and upper bounds of the inner loop, respectively; tiling interchanges loops from the tiled one inward to make the tile loop the innermost loop in the nest. The number of iterations of the tile loop is called the *tile size*. For example, in Figure 20.25, the loop in (a) has been tiled with a tile of size 2 in (b).

Tiling one or more of a nest of loops rearranges its iteration-space traversal so that it consists of a series of small polyhedra executed one after the other.[9] Figure 20.26 shows the result of tiling both loops in the code in Figure 20.21(a) with tile sizes of 2. Figure 20.27 shows the resulting iteration-space traversal, assuming that n = 6.

---

8. However, as shown in Figure 20.25(b), there may be a min operator to guarantee that the tiled version executes the proper number of iterations the last time through the outer loop.

9. Tiling is also known by three other names in the literature. It has been called "blocking," but we choose not to use that name because it has at least two other meanings in computer science already. Wolfe calls it "strip mine and interchange" because creation of a tile loop divides a given loop into a series of loops that execute "strips" of the original ones. Callahan, Carr, and Kennedy call tiling an innermost loop "unroll and jam" because it can be thought of as unrolling some number of copies and then "jamming" them together into a loop.

```
for i ← 1 by 2 to n do
   for j ← 1 by 2 to n do
      for i1 = i to min(i+1,n) do
         for j1 = j to min(j+1,n) do
            a[i1] ← a[i1+j1] + 1.0
         endfor
      endfor
   endfor
endfor
```

FIG. 20.26   The result of tiling both loops in the HIR loop nest shown in Figure 20.21(a) with a tile size of 2.

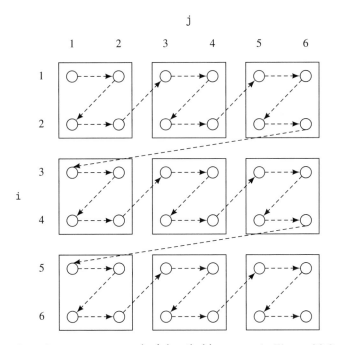

FIG. 20.27   Iteration-space traversal of the tiled loop nest in Figure 20.26, with n = 6.

Tiling a loop nest is legal exactly when the tile loops can be interchanged with the other loops to make the tile loops innermost. In particular, tiling the innermost loop is always legal.

20.4.3   Locality and Tiling

The most important technique for maximizing data-cache effectiveness for loop nests is to exploit locality of reference in areas of arrays that are larger than single elements or cache blocks. While there may be no exploitable reuse at all in a given loop nest, its pattern of cache usage may still be improvable by focusing its work on segments of the arrays.

Consider the matrix-multiplication example in Figure 20.1(a) and what we have found out about it above, namely, that any order of the loops is legal. We can apply tiling to it to cause it to operate on subarrays of any desired size. If the tile sizes are chosen optimally, each fragment of the work may be completable without any cache misses other than compulsory ones; further, if we select the best arrangement of the tiles with respect to each other in the looping structure, we may be able to reduce even the number of compulsory misses for a tile by taking advantage of reuse between consecutive tiles. Creating a tile loop for each loop results in the code in Figure 20.28(a). Now, since the original loops can be arbitrarily reordered, we can move all the tile loops to make them the innermost loops, as shown in Figure 20.28(b). The result is a loop nest that works on $T \times T$ sections of the arrays, with a traversal pattern analogous to that shown in Figure 20.27; also, of course, scalar replacement of array elements can be applied to C(ii,jj). If T is chosen judiciously, tiling reduces cache conflicts by causing fewer elements of each array to need to be present in the data cache at once to perform the given computation.

While tiling is often very valuable in reducing cache interference and hence for increasing performance, we are left with three questions:

1. What happens if a loop nest is not fully tilable?

2. How does cache organization impact the effectiveness of tiling?

3. How do we select the tile sizes for a given loop nest and loop bounds to be most effective?

Whether a loop nest is fully tilable may or may not affect its performance—it depends on where tiling is needed. Consider the HIR loop nest in Figure 20.29. The inner loop clearly will not benefit from tiling, while the outer one will if the rows of the array a[ ] may interfere with each other in the cache. Permuting the two loops in Figure 20.29 provides an example that will benefit from tiling only the inner loop. On the other hand, we may have a loop nest with an iteration space that is large in several dimensions but for which some loops are not permutable, and hence are not tilable. One may, at least, tile the loops that are permutable to be the innermost ones and there are usually performance gains to be derived from doing so.

The organization of the data cache can make a dramatic difference in the overall effectiveness of tiling and on the effectiveness of a particular tile size for a given loop size. Suppose we have a direct-mapped cache and some particular loop nest. While the cache may be large enough to hold most of the data being processed, it may not be able to do so without collisions between the contents of different arrays, or even between two parts of the same array. Even if we fully tile the loop nest, we may need to make the tile sizes surprisingly small compared to the size of the cache to avoid collisions. Having a set-associative cache obviously reduces the frequency of such collisions, but the more arrays we are processing in a single loop nest, the less effectively it does so.

```
do i = 1,N,T
  do ii = i,min(i+T-1,N)
    do j = 1,N,T
      do jj = j,min(j+T-1,N)
        do k = 1,N,T
          do kk = k,min(k+T-1,N)
            C(ii,jj) = C(ii,jj) + A(ii,kk) * B(kk,jj)
          enddo
        enddo
      enddo
    enddo
  enddo
enddo
```

(a)

```
do i = 1,N,T
  do j = 1,N,T
    do k = 1,N,T
      do ii = i,min(i+T-1,N)
        do jj = j,min(j+T-1,N)
          do kk = k,min(k+T-1,N)
            C(ii,jj) = C(ii,jj) + A(ii,kk) * B(kk,jj)
          enddo
        enddo
      enddo
    enddo
  enddo
enddo
```

(b)

FIG. 20.28 (a) Fortran matrix multiplication from Figure 20.1(a) with a tile loop for each index, and (b) the result of tiling all the loops.

```
for i ← 1 to N do
  for j ← 1 to 3 do
    a[i,j] ← (a[i-1,j-1] + a[i,j] + a[N+1-i,j+1])/j
  endfor
endfor
```

FIG. 20.29 A HIR example for which tiling may benefit at most one of the two loops.

Choosing a fixed tile size independent of the loop bounds can prove disastrous, again especially for direct-mapped caches. A particular combination of loop bounds and tile size can be very effective for reducing collision misses, while changing the loop bounds by as little as 1% or 2% and keeping the tile size fixed can dramatically increase collisions and reduce performance by a large factor. Thus, it is essential that tile sizes be allowed to change with the loop bounds and that one have either experience with their interaction to base choices on, a theory that explains their interaction, or preferably both.

Wolf ([WolL91] and [Wolf92]) provides an excellent treatment of both the theoretical and practical sides of choosing tile sizes; he also gives examples of the phenomena discussed in the preceding paragraph.

20.4.4   Using Hardware Assists: Data Prefetching

Some of the newer 64-bit RISCs—such as Alpha, PowerPC, and SPARC-V9—include data prefetching instructions that provide a hint to the data cache that the block containing a specified address is needed soon. For example, in SPARC-V9, the data prefetch instruction can specify prefetching of a block for one or several reads or writes. The meanings of the four types are as follows:

1. Several reads: fetch the data into the D-cache nearest to the processor.

2. One read: fetch the data into a data prefetch buffer and don't disturb the cache, since the data are used only once; if the data are already in the D-cache, leave them as is.

3. Several writes: fetch the data into the D-cache nearest the processor, in preparation for writing part(s) of its contents.

4. One write: fetch the data for writing, but, if possible, do it in such a way as not to affect the D-cache.

Alpha's (`fetch` and `fetch_m`) and PowerPC's (`dcbt` and `dcbtst`) data prefetching instructions hint that the block containing the given byte address should be fetched into the D-cache for reading or writing, respectively. For Alpha, the block fetched, if any, is at least 512 bytes in size, which may be too large for some applications, as discussed in the preceding section.

Note that prefetching does not reduce the latency of fetching data from memory to the cache—rather it hides it by overlapping it with other operations. Thus, the two operations are, to a degree, complementary, but we should still prefer to reduce latency by exploiting data reuse first and only then use prefetching.

Prefetching is most useful in loops that access large arrays sequentially. For loops that contain a single basic block, the generation of prefetch instructions can be driven by detecting the sequential access patterns, and the address to prefetch from can be a constant offset from an induction variable. To determine at what point a prefetch should be issued, we proceed as follows. Define the following four quantities:

1. T_{loop} is the number of cycles taken by one iteration of the loop without doing prefetching, assuming that the needed data are in the cache.

2. t_{use} is the number of cycles from the beginning of an iteration to the data's first use in the loop.

3. t_{pref} is the issue latency of the data prefetch instruction.

4. T_{pref} is the result latency of the data prefetch instruction; i.e., $t_{pref} + T_{pref}$ cycles after the prefetch instruction is issued, the data are available in the cache.

The first use of the ith block occurs at cycle $t_{use} + i * T_{loop}$ for $i = 0, 1, 2, \ldots$ without prefetching and at $t_{use} + i * (T_{loop} + t_{pref})$ for $i = 0, 1, 2, \ldots$ with prefetching. To have the data available at time $t_{use} + i * (T_{loop} + t_{pref})$, they must be prefetched $t_{pref} + T_{pref}$ cycles earlier, or

$$\left\lfloor \frac{T_{pref}}{T_{loop} + t_{pref}} \right\rfloor$$

iterations back and $T_{pref} \bmod (T_{loop} + t_{pref})$ cycles earlier than that.

For example, suppose a loop takes 20 cycles to complete an iteration and that its first use of the cached data occurs at cycle 5 within the loop. Let the prefetch instruction have a 1-cycle issue latency and a 25-cycle result latency. Then the prefetch for a given iteration should be placed $\lfloor 25/(20 + 1) \rfloor = 1$ iteration earlier and $25 \pmod{20 + 1} = 4$ cycles before the first use point, or at cycle 1 of the iteration preceding the one that uses the prefetched data, and the prefetch instruction should specify the address of the data used in the next iteration. If the first use of the data occurs at cycle 2 of each iteration, the prefetch should be placed 1 iteration and 4 cycles earlier, i.e., 2 iterations earlier and at cycle 19 of that iteration.

Note that, unlike other D-cache-oriented optimizations discussed in this chapter, this one requires that we know the number of cycles that a loop iteration takes, so it needs to be performed on low-level code. On the other hand, this optimization also needs to know what address to use for each prefetch—information that can best be determined as a base address plus a subscript value from high-level code and then passed along to the low-level code.

One complication that may occur is that the size of the block fetched may be too large for prefetching to be useful in every iteration. Loop unrolling can help in this case—unrolling by a factor of n allows us to issue one prefetch per n iterations—but even this may not be enough; in such a case, the prefetch needs to be protected by a conditional that checks the value of the induction variable modulo the size of a cache block.

Another complication is that there may be more than one array that benefits from prefetching. If the arrays and prefetches are not carefully arranged, they may increase collisions in the cache. The linker and compilers can cooperatively improve the effectiveness of sequential prefetching by proper placement of large arrays relative to cache-block boundaries.

Mowry, Lam, and Gupta ([MowL92] and [Mowr94]) describe a somewhat more sophisticated approach to data prefetching than the one given above. Their evaluation of an algorithm like the one above suggests that if all data are prefetched, approximately 60% of the prefetches are wasted effort. Since prefetches occupy the CPU, the D-cache, and the bus between the D-cache and memory, reducing them to the minimum needed is desirable.

Their approach centers on determining the leading reference to a cache line (i.e., the reference that would cause it to be loaded into the cache) and a prefetch predicate that determines whether the data need to be prefetched for each particular loop iteration i. They use the predicate to transform the loop—if the predicate is $i = 0$, they peel the first iteration of the loop, while if it is $i \equiv 0 \pmod{n}$, then they unroll the loop by a factor of n. Next they place the prefetch instructions essentially as we describe above, but only for the iterations that their analysis has shown to need them. If the loop transformation would result in the code becoming so large that it impacts I-cache performance, they either suppress the transformation or insert code that uses the prefetch predicate to control prefetching.

20.5   Scalar vs. Memory-Oriented Optimizations

Whitfield and Soffa [WhiS90] and Wolfe [Wolf90] have studied the interactions between traditional scalar optimizations and the newer parallelism- and D-cache-oriented optimizations. They show that some scalar optimizations can disable parallel optimizations; that the ordering of the optimizations is very important and needs to be varied from one program to another to achieve maximal performance; and that, in some cases, performing the inverses of some scalar optimizations is essential to enabling some D-cache optimizations.

For example, Whitfield and Soffa show that loop-invariant code motion can make loop interchange and loop fusion inapplicable, and Wolfe shows that common-subexpression elimination can inhibit loop distribution. Clearly, it follows from these results that inverting the inhibiting transformations may make the others applicable in some instances where they were not originally.

20.6   Wrap-Up

This chapter has discussed optimization techniques that take advantage of the memory hierarchy, particularly of data and instruction caches and CPU registers.

Even the earliest computer designs distinguished between main memory and registers. Main memories have been larger and slower than registers and, in many systems, operations other than loads and stores have required at least one operand (and in some cases all) to be in registers; RISC systems, of course, are in the last category.

The difference between the processor's cycle time and the memory-access time has increased to the point where it is now necessary in most systems to have caches between memory and the registers. A memory access directed to an address represented in a cache is satisfied by it rather than by main memory (or, in the case of a store, possibly in parallel with memory). Caches depend on the spatial and temporal locality properties of programs for their effectiveness. Where they can be depended on, programs run at a speed determined by the CPU and the cache(s). If they cannot be relied on, loads, stores, and instruction fetches run at main memory speeds.

To deal with the disparity in speeds, we have first discussed techniques for dealing with instruction caches; then we have considered how to improve register allocation for array elements and techniques for dealing with data caches.

The instruction-cache-related techniques include instruction prefetching, procedure sorting, procedure and block placement, procedure splitting, and combining the intra- and interprocedural methods. Prefetching allows one to provide a hint to the memory that a particular block of code is likely to be needed soon, indicating that it should be fetched into the cache when spare memory and cache cycles are available. Procedure sorting provides a way to place procedure bodies in a load module in such a way as to increase their locality of reference and to decrease their interference with each other. Intraprocedural code positioning, or block sorting, attempts to determine an order of the basic blocks in a procedure that minimizes branching by making as many of the branches as possible take the fall-through path, and secondarily by making branches forward wherever possible. In fact, loop unrolling can be thought of as a variation on block sorting, since if we unroll a loop—for simplicity's sake, a one-block loop—by a factor of n, then there is one backward branch in place of each n of them previously. Procedure splitting seeks to improve locality further by separating procedures into frequently and infrequently executed segments and by collecting segments of each type together in the load module. Finally, we briefly mentioned an approach to combining intra- and interprocedural techniques to achieve as great a gain as possible.

The most important of the I-cache-related optimizations are usually procedure sorting and procedure and block placement, with instruction prefetching next, and procedure splitting last.

Next, we focused on improving register allocation for array elements, data-cache-related techniques, and data prefetching. Scalar replacement of array elements is designed to take advantage of sequential multiple accesses to array elements by making them candidates for register allocation, as well as all the other optimizations that are typically applied to scalars. The most important of the data-related optimizations are usually the data-cache-related ones, especially tiling, with scalar replacement of array elements next, and finally data prefetching.

We gave an introduction to and overview of data-cache optimization. This is an area where there are, as yet, no clear winners among the approaches to use, although there are methods that deal effectively with various classes of problems. As a result, we have steered clear of describing any one approach in detail, providing instead a basic understanding of the problem, how it relates to the data dependence material in Chapter 9, and suggesting some candidates for effective approaches to dealing with data-cache optimization.

Finally, we discussed briefly the interaction between scalar and memory-oriented optimizations.

Most data-related optimizations for the memory hierarchy are best done on high- or medium-level code that includes representations for loops and subscript lists. Thus, they are placed in block A in the order of optimizations diagram in Figure 20.30. In contrast, data prefetching needs to be inserted into low-level code, but uses information gathered from analyzing high-level code; we put it in block D.

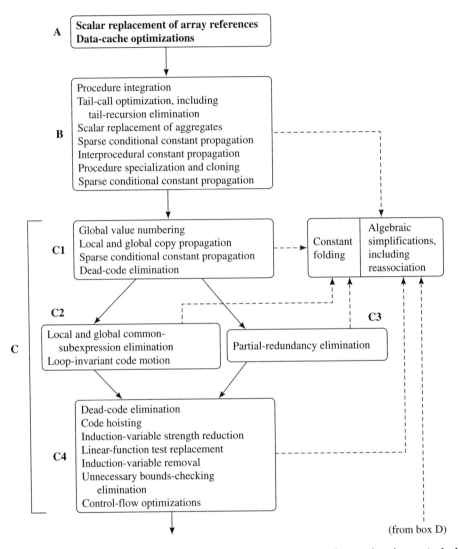

FIG. 20.30   Order of optimizations, with optimizations for the memory hierarchy shown in **bold** type.

Instruction-cache optimizations and instruction prefetching, on the other hand, benefit from being done very late in the compilation process, when the final form of the code is better comprehended. Thus, we add intraprocedural I-cache optimization and instruction prefetching to block D and the interprocedural form of the optimization to block E.

This area, and particularly data-oriented optimization, will bear careful watching over the next decade or two. There are sure to be major improvements made in the approaches to the problem, but it is difficult to say precisely where they will come

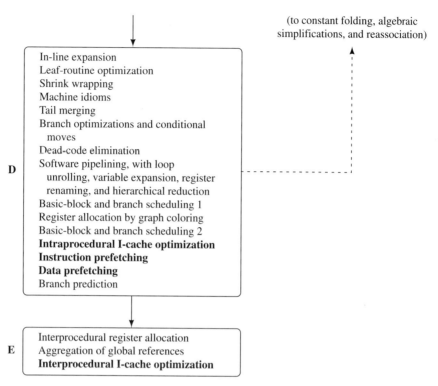

(to constant folding, algebraic
simplifications, and reassociation)

D

In-line expansion
Leaf-routine optimization
Shrink wrapping
Machine idioms
Tail merging
Branch optimizations and conditional
  moves
Dead-code elimination
Software pipelining, with loop
  unrolling, variable expansion, register
  renaming, and hierarchical reduction
Basic-block and branch scheduling 1
Register allocation by graph coloring
Basic-block and branch scheduling 2
Intraprocedural I-cache optimization
Instruction prefetching
Data prefetching
Branch prediction

E

Interprocedural register allocation
Aggregation of global references
Interprocedural I-cache optimization

FIG. 20.30 *(continued)*

from. Clearly, mathematical analysis, modeling of performance data, and brute force experimentation will all play a part, but whether any or all of them or some other insight or insights will be the sources of essential contributions is simply not clear.

20.7   Further Reading

Bell's work on the effect of tuning numerically intensive programs by hand to take better advantage of the IBM RS/6000's pipelines and caches is reported in [Bell90].

The I-cache optimization methods discussed in detail here are based on the work of Pettis and Hansen [PetH90]. McFarling's work is described in [McFa89], [McFa91a], and [McFa91b].

Scalar replacement, or register pipelining, was developed by Callahan, Carr, and Kennedy [CalC90].

Wolfe [Wolf89a] calls tiling "strip mine and interchange"; Callahan, Carr, and Kennedy [CalC90] call it "unroll and jam."

Lam, Rothberg, and Wolf's approach to D-cache optimization is described in [LamR91], [Wolf92], and [WolL91].

Gupta [Gupt90] discusses global approaches to the arrangement of data to take good advantage of D-caches.

The characterization of a large class of loop transformations as corresponding to unimodular transformations of a vector space is found in [WolL91] and [Wolf92].

Mowry, Lam, and Gupta's data prefetching algorithm is discussed in [MowL92] and further elaborated in [Mowr94].

Whitfield and Soffa's and Wolfe's studies of the interactions between scalar optimizations and parallelism- and D-cache-oriented optimizations are in [WhiS90] and [Wolf90], respectively.

See Section 9.8 for references to work on characterizing the memory use patterns of recursive data structures and pointers.

20.8   Exercises

20.1 Which of the optimizations discussed in preceding chapters are likely to enhance the effect of procedure sorting (Section 20.2.2), and why?

20.2 Which of the optimizations discussed in preceding chapters are likely to enhance the effect of intraprocedural code positioning (Section 20.2.4), and why?

20.3 Write an ICAN algorithm to perform scalar replacement of array references in a (non-nested) loop that contains only a single basic block.

20.4 Extend the algorithm in Exercise 20.3 to deal with nonlooping control-flow constructs inside the loop.

20.5 Give an example of a loop to which loop distribution applies and an optimization that makes loop distribution inapplicable.

20.6 Give an example of a doubly nested loop for which scalar replacement of array references applies to the inner loop. What happens if you unroll the inner loop by a factor of 4?

CHAPTER 21

Case Studies of Compilers and Future Trends

In this chapter, we discuss a series of commercial compiling systems and give a short list of expected trends in the future development of compilers. The compilers cover several source languages and four architectures. They represent a wide spectrum of implementation strategies, intermediate-code structures, approaches to code generation and optimization, and so on. For each compiler family, we first give a thumbnail sketch of the machine architecture or architectures for which it is targeted.

Some systems, such as the IBM XL compilers for POWER and PowerPC, do almost all traditional optimizations on a very low-level intermediate code. Other systems, such as the DEC GEM compilers for Alpha, use a medium-level intermediate code, while still others, such as Sun's SPARC compilers and Intel's 386 family compilers, split the work of optimization between a medium-level and a low-level intermediate code. Yet even the IBM compilers include a higher-level intermediate form on which to do storage-hierarchy optimizations.

In the sections that follow, we use two example programs to illustrate the effects of the various compilers. The first is the C routine in Figure 21.1. Note that in the if statement inside the loop, the value of kind is the constant RECTANGLE, so the second branch of the conditional and the test itself are dead code. The value of length * width is loop-invariant and, as a result, the accumulation of area (= 10 * length * width) can be done by a single multiplication. We should expect the compilers to unroll the loop by some factor and, of course, to do register allocation and instruction scheduling. If all the local variables are allocated to registers, there may be no need to allocate a stack frame for the routine. Also, the call to process( ) is a tail call.

The second example is the Fortran 77 routine shown in Figure 21.2. The main program simply initializes the elements of the array a( ) and calls s1( ). The second and third array references in s1( ) are to the same element, so computation of its address should be subject to common-subexpression elimination. The innermost

```
1    int length, width, radius;
2    enum figure {RECTANGLE, CIRCLE};
3    main( )
4    {  int area = 0, volume = 0, height;
5       enum figure kind = RECTANGLE;
6       for (height = 0; height < 10; height++)
7       {  if (kind == RECTANGLE)
8          {  area += length * width;
9             volume += length * width * height;
10         }
11         else if (kind == CIRCLE)
12         { area += 3.14 * radius * radius;
13           volume += 3.14 * radius * radius * height;
14         }
15      }
16      process(area,volume);
17   }
```

FIG. 21.1 A C procedure that is used as an example in this chapter.

```
1              integer a(500,500), k, l
2              do 20 k = 1,500
3                  do 20 l = 1,500
4                      a(k,l) = k + l
5        20    continue
6              call s1(a,500)
7              end
8
9              subroutine s1(a,n)
10             integer a(500,500),n
11             do 100 i = 1,n
12                 do 100 j = i+1,n
13                     do 100 k = 1,n
14                         l = a(k,i)
15                         m = a(k,j)
16                         a(k,j) = l + m
17       100   continue
18             end
```

FIG. 21.2 A Fortran 77 program that is used as an example in this chapter.

loop in s1( ) should be reduced to a sequence of at most eight instructions that load the two values, add them, store the result, update both addresses, test for termination, and branch (the termination condition should be modified by linear-function test replacement to be based on one of the array element addresses). The sequence should be shorter for those architectures that have storage-to-storage instructions, loads and stores with address update, and/or compare and branch instructions. Some of the compilers should be expected to software pipeline the innermost loop and un-roll it by some factor.

We should also expect at least some of the compilers to integrate the procedure s1( ) into the main program. In fact, there are four options for how to deal with this, as follows:

1. compile the main program and s1( ) separately (i.e., do no procedure integration),

2. integrate s1( ) into the main program and compile a separate copy of it as well,

3. integrate s1( ) into the main program and compile it to a trivial procedure that just does a return, or

4. integrate s1( ) into the main program and remove s1( ) entirely.

The latter two possibilities are reasonable alternatives because the entire call graph of the program is evident—the main program calls s1( ) and neither calls any other routines, so there can't be another use of s1( ) in the program in a separately compiled module. As we shall see, the second alternative is used by the Sun and Intel compilers, but the third and fourth are not used by any of these compilers. If the procedure is not inlined, interprocedural constant propagation could be used to determine that n has the value 500 in s1( ).

21.1   The Sun Compilers for SPARC

21.1.1   The SPARC Architecture

SPARC has two major versions of the architecture, Versions 8 and 9. SPARC Version 8 is a relatively bare-bones 32-bit RISC system. A processor consists of an integer unit, a floating-point unit, and an optional (never implemented) coprocessor. The integer unit contains a set of 32-bit general registers and executes load, store, arithmetic, logical, shift, branch, call, and system-control instructions. It also computes addresses (register + register or register + displacement) for integer and floating-point load and store instructions. The integer registers comprise eight global registers (with register r0 always delivering a zero value and discarding results written to it) and several overlapping windows of 24 registers each, consisting of eight *ins*, eight *locals*, and eight *outs*. Spilling register windows to memory and refilling them is handled by the operating system in response to traps.

The integer unit implements several specialized instructions, such as tagged adds and subtracts to support dynamically typed languages; store barrier to control the order of memory operations in multiprocessors; and save and restore, which switch register windows independently of the call and return instructions. The integer unit has condition codes that are optionally set by integer operations and by floating-point comparisons and that are used by branches to determine whether to jump or not.

Architecturally, SPARC is designed to be pipelined, with some features of the pipeline exposed to the programmer. Branch and call instructions include a following delay slot that is executed before the jump is completed,[1] and the load instructions cause an interlock if the next instruction uses the value loaded.

The floating-point unit has 32 32-bit floating-point data registers and implements the ANSI/IEEE floating-point standard, although the architectural specification allows some of the minor features to be implemented by operating-system software. The registers may be paired to hold double-precision quantities or grouped in fours to hold quad-precision values. There are no moves between the integer and floating-point register sets. The floating-point unit performs loads and stores, arithmetic instructions, square root, converts to and from integers, compares, and branches.

SPARC instructions typically have three operands—two sources and one result. The first source and the result are almost always registers, and the second source may be a register or a small constant. In the assembly language, the operand order is first source, second source, and then result. See Appendix A.1 for more details of the SPARC assembly-language syntax.

SPARC Version 9 is a newer architecture that is fully upward-compatible with Version 8. It extends the integer registers to 64 bits but provides condition codes for both 32- and 64-bit results of operations. A bit in the privileged Program Status Word indicates whether virtual address translation should produce 32- or 64-bit addresses. The integer instructions have been extended to include some that are 64-bit-specific (such as a load to a 64-bit register, in addition to the Version 8 64-bit load that sets a register pair), new branches that branch according to the 64-bit condition codes or the value in a register, and conditional register-move instructions. The privileged part of the architecture has been significantly redesigned to allow up to four trap levels and to make register-window spilling and refilling much faster.

The floating-point architecture is largely unchanged, but a new register-naming scheme has been introduced that doubles the number of double- and quad-precision registers.

Implementations of SPARC have ranged from the first, a two-chip gate array with the integer and floating-point units on separate chips (actually the slightly different Version 7 architecture), to highly integrated single-chip designs with superscalar execution.

21.1.2   The Sun SPARC Compilers

Sun provides SPARC compilers for C, C++, Fortran 77, and Pascal. The C language supported is full ANSI C, C++ conforms to AT&T's specification of the language, the Fortran 77 has DEC and Cray compatibility features, and the Pascal conforms to the ANSI standard with Apollo compatibility extensions. The compilers originated from the Berkeley 4.2 BSD UNIX software distribution and have been developed at Sun since 1982. The original back end was for the Motorola 68010 and was migrated successively to later members of the M68000 family and then to SPARC. Work on global optimization began in 1984 and on interprocedural optimization and parallelization in 1989. The organization of the optimizer follows the mixed

---

1. The annul bit in the branches provides for the delay instruction to be executed or not according to whether the instruction branches or not.

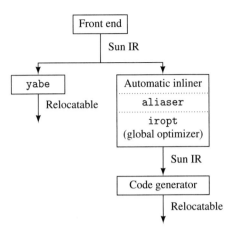

FIG. 21.3 Sun SPARC compiler structure.

```
ENTRY "s1_"  { IS_EXT_ENTRY,ENTRY_IS_GLOBAL  }
        GOTO LAB_32;
LAB_32: LTEMP.1 = ( .n { ACCESS V41});
        i = 1;
        CBRANCH (i <= LTEMP.1, 1:LAB_36, 0:LAB_35);
LAB_36: LTEMP.2 = ( .n { ACCESS V41});
        j = i + 1;
        CBRANCH (j <= LTEMP.2, 1:LAB_41, 0:LAB_40);
LAB_41: LTEMP.3 = ( .n { ACCESS V41});
        k = 1;
        CBRANCH (k <= LTEMP.3, 1:LAB_46, 0:LAB_45);
LAB_46: l = ( .a[k,i] { ACCESS V20});
        m = ( .a[k,j] { ACCESS V20});
        *(a[k,j]) = l + m { ACCESS V20, INT };
LAB_34: k = k + 1;
        CBRANCH (k > LTEMP.3, 1:LAB_45, 0:LAB_46);
LAB_45: j = j + 1;
        CBRANCH (j > LTEMP.2, 1:LAB_40, 0:LAB_41);
LAB_40: i = i + 1;
        CBRANCH (i > LTEMP.1, 1:LAB_35, 0:LAB_36);
LAB_35:
```

FIG. 21.4 Sun IR code for lines 9 through 17 in the Fortran 77 routine in Figure 21.2.

model, with two optimizers, one used before code generation and the other after. The four compilers share their back-end components, namely, the global optimizer and code generator including the postpass optimizer, as shown in Figure 21.3.

The target of the front ends is an intermediate language called Sun IR that represents a program as a linked list of triples representing executable operations and several tables representing declarative information. Figure 21.4 gives an example of Sun IR in the form produced by the front ends; it corresponds to lines 9 through 17 of the code in Figure 21.2. The operators should mostly be self-explanatory; the

CBRANCH operator tests the first expression following it, producing a 1 or 0 result, and selecting the second or third operand, respectively, as a target label.

If optimization is not enabled, the yabe ("Yet Another Back End") code generator is invoked to process the Sun IR code produced by the front end. It is designed for speed in code generation, does no optimization, and produces a relocatable object module. If optimization is enabled, the Sun IR is passed to the iropt global optimizer and the code generator for processing.

The compilers support four levels of optimization (in addition to no optimization), as follows:

O1   This level invokes only certain optimization components of the code generator.

O2   This and higher levels invoke both the global optimizer and the optimizer components of the code generator. At level O2, expressions that involve global or equivalenced variables, aliased local variables, or volatile variables are not candidates for optimization; automatic inlining, software pipelining, loop unrolling, and the early phase of instruction scheduling are not done.

O3   This level optimizes expressions that involve global variables but makes worst-case assumptions about potential aliases caused by pointers and omits early instruction scheduling and automatic inlining.

O4   This level aggressively tracks what pointers may point to, making worst-case assumptions only where necessary; it depends on the language-specific front ends to identify potentially aliased variables, pointer variables, and a worst-case set of potential aliases; it also does automatic inlining and early instruction scheduling.

If global optimization is selected, the optimizer driver reads the Sun IR for a procedure, identifies basic blocks, and builds lists of successor and predecessor blocks for each block. If the highest level of optimization (O4) is selected, the automatic inliner then replaces some calls to routines within the same compilation unit with inline copies of the called routines' bodies, as described in Section 15.2. Next, tail-recursion elimination is performed and other tail calls are marked for the code generator to optimize. The resulting Sun IR is then processed by the aliaser, which uses information that is provided by the language-specific front ends to determine which sets of variables may, at some point in the procedure, map to the same memory location. How aggressive the aliaser is at minimizing the sizes of sets of aliased variables depends on the level of optimization selected, as discussed above. Aliasing information is attached to each triple that requires it, for use by the global optimizer.

Control-flow analysis is done by identifying dominators and back edges, except that the parallelizer does structural analysis for its own purposes. All data-flow analysis is done iteratively.

The global optimizer iropt then processes each procedure body, first computing additional control-flow information; in particular, loops are identified at this point, including both explicit loops (e.g., do loops in Fortran 77) and implicit ones constructed from ifs and gotos. Then a series of data-flow analyses and transformations is applied to the procedure. Each transformation phase first computes (or recomputes) data-flow information if needed. The result of the transformations is a modified version of the Sun IR code for the procedure. The global optimizer does the following transformations, in this order:

1. scalar replacement of aggregates and expansion of Fortran arithmetic operations on complex numbers to sequences of real-arithmetic operations

2. dependence-based analysis and transformation (levels 03 and 04 only), as described below

3. linearization of array addresses

4. algebraic simplification and reassociation of address expressions

5. loop-invariant code motion

6. strength reduction and induction-variable removal

7. global common-subexpression elimination

8. global copy and constant propagation

9. dead-code elimination

The dependence-based analysis and transformation phase is designed to support parallelization and data-cache optimization and may be done (under control of a separate option) when the optimization level selected is 03 or 04. The steps comprising it (in order) are as follows:

1. constant propagation

2. dead-code elimination

3. structural control-flow analysis

4. loop discovery (including determining the index variable, lower and upper bounds, and increment)

5. segregation of loops that have calls and early exits in their bodies

6. dependence analysis using the GCD and Banerjee-Wolfe tests, producing direction vectors and loop-carried scalar du- and ud-chains

7. loop distribution

8. loop interchange

9. loop fusion

10. scalar replacement of array elements

11. recognition of reductions

12. data-cache tiling

13. profitability analysis for parallel code generation

After global optimization has been completed, the code generator first translates the Sun IR code input to it to a representation called asm+ that consists of

```
BLOCK: label = s1_
    loop level = 0
    expected execution frequency = 1
    number of calls within = 0
    attributes:  cc_alu_possible
    predecessors
    successors
        ENTRY  ! 2 incoming registers
        or     %g0,%i0,%i0
        or     %g0,%i1,%i1
BLOCK: label = .L77000081
        or     %g0,%i1,%r118
        or     %g0,%i0,%r119
        add    %r119,-2004,%r130
        ba     .L77000088
        nop
BLOCK: label = .L77000076
        add    %r125,500,%r125
        add    %r124,1,%r124
        cmp    %r124,%r132
        bg     .L77000078
        nop
        ba     .L77000085
        nop
BLOCK: label = .L77000078
        add    %r131,500,%r131
        add    %r133,1,%r133
        cmp    %r133,%r134
        bg     .L77000080
        nop
        ba     .L77000087
        nop
```

FIG. 21.5 asm+ code corresponding to lines 9 through 12 of the Fortran 77 program in Figure 21.2.

assembly-language instructions plus structures that represent control-flow and data-dependence information. Figure 21.5 shows the asm+ code, as produced by the expander phase at the beginning of code generation, corresponding to lines 9 through 12 of the Fortran 77 code in Figure 21.2. We have elided the annotations that would follow all but the first BLOCK entry. The instructions are all ordinary SPARC instructions except ENTRY, which is a higher-level operator that represents the entry-point code. Note that register numbers of the form %r*nnn* denote symbolic registers.

The code generator then performs a series of phases, in the following order:

1. instruction selection

2. inlining of assembly-language templates whose computational impact is understood (O2 and above)

3. local optimizations, including dead-code elimination, straightening, branch chaining, moving sethis out of loops, replacement of branching code sequences by

branchless machine idioms, and commoning of condition-code setting (O2 and above)

4.   macro expansion, phase 1 (expanding of switches and a few other constructs)

5.   data-flow analysis of live values (O2 and above)

6.   software pipelining and loop unrolling (O3 and above)

7.   early instruction scheduling (O4 only)

8.   register allocation by graph coloring (O2 and above)

9.   stack frame layout

10. macro expansion, phase 2 (expanding of memory-to-memory moves, max, min, comparison for value, entry, exit, etc.); entry expansion includes accommodating leaf routines and generation of position-independent code

11. delay-slot filling

12. late instruction scheduling

13. inlining of assembly-language templates whose computational impact is not understood (O2 and above)

14. macro expansion, phase 3 (to simplify code emission)

15. emission of the relocatable object code

For O1 optimization, register allocation is done by a local cost-based method like the one described in Section 16.2.

The Sun compiling system provides for both static (pre-execution) and dynamic (run-time) linking. Selection of static or dynamic linking, or some of each, is done by a link-time option.

The SPARC assembly code shown in Figure 21.6 is the listing that results from compiling the C routine in Figure 21.1 with O4 optimization. Note that the constant value of kind has been propagated into the conditional and the dead code has been eliminated (except for loading the value 3.14 stored at .L_const_seg_900000101 and storing it at %fp-8), the loop invariant length * width has been removed from the loop, the loop has been unrolled by a factor of four, the multiplication by height has been strength-reduced to additions, the local variables have been allocated to registers, instruction scheduling has been performed, and the tail call to process( ) has been optimized. On the other hand, some of the instructions preceding the first loop are unnecessary, and the accumulation of area could have been turned into a single multiplication. Also, it is somewhat strange that the loop-unrolling criteria result in the first eight iterations' being unrolled, but not the last two.

The SPARC assembly code shown in Figure 21.7 is the listing of the assembly code produced by the Sun Fortran 77 compiler for the main routine in the program in Figure 21.2 with O4 optimization (we have elided the code produced for the initialization loops and left only the code produced for the call to s1( ), which has been inlined automatically). Since s1( ) has been inlined, the compiler can make use of the information that the value of n is 500, which it does in unrolling the innermost

```
               sethi   %hi(length),%o0
               sethi   %hi(width),%o1
               sethi   %hi(.L_const_seg_900000101),%o2
               ld      [%o0+%lo(length)],%o0
               ld      [%o1+%lo(width)],%o1
               or      %g0,0,%i1
               ldd     [%o2+%lo(.L_const_seg_900000101)],%f0
               smul    %o0,%o1,%o0
               std     %f0,[%fp-8]
               or      %g0,0,%l0
               or      %g0,0,%l1
               add     %i1,%l1,%i1
               add     %l0,1,%l0
               or      %g0,0,%i0
.L900000111:   add     %l1,%o0,%o1
               add     %o1,%o0,%o2
               add     %i1,%o1,%o1
               add     %o1,%o2,%o1
               add     %o2,%o0,%o2
               add     %i0,%o0,%o3
               add     %o2,%o0,%l1
               add     %o1,%o2,%o1
               add     %o3,%o0,%o3
               cmp     %l0,3
               add     %o1,%l1,%i1
               add     %o3,%o0,%o3
               add     %l0,4,%l0
               bl      .L900000111
               add     %o3,%o0,%i0
.L900000112:   add     %l1,%o0,%l1
               cmp     %l0,10
               bge     .L77000021
               add     %i0,%o0,%i0
.L77000015:    add     %i1,%l1,%i1
               add     %l0,1,%l0
               add     %l1,%o0,%l1
               cmp     %l0,10
               bl      .L77000015
               add     %i0,%o0,%i0
.L77000021:    call    process,2    ! (tail call)
               restore %g0,%g0,%g0
```

FIG. 21.6 SPARC assembly code corresponding to the machine code produced by the Sun C compiler with 04 optimization for the program in Figure 21.1.

loop by a factor of four and producing no rolled copy. The unrolled loop, which extends from label .L900000112 to .L900000113, includes eight loads, four stores, seven adds, a compare, and a branch, which is minimal for that unrolling factor, except that linear-function test replacement could have eliminated one of the adds. The local variables have been allocated to registers and the loop has been software

```
MAIN_:          save    %sp,-120,%sp
                . . .
.L77000057: sethi   %hi(GPB.MAIN.a),%o1
            add     %o1,%lo(GPB.MAIN.a),%o1
            or      %g0,-2004,%o2
            add     %o2,%o1,%g1
            or      %g0,1,%o5
            or      %g0,500,%o7
.L77000043: add     %o5,1,%l1
            cmp     %l1,500
            bg      .L77000047
            sll     %l1,5,%o1
            sub     %o1,%l1,%o1
            sll     %o1,2,%o1
            add     %l1,%o1,%o1
            sll     %o1,2,%l0
.L77000044: add     %o7,1,%o2
            add     %l0,1,%o1
            sll     %o2,2,%o2
            add     %g1,%o2,%l2
            sll     %o1,2,%o1
            or      %g0,1,%l3
            ld      [%l2],%o2
            add     %l2,4,%l2
            add     %g1,%o1,%o0
            add     %l3,1,%l3
.L900000112:ld      [%o0],%o1
            cmp     %l3,493
            add     %o2,%o1,%o1
            st      %o1,[%o0]
            add     %o0,16,%o0
            ld      [%l2],%o2
            ld      [%o0-12],%o3
            add     %l2,16,%l2
            add     %o2,%o3,%o2
            st      %o2,[%o0-12]
            ld      [%l2-12],%o1
            add     %l3,4,%l3
            ld      [%o0-8],%o4
            add     %o1,%o4,%o1
            st      %o1,[%o0-8]
            ld      [%l2-8],%o2
            ld      [%o0-4],%o3
            add     %o2,%o3,%o2
            st      %o2,[%o0-4]
            ble     .L900000112
            ld      [%l2-4],%o2
```

(continued)

FIG. 21.7 SPARC assembly code corresponding to the machine code produced by the Sun Fortran 77 compiler with 04 optimization for the main program in Figure 21.2.

```
.L900000113:ld     [%o0],%o1
            cmp    %13,500
            add    %o2,%o1,%o1
            st     %o1,[%o0]
            bg     .L77000046
            add    %o0,4,%o0
.L77000056: ld     [%12],%o1
            add    %13,1,%13
            ld     [%o0],%o2
            cmp    %13,500
            add    %o1,%o2,%o1
            st     %o1,[%o0]
            add    %12,4,%12
            ble    .L77000056
            add    %o0,4,%o0
.L77000046: add    %11,1,%11
            cmp    %11,500
            ble    .L77000044
            add    %10,500,%10
.L77000047: add    %o5,1,%o5
            cmp    %o5,500
            ble    .L77000043
            add    %o7,500,%o7
.L77000049: ret
            restore %g0,%g0,%g0
```

FIG. 21.7 *(continued)*

pipelined (note the load just above the starting label of the loop). The temporaries have been allocated in the loop in such a way as to maximize the freedom available to scheduling. However, the compiler produces code for s1( ) as well as for the main routine, although this is unnecessary—the main routine manifestly calls only s1( ), which, in turn, calls no other routines.

21.2   The IBM XL Compilers for the POWER and PowerPC Architectures

21.2.1   The POWER and PowerPC Architectures

The POWER architecture is an enhanced 32-bit RISC machine that consists of branch, fixed-point, floating-point, and storage-control processors. Individual implementations may have multiple processors of each sort, except that the registers are shared among them and there may be only one branch processor in a system.

The branch processor includes the condition, link, and count registers and executes conditional and unconditional branches and calls, system calls, and condition-register move and logical operations. The condition register consists of eight 4-bit condition fields, one of which is set by selected fixed-point instructions and another by floating-point instructions. The other condition fields can be used to save multiple conditions, and all may be used to control branching. The link register is used primarily to hold the return address for calls and the count register to control looping, and both may be copied to and from integer registers.

The fixed-point processor contains 32 32-bit integer registers, with register gr0 delivering the value zero when used as an operand in an address computation, including in the load address instruction. The fixed-point unit has two basic addressing modes, register + register and register + displacement, plus the capability to update the base register with the computed address. It implements loads and stores (including forms that operate on halfwords with byte reversal, on multiple words, and on strings), arithmetic, logical, compare, shift, rotate, and trap instructions; and system-control instructions.

The floating-point processor has 32 64-bit data registers and implements the ANSI/IEEE floating-point standard for double-precision values only. It includes loads and stores, arithmetic instructions, convert to and from integer and single precision, compare, and some specialized operations that do a multiply followed by an add or a subtract without intermediate rounding.

The storage-control processor provides for segmented main storage, interfaces with caches and the translation-lookaside buffer, and does virtual address translation.

The PowerPC architecture is a nearly upward-compatible extension of POWER that allows for 32- and 64-bit implementations. A 64-bit implementation always allows both 64-bit and 32-bit modes of operation that differ in how effective addresses are computed and in the presence of a series of instructions. A PowerPC processor consists of branch, fixed-point, and floating-point processors and, as in POWER, a system may have one or several fixed-point and floating-point processors, but only one branch processor.

The branch processor has a 32-bit condition register and 64-bit link and count registers and provides essentially the same facilities as in POWER.

The fixed-point processor has 32 64-bit integer registers, with gr0 functioning as in POWER. It includes the same addressing modes as POWER. It implements the same categories of instructions as the POWER fixed-point unit, plus the storage-control instructions, except that some troublesome corner cases (such as using the base register as the target of a load with update, or doing a load multiple that includes the base register as a target) have been made invalid. A few instructions have been eliminated because they are difficult to implement, such as difference or zero (useful in computing maximum and minimum) and rotate left then mask insert, and others because of the change to 64-bit operation. Some new instructions have been added, many of them to deal with caches and translation-lookaside buffers.

The PowerPC floating-point processor has 32 64-bit data registers and implements the ANSI/IEEE standard for both single- and double-precision values. Aside from new instructions to deal with the 32-bit format, the instruction set is virtually identical to POWER's.

POWER and PowerPC instructions typically have three operands—two sources and one result. The first source and result are almost always registers, and the second source may be a register or a small constant. In the assembly language, the operand order is result, first source, and then second source. See Appendix A.2 for further description of the assembly language.

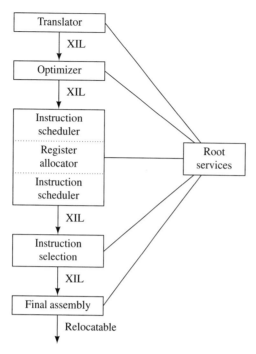

FIG. 21.8 IBM XL compiler structure.

21.2.2   The XL Compilers

IBM's compilers for the POWER and PowerPC architectures are known as the XL family and include compilers for PL.8, C, Fortran 77, Pascal, and C++, all but the first of which are available to customers. They originated from a project started in 1983 to provide compilers for an IBM RISC architecture that was an intermediate stage between the IBM 801 and POWER, but that was never released as a product. However, the first compilers based on the XL technology were, in fact, an optimizing Fortran compiler for the PC RT that was released to a selected few customers and a C compiler for the PC RT used only for internal IBM development. The compilers were written with interchangeable back ends, so as to target the IBM 370 architecture, the unreleased architecture mentioned above, the PC RT, POWER, the Intel 386 architecture, SPARC, and, more recently, PowerPC.

The structure of the XL compilers, which follows the low-level model of optimization, is shown in Figure 21.8. Each compiler consists of a front end called a translator, a global optimizer, an instruction scheduler, a register allocator, an instruction selector, and a phase called final assembly that produces the relocatable image and assembly-language listings. In addition, there is a module called root services that interacts with all the phases and serves to make the compilers compatible with multiple operating systems by, e.g., compartmentalizing information about how to produce listings and error messages. A disassembler is provided separately to enable production of assembly language from relocatables. The compilers are written in PL.8.

A translator converts the source language to an intermediate form called XIL by calling XIL library routines. The XIL generation routines do not merely generate instructions; they may, for example, generate a constant in place of an instruction that would compute the constant. A translator may consist of a front end that translates a source language to a different intermediate language, followed by a translator from the other intermediate form to XIL. The C translator for the System/370 does this, as do the C++ translators for the 370, POWER, and PowerPC, all of which translate to the 370 intermediate language first.

The compiler back end (all the phases except the source-to-XIL translator) is named TOBEY, an acronym for TOronto Back End with Yorktown, indicating the heritage of the back end as derived from the PL.8 compiler for the 801 and prerelease POWER systems development, although almost every module has since been changed significantly or replaced.

The XIL for a compilation unit consists of a *procedure descriptor table* that consists of information about each procedure, such as the size of its stack frame and information about global variables it affects, and a pointer to the representation of its code. The code representation consists of a *procedure list* that comprises pointers to the XIL structures that represent instructions, which are quite low level and source-language-independent. Each instruction is represented by an entry in the *computation table* or CT, which is an array of variable-length records that represent preorder traversals of the intermediate code for the instructions. Identical instructions in a procedure share the same CT entry. Each CT entry consists of an opcode followed by a variable number of operands, which may be integers in the range 0 through $2^{16} - 1$, indexes into tables of large and negative integers, floating-point numbers, register numbers, labels, symbol-table references, etc. The opcode may be a RISC-style operation, a load or store, a synthetic operator (such as MAX or MIN), an administrative operator (e.g., procedure header or block begin), or a control-flow operator, including unconditional, conditional, and multiway forms (the last comprising a selector and a label list). Variables and intermediate results are represented by symbolic registers, each of which comprises an entry in the *symbolic register table*; each such entry points to the CT entry that defines it. Figure 21.9 shows the relationship among the procedure list, CT, and symbolic register table.

Figure 21.10 gives an example of the external representation of the XIL code produced by the C translator for the first part of the code in Figure 21.1. Note that the external representation leaves much of the structure of the code implicit or unrepresented. The meanings of the opcodes are as follows:

1. PROC - procedure entry point

2. ST4A - store word instruction

3. L4A - load word instruction

4. C4 - compare word instruction

5. BF - branch on false instruction

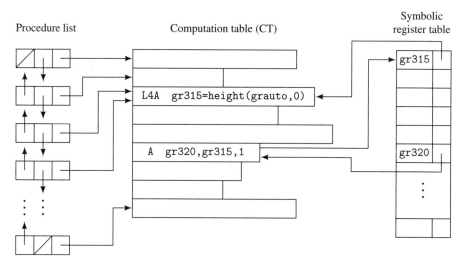

FIG. 21.9 Structure of the XIL for a procedure.

6. M - multiply instruction

7. A - add instruction

8. B - unconditional branch instruction

An operand of the form *.variable* represents the address of *variable*, gr*n* represents symbolic register *n*, and cr*n* represents symbolic condition register *n*.

Loads and stores in XIL have fully elaborated addresses. For example, a general load word instruction has a form that can be thought of as

> L4A   *reg=name(rbase,rdisp,rindex,...)*

To generate 370 code from this, the *rbase*, *rdisp*, and *rindex* components would all be used, as long as $0 < rdisp < 2^{12}$; if the inequality is not satisfied, additional instructions would be generated to put *rdisp* + *rindex* or *rbase* + *rdisp* into a register first. To generate POWER code, either *rbase* + *rdisp* (if $0 < rdisp < 2^{16}$) or *rbase* + *rindex* would be used, if the other component is zero, or additional instructions would be generated to combine components first. The optimizer is responsible for making sure that the instruction selector can generate legal instructions for the selected target architecture.

In addition to MAX and MIN, XIL includes a byte concatenate operator that takes an arbitrary number of operands, a multiplication operator, a division operator, etc. The optimizer turns MAX and MIN operators into a form from which the POWER-targeted instruction selector can generate corresponding two-instruction branchless sequences. The multiplication operator generates either a sequence of shifts, adds, and subtracts or a hardware multiply instruction, whichever is more efficient for the given operands and target. Divisions by 1, 3, 5, 7, 9, 25, 125, and products of these integers with powers of two generate a long multiply and a doubleword shift; other divisors produce a divide operation.

```
        PROC
        ST4A    area(grauto,0)=0
        ST4A    volume(grauto,0)=0
        ST4A    kind(grauto,0)=0
        ST4A    height(grauto,0)=0
        L4A     gr315=height(grauto,0)
        C4      cr316=gr315,10
        BF      CL.2,cr316,0x1/lt
CL.1:   L4A     gr317=kind(grauto,0)
        C4      cr318=gr317,0
        BF      CL.3,cr318,0x4/eq
        L4A     gr319=area(grauto,0)
        L4A     gr314=.length(gr2,0)
        L4A     gr320=length(gr314,0)
        L4A     gr313=.width(gr2,0)
        L4A     gr321=width(gr313,0)
        M       gr322=gr320,gr321
        A       gr323=gr319,gr322
        ST4A    area(grauto,0)=gr323
        L4A     gr324=volume(grauto,0)
        L4A     gr320=length(gr314,0)
        L4A     gr321=width(gr313,0)
        M       gr322=gr320,gr321
        L4A     gr315=height(grauto,0)
        M       gr325=gr315,gr322
        A       gr326=gr324,gr325
        ST4A    volume(grauto,0)=gr326
        B       CL.4
```

FIG. 21.10   XIL code for lines 1 through 10 of the C program in Figure 21.1.

The compiler back end uses a second intermediate language, called YIL, for storage-related optimization and may use it for parallelization in the future. The YIL for a procedure is generated by TOBEY from its XIL and includes, in addition to the structures in XIL, representations for looping constructs, assignment statements, subscripting operations, and conditional control flow at the level of if statements. It also represents the code in SSA form. The goal, of course, is to produce code that is appropriate for dependence analysis and loop transformations. After such analysis and transformations have been performed, the YIL is translated back to XIL.

Alias information is provided by the language-specific translators to the optimizer by calls from the optimizer to front-end routines. No further analysis is done beyond what each language definition provides.

Control-flow analysis is straightforward. It identifies basic-block boundaries within a procedure, builds the flowgraph, constructs a depth-first search tree of the flowgraph, and divides it into intervals. The basic-block structure is recorded in a table indexed by the basic-block number that includes, for each block, pointers to the first and last entries in the procedure list for the block and lists of the block numbers of this block's predecessors and successors.

Data-flow analysis is done by interval analysis, with iteration used for irreducible intervals, and the data-flow information is recorded in bit vectors. For some optimizations, such as reassociation and strength reduction, the bit vectors are converted into du- and ud-chains. The live registers and du- and ud-chains are updated as needed during these phases.

The optimizer does a series of transformations, as follows (in the order they are performed):

1. transforming multiway branches into sequences of compares and conditional branches or branches through a table of branches, according to the density of the labels

2. mapping local stack-allocated variables to register + offset addresses

3. inlining routines from the current compilation module, if requested and if warranted by several heuristic criteria

4. a very aggressive version of value numbering (more advanced than any published form)

5. global common-subexpression elimination

6. loop-invariant code motion

7. downward store motion

8. dead-store elimination

9. reassociation (see Section 12.3.1), strength reduction, and generation of update forms of the load and store instructions for POWER and PowerPC

10. global constant propagation

11. dead-code elimination

12. some architecture-specific optimizations known informally as "wand waving," such as converting MAX and MIN into branchless sequences

13. expansion of macro operators, i.e., lowering all opcodes and addressing expressions to ones supported by the target machine, turning calls into instruction sequences to address the parameters and to perform the call, turning large integer constants into sequences of instructions that generate their values, etc.

14. value numbering

15. global common-subexpression elimination

16. dead-code elimination

17. elimination of dead induction variables, including floating-point variables

Floating-point divisions are turned into three-instruction sequences that include a multiply and an add. If bounds checking is turned on in a Fortran 77 compilation, trap-motion analysis and code motion are done immediately after the reassociation and strength-reduction pass.

```
s       rx=ry,2          s.     rx=ry,2
. . .                    . . .
ci      cc0=ry,2         bt     label
bt      label
(a)                      (b)
```

FIG. 21.11   An example of coalescing condition-code setting with an arithmetic operation in POWER. The ci in (a) has been absorbed into the s. in (b) by setting its record bit.

TOBEY includes two register allocators, a "quick and dirty" local one, used when optimization is not requested, and a graph-coloring global one based on Chaitin's, but with spilling done in the style of Briggs's work (see Section 16.3). A phase just before register allocation elaborates procedure prologues and epilogues and performs tail-call simplification and leaf-routine optimization. The graph-coloring register allocator also does "*scavenging*," i.e., a version of value numbering that moves loads and stores of spilled temporaries out of loops. The allocator tries all three of the spill-code choice heuristics discussed in Section 16.3.12 for each procedure and uses the best of them for it.

The instruction scheduler is described in several papers (see Section 21.7). In addition to basic-block and branch scheduling, it does a type of global scheduling that works on acyclic flowgraphs and that uses program dependence graphs (see Section 9.5) to describe the constraints on scheduling. During optimizing compilations, it is run before register allocation (with symbolic registers) and, if any spill code has been generated, the local form is run again after register allocation.

The final assembly phase does two passes over the XIL, one pass to do a few peephole optimizations, such as coalescing condition-code setting done by compares with corresponding arithmetic operations and removing the compares (see Figure 21.11 for an example), and the other pass to output the relocatable image and listings. Final assembly calls routines in the language-specific translator to obtain debugging information to include in the relocatable.

Figure 21.12 shows the POWER assembly code produced by the XL disassembler from the object code resulting from compiling the program in Figure 21.1 with the XL C compiler with O3 optimization. The constant value of kind has been propagated into the conditional and the dead code eliminated; the loop invariant length * width has been removed from the loop; the loop has been unrolled by a factor of two; the local variables have been allocated to registers; and instruction scheduling has been performed. On the other hand, the tail call to process( ) has not been optimized, and the accumulation of area has not been turned into a single multiplication.

Figure 21.13 shows the POWER assembly code produced by the XL disassembler from the object code resulting from compiling the routine s1( ) in Figure 21.2 with the XL Fortran compiler with O3 optimization. The routine s1( ) has not been inlined. The inner loop has been unrolled by a factor of two (from label __Lfc through the next bc instruction). The unrolled loop includes four loads (two with update), two stores with update, two adds, and a branch, which is minimal for the POWER architecture. The local variables have been allocated to registers and instruction scheduling has been performed.

```
.main:  mfspr  r0,LR
        l      r5,T.22.width(RTOC)
        stu    SP,-64(SP)
        l      r4,T.26.length(RTOC)
        st     r0,72(SP)
        l      r0,0(r4)
        l      r5,0(r5)
        cal    r4,5(r0)
        muls   r0,r0,r5
        cal    r3,0(r0)
        mtspr  CTR,r4
        cal    r4,0(r3)
        cal    r5,0(r3)
__L34:  ai     r6,r5,1
        a      r3,r3,r0
        muls   r5,r5,r0
        a      r4,r4,r5
        muls   r5,r6,r0
        a      r4,r4,r5
        a      r3,r3,r0
        ai     r5,r6,1
        bc     BO_dCTR_NZERO,CR0_LT,__L34
        bl     .processPR
        cror   CR3_SO,CR3_SO,CR3_SO
        l      r12,72(SP)
        ai     SP,SP,64
        mtspr  LR,r12
        bcr    BO_ALWAYS,CR0_LT
```

FIG. 21.12 POWER assembly code produced by the XL disassembler from the object code resulting from compiling the program in Figure 21.1 with the XL C compiler with 03 optimization.

```
.s1:    l      r10,0(r4)
        st     r31,-4(SP)
        cal    r8,0(r10)
        cmpi   1,r8,0
        bc     BO_IF_NOT,CR1_FEX,__L1a4
        ai     r6,r10,-1
        cal    r12,0(r6)
        cmpi   0,r12,0
        ai     r7,r3,1996
        ai     r9,r3,-4
        cal    r11,2(r0)
        bc     BO_IF_NOT,CR0_GT,__L154
        rlinm  r3,r10,31,1,31
        rlinm. r4,r10,0,31,31
        cmpi   1,r3,0
```

FIG. 21.13 POWER assembly code produced by the XL disassembler from the object code resulting from compiling the routine s1( ) in Figure 21.2 with the XL Fortran compiler with 03 optimization.

```
                    cal      r31,0(r7)
                    mtspr    CTR,r3
      __Lec:   ai       r12,r12,-1
                    cal      r5,0(r31)
                    cal      r4,0(r9)
      __Lf8:   bc       BO_IF,CR1_VX,__L124
      __Lfc:   lu       r3,4(r4)
                    l        r0,4(r5)
                    a        r3,r3,r0
                    stu      r3,4(r5)
                    lu       r3,4(r4)
                    l        r0,4(r5)
                    a        r3,r3,r0
                    stu      r3,4(r5)
                    bc       BO_dCTR_NZERO,CR0_LT,__Lfc
                    bc       BO_IF,CR0_EQ,__L134
      __L124:  lu       r3,4(r4)
                    l        r4,4(r5)
                    a        r3,r3,r4
                    stu      r3,4(r5)
      __L134:  cmpi     0,r12,0
                    ai       r31,r31,2000
                    bc       BO_IF_NOT,CR0_GT,__L154
                    rlinm    r3,r10,31,1,31
                    rlinm.   r4,r10,0,31,31
                    cmpi     1,r3,0
                    mtspr    CTR,r3
                    b        __Lec
      __L154:  ai.      r8,r8,-1
                    ai       r9,r9,2000
                    ai       r7,r7,2000
                    ai       r11,r11,1
                    ai       r6,r6,-1
                    bc       BO_IF_NOT,CR0_GT,__L19c
                    cal      r12,0(r6)
                    cmpi     0,r12,0
                    bc       BO_IF_NOT,CR0_GT,__L154
                    rlinm    r3,r10,31,1,31
                    rlinm.   r4,r10,0,31,31
                    cal      r31,0(r7)
                    cmpi     1,r3,0
                    mtspr    CTR,r3
                    ai       r12,r12,-1
                    cal      r5,0(r31)
                    cal      r4,0(r9)
                    b        __Lf8
      __L19c:  l        r31,-4(SP)
                    bcr      BO_ALWAYS,CR0_LT
      __L1a4:  bcr      BO_ALWAYS,CR0_LT
```

FIG. 21.13 (continued)

21.3   Digital Equipment's Compilers for Alpha

21.3.1   The Alpha Architecture

Alpha is a totally new architecture that was designed by Digital Equipment to be the successor to its VAX and MIPS-based systems. It is a very streamlined 64-bit RISC design. It has 32 64-bit integer registers (with r31 delivering a zero when used as a source and discarding results written to it) and 32 64-bit floating-point registers (with f31 functioning like r31). It has only a single addressing mode, namely, register + displacement, and no condition codes.

The integer instructions include loads and stores; unconditional branches; conditional branches based on comparing the value in a register against zero; jumps that branch to and return from a subroutine and that branch between coroutines; arithmetic instructions (including adds and subtracts that scale one operand by four or eight); signed and unsigned compares that set a bit in a specified register; logical, shift, and conditional move instructions; and a rich set of byte-manipulation instructions to facilitate string handling.

The floating-point design implements the ANSI/IEEE standard but requires a lot of assistance from operating-system software for the corner cases. It implements both VAX and ANSI/IEEE single- and double-precision formats and provides instructions that include loads and stores, branches, conditional move, both VAX and ANSI/IEEE arithmetic operations, and conversions among integer and the VAX formats on one hand and the ANSI/IEEE formats on the other.

The system-control instructions provide prefetching hints, implement memory and trap barriers for the weak system storage model, and implement the so-called Privileged Architecture Library. The last of these is designed to provide facilities for an operating system that may vary from one system implementation to another.

Alpha instructions typically have three operands—two sources and one result. The first source and result are almost always registers, and the second source may be a register or a small constant. In the assembly language, the operand order is result, first source, and then second source. See Appendix A.3 for further details of the assembly language.

21.3.2   The GEM Compilers for Alpha

Digital Equipment's effort to produce compilers for Alpha is known as the GEM Project.[2] The name is not an acronym, despite being spelled uppercase, and is a carryover from the project that built the compilers for Prism, a previous DEC RISC effort that was never incorporated into a product. The GEM Project began about 1985 in parallel with several internal RISC developments. The need to provide compilers for several targets resulted in the GEM Project's producing compilers that are easily retargeted and that already have been retargeted several times. Prism was tentatively selected to be DEC's entry into the RISC market in 1987, and a GEM-based Fortran 77 compiler for it was available at that time. However, DEC soon

---

2. The GEM Project also produces compilers for Digital's VAX and MIPS-based systems.

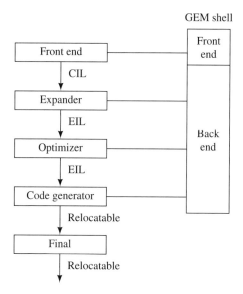

GEM shell

FIG. 21.14 DEC Alpha compiler structure.

switched to using the MIPS platform in its DECstation series, and work on retargeting GEM-based compilers for it began in summer 1988, with a GEM-based Fortran 77 compiler being first shipped for MIPS-based DECstations in March 1991.

Work on retargeting the GEM Fortran 77 compiler to Alpha began in November 1989. By summer 1990, the BLISS compiler was complete.

The compilers available for Alpha at introduction included Fortran 77 with VAX VMS and UNIX extensions, Fortran 90, ANSI C (with other dialect options), C++, Ada, COBOL, Pascal, PL/I, and BLISS. The compilers are structured as shown in Figure 21.14. A set of facilities called the GEM shell provides a common operating-system interface that is compatible with VMS, Ultrix, OSF/1, and Windows NT; it includes text input/output, diagnostic facilities, a language-sensitive editor, virtual memory management, debugging tools, and a common look and feel for all the compilers and environments.[3] Each compiler has its own front end, but all other components are shared. All compiler components are written in BLISS, except the C front end, which is written in C. BLISS macros are used to generate operator-signature tables for intermediate-language tuples and several other back-end tables.

In each compiler, the front end processes a file at a time, doing lexical, syntactic, and static-semantic analyses and producing an intermediate form called CIL (Compact Intermediate Language). All phases beyond the front end operate on a procedure-by-procedure basis.

Both CIL and EIL (Expanded Intermediate Language) represent a compilation unit as a doubly linked list of nodes. In CIL, the list corresponds to a compilation unit and the nodes have a fixed size. Each node is a record with fields that represent

---

3. Actually, there are several versions of the GEM shell in existence, one for each of several pairs of host operating systems and architectures, all providing the same facilities.

```
$1: fetch(i)                        $1: symref(; symbol=i)
                                    $2: fetch($1)
$2: subscr($1,[4],[0]; posn=1)      $3: litref(; literal=[4])
                                    $4: mul($1,$3)
$3: aref(x,$2)                      $5: symref(; symbol=x)
                                    $6: aplus($5,$4)
$4: fetch($3)                       $7: fetch($6)
                                    $8: symref(; symbol=a)
$5: store(a,$4)                     $9: store($8,$7)


(a)                                 (b)
```

FIG. 21.15 (a) Example of CIL code for the C statement a = x[i], and (b) its expansion to EIL code.

the node's kind and subkind, flags, forward and backward links, attributes, and pointers to its operand nodes. Several types of operators have comparatively high-level representations; for example, fetching a variable's value references the variable by name, and subscript lists are represented by lists that contain the subscript expressions and strides. Figure 21.15(a) shows the CIL form for the C statement a = x[i], with the minor subfields elided.

The compiler uses the mixed model of optimization, with code selection occurring between the global optimizer and register allocation and instruction scheduling. The first phase of the back end, the expander, translates CIL into the lower-level form EIL. In EIL, the list of nodes corresponds to a procedure and the sizes of nodes are variable. The nodes are tuples that represent operations with "moderately strong" machine typing. Each tuple consists of the operator, the operand and result types, its operands, an attribute list, and forward and backward links to other tuples. In comparison to CIL, the fetching of a variable's value is expanded in EIL to a symbol reference and a fetch through the symbol reference, and a subscript list is represented by a series of tuples that evaluate the subscript's linear form. Another example of the expansion in going from CIL to EIL is for procedure calls: in CIL, they are represented by elaborate tuples that describe the argument list and how each argument is to be passed and the result to be received, while in EIL, the argument list is expanded to a series of tuples that actually evaluate the arguments. EIL also includes nodes designed specifically for the optimizer, such as cseref nodes, which represent uses of common subexpressions. Figure 21.15(b) shows the EIL code that is produced by the expander for the CIL code shown in Figure 21.15(a), again with the minor subfields elided.

The compilers provide six optimization levels, as follows:

O0   This level does only peephole optimization and assigns each local variable to a distinct stack location.

O1   This level produces code that is intended to be debuggable; it does local common-subexpression elimination and lifetime analysis that results in variables sharing stack locations and registers.

O2   This level adds classic global optimizations that don't significantly increase code size.

03   This level adds loop unrolling and code replication to remove branches (the inverse of tail merging).

04   This level adds inlining of routines from within the same compilation unit.

05   This level adds dependence analysis and software pipelining.

Starting with level 01, the expander does interprocedural analysis to determine the call graph insofar as it can and does inlining of procedures within the same compilation unit. The procedures that make up the compilation unit are then optimized and have code generated for them a procedure at a time, from the leaves of the call tree toward its root.

The optimizer first constructs the flowgraph of the routine and its dominator tree, eliminating empty blocks, unreachable code, and unnecessary branches in the process. The list of basic blocks is sorted into "loop order," which resembles the depth-first search tree but keeps the blocks in the body of each loop contiguous to improve code locality. An empty preheader is inserted before each loop and a corresponding block after each loop. Also, while loops are turned into repeat loops, since the invariant-code motion phase is not designed to move code out of while loops. Data-flow analysis is done using the symbolic evaluation method of Reif and Lewis ([ReiL77] and [ReiL86]) but without constructing their global value graph. Alias analysis is done in two phases. The first phase, done before data-flow analysis, annotates data-access nodes with symbol access information and possible aliases. The second phase, done during data-flow analysis, traverses the dominator tree up and down to compute bit vectors that represent the potential side effects of assignments.

A series of peephole optimizations is done at three points in the optimization process: before control-flow analysis, after data-flow analysis, and at the end of optimization. These include algebraic simplifications, expanding multiplications and divisions by constants, expanding bit- and byte-field accesses to word fetches and extracts and the corresponding expansions for bit- and byte-field stores, and several others.

The global optimizations performed include the following:

1. induction-variable strength reduction

2. linear-function test replacement

3. loop unrolling

4. global common-subexpression elimination, including determination of those that are better recomputed than performed in common

5. loop-invariant code motion

6. global copy and constant propagation

7. dead-store elimination

8. base binding, i.e., determining address expressions that differ by a constant small enough to fit in the displacement field of a load or store

9. software pipelining

The code generator's design was inspired by the work of Wulf et al. [WulJ75] in the Production-Quality Compiler Compiler (PQCC) and the PDP-11 BLISS compiler. It consists of six phases, as follows:

1. Context 1 tiles the EIL tree for a procedure with code patterns, each with a cost per node. There may be several patterns for a particular part of a procedure's EIL tree—in practice, there are about five or six applicable patterns per node. Then Context 1 selects the set of patterns with minimal cost for the whole tree.

2. IL Scheduling next interleaves the selected code patterns for a basic block with each other sufficiently to produce high-quality register allocation. It also uses Sethi-Ullman numbers to compute the minimum number of registers that are required by each expression.

3. Next, Context 2 creates temporaries for the quantities that need them and computes their lifetimes.

4. Then Register History tracks the reloading of each temporary that has been allocated a memory location, annotating temporaries that have multiple uses so that they can be allocated to the same register.

5. TN Pack does bin packing of temporary names (as described in Section 16.2) to allocate registers, as determined by the actions contained in the patterns selected by Context 1.

6. Finally, Code emits the actual object code, based on the selected patterns and register allocation.

The code generator combines the code for the procedures in a compilation unit to produce a relocatable object module and determines where (short-displacement) branches can be used and where jumps are required.

Finally, the final phase of the compiler does peephole optimizations, such as machine idioms, jump simplifications, cross jumping, and code duplication (i.e., inverse cross jumping); and instruction scheduling using a detailed machine model and an algorithm that is based on determination of critical paths in straight-line code. The scheduler does some cross-block scheduling for safe speculative execution.[4]

Feedback of profiling results can be used to guide procedure integration and the order of the generated basic blocks and to tailor the calling conventions for frequently called routines.

Figure 21.16 shows the assembly code that is produced by the GEM C compiler with 05 optimization for the routine shown in Figure 21.1. Note that the constant value of `kind` has been propagated into the conditional and the dead code eliminated; the loop invariant `length * width` has been removed from the loop; the loop

---

4. Execution of an instruction in a particular block is *speculative* if the instruction originated from a following block with an intervening conditional. The speculative execution is *safe* if taking the other arm of the conditional does not require compensating for the effect of the speculatively executed instruction.

```
main:   ldah    gp,(r27)
        lda     gp,(gp)
        ldq     r1,8(gp)
        lda     sp,-16(sp)
        ldq     r0,16(gp)
        clr     r16
        stq     r26,(sp)
        clr     r17
        ldl     r1,(r1)
        ldl     r0,(r0)
        mull    r0,r1,r0
        clr     r1
L$3:    mull    r1,r0,r2
        ldq     r27,(gp)
        addl    r1,1,r3
        addl    r1,2,r4
        addl    r1,3,r5
        addl    r1,4,r6
        addl    r16,r0,r16
        addl    r16,r0,r16
        addl    r16,r0,r16
        addl    r1,5,r1
        addl    r16,0,r16
        addl    r16,r0,r16
        mull    r3,r0,r3
        addl    r17,r2,r2
        mull    r4,r0,r4
        addl    r2,r3,r2
        addq    r1,-10,r3
        mull    r5,r0,r5
        addl    r2,r4,r2
        mull    r6,r0,r6
        addl    r2,r5,r2
        addl    r2,r6,r17
        blt     r3,L$3
        jsr     r26,r27
        ldah    gp,(r26)
        ldq     r26,(sp)
        lda     gp,(gp)
        clr     r0
        lda     sp,16(sp)
        ret     r26
```

FIG. 21.16 Alpha assembly language produced by the GEM C compiler with 05 optimization for the routine in Figure 21.1.

```
s1_:    ldl     r17,(r17)
        mov     1,r0
        mov     2,r1
        ble     r17,L$4
L$5:    mov     r1,r2
        cmple   r2,r17,r3
        beq     r3,L$7
        nop
L$8:    sll     r2,4,r3
        ble     r17,L$13
        sll     r2,11,r5
        s4subq  r3,r3,r3
        subq    r5,r3,r3
        sll     r0,4,r5
        sll     r0,11,r6
        s4subq  r5,r5,r5
        subq    r6,r5,r5
        subl    r17,3,r6
        addq    r16,r3,r3
        addq    r16,r5,r5
        cmplt   r17,r6,r7
        mov     1,r4
        lda     r3,-2000(r3)
        lda     r5,-2000(r5)
        bne     r7,L$24
        ble     r6,L$24
```

FIG. 21.17 Alpha assembly language produced by the GEM Fortran 77 compiler with 05 optimization for the routine s1( ) in Figure 21.2.

has been unrolled by a factor of five; all the local variables have been allocated to registers; and instruction scheduling has been performed, including the safe speculative scheduling of the load of r27 in the instruction following the label L$3 from the following block. On the other hand, the allocation of the stack frame is unnecessary, the computation of area could have been reduced to a single multiplication, and the tail call to process( ) has not been optimized. Also, the multiplications to compute the terms that are added to produce volume could have been strength-reduced to additions.

Figure 21.17 shows the assembly language that is produced by the GEM Fortran 77 compiler with 05 optimization for the routine s1( ) in Figure 21.2. The code from s1_ to L$21 is initialization code for the routine and the loops, and the code from L$13 on is loop control for the outer loops and finalization code. The remaining code is for the innermost loop. It has been unrolled by a factor of four (the code beginning with L$21) and a rolled copy has also been produced, beginning at L$24. In the rolled loop, there are nine instructions, since linear-function test replacement has not been performed. The unrolled loop consists of 21 instructions, of which only one is inessential, again because linear-function test replacement has not been performed. The local variables have been allocated to registers and instruction

```
L$21:   ldl     r8,(r5)
        addl    r4,4,r4
        ldl     r19,(r3)
        addl    r8,r19,r8
        stl     r8,(r3)
        ldl     r19,4(r5)
        ldl     r8,4(r3)
        addl    r19,r8,r8
        stl     r8,4(r3)
        ldl     r19,8(r5)
        ldl     r8,8(r3)
        addl    r19,r8,r8
        stl     r8,8(r3)
        ldl     r19,12(r5)
        ldl     r8,12(r3)
        lda     r3,16(r3)
        lda     r5,16(r5)
        addl    r19,r8,r8
        cmple   r4,r6,r19
        stl     r8,-4(r3)
        bne     r19,L$21
        cmple   r4,r17,r8
        beq     r8,L$13
        nop
L$24:   ldl     r7,(r5)
        addl    r4,1,r4
        ldl     r19,(r3)
        lda     r3,4(r3)
        cmple   r4,r17,r8
        lda     r5,4(r5)
        addl    r7,r19,r7
        stl     r7,-4(r3)
        bne     r8,L$24
L$13:   addl    r2,1,r2
        cmple   r2,r17,r19
        bne     r19,L$8
L$7:    addl    r0,1,r0
        cmple   r0,r17,r7
        addl    r1,1,r1
        bne     r7,L$5
L$4:    ret     r26
```

FIG. 21.17 *(continued)*

scheduling has been performed. On the other hand, procedure integration of s1( ) into the main program has not been performed. Doing so would have saved the call and return overhead and would have propagated the value of n (= 500) into the subroutine, making the rolled copy of the innermost loop unnecessary, since 4 divides 500 evenly.

21.4   The Intel Reference Compilers for the Intel 386 Architecture Family

21.4.1   The Intel 386 Architecture

The Intel 386 architecture family includes the Intel 386 and its successors, the 486, Pentium, Pentium Pro, and so on, all of which implement essentially the same instruction set[5] but often in radically different ways (see, e.g., [Pent94]). The architecture is a thoroughly CISC design, but some of the implementations utilize RISC principles, such as pipelining and superscalarity, to achieve significant speed improvements over previous family members. The architecture is significantly constrained by the requirement that it be upwardly compatible with such early Intel processors as the 8086, which included only byte and halfword data and a rather difficult-to-use segmented addressing scheme. We discuss only a few of the compatibility features.

There are eight 32-bit integer registers named eax, ebx, ecx, edx, ebp, esp, esi, and edi. The low-order 16 bits of each register has a second name that is its name in the 8086 and that is used by the 8086 subset of the instruction set. The name of each 16-bit register is the name of the 32-bit register without the e. Each of the first four 16-bit registers is further subdivided into two byte registers, such as ah and al that comprise the high- and low-order bytes of ax, respectively. In addition, there are six 32-bit segment registers that are used in computing addresses for loads, stores, branches, and calls. Some of the registers have dedicated purposes, such as ebp and esp, which point to the base and top of the current stack frame, respectively, while others have dedicated uses in certain classes of instructions, such as ecx, esi, and edi in string-manipulation instructions.

A memory address is composed from a segment register (which is, in most cases, selected by the type of instruction), a base register, an optionally scaled (by 1, 2, 4, or 8) index register, and an eight- or 32-bit displacement, with each part optional (except that at least one must be present).

Conditional control is accomplished by compare operations that set bits in a flags register and branches based on them.

The architecture includes instructions for data movement (between registers and memory and between registers); binary and decimal arithmetic; logical, shift, and rotate operations; conditional and unconditional jumps; call and return; loop control; string manipulation; procedure entry and exit; floating point; byte translation; byte swap; and system control.

The floating-point programming model includes a stack of eight 80-bit floating-point registers. The floating-point formats are 32-bit single, 64-bit double, and 80-bit extended precision. All data are converted to extended precision upon being loaded into registers and may be converted back when stored. In addition to floating-point loads and stores, arithmetic and comparison operations, and conversions,

---

5. The Pentium Pro actually has some new instructions, including integer and floating-point conditional moves and a floating-point compare that sets the integer condition codes.

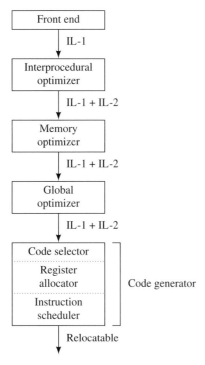

FIG. 21.18   Intel reference compiler structure.

there are instructions to load any of seven specific constants (such as π) and to perform trigonometric, exponential, and logarithmic operations.

Most Intel architecture instructions have two operands, although a significant number have one or zero. In the more typical two-operand case, the first operand is usually the first source and the second is both the second source and the destination, and operands are written in that order in the assembly language. The allowed types of the operands differ from one instruction to another, but in most cases one may be a memory address, register, or constant and the other may be a constant or register. See Appendix A.4 for further details of the assembly language.

21.4.2   The Intel Compilers

Intel provides what it calls reference compilers for C, C++, Fortran 77, and Fortran 90 for the 386 architecture family.

The structure of the compilers, which use the mixed model of optimizer organization, is as shown in Figure 21.18. Each compiler consists of a language-specific front end (derived from work done at Multiflow and the Edison Design Group); the interprocedural, memory, and global optimizers; and a three-phase code generator that does instruction selection, register allocation, and code scheduling. The interprocedural and memory optimizers were added to the compilers in 1991, along with a redesign of the code generator, called Proton, in an effort to increase the scope of optimization for the Pentium processor and its successors. Since then, the global optimizer has been extensively reworked to base much of its action on partial-redundancy elimination.

The front ends produce a medium-level intermediate code called IL-1 that includes some notable features, such as array indexes that are regenerated from pointer-based array traversal, as may occur in C and C++. Figure 21.19 shows the IL-1 code for the main routine in Figure 21.2 (as produced by the Fortran front end) as an example. The operations are organized into basic blocks with lists of predecessors and successors. The meanings of some of the operations are as follows:

1. ENTRY in instruction 1 represents the entry point to the routine.

2. SSTORE in instructions 3, 9, 25, and 29 represents storing an integer to memory.

3. VOGEN in instruction 20 and ASTORE in instruction 21 represent generating an array subscript and storing into the indexed array location, respectively.

4. LOOP_BEGIN in instructions 5 and 11 represents the beginning of a loop.

5. IF_REL.LE in lines 7 and 13 represents a loop closure test.

The result operand comes first after the operator, followed by the source operands. Note that the SI32 qualifier marks operands as 32-bit integers and that the IF_REL operations include expected execution frequencies for the two branches.

There is only one selectable level of global optimization (other than unoptimized) and separate options control invocation of the interprocedural and memory optimizers.

The interprocedural optimizer operates across file boundaries (by saving the IL-1 form of each routine) and may be driven by the results of execution profiling. It performs a series of analyses that are designed to collect information about how procedures are used and about some of their characteristics, such as their sizes, constant arguments, and uses of module-level static variables. The interprocedural optimizer then performs a series of optimizations that include inlining, procedure cloning, parameter substitution, and interprocedural constant propagation (see Section 19.3). Inlining is guided by whether a routine is called inside a loop, the size of the loop's code body, and the presence of constant-valued arguments, and it is done as much for the benefit of the memory optimizer as to reduce call-return overhead. Cloning is done to create individual copies of routines that have distinct constant parameters, thus potentially making loop and array bounds known constants. Parameter substitution tracks constant-valued arguments and propagates them to their uses as parameters. The interprocedural optimizer may also decide to pass arguments to particular routines in registers rather than on the run-time stack (except for UNIX, for which the Application Binary Interface requires that they be passed in the stack).

The output of the interprocedural optimizer is a lowered version of IL-1, called IL-2, along with IL-1's program-structure information; this intermediate form is used for the remainder of the major components of the compiler, down through input to the code generator. The IL-2 form (after optimization) of the inner loop of the main program in Figure 21.2 is shown in Figure 21.20. The result operand comes first, after the operator, followed by the source operands. Note that most of the operations

```
Entry bblocks: 0(MAIN)

BBLOCK 0:  (an entry bblock), preds: , succs: 1, stats:
    1 ENTRY.ARGS_REGS.ENT_GLOBAL
    3 SSTORE.SI32 5 1(SI32) __1.MAIN.k
BBLOCK 1:  preds: 0 6, succs: 4 2, stats:
    5 LOOP_BEGIN 5 500
    6 SLOAD.ND.NREG.SI32 5 t0 __1.MAIN.k
    7 IF_REL.LE.SI32 5 99% 0% t0 500(SI32)
BBLOCK 2:  preds: 1, succs: 3, stats:
    31 CALL.ARGS_REGS.CALLER_SAVES s1
BBLOCK 3:  preds: 2, succs:  , stats:
    33 RET.Sr
BBLOCK 4:  preds: 1, succs: 5, stats:
    9 SSTORE.SI32 6 1(SI32) __1.MAIN.l
BBLOCK 5:  preds: 4 7, succs: 7 6, stats:
    11 LOOP_BEGIN 6 500
    12 SLOAD.ND.NREG.SI32 6 t1 __1.MAIN.l
    13 IF_REL.LE.SI32 6 99% 0% t1 500(SI32)
BBLOCK 6:  preds: 5, succs: 1, stats:
    27 SLOAD.ND.NREG.SI32 5 t10 __1.MAIN.k
    28 GADD.SI32 5 t11 2 [t10,1(SI32)]
    29 SSTORE.SI32 5 t11 __1.MAIN.k
BBLOCK 7:  preds: 5, succs: 5, stats:
    15 SLOAD.ND.NREG.SI32 7 t2 __1.MAIN.k
    16 SLOAD.ND.NREG.SI32 7 t3 __1.MAIN.l
    17 GADD.SI32 7 t4 2 [t2,t3]
    18 SLOAD.ND.NREG.SI32 7 t5 __1.MAIN.k
    19 SLOAD.ND.NREG.SI32 7 t6 __1.MAIN.l
    20 VOGEN.2 7 t7 __1.MAIN.a 2
    21 ASTORE.2.SI32 7 t4 __1.MAIN.a t7 2
    23 SLOAD.ND.NREG.SI32 6 t8 __1.MAIN.l
    24 GADD.SI32 6 t9 2 [t8,1(SI32)]
    25 SSTORE.SI32 6 t9 __1.MAIN.l
```

FIG. 21.19 The IL-1 form of the main routine in Figure 21.2 as produced by the Fortran front end.

```
BBLOCK 7:  preds: 7 4, succs: 7 9, stats:
    26 LOOP_BEGIN 6 500
    30 ADD.SI32 7 t6 t4 t5
    25 ASSIGN.N32 7 t14 500(SI32)
    29 IMUL.SI32 7 t7 t14 t5
    24 ADD.SI32 7 t8 t4 t7
    23 SST.SI32 7 t6 t8 (addr(__1.MAIN.a)(P32) - 2004(SI32))(P32) __1.MAIN.a
    21 ADD.SI32 6 t5 1(SI32) t5
    2 IF_REL.GE.SI32 6 99% 0% 500(SI32) t5
```

FIG. 21.20 The IL-2 form of the inner loop in the main routine in Figure 21.2 as presented to the code generator.

have been lowered, subscripts have been expanded to address computations (note, particularly, line 23), and loop inversion and code motion have been performed.

Intraprocedural control-flow analysis is done as the first stage of either memory optimization or global optimization, whichever comes first according to the compilation options selected. It includes putting loops into a canonical form and representing their nesting structure.

The memory optimizer is concerned with improving use of memory and caches, almost entirely by performing loop transformations. It first does SSA-based sparse conditional constant propagation (see Section 12.6) and then data-dependence analysis using Banerjee's tests [Bane88] for loops with known bounds. Before the dependence analysis, a phase known as "loop cleanup" attempts to make loop nests perfectly nested and to make their bounds and strides known constants. The transformations that may be applied are loop interchange, loop distribution, strip mining, software prefetching, tiling, and creation of alternate loops. The last of these methods deals with loops that would be susceptible to significant optimization if their bodies satisfied certain dependence (or independence) relations but for which the determination of that condition depends on information available only at run time. The loop tile sizes are selected using techniques developed by Lam, Rothberg, and Wolf ([LamR91] and [WolL91]). Iteration distances computed by the memory optimizer are passed on to the code generator to control loop unrolling and code scheduling. Note that the inlining and procedure cloning that are done by the interprocedural optimizer increase the effectiveness of memory optimization by making more loops susceptible to the dependence-testing algorithms.

The global optimizer does a series of data-flow analyses and Banerjee's array-dependence test for loops with known bounds, the latter to identify ordering constraints on moves to and from memory. Control-flow analysis is done by determining dominators and back edges by the method of Lengauer and Tarjan (see Section 7.3). Data-flow analysis is done by a version of partial-redundancy elimination. Alias analysis assumes that all pointer references may conflict with each other, except for reference parameters in Fortran, as prescribed by the language standard. The optimizations performed by the global optimizer are, in order:

1. promotion of local and file-static variables to candidates for register allocation

2. constant propagation

3. dead-code elimination

4. local common-subexpression elimination

5. copy propagation

6. partial-redundancy elimination

7. a second pass of copy propagation

8. a second pass of dead-code elimination

The code generator, called Proton, uses its own intermediate form called Proton IL (PIL). The PIL code that results directly from translating the IL-2 in Figure 21.20

```
esp based stack
Stack frame size: 8

BLOCK=3 Phys_pred=2 Phys_succ=4 Loop=2
    CFlow_preds= B3 B2
    CFlow_succs= B3 B4
B3  opcode    op1      op2
1   imerge    B2.1     8
2   imerge    B1.3     B4.2
3   add       2        1
4   movi      $500
5   imul      4        1
6   add       2        5
7   st        3        ..1.MAIN.LOCALSTATIC.a-2004(6,4)
8    addi     1        $1
9   movi      $500
10  cjge      9        8        B3 p70% m0%
```

FIG. 21.21   The PIL form of the inner loop in the main routine in Figure 21.2 immediately after translation to PIL from the IL-2 form in Figure 21.20.

is shown in Figure 21.21. The operations are triples with the source operands specified after the operator and the triple number used to represent the result. Thus, for example, line 3 adds the results of lines 2 and 1, and line 7 stores the result of line 3 in the indicated memory location, which is indexed by the result of triple 6 and has an offset given by the result of triple 4. The imerge operator is an SSA-form ϕ-function.

Proton performs instruction selection, register allocation, instruction scheduling, and a series of low-level optimizations, with the four tasks intermingled to a significant degree. Formation of CISC addresses is done first. This is a nontrivial operation because an address may consist of a base register, an index register, a scaling factor, and a displacement, and address evaluation can be executed in parallel with other operations on the more advanced implementations of the architecture. The optimization is done by peephole optimization applied along du-chains. Induction-variable optimizations are also done before code selection, so as to shape the code to the architecture.

Instruction selection is relatively straightforward, except for instruction combining, which is driven by the small number of registers available and by the possibilities for running instructions in parallel in the Pentium and its successors. For example, a memory-to-memory add and a load-add-store sequence both take three cycles on Pentium, but the latter is more likely to be pairable with other instructions in the implementation's dual pipelines. As another example, PIL represents sign extension of a byte as a load followed by a shift left 24 and a shift right 24, but use of the architecture's load with sign extend instruction requires fewer cycles in some situations. Similarly, generating an effective address that includes a base, an index, and a displacement can be done in a single instruction without a result register, as indicated above, but it can also be done by two register adds with the result going to a register—which may be cheaper if the address is used more than once and if there is a register available to hold it.

Register allocation is done by a combination of local methods within basic blocks and by Chaitin-style graph coloring across basic blocks. The code generator divides the registers into local and global ones according to the loop structure of the given program. Programs with loops that have high (expected or measured) execution frequencies are allocated more registers for local use and registers are allocated from the innermost loops outward.

The stack structure of the eight floating-point registers limits the effectiveness of register allocation, since merging paths are required to have their stacks match. However, on the Pentium and Pentium Pro, the fxch (floating-point exchange register contents) instruction can be executed with zero result latency in the V pipeline, so the floating-point stack can be treated as a register set, at least within a basic block. This is in contrast to the 486 processor, in which fxch requires four cycles, so that treating the floating-point stack as a set of equivalent registers is highly unprofitable.

Global allocation of the integer registers might seem highly dubious, since there are only eight 32-bit registers and several of them have dedicated uses. However, four of the 32-bit registers have as their low-order 16 bits pairs of byte registers, thus increasing the number of registers available; also, only the stack-pointer register is permanently dedicated and unavailable for other uses. Moreover, while eight registers are certainly less useful than 32, studies of global register allocation have shown that eight are also much better than one or two.

Instruction scheduling is done by list scheduling and includes local register allocation, much in the style of the method developed by Goodman and Hsu [GooH88]. It is mostly done a block at a time, although predecessor and successor blocks are taken into account to a limited degree. Scheduling is strongly table-driven, since the architecture's implementations differ significantly in their pipeline organization and instruction timing. For example, the 386 is not pipelined at all, while Pentium has dual pipelines and the Pentium Pro has decoupled pipelines with a significant capacity for out-of-order execution.

The low-level optimizations performed in the code generator include the following:

1. induction-variable optimizations, as mentioned above, to optimize usage of addressing modes and registers; strength reduction; and linear-function test replacement, including replacing multiplications by sequences of shifts and adds

2. machine idioms, searched for along du-chains, such as using the increment and decrement instructions in place of addition and subtraction by one

3. alignment of loops on cache-block boundaries

4. converting of so-called prefix instructions that operate on halfword operands to the corresponding byte or word forms, which are faster on Pentium and newer implementations

5. code reselection to replace register-to-register instruction sequences with memory-based operations where register pressure makes it desirable or necessary to do so

6. software pipelining along the lines of window scheduling (see Section 17.4.1)

```
main:  .B1.1:
            pushl      %ebp
            movl       %esp,%ebp
            subl       $3,%esp
            andl       $-8,%esp
            addl       $4,%esp
            pushl      %edi
            pushl      %esi
            pushl      %ebx
            subl       $8,%esp
            movl       length,%esi
            xorl       %ebx,%ebx
            imull      width,%esi
            movl       %esi,%edi
            xorl       %ecx,%ecx
            movl       $-10,%edx
            xorl       %eax,%eax
       .B1.2:  addl    %esi,%ecx
            addl       %eax,%ebx
            addl       %edi,%eax
            incl       %edx
            jne        .B1.2
       .B1.3:  movl    %ecx,(%esp)
            movl       %ebx,4(%esp)
            call       process
       .B1.4:  xorl    %eax,%eax
            popl       %edx
            popl       %ecx
            popl       %ebx
            popl       %esi
            popl       %edi
            movl       %ebp,%esp
            popl       %ebp
            ret
```

FIG. 21.22 Pentium assembly code for the C program in Figure 21.1 as produced by the Intel reference compiler.

7. reassociation to collect loop-invariant operations and to move them out of the containing loop

8. loop unrolling

9. straightening and basic-block reordering to permit usage of short branch instructions

   The code generator includes an option to produce position-independent code for UNIX systems, and common-subexpression elimination applies to GOT references (see Section 5.7) as it does to other expressions.

   The Pentium assembly code for the example C program in Figure 21.1 is shown in Figure 21.22. Note that the constant value of kind has been propagated into the conditional and the dead code eliminated, the loop invariant length * width has

```
s1: .B1.1:
        . . .
 .B1.7:  movl     -2004(%ecx),%edx
         movl     -2004(%eax),%ebx
         addl     %ebx,%edx
         movl     %edx,-2004(%eax)
         movl     -2000(%ecx),%edx
         movl     -2000(%eax),%ebx
         addl     %ebx,%edx
         movl     %edx,-2000(%eax)
         movl     -1996(%ecx),%edx
         movl     -1996(%eax),%ebx
         addl     %ebx,%edx
         movl     %edx,-1996(%eax)
         movl     -1992(%ecx),%edx
         movl     -1992(%eax),%ebx
         addl     $16,%ecx
         addl     %ebx,%edx
         movl     %edx,-1992(%eax)
         movl     16(%esp),%edx
         addl     $16,%eax
         cmpl     %edx,%eax
         jle      .B1.7
.B1.17:  cmpl     %ebp,%eax
         jg       .B1.8
.B1.18:  movl     -2004(%ecx),%edx
         movl     -2004(%eax),%ebx
         addl     %ebx,%edx
         addl     $4,%ecx
         movl     %edx,-2004(%eax)
         addl     $4,%eax
         cmpl     %ebp,%eax
         jle      .B1.18
 .B1.8:  movl     8(%esp),%ebx
        . . .
```

FIG. 21.23 Pentium assembly code for the routine s1( ) in the Fortran 77 program in Figure 21.2 as produced by the Intel reference compiler.

been removed from the loop, the multiplication by height has been strength-reduced to additions, the local variables have been allocated to registers, and instruction scheduling has been performed. On the other hand, the loop has not been unrolled, the tail call to process( ) has not been optimized, and the accumulation of area could have been turned into a single multiplication.

The Pentium assembly code shown in Figures 21.23 and 21.24 is produced by the Fortran 77 compiler, with interprocedural, memory, and global optimization all enabled, for our example program in Figure 21.2, except that we have elided the initialization loops in the main program and all of s1( ) except the innermost loop.

```
MAIN: .B2.1:
         pushl      %esi
         pushl      %ebp
         pushl      %ebx
         movl       $2000,%ebx
         movl       $1,%ebp
           . . .
 .B2.5:  movl       $1,%esi
         movl       $500,%ebp
 .B2.6:  leal       1(%esi),%eax
         cmpl       $500,%eax
         jg         .B2.12
 .B2.7:  movl       %eax,%edx
         shll       $2,%edx
         subl       %eax,%edx
         leal       (%eax,%edx,8),%eax
         leal       (%eax,%eax,4),%ebx
         shll       $4,%ebx
 .B2.8:  movl       $-500,%eax
         movl       %ebp,%ecx
         shll       $2,%ecx
 .B2.9:  movl       ..1.MAIN.LOCLSTATC.a.1.0(%ecx,%eax,4),%edx
         addl       %edx,..1.MAIN.LOCLSTATC.a.1.0(%ebx,%eax,4)
         incl       %eax
         jne        .B2.9
 .B2.10: addl       $2000,%ebx
         cmpl       $1000000,%ebx
         jle        .B2.8
 .B2.12: incl       %esi
         addl       $500,%ebp
         cmpl       $500,%esi
         jle        .B2.6
 .B2.13: popl       %ebx
         popl       %ebp
         popl       %esi
         ret
```

FIG. 21.24 Pentium assembly code for the main routine in the Fortran 77 program in Figure 21.2 as produced by the Intel reference compiler.

Since s1( ) has been inlined, the compiler can make use of the information that the value of n is 500, which it does in using constant values in the loop control. The innermost loop (beginning at label .B2.9) has not been unrolled, but linear-function test replacement has been performed on it. The local variables have been allocated to registers, but otherwise the code in the innermost loop is entirely CISC-style.

However, the compiler produces code for both s1( ) and the main routine, although this is unnecessary—the main routine manifestly calls only s1( ), which in turn, calls no other routines. And, there are some interesting differences between the code produced for s1( ) and for the main program for the same loop nest.

While the code has not been unrolled and is CISC-style in the main routine, in the subroutine it has been unrolled by a factor of four (beginning at label .B1.7) and is thoroughly RISC-style code. Interprocedural constant propagation has not been done, as can be seen by noting, for example, that there is a rolled version of the loop (beginning at label .B1.18) in addition to the unrolled one. According to [Sava95], this is the case because the inlining was done and no clones of s1() were created. Also, the compiler chooses between CISC- and RISC-style code generation according to the opportunities for pairing instructions in Pentium's dual pipelines. If the RISC-like intermediate code includes nontrivial opportunities for pairing, RISC-style code is generated; if it does not, CISC-style code is produced. Unrolling the innermost loop in the subroutine created opportunities for pairing, so RISC-style code was produced for it.

21.5   Wrap-Up

In Table 21.1 we summarize the performance of each of the four compiler suites on the first (C) example program, and in Table 21.2 we summarize their performance on the second (Fortran) program.

TABLE 21.1   Comparison of the four compiler suites on the C example program.

	Sun SPARC	IBM XL	DEC GEM	Intel 386 family
constant propagation of kind	yes	yes	yes	yes
dead-code elimination	almost all	yes	yes	yes
loop-invariant code motion	yes	yes	yes	yes
strength reduction of height	yes	yes	no	yes
reduction of area computation	no	no	no	no
loop unrolling factor	4	2	5	none
rolled loop	yes	yes	no	yes
register allocation	yes	yes	yes	yes
instruction scheduling	yes	yes	yes	yes
stack frame eliminated	yes	no	no	no
tail call optimized	yes	no	no	no

TABLE 21.2 Comparison of the four compiler suites on the Fortran example program.

	Sun SPARC	IBM XL	DEC GEM	Intel 386 family
address of a(i) a common subexpression	yes	yes	yes	yes
procedure integration of s1( )	yes	no	no	yes
loop unrolling factor	4	2	4	none
rolled loop	yes	yes	yes	yes
instructions in innermost loop	21	9	21	4
linear-function test replacement	no	no	no	yes
software pipelining	yes	no	no	no
register allocation	yes	yes	yes	yes
instruction scheduling	yes	yes	yes	yes
elimination of s1( ) subroutine	no	no	no	no

21.6 Future Trends in Compiler Design and Implementation

There are several clear main trends developing for the near future of advanced compiler design and implementation:

1. SSA form is being used for more and more optimizations, primarily because it allows methods that were originally designed to apply to basic blocks or extended basic blocks to be applied to whole procedures, and because it generally results in significant additional improvements in performance.

2. Partial-redundancy elimination is being used more frequently, in part because the modern versions of it are very effective and much more efficient than the original form, and in part because its data-flow analyses provide a basis for organizing one's thinking about and performing other optimizations.

3. Techniques such as SSA form and partial-redundancy elimination are being combined to produce versions of optimizations that improve their applicability, effectiveness, and/or speed.

4. Scalar-oriented optimizations, including most of the ones we cover, are being integrated more closely with parallelization and vectorization in production compiler systems.

5. Data-dependence testing, data-cache optimization, and software pipelining will all advance significantly in the next decade.

6. The most active research area in scalar compilation is and will continue to be optimization.

Examples of all these trends can be seen in the papers presented at the annual conferences on programming language implementation.

21.7   Further Reading

The official descriptions of the processor architectures discussed in this chapter are as follows:

Architecture	Reference
SPARC Version 8	[SPAR92]
SPARC Version 9	[WeaG94]
POWER	[POWE90]
PowerPC	[Powe93]
Alpha	[Alph92]
Intel 386 family	[Pent94]

and the published descriptions of the compiler suites are as follows:

Compilers	References
Sun SPARC compilers	[Much88]
Digital's GEM compilers	[BliC92]
Intel 386 family reference compilers	[Inte93]

There is, unfortunately, no in-depth published description of the IBM XL compilers, although [BerC92], [GolR90], [OBrH90], and [Warr90] describe aspects of them. The IBM XL compilers and their intermediate languages, XIL and YIL, are discussed in [OBrO95]. [BerG89] concentrates on the register allocator, and [Warr90], [GolR90], and [BerC92] concentrate on the instruction scheduler.

AT&T's specification of C++ is [EllS90]. A bare-bones description of IBM's PL.8 language is found in [AusH82].

The IBM 801 RISC system is described in [Radi82] and [Hopk87].

Banerjee's array-dependence test for loops with known bounds is described in [Bane88]. The Banerjee-Wolfe test is found in [Wolf89b].

The description of the Sun compiling and operating systems' support for dynamic linking is found in Gingell et al. [GinL87].

Data-flow analysis in the GEM compilers is done using the symbolic evaluation method of Reif and Lewis as described in [ReiL77] and [ReiL86]. The GEM code generator was designed from the ideas in the PDP-11 BLISS compiler [WulJ75].

The UNIX System V Release 4 ABI supplement for the Intel 386 family is [UNIX93]. The Intel compilers select loop tile sizes using techniques developed by Lam, Rothberg, and Wolf (see [LamR91] and [WolL91]). Goodman and Hsu's technique for combining instruction scheduling and local register allocation is described in [GooH88].

Guide to Assembly Languages Used in This Book

In this appendix, we present succinct descriptions of the assembly language for each of the architectures we have used in examples. These descriptions are not assembly-language manuals—they provide only enough information to read our examples.

A.1 Sun SPARC Versions 8 and 9 Assembly Language

In SPARC assembly language, an instruction consists of an optional label field ending with a colon, an opcode, a series of operands separated by commas, and an optional comment field beginning with an exclamation point. The target operand is the last one. The address in a load or store is written as a bracket-enclosed sum of a register and either a register or a displacement. Register operands may be of the forms shown in Table A.1. Register r0 (equals g0) is special: it produces a zero when it is used as an operand and discards results written to it. The operators %hi( ) and %lo( ) extract the high-order 22 bits and low-order 10 bits, respectively, of their operand.

The opcodes used in the examples are listed in Table A.2. Some of the opcodes are extensions of the machine instruction set—for example, ld may produce either an integer or a floating-point load instruction, depending on the type of its target operand. The , a completer (whose value may be ",a" or absent) nullifies the branch delay slot. Branches with "i," or "x," at the beginning of the operand list branch based on the 32-bit and 64-bit condition codes, respectively.

SPARC pseudo-operations begin with a period. The ones used in the examples appear in Table A.3.

While SPARC-V9 extends Version 8 in many upward-compatible ways, such situations are, in most cases, not pertinent to our examples.

TABLE A.1   SPARC register operand forms.

Name	Meaning
%ri	Integer register i, $0 \leq i \leq 31$
%gi	Global integer register i, $0 \leq i \leq 7$
%ii	In integer register i, $0 \leq i \leq 7$
%li	Local integer register i, $0 \leq i \leq 7$
%oi	Out integer register i, $0 \leq i \leq 7$
%fi	Floating-point register i, $0 \leq i \leq 31$
%sp	Stack pointer (%o6)
%fp	Frame pointer (%i6)

TABLE A.2   SPARC opcodes used in the text.

Name	Operation
add	Add
ba, *a*	Branch always
bg, *a*	Branch on greater
bge, *a*	Branch on greater than or equal
bl, *a*	Branch on less
ble, *a*	Branch on less than or equal
bne, *a*	Branch on not equal
call	Call
cmp	Compare
faddd	Floating-point add double
fadds	Floating-point add single
fdivs	Floating-point divide single
fdtoi	Convert double to integer
fitod	Convert integer to double
fmuld	Floating-point multiply double
fsubs	Floating-point subtract single
iprefetch	Instruction prefetch (SPARC-v9 only)
ld	Load word
ldd	Load doubleword
ldf	Load word floating-point
ldh	Load halfword
mov	Move
move	Conditional move on equals
nop	No operation
or	Or

TABLE A.2 *(continued)*

Name	Operation
restore	Restore register window
ret	Return
save	Save register window
sethi	Set high-order 22 bits
sll	Shift left logical
smul	Signed multiply
st	Store word
std	Store doubleword
stf	Store word floating-point
sub	Subtract
subcc	Subtract and set condition codes
umul	Unsigned multiply
unimp	Unimplemented

TABLE A.3 SPARC pseudo-operations.

Name	Meaning
.align	Set alignment (in bytes)
.data	Switch to data segment
.double	Doubleword constant
.end	End of inlining template
.global	Global symbol
.seg	Switch segments
.template	Beginning of inlining template
.text	Switch to text segment
.word	Word constant

A.2   IBM POWER and PowerPC Assembly Language

In POWER and PowerPC assembly language, an instruction consists of an optional label field terminated by a colon, an opcode, a series of operands separated by commas, and an optional comment field beginning with a pound sign. The target operand is the first one. The address in a load or store is written as either a displacement followed by a base register in parentheses, or an index register followed by a base register separated by a comma. A general register operand is a number in the range 0 through 31 or the letter r followed by such a number, with the type of each

TABLE A.4 POWER and PowerPC opcodes used in the text.

POWER Name	PowerPC Name	Operation
a	addc	Add
ai	addic	Add immediate
b	b	Unconditional branch
bbt	bbt	Branch on condition register bit true
bc	bc	Branch conditional
bcr	bcr	Branch conditional register
bl	bl	Branch and link
cal	addi	Compute address lower
cmp	cmp	Compare
cmpi	cmpi	Compare immediate
cror	cror	Condition register or
doz	---	Difference or zero
fa	fadd	Floating add
l	lwz	Load
lbz	lbz	Load byte and zero
lhau	lhau	Load half algebraic with update
lu	lwzu	Load with update
mfspr	mfspr	Move from special register
mtspr	mtspr	Move to special register
muls	mullw	Multiply short
rlinm	rlwinm	Rotate left immediate and mask
st	stw	Store
stu	stwu	Store with update

register distinguished by the opcode. Register r0 is special: in address computations, it produces a zero when used as an operand in address computation. An operand of the form CRn, with $0 \leq n \leq 7$, represents a condition register; CR0 may be set by any integer instruction whose opcode ends in a dot. Compare instructions may set any condition register and branch instructions may test any of them.

Registers SP and RTOC are the stack pointer and the pointer to the global object table, respectively.

The opcodes used in the examples are listed in Table A.4. The difference or zero instruction (doz) in POWER has been eliminated in PowerPC.

A.3   DEC Alpha Assembly Language

In Alpha assembly language, an instruction consists of an optional label field ending with a colon, an opcode, a series of operands separated by commas, and an optional comment field beginning with a semicolon. The target operand is the last one. The address in a load or store is written as a displacement followed by a base register in parentheses. Integer register operands may be of the forms shown in Table A.5. Register r31 is special: it produces a zero when used as an operand and discards results written to it.

The opcodes used in the examples are listed in Table A.6. Some of the opcodes are extensions of the machine instruction set—for example, clr and mov both do logical ors.

Recall that DEC's "longword" and "quadword" are our "word" and "double-word," respectively.

TABLE A.5   Alpha integer register names.

Name	Meaning
ri	Integer register i, $0 \leq i \leq 31$
sp	Stack pointer (r30)
gp	Global pointer (r29)

TABLE A.6   Alpha opcodes used in the text.

Name	Operation
addl	Add longword
addq	Add quadword
beq	Branch if register equal to zero
bis	Logical or
ble	Branch if register less than or equal to zero
blt	Branch if register less than zero
bne	Branch if register not equal to zero
clr	Clear register
cmple	Compare signed longword less than or equal
cmplt	Compare signed longword less than
cvttq	Convert IEEE floating point to integer
insbl	Insert byte low
jsr	Jump to subroutine
lda	Load address
ldah	Load address high
ldl	Load longword
ldq	Load quadword
ldq_u	Load unaligned quadword
mov	Move register
mskbl	Mask byte low
mull	Multiply longword
nop	No operation

(continued)

TABLE A.6 *(continued)*

Name	Operation
ret	Return from subroutine
s4subq	Scale quadword by 4 and subtract
sll	Shift left logical
stl	Store longword
stq	Store quadword
stq_u	Store unaligned quadword
subq	Subtract quadword

A.4   Intel 386 Architecture Assembly Language

In the Intel assembly language for the 386 architecture family, an instruction consists of an optional label field terminated by a colon, an opcode, a series of operands separated by commas, and an optional comment field beginning with a semicolon. Instructions may have zero to two operands, depending on the opcode and usage (e.g., the return instruction ret may have one operand, but it is optional). For two-operand instructions, the second operand is usually both the second source and the destination.

A memory address is written as a displacement followed by a comma-separated list in parentheses; the list consists of a base register followed by an index register followed by a scaling factor (which applies to the index register), each of which is optional, except that if no index register appears there can be no scaling factor. An integer register operand is a percent sign followed by the name of the register. Constants begin with a dollar sign.

The integer register names are given in Table A.7. Some of the 32-bit registers have 16-bit subregisters and some have eight-bit subregisters also, to provide com-

TABLE A.7   Intel 386 architecture integer register names.

32-Bit Name	16-Bit Name	8-Bit Names	Usage
eax	ax	al, ah	General register
ebx	bx	bl, bh	General register
ecx	cx	cl, ch	General register
edx	dx	dl, dh	General register
ebp	bp		Base (or frame) pointer
esi	si		General register
edi	di		General register
esp	sp		Stack pointer

TABLE A.8 Intel 386 architecture opcodes used in the text.

Name	Operation
addl	Add
andl	Logical and
call	Call
cmpl	Compare
fadd	Floating-point add
imull	Multiply
incl	Increment
jg	Jump on greater than
jle	Jump on less than or equal
jne	Jump on not equal
leal	Load effective address
movl	Move
popl	Pop
pushl	Push
ret	Return
shll	Shift left logical
subl	Subtract
xorl	Logical exclusive or

patibility with earlier Intel processors. While six of the registers are general purpose, in some cases some of them are used in dedicated ways by specific instructions, such as ecx, esi, and edi for string-manipulation instructions.

The floating-point registers are 80 bits long and form a stack. They are named %st(0) (or just %st) through %st(7). Typical instructions, such as floating-point adds, may appear as follows:

```
fadd    %st(2),%st
fadd    1.0
```

The first of these instructions adds the contents of %st and %st(2) and replaces the value of %st with the result, and the second adds 1.0 to %st.

The opcodes used in examples in the text are listed in Table A.8. The suffix "l" on all the integer instructions indicates that they operate on long (i.e., 32-bit) operands.

A.5   Hewlett-Packard's PA-RISC Assembly Language

In PA-RISC assembly language, an instruction consists of an optional label field, an opcode, a series of operands separated by commas, and an optional comment field.

The target operand is the last one. The address in a load or store is written as a displacement or index register followed by a base register in parentheses. Register operands may be of the forms shown in Table A.9. The operators LR' and RR' extract the high-order and low-order 16 bits, respectively, of their constant operand.

The opcodes used in the examples are listed in Table A.10. Some of the opcodes are extensions of the machine instruction set—for example, COPY is actually a subcase of OR, and COMB is shorthand for COMBF and COMBT, compare and branch on false and true, respectively. The completer *mod* indicates a modification of the base register in a load or store instruction; in particular, MA modifies the base register by adding the displacement to it after forming the effective memory address. The completer *cond* indicates an arithmetic (or other) condition (for example, SDC indicates "some digit carry") and the completer *n* (whose value may be N) indicates nullification of the instruction following a branch.

TABLE A.9   PA-RISC register names.

Name	Meaning
%ri	Integer register i, $0 \leq i \leq 31$
%fri	Floating-point register i, $0 \leq i \leq 31$
%friL	Floating-point register i, $0 \leq i \leq 31$, left half
%friR	Floating-point register i, $0 \leq i \leq 31$, right half

TABLE A.10   PA-RISC opcodes.

Name	Operation
ADD	Add
ADDB	Add and branch
ADDBT	Add and branch on true
ADDI	Add immediate
ADDIB, *cond*	Add immediate and branch on condition
ADDIL	Add immediate left
B	Branch
BL	Branch and link
BV	Branch vectored
COMB, *cond*, *n*	Compare and branch
COMBF, *cond*	Compare and branch on false
COMIBF, *cond*, *n*	Compare immediate and branch on false
COPY	Copy
DCOR	Decimal correct
FLDWS, *mod*	Floating-point load word short

TABLE A.10 *(continued)*

Name	Operation
FSTWS, *mod*	Floating-point store word short
LDHS, *mod*	Load halfword short
LDI	Load immediate
LDO	Load offset
LDWM, *mod*	Load word and modify
LDWS, *mod*	Load word short
LDWX, *mod*	Load word indexed
MOVE	Move register
NOP	No operation
SH1ADD	Shift one and add
SH2ADD	Shift two and add
SH3ADD	Shift three and add
SHD	Shift double
STW	Store word
STWM, *mod*	Store word and modify
SUB	Subtract
XMPYU	Fixed-point multiply unsigned

Representation of Sets, Sequences, Trees, DAGs, and Functions

The choice of an appropriate concrete representation of an abstract data structure can make the difference between an algorithm's running in linear or quadratic time versus its requiring large polynomial or even exponential time. Thus, it is essential that we understand the possible choices for representing data structures, the time required by various operations performed on them, and the space they occupy if we are to turn algorithms presented here or elsewhere into code that runs efficiently.

Our goal in this appendix is not to provide a course in data structures, but primarily to remind the reader of useful concrete representations of data structures that should be considered in implementing algorithms such as those in this book.

For example, suppose we need to represent strictly increasing sequences of integers in the range 0 through $u - 1$ with at most s members in the sequences. Then, for $u = 64$,

$$1, 3, 5, 11, 23, 43, 53, 62$$

is such a sequence, and

$$3, 1, 15$$

is not, since in this second case, the first member of the sequence is larger than the second. We might represent such sequences, for example, by two-way linked lists in which the list entries contain the integers or by doubleword bit vectors in which bit position i is 1 if and only if i is in the sequence, as shown in Figure B.1(a) and (b), respectively. Let s be the number of elements that are currently in the sequence. Suppose that the operations we need to be able to perform on such sequences are (1) adding a value, (2) removing a value, (3) testing membership of a value, (4) merging sequences, and (5) determining the length of a sequence.

For the linked-list implementation, we perform each of the operations as follows:

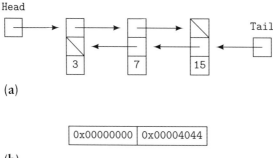

(a)

| 0x00000000 | 0x00004044 |

(b)

FIG. B.1 Representation of the three-member, strictly increasing sequence 3, 7, 15 by (a) a two-way linked list, and (b) by a doubleword bit vector (the bits are numbered from the right).

1. adding a value v: Traverse the list, comparing members to v until we (a) find v, (b) find a value larger than v, or (c), come to the end of the list. For cases (b) and (c), we insert v at the appropriate place, and for (a), we do nothing more.

2. removing a value v: Traverse the list, comparing members to v until we (a) find v, (b) find a value larger than v, or (c) come to the end of the list. For case (a), we remove the entry containing v, and for (b) and (c), we do nothing more.

3. testing membership of v: Traverse the list, comparing members to v until we (a) find v, (b) find a value larger than v, or (c) come to the end of the list. For case (a), we answer "yes," and for (b) and (c), we answer "no."

4. merging sequences: Traverse both lists in parallel, selecting elements from each list according to their relative magnitudes and combining them into one list, eliminating duplicates in the process.

5. determining the length of a sequence: Traverse the list, counting the members.

Each of these operations takes $O(u)$ time in the worst case and $O(s)$ time in the typical case, and the sequences require $3s$ words of storage.

For the bit-vector implementation, we first construct an array of $u = 64$ doublewords mask[1..64], each of which has one bit set to 1, namely, the ith bit in the ith doubleword. Call the current value of the sequence seq.

We perform the operations as follows:

1. adding a value v: Logically *or* together seq and mask[v].

2. removing a value v: Bitwise complement mask[v] and logically *and* the result with seq.

3. testing membership of v: Logically *and* together seq and mask[v]. If the result is nonzero, answer "yes," otherwise answer "no."

4. merging sequences: Logically *or* the two sequences.

5. determining the length of a sequence: For $v = 1$ to u, logically *and* together seq and mask[v], counting the number of times that the result is nonzero.

Now each operation other than (5) requires constant time, while determining length requires $O(u)$ time, and the bit vectors occupy two words each.

Thus, given the above set of operations to be performed, we would prefer the bit-vector representation, unless determining the length of the sequence is an operation that occurs very frequently. Note also that determining the length of the sequence can be sped up significantly for either representation by amortizing its cost over the other operations; i.e., we could keep a count of the length of the sequence and modify it each time an operation adds or removes an element. For the bit-vector representation, this still requires counting when we combine two sequences.

On the other hand, suppose that the range of integers allowed in the sequences is on the order of $u = 1,000,000$ but that the sequences that occur never have more than $s = 50$ elements. Now the trade-offs steer us toward the linked-list implementation: Each of the linked-list operations costs us at most 50 operations and the lists occupy at most 150 words each, while the bit-vector operations each take time that is $O(u)$, but the vectors occupy $\lceil 1,000,000/32 \rceil = 31,250$ words each.

Note that both implementations can be dynamically allocated and reallocated to deal with changes in size of the data structure, as long as they are accessed through pointers.

B.1   Representation of Sets

As is the case for most data structures, how we choose to represent sets depends on the nature of the elements, the cardinality of the universe from which the sets' elements are drawn, the typical and maximal sizes of the sets, and the operations to be performed on them.

If the universe U is a range of u integers, and preferably $0, \ldots, u - 1$ for some u, then several sorts of representations become simpler than they otherwise might be. If it is not of this form, it is often useful to map the elements of U onto the range $0, \ldots, u - 1$ by hashing.

Whether the hash function needs to be easily invertible depends on the operations to be performed on the set, e.g., if we are to union two sets and then to enumerate the members of the union, an invertible hash function is virtually necessary. If no operation requires us to enumerate the members of a set, invertibility is unnecessary.

The fundamental operations on sets are union ("$\cup$"), intersection ("$\cap$"), difference ("$-$"), equality ("$=$"), subset ("$\subset$"), and membership ("$\in$"). Some situations may require set product ("$\times$") and other operations as well.

Bit vectors are a set representation that maximizes the ease of performing the fundamental operations, especially if $U = \{0, \ldots, u - 1\}$ for some relatively small u. They are used in most data-flow analyses (see Chapter 8) because the relevant operations are fast and the representation is relatively compact. For a U with u

```
procedure Set_Union(A,B) returns set of U
   A, B: set of U
begin
   S := A: set of U
   x, y: U
   for x := first(B) to last(B) do
        for y := first(A) to last(A) do
             if x = y then
                  goto L1
             fi
             y := next(A)
             x := next(B)
        od
        S := append(S,x)
L1:     od
        return S
   end     || Set_Union
```

FIG. B.2   ICAN code to compute set union for the linked-list representation.

elements, they require $\lceil u/32 \rceil$ words per set and the fundamental operations are performed as follows:

Set Operation	Bit-Vector Operation
$c := a \cup b$	$bv(c) := bv(a) \text{ or } bv(b)$
$c := a \cap b$	$bv(c) := bv(a) \text{ and } bv(b)$
$c := a - b$	$bv(c) := bv(a) \text{ and } !bv(b)$
$t := a = b$	$t := (bv(a) \text{ xor } bv(b)) \neq \vec{0}$
$t := a \subset b$	$t := (!bv(a) \text{ and } bv(b)) \neq \vec{0}$
$t := a \in b$	$t := (\text{mask}[a] \text{ and } bv(b)) \neq \vec{0}$

where $bv(x)$ is the bit-vector representation of x; $\vec{0}$ is the bit vector of all zeros; or, and, xor, and "!" (not) are the bitwise logical operators; and mask[] is a mask such that bit i of mask[i] is a one and all other bits are zero. Thus, the typical operations can all be performed in time $O(u)$, independent of the number of elements in the sets themselves.

Linked lists are a set representation that maximizes the ease of representing sets S (of size s) that are small subsets of their universe U. A typical doubly linked representation is shown in Figure B.1(a). The size of the representation of S is $O(s)$, not $O(u)$, as it is for bit vectors. Performing the fundamental operations is harder than for bit vectors. For example, the code for computing the union of A and B is as shown in Figure B.2, where first( ), next( ), and last( ) traverse the linked list and append( ) adds its second argument to the end of its first. This requires $O(ab)$ time, where a and b are the cardinalities of A and B, respectively, or $O(s^2)$. Of course, in the worst case this is $O(u^2)$, but we are assuming that the sets A and B have many fewer than u elements. Similar routines are needed to perform the other operations, with similar time bounds, except that membership testing is $O(s)$.

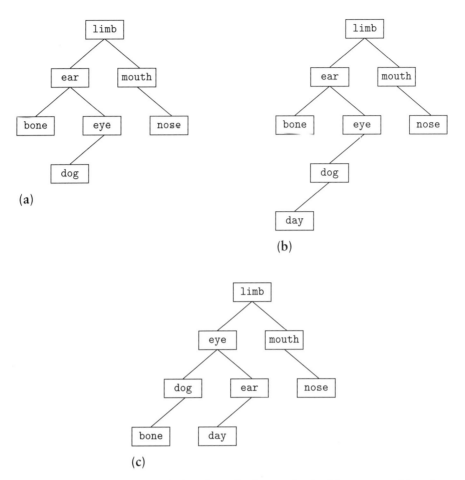

FIG. B.3 (a) A balanced binary tree of identifiers; (b) the result of adding day, making the tree unbalanced; and (c) the result of rebalancing the tree.

Balanced binary trees are an important representation of sets that have an easily computed total order among their elements (or that need to be kept ordered), such as the identifiers in a local symbol table. In such a tree, the value at each node is greater than all the values in its left subtree and less than all the values in its right subtree, and the lengths of the minimum and maximum paths from the root to a leaf differ by at most one. An example of a balanced binary tree representing the set of identifiers {bone, dog, ear, eye, limb, mouth, nose} is given in Figure B.3(a). In (b), we have added the value day to the set, resulting in the tree's becoming unbalanced. Part (c) shows the result of rebalancing the tree. Note that membership in a set S represented by a balanced binary tree can be tested in time $O(\log s)$. Computing union, intersection, difference, equality testing, and subset require $O(s \log s)$.

Hashing is another important representation for sets. As generally formulated, it involves computing a function $hash(\ )$ from elements of the set $S \subseteq U$ to a range

$c = 4$

$d[i]$	i	$s[i]$
	8	
	7	3
	6	
	5	2
4	4	4
7	3	
5	2	1
2	1	

FIG. B.4 Sparse representation of the set {2, 5, 7, 4} with $u = 8$.

$0, \ldots, u - 1$ for some appropriate u. One then finds in entry $hash(a)$ of an array Hash$[0 \cdot \cdot u\text{-}1]$ a pointer to a linked list of entries (usually called "buckets"), each corresponding to an element a of S that hashes to $hash(a)$. The efficiency of the set operations depends strongly on the choice of the hash function. Assuming that the elements are distributed so that no more than $2u/n$ elements hash to each entry, testing membership requires $O(u/n)$ time; and union, intersection, equality, and subset require $O(u)$ time if the items in each hash chain are kept ordered.

A new representation of sparse sets that requires constant time for the basic operations was developed by Briggs and Torczon [BriT94]. It represents a sparse set $S \subseteq U = \{1, \ldots, u\}$ by two u-element arrays $s[\ ]$ and $d[\ ]$ and a scalar c. The value of c is the cardinality of S. The array $d[\ ]$ holds in positions $1, \ldots, c$ the c elements of S in any order and the elements of $s[\ ]$ are set so that

$$1 \leq s[i] \leq c \text{ and } d[s[i]] = i \text{ if and only if } i \in S$$

i.e., the ith element of $s[\ ]$ gives the position of i in the array $d[\ ]$. The values in the other entries of $s[\ ]$ and $d[\ ]$ do not matter. For example, Figure B.4 shows how the set {2, 5, 7, 4} would be represented with $u = 8$. The fundamental operations are adding and removing an element, testing membership, and determining the size of the set. We perform the operations as follows:

1. adding an element v: Check whether $1 \leq s[v] \leq c$ and $d[s[v]] = v$. If not, set c to $c + 1$, $d[c]$ to v, and $s[v]$ to c.

2. removing an element v: Check whether $1 \leq s[v] \leq c$ and $d[s[v]] = v$. If so, set $d[s[v]]$ to $d[c]$, c to $c - 1$, and $s[v] := 0$.

3. testing membership of v: Check whether $1 \leq s[v] \leq c$ and $d[s[v]] = v$. If so, answer "yes," otherwise answer "no."

4. determining size: Return c.

Two mixed representations can be useful in representing sparse sets for particular kinds of problems. Linked-segment lists combine the dynamic allocation of linked

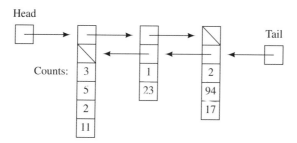

FIG. B.5 Representation of the set {5, 2, 11, 23, 94, 17} by a two-way linked-segment list.

lists with the fast traversal of arrays. For example, Figure B.5 shows a linked-segment representation of the set {5, 2, 11, 23, 94, 17}. Bit-vector linked lists are similar, except that the values stored in the list elements are bit vectors. They are useful for bit-vector problems in which most of the bits are constant throughout the analysis.

B.2   Representation of Sequences

Sequences are almost as important as sets and, in fact, many of the representations carry over from sets to sequences, as long as we keep the members of the sequences in their predetermined order.

Some of the important operations for sequences are those listed near the beginning of the appendix, namely, adding a value, removing a value, testing membership, merging sequences, and determining the length of a sequence. Concatenation is also important.

Linked lists and linked-segment lists are common representations of sequences that allow the operations to be performed in time $O(s)$, where s is the length of the sequence (note that this also includes concatenation, since all we need to do is splice the end of the first sequence to the beginning of the second).

Bit vectors, on the other hand, are not generally useful for representing sequences, since they impose an order on the elements that usually is not the desired one.

Balanced binary trees are quite useful because they allow any chosen order to be imposed on their entries (one merely adjoins to each element its position in that ordering and uses it in rebalancing the trees), and because the operations on them are fast.

B.3   Representation of Trees and DAGs

Trees are important in several areas in compiling, such as parsing, code generation, and expression optimization. In most cases, the trees are binary—particularly for code generation and optimization—so we concentrate on that variety.

Two representations of trees are frequently used, linked and linearized. The linked form usually involves nodes with at least four fields: parent, left child, right

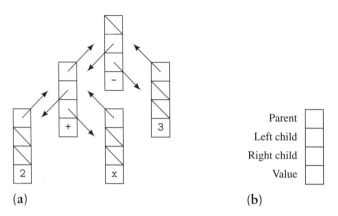

FIG. B.6 (a) Linked representation of a binary tree, namely, an expression tree that represents (2 + x) − 3; (b) the meanings of its fields.

child, and value, as shown in Figure B.6. Additional fields may represent other values in each node.

Linearized notations for trees depend on the fact that a binary tree can always be represented by its root, followed by the representation of its left subtree, followed by the representation of its right subtree, i.e., in Polish-prefix notation. The linked representation in Figure B.6 becomes − + 2 x 3 in this form. This type of representation is used as intermediate code in some compilers and is the basis for Graham-Glanville-style code generation (see Section 6.2).

DAGs, which are useful in optimizing and generating code for basic blocks and in scheduling them (see Section 17.1.2), are almost always represented by linked structures.

B.4   Representation of Functions

Functions are used to represent mappings of various sorts in compilers, such as mapping basic blocks and flowgraph edges to their execution frequencies, representing aliases, and so on.

The most efficient representation of a function requires that it have a domain that is composed of simple types and a result of a simple type, and that the function is easily computed from the domain elements, such as f(x,y,z) = x + 2 * y − z. Such functions are, of course, typically represented by code.

The next most efficient representation of a function is to use an array. For this approach to be usable, the components of the domain must be ranges of integers or easily mapped to ranges of integers and the values of the function must be of uniform size or reached by pointers stored in the array elements.

Hashing provides an attractive alternative for functions that do not easily map onto arrays. In this approach, one hashes the domain elements to determine a list of buckets and then searches the bucket list to find an entry that matches the arguments and that holds the corresponding function value.

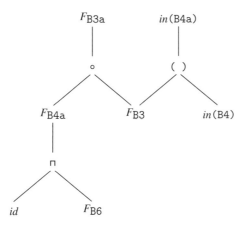

FIG. B.7 DAG representation of structural data-flow equations.

The operation most frequently performed on functions is computing a value when given a sequence of arguments, which is trivial to easy for each of the three representations discussed above.

Less frequently, one may need to compose two functions or to modify one, either by changing its domain or by changing a value or both. Composition is easiest for the code representation, of course, and only somewhat harder for the other two. Modifying a function is generally not possible for the code representation, but can be accommodated by the other two.

Another kind of function representation is one designed to be constructed by a program and then used repeatedly to compute values, such as in control-tree-based data-flow analysis (see Section 8.6). In this case, we need to construct a data structure that can then be interpreted, such as the graphs discussed in Section 8.7.3. Figure B.7 is an example of such a graph. The roots are the names of functions to be computed and the subgraph below each says how to compute it ("∘" represents function composition, "( )" represents function application, "⊓" represents the lattice operation meet, and *id* represents the identity function). Such graphs can easily be constructed and then can be interpreted as needed to compute data-flow information.

B.5   Further Reading

For the details of how to keep binary trees balanced and descriptions of other data structures that are valuable in compiler construction, see any good data structures text, such as Knuth [Knut73].

Briggs and Torczon's new representation for sparse sets is described in [BriT94].

Software Resources

This appendix describes software that is freely available on the Internet or through other means of distribution for use in student compiler-construction projects. Most of the software packages carry licenses that restrict their use to educational projects; some may be incorporated into commercial products with explicit restrictions. This entire appendix may be accessed online at the publisher's Web site, with links to all Internet, WWW, and ftp addresses in this appendix. The URL for this book is `http://www.mkp.com/books_catalog/1-55860-320-4.asp`.

C.1   Finding and Accessing Software on the Internet

The resources listed here are only a few of the many software packages available that may be useful in compiler-related projects. Information about others may be found on the World Wide Web (WWW) by means of one or another search engine, such as Yahoo, Alta Vista, Lycos, Infoseek, etc. Numerous references such as [Krol92] and [Keho93] provide information about accessing and using such search engines.

C.2   Machine Simulators

C.2.1   Spim

James Larus of the University of Wisconsin has written a MIPS R2000 and R3000 simulator called SPIM that is available for use in student projects and that is described in detail in Appendix A of [HenP94].

SPIM can read and execute files that contain assembly-language statements and MIPS a.out files. It is a self-contained system that includes a debugger and an operating-system interface and runs on at least DEC, Sun, IBM, and HP work-stations.

SPIM implements almost the entire MIPS extended assembler instruction set (excluding some of the complex floating-point comparisons and the details of page-table manipulation). It comes with complete source code and documentation of all instructions. It has both a simple, terminal-style interface and an X-Windows-based interface.

As we go to press, a DOS version and a new Windows version of SPIM are being developed. The Windows version will run under Windows 3.1, Windows 95, and Windows NT. In the fall of 1997, look for information about these new versions on the publisher's Web site at `http://www.mkp.com/cod2e.htm`.

To retrieve a compressed tar file containing the SPIM system and documentation, access the URL `http://www.cs.wisc.edu/~larus/spim.html` and follow the instructions found there. To be informed of future updates to the system, send your electronic mail address to `larus@cs.wisc.edu`.

C.2.2   Spa

Spa is a set of tools that includes a SPARC simulator and that was written by Gordon Irlam of the University of Adelaide in Australia. To find out more about it, access the file `gordoni/spa.html` at the URL `http://www.base.com`.

C.3   Compilers

C.3.1   GNU

The GNU compilers were written by contributors to the Free Software Foundation and may be freely distributed and modified. They may be included in commercial products if certain conditions are met. Contact the foundation at 675 Massachusetts Avenue, Cambridge, MA 02139 for information.

To obtain the GNU compiler source, establish an anonymous ftp connection to `prep.ai.mit.edu`, `ftp.uu.net`, or any of several other machines around the world, and retrieve the compressed tar file pub/gnu/gcc-*version*`.tar.gz` where *version* is the highest version number available. The file `GETTING.GNU.SOFTWARE` in the same directory may be helpful to the beginner.

C.3.2   LCC

`lcc` is an easily retargetable ANSI C compiler written by Christopher Fraser and David Hanson that is available by anonymous ftp from `ftp.princeton.edu` in the directory pub/lcc. It is suggested that you begin by retrieving the file README from that directory. The front end was adapted for use in the SUIF system (see below). `lcc` can also be obtained from the URL `http://www.cs.princeton.edu/software/lcc` on the World Wide Web.

The compiler contains no optimizer, but its intermediate code is suitable for most of the optimizations discussed in this book.

The compiler is described briefly in [FraH91b] and in detail in [FraH95]. If you wish to be added to the `lcc` mailing list, send e-mail with the one-line message `subscribe lcc` to `majordomo@cs.princeton.edu`. For more information, access the World Wide Web site `http://www.cs.princeton.edu/software/lcc`.

C.3.3   SUIF

SUIF is an experimental compiling system that was developed by Monica Lam and colleagues at Stanford University.[1] It consists of the intermediate format, the kernel components of a compiler, and a functional parallelizing compiler that translates C or Fortran 77 to MIPS code. The release includes, among other things:

1. C and Fortran front ends,

2. an array data-dependence analysis library,

3. a loop-transformation library (based on unimodular transformations and tiling),

4. a matrix and linear-inequality manipulation library,

5. a parallel code generator and run-time library,

6. a scalar optimizer,

7. a MIPS back end,

8. a C back end (so a native C compiler can be used as a back end for non-MIPS systems),

9. a linear-inequality calculator (for prototyping algorithms), and

10. a simplified interface that can be used for compiler courses.

SUIF is available on the World Wide Web from URL

```
http://suif.stanford.edu
```

SUIF is released without warranty and with no promise of support. It is available free for noncommercial use. Redistribution is prohibited.

SUIF is not meant to be a production-quality compiler. It does not run as fast, nor generate code as efficiently, as a production compiler such as gcc or your machine's native compiler. It does, however, compile most major benchmarks and can be used as a base for student projects or compiler research.

C.4   Code-Generator Generators: BURG and IBURG

BURG, a code-generator generator based on BURS technology (see [Pele88] and [PelG88]), was written by Christopher Fraser, Robert Henry, and Todd Proebsting and is available by anonymous ftp from `kaese.cs.wisc.edu`. It is provided as a compressed `shar` archive located in file `pub/burg.shar.Z`. [FraH91a] provides an overview of the system and how to use it.

---

1. The name SUIF stands for Stanford University Intermediate Form.

IBURG, another code-generator generator based on BURS technology, but that does dynamic programming at compile time, was written by Fraser, Hanson, and Proebsting [FraH92] and is available by anonymous ftp from

```
ftp.cs.princeton.edu
```

It is provided as a compressed `tar` archive located in file `pub/iburg.tar.Z` or `pub/iburg.tar.zip`. [FraH92] provides an overview of the system and how to use it.

C.5   Profiling Tools

C.5.1   QPT

QPT is an exact and efficient program profiler and tracing system that was written by Thomas Ball and James Larus of the University of Wisconsin. It rewrites a program's executable (`a.out`) file by inserting code to record the execution frequency or sequence of every basic block or control-flow edge. From this information, another program, called QPT_STATS, calculates the execution costs of procedures in the program. Unlike the UNIX tools `prof` and `gprof`, QPT records exact execution frequencies rather than statistical samples. When tracing a program, QPT produces a trace regeneration program that reads the highly compressed trace file and generates the full program trace. To obtain QPT and its documentation, access the URL `http://www.cs.wisc.edu/~larus/qpt.html` and follow the instructions found there.

When used for profiling, QPT operates in either of two modes. In slow mode, it places a counter in each basic block in a program. In quick mode, it places counters on an infrequently executed subset of the edges in the program's control-flow graph. This placement can reduce the cost of profiling by a factor of three or four, but increases somewhat the time required to produce a profile or trace.

QPT currently runs on SPARC-based systems and is written to be portable—all of the machine-specific features are collected in a few files. Porting the program to a new machine requires about two person-months' worth of effort. QPT is distributed with the full source and a small amount of documentation.

QPT is part of a larger project called WARTS (Wisconsin Architectural Research Tool Set), which is accessible at URL

```
http://www.cs.wisc.edu/~larus/warts.html
```

C.5.2   SpixTools and Shade

SpixTools is a collection of programs that were written by Robert Cmelik of Sun Microsystems to allow instruction-level profiling of SPARC application programs. [Cmel93] provides both a tutorial introduction to and a reference manual for Spix-Tools.

Spix creates an instrumented version of the user's program. As the instrumented program runs, it keeps track of how often each basic block is executed and writes out the block execution counts on termination. Several tools are provided for displaying and summarizing these counts. Spixstats prints tables that show opcode usage, branch behavior, register usage, function usage, etc. Sdas disassembles the application program, annotating the disassembled code with instruction execution counts. Sprint prints the source code of the application, annotating it with statement or instruction counts.

Applications that use SpixTools must be statically linked and must not use self-modifying code. A few other limitations apply.

Shade is an instruction-set simulator and custom trace generator that was written by David Keppel and Robert Cmelik. It executes and traces application programs under the control of a user-supplied trace analyzer. To reduce communication overhead, Shade and the analyzer are run in the same address space. To further improve performance, code that simulates and traces the application is dynamically generated and cached for reuse. Current implementations run on SPARC systems and, to varying degrees, simulate the SPARC Version 8 and Version 9 and MIPS I architectures. [CmeK93] describes the capabilities, design, implementation, and performance of Shade and discusses instruction-set simulation in general.

Shade provides fine-grained control over tracing, so one pays data-collection overhead only for the data actually needed. Shade is also extensible, so analyzers can examine arbitrary state and thus collect special information that Shade itself does not know how to collect.

To obtain either SpixTools or Shade (or both), request a license form from Robert Cmelik, Sun Microsystems, Inc., 2550 Garcia Avenue, Mountain View, CA 94043-1100, telephone 415-336-1709, or e-mail rfc@sun.com.

Tables

[Ada83]   *The Programming Language Ada Reference Manual, ANSI/MIL-STD-1815A-1983,* U.S. Dept. of Defense, Washington, DC, 1983.

[AdlG93]   Adl-Tabatabai, Ali-Reza and Thomas Gross. Detection and Recovery of Endangered Variables Caused by Instruction Scheduling, in [PLDI93], pp. 13–25.

[Ahal93]   Ahalt, Stanley C. and James F. Leathrum. Code-Generation Methodology Using Tree-Parsers and High-Level Intermediate Representations, *J. of Programming Languages,* Vol. 1, No. 2, 1993, pp. 103–126.

[AhoC75]   Aho, Alfred V. and M.J. Corasick. Efficient String Matching: An Aid to Bibliographic Search, *CACM,* Vol. 18, No. 6, June 1975, pp. 333–340.

[AhoG89]   Aho, Alfred V., Mahadevan Ganapathi, and Steven W.K. Tjiang. Code Generation Using Tree Pattern Matching and Dynamic Programming, *ACM TOPLAS,* Vol. 11, No. 4, Oct. 1989, pp. 491–516.

[AhoH74]   Aho, Alfred V., John Hopcroft, and Jeffrey D. Ullman. *The Design and Analysis of Computer Algorithms,* Addison-Wesley, Reading, MA, 1974.

[AhoJ76]   Aho, Alfred V. and Steven C. Johnson. Optimal Code Generation for Expression Trees, *JACM,* Vol. 23, No. 3, July 1976, pp. 488–501.

[AhoS86]   Aho, Alfred V., Ravi Sethi, and Jeffrey D. Ullman. *Compilers: Principles, Techniques, and Tools,* Addison-Wesley, Reading, MA, 1986.

[AigG84]   Aigran, Philippe, Susan L. Graham, Robert R. Henry, M. Kirk McKusick, and Eduardo Pelegri-Llopart. Experience with a Graham-Glanville Style Code Generator, in [Comp84], pp. 13–24.

[Aike88]   Aiken, Alexander. *Compaction-Based Parallelization,* Ph.D. thesis, Tech. Rept. TR-88-922, Dept. of Comp. Sci., Cornell Univ., Ithaca, NY, June 1988.

[AikN88a] Aiken, Alexander and Alexandru Nicolau. Optimal Loop Parallelization, in [PLDI88], pp. 308–317.

[AikN88b] Aiken, Alexander and Alexandru Nicolau. Perfect Pipelining: A New Loop Parallelization Technique, *Proc. of the 1988 Euro. Symp. on Programming,* Springer-Verlag, Berlin, 1988, pp. 308–317.

[AikN91]   Aiken, Alexander and Alexandru Nicolau. A Realistic Resource-Constrained Software Pipelining Algorithm, in Nicolau, Alexandru, David Gelernter, Thomas Gross, and

David Padua (eds.). *Advances in Languages and Compilers for Parallel Processing,* MIT Press, Cambridge, MA, 1991.

[AllC72a]   Allen, Frances E. and John Cocke. A Catalogue of Optimizing Transformations, in Rustin, Randall (ed.). *Design and Optimization of Compilers,* Prentice-Hall, Englewood Cliffs, NJ, 1972, pp. 1–30.

[AllC72b]   Allen, Frances E. and John Cocke. Graph Theoretic Constructs for Program Control Flow Analysis, Research Rept. RC3923, IBM Thomas J. Watson Research Ctr., Yorktown Heights, NY, 1972.

[AllC76]   Allen, Frances E. and John Cocke. A Program Data Flow Analysis Procedure, *CACM,* Vol. 19, No. 3, Mar. 1976, pp. 137–147.

[AllC81]   Allen, Frances E., John Cocke, and Ken Kennedy. Reduction of Operator Strength, in [MucJ81], pp. 79–101.

[AllC86]   Allen, J. Randy, David Callahan, and Ken Kennedy. An Implementation of Interprocedural Data Flow Analysis in a Vectorizing Fortran Compiler, Tech. Rept. COMP TR-86-38, Dept. of Comp. Sci., Rice Univ., Houston, TX, May 1986.

[Alle69]   Allen, Frances E. Program Optimization, in Halprin, Mark I. and Christopher J. Shaw (eds.). *Annual Review of Automatic Programming,* Vol. 5, Pergamon Press, Oxford, UK, 1969, pp. 239–307.

[Alph92]   *Alpha Architecture Handbook,* Digital Equipment Corp., Maynard, MA, 1992.

[AlpW88]   Alpern, Bowen, Mark N. Wegman, and F. Kenneth Zadeck. Detecting Equality of Variables in Programs, in [POPL88], pp. 1–11.

[AlsL96]   Alstrup, Stephen and Peter W. Lauridsen. A Simple Dynamic Algorithm for Maintaining a Dominator Tree, Tech. Rept. 96/3, Dept. of Comp. Sci., Univ. of Copenhagen, Copenhagen, 1996.

[AndS92]   Andrews, Kristy and Duane Sand. Migrating a cisc Computer Family onto risc via Object Code Translation, in [ASPL92], pp. 213–222.

[ANSI89]   *American National Standard X3.159-1989, The C Programming Language,* ANSI, New York, NY, 1989.

[ASPL82]   *Proc. of the Symp. on Architectural Support for Programming Languages and Operating Systems,* Palo Alto, CA, published as *SIGPLAN Notices,* Vol. 17, No. 4, Apr. 1982.

[ASPL87]   *Proc. of the 2nd Intl. Conf. on Architectural Support for Programming Languages and Operating Systems,* Palo Alto, CA, IEEE Comp. Soc. Order No. 805, Oct. 1987.

[ASPL89]   *Proc. of the 3rd Intl. Conf. on Architectural Support for Programming Languages and Operating Systems,* Boston, MA, published as *SIGPLAN Notices,* Vol. 24, special issue, May 1989.

[ASPL91]   *Proc. of the 4th Intl. Conf. on Architectural Support for Programming Languages and Operating Systems,* Santa Clara, CA, published as *SIGPLAN Notices,* Vol. 26, No. 4, Apr. 1991.

[ASPL92]   *Proc. of the Fifth Intl. Conf. on Architectural Support for Programming Languages and Operating Systems,* Boston, MA, published as *SIGPLAN Notices,* Vol. 27, No. 9, Sept. 1992.

[AusH82]   Auslander, Marc and Martin Hopkins. An Overview of the PL.8 Compiler, in [Comp82], pp. 22–31.

[BalL92]   Ball, Thomas and James R. Larus. Optimally Profiling and Tracing Programs, in [POPL92], pp. 59–70.

[BalL93]   Ball, Thomas and James R. Larus. Branch Prediction for Free, in [PLDI93], pp. 300–313.

[Bane76]   Banerjee, Utpal. *Dependence Testing in Ordinary Programs,* M.S. thesis, Dept. of Comp. Sci., Univ. of Illinois, Urbana-Champaign, IL, Nov. 1976.

[Bane88]   Banerjee, Utpal. *Dependence Analysis for Supercomputing,* Kluwer Academic Publishers, Boston, MA, 1988.

[Bane93]   Banerjee, Utpal. *Loop Transformations for Restructuring Compilers,* Kluwer Academic Publishers, Boston, MA, 1993.

[Bane94]   Banerjee, Utpal. *Loop Parallelization,* Kluwer Academic Publishers, Boston, MA, 1993.

[Bann79]   Banning, John P. An Efficient Way to Find the Side Effects of Procedure Calls and the Aliases of Variables, in [POPL79], pp. 29–41.

[Bart78]   Barth, John M. A Practical Interprocedural Data Flow Analysis Algorithm, *CACM,* Vol. 21, No. 9, Nov. 1978, pp. 724–736.

[Bell90]   Bell, Ron. IBM RISC System/6000 Performance Tuning for Numerically Intensive Fortran and C Programs, Document No. GG24-3611, IBM Intl. Tech. Support Ctr., Poughkeepsie, NY, Aug. 1990.

[BerC92]   Bernstein, David, Doron Cohen, Yuval Lavon, and Vladimir Rainish. Performance Evaluation of Instruction Scheduling on the IBM RISC System/6000, *Proc. of MICRO-25,* Portland, OR, published as *SIG MICRO Newsletter,* Vol. 23, Nos. 1 and 2, Dec. 1992.

[BerG89]   Bernstein, David, Dina Q. Goldin, Martin C. Golumbic, Hugo Krawczyk, Yishay Mansour, Itai Nahshon, and Ron Y. Pinter. Spill Code Minimization Techniques for Optimizing Compilers, in [PLDI89], pp. 258–263.

[BerG95]   Bergin, Thomas J. and Richard G. Gibson (eds.). *The History of Programming Languages-II,* ACM Press, New York, NY, 1995.

[BerK87]   Bergh, A., Keith Keilman, Daniel Magenheimer, and James A. Miller. HP 3000 Emulation on HP Precision Architecture Computers, *Hewlett-Packard J.,* Dec. 1987.

[BerR91]   Bernstein, David and M. Rodeh. Global Instruction Scheduling for Superscalar Machines, in [PLDI91], pp. 241–255.

[Bird82]   Bird, Peter. An Implementation of a Code Generator Specification Language for Table Driven Code Generators, in [Comp82], pp. 44–55.

[BliC92]   Blickstein, David S., Peter W. Craig, Caroline S. Davidson, R. Neil Faiman, Jr., Kent D. Glossop, Richard B. Grove, Steven O. Hobbs, and William B. Noyce. The GEM Optimizing Compiler System, *Digital Tech. J.,* Vol. 4, No. 4, special issue, 1992.

[BodC90]   Bodin, François and François Charot. Loop Optimization for Horizontal Microcoded Machines, *Proc. of the 1990 Intl. Conf. on Supercomputing,* Amsterdam, June 1990, pp. 164–176.

[Brad91]   David G. Bradlee. *Retargetable Instruction Scheduling for Pipelined Processors,* Ph.D. thesis, Tech. Rept. UW-CSE-91-08-07, Dept. of Comp. Sci. and Engg., Univ. of Washington, Seattle, WA, June 1991.

[BraE91]   Bradlee, David G., Susan J. Eggers, and Robert R. Henry. Integrated Register Allocation and Instruction Scheduling for RISCs, in [ASPL91], pp. 122–131.

[BraH91]   Bradlee, David G., Robert R. Henry, and Susan J. Eggers. The Marion System for Retargetable Instruction Scheduling, in [PLDI91], pp. 229–240.

[BriC89]   Briggs, Preston, Keith D. Cooper, Ken Kennedy, and Linda Torczon. Coloring Heuristics for Register Allocation, in [PLDI89], pp. 275–284.

[BriC94a] Briggs, Preston, Keith D. Cooper, and Linda Torczon. Improvements to Graph Coloring Register Allocation, ACM TOPLAS, Vol. 16, No. 3, May 1994, pp. 428–455.

[BriC94b] Briggs, Preston and Keith D. Cooper. Effective Partial Redundancy Elimination, in [PLDI94], pp. 159–170.

[BriC94c] Briggs, Preston, Keith D. Cooper, and Taylor Simpson. Value Numbering, Tech. Rept. CRPC-TR94517-S, Ctr. for Research on Parallel Computation, Rice Univ., Houston, TX, Nov. 1994.

[Brig92]   Briggs, Preston. Register Allocation via Graph Coloring, Tech. Rept. CRPC-TR92218, Ctr. for Research on Parallel Computation, Rice Univ., Houston, TX, Apr. 1992.

[BriT94]   Briggs, Preston and Linda Torczon. An Efficient Representation for Sparse Sets, ACM LOPLAS, Vol. 2, Nos. 1–4, Mar.–Dec. 1993, pp. 59–69.

[CalC86]   Callahan, David, Keith D. Cooper, Ken Kennedy, and Linda Torczon. Interprocedural Constant Propagation, in [Comp86], pp. 152–161.

[CalC90]   Callahan, David, Steve Carr, and Ken Kennedy. Improving Register Allocation for Subscripted Variables, in [PLDI90], pp. 53–65.

[CalG95]   Calder, Brad, Dirk Grunwald, Donald Lindsay, James Martin, Michael Mozer, and Benjamin G. Zorn. Corpus-Based Static Branch Prediction, in [PLDI95], pp. 79–92.

[CalK91]   Callahan, David and Brian Koblenz. Register Allocation by Hierarchical Tiling, in [PLDI91], pp. 192–203.

[Call86]   Callahan, David. Dependence Testing in PFC: Weak Separability, Dept. of Comp. Sci., Rice Univ., Houston, TX, Aug. 1986.

[Call88]   Callahan, David. The Program Summary Graph and Flow-Sensitive Interprocedural Data Flow Analysis, in [PLDI88], pp. 47–56.

[CamK93]   Campbell, Philip L., Kshccrabdhi Krishna, and Robert A. Ballance. Refining and Defining the Program Dependence Web, Tech. Rept. CS93-6, Univ. of New Mexico, Albuquerque, NM, Mar. 1993.

[Catt79]   Cattell, Roderic G.G. Code Generation and Machine Descriptions, Tech. Rept. CSL-79-8, Xerox Palo Alto Research Ctr., Palo Alto, CA, Oct. 1979.

[CF7790]   CF77 Compiling System, Volume 1: Fortran Reference Manual, Publication SR-3071 4.0, Cray Research, Inc., Mendota Heights, MN, 1990.

[ChaA81]   Chaitin, Gregory, Marc Auslander, Ashok Chandra, John Cocke, Martin Hopkins, and Peter Markstein. Register Allocation Via Coloring, Computer Languages, Vol. 6, No. 1, 1981, pp. 47–57; also in [Stal90], pp. 88–97.

[Chai82]   Chaitin, Gregory. Register Allocation and Spilling via Graph Coloring, in [Comp82], pp. 98–105.

[ChaW90]   Chase, David R., Mark Wegman, and F. Kenneth Zadeck. Analysis of Pointers and Structures, in [PLDI90], pp. 296–310.

[CheM92]   Chernoff, Anton and Maurice P. Marks. Personal communication, Digital Equipment Corp., Nashua, NH, Mar. 1992.

[Cher92]   Chernoff, Anton. Personal communication, Digital Equipment Corp., Nashua, NH, May 1992.

[ChiD89]   Chi, Chi-Hung and Hank Dietz. Unified Management of Registers and Cache Using Liveness and Cache Bypass, in [PLDI89], pp. 344–355.

[ChoH84]   Chow, Frederick and John Hennessy. Register Allocation by Priority-Based Coloring, in [Comp84], pp. 222–232; also in [Stal90], pp. 98–108.

[ChoH90]   Chow, Frederick and John Hennessy. The Priority-Based Coloring Approach to Register Allocation, *ACM TOPLAS*, Vol. 12, No. 4, pp. 501–536.

[Chow83]   Chow, Frederick. A Portable Machine-Independent Global Optimizer—Design and Measurements, Tech. Rept. 83-254, Comp. Systems Lab., Stanford Univ., Stanford, CA, Dec. 1983.

[Chow86]   Chow, Paul. MIPS-X Instruction Set and Programmer's Manual, Tech. Rept. No. CSL-86-289, Comp. Systems Lab., Stanford Univ., Stanford, CA, May 1986.

[Chow88]   Chow, Frederick. Minimizing Register Usage Penalty at Procedure Calls, in [PLDI88], pp. 85–94.

[ChoW92]   Chow, Frederick and Alexand Wu. Personal communication, MIPS Computer Systems, Inc., Mountain View, CA, May 1992.

[ChrH84]   Christopher, Thomas W., Philip J. Hatcher, and Ronald C. Kukuk. Using Dynamic Profiling to Generate Optimized Code in a Graham-Glanville Style Code Generator, in [Comp84], pp. 25–36.

[CliR91]   Clinger, William and Jonathan Rees (eds.). *Revised*[4] *Report on the Algorithmic Language Scheme,* Artificial Intelligence Lab., MIT, Cambridge, MA, and Comp. Sci. Dept., Indiana Univ., Bloomington, IN, Nov. 1991.

[CloM87]   Clocksin, W.F. and C.S. Mellish. *Programming in Prolog,* third edition, Springer-Verlag, Berlin, 1987.

[CmeK91]   Cmelik, Robert F., Shing I. Kong, David R. Ditzel, and Edmund J. Kelly. An Analysis of SPARC and MIPS Instruction Set Utilization on the SPEC Benchmarks, in [ASPL91], pp. 290–302.

[CmeK93]   Robert F. Cmelik and David Keppel. Shade: A Fast Instruction-Set Simulator for Execution Profiling, Tech. Rept. SMLI 93-12, Sun Microsystems Labs, Mountain View, CA, and Tech. Rept. UWCSE 93-06-06, Dept. of Comp. Sci. and Engg., Univ. of Washington, Seattle, WA, 1993.

[Cmel93]   Cmelik, Robert F. SpixTools User's Manual, Tech. Rept. SMLI TR-93-6, Sun Microsystems Labs, Mountain View, CA, Feb. 1993.

[CocS69]   Cocke, John and Jacob T. Schwartz. *Programming Languages and Their Compilers: Preliminary Notes,* Courant Inst. of Math. Sci., New York Univ., New York, NY, 1969.

[ColN87]   Colwell, Robert P., Robert P. Nix, John J. O'Donnell, David B. Papworth, and Paul K. Rodman. A VLIW Architecture for a Trace Scheduling Compiler, in [ASPL87], pp. 180–192.

[Comp79]   *Proc. of the SIGPLAN '79 Symp. on Compiler Constr.,* Denver, CO, published as *SIGPLAN Notices,* Vol. 14, No. 8, Aug. 1979.

[Comp82]   *Proc. of the SIGPLAN '82 Symp. on Compiler Constr.,* Boston, MA, published as *SIGPLAN Notices,* Vol. 17, No. 6, June 1982.

[Comp84]   *Proc. of the SIGPLAN '84 Symp. on Compiler Constr.,* Montreal, Quebec, published as *SIGPLAN Notices,* Vol. 19, No. 6, June 1984.

[Comp86]   *Proc. of the SIGPLAN '86 Symp. on Compiler Constr.,* Palo Alto, CA, published as *SIG-PLAN Notices,* Vol. 21, No. 7, July 1986.

[CooH92]   Cooper, Keith D., Mary W. Hall, and Linda Torczon. Unexpected Effects of Inline Substitution: A Case Study, *ACM LOPLAS,* Vol. 1, No. 1, pp. 22–32.

[CooH93]   Cooper, Keith D., Mary W. Hall, Robert T. Hood, Ken Kennedy, K.S. McKinley, J.M. Mellor-Crummey, Linda Torczon, and S.K. Warren. The ParaScope Parallel Programming Environment, *Proc. of the IEEE,* Vol. 81, No. 2, 1993, pp. 244–263.

[CooK84]   Cooper, Keith D. and Ken Kennedy. Efficient Computation of Flow Insensitive Interprocedural Summary, in [Comp84], pp. 247–258.

[CooK86]   Cooper, Keith D., Ken Kennedy, and Linda Torczon. Interprocedural Optimization: Eliminating Unnecessary Recompilation, in [Comp86], pp. 58–67.

[CooK88a] Cooper, Keith D. and Ken Kennedy. Efficient Computation of Flow Insensitive Interprocedural Summary—A Correction, *SIGPLAN Notices,* Vol. 23, No. 4, Apr. 1988, pp. 35–42.

[CooK88b] Cooper, Keith D. and Ken Kennedy. Interprocedural Side-Effect Analysis in Linear Time, in [PLDI88], pp. 57–66.

[CooK89]   Cooper, Keith D. and Ken Kennedy. Fast Interprocedural Alias Analysis, in [POPL89], pp. 49–59.

[CooS95a] Cooper, Keith D., Taylor Simpson, and Christopher Vick. Operator Strength Reduction, Tech. Rept. CRPC-TR95635-S, Ctr. for Research on Parallel Computation, Rice Univ., Houston, TX, Oct. 1995.

[CooS95b] Cooper, Keith D., and Taylor Simpson. SCC-Based Value Numbering, Tech. Rept. CRPC-TR95636-S, Ctr. for Research on Parallel Computation, Rice Univ., Houston, TX, Oct. 1995.

[CooS95c] Cooper, Keith D., and Taylor Simpson. Value-Driven Code Motion, Tech. Rept. CRPC-TR95637-S, Ctr. for Research on Parallel Computation, Rice Univ., Houston, TX, Oct. 1995.

[CouH86]   Coutant, Deborah, Carol Hammond, and John Kelly. Compilers for the New Generation of Hewlett-Packard Computers, *Proc. of COMPCON S'86,* 1986, pp. 48–61; also in [Stal90], pp. 132–145.

[Cout86]   Coutant, Deborah. Retargetable High-Level Alias Analysis, in [POPL86], pp. 110–118.

[CytF89]   Cytron, Ronald, Jean Ferrante, Barry K. Rosen, Mark N. Wegman, and F. Kenneth Zadeck. An Efficient Method of Computing Static Single Assignment Form, in [POPL89], pp. 23–25.

[CytF91]   Cytron, Ronald, Jean Ferrante, Barry K. Rosen, Mark N. Wegman, and F. Kenneth Zadeck. Efficiently Computing Static Single Assignment Form and the Program Dependence Graph, *ACM TOPLAS,* Vol. 13, No. 4, Oct. 1991, pp. 451–490.

[DamG94]   Damron, Peter C., Vinod Grover, and Shahrokh Mortazavi. Personal communication, Sun Microsystems, Inc., Mountain View, CA, May 1994.

[DanE73]   Dantzig, George and B.C. Eaves. Fourier-Motzkin Elimination and Its Dual, *J. of Combinatorial Theory* A, Vol. 14, 1973, pp. 288–297.

[DeuS84]   Deutsch, L. Peter and Allan M. Schiffman. Efficient Implementation of the Smalltalk-80 System, in [POPL84], pp. 297–302.

[Deut94]   Deutsch, Alain. Interprocedural May-Alias Analysis for Pointers: Beyond *k*-Limiting, in [PLDI94], pp. 230–241.

[Dham88]   Dhamdhere, Dhananjay M. A Fast Algorithm for Code Movement Optimization, *SIGPLAN Notices,* Vol. 23, No. 10, Oct. 1988, pp. 172–180.

[Dham91]   Dhamdhere, Dhananjay M. Practical Adaptation of the Global Optimization Algorithm of Morel and Renvoise, *ACM TOPLAS,* Vol. 13, No. 2, Apr. 1991, pp. 291–294.

[DhaR92]   Dhamdhere, Dhananjay M., Barry K. Rosen, and F. Kenneth Zadeck. How to Analyze Large Programs Efficiently and Informatively, in [PLDI92], pp. 212–223.

[DonB79]   Dongarra, Jack, James Bunch, Cleve Moler, and G. Stewart. *LINPACK Users Guide,* Society for Industrial and Applied Mathematics, Philadelphia, PA, 1979.

[EbcG94]   Ebcioğlu, Kemal, Randy Groves, Ki-Chang Kim, Gabriel Silberman, and Isaac Ziv. VLIW Compilation Techniques in a Superscalar Environment, in [PLDI94], pp. 36–46.

[EisW92]   Eisenbeis, Christine and D. Windheiser. A New Class of Algorithms for Software Pipelining with Resource Constraints, Tech. Rept., INRIA, Le Chesnay, France, 1992.

[Elli85]   Ellis, John R. *Bulldog: A Compiler for VLIW Architectures,* Ph.D. dissertation, Dept. of Comp. Sci., Yale Univ., New Haven, CT, 1985.

[EllS90]   Ellis, Margaret A. and Bjarne Stroustrup. *The Annotated C++ Reference Manual,* Addison-Wesley, Reading, MA, 1990.

[Enge75]   Engelfriet, Joost. Tree Automata and Tree Grammars, DAIMI Rept. FN-10, Dept. of Comp. Sci., Univ. of Aarhus, Aarhus, Denmark, Apr. 1975.

[FarK75]   Farrow, Rodney, Ken Kennedy, and Linda Zucconi. Graph Grammars and Global Program Flow Analysis, *Proc. of the 17th IEEE Symp. on Foundations of Comp. Sci.,* Houston, TX, Nov. 1975.

[Farn88]   Farnum, Charles. Compiler Support for Floating-Point Computation, *Software—Practice and Experience,* Vol. 18, No. 7, July 1988, pp. 701–709.

[Feau91]   Feautrier, P. Data Flow Analysis of Array and Scalar References, *Intl. J. of Parallel Programming,* Vol. 20, No. 1, Jan. 1991.

[FerO87]   Ferrante, Jeanne, Karl J. Ottenstein, and Joe D. Warren. The Program Dependence Graph and Its Use in Optimization, *ACM TOPLAS,* Vol. 9, No. 3, July 1987, pp. 319–349.

[Fish81]   Fisher, Joseph A. Trace Scheduling: A Technique for Global Microcode Compaction, *IEEE Trans. on Comps.,* Vol. C-30, No. 7, July 1981, pp. 478–490.

[FisL91]   Fischer, Charles N. and Richard J. LeBlanc, Jr. *Crafting a Compiler With C,* Benjamin-Cummings, Redwood City, CA, 1991.

[Fort78]   *Programming Language FORTRAN,* ANSI X3.9-1978 and ISO 1539-1980(E), ANSI, New York, NY, 1978.

[Fort92]   *Programming Language Fortran 90,* ANSI X3.198-1992 and ISO/IEC 1539-1991(E), ANSI, New York, NY, 1992.

[FraH91a]   Fraser, Christopher W., Robert R. Henry, and Todd A. Proebsting. BURG—Fast Optimal Instruction Selection and Tree Parsing, *SIGPLAN Notices,* Vol. 27, No. 4, Apr. 1991, pp. 68–76.

[FraH91b]   Fraser, Christopher W., David A. Hanson. A Retargetable Compiler for ANSI C, *SIGPLAN Notices,* Vol. 26, No. 10, Oct. 1991, pp. 29–43.

[FraH92]   Fraser, Christopher W., David R. Hanson, and Todd A. Proebsting. Engineering a Simple Code-Generator Generator, *ACM LOPLAS,* Vol. 1, No. 3, Sept. 1992, pp. 213–226.

[FraH95]   Fraser, Christopher W. and David R. Hanson. *A Retargetable C Compiler: Design and Implementation,* Benjamin-Cummings, Redwood City, CA, 1995.

[Frei74]   Freiburghouse, Richard A. Register Allocation via Usage Counts, *CACM,* Vol. 17, No. 11, Nov. 1974, pp. 638–642.

[GanF82]   Ganapathi, Mahadevan and Charles N. Fischer. Description-Driven Code Generation Using Attribute Grammars, in [POPL82], pp. 107–119.

[GanF84]   Ganapathi, Mahadevan and Charles N. Fischer. Attributed Linear Intermediate Representations for Code Generation, *Software—Practice and Experience,* Vol. 14, No. 4, Apr. 1984, pp. 347–364.

[GanF85]   Ganapathi, Mahadevan and Charles N. Fischer. Affix Grammar Driven Code Generation, *ACM TOPLAS,* Vol. 7, No. 4, Oct. 1985, pp. 560–599.

[GanK89]   Ganapathi, Mahadevan and Ken Kennedy. Interprocedural Analysis and Optimization, Tech. Rept. RICE COMP TR89-96, Dept. of Comp. Sci., Rice Univ., Houston, TX, July 1989.

[GarJ79]   Garey, Michael R. and David S. Johnson. *Computers and Intractability: A Guide to the Theory of NP-Completeness,* W.H. Freeman and Co., San Francisco, CA, 1979.

[GhoM86]   Ghodssi, Vida, Steven S. Muchnick, and Alexand Wu. A Global Optimizer for Sun Fortran, C, and Pascal, *Proc. of the Summer 1986 USENIX Conf.,* Portland, OR, June 1986, pp. 318–334.

[GibM86]   Gibbons, Phillip A. and Steven S. Muchnick. Efficient Instruction Scheduling for a Pipelined Processor, in [Comp86], pp. 11–16.

[GilG83]   Gill, John, Thomas Gross, John Hennessy, Norman P. Jouppi, Steven Przybylski, and Christopher Rowen. Summary of MIPS Instructions, Tech. Note 83-237, Comp. Systems Lab., Stanford Univ., Stanford, CA, Nov. 1983.

[GinL87]   Gingell, Robert A., Meng Lee, Xuong T. Dang, and Mary S. Weeks. Shared Libraries in SunOS, *Proc. of the 1987 Summer USENIX Conf.,* Phoenix, AZ, June 1987, pp. 131–146.

[GlaG78]   Glanville, R. Steven and Susan L. Graham. A New Method for Compiler Code Generation, in [POPL78], pp. 231–240.

[GofK91]   Goff, Gina, Ken Kennedy, and Chau-Wen Tseng. Practical Dependence Testing, in [PLDI91], pp. 15–29.

[Gold72]   Goldstine, Hermann H. *The Computer from Pascal to Von Neumann*, Princeton Univ. Press, Princeton, NJ, 1972.

[Gold84]   Goldberg, Adele. *Smalltalk-80: The Interactive Programming Environment*, Addison-Wesley, Reading, MA, 1984.

[Gold91]   Goldberg, David. What Every Computer Scientist Should Know About Floating-Point Arithmetic, *ACM Computing Surveys*, Vol. 23, No. 1, Mar. 1991, pp. 5–48.

[GolR90]   Golumbic, M.C. and Victor Rainish. Instruction Scheduling Beyond Basic Blocks, in [IBMJ90], pp. 93–97.

[GooH88]   Goodman, J.R. and W.-C. Hsu. Code Scheduling and Register Allocation in Large Basic Blocks, *Proc. of the Intl. Conf. on Supercomputing*, St. Malo, France, July 1988, pp. 442–452.

[GosJ96]   Gosling, James, Bill Joy, and Guy Steele. *The Java Language Specification*, Addison-Wesley, Reading, MA, 1996.

[GraH82]   Graham, Susan L., Robert R. Henry, and Robert A. Schulman. An Experiment in Table Driven Code Generation, in [Comp82], pp. 32–43.

[GraJ79]   Graham, Susan L., William N. Joy, and Olivier Roubine. Hashed Symbol Tables for Languages with Explicit Scope Control, in [Comp79], pp. 50–57.

[GriP68]   Griswold, Ralph E., James F. Poage, and Ivan P. Polonsky. *The SNOBOL4 Programming Language*, Prentice-Hall, Englewood Cliffs, NJ, 1968.

[GroF92]   Grove, Richard B. and R. Neil Faiman, Jr. Personal communication, Digital Equipment Corp., Littleton, MA, Sept. 1992.

[GroT93]   Grove, Dan and Linda Torczon. Interprocedural Constant Propagation: A Study of Jump Function Implementation, in [PLDI93], pp. 90–99.

[Grov94]   Grove, Richard B. Personal communication, Digital Equipment Corp., Littleton, MA, May 1994.

[GupS89]   Gupta, Rajiv, Mary Lou Soffa, and Tim Steele. Register Allocation via Clique Separators, in [PLDI89], pp. 264–274.

[Gupt90]   Gupta, Rajiv. *Compiler Optimization of Data Storage*, Ph.D. dissertation, California Inst. of Technology, Pasadena, CA, July 1990.

[Gupt93]   Gupta, Rajiv. Optimizing Array Bounds Checks Using Flow Analysis, *ACM LOPLAS*, Vol. 2, Nos. 1–4, Mar.–Dec. 1993, pp. 135–150.

[HalB90]   Hall, Mark and John Barry (eds.). *The SunTechnology Papers*, Springer-Verlag, New York, NY, 1990.

[Hall91]   Hall, Mary Wolcott. *Managing Interprocedural Optimization*, Ph.D. thesis, Dept. of Comp. Sci., Rice Univ., Houston, TX, Apr. 1991.

[Hay92]   Hay, William. Personal communication, IBM Canada Lab., Toronto, Canada, May 1992.

[Hay94]   Hay, William. Personal communication, IBM Canada Lab., Toronto, Canada, June 1994.

[Hech77] Hecht, Matthew S. *Flow Analysis of Computer Programs,* Elsevier North-Holland, New York, NY, 1977.

[HecU75] Hecht, Matthew S. and Jeffrey D. Ullman. A Simple Algorithm for Global Data Flow Problems, *SIAM J. of Computing,* Vol. 4, No. 4, Dec. 1975, pp. 519–532.

[HenD89a] Henry, Robert R. and Peter C. Damron. Performance of Table-Driven Code Generators Using Tree-Pattern Matching, Tech. Rept. 89-02-02, Comp. Sci. Dept., Univ. of Washington, Seattle, WA, Feb. 1989.

[HenD89b] Henry, Robert R. and Peter C. Damron. Algorithms for Table-Driven Code Generators Using Tree-Pattern Matching, Tech. Rept. 89-02-03, Comp. Sci. Dept., Univ. of Washington, Seattle, WA, Feb. 1989.

[Hend90] Hendren, Laurie J. Parallelizing Programs with Recursive Data Structures, *IEEE Trans. on Parallel and Distributed Systems,* Vol. 1, No. 1, Jan. 1990, pp. 35–47.

[HenG83] Hennessy, John and Thomas Gross. Postpass Code Optimization of Pipeline Constraints, *ACM TOPLAS,* Vol. 5, No. 3, July 1983, pp. 422–448.

[HenP94] Hennessy, John L. and David A. Patterson. *Computer Organization and Design: The Hardware/Software Interface,* Morgan Kaufmann, San Francisco, CA, 1994.

[Henr84] Henry, Robert R. Graham-Glanville Code Generators, Rept. UCB/CSD 84/184, Comp. Sci. Division, Dept. of Elec. Engg. and Comp. Sci., Univ. of California, Berkeley, CA, May 1984.

[HewP91] *PA-RISC Procedure Calling Conventions Reference Manual,* HP Part No. 09740-90015, Hewlett-Packard, Palo Alto, CA, Jan. 1991.

[HimC87] Himelstein, Mark I., Fred C. Chow, and Kevin Enderby. Cross-Module Optimization: Its Implementation and Benefits, *Proc. of the Summer 1987 USENIX Conf.,* Phoenix, AZ, June 1987, pp. 347–356.

[Hime91] Himelstein, Mark I. Compiler Tail Ends, tutorial notes, *ACM SIGPLAN '91 Conf. on Programming Language Design and Implementation,* Toronto, Ontario, June 1991.

[HofO82] Hoffman, C.W. and Michael J. O'Donnell. Pattern Matching in Trees, *JACM,* Vol. 29, No. 1, Jan. 1982, pp. 68–95.

[Hopk87] Hopkins, Martin. A Perspective on the 801/Reduced Instruction Set Computer, *IBM Systems J.,* Vol. 26, No. 1, 1987, pp. 107–121; also in [Stal90], pp. 176–190.

[HumH94] Hummel, Joseph, Laurie J. Hendren, and Alexandru Nicolau. A General Data Dependence Test for Dynamic, Pointer-Based Data Structures, in [PLDI94], pp. 218–229.

[IBMJ90] *IBM J. of Research and Development,* special issue on the IBM RISC System/6000 Processor, Vol. 34, No. 1, Jan. 1990.

[IEEE83] *IEEE Standard Pascal Computer Programming Language,* Inst. of Elec. and Electronic Engrs., New York, NY, 1983.

[IEEE85] *IEEE Standard for Binary Floating-Point Arithmetic,* ANSI/IEEE Std 754-1985, Inst. of Elec. and Electronic Engrs., New York, NY, 1985.

[Inge61] Ingerman, Peter Z. Thunks, *CACM,* Vol. 4, No. 1, Jan. 1961, pp. 55–58.

[Inte93] *Intel Reference Compiler for the Intel 386, Intel 486, and Pentium Microprocessor Family: An Overview,* Intel Corporation, Santa Clara, CA, 1993.

[Jain91]   Jain, Sunil. Circular Scheduling: A New Technique to Perform Software Pipelining, in [PLDI91], pp. 219–228.

[JaiT88]   Jain, Sunil and Carol Thompson. An Efficient Approach to Data Flow Analysis in a Multiple Pass Global Optimizer, in [PLDI88], pp. 154–163.

[JohM86]   Johnson, Mark S. and Terrence C. Miller. Effectiveness of a Machine-Level, Global Optimizer, in [Comp86], pp. 99–108.

[John78]   Johnson, Steven C. A Portable Compiler: Theory and Practice, in [POPL78], pp. 97–104.

[JohP93]   Johnson, Richard and Keshav Pingali. Dependence-Based Program Analysis, in [PLDI93], pp. 78–89.

[JonM76]   Jones, Neil D. and Steven S. Muchnick. Binding Time Optimization in Programming Languages: Some Thoughts Toward the Design of an Ideal Language, in [POPL76], pp. 77–94.

[JonM78]   Jones, Neil D. and Steven S. Muchnick. TEMPO: A Unified Treatment of Binding Time and Parameter Passing Concepts in Programming Languages, *Lecture Notes in Comp. Sci.,* Vol. 66, Springer-Verlag, Berlin, 1978.

[JonM81a] Jones, Neil D. and Steven S. Muchnick. Flow Analysis and Optimization of LISP-Like Structures, in [MucJ81], pp. 102–131.

[JonM81b] Jones, Neil D. and Steven S. Muchnick. Complexity of Flow Analysis, Inductive Assertion Synthesis, and a Language Due to Dijkstra, in [MucJ81], pp. 380–393.

[KamU75]   Kam, J.B. and Jeffrey D. Ullman. Monotone Data Flow Analysis Frameworks, Tech. Rept. No. 169, Dept. of Elec. Engg., Princeton Univ., Princeton, NJ, 1975.

[KanH92]   Kane, Gerry and Joe Heinreich. *MIPS RISC Architecture,* Prentice-Hall, Englewood Cliffs, NJ, 1992.

[Karr84]   Karr, Michael. Code Generation by Coagulation, in [Comp84], pp. 1–12.

[Keho93]   Kehoe, Brendan P. *Zen and the Art of the Internet,* Prentice-Hall, Englewood Cliffs, NJ, 1993.

[Keil94]   Keilman, Keith. Personal communication, Hewlett-Packard, Cupertino, CA, June 1994.

[Kenn71]   Kennedy, Ken. *Global Flow Analysis and Register Allocation for Simple Code Structures,* Ph.D. thesis, Courant Inst., New York Univ., New York, NY, Oct. 1971.

[Kenn75]   Kennedy, Ken. Node Listing Applied to Data Flow Analysis, in [POPL75], pp. 10–21.

[Kenn81]   Kennedy, Ken. A Survey of Data Flow Analysis Techniques, in [MucJ81], pp. 5–54.

[Kenn86]   Kennedy, Ken. PTOOL, Tech. Rept., Dept. of Math. Sci., Rice Univ., Houston, TX, 1986.

[KerE93]   Kerns, Daniel R. and Susan J. Eggers. Balanced Scheduling: Instruction Scheduling When Memory Latency Is Uncertain, in [PLDI93], pp. 278–289.

[Kild73]   Kildall, Gary A. A Unified Approach to Global Program Optimization, in [POPL73], pp. 194–206.

[KnoR92]   Knoop, Jens, Oliver Rüthing, and Bernhard Steffen. Lazy Code Motion, in [PLDI92], pp. 224–234.

[KnoR93]   Knoop, Jens, Oliver Rüthing, and Bernhard Steffen. Lazy Strength Reduction, *J. of Programming Languages,* Vol. 1, No. 1, 1993, pp. 71–91.

[KnoR94]   Knoop, Jens, Oliver Rüthing, and Bernhard Steffen. Partial Dead Code Elimination, in [PLDI94], pp. 147–158.

[KnoZ92]   Knobe, Kathleen and F. Kenneth Zadeck. Register Allocation Using Control Trees, Tech. Rept. No. CS-92-13, Dept. of Comp. Sci., Brown Univ., Providence, RI, Mar. 1992.

[Knut62]   Knuth, Donald E. A History of Writing Compilers, *Computers and Automation,* Dec. 1962, pp. 8–10, 12, 14, 16, 18.

[Knut71]   Knuth, Donald E. An Empirical Study of Fortran Programs, *Software—Practice and Experience,* Vol. 1, No. 2, 1971, pp. 105–134.

[Knut73]   Knuth, Donald E. *The Art of Computer Programming, Vol. 3: Sorting and Searching,* Addison-Wesley, Reading, MA, 1973.

[KolW95]   Kolte, Pryadarshan and Michael Wolfe. Elimination of Redundant Array Subscript Checks, in [PLDI95], pp. 270–278.

[Kou77]   Kou, Lawrence T. On Live-Dead Analysis for Global Data Flow Problems, *JACM,* Vol. 24, No. 3, July 1977, pp. 473–483.

[Kris90]   Krishnamurthy, Sanjay. *Static Scheduling of Multi-Cycle Operations for a Pipelined RISC Processor,* M.S. paper, Dept. of Comp. Sci., Clemson Univ., Clemson, SC, May 1990.

[Krol92]   Krol, Ed. *The Whole Internet User's Guide and Catalog,* O'Reilly & Associates, Sebastopol, CA, 1992.

[Kuck74]   Kuck, David J. Measurements of Parallelism in Ordinary Fortran Programs, *Computer,* Vol. 7, No. 1, Jan. 1964, pp. 37–46.

[Lam88]   Lam, Monica S. Software Pipelining: An Efficient Scheduling Technique for VLIW Machines, in [PLDI88], pp. 318–328.

[Lam90]   Lam, Monica S. Instruction Scheduling for Superscalar Architectures, in Joseph F. Traub (ed.). *Annual Review of Comp. Sci.,* Vol. 4, Annual Reviews, Inc., Palo Alto, CA, 1990, pp. 173–201.

[LamR91]   Lam, Monica, Edward E. Rothberg, and Michael E. Wolf. The Cache Performance and Optimization of Blocked Algorithms, in [ASPL91], pp. 63–74.

[LanJ82]   Landwehr, Rudolf, Hans-Stephan Jansohn, and Gerhard Goos. Experience with an Automatic Code Generator Generator, in [Comp82], pp. 56–66.

[LarH86]   Larus, James and Paul Hilfinger. Register Allocation in the SPUR Lisp Compiler, in [Comp86], pp. 255–263.

[Laru89]   Larus, James R. Restructuring Symbolic Programs for Correct Execution on Multiprocessors, Tech. Rept. UCB/CSD/89/502, Comp. Sci. Division, Univ. of California, Berkeley, CA, May 1989.

[Laru90]   Larus, James R. Abstract Execution: A Technique for Efficiently Tracing Programs, *Software—Practice and Experience,* Vol. 20, No. 12, Dec. 1990, pp. 1241–1258.

[LawL87]   Lawler, Eugene, Jan Karel Lenstra, Charles Martel, and Barbara Simons. Pipeline Scheduling: A Survey, Comp. Sci. Research Rept. RJ 5738, IBM Research Division, San Jose, CA, July 1987.

[Lee89]   Lee, Peter H. *Realistic Compiler Generation,* MIT Press, Cambridge, MA, 1989.

[Lee91]   Lee, Peter H. (ed.). *Topics in Advanced Language Implementation,* MIT Press, Cambridge, MA, 1991.

[LenT79] Lengauer, Thomas and Robert E. Tarjan. A Fast Algorithm for Finding Dominators in a Flowgraph, *ACM TOPLAS,* Vol. 1, No. 1, July 1979, pp. 121–141.

[LevC80] Leverett, Bruce W., Roderic G.G. Cattell, Steven O. Hobbs, Joseph M. Newcomer, Andrew H. Reiner, Bruce R. Schatz, and William A Wulf. An Overview of the Production-Quality Compiler-Compiler Project, *Computer,* Vol. 13, No. 8, Aug. 1980, pp. 38–49.

[LoEg95] Lo, Jack L. and Susan Eggers. Improving Balanced Scheduling with Compiler Optimizations that Increase Instruction-Level Parallelism, in [PLDI95], pp. 151–162.

[LowM69] Lowry, E. and C.W. Medlock. Object Code Optimization, *CACM,* Vol. 12, No. 1, 1969, pp. 13–22.

[MahC92] Mahlke, Scott A., Pohua P. Chang, William Y. Chen, John C. Gyllenhaal, Wen-mei W. Hwu, and Tokuzo Kiyohara. Compiler Code Transformations for Superscalar-Based High-Performance Systems, *Proc. of Supercomputing '92,* Minneapolis, MN, Nov. 1992, pp. 808–817.

[MahR94] Mahadevan, Uma and Sridhar Ramakrishnan. Instruction Scheduling over Regions: A Framework for Scheduling Across Basic Blocks, *Proc. of Compiler Constr. '94,* Edinburgh, *Lecture Notes in Comp. Sci.,* Vol. 786, Springer-Verlag, Berlin, 1994.

[MauF81] Mauney, John and Charles N. Fischer. ECP—An Error Correcting Parser Generator: User Guide, Tech. Rept. 450, Comp. Sci. Dept., Univ. of Wisconsin, Madison, WI, Oct. 1981.

[MayH91] Maydan, Dror E., John L. Hennessy, and Monica S. Lam. An Efficient Method for Exact Dependence Analysis, in [PLDI91], pp. 1–14.

[McFa89] McFarling, Scott. Program Optimization for Instruction Caches, in [ASPL89], pp. 183–191.

[McFa91a] McFarling, Scott. Procedure Merging with Instruction Caches, in [PLDI91], pp. 71–79.

[McFa91b] McFarling, Scott. *Program Analysis and Optimization for Machines with Instruction Cache,* Ph.D. dissertation, Tech. Rept. CSL-TR-91-493, Comp. Systems Lab., Stanford Univ., Stanford, CA, Sept. 1991.

[Mill92] Miller, James A. Personal communication, Hewlett-Packard, Cupertino, CA, Apr. 1992.

[MilT90] Milner, Robin, M. Tofte, and R. Harper. *The Definition of Standard ML,* MIT Press, Cambridge, MA, 1990.

[MitM79] Mitchell, James G., William Maybury, and Richard Sweet. Mesa Language Manual, Version 5.0, Tech. Rept. CSL-79-3, Xerox Palo Alto Research Ctr., Palo Alto, CA, Apr. 1979.

[MorR79] Morel, Etienne and Claude Renvoise. Global Optimization by Suppression of Partial Redundancies, *CACM,* Vol. 22, No. 2, Feb. 1979, pp. 96–103.

[MorR81] Morel, Etienne and Claude Renvoise. Interprocedural Elimination of Partial Redundancies, in [MucJ81], pp. 160–188.

[Morr91] Morris, W.G. CCG: A Prototype Coagulating Code Generator, in [PLDI91], pp. 45–58.

[MowL92]   Mowry, Todd C., Monica S. Lam, and Anoop Gupta. Design and Evaluation of a Compiler Algorithm for Prefetching, in [ASPL92], pp. 62–73.

[Mowr94]   Mowry, Todd C. *Tolerating Latency Through Software-Controlled Prefetching*, Ph.D. dissertation, Dept. of Elec. Engg., Stanford Univ., Stanford, CA, Mar. 1994.

[Much88]   Muchnick, Steven S. Optimizing Compilers for SPARC, *SunTechnology*, Vol. 1, No. 3, summer 1988, pp. 64–77; also appeared in [HalB90], pp. 41–68, and in [Stal90], pp. 160–173.

[Much91]   Muchnick, Steven S. Optimization in the SPARCompilers, *Proc. of the Sun Users' Group Conf.*, Atlanta, GA, June 1991, pp. 81–99; also appeared in *Proc. of Sun USER '91*, Birmingham, England, Sept. 1991, pp. 117–136, and in *README*, Sun Users' Group, 1991, pp. 1–13 and 20–23.

[MucJ81]   Muchnick, Steven S. and Neil D. Jones (eds.). *Program Flow Analysis: Theory and Applications*, Prentice-Hall, Englewood Cliffs, NJ, 1981.

[Myer81]   Myers, E.A. Precise Interprocedural Data Flow Analysis Framework, in [POPL81], pp. 219–230.

[Nick90]   Nickerson, Brian. Graph Coloring Register Allocation for Processors with Multi-Register Operands, in [PLDI90], pp. 40–52.

[Nico86]   Nicolau, Alexandru. A Fine-Grain Parallelizing Compiler, Tech. Rept. TR-86-792, Dept. of Comp. Sci., Cornell Univ., Ithaca, NY, Dec. 1986.

[OBrH90]   O'Brien, Kevin, Bill Hay, Joanne Minish, Hartmann Schaffer, Bob Schloss, Arvin Shepherd, and Matthew Zaleski. Advanced Compiler Technology for the RISC System/6000 Architecture, in Misra, Mamata (ed.). *IBM RISC System/6000 Technology*, Publication SA23-2619, IBM Corp., Austin, TX, 1990, pp. 154–161.

[OBrO95]   O'Brien, Kevin, Kathryn M. O'Brien, Martin Hopkins, Arvin Shepherd, and Ron Unrau. XIL and YIL: The Intermediate Languages of TOBEY, *Proc. of the ACM SIGPLAN Workshop on Intermediate Representations*, San Francisco, CA, Jan. 1995, published as Microsoft Tech. Rept. MSR-TR-95-01, Microsoft Corp., Redmond, WA, Jan. 1995, and as *SIGPLAN Notices*, Vol. 30, No. 3, Mar. 1995, pp. 71–82.

[PaiS77]   Paige, Bob and Jack T. Schwartz. Expression Continuity and the Formal Differentiation of Algorithms, in [POPL77], pp. 58–71.

[Patt95]   Patterson, Jason R.C. Accurate Static Branch Prediction by Value Range Propagation, in [PLDI95], pp. 67–78.

[Pele88]   Pelegri-Llopart, Eduardo. *Rewrite Systems, Pattern Matching, and Code Generation*, Ph.D. dissertation, Rept. No. UCB/CSD 88/423, Comp. Sci. Division, Univ. of California, Berkeley, CA, June 1988.

[PelG88]   Pelegri-Llopart, Eduardo and Susan L. Graham. Code Generation for Expression Trees: An Application of BURS Theory, in [POPL88], pp. 294–308.

[Pent94]   *Pentium Family User's Manual, Volume 3: Architecture and Programming Manual*, Intel Corp., Mount Prospect, IL, 1994.

[PetH90]   Pettis, Karl and Robert C. Hansen. Profile Guided Code Positioning, in [PLDI90], pp. 16–27.

[Pint93]   Pinter, Shlomit S. Register Allocation with Instruction Scheduling: A New Approach, in [PLDI93], pp. 248–257.

[PLDI88]   *Proc. of the SIGPLAN '88 Symp. on Programming Language Design and Implementation,* Atlanta, GA, published as *SIGPLAN Notices,* Vol. 23, No. 7, June 1988.

[PLDI89]   *Proc. of the SIGPLAN '89 Symp. on Programming Language Design and Implementation,* Portland, OR, published as *SIGPLAN Notices,* Vol. 24, No. 7, July 1989.

[PLDI90]   *Proc. of the SIGPLAN '90 Symp. on Programming Language Design and Implementation,* White Plains, NY, published as *SIGPLAN Notices,* Vol. 25, No. 6, June 1990.

[PLDI91]   *Proc. of the SIGPLAN '91 Symp. on Programming Language Design and Implementation,* Toronto, Ontario, published as *SIGPLAN Notices,* Vol. 26, No. 6, June 1991.

[PLDI92]   *Proc. of the SIGPLAN '92 Symp. on Programming Language Design and Implementation,* San Francisco, CA, published as *SIGPLAN Notices,* Vol. 27, No. 7, July 1992.

[PLDI93]   *Proc. of the SIGPLAN '93 Symp. on Programming Language Design and Implementation,* Albuquerque, NM, published as *SIGPLAN Notices,* Vol. 28, No. 7, July 1993.

[PLDI94]   *Proc. of the SIGPLAN '94 Conf. on Programming Language Design and Implementation,* Orlando, FL, published as *SIGPLAN Notices,* Vol. 29, No. 6, June 1994.

[PLDI95]   *Proc. of the SIGPLAN '95 Conf. on Programming Language Design and Implementation,* La Jolla, CA, published as *SIGPLAN Notices,* Vol. 30, No. 6, June 1995.

[PLDI96]   *Proc. of the SIGPLAN '96 Conf. on Programming Language Design and Implementation,* Philadelphia, PA, published as *SIGPLAN Notices,* Vol. 31, No. 5, May 1996.

[POPL73]   *Conf. Record of the ACM SIGACT/SIGPLAN Symp. on Principles of Programming Languages,* Boston, MA, Oct. 1973.

[POPL75]   *Conf. Record of the 2nd ACM SIGACT/SIGPLAN Symp. on Principles of Programming Languages,* Palo Alto, CA, Jan. 1975.

[POPL76]   *Conf. Record of the 3rd ACM SIGACT/SIGPLAN Symp. on Principles of Programming Languages,* Atlanta, GA, Jan. 1976.

[POPL77]   *Conf. Record of the 4th ACM SIGACT/SIGPLAN Symp. on Principles of Programming Languages,* Los Angeles, CA, Jan. 1977.

[POPL78]   *Conf. Record of the 5th ACM SIGACT/SIGPLAN Symp. on Principles of Programming Languages,* Tucson, AZ, Jan. 1978.

[POPL79]   *Conf. Record of the 6th ACM SIGACT/SIGPLAN Symp. on Principles of Programming Languages,* San Antonio, TX, Jan. 1979.

[POPL80]   *Conf. Record of the 7th ACM SIGACT/SIGPLAN Symp. on Principles of Programming Languages,* Las Vegas, NV, Jan. 1980.

[POPL81]   *Conf. Record of the 8th ACM SIGACT/SIGPLAN Symp. on Principles of Programming Languages,* Williamsburg, VA, Jan. 1981.

[POPL82]   *Conf. Record of the 9th ACM SIGACT/SIGPLAN Symp. on Principles of Programming Languages,* Albuquerque, NM, Jan. 1982.

[POPL84]   *Conf. Record of the 11th ACM SIGACT/SIGPLAN Symp. on Principles of Programming Languages,* Salt Lake City, UT, Jan. 1984.

[POPL86]   *Conf. Record of the 13th ACM SIGACT/SIGPLAN Symp. on Principles of Programming Languages,* St. Petersburg Beach, FL, Jan. 1986.

[POPL88]   *Conf. Record of the 15th ACM SIGACT/SIGPLAN Symp. on Principles of Programming Languages,* San Diego, CA, Jan. 1988.

[POPL89]   *Conf. Record of the 16th ACM SIGACT/SIGPLAN Symp. on Principles of Programming Languages,* Austin, TX, Jan. 1989.

[POPL90]   *Conf. Record of the 17th ACM SIGACT/SIGPLAN Symp. on Principles of Programming Languages,* San Francisco, CA, Jan. 1990.

[POPL91]   *Conf. Record of the 18th ACM SIGACT/SIGPLAN Symp. on Principles of Programming Languages,* Orlando, FL, Jan. 1991.

[POPL92]   *Conf. Record of the 19th ACM SIGACT/SIGPLAN Symp. on Principles of Programming Languages,* Albuquerque, NM, Jan. 1992.

[POPL94]   *Conf. Record of the 21st ACM SIGACT/SIGPLAN Symp. on Principles of Programming Languages,* Portland, OR, Jan. 1994.

[POWE90]   *POWER Processor Architecture, Version 1.52,* IBM Corp., Austin, TX, Feb. 1990.

[Powe93]   *PowerPC Architecture,* first edition, IBM Corp., Austin, TX, May 1993.

[ProF94]   Proebsting, Todd A. and Christopher W. Fraser. Detecting Pipeline Structural Hazards Quickly, in [POPL94], pp. 280–286.

[PugW92]   Pugh, William and David Wonnacott. Eliminating False Data Dependences Using the Omega Test, in [PLDI92], pp. 140–151.

[Radi82]   Radin, George. The 801 Minicomputer, in [ASPL82], pp. 39–47.

[RaoS95]   Rao, Suresh, William A. Savage, and Kevin J. Smith. Personal communication, Intel Corp., Santa Clara, CA, Mar. 1995.

[RauG81]   Rau, B.R. and C.D. Glaeser. Some Scheduling Techniques and an Easily Schedulable Horizontal Architecture for High Performance Scientific Computing, *Proc. of the 14th Annual Microprogramming Workshop,* Chatham, MA, published as *SIGMicro Newsletter,* Vol. 12, No. 4, Dec. 1981, pp. 183–198.

[ReiL77]   Reif, John R. and Harry R. Lewis. Symbolic Evaluation and the Global Value Graph, in [POPL77], pp. 104–118.

[ReiL86]   Reif, John R. and Harry R. Lewis. Efficient Symbolic Analysis of Programs, *J. of Comp. and System Sci.,* Vol. 32, No. 3, June 1986, pp. 280–313.

[Reyn68]   Reynolds, John C. Automatic Computation of Data Set Definitions, *Proc. of the IFIP Congress 1968,* Aug. 1968, pp. B69–B73.

[RicG89a]   Richardson, Stephen E. and Mahadevan Ganapathi. Interprocedural Optimization: Experimental Results, *Software—Practice and Experience,* Vol. 19, No. 2, Feb. 1989, pp. 149–169.

[RicG89b]   Richardson, Stephen E. and Mahadevan Ganapathi. Interprocedural Analysis vs. Procedure Integration, *Information Processing Letters,* Vol. 32, Aug. 1989, pp. 137–142.

[Rich91] Richardson, Stephen C. *Evaluating Interprocedural Code Optimization Techniques,* Ph.D. dissertation, Tech. Rept. CSL-TR-91-460, Comp. Sci. Lab., Stanford Univ., Stanford, CA, Feb. 1991.

[RogL92] Rogers, Anne and Kai Li. Software Support for Speculative Loads, in [ASPL92], pp. 38–50.

[Rose77] Rosen, Barry K. High-Level Data Flow Analysis, *CACM,* Vol. 20, No. 10, Oct. 1977, pp. 712–724.

[Rose79] Rosen, Barry K. Data Flow Analysis for Procedural Languages, *JACM,* Vol. 26, No. 2, Apr. 1977, pp. 322–344.

[Rose81] Rosen, Barry K. Degrees of Availability as an Introduction to the General Theory of Data Flow Analysis, in [MucJ81], pp. 55–76.

[RutG96] Ruttenberg, John, G.R. Gao, A. Stoutchinin, and W. Lichtenstein. Software Pipelining Showdown: Optimal vs. Heuristic Methods in a Production Compiler, in [PLDI96], pp. 1–11.

[Ryma82] Rymarczyk, J.W. Coding Guidelines for Pipelined Processors, in [ASPL82], pp. 12–19.

[SanO90] Santhanam, Vatsa and Daryl Odnert. Register Allocation Across Procedure and Module Boundaries, in [PLDI90], pp. 28–39.

[Sava95] Savage, William A. Personal communication, Intel Corp., Santa Clara, CA, Sept. 1995.

[Schl91] Schlansker, Michael. Compilation for VLIW and Superscalar Processors, tutorial notes, Fourth Intl. Conf. on Architectural Support for Programming Languages and Operating Systems, Santa Clara, CA, Apr. 1991.

[SchS79] Schwartz, Jacob T. and Micha Sharir. A Design for Optimizations of the Bitvectoring Class, Comp. Sci. Rept. No. 17, Courant Inst. of Math. Sci., New York Univ., New York, NY, 1979.

[Schw73] Schwartz, Jacob T. *On Programming: An Interim Rept. on the SETL Project,* Installment II, Comp. Sci. Dept., Courant Inst. of Math. Sci., New York Univ., New York, NY, 1973.

[SetU70] Sethi, Ravi and Jeffrey D. Ullman. The Generation of Optimal Code for Arithmetic Expressions, *JACM,* Vol. 17, No. 4, Oct. 1970, pp. 715–728.

[Shar80] Sharir, Micha. Structural Analysis: A New Approach to Flow Analysis in Optimizing Compilers, *Computer Languages,* Vol. 5, Nos. 3/4, 1980, pp. 141–153.

[ShaS69] Shapiro, R.M. and H. Saint. The Representation of Algorithms, Tech. Rept. RADC-TR-69-313, Volume II, Rome Air Development Center, Griffiss Air Force Base, NY, Sept. 1969; also published as Tech. Rept. CA-7002-1432, Massachusetts Computer Associates, Wakefield, MA, Feb. 1970.

[ShiP89] Shieh, J.J. and C.A. Papachristou. On Reordering Instruction Streams for Pipelined Processors, *Proc. of the 22nd Annual Intl. Symp. on Microarchitecture,* Dublin, Ireland, Aug. 1989, pp. 199–206.

[Simp96] Simpson, Loren Taylor. *Value-Driven Redundancy Elimination,* Ph.D. thesis, Dept. of Comp. Sci., Rice Univ., Houston, TX, Apr. 1996.

[SitC92] Sites, Richard L., Anton Chernoff, Matthew B. Kirk, Maurice P. Marks, and Scott G. Robinson. Binary Translation, *Digital Tech. J.,* Vol. 4, No. 4, special issue, 1992; also appeared in slightly different form in *CACM,* Vol. 36, No. 2, Feb. 1993, pp. 69–81.

[SmoK91] Smotherman, Mark, Sanjay Krishnamurthy, P.S. Aravind, and David Hunnicutt. Efficient DAG Construction and Heuristic Calculation for Instruction Scheduling, *Proc. of the 24th Annual Intl. Symp. on Microarchitecture,* Albuquerque, NM, Nov. 1991, pp. 93–102.

[SPAR92] *The SPARC Architecture Manual, Version 8,* Prentice-Hall, Englewood Cliffs, NJ, 1992.

[SPEC89] *SPEC newsletter,* Vol. 1, No. 1, Systems Performance Evaluation Cooperative, Fremont, CA, 1989.

[SriW93] Srivastava, Amitabh and David W. Wall. A Practical System for Intermodule Code Optimization at Link-Time, *J. of Programming Languages,* Vol. 1, No. 1, 1993, pp. 1–18.

[SriW94] Srivastava, Amitabh and David W. Wall. Link-Time Optimization of Address Calculation on a 64-Bit Architecture, in [PLDI94], pp. 49–60.

[Stal90] Stallings, William. *Reduced Instruction Set Computers,* second edition, IEEE Comp. Society Press, Los Alamitos, CA, 1990.

[Stee84] Steele, Guy L., Jr. *COMMON LISP: The Language,* Digital Press, Burlington, MA, 1984.

[SteH89] Steenkiste, Peter and John Hennessy. A Simple Interprocedural Register Allocation Algorithm and Its Effectiveness for LISP, *ACM TOPLAS,* Vol. 11, No. 1, Jan. 1989, pp. 1–32.

[Stro88] Stroustrup, Bjarne. Type-Safe Linkage for C++, *Computing Systems,* Vol. 6, No. 4, 1988, pp. 371–404.

[Tarj72] Tarjan, Robert Endre. Depth First Search and Linear Graph Algorithms, *SIAM J. of Computing,* Vol. 1, No. 2, 1972, pp. 146–160.

[Tarj74] Tarjan, Robert Endre. Testing Flow Graph Reducibility, *J. of Comp. and System Sci.,* Vol. 9, No. 4, Dec. 1974, pp. 355–365.

[Tarj81] Tarjan, Robert Endre. Fast Algorithms for Solving Path Problems, *JACM,* Vol. 28, No. 3, July 1981, pp. 591–642.

[Tene74a] Tenenbaum, Aaron. Type Determination for Very High Level Languages, Rept. NSO-3, Comp. Sci. Dept., New York Univ., New York, NY, Oct. 1974.

[Tene74b] Tenenbaum, Aaron. Compile Time Type Determination in SETL, *Proc. of the ACM Annual Conf.,* San Diego, CA, Nov. 1974, pp. 95–100.

[Thom92] Thompson, Carol. Personal communication, Hewlett-Packard, Cupertino, CA, May 1992.

[Tiem89] Tiemann, Michael D. The GNU Instruction Scheduler, CS 343 Report, Dept. of Comp. Sci., Stanford Univ., Stanford, CA, June 1989; also appeared in an updated form as Cygnus Tech. Rept. CTR-0, Cygnus Support, Mountain View, CA, 1989.

[Tjia93] Tjiang, Steven W.K. *Automatic Generation of Data-Flow Analyzers: A Tool for Building Optimizers,* Ph.D. dissertation, Dept. of Comp. Sci., Stanford Univ., Stanford, CA, July 1993.

[TjiH92] Tjiang, Steven W.K. and John L. Hennessy. Sharlit—A Tool for Building Optimizers, in [PLDI92], pp. 82–93.

[TjiW91] Tjiang, Steven W.K., Michael E. Wolf, Monica S. Lam, K.L. Pieper, and John L. Hennessy. Integrating Scalar Optimization and Parallelization, *Proc. of 4th Workshop on Languages and Compilers for Parallel Computing,* Santa Clara, CA, Aug. 1991, pp. 137–151.

[Towl76]   Towle, Robert A. *Control and Data Dependence for Program Transformations*, Ph.D. thesis, Dept. of Comp. Sci., Univ. of Illinois, Champaign-Urbana, IL, Mar. 1976.

[Ullm73]   Ullman, Jeffrey D. Fast Algorithms for the Elimination of Common Subexpressions, *Acta Informatica*, Vol. 2, Fasc. 3, July 1973, pp. 191–213.

[Unga87]   Ungar, David M. *The Design and Evaluation of a High Performance Smalltalk System*, MIT Press, Cambridge, MA, 1987.

[UngS91]   Ungar, David M. and Randall B. Smith. SELF: The Power of Simplicity, *Lisp and Symbolic Computation*, Vol. 4, No. 3, June 1991, pp. 187–205.

[Unic90]   Unicode Consortium. *The Unicode Standard: Worldwide Character Encoding, Version 1.0*, Addison-Wesley, Reading, MA, 1990.

[UNIX90a] UNIX Software Operation. *System V Application Binary Interface*, UNIX Press/Prentice-Hall, Englewood Cliffs, NJ, 1990.

[UNIX90b] UNIX Software Operation. *System V Application Binary Interface: Motorola 88000 Processor Supplement*, UNIX Press/Prentice-Hall, Englewood Cliffs, NJ, 1990.

[UNIX90c] UNIX Software Operation. *System V Application Binary Interface: SPARC Processor Supplement*, UNIX Press/Prentice-Hall, Englewood Cliffs, NJ, 1990.

[UNIX91]   UNIX System Labs. *System V Application Binary Interface: Intel i860 Processor Supplement*, UNIX Press/Prentice-Hall, Englewood Cliffs, NJ, 1991.

[UNIX93]   UNIX System Labs. *System V Application Binary Interface: Intel 386 Architecture Processor Supplement*, UNIX Press/Prentice-Hall, Englewood Cliffs, NJ, 1993.

[Wall86]   Wall, David W. Global Register Allocation at Link Time, in [Comp86], pp. 264–275.

[Wall88]   Wallace, David R. Dependence Among Multi-Dimensional Array References, *Proc. of the 1988 ACM Intl. Conf. on Supercomputing*, St. Malo, France, July 1988, pp. 418–428.

[Wall91]   Wall, David W. Predicting Program Behavior from Real or Estimated Profiles, in [PLDI91], pp. 59–70.

[Wall92]   Wallace, David R. Cross-Block Scheduling Using the Extended Dependence Graph, *Proc. of the 1992 Intl. Conf. on Supercomputing*, Washington, DC, July 1992, pp. 72–81.

[WanE93]   Wang, Jian and Christine Eisenbeis. Decomposed Software Pipelining, Tech. Rept. No. 1838, INRIA, Le Chesnay, France, Jan. 1993.

[Warr90]   Warren, Henry S. Instruction Scheduling for the IBM RISC System/6000, in [IBMJ90], pp. 85–92.

[WeaG94]   Weaver, David L. and Tom Germond. *The SPARC Architecture Manual, Version 9*, Prentice-Hall, Englewood Cliffs, NJ, 1994.

[WegZ91]   Wegman, Mark N. and F. Kenneth Zadeck. Constant Propagation with Conditional Branches, *ACM TOPLAS*, Vol. 13, No. 2, Apr. 1991, pp. 181–210.

[Weic84]   Weicker, Reinhold P. Dhrystone: A Synthetic Systems Programming Benchmark, *CACM*, Vol. 27, No. 10, Oct. 1984, pp. 1013–1030.

[WeiC94]   Weise, Daniel, Roger F. Crew, Michael Ernst, and Bjarne Steensgaard. Value Dependence Graphs: Representation Without Taxation, in [POPL94], pp. 287–296.

[Weih80] Weihl, William E. Interprocedural Data Flow Analysis in the Presence of Pointers, Procedure Variables, and Label Variables, in [POPL80], pp. 83–94.

[Wexe81] Wexelblat, Richard L. *History of Programming Languages,* Academic Press, New York, NY, 1981.

[WhiS90] Whitfield, Debbie and Mary Lou Soffa. An Approach to Ordering Optimizing Transformations, *Proc. of the Second ACM Symp. on Principles and Practice of Parallel Programming,* Seattle, WA, published as *SIGPLAN Notices,* Vol. 25, No. 3, Mar. 1990, pp. 137–146.

[Wism94] Wismüller, Roland. Debugging Globally Optimized Programs Using Data Flow Analysis, in [PLDI94], pp. 278–289.

[Wolf89a] Wolfe, Michael R. More Iteration Space Tiling, Tech. Rept. No. CS/E 89-003, Dept. of Comp. Sci. and Engg., Oregon Graduate Inst., Beaverton, OR, May 1989.

[Wolf89b] Wolfe, Michael R. *Optimizing Supercompilers for Supercomputers,* MIT Press, Cambridge, MA, 1989.

[Wolf90] Wolfe, Michael R. Scalar vs. Parallel Optimizations, Tech. Rept. No. CS/E 90-010, Dept. of Comp. Sci. and Engg., Oregon Graduate Inst., Beaverton, OR, July 1990.

[Wolf92] Wolf, Michael E. *Improving Locality and Parallelism in Nested Loops,* Ph.D. dissertation, Tech. Rept. CSL-TR-92-538, Comp. Systems Lab., Stanford Univ., Stanford, CA, Aug. 1992.

[Wolf96] Wolfe, Michael R. *High-Performance Compilers for Parallel Computing,* Addison-Wesley, Redwood City, CA, 1996.

[WolH90] Wolfe, Michael R. and Robert Halstead (eds.). *Proc. of a Workshop on Parallelism in the Presence of Pointers and Dynamically Allocated Objects,* Tech. Note SRC-TN-90-292, Inst. for Defense Analyses Supercomputing Research Ctr., Bowie, MD, Mar. 1990.

[WolL91] Wolf, Michael E. and Monica S. Lam. A Data Locality Optimizing Algorithm, in [PLDI91], pp. 30–44.

[WolT90] Wolfe, Michael R. and Chau-Wen Tseng. The Power Test for Data Dependence, Tech. Rept. No. CS/E 90-015, Dept. of Comp. Sci. and Engg., Oregon Graduate Inst., Beaverton, OR, Aug. 1990.

[WulJ75] Wulf, William A., Richard K. Johnsson, Charles B. Weinstock, Steven O. Hobbs, and Charles M. Geschke. *The Design of an Optimizing Compiler,* American Elsevier, New York, NY, 1975.

[WulR71] Wulf, William A., David B. Russell, and A. Nico Habermann. BLISS: A Language for Systems Programming, *CACM,* Vol. 14, No. 12, Dec. 1971, pp. 780–790.

[Zade84] Zadeck, F. Kenneth. Incremental Data Flow Analysis in a Structured Program Editor, in [Comp84], pp. 132–143.

[ZimC91] Zima, Hans with Barbara Chapman. *Supercompilers for Parallel and Vector Machines,* ACM Press/Addison-Wesley, Reading, MA, 1991.

'Begin at the beginning, the King said, gravely,
'and go until you come to the end; then stop.'
—Carrol, Lewis, *Alice in Wonderland*, Chap. 11.

Mathematical Formulas
ICAN Procedures
Major ICAN Data Structures